Presidency 1976

**Timely Reports to Keep
Journalists, Scholars and the Public
Abreast of Developing Issues, Events and Trends**

April 1977

CONGRESSIONAL QUARTERLY INC.
1414 22ND STREET, N.W., WASHINGTON, D.C. 20037

Congressional Quarterly Inc.

Congressional Quarterly Inc., an editorial research service and publishing company, serves clients in the fields of news, education, business and government. It combines specific coverage of Congress, government and politics by Congressional Quarterly with the more general subject range of an affiliated service, Editorial Research Reports.

Congressional Quarterly was founded in 1945 by Henrietta and Nelson Poynter. Its basic periodical publication was and still is the CQ *Weekly Report,* mailed to clients every Saturday. A cumulative index is published quarterly.

The CQ *Almanac,* a compendium of legislation for one session of Congress, is published every spring. *Congress and the Nation* is published every four years as a record of government for one presidential term.

Congressional Quarterly also publishes books on public affairs. These include the twice-yearly *Guide to Current American Government* and such recent titles as *Origins and Development of Congress* and *Powers of Congress.*

CQ Direct Research is a consulting service which performs contract research and maintains a reference library and query desk for the convenience of clients.

Editorial Research Reports covers subjects beyond the specialized scope of Congressional Quarterly. It publishes reference material on foreign affairs, business, education, cultural affairs, national security, science and other topics of news interest. Service to clients includes a 6,000-word report four times a month bound and indexed semi-annually. Editorial Research Reports publishes paperback books in its fields of coverage. Founded in 1923, the service merged with Congressional Quarterly in 1956.

Editor: Patricia Ann O'Connor.
Contributors: James R. Berger, Elizabeth Bowman, Rhodes Cook, Prudence Crewdson, Mercer Cross, Harrison H. Donnelly, Mary Eisner Eccles, Alan Ehrenhalt, Judy Gardner, Mary Link, David M. Maxfield, Lynda McNeil, Thomas P. Southwick, David Tarr, Pat Towell, Ted Vaden, Wayne Walker.
Editorial Assistant: Michael L. Pleasants.
Cover Design: Howard Chapman.
Production Manager: I.D. Fuller. **Assistant Production Manager:** Kathleen E. Walsh.

Cover Photo: Wide World Photos.

Library of Congress Cataloging in Publication Data

Congressional Quarterly, Inc.
　　Presidency 1976.
　　Includes Index.

　　　1. United States—Politics and government—1976—Addresses, essays, lectures. 2. United States—Economic policy—1976—Addresses, essays, lectures. 3. United States—Foreign relations—1976—Addresses, essays, lectures. I. Title.
E865.C66　　1977　　320.9'93'0925　　74-4270
ISBN 0-87187-108-4

Table of Contents

Editor's Note

Presidency 1976 provides researchers with an overview of Gerald R. Ford's last year in the White House. This volume, the eighth in Congressional Quarterly's *Presidency* series, contains summaries of White House and congressional action in all major legislative fields, as well as details on congressional action on Ford's legislative proposals and his executive and judicial nominations.

The political section of this book follows Ford's fortunes from the Republican primaries through the convention and the 1976 presidential election. This narrative material is supplemented by the primary returns, presidential and vice presidential ballots at the Republican Convention, presidential election returns by region and state, electoral college votes and voter turnout statistics. Also included are transcripts of the presidential and vice presidential nomination acceptance speeches, the Republican Party platform and the three Ford-Carter debates.

Other documents included in this volume are the texts of key presidential messages to Congress, legislative veto messages and White House news conferences.

Introduction

Presidency 1976: Ford Clashes
With Congress, Loses Presidential Race

Gerald R. Ford joined an elite group in 1976. He became the third incumbent President of the 20th century to be denied a second term by the voters.

Ford had already made his share of history. In 1973 he had become the first Vice President appointed under the provisions of the Twenty-fifth Amendment to the Constitution. In 1974 he had become the first Vice President to replace a President who had resigned.

As 1976 began, the affable man who had spent 25 years as a Republican representative from Michigan wanted very much to make it on his own, to be elected to a full term in the presidency. He had never lost an election before. He had no desire to be the third member of a trio with the fellow Republicans who had lost their jobs after one term: William Howard Taft in 1912 and Herbert Hoover in 1932.

Ford nearly succeeded. After the most dramatic comeback in the history of public-opinion polling, he lost the presidency to Democrat Jimmy Carter by only 2.1 percentage points.

It was uphill from the beginning. Ford entered his last year in office with a discouraging approval rating of only 39 per cent in the Gallup Poll. Forty-six per cent disapproved of his performance as President.

Ford's Gallup ratings improved somewhat as the year went on, but they remained unimpressive. His approval score rose to 50 in February and March but sank to 47 in May, as the primary election season drew to a close. Gallup noted that during the same period in 1972, President Nixon's rating had been 15 points higher.

Throughout his presidency, Ford seemed more often to be liked rather than admired. He also had to struggle with the perception of him, encouraged by his political enemies and enhanced by caricaturists, as a dull-witted, fumble-tongued bumbler. He and his staff were unhappy over the seemingly endless press reports of his head-bumpings and ski tumblings.

While his awkwardness might have been imaginary, the opposition to his programs from the heavily Democratic Congress was an ever-present reality. Few of the administration's legislative initiatives, which were limited, were favorably received on Capitol Hill. Ford, far more conservative than the majority in Congress, greeted many of the year's congressional initiatives with hostility.

The result was stalemate. Ford vetoed 20 public bills during the second session of the 94th Congress. High inflation and high unemployment added to the administration's troubles, and Ford differed with Congress on the best solutions. The embattled incumbent made Congress one of the main targets of his campaign. "If

Congress has its way," he said in an April speech to the U.S. Chamber of Commerce, "there is every reason to expect that our present recovery will be followed by a new round of inflation and then another recession, with higher unemployment on the same old roller-coaster pattern of the postwar years."

While Ford was doing his best to withstand congressional pressures from the left, he was being challenged from the right for the Republican nomination. The threat from former California Gov. Ronald Reagan, who came close to taking the nomination away from Ford in the primaries, had the effect of pushing the administration toward more conservative positions than it might otherwise have taken, on both domestic and foreign issues.

Conflicts with Congress

The foundations for confrontation were established early in the year. In his budget message Jan. 21, Ford rejected an election-year "quick-fix" policy for reducing inflation and unemployment. "The combination of the tax and spending messages I propose will set us on a course that not only leads to a balanced budget within three years, but also improves the prospects for the economy to stay on a growth path that we can sustain," he said. *(Text, p. 6-A)*

Warning against continued "drifting in the direction of bigger and bigger government," Ford proposed a reduced growth rate of 5.5 per cent in federal spending for fiscal 1977, with outlays of $394.2-billion, receipts of $351.3-billion and a deficit of nearly $43-billion. "If we try to stimulate the economy beyond its capacity to respond, it will lead only to a future whirlwind of inflation and unemployment," he said.

Democratic leaders of both houses of Congress took immediate issue with Ford's message. Sen. Hubert H. Humphrey (D Minn.), chairman of the Joint Economic Committee, said the proposed budget would neither create jobs nor reduce inflation. "After the rhetoric has faded, we find that the tough questions remain unanswered by this President," said House Speaker Carl Albert (D Okla.).

States of the Union, Economy

The line between the Hill and the White House was drawn just as clearly when Ford delivered his State of the Union address Jan. 19. He emphasized orthodox Republican themes such as the importance of the individual and the

1

Ford's Positions on Important Issues

During the 1976 presidential campaign, Congressional Quarterly published a series of articles comparing the positions of President Ford and Jimmy Carter on several major issues. Following is a summary of some of Ford's positions:

Foreign Policy

Ford and his Secretary of State, Henry A. Kissinger, followed a policy of flexibility based on day-to-day overseas developments. The choice, said Kissinger in 1975, "is not between morality and pragmatism." The United States, he said, must be true to its own beliefs, but it must also survive in a world of sovereign nations and competing wills.

Ford opposed an annual ceiling on U.S. arms sales abroad. Vetoing a foreign military aid bill in May 1976 that would have imposed a $9-billion limit, he said that it "limits our ability to respond to the legitimate defense needs of our friends and obstructs U.S. industry from competing fairly with foreign suppliers."

In the same veto message, Ford defended his administration's support for human rights, but said provisions in the bill (S 2662) to terminate assistance to violator countries "ignore important and complex policy considerations" and probably would be "counterproductive as a means for promoting human rights."

Social Security and Welfare

In his fiscal 1977 budget request, Ford called for an increase in Social Security payroll tax rates. "Simple arithmetic warns all of us that the Social Security trust fund is headed for trouble," he said in his 1976 State of the Union message. "Unless we act soon to make sure the fund takes in as much as it pays out, there will be no security for young or old."

Maintaining that "complex welfare programs cannot be reformed overnight," Ford also expressed doubts that the economy could absorb any major new expenditures for welfare before the end of the decade. "I have never believed that a guaranteed annual income was the answer to our problems," he said in a campaign speech.

Jobs and Inflation

Describing inflation as "public enemy number one," Ford attacked it with proposals for reduced government spending. The way to continue lowering the inflation rate, he asserted, was to pursue "balanced economic policies which encourage the growth of the private sector without risking a new round of inflation."

When he vetoed the Public Works Employment Act of 1976 (S 3201) in July, Ford said that "basic to job creation in the private sector is reducing the ever-increasing demand of the federal government for funds."

Taxes and Spending

Ford's approach to taxes and federal spending was closely linked to his philosophy on inflation.

He proposed a $10-billion tax cut in his State of the Union message, offset by an equal slash in federal spending. "For many Americans," he said, "the way to a healthy, non-inflationary economy has become increasingly clear. The government must stop spending so much and borrowing so much of our money. To hold down the cost of living we must hold down the cost of government."

"I favor giving greater tax relief to the so-called middle-income taxpayers—those in the earning brackets of $8,000 to $30,000 a year," Ford said in an October *Reader's Digest* interview. "I believe we need to simplify the system, but I don't think eliminating all deductions is the way to achieve reform."

"The best income tax reform that I know of is the kind of program I recommended to the Congress in January of last year, where I recommended an increase in the personal exemption for every individual taxpayer from $750 to $1,000," Ford said in April.

Health Insurance

Ford was an opponent of national health insurance. He believed that the federal government should not step in if private enterprise could handle the job.

Although he had indicated willingness to compromise with the Democratic Congress on a health insurance proposal when he took office in 1974, his attitude had hardened by 1976. "We cannot realistically afford federally dictated national health insurance coverage for all 215 million Americans," he said in his State of the Union address.

Energy

As in his approach to medical care, Ford saw private industry as a colleague of government in working toward energy independence. "Greater utilization must be made of nuclear energy in order to achieve energy independence and maintain a strong economy," he said in his 1976 energy message.

Agriculture

"The last three years have registered the highest net farm income in America's history," said Ford May 2 in Indiana. "American farmers have been relieved of heavy and costly burdens of government intervention. They have been given new freedom to meet the challenge of the open market and been rewarded for it."

Because of his support for the open-market orientation of the farm program, Ford favored relatively low target prices for crops. The reasoning behind the administration stand on the low prices was that raising support prices makes the federal program more attractive to farmers, leading to the return of such policies as government acquisition of commodities, followed by acreage restrictions and other rigid controls.

Ford, stung by farm-state resentment of his 1975 embargo on U.S. grain shipments to the Soviet Union, promised "no more embargoes" in his August speech accepting the presidential nomination. He also promised that "we will never use the bounty of America's farmers as a pawn in international diplomacy."

danger of big government and its attendant high spending:

"Five out of six jobs in this country are in private business and industry. Common sense tells us this is the place to look for more jobs and to find them faster.... We must introduce a new balance in the relationship between the individual and the government, a balance that favors greater individual freedom and self-reliance." *(Text, p. 2-A)*

Two days later, congressional Democrats countered with their opposing views in a speech by Sen. Edmund S. Muskie of Maine. "We must reject those of timid vision who counsel us to go back—to go back to simpler times now gone forever," he said. "...I do not believe most Americans want their government dismantled. We can't very well fire the mailmen, discharge our armed forces or lay off the people who run the computers that print our Social Security checks."

Ford struck back in a political speech to midwestern Republicans Jan. 31 in Dearborn, Mich. He decried what he described as the Democratic idea "that the federal government can effectively control the economy, provide everybody not only with their needs but also with their wants, decide what is best for Michigan in the same sweeping law that decides what is best for Mississippi."

Foreign Affairs

Ford's disagreements with Congress were not limited to domestic matters. The quarrels extended to foreign and defense policies as well.

Angola was a case in point. Ford and Secretary of State Henry A. Kissinger were alarmed over Russian intervention in the Angolan civil war, and wanted to send further aid to anti-Soviet forces in the African country. Congress, mindful of earlier U.S. involvement in another faraway land, Vietnam, said no. When Ford signed the $112.3-billion defense appropriations bill—minus aid to Angola—on Feb. 10, he accused members who voted against the money of having "lost their guts." He said their action "was a serious mistake, and they will live to regret it."

Reagan took a hard line on defense and foreign policy which affected some of Ford's positions. Reagan, for example, emphasized the danger of the United States slipping behind the Soviet Union in defense capability. Ford, in a March 24 statement, criticized not Reagan, but Democrats in the House who recommended trimming the defense budget, for "playing politics with world peace and national security interests."

Ford reacted angrily to Reagan's charge that he was about to "give away" the Panama Canal. "We bought it, we paid for it, we built it and we intend to keep it," said Reagan in an appeal to his right-wing constituency. It was one of the most effective themes of his primary campaign.

Failure to continue negotiations for a treaty with Panama would, Ford responded, cause "the alienation of the whole of Latin and South America, the need to send more U.S. personnel down there to protect it [the canal]. These are just irresponsible acts that we can avoid and we are avoiding right now."

On Feb. 17, Ford announced plans to restructure the country's foreign intelligence operations. "As Americans," he said, "we must not and will not tolerate actions by our government which will abridge the rights of our citizens. At the same time, we must maintain a strong, effective intelligence capability.... I will not be a party to the dismantling of the CIA or other intelligence agencies."

Frank Church (D Idaho), chairman of the Senate Select Intelligence Committee, said Feb. 20, "Overall, the President's proposal is clearly to give the CIA a bigger shield and a longer sword with which to stab about within as well as without the country."

Ford's 1976 travels, in contrast to those of his Secretary of State, were confined almost entirely to the United States. He departed the continental shores only once: to serve as host to a two-day, seven-nation economic summit conference in June in Puerto Rico.

The Veto Record

Ford's chief weapon against Congress was the veto. On Jan. 2, the day before the second session of the 94th Congress convened, he vetoed his first bill of the year: a holdover from the previous session, HR 5900, the common-site picketing bill. The bill, strongly supported by organized labor, would have permitted a local union with a grievance against one contractor to picket all other contractors and subcontractors on a building site. In his veto message, Ford said such a law could lead to "greater, not lesser, conflict in the construction industry."

The veto caused more repercussions than usual. Labor Secretary John T. Dunlop had originally convinced Ford to sign the bill. Ford's reversal, under pressure from contractors and conservatives, left Dunlop in an untenable position. He announced his resignation Jan. 14 and was replaced by W. J. Usery Jr.

The conflict between the President and Congress was summed up by the issue of finding jobs for the unemployed. In February, Ford vetoed a $6.1-billion public works jobs and anti-recession bill (HR 5247), calling it "little more than an election-year pork barrel." The measure did little to create jobs, he said, arguing that the best way to do so was "to pursue balanced economic policies that encourage the growth of the private sector without risking a new round of inflation." *(Text, p. 32-A)*

Congress failed to override Ford's veto. Another bill (S 3201) was passed in June. Although it had a more modest price tag of $3.95-billion, Ford vetoed again, calling the proposal inflationary and unproductive. *(Text, p. 37-A)*

This time Congress overrode. When the vote was taken late in July, Sen. Humphrey of Minnesota reminded Democrats of their national convention pledge to give jobs top priority. "This will be the acid test," he said. "If the American people find out that this party cannot keep its word, we do not deserve to win elections."

Ford's Initiatives

All was not vetoes, however. In several of his messages to Congress, Ford proposed the "block grant" concept—replacing categorical programs with blocks of money to state and local governments which they could use as they chose for various programs. Congress responded negatively to the concept, and no block-grant proposals got out of committee.

In January, Ford proposed spending nearly $18-billion in block grants for four programs: health, education, child nutrition and social services. He sent his health legislation to Congress in February. In a speech which summed up his attitude toward block grants, he said, "The hard choices of how best to meet the health needs of your state will no longer be defined by a complicated and categorical tangle of federal regulations. They will be for you and your citizens to determine in an open and locally responsive process."

Several times during the year, Ford showed interest in doing something to weaken court-ordered busing of students to desegregate public schools. In May he reportedly asked Attorney General Edward H. Levi to "look for an appropriate case" to test the Supreme Court ruling. The outcry from civil rights leaders was sharp and immediate. Levi said a few days later that he did not plan to intervene at that time.

The Campaign

Hanging over everything the Ford administration did throughout the year was the Nov. 2 election. Before he could concentrate on being elected to a full term, Ford had to win his party's nomination. No other incumbent President in the century had been denied nomination for a second term.

But Ford nearly earned that distinction. Reagan waged an effective campaign and aroused a passion in his supporters which Ford could not match. This made the nomination contest a nip-and-tuck battle which was not decided until the August convention in Kansas City, Mo. When it was decided, only 117 votes out of 2,259 separated Ford from Reagan. *(Campaign, p. 64)*

The President, never renowned for his oratorical prowess, delivered what was generally thought to be the best speech of his career when he accepted the nomination. Indirectly attacking Carter, who had won the Democratic nomination a month earlier, Ford said: "We will build on performance, not promises; experience, not expediency; real progress instead of mysterious plans to be revealed in some dim and distant future." *(Text, p. 70)*

To win, Ford had to overcome what appeared to be an insurmountable Carter lead in the opinion polls. Gallup found Carter to be an inflated 33 points ahead just after the Democratic convention. Just after Ford's nomination, the gap narrowed to 10 points. It dwindled to just one point on the eve of the election—too close to call, said the pollsters.

When the returns were in, Ford had lost to Carter by only 2.1 percentage points, 48 to 50.1. *(Results, p. 62)*

The Debates

The dominant feature of the 1976 campaign was the three debates between Ford and Carter sponsored by the League of Women Voters. Television brought one or more of the debates into 100 million living rooms. Millions also watched the two vice presidential nominees, Republican Sen. Robert Dole of Kansas and Democratic Sen. Walter F. Mondale of Minnesota, in a fourth debate. *(Presidential debate texts, p. 93)*

It was the first time since 1960 that the American electorate had been given the opportunity to view presidential candidates, standing face to face, being asked questions by panels of journalists. More than any other single factor, the debates shaped the public's perception of Carter and Ford. They had been proposed by Ford in Kansas City.

Pollsters measured public reaction after each encounter. Ford was seen as the winner of the first one only; Carter, of the second two. Mondale was generally considered the decisive winner over Dole. Dole's gut-fighting approach, including charges of "Democrat wars," was credited with sending some wavering Democrats back to the Carter camp.

The presidential debates were Sept. 23 in Philadelphia, Oct. 6 in San Francisco and Oct. 22 in Williamsburg, Va. The vice presidential debate was Oct. 15 in Houston.

The Gaffe Factor

Ford's basic campaign strategy was to portray himself as an experienced leader, a calm and reasonable man who had restored openness and respect to the presidency. During the early part of the campaign Ford followed his campaign advisers' advice to stay in the White House and act presidential, emerging for carefully staged bill-signing ceremonies in the rose garden. Carter's strategy was to attack Ford as an inept leader who lacked the imagination and instincts to move the country forward.

For the first time ever, public funds paid for both presidential campaigns, in accordance with a law enacted in 1974. The spending limit for each was $21.8-million, far less than the amounts spent on campaigns of the recent past.

Because of tight budgets, many of the trappings of past campaigns were missing. Gone, except for the few partisans who cared to pay for them, were the buttons and bumper stickers of the past. The limited money made free exposure, such as that provided by the debates, more important than ever before. Neither Ford nor Carter could afford all the television ads he would have liked.

Ill-chosen words in free forums had a great impact on both campaigns. Ford's most serious blunder was made during the second television debate on Oct. 6, when he said that "there is no Soviet domination of Eastern Europe." Under heavy pressure from Carter and from ethnic organizations, the President was forced to recant his position.

Carter's most devastating gaffes were contained in an interview with *Playboy* magazine, released Sept. 20. The Baptist fundamentalist admitted he had "looked on a lot of women with lust. I've committed adultery in my heart many times." And he said, "I don't think I would ever take on the same frame of mind that Nixon or [President] Johnson did—lying, cheating and distorting the truth." The statements plagued Carter for the rest of the campaign. He apologized to Johnson's widow and later admitted that granting the interview at all had been a mistake.

Right Track, Wrong Result

At the start, Ford had problems with his campaign organization. His first two campaign chairmen resigned for different reasons. The campaign did not start functioning efficiently until James A. Baker III took over as chairman, assisted by campaign consultant Stuart Spencer. Contributing to Ford's late-blooming momentum was a well-conceived television advertising campaign.

But the bloom came too late. Despite Carter's mistakes and his less efficient campaign structure, he fought off Ford's charge.

Although Ford would be President for 10 more weeks, his time for effective leadership terminated with an informal but poignant ceremony Nov. 3, the day after the election. Ford himself could not read the telegram he had sent Carter; he had all but lost his voice at the end of the campaign. Surrounded by her husband and children, Ford's wife, Betty, fought back tears as she read the message. The telegram congratulated Carter and pledged "my complete and wholehearted support" to the President-elect.

It was, said Carter, a "characteristically gracious statement."

Economic Policy

Uncertain was the key adjective to describe the state of the economy in the closing months of 1976.

The course of the recovery from the deepest recession since the 1930s had been an issue between the Democratic Congress and the Republican White House all year long, with members on Capitol Hill advocating more fiscal stimulus to combat the persistently high rate of unemployment, one of the legacies of the 1974-75 recession. The administration of President Ford, on the other hand, warned of the dangers of inflation that could be set off by excessive deficit spending, and it was successful in thwarting, by vetoes, the most ambitious of the congressionally initiated economic plans on the grounds they were too costly or were ineffective.

The economic statistics were not conclusive in proving or disproving the correctness of the positions of either side. The recovery that had begun in 1975 continued throughout the first nine months of 1976, but then appeared to falter. After a booming first quarter, the rate of growth in the nation's economy as measured by the gross national product (GNP) slowed dramatically in the next three months to a near standstill that raised concern among Democrats, but was considered merely a pause by administration economists. Preliminary data for the third quarter showed a further slight decline in the rate of growth, fueling debate over whether the economy was still in a pause before moving upward once again or in a stagnant condition preceding a downward trend.

Alan Greenspan, chairman of the President's Council of Economic Advisers, gave his view that the normal pace of recovery was a pattern of "spurt, pause, spurt," implying that the "pause" was temporary, the economy was basically healthy, and the recovery would continue in 1977.

But the slowed growth did nothing to lower already high unemployment, and both consumers and business showed caution in spending and investment plans, casting a pall over the outlook and raising doubts among Democrats whether the recovery would continue without new economic stimulus.

Campaign Issue

In a presidential election campaign in which the two candidates found few issues to capture the voters' attention, Democratic candidate Jimmy Carter and Republican incumbent Gerald Ford used the economic statistics to bolster their respective positions and priorities.

Ford defended his administration's policies, saying they would lead to long-term stability and economic health, that the monthly statistics showed gradual improvement and that his policy of fiscal restraint was paying dividends.

Nevertheless, the administration's earlier optimism that the economy would be much improved by the November elections clearly had gone awry, particularly as reflected in the economic indicators announced in the month preceding election day.

Carter used the data to argue his case that the Republican's handling of the economy was having the effect of worsening unemployment and inflation, and that a change was needed in the White House.

Uneven Recovery

The economy took off at a booming rate early in the year, a spurt of such proportions that few analysts believed it could, or should, continue.

Following a sluggish final quarter in 1975 in which the gross national product grew at a 3.3 per cent annual rate after adjustments for seasonal variations and for inflation, "real" GNP showed a 9.2 per cent annual growth rate in the first three months of 1976. The GNP price deflator, an indicator of inflation, showed only a 3.2 per cent annual increase over the preceding quarter, a marked improvement from the 7.1 per cent increase of the last quarter of 1975.

Other indicators showed a lessening of inflation in the first quarter as well. The wholesale price index continued a trend of either small declines or increases that had begun in November 1975. Prices, as measured by the consumer price index (CPI), rose on a seasonally adjusted basis at an annual rate under 3 per cent, in contrast to the 12.2 per cent annual rate in 1974 and 7 per cent in 1975. Unemployment declined too from the record levels of the recession near 9 per cent, falling to 7.5 per cent by March.

The various figures were so encouraging that some Ford administration economists predicted that their original estimates for the economy's performance would be reached sooner than first anticipated. The short-term economic assumptions presented in the President's fiscal 1977 budget in January 1976 were revised in the mid-year review to reflect the "stronger economy." The 1976 average unemployment rate was revised downward to 7.3 per cent from 7.7 per cent, and the rise in the consumer price index from December 1975 to December 1976 was projected to be 5 per cent rather than 5.9 per cent. The "real" growth in GNP for calendar 1976, estimated in January to be 6.2 per cent, was revised upward to 6.8 per cent. Those estimates, however, were subject to later revision as the year progressed.

Economic Pause

The expected slowdown did indeed come, with second quarter GNP growth, after accounting for inflation, at a 4.5 per cent annual rate over the first quarter. Adjusted figures for the third quarter, announced Nov. 18, showed a 3.8 per cent growth rate, barely enough to keep the economy expanding sufficiently to keep up with inflation and the increasing labor force.

The unemployment figures for the two quarters reflected the slowed expansion, with the unemployment rate rising from a seasonally adjusted 7.5 per cent rate in April to 7.8 per cent in September.

Another discouraging sign was a decline in the index of key economic indicators in both August and September.

Wholesale prices spurted in September by nearly a percentage point from the previous month, and other indicators of inflation were rising as well during the second and third quarters, including the consumer price index and the GNP deflator.

Continuing Optimism

Despite the weakness indicated by the statistics, many economic analysts both inside and outside the administration remained optimistic about the final quarter of 1976 and the prospects for healthy economic growth continuing in 1977. The signs were not so bad, the Commerce Department's chief economist told reporters Oct. 20, that new policies were needed. Administration economists warned that plans aimed at quickly reducing the high unemployment rate would put the nation back in a boom-bust cycle.

In Congress, the Democratic-controlled Budget Committees had made clear, in setting their spending ceiling and revenue floor for fiscal 1977, that they considered the recovery uncertain and would act early in 1977 to provide greater stimulus if conditions warranted it. And President-elect Carter emphasized that lowering unemployment was one of his priorities.

Government Policy

Through its fiscal (spending and taxing) policies, and through buffers such as unemployment benefits and income transfer payments, the government played its traditional role in trying to cushion downturns and spur the recovery.

Fiscal Policy

The largest tax cut in U.S. history, enacted in 1975 and then continued through the first six months of 1976, was extended by Congress through calendar 1977 as an imperative stimulus to the economy.

By any measure federal budget policy was stimulative in 1976, which covered the last half of fiscal 1976, the July 1-Sept. 30 transition quarter preceding the switch to a new beginning date of Oct. 1 for the fiscal year, and the first three months of fiscal 1977.

The Office of Management and Budget (OMB) had estimated in January 1976 that the fiscal 1976 budget deficit could reach a record $76-billion, and Congress set a ceiling of $74.1-billion. At mid-year, OMB set the fiscal 1976 actual deficit at $65.6-billion, a substantial decrease but still stimulative compared to the $43.6-billion deficit in fiscal 1975.

Spending was down as well in the July 1-Sept. 30 transition quarter, $7.6-billion, or more than 7 per cent, of the outlays of $102.1-billion estimated by OMB in its mid-year review. The actual deficit was $12.7-billion for the transition quarter; Congress had set a ceiling of $16.2-billion.

Ironically, in light of the Ford administration's warnings of the dangers of excessive federal spending, those decreases in government spending, which could not be immediately explained, were suspected by some economists as a contributing factor in the slowing in economic growth during the second and third quarters.

Through its new budget process, Congress tried its hand at playing a more reasoned role in setting economic policy. The procedures were designed to bring a greater degree of rationality and overall strategy to the frequently fragmented and haphazard enactment of spending legislation in the past. In setting its broad economic plan, the Democratic-controlled Congress differed sharply from the Ford administration, choosing to spend more and to direct the extra outlays at jobs-stimulus programs. It largely ignored Ford's proposals for consolidations and cuts in domestic programs and for deeper tax cuts than enacted in 1975. By rejecting those further cuts, Congress kept the proposed deficits of its budget and the administration's very close for fiscal 1977, a difference of only $3.1-billion.

The two branches clashed time and again throughout 1976 over legislation aimed at spurring the economy, with Ford vetoing Democratic-backed programs as too expensive and hence inflationary. The lopsided Democratic majority was frequently thwarted when the vetoes were sustained by the combined votes of Republicans and conservative Democrats, forcing delays or reductions in the ambitious economic programs.

Monetary Policy

Despite the grumbling of some in Congress, the Federal Reserve Board maintained its independence in setting monetary policy by regulating the growth of the money supply. Some members of Congress, including Brock Adams (D Wash.), chairman of the House Budget Committee, feared that the growth rates targeted by the board would undermine the basis of the congressional fiscal policies, throwing the recovery off course. But as in the past, various legislative efforts to bring the Federal Reserve under closer control came to nothing.

In his required quarterly appearances before the congressional banking committees, Federal Reserve Board Chairman Arthur F. Burns gave the goals for annual growth rates in the nation's money supply. He made clear in those appearances that while the nation had made "notable" progress in reducing the rate of inflation since 1974, it was his view that the underlying rate had not decreased since mid-1975 and could still be about 6 or 7 per cent. That rate, he emphasized, was a serious threat to the economy and its reduction should be a major objective of economic policy.

The aim of the board, Burns testified, was to support further growth of output and employment while avoiding excesses that would aggravate underlying inflation. Its goal for the year ending in the first quarter of 1977 was a growth rate of 4½ to 7 per cent for the narrowly defined money supply, consisting of currency and demand deposits. That was lowered to 4½ to 6½ per cent for the year ending in the third quarter of 1977. The growth targets for a more broadly defined money supply including bank time deposits was 7½ to 10 per cent for the year ending in both the first and third quarters of 1977 after a slight dip in the second quarter.

The board reported that on the basis of quarterly-average data, the narrowly defined money supply had grown at an annual rate of 2.7 per cent in the first quarter of 1976, and 4.1 per cent in the third quarter. The broader money supply had grown at 9.7 per cent in the first quarter and 9.2 per cent the third.

While short-term interest rates had vacillated in the first half of 1976, they had gradually declined between June and October, as had long-term rates.

Energy and Environment

America's energy crisis quietly worsened in 1976. Three years after President Richard M. Nixon called for a total commitment to make the United States energy independent, this country was more dependent than ever upon foreign powers for fuel.

Rather than generating more energy, America was producing less. For the year's first seven months, average daily domestic energy production hung about 1 per cent below the comparable 1975 level. While domestic energy production lagged, consumption grew. Americans used about 1.6 per cent more energy each day during the first six months of 1976 than during the first half of 1975.

With demand growing while domestic supplies fell, America was forced to look elsewhere for fuel to turn its turbines, power its plants and heat its homes. Inevitably, that meant increasing reliance on the oil-rich Arab nations—the same nations that had imposed the 1973 oil embargo.

"We must reduce our vulnerability to the economic disruption which a few countries can cause by cutting off our energy supplies or by arbitrarily raising prices," President Ford declared in a Feb. 26 message to Congress.

But Congress at the close of its 94th term had failed to take many far-reaching energy initiatives in 1976. "We have dabbled with oil and gas pricing. We have made more money available for long-range research, for things like solar energy, that may help us 30 or 40 years from now. But as far as doing anything practical to increase the supply of energy and reduce our dependence upon foreign sources in the foreseeable future, we have done nothing," concluded Rep. Jim Wright (D Texas) shortly before Congress adjourned.

The Problem—Oil

A steadily shrinking oil supply lay at the heart of America's energy troubles. Average daily domestic crude oil output reached its lowest level in more than a decade in March at 8.1 million barrels per day, a level which held roughly steady through July. Almost twice that amount was being consumed daily. America demanded 15.911 million barrels of refined petroleum products daily. To meet demand, imports increased. Total imports averaged 6.8 million barrels per day during the first half of 1976—40 per cent of the nation's total oil supply. In 1975, only 37 per cent was imported. The Federal Energy Administration (FEA) projected a total 1976 import figure of 41 per cent.

The Arab nations of the Organization of Exporting Countries (OPEC) continued to manipulate America's energy fate. Through the first half of 1976, the Arabs supplied about 38 per cent of the nation's oil imports. The OPEC nations met in Qatar in December and emerged with a surprising two-tier pricing system. Eleven member nations agreed to raise the benchmark price of crude oil 15 per cent in two steps, but Saudi Arabia and the United Arab Emirates insisted on raising their prices only 5 per cent

through 1977. The benchmark price was $11.51 per barrel. A 15 per cent hike would raise it to $13.30, and a 5 per cent hike would make the price $12.09.

The Alaska Pipeline

America's petroleum outlook was not rosy at year's end. The only relief in sight lay in Alaska. Initial estimates were that 1.2 million barrels of oil would flow each day from the rich lode beneath the North Slope when the Alaska pipeline went into operation. Production eventually could increase to 2 million barrels per day. The Alyeska Pipeline Service Co., contractors for the pipeline, continued to promise delivery of the oil beginning in mid-1977, but others were skeptical.

Congressional investigators reported "serious doubts" in early September that Alyeska's 800-mile pipeline would be finished on schedule. A delay of up to one year was possible, they said. Investigations also alleged that the line was plagued with sloppy workmanship. An audit revealed 3,955 "irregularities" in the pipeline's welds, all but a few of which had to be repaired, sometimes at great cost. Sporadic reports of accidents—such as when a section of the line laid beneath a river was found broken loose and floating at the surface—also raised doubts about the pipeline's integrity.

Yet another problem concerning the pipeline surfaced in September. When the project was approved, plans called for Alaska's oil to be used by western states, where the oil was to be shipped. In September, however, FEA officials announced that the West Coast had no need for Alaskan oil. They predicted that up to 600,000 barrels of oil might pile up unused on western shores each day by 1978 if some alternate final destination was not selected. The government had not decided what to do with the excess oil as of early 1977. Proposals ranged from piping it to oil-starved eastern states, which would require expensive new pipelines, to selling it to Japan, a politically explosive alternative.

Other Energy Sources

Natural Gas. For the first seven months of the year, domestic marketed production and consumption of natural gas declined roughly 2 per cent below 1975 levels. Imports rose about 2 per cent. The FEA did not expect those trends to change in the next several years unless the industry was deregulated. During the 1975-76 heating season, 31 of the 48 major interstate pipelines experienced curtailments, and more were expected during the 1976-77 season, especially in Mid-Atlantic and Midwest states.

Coal. Coal production continued the slow but steady increase which had been evident for five years. Production in 1976 reached 665.4 million tons, up from the 640 million total for 1975. Coal consumption was up also. During the year's first six months, coal accounted for 18.5 per cent of the total energy consumed, compared with 17.9 per cent for the same period in 1975.

Increasing demands for coal made some coal-rich western states nervous. "We're not interested in being a colony for the rest of the country," commented New Mexico Gov. Jerry Apodaca. Several western states banded together in organizations to ensure that the nation's need for coal did not lead to unfair exploitation of their lands.

Meanwhile, on May 11 the Interior Department adopted revised regulations governing reclamation of federal lands strip-mined for coal. Secretary Thomas S. Kleppe said the new rules would protect the environment while allowing increased coal production, but environmentalists called them too lenient.

Nuclear Energy. As of October, 61 nuclear power plants were operating in the United States. Another 75 were being built. Nineteen more had limited site authorizations and 63 reactors were on order—a total of over 200 nuclear power plants operating, under construction or planned. The total capacity of all those would be equal to about one half of the nation's fossil fuel generating plants.

From its inception, nuclear power prompted controversy and 1976 was no exception. In June, Californians by better than a 2-1 margin rejected a referendum initiative that would have limited severely existing and future nuclear plants. The proposal stimulated tremendous campaigns on both sides. Voters in six other states made similar decisions in referenda in the November elections.

Concerns about the safety of nuclear power plants were dramatized in February when three managing engineers from the General Electric Co. division that builds nuclear reactors quit their jobs and volunteered to work for the movement to halt nuclear power. Their action followed the January resignation of a Nuclear Regulatory Commission (NRC) engineer who also said there was a lack of safety in the industry. A second NRC engineer resigned in late October, declaring that the agency covers up safety problems "of far-reaching significance" at the nation's atomic power plants.

THE PRESIDENT'S PROGRAM

Against that backdrop, President Ford Feb. 26 outlined his ideas on how to cure the country's energy ills. Most of his proposals were the same ones he had offered to a largely unresponsive Congress in 1975.

"During the past year, we have made some progress toward achieving our energy independence goals," he said, "but the fact remains that we have a long way to go."

Foremost among Ford's priorities was a call to deregulate the price of natural gas. He termed deregulation "the most important action that can be taken by the Congress to improve our future gas supply situation."

Ford reemphasized his strong commitment to nuclear power. "Greater utilization must be made of nuclear energy," he said. "It is likewise vital that we continue our world leadership as a reliable supplier of nuclear technology...." The President urged increased funding for nuclear development and nuclear safety programs. He called for streamlined licensing procedures to speed construction of new nuclear reactors. And he strongly urged passage of his proposed Nuclear Fuel Assurance Act, which would have allowed private investment to enter the government-controlled industry of producing enriched uranium to fuel nuclear reactors.

In other energy areas, Ford asked Congress to amend the Clean Air Act to extend air quality control deadlines to encourage use of coal and to improve auto mileage; allow production of oil from the Naval Petroleum Reserves; create a $100-billion government corporation to stimulate private sector development of new energy sources; authorize $6-billion in loan guarantees for private production of synthetic fuels; establish thermal efficiency standards for new buildings and to pass a series of other energy conservation proposals; authorize a $1-billion program to help local governments adjust to the economic and social impacts of developing energy resources on federal lands, including off-shore areas; and increase funding for energy research by 30 per cent.

THE CONGRESSIONAL RESPONSE

Congress approved only a small portion of the energy legislation which President Ford requested. The end result was that the nation lacked a coordinated energy policy when the 94th Congress adjourned.

Oil. Ford signed one important energy-environment measure (S 586) authorizing $1.2-billion in federal aid to coastal states to help them adjust to the impact of offshore oil and gas development. His proposal (HR 49) to allow production from three oil reserves previous held exclusively by the Navy was also enacted.

A series of FEA proposals to decontrol the prices of jet fuel, residual oil, diesel fuel and a variety of special petroleum products went into effect during the year, not because Congress approved them but because it did not block them. With those controls lifted, more than one-half of the products of a barrel of crude oil were exempted from controls, and no significant price increases or shortages developed.

The administration claimed another victory when the House killed a bill (S 521) revising procedures guiding development of federal offshore oil and gas resources. The administration and the oil industry opposed the bill, arguing that it would cause unnecessary delays.

The one oil measure provoking the most sound and fury never got to the floor of either chamber, but it advanced far enough to throw a major scare into the oil industry and the White House. The measure (S 2387) would have forced the break-up of the nation's 18 largest oil companies. The Senate Judiciary Committee approved it despite intense industry lobbying, but late in the session the bill was shelved. Both sides were preparing to resume the battle in 1977.

Natural Gas. The Ford administration failed to persuade Congress to deregulate the price of natural gas, its primary energy objective in 1976. However, the pressure for deregulation was eased by a July Federal Power Commission decision to allow a substantial increase in the regulated price of natural gas.

Nuclear Power. Congress did not clear one major nuclear energy measure strongly urged by the Ford administration—the proposed Nuclear Fuel Assurance Act (HR 8401). The bill passed the House narrowly in August, but the Senate refused to bring it to the floor late in the session.

Both houses of Congress approved Ford's requests for increased funding of nuclear development and safety programs in passing separate versions of HR 13350, the fiscal 1977 authorization for the Energy Research and Development Administration (ERDA). The measure died an unnatural death in the Senate just before adjournment, however, when Sen. Mike Gravel (D Alaska) vowed to filibuster against it, forcing its abandonment so the Senate could adjourn on schedule.

Coal. There were two major coal-related battles in 1976. Congress won one and the administration won the other, with help from the House Rules Committee.

Congress won on Aug. 4 when it overrode a Ford veto of S 391, which revised procedures for leasing and development of federal coal deposits. Ford had vetoed the bill because he said it would unnecessarily delay coal production.

In the other critical coal policy battle, two attempts to resurrect the twice-vetoed strip mining control bill proved fruitless when the House Rules Committee refused to send the measures to the floor.

Solar. The administration requested $162.5-million for solar energy research and development, a substantial increase over the fiscal 1976 request. Congress was eager to raise the amount further. The ERDA authorization bill blocked by Sen. Gravel included $319.7-million for solar energy development. The public works appropriations bill (HR 14236) included $290.4-million for solar projects.

FEA Extension. Congress in HR 12169 extended the life of the FEA for 18 months and required Congress to develop plans for general federal energy policy reorganization. The measure included terms providing financial incentives for energy efficient buildings and empowered the FEA to collect financial data from oil companies.

Other. Other important energy battles between White House and Congress in 1976 included:

● House refusal to take up a bill (HR 12112) backed by the administration providing $4-billion in loans and price supports for synthetic fuels development;

● Enactment over a Ford veto of HR 8800, a bill providing $160-million to develop electric cars;

● Failure to overturn a Ford veto of a bill (HR 13655) authorizing ERDA to develop automobiles that ran on other than petroleum-based fuels;

● Senate refusal to confirm four Ford nominees to energy-related agencies, two to the Tennessee Valley Authority and one each to the Federal Power Commission and the Nuclear Regulatory Commission.

The Environmental Picture

Efforts to protect the nation's air, water, land and wildlife continued to conflict with economic and energy goals in 1976. The environmental movement stepped up its campaign to convince Congress and the public that strong environmental controls could coexist with a healthy economy and adequate energy production.

Congress

Congress' 1976 record on environmental issues was mixed. It passed a long-debated toxic substances control bill, expanded solid waste management programs, substantially increased funding for the national parks and recreation lands system, and blocked construction of a giant electric power project that threatened to flood a section of North Carolina's beautiful New River.

Major environmental bills that did not make it through in 1976, largely because of industry and Ford administration opposition, included a complex clean air amendments measure, and the energy-related bills to control strip mining and set standards for offshore oil leasing.

Compromises were worked out on measures increasing federal controls on public lands, allocating federal funds for states affected by offshore drilling and revising federal policies on forest management.

Congress failed to pass several bills opposed by environmentalists. One was a water pollution measure that would have put new restrictions on wetlands protection regulations. Environmentalists also opposed the administration-backed energy bills which would have provided federal loan guarantees for private development of synthetic fuels and permitted private industry to begin producing enriched uranium.

"The environment just isn't the sexy issue it once was," one environmental lobbyist commented, reviewing the session.

Recognizing this, environmentalists showed a new willingness to compromise. On the toxic substances bill (S 3149), for example, environmental and industry lobbyists worked out solutions to their past disagreements. Both sides endorsed the final version even though neither was entirely satisfied.

The Environmental Study Conference, a bipartisan group organized by House members in 1975, helped draw attention to environmental issues with an expanded weekly bulletin that provided details of House and Senate hearings, committee markup sessions and floor action on a broad range of bills.

Pollution Progress

The quality of the nation's air and water was improving rapidly, the President's Council on Environmental Quality (CEQ) reported in September. Although strict clean-up deadlines set by Congress early in the decade would not be met in many cases, the council predicted that the country would enjoy relatively clean air and water by the early 1980s.

The council found "significant progress" in cleaning up air pollution. It singled out Los Angeles, Calif., and New York City as particular problem areas that would require "unique control programs" to cope with auto pollution.

The effort to "force technology" by putting industry on specific clean-up timetables remained extremely controversial, as was demonstrated by the heavy lobbying of auto companies, electric utilities and other industries on the clean air bill (S 3219) that died on the last day of the session.

Environmentalists generally supported the 1976 clean air bill, although they would have preferred a stronger measure. The bill's death left hanging the questions of how quickly auto companies would have to comply with stiffer tailpipe controls—and to what degree the federal government should regulate industrial growth in regions where the air remained relatively pristine.

The supporters of controlling such growth scored a victory in April, when three utility companies cancelled plans to build a huge coal-fired power complex on the Kaiparowits plateau in southern Utah.

Another important development on air pollution came in October, when the U.S. Steel Corporation agreed to a complex plan for cleaning up emissions at its Clairton Coke Works in Pennsylvania, one of the nation's largest and dirtiest industrial plants.

The CEQ was impressed with the progress in cleaning up water pollution from industrial and municipal sources, even though the federal grant program for construction of municipal sewage treatment facilities was behind schedule.

But the council warned that the difficult task of controlling "nonpoint" sources of water pollution—such as agricultural runoff contaminated with pesticides—had hardly begun.

Congress had several preliminary skirmishes on water pollution issues in 1976 but little was resolved. The National Commission on Water Quality published a long, detailed report recommending "mid-course" corrections in the 1972 water pollution law—issues Congress was planning to tackle in 1977.

Toxic Chemicals

The potential dangers of industrial and commercial chemicals, and the difficulty of coping with toxic substances once they got into the environment, came home to Americans dramatically in 1976. A pesticide called kepone, industrial chemicals known as PCBs and aerosol propellants called fluorocarbons shared the spotlight.

In October, a federal judge in Richmond, Va., levied the largest fine ever imposed on an industrial polluter in the country—$13.2-million against the Allied Chemical Corporation for illegally discharging the pesticide kepone and other toxic chemicals into Virginia's James River over a three-year period.

Fines also were levied against the Life Sciences Products Company, a small spin-off firm in Hopewell, Va., that produced kepone for Allied. The Life Sciences plant was closed down in 1975 after it was discovered that about 70 employees at the plant were ill and 28 of them were hospitalized with complications including brain and liver damage, loss of memory, slurred speech, tremors and sterility.

Aside from that human tragedy, the kepone pollution forced officials to ban commercial fishing in the James River and lower Chesapeake Bay.

Congressional committees and reporters tried to trace the links in the kepone disaster and pinpoint why no federal, state or local agency had acted sooner. Allied summed up the general conclusion in a full-page newspaper ad it ran after the trial ended. "The...entire Kepone story has been a succession of errors in which many persons and organizations, both public and private, have played a part and must share responsibility," the company said.

Kepone, like the banned pesticide DDT, was considered particularly dangerous because it persisted in the environment and could accumulate in human and animal tissues. Polychlorinated biphenyls (PCBs), a class of synthetic chemicals with similar persistent and toxic properties, posed another menace recognized fully in 1976.

PCBs were used as insulators in electric equipment and in other commercial and industrial products. High levels of the chemical were found in the Great Lakes, the Hudson River in New York and other U.S. waters. Commercial fishing was banned in the Hudson. The substance even turned up in milk from some Indiana cows that had grazed on land treated with PCB-contaminated sludge.

U.S. companies pledged to phase out PCB use and Congress attached a provision to the toxic substances bill calling for a complete ban on their manufacture and distribution by early 1979. But even if all PCB use was ended, officials warned, the substance already had pervaded the environment and would be around for years.

A less immediate but potentially devastating problem was posed by fluorocarbons, which were used as propellants in aerosol spray cans and as coolants in refrigerators and air conditioners. A National Academy of Sciences panel confirmed in September the popular theory that fluorocarbon gases were slowly breaking down the atmospheric ozone layer that protected the earth from harmful ultraviolet rays.

It was thought that increased ultraviolet exposure could cause skin cancer and even modify the earth's climate.

The academy committee stopped short of recommending the immediate ban on aerosol products some environmentalists wanted, calling instead for more study of the problem to be followed by federal regulations within two years.

The defeated clean air bill contained a provision that would have prodded the Environmental Protection Agency (EPA) to act on the ozone threat. In the absence of that law, the Food and Drug Administration (FDA) in October announced that it would begin "an orderly phase-out" of all nonessential uses of fluorocarbon propellants in food, drug and cosmetic products—and require warning labels on those products in the meantime.

Jobs and the Environment

Environmentalists intensified their efforts in 1976 to counter the standard industry argument that strict pollution controls imposed too quickly led to unemployment and economic stagnation.

The environmentalists responded that pollution control expenditures represented only a small percentage of overall industry outlays, and that they actually increased employment in the nation as a whole. In contrast, environmentalists contended, big new energy facilities would provide far fewer jobs than industry spokesmen promised.

Several activists set up a new group in Washington, D.C., "Environmentalists for Full Employment," to promote those counterarguments.

The first concrete effort to forge an alliance of environmentalists, labor unions and community action groups took place at Black Lake, Mich., in May at a conference sponsored by the United Auto Workers Union (UAW) and other organizations.

"Contrary to what corporate America and the Ford administration would have the public believe," UAW President Leonard Woodcock told the gathering, "there is today more than ever before a common cause between union members and environmentalists, between workers, poor people, minorities and those seeking to protect our natural resources."

In spite of the efforts at detente, environmental and labor forces often clashed, as in battles in a number of states over mandatory deposit proposals for soda cans and bottles. Environmentalists said the requirement would clean up roadside litter, but industry and labor spokesmen warned that it would cost jobs and profits.

Another demonstration of the conflict came in March, when the EPA raised the hackles of environmentalists by granting an unusual extension of deadlines for water pollution abatement at several iron and steel plants along Ohio's Mahoning River Basin. The agency said the delay would save as many as 25,000 jobs.

Foreign Policy

Relations between the legislative and executive branches on foreign policy issues were far less turbulent in 1976 than in 1975. But when Congress did clash with executive branch objectives, lawmakers offered only the broadest outline of goals for the post-Vietnam War period.

Although the record of the second session suggested that a broad consensus on the U.S. role in the world had not yet emerged to replace the shattered 25-year-old policy of containment of communism, Congress on occasion tried to check presidential discretion in foreign affairs by foreclosing specific policy alternatives and by demanding a greater role in executive branch decisions.

Both strategies were embodied in the fiscal 1976-77 foreign military aid bill (HR 13680—PL 94-329) signed by President Ford June 30. The bill gave Congress authority to block by concurrent resolution proposed major weapons sales by the U.S. government, and it banned outright any military assistance or weapons sales to Chile. An even stronger version of the legislation (S 2662) had been vetoed by President Ford because of provisions that he said interfered with the executive branch's constitutional responsibilities for the conduct of foreign affairs.

But Congress in 1976 clearly demonstrated that it was uncertain under what circumstances the new tools for blocking the sales should be used. Lacking explicit foreign policy guidance from the administration, and unable to agree on a course of its own, Congress floundered.

Late in the session, for example, it backed away from a tentative decision by the Senate Foreign Relations Committee to prohibit the sale of Maverick air-to-ground missiles to Saudi Arabia after Secretary of State Henry A. Kissinger warned the committee that its action might precipitate a major increase in petroleum prices for American consumers. The reversal on this issue revealed that Congress chose to avoid taking action when political and economic consequences loomed costly.

The Senate committee also had demanded that the administration offer a comprehensive policy on U.S. alliances and on future arms sales to the Middle East by April 1, 1977. Divided over these policies itself, the panel was unanimous in calling on the executive branch to take the lead.

Confrontations With Ford

If Congress was unwilling to reduce the level of arms shipments to U.S. allies and friends because of possible economic reprisals, just as clearly neither house was willing to tolerate any substantial risk of military involvement in areas where no tangible U.S. strategic interest was at stake. When confronted with the risk of direct U.S. military or paramilitary involvement in Angola, Congress firmly rejected the administration's policy there, even though the White House had insisted it was essential to the national interest.

A Senate vote to ban U.S. aid to factions in the Angolan civil war succeeded by a wide margin in 1975, and the House sealed the ban in January 1976 by a decisive 323-99 vote. Without a direct threat to U.S. security, Congress was unwilling to risk another commitment reminiscent of the Vietnam experience.

Against White House wishes, Congress also clamped prohibitions on U.S. military assistance to Chile and Uruguay in 1976 because of alleged human rights violations perpetrated by those Latin American nations. But here the potential repercussions for the American public of a congressional ban were minimal.

The Election Year Factor

The session lacked the heated confrontations between the executive and legislative branches evident in 1975 on foreign policy matters. Both branches seemed reluctant to take bold positions that might antagonize any segment of the electorate during the election year.

At mid-year, Congress and the White House quietly resolved a dispute over aid levels for Israel for fiscal 1976 and the budget transition period, compromising on an issue fraught with danger for both political parties. And President Ford looked with favor on the Senate's decision to establish a permanent select intelligence committee to monitor the activities of the CIA, FBI and other components of the federal intelligence gathering apparatus.

Congress, in fact, came to the administration's rescue on at least three occasions during the strident Republican presidential primary race. The Panama Canal negotiations, U.S.-Soviet detente and the administration's new African policy were subjected to intense criticism by Republican presidential contender Ronald Reagan. In all three areas, Congress backed Ford's positions.

Detente Defended

Early in the 1976 primary campaign Reagan began denouncing detente as a "one way street," telling a New Hampshire audience that the United States had received no benefits from the policy more substantial than the "right to sell Pepsi-Cola in Siberia." Citing government estimates of higher Soviet military production, he challenged administration claims that U.S. military strength was second to none.

Ford's response was to emphasize his determination to "keep cool" in foreign affairs, "keep our powder dry" and avoid "nuclear holocaust." The implication was that a harder line in foreign policy could have catastrophic results.

On March 11 Secretary Kissinger struck back at Reagan. He charged that politically motivated criticism of American policy would wreck the nation's foreign policy. He declared that there was no alternative to the administration's policy of imposing penalties for Soviet adventurism while offering incentives to them for restraint.

"What do those who speak so glibly about one-way streets or pre-emptive concessions propose concretely that this country do?" Kissinger asked. "What precisely has been given up? What level of confrontation do they seek? What threats would they make...?"

On May 5 the Senate gave its support to the Ford-Kissinger policy toward the Soviet Union by approving a bipartisan resolution registering support for U.S.-Soviet negotiations on issues dividing Moscow and Washington.

But the so-called pro-detente measure initially had been debated by the Senate March 22 and then referred to the Foreign Relations Committee after Senate conservatives complained that the resolution's language indirectly criticized Reagan's presidential campaign. Language referring to "strident voices" critical of detente was expurgated from the resolution by the committee.

Panama Canal

Congress came to Ford's defense a second time in 1976 after Reagan charged that the Ford administration was about to "give away" the Panama Canal. The subject of quiet diplomatic talks in recent years, the canal became a full-blown issue in the Republican primaries when Reagan insisted that he intended "to keep it"; the White House responded that unless negotiations with the Panamanians continued on a new treaty that would grant some control over the operation of the Canal Zone to the Panamanians, violence and rioting like that which occurred in 1964 along the waterway might erupt again.

On June 18 the House stepped into the fray by voting 229-130 that the negotiations must "preserve the vital interests" of the United States. This was viewed as a vote of confidence in the administration's policy. Those who opposed the talks unsuccessfully attempted to win approval of language declaring that any new treaty must "perpetuate the sovereignty and control" of the United States over the canal—Reagan's position.

African Policy

Even some of the President's closest political advisers publicly suggested that Ford probably had picked the worst possible time for Secretary Kissinger to outline a new U.S. policy for southern Africa. On May 1, four days after Kissinger announced in Lusaka, Zambia, the administration's intention to support black majority rule on the continent, Ford was crushed by Reagan in the Texas Republican primary.

Reagan and his supporters had denounced Kissinger's April 26-May 6 African mission, leaving it once again for a bipartisan majority on Capitol Hill to back Ford by giving his African policy protection against the outcry from the conservative wing of the Republican Party. Throughout the remainder of the 94th Congress, Senate and House moderates and liberals clashed with conservatives over Kissinger's pledges of aid to revolution-torn African nations and his commitments to support majority rule in Rhodesia, Namibia and South Africa.

Carter-Ford Policy Debate

Stripped of its verbal punches, the Oct. 6 foreign policy debate between President Ford and Democratic presidential contender Jimmy Carter revealed that on the substance of foreign policy, the two candidates agreed on many issues. Both were blunt in insisting on preserving American military strength, supporting Israel, maintaining U.S. control over the operation of the Panama Canal and refusing to sacrifice commitments to Taiwan in the quest for detente with the People's Republic of China.

Although Carter and Ford differed completely on the level of arms the United States should sell abroad, an issue on which Ford became defensive during the debate, it was a difference in style that separated the two men most. Carter labeled the President a weak leader whose foreign policy decisions were made in secret, by his Secretary of State, without moral principles. Ford tried to picture the Democratic candidate as a person who totally lacked experience in foreign relations.

During the debate and throughout the campaign, Carter called for a "new moral authority"—a dedication to humanitarian principles and opposition to human injustice abroad—as the guidepost for the United States to follow in mapping relations with other nations.

But the Ford administration claimed that it conducted foreign policy on a moral basis as circumstances realistically allowed.

Defending the President's decision to intervene in Angola, Kissinger told the Senate Foreign Relations Committee Jan. 29 that "we chose covert means because we wanted the greatest possible opportunity for an African solution."

Although the American public was not told of the administration's covert activities in Angola, which Congress subsequently terminated, Kissinger noted that "eight congressional committees were briefed on 24 separate occasions" about administration plans.

Arab Boycott

After the foreign policy debate, Carter told a Salt Lake City audience that the President had always "shown a weakness in yielding to pressure." Carter then accused Ford of acquiescing to an Arab boycott of American companies that traded with Israel, or were owned by Jews, because of Arab threats to embargo or raise the price of oil shipped to the United States if it interfered.

The administration, he contended, had blocked legislation that would have required disclosure of information about companies taking part in the boycott. Ford, in a rebuttal statement during the debate, argued that his administration had taken decisive action against the boycott. The previous week, he said, "my administration went to Capitol Hill and tried to convince the House and Senate that we should have an amendment which would take strong and effective action against those [American firms] who participate or cooperate in the Arab boycott [of Israel]." (Ford had announced during the debate that he was ordering the Commerce Department to publish a list of all U.S. firms that had complied with Arab demands to boycott Israel. The directive took effect Oct. 7.)

Sen. William Proxmire (D Wis.), a leader of the anti-boycott fight in the Senate, said Oct. 7 that the President had tried to "seriously mislead the American people.... It was Congress that took the initiative on legislation to outlaw the boycott...and it was the Ford administration that blocked us at every step of the way."

But Congress did achieve some success in trying to diminish the effect of the boycott. A prohibition on taking certain tax deductions by U.S. firms that cooperated with the boycott was enacted as part of the 1976 tax revision bill (PL 94-455).

National Security

In response to a continuing Soviet military buildup and less resistance than in recent years to defense spending, Congress in 1976 endorsed the basic themes of the Ford administration's national security policy. To support U.S. commitments in Western Europe, Asia and the Middle East, President Ford called for—and Congress approved—a Pentagon budget that contained more than $7-billion in "real growth"—defined as an increase beyond that necessary to offset inflation.

Some major weapons were challenged on grounds of cost, particularly the B-1 bomber and additional nuclear-powered warships, and some congressional prerogatives were asserted in national security affairs. Congress insisted on having a voice in Pentagon decisions to close or substantially reduce civilian personnel at U.S. military bases, and the Senate established a new committee to oversee the operation of the CIA and other intelligence agencies. The House Armed Services Committee continued to support the uniformed services in disputes with Pentagon civilians over the management of Navy shipbuilding contracts and the development of a new Army tank.

But there was no serious congressional challenge to the administration argument that U.S. global commitments could be met only by expansion and continued upgrading of U.S. nuclear and conventional forces.

$14-Billion Increase Requested

In January the administration requested a $112.7-billion budget for the Pentagon for fiscal 1977, $8-billion more than the previous year's request and $14.4-billion more than the amount approved by Congress. Allowing for inflation, the 1977 request represented an estimated $7.2-billion increase in real spending for military programs. The final fiscal 1976 appropriation had provided $2-billion in real growth over the previous year's funding, but administration spokesmen conceded that approximately $1.5-billion of that amount was due to an overestimate of inflation in the fiscal 1976 budget request.

Beyond the increase necessary to compensate for anticipated inflation, the administration insisted that the requested real growth in the budget request was necessary to offset increases in Soviet military spending. The largest increase, proportionally, was in the request for weapons procurement: $29.3-billion, up 38 per cent from the fiscal 1976 request. According to the Pentagon, the surge in procurement spending, which included funds to begin production of the B-1 bomber, the Trident submarine-launched missile and the F-16 fighter plane, was in part a consequence of the Vietnam War. During that period, existing weapons were subjected to hard use, and new programs were deferred because of the cost of fighting the war.

To compensate in part for the programmed increases, President Ford proposed to restrain manpower costs by a series of changes in military fringe benefits that was to save $2-billion to $4-billion in fiscal 1977 and yield savings over five years of $13-billion to $28-billion. In each of the three fiscal years 1974-76, personnel related costs, including military retired pay, had comprised more than 54 per cent of the defense budget. Even with Ford's proposed changes, manpower costs made up over 51 per cent of the fiscal 1977 budget.

Supplemental Requests

On April 27 the President requested an additional $317-million to procure 60 Minuteman III intercontinental ballistic missiles and to equip them with a new, larger and more accurate warhead, the Mark 12A. Production of the missile had been scheduled to end in September 1976, but the administration had warned in January that it might request funds to continue Minuteman production if arms limitation talks with the Soviet Union bogged down. Congressional Democrats charged that the additional request, which was made four days before the Texas presidential primary election, was aimed less at the diplomatic intransigence of the Soviet Union than at the political success of Republican presidential candidate Ronald Reagan, who was belaboring Ford for allowing U.S. military strength to deteriorate. Despite some opposition, Congress approved the additional amount.

On May 4, three days after the Texas primary, in which Reagan overwhelmed Ford, the administration again amended its request by adding $974-million for five more warships—four antiaircraft escorts and an oiler—and $200-million for Navy research on combat aircraft capable of taking off and landing within a very short space, thus obviating the need for giant aircraft carriers.

Administration spokesmen denied Democratic charges that the additional request was politically motivated, insisting that it was based on a high-level study that had been underway for months and that the specific request was decided on by Ford at a White House meeting May 1, the day of the Texas primary.

On Aug. 23, after Congress had refused to fund two warships in the initial budget request and the four escort ships that had been requested in May, the President submitted a supplemental appropriations request of $1.1-billion for the six ships. But the House Democratic leadership insisted that the request could not be considered because it exceeded the already enacted fiscal 1977 congressional budget. On Sept. 27 the House Armed Services Committee tabled, and thus killed, the supplemental funds requested.

Congressional Support

Underlying Congress' support of the general outlines of the administration's defense budget was concern over the rapid growth of Soviet forces and growing suspicion of

Soviet intentions in the global arena. Reinforcing these attitudes were the rise of pro-defense attitudes by the public and the impact of the 1976 elections.

Military Balance

Early in 1975 administration warnings of growing Soviet military power, typically dismissed by critics as budgetary maneuvers, were effectively buttressed by three analyses of the Soviet military buildup:

● The "dollar model." It would cost the United States $114-billion (1974 dollars) to pay for the Soviet Union's 1975 military machine—40 per cent more than the United States actually spent on defense that year—according to a CIA analysis released in February. If the costs of military pensions were disregarded, the "dollar gap" was 50 per cent in favor of the Soviet Union. The analysis concluded that in real terms, Soviet military spending had increased by nearly 3 per cent annually since 1965, while U.S. spending had declined.

● The "ruble model." Roughly 15 per cent of the Soviet Union's $900-billion annual gross national product (GNP)—twice the proportion estimated earlier—went to military purposes, according to another CIA study. The U.S. military effort consumed about 6 per cent of its $1.5-trillion GNP. The new analysis added to the earlier estimates of Soviet defense costs the heavy burden of the Soviet policy of "hardening" and geographically dispersing industrial facilities to speed economic recovery from a nuclear attack.

● A Library of Congress study. "The quantitative military balance since 1965 had shifted substantially in favor of the Soviet Union," according to a Library of Congress study released Feb. 11 by the Senate Armed Services Committee. The study concluded that "U.S. qualitative superiority never compensated completely and, in certain respects, was slowly slipping away." The analysis, requested by committee member John C. Culver (D Iowa), reported Soviet advantages over the United States in numbers of men (4.8 million to 2.1 million), tanks (35,000 to 9,000) and armored personnel carriers (40,000 to 19,000).

Pentagon critics in Congress did not deny that the Soviet buildup required a U.S. response. But they maintained that the administration exaggerated the situation by assuming that the Soviet Union directed its military activity exclusively against the United States, ignoring their heavy commitments on the Chinese border and the need to police Eastern Europe.

They also insisted that the administration's argument understated the technological superiority of U.S. weaponry. Cost comparisons of U.S. and Soviet forces were meaningless since many U.S. technical advantages were beyond Soviet reach at any cost, they added.

But many of the leading congressional critics accepted the administration argument that military spending had to increase at a rate sufficient to offset the cost of inflation and, in addition, show some real growth in order to counter the Soviet buildup.

Doubting Detente

The perception of a rising Soviet military threat fed on a growing congressional suspicion of Soviet intentions. This hardening attitude followed a long sequence of Soviet actions, including incitement of the Arab combatants in the 1973 Middle East war, intransigence toward internal dissidents and toward Jews wishing to emigrate to Israel, and diplomatic and financial support of leftist revolutionary movements in Angola and elsewhere in southern Africa.

When Under Secretary of State Joseph J. Sisco explained to the Senate Budget Committee March 5 that such actions were not precluded by the concept of detente, committee Chairman Edmund S. Muskie (D Maine) demanded to know: "What in heaven's name is the difference between this and the Cold War?" And when Defense Secretary Rumsfeld appeared before the committee March 9, Henry Bellmon (R Okla.) suggested that the fiscal 1977 defense budget "recognizes the end of detente."

Reinforcing the skepticism about Soviet aims was a broader congressional concern triggered by the collapse of U.S. policy in Southeast Asia: that America's allies and adversaries might conclude that the United States lacked the will to maintain its other commitments. One result was strong and widespread congressional support for the administration's swift recourse to military force when Cambodian gunboats seized the U.S. merchant ship *Mayaguez* in 1975; another was widespread acceptance of the administration argument that cuts in the Pentagon budget could have a symbolically weakening effect on the international image of U.S. will.

Political Milieu

In 1976, as in 1972, relations with the Soviet Union were central issues in the election campaign, but the focus was different. In 1972 the policy of detente—Secretary of State Henry A. Kissinger's cultivation of a web of U.S.-Soviet cooperative ties—was the centerpiece of President Richard M. Nixon's carefully crafted image of statesmanship. Four years later, there was strong criticism in both major parties about what detente might be costing the United States in its continuing competition with the Soviet Union for political and military influence.

Conservatives of both parties had never been entirely comfortable with detente. In 1972 they questioned the sale of 400 million bushels of wheat to the Soviet Union on favorable terms and the arms agreement that allowed the Soviet Union a numerical superiority in land-based and sea-based ballistic missiles. During the 1970s there was increasing concern over Soviet reluctance to permit large-scale Jewish emigration. By late 1975, evidence of a Soviet military buildup, plus the continued Soviet commitment to leftist forces in the developing world, had fostered a suspicion of Soviet global intentions that was not limited to the political right wing.

These suspicions were amplifed by the presidential campaigns of Sen. Henry M. Jackson (D Wash.) and Republican hopeful Ronald Reagan. Both were long-time opponents of any accommodation with the Soviet Union on terms that they deemed too soft; both attacked the Ford administration for permitting what they viewed as the erosion of the nation's military strength.

Early in the campaign, Reagan began denouncing detente as "a one-way street," telling a New Hampshire audience that the United States had received no benefits more substantial than "the right to sell Pepsi-Cola in Siberia." Citing U.S. estimates of Soviet military production, he challenged administration claims that U.S. military strength was second to none. Jackson hit at the same themes, calling detente "a coverup for the gross mismanagement of the foreign policy of the United States."

Ford's response was to emphasize his determination to avoid "nuclear holocaust," implying that a harder line in foreign policy could have catastrophic results. He stressed his experience in foreign affairs and lamented that "nit-picking" challenges to the administration's foreign policy were not helpful to the country.

Although Ford was adamant in defense of his policies, there was evidence of a hardening of the administration's line on U.S.-Soviet relations. Critics charged that major areas of national security policy, including negotiations on a new strategic arms limitation (SALT) agreement with the Soviet Union, were being sacrificed to the President's renomination strategy. To avoid any last minute alienation of the Republican party's right wing, Ford acquiesced in changes in the party's 1976 campaign platform drafted by Reagan delegates that repudiated aspects of the Kissinger foreign policy.

In the campaign for the Democratic nomination, the "hard line" on national security policy was muted by the early failure of Jackson's campaign (the Washington senator withdrew from the race after losing to Jimmy Carter in the April 27 Pennsylvania primary). But the party showed no desire to challenge Ford on defense spending or on any other major aspect of the administration's national security policy.

The party's campaign platform adopted at its July convention called for a reduction of $5-billion to $7-billion in "present defense spending," a figure that had been used by nominee Jimmy Carter. But in the election campaign, Carter was careful always to emphasize that the reductions would be made by cutting fat and waste from the Pentagon budget rather than by reducing force levels or procurement programs.

Throughout the presidential campaign, independent candidate Eugene J. McCarthy was essentially alone in his position that "it's not the fat [in defense spending] that worries me; it's the lean that is causing all the trouble."

Whether as a cause or an effect of the campaign oratory, public support of defense spending showed a clear increase over past years. A Gallup Poll released March 7 reported that since September 1974 the proportion of respondents who felt that too much was being spent on defense dropped from 44 per cent to 36 per cent. The proportion responding that defense spending was too low rose from 12 per cent to 22 per cent. In both polls, 32 per cent of the samples said the level of defense spending was "about right."

In a May 1976 poll conducted for Potomac Associates by the Gallup organization, a national sample agreed by a margin of 52 per cent to 41 per cent that "the United States should maintain its dominant position as the world's most powerful nation at all costs, even going to the very brink of war if necessary." National samples had rejected the same statement in 1974 (42 per cent to 43 per cent) and in 1972 (39 per cent to 50 per cent).

The same series of polls showed an increase in the proportion of respondents supporting higher defense spending—from 9 per cent in 1972 to 17 per cent in 1974 and to 28 per cent in 1976.

A Louis Harris survey released in early October showed an even wider margin of support for defense spending. By a margin of 61 per cent to 23 per cent (14 per cent not sure), a national sample agreed that the United States should "make sure that our defense preparations and weapons are better than those of any other country, even if this means increasing defense spending."

The same Harris poll showed a narrow plurality (38 per cent to 43 per cent) rejecting a $5-billion to $7-billion cut in military spending.

"National Security" Aura

Despite the abuses of Nixon and previous Presidents, the exigencies of national security retained an aura of great political potency for Congress in 1976. To an overwhelming degree, Congress and the nation held the position that national security policy involved a special kind of risk that made it preferable to err on the side of too much rather than too little.

Symptomatic was the termination of the House investigation of alleged improprieties by the U.S. intelligence community and the stringent secrecy rules adopted by the Senate's newly created intelligence oversight panel. Another indication of the current attitude was the overwhelming rejection in both houses of moves to impose modest cuts in the congressional budget ceiling for defense (S Con Res 109) and in the actual amounts contained in the fiscal 1977 defense appropriations bill (HR 14262—PL 94-419).

Highlights of congressional action on national security policy in 1976 were:

● **Nuclear Strategy.** The administration continued without major congressional opposition to develop larger and more accurate intercontinental and submarine-launched ballistic missiles intended to give the United States a "flexible response," including the ability to make narrowly circumscribed nuclear strikes, to deter Soviet aggression short of a major attack on U.S. cities. Congress did defer advanced development of the sea-launched cruise missile, one of the major outstanding issues in strategic arms negotiations with the Soviet Union, and it delayed until Feb. 1, 1977, obligation of most of the funds requested to begin production of the B-1 bomber. But the B-1 delay—the year's only significant success for Pentagon spending critics—left to the winner of the November presidential election the decision on whether to go ahead with production of the $87-million plane.

● **Navy Rebuilding.** The administration won approval of its naval expansion program, although some projects were delayed by disagreement between the Senate and House over the proper emphasis to give nuclear-propulsion for surface warships. Funds were provided for the downpayment on a fifth giant nuclear-powered aircraft carrier after the ship survived by a 13-vote margin a move in the House to delay it for one year.

Emphasizing the necessity for budgetary restraint, the administration had requested a naval building program that included a mix of very costly nuclear-powered ships and less expensive conventional vessels that could be purchased in larger numbers. The Armed Services Committees of the Senate and House became deadlocked on the issue after the House panel had altered the administration's program to include more nuclear ships. A compromise shipbuilding program was finally approved, with the dispute over the future role of nuclear power for the surface fleet being deferred.

● **Intelligence Oversight.** The House investigation of alleged improprieties by the U.S. intelligence community did not lead to any institutional reforms in 1976.

Yielding to administration warnings that the House Select Intelligence Committee's draft report contained information that could, if released, endanger the national security, the House voted to embargo its publication (H Res 982). When a draft version was leaked to the press through CBS News reporter Daniel Schorr, the House directed its Committee on Standards of Official Conduct, the ethics committee, to investigate the disclosure (H Res 1042).

The Senate, following its probe of the intelligence agencies, created an intelligence oversight committee and, over administration objections, established a procedure allowing the full Senate, by majority vote, to disclose secret information over the objections of the executive branch (S Res 400). But the new Senate committee demonstrated its overriding concern for the protection of government secrets by adopting such stringent rules for handling classified information that committee members were prohibited from even discussing with senators not on the panel any information that was classified secret.

Housing and Urban Affairs

The nation's housing industry crawled out of its worst slump since World War II in 1976, but the modest recovery still left hundreds of thousands of construction workers without jobs.

The construction spurt coincided with the start-up of federally subsidized housing programs replacing those halted by the Nixon administration in 1973. But an increase in private homebuilding played the biggest part in the improvement, and federal housing policy remained basically unchanged.

The Ford administration continued to promote general economic recovery as the best way to stimulate construction. The Department of Housing and Urban Development (HUD) concentrated on the implementation of previously proposed programs. During his campaign, President Ford offered some proposals aimed at young families who wanted to own homes, but they were not expected to have a major impact on homebuying.

For their part, Democrats in Congress heaped election-year criticism on the Republican administration's housing record, but decided to wait until 1977 to consider new ways to meet the nation's housing needs. In fact, Congress decided that the old ways worked as well as any in some respects. It mandated a limited return to the public housing program begun in 1937 and abandoned as a failure by the Nixon administration in 1973.

Recovery

The new construction recovery moved along at a slow but steady pace in the early months of the year. Forecasts suggested that new housing starts might reach 1.5 million units in 1976, compared to 1.17 million units in 1975. Activity still remained far below the boom years of 1971-73 when construction began on more than 2 million units.

The building rate in September, announced two weeks before the Nov. 2 presidential election, was the highest since February 1974. The annual rate of starts that month was 1.81 million, 39 per cent higher than the pace in the same month in 1975. The number of construction permits issued in September, at an annual rate of 1.43 million units, also pointed to continued construction recovery.

The construction comeback was spotty. Starts of new single-family homes returned close to normal levels, but new apartment construction remained extremely sluggish during the first half of the year. Signs were more encouraging by September when the annual rate of multi-family housing starts jumped 46 per cent above the August rate.

Some analysts saw a connection between this improvement and a push by HUD just before the election for a speed-up in construction starts of federally subsidized and federally insured apartment projects. But HUD officials denied that the push had anything to do with politics.

HUD also used a program approved by Congress in 1974 to provide special support for apartment construction. The program authorized HUD to buy up mortgage loans at subsidized interest rates then passed on to private homebuyers.

The administration released $3-billion of the $5-billion appropriated by Congress in early January and the rest of the funding in September. HUD limited the purchases to mortgages on multi-family housing insured by the Federal Housing Administration (FHA).

The recovery also was uneven geographically. Starts in the Northeast showed the slowest and weakest improvement.

Demand, Costs, Credit

Demand for single-family homes was strong in many parts of the country, although some areas reported a continued backlog of unsold homes and condominiums. Buying reached frenzied levels in southern California; developers had to resort to lotteries in some cases to determine who could and could not buy new homes offered for sale.

But the steady march of increases in housing prices remained a problem for many. The median sales price of a new single-family home in August was $44,100, up $2,000 since the end of 1975. The average sales price of a new home reached a record high of $50,500 in September. Homebuyers paid a median sale price of $39,400 for an existing home in August, a $3,600 boost since December 1975.

And although mortgage credit was generally available, interest rates did not come down. Federal Home Loan Bank Board figures showed the effective interest rate on mortgages stuck at 9 per cent over the year. HUD did lower the rate on FHA-insured loans for single-family homes to 8 per cent in October; the rate was 9 per cent at the beginning of the year.

Arguing that these high prices and interest rates made it most difficult for young families to own homes, President Ford told HUD in September to implement an experimental mortgage payment program. The program, approved by Congress in 1974, allowed the FHA to insure mortgages requiring artificially low payments at the beginning that would increase gradually at the same time a family's income theoretically grew. But the program was expected to help only 3,000 families a year, according to HUD estimates.

The President also announced in September that he would try to help out these young families by asking Congress to lower the cash downpayments required to buy a home backed by an FHA loan. The proposal came too late for any congressional consideration in 1976.

Jobs

Unemployment in the building trades remained a persistent problem in 1976.

In October, the jobless rate in the construction industry still stood at 14.9 per cent, nearly twice the general unemployment rate of 7.9 per cent. Almost 700,000 construction workers were unemployed. Labor unions estimated that unemployment ranged as high as 60 per cent in some cities, due in part to cutbacks in capital spending by local governments.

Congress tried to remedy this problem by approving a special public works program, but President Ford vetoed the bill in February. Ford said he could support a proposal using the community development block grant program to channel more aid to areas with high unemployment rates. But Congress insisted on the public works approach, enacting a new bill (PL 94-369) in July over a second Ford veto.

There were glimmers of some improvement in the unemployment situation near the end of the year. The October jobless rate of 14.9 per cent, while high, was nearly three points below the July level.

Policy Clashes

While neither came up with any bold new solutions to the nation's housing problems, Congress and the Ford administration continued to clash over the operation of existing programs. Much of the dispute centered on a new rental subsidy program (Section 8) for low- and moderate-income families approved in 1974.

Congressional critics wanted the program accelerated and focused more on new construction instead of subsidies for existing housing. By the end of August, HUD had reserved contracts to provide subsidies on 376,000 units of housing, including roughly 145,000 units of newly built housing. Construction had started, however, on only 14,000 units and only 66,500 units were occupied. By Sept. 30, the number of occupied units had reached almost 90,000.

HUD officials argued that the pace of the program was on target and picking up all the time. They also defended the use of existing housing, pointing out that it was cheaper to subsidize old units than construct new units.

The critics also attacked slow progress under a homeownership subsidy program (Section 235) reactivated by HUD under court pressure in 1975. By the end of September, HUD had reserved contracts to subsidize mortgage interest rates on 17,800 homes.

The discontent prompted Congress to revive the old public housing program. Public housing supporters admitted that the program was not perfect, but maintained that it had built 1.2 million units while the Section 8 program had yet to prove its production potential.

HUD strongly opposed the revival, arguing that the "warehousing" approach of public housing was thoroughly discredited. The department also maintained that building public housing was more expensive than subsidizing rents.

Eventually, the two sides reached a compromise setting aside $85-million in fiscal 1977 appropriations for newly built housing projects. While it ordered the department to respect local desires for new construction subsidies, Congress agreed to let HUD spend most of its housing money on the rental subsidy program.

HUD went part way toward honoring another congressional policy during the year. In June, it announced a limited implementation of a mortgage aid program for the jobless approved by Congress in 1975.

HUD said it would take over payments for jobless homeowners only if they held federally insured mortgages while Congress approved a program for all unemployed satisfying certain conditions. Preliminary estimates through

September put applications for relief at 6,000; HUD had accepted 400 of the 3,000 applications it had processed.

Housing Discrimination

Racial discrimination in the housing field came under attack from several quarters in 1976.

In April, the Justice Department filed suit charging national lending and real estate appraisers' groups with following practices that effectively denied home loans to black and other minority applicants. Later the same month, a coalition of civil rights groups accused four federal bank regulatory agencies with taking inadequate steps to combat racial discrimination in mortgage lending practices. A June report by the Senate Banking, Housing and Urban Affairs Committee also gave an unsatisfactory rating to the agencies' enforcement of fair lending laws.

While these cases were aimed at private lending practices, the Supreme Court ruled in April that the federal government also could be required to remedy past racial segregation in public housing programs by offering subsidized housing to blacks in mostly white suburbs, HUD argued that any remedy must be confined to the city—in this case, Chicago—and could not involve the suburbs.

In return for a delay in full implementation of the ruling, HUD agreed in June to provide subsidized rental housing for 400 inner-city black families in mostly white areas of Chicago.

Aid to Communities

Like the housing comeback, the economic recovery of the cities was spotty in 1976. Some cities, mostly in the "Sun Belt," were booming. But other older cities continued to face economic problems like the ones that forced New York City to the brink of financial disaster in 1975.

Congress provided two bits of good news for these cities in 1975. It agreed to extend the general revenue-sharing program through Sept. 30, 1980, giving state and local government another $25.6-billion. It also enacted, over President Ford's veto, a $1.25-billion "countercyclical" aid program to help state and local governments avoid cutbacks in public services.

The New York City loan program approved by Congress during 1975 also ran fairly smoothly. While some members of Congress still wondered if the city could make it once it loses federal loan assistance in mid-1978, they found themselves impressed by the city's drastic sacrifices by the end of the year. The city repaid all federal loans it received in fiscal 1976 on time.

The government also continued operation of the community development block grant program, providing $3.25-billion for grants in fiscal 1977.

The block grant program, set to expire in October 1977, came under intense scrutiny by private groups during the year. Civil rights groups maintained that communities did not concentrate enough spending on the poor and did not offer enough opportunity for citizen participation in spending decisions.

Labor and Manpower

Confounding many economists and forecasters, unemployment during the first nine months of 1976 did not decline as much or as steadily as expected.

In his fiscal 1977 budget message, President Ford anticipated decreasing unemployment through 1976, with the jobless rate dipping below 7 per cent by 1977. The Congressional Budget Office, in conjunction with preliminary spending targets adopted by Congress in May, projected a downward trend settling in the range of 6.9 per cent to 7.3 per cent by the year's end.

Instead, the Labor Department's statistics, subject to revision at the end of the year, showed less encouraging conditions. The September unemployment rate of 7.8 per cent matched the figure recorded in January; after inching down to 7.3 per cent in May, the unemployment rate began to climb over the summer and hovered around 7.8 per cent for most of the third quarter. With the exception of the 1974-1975 recession—which officially "bottomed out" in May 1975 when the unemployment rate hit 8.9 per cent—the picture in 1976 still showed joblessness higher than at any time since World War II.

When Congress adjourned Oct. 2, 7.4 million persons—including 3.1 million men, 2.6 million women and 1.7 million teenagers—were unemployed. Throughout the year, all groups had exhibited higher than usual rates of joblessness: white males and household heads—although less prone to unemployment than other categories of workers—continued to experience unemployment rates above 5 per cent. Women, minority groups and young workers, however, were consistently least likely to find jobs.

Unemployment Trends

During the first three quarters of 1976, unemployment among adult women ranged from 7.1 to 7.6 per cent, compared to rates of 6 per cent or less for men. More adult women, especially those considered heads of households, were counted unemployed in 1976 than in 1975—the reverse of the trend among males.

As in the past, blacks were nearly twice as likely as whites to find themselves looking for work in 1976. Black unemployment rates fluctuated around 13 per cent, as compared with an average of about 7 per cent for whites. The jobless ranks also claimed around 19 per cent of teenaged workers, including between 35 per cent and 40 per cent of minority youth. And while unemployment among white teenagers tended to decline from 1975 to 1976, employment prospects for minority youth deteriorated.

Overall, against an annual average unemployment rate of 8.5 per cent for 1975, job markets in 1976 looked less bleak. The 1976 figures, nonetheless, threw assessments of the strength of recovery from the recession into doubt and continued to signal considerable economic hardship. On the basis of past trends, Bureau of Labor Statistics analysts estimated that the number of workers experiencing some unemployment (at least one week) during the course of a year was about 2½ to 3½ times as great as the average level. In the construction industry, where jobless rates stayed in the 15 to 17 per cent range over the first nine months of the year, at least one worker in three was expected to spend significant time without a job.

In addition to those officially counted unemployed, large numbers of Americans lacked jobs and gave up looking for them. Since mid-1975, however, the discouraged worker category shrank from well over one million to 800,000 workers, reflecting growing optimism about the availability of jobs.

But even as overall employment increased, millions of workers settled for less satisfactory arrangements than they originally had sought. For example, during the first three quarters of 1976, between three million and 3.3 million persons worked part-time despite preferences for full-time employment—about the same as the average numbers for 1975.

The full extent of underemployment was not apparent from the Labor Department figures, however, and a more complete profile would include information not currently compiled on how many workers accepted jobs with less pay, skill or status as their only alternative to unemployment.

Election Issue

As bad as the job figures looked, the 1976 election was no depression-era Democratic landslide. Though Jimmy Carter attempted to make the Ford administration's economic record a key issue throughout the campaign, he apparently had trouble getting the message across to the vast majority of Americans who still had jobs—and were not overly concerned about losing them.

According to a CBS News poll conducted on election day, 54 per cent of American voters considered "trust in government" the overriding issue of the election. Another 28 per cent named inflation, while jobs—the priority issue for only 17 per cent of the voters—finished a poor third.

Carter's speeches on unemployment may have sounded like a broken record to some of the American electorate—but not to organized labor. Unlike 1972, when the AFL-CIO remained neutral in the presidential race and several large unions backed Nixon, labor showed solid support for Carter.

With voter turnout low in most parts of the country, labor's efforts to bring out the union vote in key industrial states clearly helped save Carter from defeat. The same efforts also paved the way for a relatively easy sweep of the congressional races by the Democrats—and the election of most labor-supported House and Senate candidates. The choices of the AFL-CIO's Committee on Political Education (COPE), for example, won 19 Senate seats and 257 House seats in 1976. COPE had taken a side in 28 Senate races and 362 races in the House.

Labor's Image

Election results aside, 1976 did little to enhance the public image of organized labor. Federal investigations of the Teamsters' Union pension system unearthed serious mismanagement of its Central States Pension Fund—involving several hundred million dollars' worth of potentially "imprudent" loans to real estate, gambling and underworld enterprises. Although the Internal Revenue Service (IRS) revoked the fund's tax-exempt status in June, the union hoped that a thorough "housecleaning"— including replacement of most of the current trustees and adoption of new investment practices—might cause the government to reconsider. If put into effect, the IRS order would make the $1.4-billion fund liable for taxes on its earnings dating back to 1965.

In another sphere, members of the United Mine Workers (UMW) embarked on a housecleaning venture of a different sort. In an action reminiscent of the McCarthy period during the 1950s, UMW delegates attempted to purge their annual convention of Communist and leftist elements. The tactics, encouraged by challengers to the leadership of union president Arnold Miller, resulted in the expulsion of reporters from some publications amid threats of violence.

Collective Bargaining

At the bargaining table, labor took a sober, no-nonsense approach. During 1976, unions negotiated new agreements affecting an estimated 4.5 million workers—about twice the number covered by new contracts in 1975. Tough bargaining sessions were expected, as most contracts expiring in 1976 had last been negotiated in 1973 under wage and price controls—before the periods of "double digit" inflation and recession.

Despite fears of expensive, potentially inflationary labor demands, collective bargaining settlements in 1976 on the whole contained fairly moderate terms. During the first nine months of the year, wage increases averaged 8.9 per cent for the first year and 7 per cent annually over the life of the contract, compared to 1975 averages of 10.2 per cent and 7.8 per cent, respectively. In addition, major agreements in the construction, trucking and electrical equipment industries were reached quickly with a minimum of labor strife.

Prolonged strikes did occur over the summer in certain key industries—idling 60,000 rubber workers, 170,000 auto workers and about two-thirds of the nation's miners. The coal strikes, which the UMW leadership did not support, arose in protest over federal court "interference" in local disputes and only indirectly involved bargaining issues.

The striking rubber and auto workers, however, secured landmark contracts. Under the rubber workers' agreement, pay raises sharply exceeded the national averages, with wages increasing by 17.1 per cent during the first year and by an annual rate of 11.7 per cent over the three-year contract period. In contrast, the United Auto Workers sought smaller improvements in wages and benefits and aimed chiefly at a shorter work week, to encourage greater sharing of available employment within the auto industry. The model pact, negotiated with Ford Motor Co., guaranteed to phase in, by the end of the contract period, 12 new days off on top of the annual average of nearly 33 days of paid vacations and holidays already received.

Supreme Court Decisions

In key 1976 decisions affecting labor, the Supreme Court:

● By a 5-4 vote June 24 struck down provisions of 1974 legislation extending federal minimum wage and overtime coverage to state and local government employees. The 1974 amendments to the Fair Labor Standards Act had lifted the exemption from this coverage which state and local governments had previously enjoyed.

The ruling came in a pair of cases brought by 19 states, four cities, the National League of Cities and the National Governors' Conference. The states and cities had challenged the 1974 amendments as unconstitutional interference in their affairs. *(National League of Cities v. Usery, California v. Usery)*

● By a 5-3 vote March 24 upheld the right of courts to award retroactive seniority to persons who were denied jobs because of illegal sex or racial discrimination. Such a remedy would allow employees' seniority to date back to the time at which the company discriminatorily refused to hire or place them. The majority held that such awards were intended by Congress in passing the 1964 Civil Rights Act and should be made in most cases where they were sought by the victim of discrimination. *(Frank v. Bowman Transportation Co.)*

● By a 7-2 vote June 7 outlined stiffer standards for proving that job qualifications tests discriminate against minority applicants. The court held that as long as employers could show that written or other personnel tests bore a direct relation to job performance and did not intend to exclude particular groups, higher failure rates for minority applicants did not by themselves constitute sufficient evidence of job discrimination. *(Washington v. Davis)*

Agriculture

Agriculture programs were more affected in 1976 by the politics of a presidential election year than by major congressional action. As President Ford wooed the farm vote that he knew was essential for a Republican victory, he raised grain price support loan rates, cut off meat imports and lost his controversial Secretary of Agriculture.

Congress cleared only two pieces of major agriculture legislation in 1976. The first (HR 8529—PL 94-214) freed rice growers from the production restrictions of the old quota system and placed rice on the same "target price" system that was set up in 1973 for wheat, corn and other feed grains. The second measure (HR 12572—PL 94-582) tightened up the scandal-plagued U.S. grain inspection process by requiring federal inspection of grain at most export port locations and requiring private and state inspection agencies at inland locations to meet strict federal criteria.

Personnel Problems

As President Ford struggled to win the Republican nomination and then the presidency, several personnel problems affected both his campaign and agricultural matters.

The most publicized incident involved Agriculture Secretary Earl L. Butz, who was forced to resign Oct. 4 as a result of what he termed a "gross indiscretion" on his part.

Butz, who had served as Secretary of Agriculture since Dec. 2, 1971, was quoted in several national magazines as having made a disparaging remark about black Americans following the Republican national convention. It was not the first time Butz had misspoken; in 1974 President Ford reprimanded him for telling a joke about the Pope and birth control methods that offended numerous Catholics. Ford again reprimanded Butz Oct. 3 for his most recent comment, but the severe public outcry, combined with criticism by Democratic candidate Jimmy Carter, proved to be too much, and Butz submitted his resignation.

Farm groups and individual farmers expressed regret at Butz's departure. He had overseen the changes in agricultural policy that, since 1973, moved farmers away from government subsidies and toward bigger incomes, and they saw him as one of their strongest supporters. He was replaced by Under Secretary of Agriculture John A. Knebel.

Another loss to Ford earlier in the campaign year was the resignation of his campaign manager, Howard H. (Bo) Callaway Jr. Callaway quit in March after accusations surfaced that he had used his previous position as Secretary of the Army to pressure the U.S. Forest Service, a branch of the Agriculture Department, into aiding his Colorado ski resort.

The Senate Interior Subcommittee on the Environment and Land Resources held hearings on the matter and concluded by a 5-4 party-line vote that Callaway had indeed done so; the five Republican members of the Interior Committee submitted minority views to the subcommittee's September report, saying the whole inquiry was politically motivated.

Farm Vote Sweeteners

The Ford campaign, finding disaffection in the traditionally Republican farm areas, set out to win farmers back into the Republican fold.

Ford's selection of a farm state senator, Robert Dole of Kansas, as his vice presidential running mate was viewed as one effort to make points in the farm belt.

One of Ford's most startling actions in his wooing of the farm vote was the increase in loan rates for wheat, corn and other feed grains he announced on Oct. 13. The administration had opposed large increases in loan rates since Ford vetoed the emergency farm bill in 1975, and as late as September 1976 the Agriculture Department said there would be no raises in loan rates.

But with bumper crops expected in both corn and wheat and commodity prices dropping as a result of the expected surplus, farmers, along with challenger Carter, began calling for higher loan rates to protect their investments. In the middle of November, wheat was selling for under $3 a bushel, as compared to more than $4 a bushel a year earlier. Corn, while not down as much as wheat, was still lower than the year before.

Denying that the move was politically motivated, Knebel announced the new loan rates Oct. 13 for 1976 and 1977 crops: a 50 per cent jump for wheat, to $2.25 a bushel from $1.50, and a 20 per cent hike for corn, to $1.50 from $1.25 a bushel. The loans are sought by farmers when they need cash for production expenses and cannot get the market prices they want. They can borrow at the government rates and have a year to repay the loan, with interest and storage costs added, before the government takes possession of the grain.

Additional sweeteners were offered to livestock producers, dairy farmers and sugar producers in September and October. The administration tripled the duty on imported sugar, raised dairy price supports for the quarter beginning Oct. 1 and established a 1976 quota for imported meat of 1.23 million pounds. It was the first time a quota had been instituted since the 1964 meat act was passed and represented an effort to keep foreign supplies from further harming an already depressed American livestock market.

Drought

One of the most serious problems affecting American agriculture during 1976 was a severe drought in the upper Midwest. As of the last week in August, 188 counties in North Dakota, South Dakota, Minnesota and Wisconsin had been declared disaster areas. Unable to grow feed for their livestock, farmers were slaughtering herds in record numbers. Congressional leaders from the affected states charged the administration with inadequate disaster efforts and criticized the proliferation of federal disaster programs, each with such particular eligibility requirements that many farmers found themselves unable to participate.

In response to the drought, Congress extended through fiscal 1978 the provisions of the Emergency Livestock Credit Act of 1974, which authorized federal guarantees of loans by private lenders to financially troubled livestock producers. In addition, Congress increased the federal payment for costs of transporting hay to disaster areas.

On Oct. 15 the administration eased the rules allowing farmers to borrow money at low emergency interest rates to cover natural disaster losses. At the end of October a special Cabinet-level committee was formed to coordinate and speed up aid to the drought areas.

Crop Reports, Prices

Despite the severe Midwest drought, American farmers again produced bumper wheat and corn crops in 1976. In its November report, the Agriculture Department predicted that U.S. farmers would harvest 6.06 billion bushels of corn, 5 per cent more than the 1975 record crop. The wheat crop was estimated at 2.13 billion bushels, slightly less than 1975. Soybeans, however, were expected to be 18 per cent less than last year.

The department said the huge crops would mean more than enough grain for domestic and export needs and an increase in the carryover of stocks for 1977. Such surpluses, the department said, should hold retail food price rises down to 3 per cent through mid-1977.

But those bumper crops caused concern among farmers. The large carryover and the drop in exports predicted by the department caused prices received by farmers to drop successively each month between July and October.

As of Oct. 1, farmers were holding a record amount of wheat off the market, trying to drive the price up. In addition, the amount of wheat under government loan nearly doubled during the month of October—the month Ford announced the increase in federal loan rates—to 80.4 million bushels from 42.7 million bushels. In October 1975 only 18.3 million bushels were under loan.

One of the contributing factors to this surplus so despised by farmers was the reduced export demand for U.S. commodities. Despite a severe drought in Western Europe, the Food and Agriculture Organization of the United Nations predicted that total world cereal production in 1976 would be 6 per cent more than 1975, with the harvest in the Soviet Union again providing a key to the world grain situation.

In 1975, the Soviet Union produced only 140 million tons of grain, while the 1976 harvest was estimated to be more than 215 million tons. As a result, the Soviets were expected to import only about eight million tons of U.S. grain, compared to 26 million tons in 1975-76. Under terms of the grain agreement that became effective Oct. 1, 1976, the Soviet Union must import between six and eight million tons of U.S. grain a year.

Law Enforcement and Judiciary

As in the previous year, Congress during 1976 cleared few bills in the law enforcement area. The only major piece of legislation enacted was a three-year extension of the Law Enforcement Assistance Administration (LEAA).

The two biggest issues held over from 1975—gun control and revision of the federal criminal code—ran into roadblocks by the summer of 1976 that were never overcome. Legislation on domestic intelligence activity and wiretapping drew congressional attention but also did not pass either chamber during the session.

Gun Control

The intense interest and drive in early 1975 for legislation to curb the proliferation of handguns sputtered into 1976 but ultimately succumbed to election-year jitters. After a number of delays, the House Judiciary Committee reported a handgun bill (HR 11193) on May 6, but the bill was never brought to the House floor. Many House members were not eager to face gun control legislation in an election year, and reports in early summer indicated that Senate Majority Leader Mike Mansfield (D Mont.) had ruled out Senate consideration of gun control legislation so close to the election.

However, the House was almost caught by a strict handgun bill passed by the District of Columbia government. Under existing law, the District bill would automatically become law unless disapproved by Congress. Rep. Ron Paul (R Texas) introduced a disapproving resolution in August, but was unsuccessful in bringing it to the House floor and House members avoided a controversial vote.

Criminal Code Revision

The 750-page bill (S 1) codifying and revising the federal criminal code was also a victim of congressional inaction in 1976. In this case the roadblock was a disagreement between liberals and conservatives over several key sections of the revised code.

A draft bill had been reported by the Senate Judiciary Subcommittee on Criminal Laws and Procedures in 1975, but a number of provisions were strongly opposed by the American Civil Liberties Union and other groups. Senate leaders proposed deleting the most controversial provisions, which involved espionage, wiretapping and the death sentence, which they said constituted only about 10 per cent of the entire code. They hoped that this compromise would save the rest of the badly needed revised code, which would replace the existing jumble of federal criminal statutes. The liberals and conservatives on the committee, however, chose to negotiate on the controversial provisions. Despite numerous meetings, the two groups never reached agreement and the bill stayed in the Senate Judiciary Committee.

Wiretapping and Intelligence Activities

During 1976, both House and Senate also spent considerable time investigating domestic intelligence activities, although no legislation resulted.

The temporary Senate Select Committee on Intelligence Operations issued a lengthy report April 28, detailing its recommendations for curbing intelligence activities by federal agencies within the United States. Citing a broad range of spying activity in past years against U.S. citizens by those agencies, the committee stated, "Too many people have been spied upon by too many government agencies and too much information has been collected." The committee recommended that most domestic intelligence activity be handled by the FBI, subject to a legislative charter and stronger oversight within the Justice Department and also by Congress. The committee also recommended more stringent control of intrusive investigative techniques, such as wiretapping, mail surveillance and the use of informants.

Two days later the National Wiretap Commission released its final report urging that the use of wiretaps be expanded in order to aid law enforcement agencies in domestic criminal cases and that regulations for obtaining those wiretaps be eased.

Existing law has no requirement for judicial warrants for wiretapping in the United States to obtain foreign intelligence information. Legislation (S 3197) detailing requirements for warrants in such situations was introduced March 23 with the support of the administration and congressional members of both political parties. Both the Senate Judiciary Committee and the permanent Intelligence Committee created in May reported the bill during the summer, but opposition led by John V. Tunney (D Calif.) and civil liberties groups stalled the bill and prevented its reaching the floor before the end of the session.

In other activity relating to wiretapping, Congress again ran into administration roadblocks caused by claims of executive privilege. The House Government Operations Subcommittee on Government Information and Individual Rights subpoenaed records and testimony regarding federal interception of commercial overseas cables and telex messages. Five subpoenaed agents of the FBI and the National Security Agency refused to testify under an administration order of executive privilege and the subcommittee Feb. 25 recommended they be cited for contempt of Congress. The full committee took no action on the recommendation.

Later in the year, the House Interstate and Foreign Commerce Subcommittee on Oversight and Investigations subpoenaed records of the American Telephone and Telegraph Company (AT&T) regarding national security wiretaps. U.S. District Court Judge Oliver Gasch granted a permanent injunction July 30 prohibiting release of the records, thereby upholding the administration claim that release of the records would jeopardize national security. When the subcommittee appealed that decision, the U.S. Court of Appeals urged the parties involved to try for a better compromise. Negotiations were underway in early 1977.

Assassination Committee

At the end of 1976, the House opened still another investigation into the 1963 and 1968 assassinations of President John F. Kennedy and civil rights leader Rev. Dr. Martin Luther King Jr. On Sept. 29, the House voted to appropriate $150,000 for initial staff activities of the new Select Committee on Assassinations. Supporters of the committee said that further investigation of the two assassinations was "badly needed...at the earliest possible time."

The committee will have to be re-created by the 95th Congress, given additional funding and a new chairman. The former chairman, Thomas N. Downing (D Va.), retired at the end of the 94th Congress.

On Oct. 4, Downing named Philadelphia lawyer Richard A. Sprague as chief counsel of the new committee. Sprague led the investigation and prosecution of former United Mine Workers Union President W. A. (Tony) Boyle for the 1969 murder of Boyle's UMW rival Joseph A. Yablonski.

Judiciary

The Supreme Court ended its 1975-76 term on July 6—a term that included major decisions on the death penalty, criminal law rulings, libel and Congress' power to limit campaign contributions as well as the first participation of the newest justice, John Paul Stevens.

On July 2, just before adjournment, the court finally ruled on several cases involving the death penalty that had been held over from the previous term. By a 7-2 vote the court ruled that a sentence of death is not in itself cruel and unusual punishment in violation of the Constitution. In a separate vote, the court upheld the death penalty laws of Georgia, Texas and Florida, which provided for a two-part sentencing procedure allowing for consideration of the character and record of the defendant separate from the finding of the guilty verdict. The court overturned the laws of North Carolina and Louisiana, which provided for a mandatory death sentence in certain cases.

In the criminal rulings, also handed down at the end of the term, the court restricted the right of state prisoners to request federal courts to release them or request a new trial, based on a writ of habeus corpus, and held that several types of search and seizure were not in violation of defendants' constitutional rights.

Stevens' participation in court rulings did not become apparent until late in the 1975-76 term; observers noted that his decisions fit the moderate description that had been given at the time of his nomination. In some instances Stevens sided with the liberal contingent on the court, in others with the conservative side. He wrote several opinions and dissented more frequently than several of his colleagues, though he participated in fewer cases.

During 1976 Congress delayed several bills creating new federal judgeships. The Senate on April 1 finally passed the bill (S 287) creating additional federal district judgeships, after media charges that the delay was strictly a partisan move to hold onto the important judicial appointments for a possible Democratic president. The House never acted on the bill, however, nor on a bill (S 286) passed in 1975 creating additional federal appellate judgeships.

Crime Statistics

The FBI reported Sept. 23 that thefts increased 11 per cent and violent crimes declined 6 per cent during the first six months of 1976. The result was a 3 per cent increase in the overall crime rate compared with an 11 per cent increase for the comparable period in 1975.

Some of the increase in theft was considered to be drug related, but there were no major changes in the government's war on drugs in 1976. The Permanent Subcommittee on Investigations of the Senate Government Operations Committee July 18 released an interim report (S Rept 94-1039) on its continuing investigation of federal narcotics enforcement.

The 200-page report explained in great detail the problems encountered by federal law enforcement agencies involved with narcotics control since the Drug Enforcement Administration (DEA) was created by executive order on July 1, 1973. The report was issued to consolidate conclusions reached by the subcommittee after hearings held in the summer of 1975, as it prepared for additional hearings in July 1976.

The subcommittee found that during the three years of DEA's existence the drug trade had grown. It said DEA's "track record had not been good" and Congress had no assurance that it would improve.

Consumer Policy

Consumer protection issues continued to take a back seat to economic problems on the congressional agenda in 1976, leaving consumer groups hoping for a Democratic administration in 1977 to give their proposals new impetus.

The long-time legislative priority of consumer groups—creation of a federal agency to represent consumer interests before other agencies and the courts—died once again at the end of the 94th Congress.

The House and Senate passed slightly different versions of the consumer agency proposal in 1975, but sponsors abandoned it at the end of 1976 without even sending it to conference. It appeared unlikely that they could have mustered the votes to override President Ford's promised veto in an election year in which "big government" had become the number one enemy.

Ford, meanwhile, proceeded to put into effect his counterproposal—a series of "consumer representation plans" that involved appointing one official in each of 17 executive branch departments to listen to consumer complaints and represent their interests in the departments' policy deliberations.

Ford said his approach recognized "the consumer's right to be heard" without adding an expensive new layer to the federal bureaucracy. Consumer spokesmen were nearly unanimous in denouncing the plans as a meaningless gesture designed to cover up the President's insensitivity to consumer issues.

Another long-debated legislative goal of the consumer forces, a national no-fault auto insurance plan, was defeated by a narrow margin in the Senate in March. Its popularity was diminished by reports that many state no-fault laws were not working as well as expected, and by opposition from the Ford administration and lawyers' organizations.

Congress did pass a major antitrust enforcement bill hailed by supporters as a boon to consumers. The key provision authorized state attorneys general to bring triple damage antitrust suits on behalf of citizens.

These *"parens patriae"* suits were considered especially effective in deterring or remedying price-fixing violations that hike up the price of everyday items like soda pop, bread and toothpaste—costing individual consumers only a few cents or dollars extra, but adding up to millions of dollars in overcharges.

The Ford administration sided with business groups in opposing some features of the bill, and the measure was modified in response. The President agreed to sign the final version in October, citing his administration's firm "commitment to antitrust enforcement."

Political Activity

The consumer groups' frustration with Ford administration policies and their desire to increase their influence on a wide range of national issues led them deeper into politics in 1976.

The Consumer Federation of America, the largest national organization, endorsed congressional candidates for the first time—a move facilitated by a change in the tax code. The federation based its endorsements on ratings of incumbents' voting records. Ralph Nader's Public Citizen group also rated members' voting records in 1976.

Most consumer groups stopped short of endorsing presidential candidates, but Democratic nominee Jimmy Carter was their obvious favorite. He pledged support for the consumer protection agency, called for an end to the close relationship between industry and federal regulatory agencies and promised to listen to consumer spokesmen.

To dramatize their frustration with Ford, a coalition of eight national and state consumer groups in September issued a mock indictment accusing the President of conspiring with business groups to "endanger the health and safety and rip off the wallets of the consumers of the United States...in violation of the most basic principles of fairness and participatory democracy."

The 82 counts of the "indictment" reflected the expanding interests of consumer groups. They ranged from traditional concerns such as food additives and auto safety to complex economic and energy policy questions such as oil company divestiture and tax breaks for big companies.

Consumer and public interest groups had their usual problems raising sufficient funds to support their activities. The Citizen Action Fund, organized in 1976 by several national groups to alleviate that problem, began channeling money to consumer and environmental groups around the country. The fund got started with money raised at benefit showings of the Watergate movie, "All the President's Men."

The U.S. Chamber of Commerce established its own citizen lobby group in 1976, called Citizens' Choice, to press for restrictions on federal regulations and oppose proposals like the consumer agency which the chamber viewed as an expensive, bureaucratic response to problems that are "largely individual."

Regulatory Agencies

The complex and controversial issue of "regulatory reform," a subject of interest to consumer groups, continued to be studied and discussed in 1976, but major initiatives were put off for the new administration.

House and Senate committees began to issue findings and make recommendations resulting from studies of regulatory reform begun in 1975. The House Interstate and Foreign Commerce Subcommittee on Oversight and Investigations issued a series of reports in October analyzing the performance of nine key independent agencies.

The panel found all of the agencies guilty of the "critical defect" of paying too much attention to "the special interests of regulated industry" at the expense of the broader public interest. It gave the highest marks for efficiency and responsiveness to the public interest to the Securities and Exchange Commission, the Federal Trade Commission (FTC) and the Environmental Protection Agency. At the bottom of the list were the Interstate Commerce Commission and the Federal Power Commission.

The subcommittee's recommendations for improving the agencies included proposals to increase public participation, isolate agency officials from White House and industry pressures and open more agency proceedings to public view.

The proposal for a "congressional veto" over federal regulations was debated repeatedly in Congress in 1976. The Ford administration said it violated constitutional principles, while consumer and environmental groups opposed it on grounds that it would interfere with agency procedures and give industry lobbyists a second chance to defeat health and safety regulations designed to protect the public.

A proposal to require top regulatory officials to disclose financial holdings that might pose a conflict of interest gained popularity and was attached as an amendment to several bills during the year.

Three of the federal agencies most closely concerned with consumer issues—the FTC, Food and Drug Administration and Consumer Product Safety Commission—experienced leadership changes in 1976 and felt "regulatory reform" pressures.

Consumer Product Safety Commission. Congress completed action in April on legislation authorizing funds for the Consumer Product Safety Commission and revising the 1972 law that created the newest federal regulatory agency.

The measure increased the commission's authority to conduct its own litigation and also specifically barred it from regulating cigarettes, guns or ammunition—touchy issues the young agency preferred to avoid.

The Senate confirmed S. John Byington, President Ford's nominee to replace the first chairman of the commission, after a long and bitter battle over his qualifications.

Consumer groups opposed the nomination, arguing that Byington was a Ford administration loyalist who lacked the independence and experience to lead the commission—especially during a period of growing pains. The Senate finally approved Byington after the President agreed to nominate him for a two-and-one-half-year term instead of a seven-year term.

Echoing consumer complaints, the General Accounting Office reported in July that the commission had not been "timely and systematic in assuring industry compliance with safety requirements." Byington agreed that there was room for improvement, and appointed a special task force which came up with a reorganization plan in September.

Food and Drug Administration. The Food and Drug Administration (FDA) continued to draw criticism from Congress and consumer activists dissatisfied with its drug approval and other procedures.

Sen. Edward M. Kennedy (D Mass.) held follow-up hearings on charges first publicized by two subcommittees in 1974 that the FDA often was swayed by industry pressures to approve new drugs for marketing and had punished employees who resisted those pressures.

Kennedy and other critics were unconvinced that the charges had been adequately investigated. A second report on the charges, issued by a Department of Health, Education and Welfare panel, called for further investigation—so yet another report was expected in 1977.

The agency also was criticized during the year for relying too heavily on advisory panels in an effort to escape responsibility for hard decisions, and for laxity in supervising testing of new drugs.

Hearings and preliminary discussions got underway in the House and Senate on proposed legislation to require more detailed labeling of prescription drugs and increase the FDA's power to halt sales of potentially dangerous drugs and food additives.

Also under discussion was a proposal by Kennedy to split the FDA into two separate agencies—one dealing with food and cosmetics, the other with drugs and medical devices—on the theory that two units would be more efficient and manageable. The House subcommittee's regulatory reform report proposed merging the FDA with the Consumer Product Safety Commission and National Highway Traffic Safety Administration to form one consumer safety and health agency.

Congress cleared legislation in 1976 increasing the FDA's authority to control medical devices but did not finish action on two Senate-passed measures on cosmetics and food regulation.

Alexander M. Schmidt, FDA commissioner since 1973, announced he would retire at the end of 1976, but insisted that the many controversies surrounding the agency had not contributed to his decision.

Federal Trade Commission. Calvin J. Collier, a former administration budget official and FTC general counsel, was confirmed for a seven-year term on the commission in March and appointed chairman. Collier was expected to continue the emphasis on antitrust enforcement established by his predecessor, Lewis F. Engman.

The commission began antitrust investigations of the auto industry, women's apparel industry and industry trade associations. It continued to fight large companies in court for access to information about profits, sales and advertising expenditures by product ("line-of-business") and to seek other corporate data useful in determining the degree of competition in the economy.

The U.S. Chamber of Commerce told Congress that the commission, with the new regulatory powers granted to it in recent years, had become "the second most powerful legislative body in the United States."

The Senate passed a bill aimed at beefing up the commission's antitrust program and assuring its independence from the White House. The House took no action on the measure.

Congress and Government

Events in the executive and congressional branches of the federal government were heavily influenced in 1976 by the fall elections for the House, Senate and presidency.

With government credibility an important voter concern, Congress passed legislation opening up the activities of many federal agencies to closer public scrutiny and began serious consideration of another proposal that, if enacted in later years, would require periodic re-evaluation of ongoing programs.

Politics also was the motivating force behind quick action to correct deficiencies found by the Supreme Court in the 1974 campaign finance law that halted federal subsidies to presidential aspirants. A second bill with an important political impact would have allowed thousands of federal workers to participate in partisan political activities, but it died under a presidential veto. And a third, which was never passed, would have allowed mass-mailing of postcards to build up voter registration.

The political year was evident too in several internal congressional matters. A sex and payroll scandal involving a powerful House member, which unleashed charges by some employees of similar hanky-panky in other Hill offices, caused much embarrassment in Congress and threatened the political lives of members—at least in their own eyes. The extent of the potential or imagined political threat was seen in the swiftness with which pressure was brought by House members on the congressman, Rep. Wayne L. Hays (D Ohio), to resign his positions of influence (he eventually even resigned his seat in Congress). It was also seen in the speed at which Democrats developed, unfurled and publicized a set of changes in House procedures designed to prevent future power abuses of the type for which Hays was well known. However, Congress did nothing to change the fundamental employment practices that many observers believed were at the root of the problem exemplified by the Hays controversy.

In related matters with an election-year connection, Congress killed an automatic pay raise it granted itself just a year earlier, refused to sanction televising of Senate and House proceedings and never quite got around to passing a bill requiring extensive disclosure of members' outside income and other financial holdings.

Government

Congress in 1976 made no fundamental changes in the operation of the federal government, but it enacted an important law that required some federal agencies—primarily the independent regulatory bodies—to open more of their proceedings to public view. Congress also began serious consideration of proposals to terminate outdated or unproductive government programs.

But the legislators did not pass major proposals to strengthen the loophole-ridden lobby regulation law and to increase voter registration for federal elections through the use of postcards. The latter was a victim of election-year pressures.

The 1976 elections, however, were the motive force behind Congress' early-year action to reconstitute the Federal Election Commission after the Supreme Court ruled that the law creating the body was defective.

Open Government. After four years of debate on the issue of secrecy in government, Congress passed a bill, popularly known as the "sunshine law," which required more than 50 agencies and commissions to open their meetings to the public. The legislation had been given its most vigorous push by Washington-based "citizens" organizations which charged that excessive secrecy was a major reason for the public's declining confidence in the federal government.

Program Reauthorization. This proposal, popularly called the "sunset" bill and also strongly backed by "citizens" groups, required many government programs to be reauthorized periodically by Congress or die. The bill was reported by a Senate committee but got no further before Congress adjourned.

Lobby Regulation. A bill to strengthen the federal lobby disclosure law died in the last moments of the 94th Congress, a victim of procedural moves in the Senate. The bill, strongly opposed by major lobby organizations in Washington, required extensive public disclosure of lobbying activities.

Postcard Registration. Election-year pressures were the key factor in the death of this bill, which was backed largely by the Democrats. The bill would have allowed persons to register to vote in federal elections by sending a postcard with necessary information on it to local registration officials. Under the original bill, the postcards were to be mass-mailed to all persons of voting age. That provision was dropped in the House. Nevertheless, the postcards would have been available in post offices and for door-to-door voter registration drives, and even that possibility was more than Republicans could accept. Republicans publicly said they feared widespread fraud but privately they acknowledged that mass registration efforts were more likely to benefit Democrats than the GOP. The bill never came up in the Senate where a filibuster was expected.

Hatch Act. This bill also was a victim of the 1976 election year. Much desired by organized labor, it removed the long-standing legal prohibition on partisan election work by federal employees. The bill passed Congress but was vetoed by the President; an override attempt failed. Critics said the bill would politicize the civil service, but Republicans also feared that the ranks of federal employees were heavily Democratic and would hurt GOP efforts.

Federal Election Commission. In early 1976, Congress rewrote large parts of the 1974 federal election law after the Supreme Court ruled in January that the Federal Election Commission could not be appointed partly by Congress and partly by the President, as the law stipulated. This decision halted the commission's authority to implement the law, including the distribution of tax dollars to presidential candidates under the campaign financing sections. Both parties, and the Democrats in particular, thus had a special incentive to reconstitute the commission quickly as a strictly presidentially appointed body. But Congress went beyond that action and made numerous other changes in the 1974 law.

Copyright Law. In another major action, Congress passed legislation overhauling the nation's copyright law for the first time since 1909. The existing body of law had long been outdated by technological developments in such areas as motion pictures, recording and photocopying.

Congress

It was not a particularly good year for Congress as an institution.

This branch of government was troubled and embarrassed by sex and payroll scandals, by abuses of House travel allowances benefits by a few members, by allegations of campaign finance law violations, by conflict of interest charges and by inaction on various proposals to halt these problems.

Some of the bad press Congress received was due to normal election year pressures, some to the lack of strong leadership in both chambers and some simply to the expected foibles of a body composed of diverse personalities and interests.

Moreover, the year was not without some redeeming events for Congress. Both chambers completed the first full year under stringent open meeting requirements for committee work sessions. In the Senate, two special committees began to examine the procedural and management problems of the chamber as well as the all-important committee structure. In the House, special committees studied the chamber's housekeeping and administrative practices and other rules to see whether additional changes beyond those made in recent years were called for.

Nevertheless, the image Congress projected to the public was not favorable. The principal element in this picture was the revelation in the spring that powerful Rep. Wayne L. Hays (D Ohio) maintained a woman on his official payroll to serve as his mistress. The woman, Elizabeth Ray, said she did no congressional work for the pay and possessed no office skills.

The revelations, which were first made by Ray to newspaper reporters, led initially to Hays resignation as chairman of the House Administration Committee and the Democratic Congressional Campaign Committee, which hands out campaign money to Democratic candidates, and eventually, on Sept. 1, from his seat in Congress.

More significant than his departure, however, were House reforms that followed the publicity about the sex-payroll controversy. Over the years, Hays had built his Administration Committee into a power base by getting the House to grant it authority to provide allowances and other perquisites (such as office space, mechanical equipment and so on) that make life more comfortable for members.

A few months after the Hays-Ray scandal broke, the House took back from the committee many of these powers and vested final decisions on them in the full House. The legislators also made other changes in internal procedures designed to prevent similar abuses of power and to make the House look better in the public's eye. The changes were

engineered by Democrats and criticized by Republicans who charged that they were a whitewash of the scandal and were inadequate as reforms.

Elizabeth Ray's revelations brought forth from some other women complaints that they, too, had had to submit to sexual advances by members to retain their jobs or to advance to better positions and higher salaries. These charges were supplemented by broader-based complaints that Hill working conditions were among the most unpleasant in Washington. Women charged that they seldom could rise to top-paying positions and often were required to do equal work with men for much less pay. For all employees, it was widely acknowledged that Hill staffers often were hired for political rather than merit reasons, had no job protection whatsoever, usually worked extremely long hours and often were required to undertake tasks with little if any relation to the professional duties for which they were hired. It was pointed out that over the years Congress had exempted itself from all the worker protection laws, such as equal employment opportunities and equal pay, that it had imposed on private employers and other branches of the government.

Partly as a result of this, a small group of House members during the summer set up a volunteer committee to investigate complaints of unfair treatment brought by congressional staff members. The idea of Reps. Charles G. Rose III (D N.C.) and Patricia Schroeder (D Colo.), the group numbered only about two dozen members.

The Hays-Ray affair was the most spectacular event in Congress in 1976, but equally serious were charges that some members, including Senate Minority Leader Hugh Scott (R Pa.), accepted more than $5-million in illegal campaign contributions over the past decade from Gulf Oil Corporation. And the House was forced by the self-styled "citizens lobby" Common Cause to investigate conflict-of-interest charges against one of its most senior members, Rep. Robert L. F. Sikes (D Fla.). After a lengthy delay, the House ethics committee investigated the charges and the House reprimanded Sikes.

Although the ethics controversies dominated the news about Congress, there were a number of other important matters in 1976 that concerned the way in which Congress functioned.

Congressional Veto. An issue that was at the center of the traditional executive-congressional power struggle over control of government programs, the congressional veto, was not resolved in 1976. The veto is legislative language that can be added to bills and allows Congress to review and reject regulations promulgated by executive agencies.

The device has been around since the early 1930s, although used sparingly. But in the 1970s, as Congress sought to regain lost influence over governmental affairs, the veto provision was inserted in more and more pieces of legislation. It was inserted in several bills in 1976 and prompted President Ford to veto one measure, a pesticides control bill, because of its presence.

On a broader scale, the House attempted to pass a general congressional veto bill which would have established this power over virtually all federal agencies. That bill failed by two votes under a parliamentary procedure that requires a two-thirds majority; but it received a substantial majority, 265-135, nevertheless.

Pay Raise Repeal. Election-year considerations were behind Congress' repeal late in the session of an automatic cost-of-living pay hike it granted itself, as well as judges and top-ranking executive branch employees, in 1975. The 1975 action made these persons eligible for the automatic hikes along with lower level civil servants who already got the increases. The reversal action came in the fiscal 1977 legislative appropriations bill. An effort to keep the pay hike for judges and other top-level government officials, but repeal it for members of Congress, failed. Congress in that same bill also repealed the 1 per cent bonus which had been given to federal retirees each time they received a cost-of-living increase in their pensions.

Televising Congress. Efforts to bring television cameras into Senate and House chambers to record the proceedings failed in 1976. Pressure for this change built in the spring, but opposition from the Democratic leadership doomed the idea. In the House, the Rules Committee March 24 voted 9-6 to kill a proposal (H Res 875) that would have permitted live broadcast coverage of House activities. Although some participants in the controversy attributed the rejection to disagreements over who should control the televising, others said the real reason was the reluctance of House leaders and many members to have their activities broadcast on the powerful communications medium. Rep. Richard Bolling (D Mo.), a Rules Committee member, told a reporter: "There are many members who feel uncomfortable with all this exposure. They're anxious. They fear the unknown. Many of them won't come out and say that."

Financial Disclosure. Congress moved further in 1976 than in any recent year toward requiring extensive disclosure of financial information by high level federal employees. The Senate approved stiff disclosure requirements as part of a Watergate reform bill establishing a permanent independent special prosecutor. They applied to the President and Vice President, members of Congress, Supreme Court justices and federal judges and high-ranking executive branch officials. A similar bill in the House never emerged from committee.

Members of Congress currently had to file certain financial information on outside income, stock and property holdings. But the information was limited and left much unknown about members' financial relationships with organizations that might have an interest in legislation on which the members pass judgment.

Maryland Taxes. President Ford vetoed a bill (S 2447) that would have exempted members of Congress who reside in Maryland from paying state and local income taxes. Critics, including Ford, said the bill unfairly created a special class of citizens with special privileges. Supporters said it was necessary to provide uniform tax treatment of members. Virginia and the District of Columbia already exempted members from these taxes. S 2447 also wrote those exemptions into federal law. Supporters also argued that members residing in the Washington area already paid taxes to their home states. The veto came Aug. 3.

Rule 22 Change. The Senate April 6 amended its cloture rule (Rule 22), under which filibusters can be stopped, to allow the introduction of amendments to pending legislation until the announcement of the outcome of a cloture vote. No amendment can be considered after cloture is invoked unless it was formally read or considered read before the cloture vote was taken. In practice, the Senate routinely granted unanimous consent to consider read all amendments at the Senate desk at the time of the cloture vote. Supporters said the change merely formalized the existing informal practice, but opponents said it could

allow bill foes to introduce many more amendments that could delay action on a measure even after cloture was invoked.

Proxmire Legal Fees. The Senate Aug. 9 voted to pay legal expenses incurred by Sen. William Proxmire (D Wis.) in defending himself against a $6-million libel and slander suit.

The suit was brought by Dr. Ronald R. Hutchinson of Kalamazoo State Hospital in Michigan after Proxmire criticized government-financed research awards to him as a waste of money. Proxmire was sued after he presented one of his "Golden Fleece" awards for the $500,000 given to Hutchinson for studying why animals and humans gnash their teeth. Proxmire issued Golden Fleece awards monthly to spotlight government projects he believed to be wasteful. The vote to reimburse Proxmire for legal expenses, to be paid from the Senate's contingent fund, was 56-20. The payment would not include any money judgment against Proxmire.

Assassination Committee. The House Sept. 17 set up a select committee to investigate the killing of President John F. Kennedy and civil rights leader Martin Luther King Jr. and any other political assassinations the panel wished to look into. Backers of the committee said that new evidence had been discovered in recent years that cast doubt on the accepted explanations of events behind both killings. [In February 1977 the House agreed on a temporary reconstitution of the panel.]

Congressional Immunity. As the result of a Justice Department ruling, members of Congress were no longer immune to arrest for crimes such as drunk driving and soliciting prostitutes in Washington, D.C. The change stemmed from a case in which Rep. Joe D. Waggonner Jr. (D La.) was apprehended for allegedly soliciting a District of Columbia policewoman posing as a prostitute. He was released when police identified him as a member of Congress.

That occurred in January. On July 23, the D.C. police chief, Maurice J. Cullinane, said that members as well as other elected and appointed federal, state or local officials "are subject to arrest for the commission of criminal offenses to the same extent and in the same manner as all other citizens." Cullinane said that the previous non-arrest policy for members, which had been in effect for more than 100 years, was based on a "misinterpretation" of constitutional provisions. Cullinane had requested the Justice Department ruling on the issue.

House Two-Hour Rule. In an effort to improve its operations, the House Feb. 26 changed its rules to prevent consideration of a legislative proposal unless copies of the legislation had been available to members at least two hours before it was taken up on the floor. The change, adopted 258-107, applied to bills, resolutions and conference committee reports.

Under existing rules, legislation had to be available in printed form for members to study at least three days before the House could consider it. H Res 868 did not eliminate the three-day layover rule, but gave the House the alternative of taking up legislation two hours after copies of it became available. However, the Rules Committee and the House would have to sanction use of the two-hour period by voting to waive the three-day rule. (Existing rules allowed waiver of the three-day requirement by majority vote of the House.)

H Res 868 also allowed the Rules Committee and the full House by majority vote to suspend the two-hour rule entirely. If this were done, the legislation under consideration would not have to be delayed at all and conceivably could be considered before printed copies were available. Such situations might occur in hectic final days of congressional sessions as both houses attempt to pass many bills.

H Res 868 was sponsored by Rep. John L. Burton (D Calif.) who said he wanted to protect members against legislating blindly without a bill to study.

The change was strongly opposed by Rep. John B. Anderson (R Ill.), Republican Conference chairman. Anderson's basic concern was that committees might be encouraged to utilize the new two-hour rule in lieu of the three-day requirement. He said that committees could slip in controversial items that members might not notice if they had only two hours to examine the bill or conference report before a House vote.

Health Policy

The 1976 election year saw little change in federal health policy.

Preoccupied with a massive "swine flu" immunization program proposed by President Ford, the Department of Health, Education and Welfare (HEW) offered few new health policy initiatives. Congress approved a batch of health bills, but most of them just extended old programs. The complex problems affecting the nation's health care system continued to defy easy remedy.

Skyrocketing health costs remained a top concern. Health spending reached an estimated $134.9-billion in fiscal 1976 according to an HEW projection, a $16.4-billion jump from the previous year. The federal government alone expected to pay more than $31-billion in fiscal 1977—a 40 per cent increase in two years—for the Medicare program for the elderly and Medicaid program for the poor.

Investigations during the year repeatedly revealed that the federal government paid too much of this money to doctors and others cheating the two programs. A study by the Senate Special Committee on Aging estimated that fraud and abuse cost the $15-billion Medicaid program $1.8-billion a year and denied many patients proper medical care. Experts also agreed that overuse of health services under Medicare and Medicaid cost the taxpayers too much.

The two major health proposals promoted by the Ford administration reflected its fiscal concerns. Calling a national health insurance program too expensive and ill-advised, the President proposed instead to cover the elderly against the high cost of a "catastrophic" illness. But the proposal more than paid for itself by requiring elderly Medicare patients to pay more for short-term care.

A second proposal prepared by Ford's budget planners would have put a lid on federal spending for the uncontrollable Medicaid program and 15 federal programs focused on specific health problems. The proposal would have given states a single block grant for these activities, eliminating the federal government's open-ended commitment under existing law to match whatever the states spend on Medicaid services for the needy.

To no one's surprise, these proposals proved immediately unpopular on Capitol Hill. While Ford frequently referred to them during his campaign, the administration mounted no serious push for these proposals in Congress.

Congress also was unwilling to live with the President's health budget. Twice in 1976 it overrode vetoes of appropriations bills boosting health spending.

But Congress appeared more cautious about moving to any national health scheme. To some extent, Congress did not bother to consider national health insurance proposals in 1976 because it wanted to see whether Jimmy Carter, a health insurance supporter, would win the November presidential election. But the cost of a national program, coupled with public disenchantment with federal regulatory efforts, also weighed against quick action.

And many key members of Congress questioned whether it made any sense to set up a universal health insurance program until the federal government learned to control the costs and abuses of Medicaid and Medicare. House and Senate committees began to look at proposed program changes in 1976 but took no formal action.

Congress did finish work in 1976 on legislation that experts had called for before the country moved to a national health insurance system. The measure revised medical education programs in ways encouraging more young doctors to practice in rural and inner-city areas and in primary care fields.

Swine Flu

Medical history books probably will record 1976 as the year of the swine flu immunization program, perhaps the most widely publicized federal health effort ever undertaken.

President Ford proposed the program in March after flu usually found in swine broke out at Ft. Dix, N.J. Scientists suggested that the flu was related to a strain that caused a worldwide epidemic taking 20 million lives in 1918-19.

President Ford urged everyone to get a shot. Government health officials enthusiastically promoted the program as an important opportunity to take a preventive step that could avert a major health disaster. But after the flu failed to show up anywhere else in a few months, critics accused the administration of overreacting and using scare tactics to encourage participation in the program. (During the winter a small number of swine flu cases were reported in the Midwest.)

The program ran into a host of other problems delaying its initial starting date six weeks, until Oct. 1. A lack of insurance protection for drug companies making swine flu vaccine caused a major snag. Congress initially balked at resolving this problem, but agreed to do so in August after a mysterious "Legionnaires' disease" started killing persons who attended an American Legion convention in Philadelphia.

On Dec. 16 all flu immunizations were halted when the swine flu vaccine was linked with an increased incidence of a rare paralytic disease called Guillain-Barre syndrome. After an outbreak of A-Victoria strain flu in January 1977, the moratorium on the combined A-Victoria-swine flu shots was lifted for high-risk individuals.

HEW Program Actions

HEW's operation of the swine flu program was closely scrutinized. The department's implementation of four existing programs designed to control health costs proceeded more quietly, but organized medicine remained militantly opposed to some of them.

Medical Peer Review. A medical peer review system, approved by Congress in 1972, continued to move into place in 1976. The 1972 law created a network of doctor organizations, called professional standards review organizations (PSROs), to monitor the quality and necessity of care received by Medicare and Medicaid patients.

By February 1977, HEW had designated 106 groups as conditional PSROs and expected to name at least 20 more groups by the end of the year. It also sought in February applications from groups planning to become PSROs in the rest of the 203 PSRO regions in the country. Several preliminary studies suggested that PSRO review reduced the length of hospital stays for the elderly in some cases and decreased the number of shots given by doctors.

Health Planning. A health planning network also moved toward the operational stage in 1976. A 1974 law called for local planning agencies to prevent unnecessary or overlapping development of health facilities or services, to set priorities for new development and to monitor use of federal health funds.

During the course of the year, HEW named organizations to serve as the local planning agency in almost all of the 204 health service areas across the country. The overwhelming majority of the organizations were private, nonprofit groups rather than local or regional government agencies.

The planning program continued to face heavy criticism from organized medicine and state and local governments. The National Association of Regional Councils, American Medical Association (AMA) and the state of North Carolina filed lawsuits during the year charging that the planning act gave too much power to private groups and the federal government.

Health Maintenance Organizations. The federal government also continued to aid alternative medical groups called health maintenance organizations (HMOs) that provided a range of services for a periodic fee paid in advance. Proponents claimed that this approach gave HMOs incentives to catch health problems early, before they required costly treatment, thus holding down health spending in general.

Congress approved legislation in 1976 making it easier for HMOs to qualify for federal aid and to compete with traditional health insurance plans. As of early 1977, HEW had provided $47.5-million in grants to 168 separate HMO projects; 28 HMOs had won federal approval qualifying them for inclusion in employers health benefit plans. The law required employers to offer their workers HMO care if they offered traditional health insurance.

Drug Cost Controls. HEW went ahead in 1976 with a controversial proposal to limit payments under Medicare and Medicaid for prescription drugs. The plan, first proposed by former HEW Secretary Caspar W. Weinberger in 1973, would restrict government payments for some drugs to the lowest price at which they were generally available.

The proposal was expected to stimulate prescription of drugs by their generic, chemical names, which generally cost less than their brand-name equivalents. HEW chose ampicillin, a commonly prescribed antibiotic, as the first drug to be covered under the program.

The AMA and the Pharmaceutical Manufacturers Association had filed suit challenging the program.

Medical Competition

While HEW went forward with these programs, other federal agencies looked at possible barriers to cost competition in the health care industry. The Antitrust Division of the Justice Department disclosed in June that it had launched a broad review of the health services industry.

The Federal Trade Commission (FTC) announced a major investigation of the AMA in April to determine whether the group had illegally restrained the supply of doctors and health services. The FTC said it was concentrating its inquiry on the AMA's role in the accreditation of medical schools and advanced training programs, definitions of fields of medical practice and limitations on the development of HMOs.

The FTC's action was the agency's second decision in six months affecting the AMA. In late 1975, the commission accused the group of hindering competition illegally because its code of ethics barred its members from advertising their fees. The case was pending in early 1977.

In February, the FTC also announced an investigation to determine whether physician control of Blue Shield health insurance plans hindered cost competition.

Abortion

Abortion emerged as one of the touchiest health-related issues during the year.

Abortion opponents worked hard to make it an issue in the presidential campaign. Ellen McCormack, a Long Island housewife, ran on a right-to-life platform in 18 presidential primary contests. Jimmy Carter's and President Ford's early September meetings with Catholic bishops to discuss the issue also kept abortion in the news.

The two presidential candidates took positions that did not entirely please those on either side of the issue. Carter said he personally opposed abortion, but did not propose any constitutional amendment to overturn the Supreme Court's 1973 decision striking down state restrictions on abortion. Ford said he could support an amendment giving each state the right to set its own abortion laws.

Abortion opponents also won an important symbolic victory in September when Congress agreed after a summer of debate to cut off federal funding of abortions for women unless they were medically necessary. But federal judges temporarily blocked the ban as soon as it became law, pending further legal action.

Other developments during the year were less to the liking of the determined right-to-life lobby. Proposed constitutional amendments overturning the Supreme Court decision remained firmly lodged in committee. The Senate voted 47-40 against a move to bypass committee action.

On July 1, the Supreme Court also strengthened the rights of a woman seeking abortion. It struck down Missouri laws requiring a husband's or parent's consent for an abortion for married or teenage single women. The court also agreed to decide during its 1976-77 term whether the states could limit abortion payments under Medicaid.

Medical Malpractice

The medical malpractice insurance "crisis," prominent in the news in 1975, captured less attention in 1976. The federal government continued to play no role, but states and doctors themselves took steps to cope with the growing unavailability and soaring cost of insurance protecting physicians against claims.

By late 1976, 41 states had enacted laws to make sure that insurance would be available; many also changed legal procedures affecting malpractice cases. Physician groups set up their own malpractice insurance companies in nine states and seven other state medical societies were considering similar moves.

While helping to make insurance available, these actions had little effect on high premium costs.

Education and Science

Although Congress in 1976 passed a multi-faceted bill to overhaul most programs of federal aid to higher and vocational education, the year was notable as much for legislation which was not considered as for that which did come up.

Two major presidential initiatives in the field—anti-busing legislation and a proposal to consolidate grants for elementary and secondary education programs into a single block grant—were all but ignored by the 94th Congress.

In education, as in a number of other areas, the tension between a Democratic Congress and a Republican President produced legislation which President Ford often was reluctant to sign as well as presidential proposals which were snubbed on the Hill.

Congressional action on education issues in 1976 was taken against a background of declining enrollment at many levels of education, renewed emphasis on the teaching of basic skills, reduced racial tensions and a growing demand for equality of the sexes in education.

Enrollments

Enrollments in public schools dropped for the fourth year in a row in 1975, according to the National Center for Education Statistics. Between 1971 and 1975 the number of pupils in public elementary and high schools dropped by 2.7 per cent to 44.8 million.

This decline had been expected, but education statisticians were shocked at indications that college enrollments also dropped in 1976. Preliminary results of a survey taken by the American College Testing organization indicated that college enrollments in the fall of 1976 may have dropped about 1 per cent from the previous year. Statisticians had predicted an increase of about 4.5 per cent.

If the early findings of the survey were confirmed by the final study, to be published early in 1977, it would mean a drop in college enrollment for the first time since 1951.

Minority enrollment in the nation's colleges and universities appeared to be rising, however. The Office for Civil Rights in the Department of Health, Education and Welfare (HEW) reported in late October that minority enrollment rose 11.7 per cent between 1972 and 1974. The sharpest increase was in private institutions—37.7 per cent; the increase in public colleges was 4.1 per cent. Minority students represented 13.1 per cent of the total higher education enrollment in 1974, compared to 11.9 per cent in 1972.

Total enrollment in U.S. colleges and universities was 6,227,796 in 1974, the survey showed.

Back to Basics

While the school enrollment explosion of the 1960s began to dissipate in the mid-1970s, so too did the demands of students for greater freedom in selection of courses. Instead, the idea of general education, which requires each student to take courses in each of the major branches of knowledge, began to make a comeback.

A *New York Times* survey published in October found that a number of the pace-setting liberal arts colleges which had abandoned course distribution requirements in the 1960s were returning to this concept in 1976. Other surveys indicated that a number of high schools were following suit.

One possible reason for this trend was concern among educators about declining verbal and mathematics scores among college applicants documented in 1976. The average Scholastic Aptitude Test (SAT) score declined 41 per cent in the verbal test and 29 per cent in the mathematics test between 1962 and 1976, according to the College Entrance Examination Board.

Board member Albert G. Sims said in August that the declining SAT scores offered "an occasion for a hard look at what's happening in the schools and society that has a cumulative effect on students' performance."

Officials of the National Assessment of Education Progress attributed improved scores on reading tests by younger school children in 1976 to "back-to-basics" programs in many public school systems.

Sex Equality

Women continued to push for equal rights in the education field, but there were indications that their progress was slow.

The National Center for Education Statistics reported in February that in U.S. colleges and universities women faculty members had made little or no headway in 1975 in increasing their salaries or rank in comparison to men.

The Department of Health, Education and Welfare continued to issue anti-sex-discrimination rulings and guidelines, but was forced to withdraw several of them—such as one that would have barred father-son and mother-daughter functions at schools—when they drew cries of outrage from the public, members of Congress and the President.

However, Congress did include in its big higher and vocational education bill several provisions designed to provide women with equal opportunity and to eliminate sex stereotyping in federally funded education programs.

Legislative Action

Passage of the higher and vocational education bill (S 2657) was the major congressional action of the year in the education field. Although the bill made no revolutionary departures from traditional federal aid to education policies, it did mandate several changes in the scope, direction and administration of some of the programs.

The sections of the bill with the most widespread impact increased the maximum Basic Educational Opportunity Grants for college students and raised the ceiling on family income for eligibility for federal-interest subsidies on college loans. Both changes were aimed at meeting the increased costs of higher education and bringing relief to middle-income families with college-age students.

The measure also included provisions designed to open up the vocational education planning process to community colleges and other institutions newly involved in vocational education, to eliminate sex discrimination in federally funded programs, to provide new programs for part-time students and students beyond the traditional age of college attendance, and to reduce the number of defaults on federally guaranteed college tuition loans.

President Ford signed the bill on Oct. 12 (PL 94-482) but said he did so "with some reluctance." He said he opposed the increase in the basic grants.

Busing

Throughout 1976, Ford sought a way to dramatize his opposition to court-ordered busing for racial desegregation. In the spring, he ordered Attorney General Edward H. Levi to seek a "clarification" of the Supreme Court's busing rulings.

But Levi announced on June 2 that he would not order the Justice Department to intervene in the Boston school busing case, the most readily available vehicle for a clarification of the Supreme Court rulings, and Ford turned to another arena.

On June 24 Ford sent Congress proposed legislation to limit busing orders by the courts to a maximum of five years, to confine the orders to cases where segregation resulted from illegal actions by government bodies, and to limit the orders to specific cases of discrimination rather than allowing the courts to apply the orders to entire school districts.

Ford said he was asking for the legislation because "it is my belief that in their earnest desire to carry out the decisions of the Supreme Court, some judges of lower federal courts have gone too far."

But civil rights leaders denounced the proposal in bitter terms, and the measure never even received a hearing in Congress.

Congress also continued to rebuff attempts to write an anti-busing amendment to the Constitution and defeated several attempts to strengthen anti-busing provisions of existing law.

Part of the reason for congressional inaction in the busing field in 1976 may have been the declining number of violent incidents related to school busing orders. Despite continued incidents of violence in Boston, many cities were able to begin or to continue busing orders without disturbance. In the fall of 1976 classes opened in previously troubled Detroit and Louisville without disturbance, and new school desegregation plans were implemented smoothly in Dayton, Milwaukee, Omaha and St. Louis.

But while overt resistance to busing decreased in 1976, there were also signs that the court orders were not always achieving their goal. A study by HEW's Office for Civil Rights revealed in June that while segregation of schools in the South continued to decrease from 1970-1974, in the Northeast segregation increased sharply.

Block Grants

Another Ford proposal which ran up against a stone wall of congressional opposition would have consolidated 24 federal categorical grant programs for elementary and secondary education programs into a single block grant for the states.

Ford sent Congress his proposal on March 1, arguing that consolidation would give state and local school districts greater flexibility.

But opponents of the proposal said it would reduce spending on education, result in a loss of federal control over the use of federal funds and kill a number of programs that would be unable to compete for dollars in a block grant.

The President's proposal never got beyond the hearing stage.

Politics, Personnel

Recognizing that the presidential election would have a dramatic impact on a number of education programs, education groups became more directly involved in the political process in 1976 than ever before.

The National Education Association, with 1.7 million members, endorsed a presidential candidate for the first time in its history when it voted to back the Carter-Mondale ticket. The Democratic nominees also won the endorsement of the 460,000 member American Federation of Teachers.

The endorsements reflected the long-standing distaste of many teachers and education officials for the Ford administration and their delight at the place of Mondale, a longtime education backer in Congress, on the Democratic ticket.

Personnel Changes

The year witnessed some changes in the top administration posts in both education and science. U.S. Commissioner of Education Terrel H. Bell, the second highest ranking education officer in the government, left his post Aug. 1. He was succeeded in September by Edward G. Aguirre, 47, who had been the Office of Education's regional commissioner of education in San Francisco since 1973.

Bell said he resigned because he could no longer afford to live on his $37,800-a-year government salary. He took the top education post with the state of Utah at a salary of about $50,000. His deputy, Duane J. Mattheis, also left the government in July to take a $50,000-a-year job with the Education Research Council of America.

Science

The U.S. scientific community saw one of its important goals fulfilled in 1976 when Congress voted to revive the position of presidential science adviser. Former President Richard M. Nixon had alienated scientists in 1973 by abolishing the post.

President Ford named H. Guyford Stever to assume the position. Stever had been director of the National Science Foundation since 1972.

There were several dramatic moments for the scientific community in 1976. Americans won all three Nobel prizes in scientific fields. And two unmanned U.S. spacecraft, Viking I and Viking II, landed on Mars—the first man-made objects to reach the planet in working condition. Initial tests neither confirmed nor ruled out the possibility of life on Mars.

Welfare Policy

While outside groups called for changes, the federal government continued to show little interest in 1976 in overhauling the nation's fragmented welfare system.

The Ford administration took the same tone it had in 1975: something should be done, but not necessarily right away.

"Complex welfare programs cannot be reformed overnight," said President Ford in January. "Surely we cannot simply dump welfare into the laps of the 50 states, their local taxpayers or private charities, and just walk away. Nor is it the right time for massive and sweeping changes while we are still recovering from a recession."

Congress was in no mood, either, to tackle comprehensive revision of the welfare system in an election year. The cost and complexity of proposed changes also doused any legislative interest in welfare reform.

To some extent, Congress was waiting to see who would win the November presidential election. Democrat Jimmy Carter advocated consolidation of some welfare programs, establishment of basically uniform benefit levels and strengthening of work incentives. Carter also foresaw a reduction in local and some state welfare costs.

Other Proposals

While the federal government sat out the debate, outside groups came up with welfare proposals that could spark congressional discussion in 1977.

After some wrangling, the nation's governors voted in July to endorse a plan setting up a single welfare program paying minimum benefits to all. The plan called for the federal government to pay all of the basic minimum benefits and 75 per cent of any state supplemental payments or administrative costs.

A nonpartisan panel of business leaders, the Committee for Economic Development, also called for a full federal takeover of public assistance programs during the year. The group argued that federal administration "puts assistance directly into the hands of people who need it most, and it eliminates expensive, overlapping and inequitable administration of such assistance." In a departure from other welfare proposals, the committee recommended that the government pay for the program by eliminating general revenue sharing. Congress, however, voted to extend the revenue sharing program through 1980 before it adjourned in 1976.

The American Public Welfare Association also called for welfare consolidation in September, proposing a single program with a national minimum payment fully funded by the federal government.

Costs, Controls

While the administration eschewed such sweeping proposals, the Department of Health, Education and Welfare (HEW) continued to implement other programs designed to control the cost of the Aid to Families with Dependent Children (AFDC) program—the most expensive welfare program.

Because of high unemployment levels, the number of persons receiving AFDC payments reached a record 11.5 million in fiscal 1976, according to preliminary government estimates. HEW estimated that the number would drop to 11.3 million recipients in fiscal 1977.

HEW attributed the dip to general economic improvement, its continuing drive to lower the payment error rate in the AFDC program and implementation of a new child support program.

HEW began the campaign to reduce payment errors in 1973. By the end of 1975, the department reported that states had lowered the rate of payment to ineligible recipients to 6.4 per cent from 7.5 per cent six months earlier and cut the rate of overpayments to 14.7 per cent from 17.5 per cent over the same period. Further reductions were expected for 1976.

Initially, HEW had proposed to withhold AFDC funding from states that did not reach error rates of 5 per cent overpayment and 3 per cent ineligible by June 30, 1975. In May 1976, however, several states secured a court ruling holding the target rates arbitrary. In the wake of the court decision, HEW continued to work with the states to cut errors, but did not actually withhold any funds.

Stepped-up collection of child support payments also helped control welfare costs in 1976. A 1974 act (PL 94-647) required states to establish programs to obtain child support from fathers who deserted their families.

HEW reported that the states collected $280-million in child support payments on behalf of welfare families during the year ending June 30, 1976, while spending $134-million to put the program into place. The department estimated that half of the parents who desert welfare families could afford to make child support payments, thus cutting welfare costs by more than $1-billion a year.

Despite these efforts and the anticipated drop in the welfare caseload, HEW still expected welfare costs to increase as benefits went up. The federal cost of the AFDC program, for instance, was expected to rise to $6.2-billion in fiscal 1977, compared to $5.9-billion in fiscal 1976.

The average AFDC payment to a family was $230.38 a month in June 1976, up nearly $20 from a year earlier.

Supplemental Security Income

Errors rather than costs remained the top concern in the administration of the federal Supplemental Security Income (SSI) program for the needy aged, blind and disabled. The program paid benefits to more than four million recipients in 1976.

Computer foul-ups and other problems had resulted in overpayment and underpayment of SSI benefits as well as payments to ineligible recipients. The payment error rate was running about 25 per cent in 1975; HEW's target rate for the end of 1976 was 19 per cent. Because of the program's complexities, HEW officials more or less conceded that the program would never be error-free. They also admitted that the cost of errors in 1974 and 1975—the program's first two years—could reach $800-million to $900-million.

While a House Ways and Means Oversight Subcommittee closely followed the operations of the SSI program, Congress decided to postpone action on proposals designed to reduce the impact of payment delays and errors.

Social Services

Congress also took no action on an administration proposal to untie federal strings attached to social services programs for welfare recipients and other needy families. The federal government provided $2.5-billion a year to help states run a variety of social services programs ranging from day care to job counseling.

The administration plan would have eliminated many federal restrictions on the use of funds. In its original form, the proposal also kept federal funding at the $2.5-billion annual level while dropping a requirement that states put up some of their own matching money. Social welfare groups concluded that this approach added up to fewer dollars and feared that states might divert social services funds to more general-purpose uses.

HEW then offered a compromise increasing social services funding by $800-million over four years, but most social welfare groups still found the proposal unacceptable. The outside opposition stifled any congressional interest in the proposal.

Food Stamps

Efforts by both Congress and the administration to overhaul the food stamp program were unsuccessful in 1976.

The program had received an enormous amount of attention during the 94th Congress as unemployment resulting from the economic recession contributed to a peak enrollment of more than 19 million recipients in 1975 and fears were raised that the program cost would exceed $6-billion in 1976. Constituents complained that fraud and program misuse were allowing middle-class Americans to buy food stamps, thereby wasting taxpayers' money.

President Ford warned Congress early in 1976 that if it did not change the program legislatively to force middle-income persons out of the program and focus aid to the neediest recipients, he would make sharp administrative changes.

The Senate responded April 8 by passing a bill (S 3136) that the administration viewed as too liberal. With the House far from completing its version of food stamp reform, the administration proposed new regulations to be effective June 1, claiming they would save more than $1-billion a year in program costs. However, the regulations were never implemented because a coalition of food stamp recipients, religious groups and state and local governments successfully blocked the regulations in court. They said in their suit that the regulations would cause administrative chaos in the states and would hurt many food stamp recipients.

The House Agriculture Committee later reported out a food stamp bill (HR 13613) Sept. 1 by a narrow 21-19 vote, but the bill was deemed too controversial to bring to the House floor before the end of the session. This forced food stamp reform into the 95th Congress, where action must be taken to avoid the program's expiration in 1977.

Transportation and Communications

Constrained by election year considerations and the time limitations of a short session, Congress eschewed major initiatives in the transportation field and undertook instead only legislation necessary to maintain existing programs. The year's most important legislative products were bills extending the federal highway and airport aid programs and increasing federal aid to the National Railroad Passenger Corp. (Amtrak). The Amtrak bill also patched cracks in the law, put together hurriedly in 1975, that provided for reorganization of the major railroads in the Northeast and Midwest.

More notable than what Congress did in 1976 was what it did not do. It did not take more than tentative steps toward deregulating the nation's airline and trucking industries, despite strong urgings from the Ford administration. And it declined to tamper with the Highway Trust Fund, the highway construction funding mechanism that liberal and urban members of Congress for years had sought to either kill or open up to mass transit programs.

A transportation dispute that had divided Congress for years was settled at least temporarily in March when the Senate rejected a House-passed ban on landings in the United States by the Concorde supersonic transport (SST) jet. Clearing the way for Concorde service to Washington, D.C., and possibly, New York City, the Senate action followed a decision in February by Transportation Secretary William T. Coleman Jr. to allow SST flights on a trial basis for 16 months.

Later in 1976, Coleman again assumed the arbiter's role in an automobile safety dispute that, at year's end, remained unresolved. His department's National Highway Traffic Safety Administration had been trying for seven years to decide whether to require auto-makers to install in new cars "passive restraint systems" such as self-inflating air cushions. The issue had sparked a bitter fight between insurance companies, which supported the air bag concept, and car-makers, who opposed it.

Coleman's Dec. 6 rejection of mandatory air bags and proposal for a demonstration program was subject to congressional review and possible revision by the new administration.

Transportation

Railroad Policy

Plagued by financial ills and mounting competition on all fronts, the troubled railroad industry—freight and passenger—dominated the list of transportation problems considered by Congress in 1976. In what was widely regarded as a last-ditch effort to avert nationalization of the railroads, Congress at the beginning of the year gave final approval to an ambitious $6.4-billion railroad reorganization act (S 2718—PL 94-210). The measure provided for the consolidation of medium-to-large bankrupt railroads in the Northeast and Midwest into a single government-subsidized corporation called the Consolidated Rail Corporation (ConRail). It also authorized money for those lines not included in ConRail and for modernization of the railroad industry's deteriorating track and plant network.

Hindered at the outset by labor difficulties, ConRail began operations April 1 amid forecasts of failure from railroad industry observers. But in its early stages at least, the new system surprised the experts, winning high marks from shippers for service and recording a respectable financial performance in its first quarterly report. The new company's future would rest, it was expected, upon the decisions of a special bankruptcy court that had been set up to judge the claims of the thousands of creditors of the bankrupt railroads that ConRail replaced.

Even as Congress was setting up the new freight railroad network, it was casting a worrisome eye to ConRail's passenger counterpart, Amtrak. Amtrak had been set up as a government-funded corporation by Congress in 1970 to relieve the nation's private railroads of their costly passenger service. By 1976, its fifth year of operation, Amtrak was deeply in debt with no realistic prospect of meeting Congress' mandate to become profitable.

To relieve the problem, the Ford administration proposed that Amtrak be cut back drastically from the existing nationwide system to pockets of service in more profitable urban corridors. To force that result, it proposed a tight ceiling on federal grants to Amtrak for operating expenses in 1977.

But in Congress, curtailment of service meant removing trains from members' districts. Congress rejected the administration's tight budget and instead passed a bill (S 3131—PL 94-555) increasing Amtrak's operating subsidy for 1977 by $100-million over the previous year. The bill also included funds to permit Amtrak to purchase from ConRail the Washington-to-Boston Northeast Corridor, thus giving Amtrak its first actual ownership of right-of-way. It previously had used the facilities of other railroads.

The Amtrak bill also included a smattering of amendments designed to remove irritations that had appeared in the ConRail reorganization after the April 1 takeover. The most important provided $350-million in loan guarantee authority to permit ConRail and other railroads to pay off claims on the system they had taken over from the bankrupt railroads. The administration strongly opposed both the Amtrak subsidy and the generous loan guarantee, but the President signed the bill anyway.

Aviation

There was a lot of talk but little action in 1976 on deregulation of the airline industry. The focus of the attention was legislation introduced late in 1975 by the Ford administration that would have given airlines greater flexibility in rate-setting and route selection, permitted easier entry into and exit from the industry and removed some anti-trust protections enjoyed by airlines. Subsequently, related deregulation plans were sponsored by Sen. Edward M. Kennedy (D Mass.) and by the Civil Aeronautics Board (CAB), which regulates the airline industry.

Committees in both the House and Senate that oversee air transportation held extensive hearings in 1976 on several versions, with the industry generally opposing deregulation and the public supporting it. The volatility of the issues, and the short time that was left in the session to consider them, made further legislative action unrealistic in an election year.

There were indications of early action in 1977, however. At the end of the 94th Congress, Sen. Howard W. Cannon (D Nev.), chairman of the Senate Commerce Subcommittee on Aviation, introduced a far-ranging bill (S 3860) that went beyond the other measures by mandating an across-the-board deregulation of the industry and stripping the CAB of most of its power. Given the firm entrenchment of the CAB and the industry's resistance to such drastic change, Cannon's bill was seen not so much as a serious legislative proposal as a signal to the CAB to cooperate more with deregulation efforts.

In another sign of sentiment on the issue, President Ford in an October campaign speech criticized the Democratic-dominated Congress for dragging its heels on deregulation. He said it was "imperative" that an airline deregulation measure be enacted in the first 90 days of the next Congress.

Also during the campaign, Ford for the first time declared his position on an issue that had been building all year—muffling jet engine noise. During Senate consideration of an airport aid bill (HR 9971—PL 94-353), some senators unsuccessfully offered an amendment that would have required airlines to "retrofit" their jets with quieter engines so they could meet federal noise standards. Some 80 per cent of existing jets, mostly older ones, emitted noise considered too loud by the Federal Aviation Administration (FAA).

Subsequently, Secretary Coleman in June forwarded to the White House a plan to finance retrofitting of jets through a surcharge on the price of airplane tickets. That proposal, opposed by the airlines, languished in the White House until October, when Ford announced that he had ordered the FAA to enforce its noise standards for all planes, beginning Jan. 1, 1977. He said Coleman would hold public hearings to determine how best to finance either retrofitting or replacement of the existing fleet of noisy jets.

The year 1976 also saw the temporary resolution of the long-standing debate over whether to permit landings of the supersonic Concorde transport in the United States. After a widely publicized set of hearings, Coleman in February announced that the British and French plane would be allowed to make regular commercial flights to Washington, D.C., for a 16-month trial period, beginning in May.

Flights to New York City, which also had been approved by Coleman in February, were held up pending resolution of complicated legal action over the refusal of local New York authorities to permit such landings at John F. Kennedy International Airport.

Although Concorde had generated tremendous controversy as a potential noise and health hazard, its flights to Washington achieved some success, and some U.S. airplane companies at the end of the year were considering joining Britain in construction of a second generation of Concordes.

One of the few major transportation accomplishments of 1976 was Congress' final passage of a bill (HR 9971—PL 94-353) providing $5.6-billion for airport construction over the five-year period, 1976-80. The measure rescued from limbo a program that had gone unfunded since June 30, 1975, when the previous authorization expired.

About half the new authorization—$2.7-billion—was for capital projects at air carrier and general aviation airports. The balance was for Federal Aviation Administration programs, including air navigation and research and development. For the first time, the bill permitted use of capital funds for operating expenses—specifically for maintenance of federally owned facilities at airports. Deferring to Coleman's decision in February, sponsors dropped from the bill a House-passed ban on Concorde landings.

At the end of the year another aviation controversy was brewing over international airline traffic. Dissatisfied with the share of trans-Atlantic traffic allotted it by accords with the United States, Britain in the summer declared its withdrawal from existing agreements. In September, Coleman issued an aviation policy statement for the United States declaring that it was America's desire to reduce the overall number of overseas flights and to award service to airlines on the basis of efficiency. This was considered a direct jab at Britain, which subsidizes its airlines. At year's end, the two countries were engaged in discussions to renegotiate their air service agreements.

Highways

Of the Ford deregulation plans aimed at various transportation industries, the proposed changes for trucking were likely to draw the most resistance. Introduced in 1975 as part of the overall deregulation package, they drew loud and bitter criticism from the nation's very powerful trucking industry and unions. The House held two days of hearings in 1976 on the proposal, which was similar to the other deregulation plans.

Especially resented by the truckers was a provision in the administration bill (S 2929, HR 10909) permitting easier entry into the business. Truckers pay thousands of dollars for the certificates that entitled them to operate as common carriers, and some of them were afraid that deregulation would make their certificates worthless.

Shortly before the election, the administration indicated that it might back down somewhat on its proposal. Speaking to a truckers convention in Washington, D.C., Secretary Coleman said that he had talked to President Ford about truck deregulation and that the 1977 version of the bill would be more "sophisticated," with greater sensitivity to the value of certificates.

In another highway action, Congress in April finally cleared a major highway-aid bill (HR 8235—PL 94-280) that had been tied up since 1975 by differences between House and Senate versions. The enacted measure authorized $17.6-billion for highway construction for fiscal 1977 and 1978. It also extended the completion date for the Interstate Highway System to 1990, from 1978, and raised its funding level to $3.625-billion annually, from $3.250-billion under existing law.

The bill also extended for two years the Highway Trust Fund, long a target of members who wanted to use its money for other transportation needs besides highway construction. Sponsors of the bill said the extension was an interim step and promised major hearings on the trust fund in the next Congress.

Other Legislative Action

Following are other transportation developments of 1976:

● Doubling the administration's budget, Congress cleared a bill (HR 11670—PL 94-406) authorizing $284.9-billion for the Coast Guard for fiscal 1977. The total included $100-million to permit the Coast Guard to buy ships and planes to patrol the new 200-mile commercial fishing limit enacted by Congress in March.

● Congress dropped from an omnibus rivers and harbors bill (S 3823—PL 94-587) a section that would have permitted construction of a major new locks and dam navigation facility on the Mississippi River. The controversial project had been opposed by environmentalists and the railroad industry.

● There was little movement either in Congress or by the administration on a proposal submitted in 1975 by Secretary Coleman to force barge operators for the first time to pay user fees or taxes on the system of waterways that they traditionally had used at no cost. Efforts in the Senate to tie such a requirement to tax revision and public works bills were unsuccessful.

● Congress did not complete action on legislation (HR 10841) to ease Federal Maritime Commission regulation of ocean shipping to Guam, Hawaii and other domestic ports. The bill did not address the more important overseas shipping trade, which was heavily subsidized by the federal government. In its fiscal 1978 budget, the Ford administration said the subsidies were anticompetitive and suggested that Congress consider dropping them. The Justice Department in January 1977 recommended that Congress remove some, if not all, of the antitrust immunity that permits shipowners to set rates by mutual agreement.

Communications

In the communications field, 1976 was a year of uncertainty and inaction. For the second year in a row, the major issues that troubled the communications industry—broadcast license renewal, television violence and sex, the fairness doctrine, the equal time law, cable television—were left unresolved at session's end.

The major reason for the lack of progress on these issues was a sweeping change in congressional leadership in communications. The very assertive chairman of the Senate Commerce Subcommittee on Communications, John O. Pastore (D R.I.), announced even before the beginning of the session that he would not run for re-election in 1976. And he let it be known early that he would not tackle major issues that would be likely to carry the subcommittee into the next Congress.

On the House side, Torbert H. Macdonald (D Mass. 1955-76), the chairman of the Interstate and Foreign Commerce Subcommittee on Communications, died in May after a long illness during which the subcommittee lay dormant. He was replaced by Lionel Van Deerlin (D Calif.), a former television broadcaster who brought new vigor to the subcommittee through hearings on various issues. But Van Deerlin was prevented by time constraints from taking up any important legislation.

Major communications developments in 1976:

Cable Television. Igniting a long-simmering broadcast industry fight, Van Deerlin in May began a series of hearings into the effect of Federal Communications Commission (FCC) regulations on the cable television industry. An important touchstone for the hearings, which continued off and on for the rest of the session, was a communications subcommittee staff study suggesting that the FCC had stifled the growth of cable TV in order to protect the competing over-the-air broadcasting industry. The hearings produced a confrontation between the cable and broadcast industries and set the stage for likely cable deregulation legislation in the 95th Congress.

AT&T. Taking on another explosive issue, Van Deerlin late in the session conducted three days of hearings on legislation proposed by the American Telephone and Telegraph Co. (AT&T) and other companies that would have had the effect of writing AT&T's virtual telecommunications monopoly into law. The legislation was prompted by a series of FCC decisions opening small segments of the industry to competition.

Communications Act. Van Deerlin and ranking subcommittee minority member Louis Frey Jr. (R Fla.) announced late in the session that a major priority in the next Congress would be to completely rewrite the Communications Act of 1934. The law had been rendered unwieldy by the development of television, cable television, computer communications, and other forms of technology.

Fairness Doctrine. Pastore's subcommittee held hearings, but took no action, on bills that would abolish the fairness doctrine. Long the target of the broadcast industry, the fairness doctrine required broadcast stations—if they aired one side of a controversial issue—to broadcast the other side as well.

License Renewal. The House Communications Subcommittee left unconsidered some 70 bills that, in one way or another, would have extended the length of the license period for broadcast stations. Listed by the broadcasting industry as its number one priority, license renewal legislation was passed by both houses in the 93rd Congress, but ultimately fell victim to intramural disputes.

Sports Anti-blackout Rule. For the second consecutive year, House and Senate conferees were unable to reach agreement on legislation to extend a ban, originally enacted in 1973, on blackouts by television stations of home professional sports games that were sold out three days in advance. Although the House and Senate passed separate bills in 1975, conferees remained deadlocked throughout the second session over 1) how long to extend the ban, and 2) the size of the area that could be blacked out for games that were not sold out. The National Football League continued to operate under a voluntary blackout rule pending extension of the original law, which expired at the end of 1975.

Equal Time Law. The 1976 presidential debates focused new attention on the FCC's administration of the equal time law, which requires broadcasters to afford air time to all candidates for an office, including those of minor parties, if they give it to one. In 1975 the FCC relaxed its interpretation of the rule to exempt coverage of bona fide news events, which it said could include presidential news conferences and political debates sponsored by a third party. That interpretation allowed sponsors of the Ford-Carter debates to exclude participation by third-party candidates and independents such as Eugene J. McCarthy. The Supreme Court in October refused to review a federal appeals court decision upholding the FCC position.

Family Viewing. In a decision with great potential impact on television programming, a federal judge in November ruled unconstitutional the television networks' so-called "family viewing" policy. Under the policy, worked out voluntarily between the FCC and broadcasters in 1975, the three major networks agreed not to air shows "inappropriate for a family audience" during early evening prime time. But the court rejected that policy on the ground that it violated the first amendment right of free speech of program producers whose shows were arbitrarily banned during the family viewing hours. Some of the networks appealed the ruling.

Postal Service

The U.S. Postal Service, staggering under a mounting debt, was rescued by Congress in 1976 from a financial crisis. But the congressional debate over the bailout was bitter. Responding to warnings from Postal Service officials that it could go bankrupt by the spring of 1977, Congress in September passed a bill (HR 8603—PL 94-421) advancing the Postal Service an emergency $1-billion subsidy for fiscal 1977 and 1978.

With the money, however, came some tight federal strings—the Postal Service could neither raise postage rates nor cut back mail services until March 15, 1977. The bill also included a provision making it very difficult for the agency to continue its practice of closing small post offices to save money.

The rescue package was cleared only after long and often acrimonious negotiations between Congress and the administration, which at first opposed any new subsidy at all. Under existing law, the Postal Service already received an automatic $920-million annual subsidy. In the face of growing public concern about mail service, the administration compromised, but only with a subsidy figure much lower than had been sought by Senate leaders.

In addition to the subsidy, which was intended to meet short-term problems, the bill also set up a seven-member Commission on Postal Service to study the problems of the agency and make recommendations for the future. The commission's report, due March 15, 1977, was expected to set off a major congressional reappraisal of the Postal Reorganization Act of 1970 (PL 91-375), which removed the Postal Office Department from the government and set it up as a semi-independent corporation. At year's end, a growing body of opinion in Congress was expressing sympathy with a proposal to bring the U.S. Postal Service back under congressional control.

Ford's Support in Congress Dropped in 1976

President Ford lost on almost half of the votes before Congress in 1976 where he staked out a clear position. Ford won only 53.8 per cent of those votes, his lowest annual mark since becoming President on Aug. 9, 1974.

Only two lower presidential support scores have been recorded since Congressional Quarterly began keeping the record in 1953. The lowest score of any President was 50.6 per cent set by Richard M. Nixon in 1973. The second lowest score came in 1959 when President Eisenhower received only 52.0 per cent support. *(Success rates, box, this page)*

Ford dropped significantly from the 61 per cent score he attained in 1975. That year's mark had been an improvement over his five-month debut in 1974, when Ford received only 58.2 per cent support.

Ford's luck in 1976 was toughest in the chamber where he served 24 years—the House gave him only 43.1 per cent support. His positions fared better in the Senate, where he won 64.2 per cent.

Four House Democrats racked up scores of 78 per cent in opposition to the President's positions. Two of them were freshmen: William M. Brodhead (Mich.) and Richard L. Ottinger (N.Y.), who had served in the House previously, 1965-71. The other two were Don Edwards (Calif.) and Edward Mezvinsky (Iowa).

Seven Senate Democrats opposed the President on 60 per cent or more of the votes, with no senator opposing him on more than 62 per cent.

The President's biggest Republican supporters were John N. Erlenborn (Ill.) in the House with 86 per cent and Paul J. Fannin (Ariz.) and Pete V. Domenici (N.M.) in the Senate, each with 83 per cent. His most consistent

Democratic supporters were James B. Allen (Ala.) in the Senate with 77 per cent and four southern representatives in the House with 75 per cent.

The study was based upon 104 votes in 1976 where the President's position was publicly stated. Ford or one of his aides speaking for him took clear stands on 53 Senate votes and 51 House votes, according to Congressional Quarterly's study. *(Ground rules, box, p. 43)*

Congress took 1,349 roll call votes in 1976, 661 in the House and 688 in the Senate. Max L. Friedersdorf, assistant to the President for legislative affairs, was unavailable for comment in late October on the President's low support score and Friedersdorf's subordinates declined to comment.

Support and Opposition Breakdown

Ford drew less support in 1976 in the Senate from Democrats and Republicans alike than he had in 1975. The average Senate Democrat supported Ford's positions 39 per cent in 1976, down from 47 per cent in 1975. The average Senate Republican supported Ford on 62 per cent of his 1976 stands, a drop of six percentage points from 1975.

The composite House Democratic score showed less support for Ford in 1976 than in previous years, but House Republicans were steady at 63 per cent for both sessions of the 94th Congress. The average House Democrat supported Ford on 32 per cent of his stands in 1976, compared with 38 per cent in 1975.

Cumulatively over the two sessions of the 94th Congress, Senate Democrats supported Ford 44 per cent and their Republican colleagues backed him 66 per cent. House Democrats gave Ford 36 per cent support and Republicans 63 per cent on his stands during the 94th Congress.

Opposition to the President's positions was more frequent among both parties in the Senate and among Democrats in the House than it was in 1975.

The average Senate Democrat in 1976 opposed the President on 44 per cent of his stands, up from 41 per cent in 1975. The average Senate Republican opposed the President on 23 per cent of the eligible 1976 votes, compared with 22 per cent in 1975. His House Republican counterpart opposed Ford on only 31 per cent in 1975 and on only 27 per cent in 1976.

Regional Divisions

President Ford drew his most consistent support from the South and faced his most inflexible antagonism from the East.

In 1976, southern Senate Democrats gave Ford an average support score of 53 per cent. Their fellow Democrats from the Midwest supported Ford 34 per cent; from the West, 31 per cent; and from the East 36 per cent.

Ford received support 70 per cent of the time from the average Senate Republican if he was from the South, 69 per cent if from the Midwest, 67 per cent if from the West and 48 per cent if from the East.

The House breakdown reflected less regional variation. The average southern Democrat in the House supported the

Success Rates

Following are the annual percentages of presidential victories since 1953 on congressional votes where the Presidents took clear-cut positions:

Eisenhower		1966	79.0
1953	89.0%	1967	79.0
1954	82.8	1968	75.0
1955	75.0		
1956	70.0	**Nixon**	
1957	68.0	1969	74.0%
1958	76.0	1970	77.0
1959	52.0	1971	75.0
1960	65.0	1972	66.0
		1973	50.6
Kennedy		1974	59.6
1961	81.0		
1962	85.4	**Ford**	
1963	87.1	1974	58.2
Johnson		1975	61.0
1964	88.0	1976	53.8
1965	93.0		

President 46 per cent, while Democrats from each of the other three regions scored 26 per cent.

Among Republicans in the House, Southerners gave Ford 71 per cent support, while Midwesterners supported him 68 per cent, Westerners 59 per cent, and Easterners 52 per cent.

The measurements of opposition to the President's stands reflected almost a mirror image of the support figures. For example, the average Senate Democrat from the East opposed the President 53 per cent while his southern Democratic counterpart opposed him 34 per cent. The average Senate Republican from the East opposed the President 38 per cent while southern GOP senators opposed him only 16 per cent.

Individual Support Scores

Close behind Fannin and Domenici as Ford's most consistent GOP supporters in the Senate were Robert P. Griffin (Mich.) and Strom Thurmond (S.C.) with 81 per cent and Dewey F. Bartlett (Okla.) with 79 per cent.

On the other side of the Senate aisle, Ford found Alabama's Democratic Sen. Allen the most sympathetic to his point of view, with a support figure of 77 per cent. Other friendly votes usually could be counted upon from Sens. Harry F. Byrd Jr. (Ind. Va.), 75 per cent; John L. McClellan (D Ark.), 74 per cent; John C. Stennis (D Miss.), 66 per cent; and Sam Nunn (D Ga.), 64 per cent.

In the House, Rep. Erlenborn's high support score of 86 per cent was followed by Republican Reps. Edward Hutchinson (Mich.), Elford A. Cederberg (Mich.), Delbert L. Latta (Ohio) and Samuel L. Devine (Ohio), all of whom

tallied scores of 84 per cent. Close behind were Republicans Robert McClory (Ill.), John Jarman (Okla.) and Robin L. Beard Jr. (Tenn.), with 82 per cent scores.

House Democrats lending consistent support to President Ford were led by Larry P. McDonald (Ga.), David E. Satterfield III (Va.), W. C. (Dan) Daniel (Va.) and W. R. Poage (Texas), all with scores of 75. Not far behind were G. V. (Sonny) Montgomery (Miss.) and Omar Burleson (Texas) with scores of 73, and George Mahon (Texas) with 71.

Individual Opposition Scores

Three Democrats led the Senate in opposing President Ford in 1976. They were John A. Durkin (N.H.), Lee Metcalf (Mont.) and Harrison A. Williams Jr. (N.J.), all with opposition scores of 62 per cent.

Other Democratic Senators close behind with opposition scores of 60 per cent were James Abourezk (S.D.), Quentin N. Burdick (N.D.), Edward M. Kennedy (Mass.) and Gaylord Nelson (Wis.).

The Senate Republican most opposed to President Ford's stands was Clifford P. Case (N.J.), with a score of 58 per cent. Not far behind were Republican Sens. Richard S. Schweiker (Pa.), 55 per cent; Edward W. Brooke (Mass.), 51 per cent; Jacob K. Javits (N.Y.), 47 per cent; Charles McC. Mathias Jr. (Md.), 42 per cent; and Mark O. Hatfield (Ore.), 40 per cent.

Just below the four House Democrats recording opposition scores of 78 per cent were 13 Democrats scoring 76 per cent. They were Phillip Burton (Calif.), George Miller (Calif.), Fortney H. (Pete) Stark (Calif.), Norman Y. Mineta (Calif.), John Krebs (Calif.), Gerry E. Studds

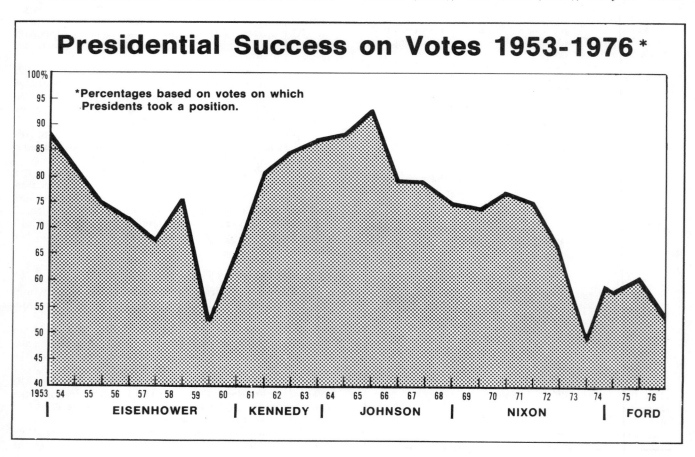

Presidential Success on Votes 1953-1976 *

*Percentages based on votes on which Presidents took a position.

Ground Rules for CQ Presidential Support-Opposition

Presidential Issues—CQ tries to determine what the President personally, as distinct from other administration officials, does and does not want in the way of legislative action by analyzing his messages to Congress, press conference remarks and other public statements and documents.

Borderline Cases—By the time an issue reaches a vote, it may differ from the original form on which the President expressed himself. In such cases, CQ analyzes the measure to determine whether, on balance, the features favored by the President outweigh those he opposed or vice versa. Only then is the vote classified.

Some Votes Excluded—Occasionally, important measures are so extensively amended on the floor that it is impossible to characterize final passage as a victory or defeat for the President.

Procedural Votes—Votes on motions to recommit, to reconsider or to table often are key tests that govern the legislative outcome. Such votes are necessarily included in the presidential support tabulations.

Appropriations—Generally, votes on passage of appropriation bills are not included in the tabulation, since it is rarely possible to determine the President's position on the overall revisions Congress almost invariably makes in the sums allowed. Votes on amendments to cut or increase specific funds requested in the President's budget, however, are included.

Failures to Vote—In tabulating the support or opposition scores of members on the selected presidential-issue votes, CQ counts only "yea" and "nay" votes on the ground that only these affect the outcome. Most failures to vote reflect absences because of illness or official business. Failures to vote lower both support and opposition scores equally.

Weighting—All presidential-issue votes have equal statistical weight in the analysis.

Changed Positions—Presidential support is determined by the position of the President at the time of a vote, even though that position may be different from an earlier position, or may have been reversed after the vote was taken.

(Mass.), John D. Dingell (Mich.), James L. Oberstar (Minn.), Norman E. D'Amours (N.H.), William J. Hughes (N.J.), Helen Meyner (N.J.), Ken Hechler (W.Va.) and Dominick V. Daniels (N.J.).

House Republicans registering high opposition scores included Benjamin A. Gilman (N.Y.), 71 per cent; Charles W. Whalen Jr. (Ohio), 69 per cent; Matthew J. Rinaldo (N.J.), 65 per cent; Silvio O. Conte (Mass.), 61 per cent; Edward G. Biester Jr. (Pa.), 59 per cent; William S. Cohen (Maine), Gilbert Gude (Md.) and Margaret M. Heckler (Mass.), each 57 per cent; David F. Emery (Maine) and Millicent Fenwick (N.J.), both 55 per cent.

State Rankings

In the Senate, the state delegations which, on the average, showed the most consistent support for the President in 1976 were Arizona, 77 per cent; Nebraska, 77; Oklahoma, 76; Virginia, 71; Alabama, 69; North Carolina, 65; South Carolina, 65; Kansas, 63; Mississippi, 59; Arkansas, 58.

The Senate delegations that averaged the most consistent presidential opposition were New Jersey, 60 per cent; Maine, 58; Wisconsin, 58; Colorado, 57; Kentucky, 57; Massachusetts, 56; Iowa, 55; Montana, 55; New Hampshire, 55; Minnesota, 54.

The House delegations that averaged the most consistent support for the President's stands were Nebraska, 66 per cent; Virginia, 65; Idaho, 61; Kansas, 60; Mississippi, 60; South Dakota, 59; Alabama, 58; Louisiana, 56; New Mexico, 56; Oklahoma, 56.

Most consistent House opposition to the President was provided by Rhode Island, 72 per cent; Montana, 69; Iowa, 67; Massachusetts, 67; New Jersey, 67; Hawaii, 63; West Virginia, 62; Washington, 61; Oregon, 59; Wisconsin, 59.

Average Scores

Following are composites of Republican and Democratic scores for 1976 and 1975:

	1976		1975	
	Dem.	Rep.	Dem.	Rep.
SUPPORT				
Senate	39%	62%	47%	68%
House	32	63	38	63
OPPOSITION				
Senate	44	23	41	22
House	58	27	57	31

The following are composite party scores for the 94th and 93rd Congress:

	94th Congress		93rd Congress	
	Dem.	Rep.	Dem.	Rep.
SUPPORT				
Senate	44%	66%	39%	55%
House	36	63	41	51
OPPOSITION				
Senate	42	22	47	27
House	57	30	45	35

Regional Averages

SUPPORT

Regional presidential support scores for 1976; scores for President Ford in the 94th Congress are in parentheses:

	East	West	South	Midwest
DEMOCRATS				
Senate	36%(41)	31%(39)	53%(56)	34%(38)
House	26 (31)	26 (32)	46 (45)	26 (32)
REPUBLICANS				
Senate	48 (53)	67 (70)	70 (72)	69 (72)
House	52 (57)	59 (61)	71 (66)	68 (67)

OPPOSITION

Regional presidential opposition scores for 1976; scores for President Ford in the 94th Congress are in parentheses:

	East	West	South	Midwest
DEMOCRATS				
Senate	53%(50)	43%(42)	34%(31)	49%(48)
House	67 (63)	64 (60)	43 (46)	63 (60)
REPUBLICANS				
Senate	38 (36)	16 (17)	16 (18)	17 (16)
House	39 (36)	22 (26)	23 (29)	24 (27)

High Scorers—Support

Highest individual scorers in presidential support—those who voted for the President's position most often in 1976.

SENATE

Democrats		Republicans	
Allen (Ala.)	77%	Fannin (Ariz.)	83%
Byrd (Va.)#	75	Domenici (N.M.)	83
McClellan (Ark.)	74	Griffin (Mich.)	81
Stennis (Miss.)	66	Thurmond (S.C.)	81
Nunn (Ga.)	64	Bartlett (Okla.)	79

 # Elected as independent.

HOUSE

Democrats		Republicans	
McDonald (Ga.)	75%	Erlenborn (Ill.)	86%
Satterfield (Va.)	75	Hutchinson (Mich.)	84
Daniel (Va.)	75	Cederberg (Mich.)	84
Poage (Texas)	75	Latta (Ohio)	84
Montgomery (Miss.)	73	Devine (Ohio)	84

1976 Presidential Position Votes

Following is a list of all Senate and House recorded votes in 1976 on which President Ford took a position. The votes, listed by CQ vote number, appear in the Roll Call charts.

Senate Votes (53)

Presidential Victories (34)—2, 5, 6, 9, 19, 22, 23, 37, 50, 93, 94, 95, 96, 103, 161, 180, 185, 190, 192, 203, 301, 368, 390, 398, 444, 501, 504, 508, 511, 535, 582, 661, 662, 671.

Presidential Defeats (19)—1, 8, 11, 31, 65, 66, 99, 147, 149, 153, 181, 186, 377, 391, 443, 448, 507, 594, 672.

House Votes (51)

Presidential Victories (22)—19, 20, 106, 124, 131, 142, 150, 236, 263, 409, 410, 416, 446, 449, 454, 455, 458, 478, 483, 557, 651, 659.

Presidential Defeats (29)—13, 14, 17, 25, 26, 27, 28, 37, 38, 42, 81, 101, 138, 145, 146, 170, 349, 403, 404, 420, 422, 436, 459, 473, 527, 530, 563, 645, 649.

Burleson (Texas)	73	McClory (Ill.)	82
Mahon (Texas)	71	Jarman (Okla.)	82
		Beard (Tenn.)	82

High Scorers—Opposition

Highest individual scorers in Ford opposition—those who voted against the President's position most often in 1976:

SENATE

Democrats		Republicans	
Durkin (N.H.)	62%	Case (N.J.)	58%
Metcalf (Mont.)	62	Schweiker (Pa.)	55
Williams (N.J.)	62	Brooke (Mass.)	51
Abourezk (S.D.)	60	Javits (N.Y.)	47
Burdick (N.D.)	60	Mathias (Md.)	42
Kennedy (Mass.)	60	Hatfield (Ore.)	40
Nelson (Wis.)	60		

HOUSE

Democrats		Republicans	
Edwards (Calif.)	78%	Gilman (N.Y.)	71%
Mezvinsky (Iowa)	78	Whalen (Ohio)	69
Brodhead (Mich.)	78	Rinaldo (N.J.)	65
Ottinger (N.Y.)	78	Conte (Mass.)	61
		Biester (Pa.)	59

The following Democrats had opposition scores of 76 per cent: P. Burton (Calif.), Miller (Calif.), Stark (Calif.), Mineta (Calif.), Krebs (Calif.), Studds (Mass.), Dingell (Mich.), Oberstar (Minn.), D'Amours (N.H.), Hughes (N.J.), Meyner (N.J.), Hechler (W.Va.), Daniels (N.J.).

	1	2	3	4		1	2	3	4		1	2	3	4
ALABAMA					**IOWA**					**NEW HAMPSHIRE**				
Allen	77	23	65	30	Clark	36	55	38	58	Durkin	32	62	31*	60*
Sparkman	60	32	53	28	Culver	32	55	38	52	McIntyre	36	47	36	49
ALASKA					**KANSAS**					**NEW JERSEY**				
Gravel	34	40	32	39	*Dole*	66	17	72	16	Williams	30	62	42	53
Stevens	57	25	66	20	*Pearson*	60	32	63	25	*Case*	38	58	47	49
ARIZONA					**KENTUCKY**					**NEW MEXICO**				
Fannin	83	8	82	9	Ford	36	57	49	46	Montoya	25	34	44	29
Goldwater	72	2	65	7	Huddleston	40	57	48	42	*Domenici*	83	11	82	14
ARKANSAS					**LOUISIANA**					**NEW YORK**				
Bumpers	42	51	45	42	Johnston	45	43	56	31	*Buckley#*	51	15	62	14
McClellan	74	15	71	21	Long	49	34	60	26	*Javits*	42	47	44	50
CALIFORNIA					**MAINE**					**NORTH CAROLINA**				
Cranston	34	58	38	58	Hathaway	38	58	41	56	Morgan	53	30	49	31
Tunney	9	21	30	36	Muskie	36	57	40	52	*Helms*	77	23	71	26
COLORADO					**MARYLAND**					**NORTH DAKOTA**				
Hart	40	55	43	52	Beall	55	32	66	27	Burdick	38	60	39	57
Haskell	26	58	36	56	*Mathias*	40	42	42	36	*Young*	72	13	79	14
CONNECTICUT					**MASSACHUSETTS**					**OHIO**				
Ribicoff	36	51	42	51	Kennedy	21	60	35	51	Glenn	53	38	56	38
Weicker	51	38	55	38	*Brooke*	34	51	40	46	*Taft*	60	25	58	19
DELAWARE					**MICHIGAN**					**OKLAHOMA**				
Biden	28	49	27	53	Hart	28	32	28	40	*Bartlett*	79	11	79	16
Roth	66	28	64	32	*Griffin*	81	8	84	8	*Bellmon*	74	21	73	21
FLORIDA					**MINNESOTA**					**OREGON**				
Chiles	45	34	58	29	Humphrey	34	53	42	50	*Hatfield*	40	40	43	42
Stone	49	47	55	39	Mondale	19	55	34	50	*Packwood*	64	26	67	27
GEORGIA					**MISSISSIPPI**					**PENNSYLVANIA**				
Nunn	64	36	68	30	Eastland	53	19	49	18	Schweiker	42	55	42	55
Talmadge	49	32	52	34	Stennis	66	17	65	19	*Scott*	53	17	67	17
HAWAII					**MISSOURI**					**RHODE ISLAND**				
Inouye	28	28	31	32	Eagleton	36	51	43	44	Pastore	40	40	46	44
Fong	58†	12†	67*	9*	Symington	36	36	42	36	Pell	34	51	38	51
IDAHO					**MONTANA**					**SOUTH CAROLINA**				
Church	23†	44†	34*	41*	Mansfield	28	47	37	47	Hollings	49	40	49	43
McClure	72	15	73	17	Metcalf	30	62	36	49	*Thurmond*	81	8	80	12
ILLINOIS					**NEBRASKA**					**SOUTH DAKOTA**				
Stevenson	51	45	45	47	*Curtis*	77	8	76	10	Abourezk	23	60	28	62
Percy	57	32	64	27	*Hruska*	77	6	81	8	McGovern	28	36	29	45
INDIANA					**NEVADA**					**TENNESSEE**				
Bayh	21	49	24	35	Cannon	49	42	53	33	*Baker*	64	15	68	14
Hartke	26	38	33	44	*Laxalt*	53	15	65	16	*Brock*	42	19	58	16

- KEY -

† Not eligible for all recorded votes in 1976.

* Not eligible for all recorded votes in 94th Congress.

	1	2	3	4
TEXAS				
Bentsen	32	30	48	27
Tower	75	15	82	12
UTAH				
Moss	36	42	45	39
Garn	77	13	75	15
VERMONT				
Leahy	36	51	40	51
Stafford	60	34	57	37
VIRGINIA				
Byrd**	75	21	73	23
Scott	66	17	66	25
WASHINGTON				
Jackson	36	40	48	38
Magnuson	36	49	41	51
WEST VIRGINIA				
Byrd	47	53	59	41
Randolph	49	45	53	43
WISCONSIN				
Nelson	34	60	38	55
Proxmire	43	57	47	53
WYOMING				
McGee	26	30	34	27
Hansen	75	9	81	10

Democrats   **Republicans**   #Buckley elected as Conservative.   **Byrd elected as independent.

Presidential Support and Opposition: Senate

1. Ford Support Score, 1976. Percentage of 53 Ford-issue roll calls in 1976 on which senator voted "yea" or "nay" *in agreement* with the President's position. Failures to vote lower both Support and Opposition scores.

2. Ford Opposition Score, 1976. Percentage of 53 Ford-issue roll calls in 1976 on which senator voted "yea" or "nay" *in disagreement* with the President's position. Failures to vote lower both Support and Opposition scores.

3. Ford Support Score, 94th Congress. Percentage of 146 Ford-issue roll calls in 1975 and 1976 on which senator voted "yea" or "nay" *in agreement* with the President's position. Failures to vote lower both Support and Opposition scores.

4. Ford Opposition Score, 94th Congress. Percentage of 146 Ford-issue roll calls in 1975 and 1976 on which senator voted "yea" or "nay" *in disagreement* with the President's position. Failures to vote lower both Support and Opposition scores.

Presidential Support and Opposition: House

1. Ford Support Score, 1976. Percentage of 51 Ford-issue roll calls in 1976 on which representative voted "yea" or "nay" *in agreement* with the President's position. Failures to vote lower both Support and Opposition scores.

2. Ford Opposition Score, 1976. Percentage of 51 Ford-issue roll calls in 1976 on which representative voted "yea" or "nay" *in disagreement* with the President's position. Failures to vote lower both Support and Opposition scores.

3. Ford Support Score, 94th Congress. Percentage of 140 Ford-issue roll calls in 1975 and 1976 on which representative voted "yea" or "nay" *in agreement* with the President's position. Failures to vote lower both Support and Opposition scores.

4. Ford Opposition Score, 94th Congress. Percentage of 140 Ford-issue roll calls in 1975 and 1976 on which representative voted "yea" or "nay" *in disagreement* with the President's position. Failures to vote lower both Support and Opposition scores.

1. Rep. Torbert H. Macdonald (D Mass.) died May 21, 1976.

2. Rep. Jerry Litton (D Mo.) died Aug. 3, 1976.

3. Rep. James F. Hastings (R N.Y.) resigned Jan. 20, 1976. He was not eligible for any presidential support votes in 1976. His Presidential support score in 1975 was 71 per cent, his opposition score 24 per cent. Rep. Stanley N. Lundine (D) sworn in March 8, 1976, to replace Hastings.

4. Rep. Wayne L. Hays (D Ohio) resigned Sept. 1, 1976.

5. Rep. Carl Albert (D Okla.), as Speaker, votes at his own discretion.

6. Rep. William A. Barrett (D Pa.) died April 12, 1976.

7. Rep. Wright Patman (D Texas) died March 7, 1976. His 1976 presidential support score was 42 per cent, his opposition score 33 per cent; for the 94th Congress his presidential support score was 35 per cent, his opposition score 46 per cent. Rep. Sam B. Hall Jr. (D) sworn in June 28, 1976, to replace Patman.

8. Rep. Bob Casey (D Texas) resigned Jan. 22, 1976. He was not eligible for any presidential support votes in 1976. His presidential support score in 1975 was 57 per cent, his opposition score 40 per cent. Rep. Ron Paul (R) sworn in April 7, 1976, to replace Casey.

- KEY -

† Not eligible for all recorded votes in 1976.

* Not eligible for all recorded votes in 94th Congress.

	1	2	3	4
ALABAMA				
1 Edwards	80	14	76	16
2 Dickinson	76	18	69	24
3 Nichols	49	37	49	44
4 Bevill	43	43	42	51
5 Jones	39	51	39	48
6 Buchanan	67	27	70	26
7 Flowers	49	37	54	38
ALASKA				
AL Young	49	27	49	31
ARIZONA				
1 Rhodes	76	6	81	9
2 Udall	16	41	13	35
3 Steiger	31	6	48	23
4 Conlan	41	14	54	23
ARKANSAS				
1 Alexander	37	39	40	45
2 Mills	43	39	43	34
3 Hammerschmidt	65	33	64	36
4 Thornton	45	49	48	49
CALIFORNIA				
1 Johnson	37	61	39	59
2 Clausen	63	33	60	33
3 Moss	16	71	21	67
4 Leggett	22	63	29	62
5 Burton, J.	20	71	22	69
6 Burton, P.	18	76	22	70
7 Miller	24	76	26	73
8 Dellums	24	73	28	71
9 Stark	16	76	25	69
10 Edwards	20	78	26	70
11 Ryan	20	67	32	55
12 McCloskey	37	49	54	34
13 Mineta	20	76	31	66
14 McFall	29	67	41	58
15 Sisk	33	43	34	44
16 Talcott	65	25	69	24
17 Krebs	24	76	26	74
18 Ketchum	65	25	60	31
19 Lagomarsino	67	31	67	32
20 Goldwater	69	20	63	24
21 Corman	14	75	27	66
22 Moorhead	69	31	63	33
23 Rees	25	43	40	44
24 Waxman	18	75	26	65
25 Roybal	20	73	28	68
26 Rousselot	67	25	61	29
27 Bell	47	16	50	20
28 Burke	20	71	26	66
29 Hawkins	20	65	29	62
30 Danielson	29	67	39	55
31 Wilson	25	57	33	48
32 Anderson	25	71	26	69
33 Clawson	76	14	65	24
34 Hannaford	31	69	33	64
35 Lloyd	37	63	34	66
36 Brown	31	59	35	59
37 Pettis	67	27	70*	28*
38 Patterson	25	67	28	66
39 Wiggins	65	12	71	11
40 Hinshaw	0	0	30	9
41 Wilson	78	18	71	18
42 Van Deerlin	24	73	34	59
43 Burgener	75	22	66	30
COLORADO				
1 Schroeder	27	71	30	69
2 Wirth	27	67	31	65
3 Evans	20	65	36	57
4 Johnson	59	29	60	34

	1	2	3	4
5 Armstrong	78	14	70	25
CONNECTICUT				
1 Cotter	29	61	32	61
2 Dodd	24	71	26	69
3 Giaimo	37	59	36	59
4 McKinney	53	39	56	36
5 Sarasin	51	47	56	42
6 Moffett	22	75	24	74
DELAWARE				
AL du Pont	39	45	57	34
FLORIDA				
1 Sikes	51	35	49	36
2 Fuqua	47	45	45	49
3 Bennett	57	43	51	49
4 Chappell	43	39	47	40
5 Kelly	80	14	71	25
6 Young	69	29	60	36
7 Gibbons	35	55	45	47
8 Haley	63	31	54	41
9 Frey	65	29	66	31
10 Bafalis	67†	31†	60*	38*
11 Rogers	37	63	39	60
12 Burke	63	31	50	29
13 Lehman	29	63	31	64
14 Pepper	18	37	31	44
15 Fascell	25	69	35	61
GEORGIA				
1 Ginn	53	47	42	56
2 Mathis	59	29	54	36
3 Brinkley	43	43	44	50
4 Levitas	43	55	39	59
5 Young	12	65	26	62
6 Flynt	41	20	46	25
7 McDonald	75	24	66	32
8 Stuckey	41	29	49	34
9 Landrum	53	16	49	25
10 Stephens	33	22	45	33
HAWAII				
1 Matsunaga	20	55	31	56
2 Mink	14	71	24	66
IDAHO				
1 Symms	71	18	64	31
2 Hansen, G.	51	10	55	25
ILLINOIS				
1 Metcalfe	24	55	24	55
2 Murphy	31	55	36	55
3 Russo	27	73	32	68
4 Derwinski	73	24	74	21
5 Fary	37	59	30*	45*
6 Hyde	76	22	78	21
7 Collins	24	57	29	50
8 Rostenkowski	27	55	33	51
9 Yates	31	69	36	63
10 Mikva	18	75	29	63
11 Annunzio	35	65	37	55
12 Crane	71	20	64	28
13 McClory	82	18	77	19
14 Erlenborn	86	10	83	12
15 Hall	39	57	39	59
16 Anderson	53	25	65	20
17 O'Brien	69	27	69	25
18 Michel	78	12	84	9
19 Railsback	51	43	60	34
20 Findley	51	24	66	21
21 Madigan	71	22	67	25
22 Shipley	41	51	47	48
23 Price	33	67	40	56
24 Simon	25	67	39	58
INDIANA				
1 Madden	25	61	31	60
2 Fithian	22	73	26	70
3 Brademas	24	75	30	66
4 Roush	33	65	33	66
5 Hillis	57	29	61	29
6 Evans	31	57	29	66
7 Myers	75	24	68	31
8 Hayes	22	45	26	61
9 Hamilton	33	67	44	55
10 Sharp	33	67	36	64
11 Jacobs	27	67	31	64
IOWA				
1 Mezvinsky	22	78	26	73
2 Blouin	25	75	28	72
3 Grassley	63	37	57	43
4 Smith	29	69	35	64
5 Harkin	24	69	26	68
6 Bedell	25	75	26	71

Democrats   **Republicans**

	1	2	3	4
KANSAS				
1 Sebellus	71	14	67	24
2 Keys	22	71	26	71
3 Winn	63	31	64	31
4 Shriver	73	22	67	24
5 Skubltz	73	20	71	24
KENTUCKY				
1 Hubbard	53	47	41	57
2 Natcher	43	57	34	66
3 Mazzoli	31	67	36	61
4 Snyder	67	27	57	39
5 Carter	69	27	65	33
6 Breckinridge	39	55	40	54
7 Perkins	37	63	37	61
LOUISIANA				
1 Hebert	41	14	33	19
2 Boggs	39	43	42	47
3 Treen	80	14	71	21
4 Waggonner	67	27	66	29
5 Passman	45	24	49	35
6 Moore	75	25	68	30
7 Breaux	53	39	54	40
8 Long	45	51	49	49
MAINE				
1 Emery	45	55	48	52
2 Cohen	43	57	55	44
MARYLAND				
1 Bauman	76	22	64	34
2 Long	31	69	38	59
3 Sarbanes	18	71	30	64
4 Holt	71	24	63	34
5 Spellman	25	71	32	66
6 Byron	51	43	54	42
7 Mitchell	25	75	31	66
8 Gude	33	57	41	54
MASSACHUSETTS				
1 Conte	37	61	49	48
2 Boland	25	75	36	62
3 Early	25	71	27	70
4 Drinan	24	73	30	69
5 Tsongas	24	75	30	69
6 Harrington	24	61	24	64
7 Macdonald [1]	0†	52†	21*	54*
8 O'Neill	33	59	38	57
9 Moakley	24	75	29	69
10 Heckler	41	57	46	50
11 Burke	35	61	34	64
12 Studds	22	76	29	71
MICHIGAN				
1 Conyers	8	61	20	55
2 Esch	16	12	42	22
3 Brown	73	14	75	17
4 Hutchinson	84	14	79	19
5 Vander Veen	24	67	32	64
6 Carr	25	73	25	74
7 Riegle	10	47	20	56
8 Traxler	20	75	26	70
9 Vander Jagt	75	16	71	17
10 Cederberg	84	10	84	12
11 Ruppe	59	29	65	24
12 O'Hara	18	55	32	56
13 Diggs	22	49	25	46
14 Nedzi	29	67	34	62
15 Ford	22	65	26	59
16 Dingell	16	76	27	65
17 Brodhead	20	78	24	73
18 Blanchard	29	71	32	68
19 Broomfield	65	24	66	21
MINNESOTA				
1 Quie	78	18	73	23
2 Hagedorn	71	25	64	31
3 Frenzel	73	25	75	21
4 Karth	10	37	26	50
5 Fraser	22	67	28	49
6 Nolan	24	67	26	69
7 Bergland	27	63	36	60
8 Oberstar	24	76	31	69
MISSISSIPPI				
1 Whitten	53	43	49	44
2 Bowen	51	45	52	42
3 Montgomery	73	27	63	34
4 Cochran	63	33	61	36
5 Lott	59	37	54	40
MISSOURI				
1 Clay	12	47	26	56
2 Symington	16	45	31	48
3 Sullivan	22	45	25	57

	1	2	3	4
4 Randall	53	31	46	46
5 Bolling	20	67	39	54
6 Litton 2	11†	53†	27*	55*
7 Taylor	73	25	64	31
8 Ichord	65	27	54	37
9 Hungate	29	71	36	59
10 Burlison	45	49	44	54
MONTANA				
1 Baucus	25	73	26	71
2 Melcher	29	65	31	62
NEBRASKA				
1 Thone	69	31	63	37
2 McCollister	59	16	62	26
3 Smith	71	27	66	30
NEVADA				
AL Santini	35	53	32	61
NEW HAMPSHIRE				
1 D'Amours	20	76	25	73
2 Cleveland	73	27	66	29
NEW JERSEY				
1 Florio	24	73	26	70
2 Hughes	24	76	31	69
3 Howard	22	71	28	66
4 Thompson	24	67	28	63
5 Fenwick	39	55	56	34
6 Forsythe	67	25	68	24
7 Maguire	27	71	30*	68*
8 Roe	29	71	31	69
9 Helstoski	16	59	24	60
10 Rodino	18	73	29	61
11 Minish	24	75	31	66
12 Rinaldo	31	65	41	55
13 Meyner	20	76	31	65
14 Daniels	20	76	30	65
15 Patten	29	69	39	58
NEW MEXICO				
1 Lujan	55	27	56	34
2 Runnels	57	39	54	41
NEW YORK				
1 Pike	25	75	34	66
2 Downey	29	67	31	66
3 Ambro	25	75	26	71
4 Lent	61	35	63	31
5 Wydler	69	29	68	29
6 Wolff	27	71	26	68
7 Addabbo	25	71	31	64
8 Rosenthal	24	75	26	66
9 Delaney	33	67	37	63
10 Biaggi	29	61	30	60
11 Scheuer	22	71	27	61
12 Chisholm	16	61	24	64
13 Solarz	22	75	32	61
14 Richmond	18	73	24	70
15 Zeferetti	25	65	26	67
16 Holtzman	29	71	33	66
17 Murphy	39	45	36	48
18 Koch	24	73	31	67
19 Rangel	24	75	31	63
20 Abzug	14	55	25	59
21 Badillo	14	67	23	66
22 Bingham	24	75	34	64
23 Peyser	16	41	34	41
24 Ottinger	20	78	27	70
25 Fish	51	43	58	39
26 Gilman	27	71	43	55
27 McHugh	24	75	31	67
28 Stratton	43	43	48	46
29 Pattison	27	71	31	66
30 McEwen	71	10	63	24
31 Mitchell	55	39	59	36
32 Hanley	29	69	34	65
33 Walsh	49	47	53	42
34 Horton	53	39	59	32
35 Conable	80	8	81	14
36 LaFalce	27	55	33	58
37 Nowak	27	71	33	66
38 Kemp	73	22	69	27
39 Lundine 3	36†	59†	36*	59*
NORTH CAROLINA				
1 Jones	45	35	39	51
2 Fountain	45	31	43	44
3 Henderson	51	33	44	44
4 Andrews	41	45	39	46
5 Neal	39	53	31	65
6 Preyer	36†	60†	42*	56*
7 Rose	43	53	35	59
8 Hefner	43	45	33	62

	1	2	3	4
9 Martin	76	22	68	28
10 Broyhill	80	18	71	26
11 Taylor	63	31	55	43
NORTH DAKOTA				
AL Andrews	49	43	49	46
OHIO				
1 Gradison	76	22	78	21
2 Clancy	67	16	61	29
3 Whalen	31	69	39	59
4 Guyer	65	22	68	27
5 Latta	84	14	71	26
6 Harsha	53	31	45	45
7 Brown	80	16	78	17
8 Kindness	76	18	70	24
9 Ashley	37	59	44	51
10 Miller	80	20	69	30
11 Stanton	80	18	79	20
12 Devine	84	14	74	24
13 Mosher	57	35	60	29
14 Seiberling	25	71	33	64
15 Wylie	69	20	66	27
16 Regula	71	25	71	28
17 Ashbrook	69	20	62	33
18 Hays 4	26†	51†	30*	55*
19 Carney	25	67	26	69
20 Stanton	14	49	21	60
21 Stokes	24	69	28	64
22 Vanik	24	73	30	65
23 Mottl	25	67	26	69
OKLAHOMA				
1 Jones	51	43	54	39
2 Risenhoover	39	45	41	42
3 Albert 5				
4 Steed	47	43	46	45
5 Jarman	82	10	77	10
6 English	61	39	56	44
OREGON				
1 AuCoin	29	53	32	54
2 Ullman	31	63	41	54
3 Duncan	35	59	47	48
4 Weaver	25	63	28	66
PENNSYLVANIA				
1 Barrett 6	11†	50†	26*	54*
2 Nix	16	55	28	58
3 Green	6	53	21	60
4 Eilberg	24	71	26	69
5 Schulze	63	35	64	34
6 Yatron	37	57	31	63
7 Edgar	27	73	30	67
8 Biester	27	59	47	47
9 Shuster	76	24	66	34
10 McDade	45	49	51	46
11 Flood	35	59	34	60
12 Murtha	37	61	40	54
13 Coughlin	51	47	61	36
14 Moorhead	27	65	35	56
15 Rooney	43	53	41	57
16 Eshleman	45	8	48	18
17 Schneebeli	75	8	76	14
18 Heinz	18	41	38	41
19 Goodling, W.	65	29	59	38
20 Gaydos	20	75	26	61
21 Dent	29	57	33	58
22 Morgan	27	67	38	58
23 Johnson	59	22	70	21
24 Vigorito	29	63	30	64
25 Myers	65	35	70	30
RHODE ISLAND				
1 St Germain	24	71	29	67
2 Beard	22	73	26	67
SOUTH CAROLINA				
1 Davis	39	61	35	62
2 Spence	75	25	61	36
3 Derrick	37	61	39	56
4 Mann	63	33	57	36
5 Holland	22	45	28	53
6 Jenrette	31	67	31	59
SOUTH DAKOTA				
1 Pressler	47	51	43	56
2 Abdnor	71	27	61	38
TENNESSEE				
1 Quillen	76	20	66	25
2 Duncan	67	31	61	36
3 Lloyd	41	59	34	66
4 Evins	25	47	27	52
5 Allen	33	63	33*	64*
6 Beard	82	18	71	26

	1	2	3	4
7 Jones	37	27	34	48
8 Ford	24	61	27	61
TEXAS				
1 Hall 7	65†	35†	65*	35*
2 Wilson	45	39	49	33
3 Collins	78	22	70	30
4 Roberts	53	33	51	39
5 Steelman	29	8	49	26
6 Teague	57	18	44	22
7 Archer	73	27	70	29
8 Eckhardt	20	75	30	66
9 Brooks	33	61	37	53
10 Pickle	53	39	53	44
11 Poage	75	25	66	33
12 Wright	45	49	49	46
13 Hightower	65	33	56	41
14 Young	41	45	49	46
15 de la Garza	37	39	48	41
16 White	41	43	46	48
17 Burleson	73	27	68	30
18 Jordan	31	63	32	64
19 Mahon	71	29	64	35
20 Gonzalez	35	63	34	56
21 Krueger	47	47	49	42
22 Paul 8	66†	31†	66*	31*
23 Kazen	53	45	53	46
24 Milford	67	27	60	32
UTAH				
1 McKay	45	51	50	48
2 Howe	20	39	29	54
VERMONT				
AL Jeffords	35	53	54	41
VIRGINIA				
1 Downing	57	33	59	36
2 Whitehurst	71	20	64	31
3 Satterfield	75	25	65	34
4 Daniel	76	24	70	30
5 Daniel	75	25	71	29
6 Butler	76	18	74	24
7 Robinson	80	20	71	29
8 Harris	31	69	32	67
9 Wampler	69	25	63	30
10 Fisher	39	61	36	63
WASHINGTON				
1 Pritchard	57	39	64	28
2 Meeds	22	75	35	61
3 Bonker	27	67	31	62
4 McCormack	43	47	41	51
5 Foley	37	61	41	53
6 Hicks	33	63	39	59
7 Adams	20	73	31	63
WEST VIRGINIA				
1 Mollohan	35	63	35	51
2 Staggers	31	63	35	55
3 Slack	51	47	50	49
4 Hechler	22	76	29	70
WISCONSIN				
1 Aspin	29	59	35	58
2 Kastenmeier	33	67	32	66
3 Baldus	33	65	38	61
4 Zablocki	35	65	41	58
5 Reuss	25	75	31	66
6 Steiger	76	22	76	19
7 Obey	25	71	36	62
8 Cornell	27	73	31	69
9 Kasten	63	35	66	31
WYOMING				
AL Roncalio	33	59	34	59

Democrats   **Republicans**

Ford Appointments Stir Little Controversy

Presidential nominations generated few major controversies in 1976. None of President Ford's nominations was rejected on the Senate floor, although several met defeat in committee and no action was taken on others in order to delay filling of the vacancies until a new administration took office in 1977.

Meanwhile, as President Ford's term drew to a close, only two Cabinet officials inherited from the Nixon administration remained in office. One holdover, Treasury Secretary William E. Simon, had assumed his post only three months before Nixon resigned in August 1974. But the other, Secretary of State Henry A. Kissinger, had been associated with the Nixon administration from its earliest days, first as national security adviser and, since September 1973, as Secretary of State.

Cabinet Changes in 1976

A third Nixon appointee, Agriculture Secretary Earl L. Butz, resigned Oct. 4, three days after receiving a "severe reprimand" from Ford for making derogatory remarks about blacks that were reported in the press. "By taking this action," Butz wrote, "I hope to remove even the appearance of racism as an issue in the Ford campaign." Butz was succeeded by Under Secretary John A. Knebel on an interim appointment announced Nov. 4.

Two other Cabinet changes occurred earlier in the year.

The Senate Feb. 4 confirmed the nomination of W. J. Usery Jr. as Secretary of Labor to succeed John T. Dunlop, who resigned Jan. 14 because of Ford's veto of common-site picketing legislation. Usery, a Democrat who had been director of the Federal Mediation and Conciliation Service since 1973, was confirmed by a 79-7 vote.

The other Cabinet shift involved Elliot L. Richardson, who was confirmed as Secretary of Commerce in 1975 but did not assume office until February 1976, following the resignation of Rogers C. B. Morton.

Nominations That Failed

Of the 2,691 civilian nominations submitted by President Ford in 1976, 2,599 were confirmed by the Senate, while 77 were not confirmed and 15 were withdrawn. Election-year politics figured in the failure of some nominations, as Democratic leaders sought delays in the hope that vacancies could be filled by a President of their own party in 1977.

TVA Nominations Rejected

The Senate Public Works Committee rejected two Ford nominations to the three-member board of directors of the Tennessee Valley Authority (TVA).

By an 11-1 vote, the committee Feb. 24 indefinitely postponed action on the nomination of Mississippi dairyman James F. Hooper III to the TVA board. Only Sen. Robert Morgan (D N.C.) opposed the postponement. The nomination originally had been submitted June 12, 1975, but was returned to the White House on adjournment of the first session of the 94th Congress and resubmitted in 1976.

Hooper's nomination had been protested by Sen. Bill Brock (R Tenn.), unions, environmentalists and other officials from the seven states where the TVA supplied electric power. Critics contended that his record of business failures made him unqualified for the post. It also was noted that Hooper's wife was the Republican national committeewoman for Mississippi.

Ford subsequently nominated Thomas L. Longshore, an executive with the Alabama Power Company, to the TVA post. The committee Aug. 24 rejected, by a 6-8 vote, a motion to send that nomination to the full Senate with the recommendation that it be confirmed.

ICC Nomination Withdrawn

A nomination that critics had attacked as politically motivated backfired on the White House June 11 when the nominee asked that his name be withdrawn.

Warren B. Rudman, former attorney general of New Hampshire, was named by President Ford to succeed George M. Stafford as chairman of the Interstate Commerce Commission (ICC) on Feb. 4, 20 days before the Feb. 24

Ford Cabinet Members

Following is a list of Cabinet members serving during the Ford administration. By the end of the Ford presidency, only two Cabinet Secretaries remained from the Nixon administration: State and Treasury. Dates show the period actually served by each official.

Agriculture. Earl L. Butz (12/2/71-10/4/76); John A. Knebel (11/5/76-1/20/77).

Commerce. Frederick B. Dent (2/2/73-3/26/75); Rogers C. B. Morton (5/1/75-1/31/76); Elliot L. Richardson (2/2/76-1/20/77).

Defense. James R. Schlesinger (7/2/73-11/19/75); Donald H. Rumsfeld (11/20/75-1/20/77).

Health, Education and Welfare. Caspar W. Weinberger (2/12/73-8/8/75); F. David Mathews (8/8/75-1/20/77).

Housing and Urban Development. James T. Lynn (2/2/73-2/9/75); Carla A. Hills (3/10/75-1/20/77).

Interior. Rogers C. B. Morton (1/29/71-5/1/75); Stanley K. Hathaway (6/13/75-7/25/75); Thomas S. Kleppe (10/17/75-1/20/77).

Justice. William B. Saxbe (1/4/74-2/3/75); Edward H. Levi (2/7/75-1/20/77).

Labor. Peter J. Brennan (2/2/73-3/15/75); John T. Dunlop (3/18/75-2/1/76); W. J. Usery Jr. (2/10/76-1/20/77).

State. Henry A. Kissinger (9/22/73-1/20/77).

Transportation. Claude S. Brinegar (2/2/73-2/1/75); William T. Coleman (3/7/75-1/20/77).

Treasury. William E. Simon (5/8/74-1/20/77).

New Hampshire presidential primary. Democratic and Republican opponents of the nomination claimed it was a tactic to boost Ford's chances in the primary.

Martin Nomination Killed

The Senate Foreign Relations Committee Sept. 10 indefinitely postponed hearings on the nomination of Graham A. Martin to be the President's personal representative for negotiating the future political status of Micronesia, a U.S. trust territory.

The 64-year-old Foreign Service officer was ambassador to South Vietnam from 1973 to 1975, when the country fell to North Vietnamese control. During the April 1975 Communist siege of Saigon, Martin had been criticized for his role in the American evacuation, including charges that he procrastinated in evacuating U.S. personnel.

Hall Nomination Withdrawn

Conflict-of-interest charges led to withdrawal March 25 of Ford's nomination of Albert C. Hall as assistant secretary of the Air Force, at the nominee's request. Hall also resigned his position as assistant secretary of Defense because of a controversy over his relationship with his previous employer, Martin-Marietta Corp.

Judgeship: Senatorial Courtesy

The Senate Judiciary Committee May 5 tabled, and thus killed, the nomination of William B. Poff to a U.S. district court judgeship for the western district of Virginia. Poff fell victim to the tradition of "senatorial courtesy," an unwritten custom that makes it possible for one senator to block a nomination for a federal office within his state.

Poff's nomination was opposed by Sen. William Lloyd Scott (R Va.). Scott's preferred candidate for the judgeship was Glen M. Williams, whose philosophy, Scott said, "is a little bit closer to my own." Williams subsequently was nominated and confirmed by voice vote of the Senate Sept. 17.

Killed by Inaction

The threat of a filibuster during the waning hours of the 94th Congress blocked Senate action on the nomination of George F. Murphy Jr. as a member of the Nuclear Regulatory Commission. Confirmation of Murphy, executive director of the Joint Committee on Atomic Energy, was recommended by the committee Oct. 1 following a short closed-door meeting.

Other nominees for whom inaction spelled defeat included:

● Patrick J. Delaney, Securities and Exchange Commission. Delaney, son of Rep. James J. Delaney (D N.Y.), had been associate director of the Domestic Council since January 1976.

● Stanley E. Shirk, Comptroller of the Currency. Offered an interim appointment pending election of a new President, Shirk declined, saying such an action would further politicize the office.

● Thaddeus A. Garrett Jr., Consumer Product Safety Commission. Garrett, a black who served on the staff of Vice President Nelson A. Rockefeller, was given an interim appointment Nov. 17.

● Barbara Ann Simpson, Federal Power Commission. If confirmed, Simpson would have served only until June 22, 1977.

Other Controversies

Despite controversies over their nominations, several other Ford appointees won Senate confirmation in 1976.

Byington: Consumer Product Safety

Ending the year's most spirited confirmation struggle, the Senate May 26 approved S. John Byington as a member of the Consumer Product Safety Commission despite objections from consumer spokesmen who said he was unqualified. Byington, who was named commission chairman by Ford, won confirmation on a 45-39 vote. Only two days earlier the Senate had rejected the nomination 33-37.

A 38-year-old attorney from Grand Rapids, Mich., Byington had been deputy director of the Office of Consumer Affairs in the Department of Health, Education and Welfare since March 1974. He was a one-time business partner of Ford economic adviser L. William Seidman.

Byington was to fill a vacancy in a term ending in October 1978. The Senate Commerce Committee had shelved Ford's original nomination of Byington to a seven-year term as commission chairman.

Bush: CIA

The Senate Jan. 27 confirmed the nomination of George Bush to succeed William E. Colby as director of Central Intelligence. The vote was 64-27.

Some Democrats opposed the nomination because of Bush's past role in Republican Party affairs, including his service as national chairman in 1973-74.

Bush was serving as U.S. envoy to Peking when President Ford nominated him Nov. 3, 1975, to head the CIA. The Armed Services Committee approved the nomination Dec. 18 by a 12-4 vote after Ford assured Chairman John C. Stennis (D Miss.) by letter that he would not propose Bush as his 1976 running mate.

Brown: Joint Chiefs

By a vote of 57-34 the Senate July 1 confirmed Air Force Gen. George S. Brown's nomination to a second two-year term as chairman of the Joint Chiefs of Staff.

The nomination was strongly opposed by senators who condemned statements by Brown alleging that the U.S. Jewish community had "undue" influence on Congress in matters of policy affecting the Middle East.

Brown had come under fire in November 1974 for remarks at Duke University in which he criticized the power of the "Jewish lobby." Some members of Congress called for Brown's resignation, and President Ford reprimanded him Nov. 13.

Fogarty, White: FCC

Resolving a dispute that had become embroiled in election-year politics, the Senate Commerce Committee Sept. 8 approved, and the Senate by voice vote confirmed, the nominations of one Democrat and one Republican to the Federal Communications Commission.

Joseph R. Fogarty, the Democratic nominee, won a full seven-year term, while Republican Margareta E. White was to fill an uncompleted term for two years. Ford originally had nominated White for the full term and Fogarty for the two-year term.

Membership of Federal Regulatory Agencies, 1976

Civil Aeronautics Board

(Five members appointed for six-year terms; not more than three members from one political party)

Member	Party	Term Expires	Nominated	Confirmed by Senate
R. Tenney Johnson*	R	12/31/76	2/2/76	3/22/76
John E. Robson (C)*	R	12/31/77	2/28/75	4/18/75
Lee R. West	D	12/31/78	3/12/73	11/20/73
G. Joseph Minetti	D	12/31/79	11/26/73	12/12/73
Richard J. O'Melia**	R	12/31/80	5/16/74	9/19/74

Consumer Product Safety Commission

(Five members appointed for seven-year terms; not more than three members from one political party)

Member	Party	Term Expires	Nominated	Confirmed by Senate
Lawrence M. Kushner‡	D	10/26/76		
R. David Pittle	D	10/26/77	9/5/73	9/13/73
S. John Byington (C)*	R	10/26/78	1/20/76	5/26/76
Barbara H. Franklin	R	10/26/79	4/9/73	5/10/73
Thaddeus A. Garrett Jr.	R†	10/26/82		

Federal Communications Commission

(Seven members appointed for seven-year terms; not more than four members from one political party)

Member	Party	Term Expires	Nominated	Confirmed by Senate
Richard E. Wiley (C)	R	6/30/77	1/24/72	5/30/72
Margareta E. White*	R	6/30/78	7/19/76	9/8/76
Benjamin L. Hooks	D	6/30/79	4/12/72	5/30/72
James H. Quello	D	6/30/80	1/22/74	4/22/74
Robert E. Lee	R	6/30/81	5/17/74	6/27/74
Abbott Washburn**	R	6/30/82	6/18/75	9/26/75
Joseph R. Fogarty*	D	6/30/83	6/21/76	9/8/76

Federal Election Commission

(Six members appointed for six-year terms; not more than three members from one political party)[1]

Member	Party	Term Expires	Nominated	Confirmed by Senate
William L. Springer*	R	4/30/77	5/17/76	5/21/76
Neil Staebler*	D	4/30/77	5/17/76	5/18/76
Thomas E. Harris*	D	4/30/79	5/17/76	5/18/76
Vernon W. Thomson (C)*	R	4/30/79	5/17/76	5/18/76
Joan D. Aikens*	R	4/30/81	5/17/76	5/18/76
Robert O. Tiernan*	D	4/30/81	5/17/76	5/18/76

[1] Sitting members of the commission in 1976 were reconfirmed after the commission was reconstituted by order of the Supreme Court Jan. 30.

Federal Power Commission

(Five members appointed for five-year terms; not more than three members from one political party)

Member	Party	Term Expires	Nominated	Confirmed by Senate
Vacancy		6/22/77		
Don S. Smith	D	6/22/78	11/2/73	11/28/73
James G. Watt*	R	6/22/79	4/9/75	11/3/75
Richard L. Dunham (C)*	R	6/22/80	9/10/75	10/7/75
John Holliday Holloman*	D	6/22/81	5/7/76	6/18/76

Federal Reserve System Governors

(Seven members appointed for 14-year terms; no statutory limitation on political party membership)

Member	Party	Term Expires	Nominated	Confirmed by Senate
David M. Lilly*	R	1/31/78	4/26/76	5/28/76
Philip E. Coldwell	D	1/31/80	9/26/74	10/9/74
Philip C. Jackson Jr.*	D	1/31/82	5/22/75	6/25/75
Arthur F. Burns (C)	R	1/31/84	10/22/69	12/18/69
J. Charles Partee*	I	1/31/86	12/8/75	12/19/75
Henry C. Wallich	R	1/31/88	1/11/74	2/8/74
Stephen S. Gardner*	R	1/31/90	1/20/76	1/29/76

Federal Trade Commission

(Five members appointed for seven-year terms; not more than three members from one party)

Member	Party	Term Expires	Nominated	Confirmed by Senate
Vacancy		9/25/77		
Mary E. Hanford-Dole	I	9/25/80	9/5/73	11/20/73
Paul Rand Dixon**	D	9/25/81	9/5/74	9/26/74
Calvin Joseph Collier (C)*	R	9/25/82	2/23/76	4/18/76
David A. Clanton*	R	9/25/83	7/20/76	7/29/76

Interstate Commerce Commission

(Eleven members appointed for seven-year terms; not more than six members from one political party)

Member	Party	Term Expires	Nominated	Confirmed by Senate
Robert J. Corber*	R	12/31/76	1/16/75	3/3/75
Virginia Mae Brown	D	12/31/77	4/14/71	6/30/71
Dale W. Hardin	R	12/31/77	4/14/71	6/30/71
Rupert L. Murphy	D	12/31/78	3/23/72	10/5/72
Alfred T. MacFarland	I	12/31/78	2/7/73	4/6/73
Betty Jo Christian*	D	12/31/79	12/8/75	3/18/76
A. Daniel O'Neal Jr.	D	12/31/79	3/6/73	4/6/73
George M. Stafford (C)	R	12/31/80	1/15/74	2/27/74
Charles L. Clapp	R	12/31/80	1/22/74	2/27/74
Robert C. Gresham	R	12/31/81	6/3/74	9/19/74
Vacancy		12/31/82		

National Labor Relations Board

(Five members appointed for five-year terms; no statutory limitation on political party membership)

Member	Party	Term Expires	Nominated	Confirmed by Senate
John H. Fanning	D	12/16/77	1/11/73	1/31/73
Howard Jenkins Jr.	R	8/27/78	9/5/73	10/11/73
Betty Southard Murphy (C)*	R	12/16/79	1/27/75	2/5/75
Peter D. Walther*	R	8/27/80	10/28/75	11/20/75
John A. Penello**	D	8/27/81	5/28/76	8/4/76

Nuclear Regulatory Commission

(Five members appointed for five-year terms; not more than three members from one political party)

Member	Party	Term Expires	Nominated	Confirmed by Senate
Marcus A. Rowden (C)*	I	6/30/77	12/12/74	12/19/74
Edward A. Mason	R	6/30/78	12/12/74	12/19/74
Victor Gilinsky*	D	6/30/79	12/12/74	12/19/74
Richard T. Kennedy*	R	6/30/80	12/12/74	12/19/74
Vacancy		6/30/81		

Securities and Exchange Commission

(Five members appointed for five-year terms; not more than three members from one political party)

Member	Party	Term Expires	Nominated	Confirmed by Senate
Roderick M. Hills (C)*	R	6/5/77	10/2/75	10/9/75
John R. Evans	R	6/5/78	5/29/73	6/1/73
Philip A. Loomis Jr.	R	6/5/79	7/15/74	8/8/74
Irving M. Pollack**	D	6/5/80	7/1/75	8/1/75
Vacancy		6/5/81		

* Ford appointment   (C) Chairman
** Reappointed by Ford; first appointed in a previous administration.
† Interim appointment pending filling of vacancy.
‡ Continuing to serve pending filling of vacancy.

1976 CONFIRMATIONS

Listed below are the names of 131 persons named to major federal posts and confirmed by the Senate in 1976. Information is given in the following order: name of office; salary; appointee; voting residence; last occupation before appointment; date and place of birth; party affiliation (when available); date of Senate confirmation.

Ambassadorial confirmations are listed only if the appointment was of more than routine interest.

EXECUTIVE OFFICE OF THE PRESIDENT

Central Intelligence Agency

Director of Central Intelligence, $44,600—**George Bush;** Columbus, Ohio; chief of the U.S. liaison office, People's Republic of China (1974-76); former U.S. Representative (R Texas 1967-71); June 12, 1924, in Milton, Mass.; Rep.; Jan. 27.

Deputy Director of Central Intelligence, $42,000—**E. Henry Knoche;** Fairfax, Va.; associate deputy to the director (1975-76); Jan. 14, 1925, in Charleston, W.Va.; July 1.

Office of Science and Technology Policy

Director, $44,600—**H. Guyford Stever;** Washington, D.C.; director, National Science Foundation (1972-76); Oct. 24, 1916, in Corning, N.Y.; Rep.; Aug. 9.

Office of Telecommunications Policy

Director, $42,000—**Thomas J. Houser;** Woodstock, Ill.; partner in the law firm of Sidley and Austin in Chicago, Ill. (1973-76); former member, Federal Communications Commission (1971); June 28, 1929, in Chicago, Ill.; Rep.; July 1.

DEPARTMENTS

Department of Commerce

Under Secretary, $42,000—**Edward O. Vetter;** Dallas, Texas; executive vice president and chief financial officer of Texas Instruments Inc., Dallas (1972-75); Oct. 20, 1920, in Rochester, N.Y.; June 30.

Assistant Secretary for Administration, $39,900—**Joseph E. Kasputys;** Jamaica, N.Y.; assistant administrator, Maritime Administration (1975-76); Aug. 12, 1936, in Jamaica, N.Y.; Feb. 26.

Assistant Secretary for Domestic and International Business, $39,900—**Leonard S. Matthews;** Kenilworth, Ill.; consultant to the Leo Burnett Co. Inc., Chicago, Ill. (1976) and president and vice chairman of the board (1970-75); Jan. 2, 1922, in Glen Dean, Ky.; June 30.

Assistant Secretary for Economic Development, $39,900—**John W. Eden;** York, Pa.; deputy under secretary for field programs, and special assistant to the secretary for regional coordination (1975-76); July 30, 1927, in Cleveland, Ohio; Rep.; Aug. 3.

Assistant Secretary for Policy, $39,900—**Richard G. Darman;** Wellesley Hills, Mass.; principal and director of IFC Inc., Washington, D.C. (1975-76); May 10, 1943, in Charlotte, N.C.; Feb. 26.

General Counsel, $39,900—**John Thomas Smith III;** Washington, D.C.; associate in the law firm of Covington and Burling, Washington, D.C. (1974-76); Nov. 22, 1943, in New York, N.Y.; Rep.; Feb. 26.

Department of Defense

Assistant Secretary/Comptroller, $39,900—**Fred P. Wacker;** McLean, Va.; principal deputy assistant secretary/comptroller; Dec. 3, 1926, in Washington, D.C.; Aug. 6.

Assistant Secretary for Health Affairs, $39,900—**Robert Nelson Smith;** Toledo, Ohio; anesthesiologist in private practice, Toledo; April 2, 1920, in Toledo, Ohio; Rep.; Aug. 6.

Assistant Secretary for Installations and Logistics, $39,900—**Frank A. Shrontz;** McLean, Va.; assistant secretary of the Air Force for installations and logistics (1973-76); Dec. 14, 1931, in Boise, Idaho; Rep.; Feb. 6.

Assistant Secretary for International Security Affairs, $39,900—**Eugene V. McAuliffe;** Jamaica Plain, Mass.; ambassador to Hungary (1975-76); Nov. 25, 1918, in Boston, Mass.; May 3.

Assistant Secretary for Legislative Affairs, $39,900—**William K. Brehm;** Dearborn, Mich.; assistant secretary for manpower and reserve affairs (1973-76); March 29, 1929, in Dearborn, Mich.; March 18.

Assistant Secretary for Manpower and Reserve Affairs, $39,900—**David P. Taylor;** McLean, Va.; assistant secretary of the Air Force for manpower and reserve affairs (1974-76); April 7, 1934, in Chicago, Ill.; June 30.

Assistant Secretary for Public Affairs, $39,900—**M. Alan Woods;** Mexico, Mo.; special assistant to the secretary and deputy secretaries (1976); Oct. 13, 1945, in St. Louis, Mo.; Rep.; Aug. 6.

Air Force

Assistant Secretary for Financial Management $39,900—**Francis Hughes;** Hilton Head Island, S.C.; independent consultant in Hilton Head (1975-76); Aug. 12, 1921, in Washington, D.C.; March 10.

Assistant Secretary for Financial Management, $39,900—**Everett T. Keech;** Washington, D.C.; deputy associate director of the Office of Management and Budget (1974-76); Feb. 23, 1940, in Rochester, N.Y.; Sept. 10.

Assistant Secretary for Installations and Logistics, $39,900—**James Gordon Knapp;** Atherton, Calif.; president, Calso Water Co., Menlo Park, Calif. (1952-76); March 19, 1922, in San Francisco, Calif.; March 10.

Assistant Secretary for Manpower and Reserve Affairs, $39,900—**Juanita Ashcraft;** San Francisco, Calif.; member of the

---

Judgeships

The prestige of a federal judgeship is high, and appointment to the judiciary is considered by most attorneys and politicians to be the apex of a legal and public career.

Federal judgeships are lifetime appointments and pay $44,600 in the circuit court and $42,000 in the district court annually. There is no mandatory retirement age, but judges may retire at full salary at age 65 after 15 years or at 70 after 10 years on the bench.

The following list gives the number of confirmed federal circuit and district court judges appointed by President Ford in 1976 and by his six immediate predecessors.

	Democrats	Republicans
Roosevelt	188	6
Truman	116	9
Eisenhower	9	165
Kennedy†	111	11
Johnson	159	9
Nixon‡	15	198
Ford (1974-75)	5	28
Ford (1976)	7	24

† One New York liberal also was appointed
‡ No party affiliation was available for one judge from Puerto Rico, and one independent was chosen.

California State Personnel Board (1967-76); June 25, 1921, in Amarillo, Texas; Rep.; Aug. 6.

Assistant Secretary for Research and Development, $39,900—**John J. Martin;** Bethesda, Md.; principal deputy assistant secretary for research and development (1974-76); Oct. 19, 1922, in Detroit, Mich.; unaffiliated; June 30.

Navy

Under Secretary, $39,900—**David Robert Macdonald;** Winnetka, Ill.; assistant secretary of the Treasury for enforcement, operations and tariff affairs (1974-76); Nov. 1, 1930, in Chicago, Ill.; Rep.; Sept. 14.

Assistant Secretary for Installation and Logistics, $39,900—**John J. Bennett;** Alexandria, Va.; principal deputy assistant secretary of defense for installations and logistics (1975-76); Sept. 4, 1923, in Camden, N.J.; Sept. 10.

Joint Chiefs of Staff

Chairman for the term expiring July 3, 1978, $37,800—**George S. Brown;** Del Ray Beach, Fla.; reappointment (1974-76); Aug. 17, 1918, in Montclair, N.J.; July 1.

Department of Health, Education and Welfare

Assistant Secretary for Legislation, $39,900—**Thomas L. Lias;** Akron, Iowa; special assistant to the secretary for external affairs (1975-76); Sept. 27, 1934, in Akron, Iowa; Rep.; Aug. 27.

Assistant Secretary for Public Affairs, $39,900—**Susan B. Gordon;** Albuquerque, N.M.; assistant commissioner for public affairs, U.S. Office of Education (1975-76); April 6, 1940, in Brooklyn, N.Y.; Sept. 23.

General Counsel, $39,900—**William H. Taft IV;** Alexandria, Va.; assistant to the secretary (1973-76); Sept. 13, 1945, in Washington, D.C.; Rep.; April 5.

Office of Education

Commissioner, $37,800—**Edward Aguirre;** San Mateo, Calif.; regional commission of education in San Francisco (1973-76); Sept. 14, 1929, in Miami, Fla.; Dem.; Sept. 30.

Social and Rehabilitation Service

Administrator, $39,900—**Robert Fulton;** Winchester, Mass.; region I director, Boston, Mass. (1973-76); Sept. 8, 1931, in Patton, Mo.; Rep.; June 16.

Department of Housing and Urban Development

Assistant Secretary for Consumer Affairs and Regulatory Functions, $39,900—**Constance B. Newman;** Washington, D.C.; vice chairman, Consumer Product Safety Commission (1975-76), July 8, 1935, in Chicago, Ill.; Rep.; Feb. 24.

Assistant Secretary for Housing/Federal Housing Commissioner, $39,900—**James L. Young;** Bellevue, Wash.; regional administrator in Seattle, Wash. (1974-76); Sept. 8, 1932, in Swain, Ark.; Rep.; March 11.

Department of the Interior

Assistant Secretary for Administration and Management, $39,900—**Albert C. Zapanta;** Los Angeles; southwest coordinator of the President Ford Committee (1975-76); March 8, 1941, in Los Angeles, Calif.; Rep.; June 29.

Assistant Secretary for Energy and Minerals, $39,900—**William L. Fisher;** Austin, Texas; deputy assistant secretary for energy and minerals (1975-76); Sept. 16, 1932, in Marion, Ill.; Rep.; March 23.

Assistant Secretary for Program Development and Budget, $39,900—**Ronald G. Coleman;** Annandale, Va.; executive assistant to the secretary (1975-76); Nov. 14, 1935, in Royal Oak, Mich.; Rep.; May 21.

Department of Justice

Assistant Attorney General (Antitrust), $39,900—**Donald I. Baker;** Ithaca, N.Y.; special counsel for Cadwalader, Wickersham and Taft in New York City (1975-76) and part-time consultant for the antitrust division (1976); June 4, 1934, in Englewood, N.J.; unaffiliated; Aug. 26.

Drug Enforcement Administration

Administrator, $42,000—**Peter B. Bensinger;** Chicago, Ill.; chief, crime victims division, Illinois attorney general's office, Chicago (1974-76); March 24, 1936, in Chicago, Ill.; Rep.; Feb. 5.

Department of Labor

Secretary, $63,000—**W. J. Usery Jr.;** Macon, Ga.; special assistant to the President for labor-management negotiations (1975-76) and director, Federal Mediation and Conciliation Service (1973-76); Dec. 21, 1923, in Hardwick, Ga.; Dem.; Feb. 4.

Under Secretary, $42,000—**Michael H. Moskow;** Paterson, N.J.; director, Council on Wage and Price Stability (1975-76); Jan. 7, 1938, in Paterson, N.J.; Rep.; May 12.

Assistant Secretary for Employment Standards Administration $39,900—**John Conyers Read;** Reston, Va.; counselor and executive assistant to the secretary (1975-76); May 21, 1947, in New York, N.Y.; Rep.; May 12.

Department of State

Deputy Secretary, $44,600—**Charles W. Robinson;** San Francisco, Calif.; under secretary for economic affairs (1975-76); Sept. 7, 1919, in Long Beach, Calif.; April 7.

Under Secretary for Economic Affairs, $42,000—**William D. Rogers;** Great Falls, Va.; assistant secretary for inter-American affairs (1974-76); May 12, 1927, in Wilmington, Del.; Dem.; June 16.

Under Secretary for Political Affairs, $42,000—**Philip C. Habib;** San Francisco, Calif.; assistant secretary for East Asian and Pacific Affairs (1974-76); Feb. 26, 1920, in Brooklyn, N.Y.; unaffiliated; June 16.

Deputy Inspector General, Foreign Assistance, $39,900—**Joseph Z. Taylor;** Alexandria, Va.; assistant inspector general (1974-76); June 10, 1927, in East Greenwich, R.I.; June 16.

Assistant Secretary for East Asian and Pacific Affairs, $39,900—**Arthur W. Hummel Jr.;** Chevy Chase, Md.; ambassador to Ethiopia (1975-76); June 1, 1920, in China; unaffiliated; June 16.

Assistant Secretary for Economic and Business Affairs, $39,900—**Joseph A. Greenwald;** Chicago, Ill.; minister to the European Communities (1972-76); Sept. 18, 1918, in Chicago, Ill.; Jan. 28.

Assistant Secretary for Economic and Business Affairs, $39,900—**Julius L. Katz;** Bethesda, Md.; deputy assistant secretary for economic and business affairs (1974-76); March 9, 1925, in New York, N.Y.; Sept. 15.

Assistant Secretary for Inter-American Affairs, $39,900—**Harry W. Shlaudeman;** San Marino, Calif.; ambassador to Venezuela (1975-76); April 17, 1926, in Los Angeles, Calif.; June 16.

Assistant Secretary for Oceans and International Environmental and Scientific Affairs, $39,900—**Frederick Irving;** Providence, R.I.; ambassador to Iceland (1972-76); May 2, 1921, in Providence, R.I.; March 24.

Agency for International Development

Assistant Administrator for Interagency Development Coordination, $39,900—**Christian A. Herter Jr.;** Washington, D.C.; deputy assistant secretary of state for environmental and population affairs (1975-76); Jan. 29, 1919, in New York, N.Y.; Rep.; April 1.

Assistant Administrator for Latin America, $39,900—**Eugene N. S. Girard II;** Clarksdale, Miss.; administration and marketing vice president, financial institutions division of Citibank, New York City (1976); March 20, 1938, in Hazleton, Pa.; Sept. 30.

Assistant Administrator for Population and Humanitarian Assistance, $39,900—**Frederick O. Pinkham;** Old Greenwich, Conn.; vice president of the World Business Council, New York City (1970-76); June 16, 1920, in Ann Arbor, Mich.; Rep.; April 1.

Ambassadors

(Dollar figures in parentheses reflect 5 per cent pay raise that took effect Oct. 1.)

At Large and Chief of Protocol, $39,900 ($41,800)—**Shirley Temple Black;** Woodside, Calif.; ambassador to Ghana (1974-76); April 23, 1928, in Santa Monica, Calif.; Rep.; June 23.

China, People's Republic (Chief of Liaison Office), $37,800 ($39,600)—**Thomas S. Gates Jr.;** Devon, Pa.; chairman of the executive committee, Morgan Guaranty Trust Co.; New York City (1969-76), former Secretary of Defense (1959-60); April 10, 1906, in Philadelphia, Pa.; Rep.; April 1.

Germany, Federal Republic, $44,600 ($46,800)—**Walter J. Stoessel;** Santa Monica, Calif.; ambassador to Russia (1973-76); Jan. 24, 1920, in Manhattan, Kan.; Sept. 15.

Great Britain, $44,600 ($46,800)—**Anne Legendre Armstrong;** Armstrong, Texas; counselor to the President (1973-74); Dec. 27, 1927, in New Orleans, La.; Rep.; Jan. 28.

Norway, $39,900 ($41,800)—**William A. Anders;** McLean, Va.; chairman, Nuclear Regulatory Commission (1975-76); Oct. 17, 1933, in Hong Kong; Rep.; April 1.

European Communities, $41,800 ($42,000)—**Deane R. Hinton;** Chicago, Ill.; senior adviser to the under secretary for economic affairs (1975-76); March 12, 1923, in Fort Missoula, Mont.; Jan. 28.

North Atlantic Treaty Organization, $44,600 ($46,800)—**Robert Strausz-Hupé;** Newton Square, Pa.; ambassador to Sweden (1974-76); March 25, 1903, in Vienna, Austria; Rep.; March 3.

United Nations, $44,600 ($46,800)—**William W. Scranton,** Dalton, Pa.; former governor of Pennsylvania (R 1963-67), former U.S. Representative (R Pa. 1961-63); July 19, 1917, in Madison, Conn.; Rep.; March 3.

United Nations' European Office, $41,800 ($44,000)—**Henry E. Catto Jr.;** San Antonio, Texas; chief of protocol (1974-76); Dec. 6, 1930, in Dallas, Texas; Rep.; June 23.

Department of Transportation

Administrator, National Highway Traffic Safety Administration, $39,900—**John W. Snow;** Washington, D.C.; deputy under secretary of transportation (1975-76); Aug. 2, 1939, in Toledo, Ohio; Rep.; July 2.

Department of the Treasury

Deputy Secretary, $44,600—**George H. Dixon;** Minneapolis, Minn.; chairman and president, First National Bank of Minneapolis (1968-76); Oct. 7, 1920, in Rochester, N.Y.; March 2.

Under Secretary, $42,000—**Jerry Thomas;** Jupiter, Fla.; president and chairman of the board, General Financial Systems Inc., Riviera, Fla. (1964-76); April 30, 1929, in West Palm Beach, Fla.; Rep.; April 13.

Assistant Secretary for Capital Markets and Debt Management, $39,900—**Robert A. Gerard;** Washington, D.C.; deputy assistant secretary for financial resources policy (1975-76); Oct. 19, 1944, in New York, N.Y.; Rep.; April 13.

INDEPENDENT AGENCIES

Civil Aeronautics Board

Member for the term expiring Dec. 31, 1976, $39,900—**R. Tenney Johnson;** Bethesda, Md.; general counsel, Energy Research and Development Administration (1975-76); March 24, 1930, in Evanston, Ill.; Rep.; March 22.

Civil Service Commission

Vice chairman for the term expiring March 1, 1977, $39,900—**Georgiana H. Sheldon;** Arlington, Va.; foreign disaster relief coordinator, Agency for International Development (1975-76); Dec. 2, 1923, in Lawrenceville, Pa.; Rep.; Feb. 26.

Commodity Futures Trading Commission

Member for the term expiring June 19, 1981, $39,900—**Robert L. Martin;** Arlington Heights, Ill.; reappointment (1975-76); Oct. 30, 1914, in Vancouver, B.C., Canada; Rep.; June 17.

Community Services Administration

Director, $44,600—**Samuel R. Martinez;** Lakewood, Colo.; Department of Labor regional director, Denver, Colo. (1973-76); April 30, 1933, in Del Norte, Colo.; April 7.

Deputy Director, $42,000—**Robert C. Chase;** Alexandria, Va.; deputy assistant secretary of labor for employment standards (1974-76); Oct. 27, 1937, in Westwood, Mass.; July 23.

Consumer Product Safety Commission

Chairman for the term expiring Oct. 26, 1978, $42,000—**S. John Byington;** Annandale, Va.; deputy director, Office of Consumer Affairs, Department of Health, Education and Welfare (1974-76); Oct. 9, 1937, in Kalamazoo, Mich.; Rep.; May 26.

Energy Research and Development Administration

Assistant Administrator for Solar, Geothermal and Advanced Energy Systems, $39,900—**Robert L. Hirsch;** Potomac, Md.; director, division of controlled thermonuclear research, AEC-ERDA (1972-76); March 6, 1935, in Evanston, Ill.; Rep.; March 23.

Equal Employment Opportunity Commission

Member for the term expiring July 1, 1979, $39,900—**Daniel Edward Leach;** Alexandria, Va.; associate chief counsel, Democratic Policy Committee of the U.S. Senate (1966-76); April 2, 1937, in Detroit, Mich.; Dem.; March 3.

Federal Communications Commission

Member for the term expiring June 30, 1983, $39,900—**Joseph R. Fogarty;** Middletown, R.I.; communications counsel for the U.S. Senate Committee on Commerce (1975-76); Jan. 12, 1931, in Newport, R.I.; Dem.; Sept. 8.

Member for the term expiring June 30, 1978, $39,900—**Margareta E. White;** McLean, Va.; assistant press secretary to the President (1975-76) and director, office of communications (1975-76); June 27, 1937, in Sweden; Rep.; Sept. 8.

Federal Deposit Insurance Corporation

Chairman of the Board of Directors for the term expiring March 18, 1982, $42,000—**Robert E. Barnett;** Washington, D.C.; deputy to the chairman (1970-76); Dec. 4, 1935, in Lincoln, Neb.; Rep.; March 17.

Federal Election Commission

Chairman for the term expiring April 30, 1979, $39,900—**Vernon W. Thomson;** Richmond Center, Wis.; reappointment, former U.S. Representative (R Wis. 1961-75), former governor of Wisconsin (R 1957-59); Nov. 5, 1905, in Richmond Center, Wis.; Rep.; May 18.

Vice chairman for the term expiring April 30, 1979, $39,900—**Thomas E. Harris;** Washington D.C.; reappointment; May 25, 1912, in Little Rock, Ark.; Dem.; May 18.

Member for the term expiring April 30, 1981, $39,900—**Joan D. Aikens;** Swarthmore, Pa.; reappointment; May 1, 1928, in Lansdowne, Pa.; Rep.; Jan. 29, May 18.

Member for the term expiring April 30, 1977, $39,900—**William L. Springer;** Champaign, Ill.; commissioner, Federal Power Commission (1974-75), former U.S. Representative (R Ill. 1951-73); April 12, 1909, in Sullivan, Ill.; Rep.; May 21.

Member for the term expiring April 30, 1977, $39,900—**Neil Staebler;** Ann Arbor, Mich.; reappointment; former U.S. Representative (D Mich. 1963-65); July 11, 1905, in Ann Arbor, Mich.; Dem.; May 18.

Member for the term expiring April 30, 1981, $39,900—**Robert O. Tiernan;** Providence, R.I.; reappointment; former U.S. Representative (D R.I. 1967-75); Feb. 24, 1929, in Providence, R.I.; Dem.; May 18.

Federal Energy Administration

Assistant Administrator for Energy Conservation and Environment, $39,900—**Samuel J. Tuthill;** McLean, Va.; adviser to the administrator (1976); Sept. 6, 1925, in San Diego, Calif.; Rep.; June 29.

Assistant Administrator for Energy Information and Analysis, $39,900—**John D. Christie;** Arlington, Va.; principal deputy assistant secretary of defense for program analysis and evaluation (1972-76); April 20, 1937, Greensburg, Pa.; unaffiliated; March 23.

Assistant Administrator for International Energy Affairs, $39,900—**Clement B. Malin;** Falls Church, Va.; deputy assistant administrator for international energy affairs (1974-76); April 4, 1934, in Drexel Hill, Pa.; Rep.; June 29.

Federal Maritime Commission

Member for the term expiring June 30, 1978, $39,900—**Bob Casey;** Houston, Texas; former U.S. Representative (D Texas 1959-76); July 27, 1915, in Joplin, Mo.; Dem.; Jan. 21.

Federal Mediation and Conciliation Service

National Director, $42,000—**James F. Scearce;** McLean, Va.; deputy director (1974-76); Oct. 11, 1932, in High Point, N.C.; April 7.

Federal Power Commission

Member for the term expiring June 22, 1981, $39,900—**John Holliday Holloman III;** Jackson, Miss.; reappointment (1975-76); March 5, 1937, in Columbus, Miss.; Dem.; June 18.

Federal Reserve System

Vice Chairman of the Board of Governors for the term expiring Jan. 31, 1990, $42,000—**Stephen S. Gardner;** Wawa, Pa.; deputy secretary of the Treasury (1974-76); Dec. 26, 1921, in Wakefield, Mass.; Rep.; Jan. 29.

Member of the Board of Governors for the term expiring Jan. 31, 1978, $42,000—**David M. Lilly;** St. Paul, Minn.; president and chairman of the board of the Toro Co.; Minneapolis, Minn.; June 14, 1917, in St. Paul, Minn.; Rep.; May 28.

Federal Trade Commission

Chairman for the term expiring Sept. 25, 1982, $42,000—**Calvin Joseph Collier,** McLean, Va.; associate director for economics and government, Office of Management and Budget (1975-76); Jan. 6, 1942, in Berwyn, Ill.; Rep.; March 18.

Member for the term expiring Sept. 25, 1976, $39,900—**David A. Clanton;** Arlington, Va.; legislative assistant to the minority leader of the U.S. Senate (1975-76); May 31, 1944, in Santa Barbara, Calif.; Rep.; July 29.

Member for the term expiring Sept. 25, 1983, $39,900—**David A. Clanton;** Arlington, Va.; reappointment (1976); May 31, 1944, in Santa Barbara, Calif.; Rep.; July 29.

Interstate Commerce Commission

Member for the term expiring Dec. 31, 1979, $39,900—**Betty Jo Christian;** Washington, D.C.; associate general counsel for litigation (1971-76); July 27, 1936, in Smithville, Texas; Dem.; March 18.

National Aeronautics and Space Administration

Deputy Administrator, $42,000—**Alan M. Lovelace;** Severna Park, Md.; associate administrator for aeronautics and space technology (1974-76); Sept. 4, 1929, in St. Petersburg, Fla.; June 25.

National Labor Relations Board

Member for the term expiring Aug. 27, 1981, $39,900—**John A. Penello;** Severna Park, Md.; reappointment (1972-76); Aug. 26, 1909, in Norfolk, Va.; Dem.; Aug. 4.

National Mediation Board

Member for the term expiring July 1, 1979, $39,900—**David H. Stowe;** Bethesda, Md.; reappointment (1970-76); Sept. 10, 1910, in New Canaan, Conn.; Dem.; July 21.

National Transportation Safety Board

Chairman and member for the term expiring Dec. 31, 1980, $42,000—**Webster B. Todd Jr.;** Far Hills, N.J.; inspector general of foreign assistance, Department of State (1974-76); Dec. 1, 1938, in New York, N.Y.; Rep.; Feb. 5.

Vice Chairman and member for the term expiring Dec. 31, 1979, $39,900—**Kay Bailey;** Houston, Texas; former Texas State Representative (R 1972-76); July 22, 1943, in Galveston, Texas; Rep.; June 25.

Member for the term expiring Dec. 31, 1978, $39,900—**Philip Allison Hogue;** Springfield, Va.; deputy chief officer of operations of the Coast Guard, Washington, D.C. (1974-76); Sept. 12, 1920, in Kansas City, Mo.; independent; April 12.

Small Business Administration

Administrator, $42,000—**Mitchell P. Kobelinski;** Chicago, Ill.; member of the board of directors, Export-Import Bank (1973-76); Aug. 1, 1928, in Chicago, Ill.; Rep.; Feb. 6.

JUDICIARY

U.S. Circuit Court of Appeals

Judge for the fourth circuit, $44,600—**Kenneth K. Hall;** Charleston, W.Va.; U.S. district court judge for the southern district of West Virginia (1971-76); Feb. 24, 1918, in Greenview, W.Va.; Dem.; Sept. 1.

Judge for the fifth circuit, $44,600—**Peter T. Fay;** Miami, Fla.; U.S. district court judge for the southern district of Florida (1970-76); Jan. 18, 1929, in Rochester, N.Y.; Rep.; Sept. 17.

Judge for the fifth circuit, $44,600—**James C. Hill;** Atlanta, Ga.; U.S. district court judge for the northern district of Georgia (1974-76); Jan. 8, 1924, in Darlington, S.C.; Dem.; May 19.

Judge for the seventh circuit, $44,600—**Harlington Wood Jr.;** Springfield, Ill.; U.S. district court judge for the southern district of Illinois (1973-76); April 17, 1920, in Springfield, Ill.; Rep.; May 6.

Judge for the ninth circuit, $44,600—**J. Blaine Anderson;** Boise, Idaho; U.S. district court judge for the district of Idaho (1971-76); Jan. 19, 1922, in Trenton, Utah; Rep.; July 2.

U.S. District Courts

Judge for the district of Arizona, $42,000—**Mary Anne Richey;** Tucson, Ariz.; judge, Superior Court of Arizona (1964-76); Oct. 24, 1917, in Shelbyville, Ind.; Rep.; June 16.

Judge for the central district of California, $42,000—**Robert M. Takasugi;** Montebello, Calif.; judge, Los Angeles Superior Court (1975-76); Sept. 12, 1930, in Tacoma, Wash.; Dem.; May 6.

Judge for the central district of California, $42,000—**Laughlin E. Waters;** Los Angeles, Calif.; partner in the law firm of Nossaman, Waters, Krueger and Marsh, Los Angeles (1961-76); Aug. 16, 1914, in Los Angeles, Calif.; Rep.; May 11.

Judge for the northern district of California, $42,000—**William A. Ingram;** Palo Alto, Calif.; judge, Superior Court of California (1971-76); July 6, 1924, in Jeffersonville, Ind.; Rep.; July 23.

Judge for the northern district of California, $42,000—**Cecil F. Poole;** San Francisco, Calif.; counsel in the law firm of Jacobs, Sills and Coblentz, San Francisco (1970-76); July 25, 1914, in Birmingham, Ala.; Dem.; July 23.

Judge for the northern district of California, $42,000—**William W. Schwarzer;** Mill Valley, Calif.; member of the law firm of McCutchen, Doyle, Brown and Enersen, San Francisco (1952-76); April 30, 1925, in Berlin, Germany; Rep.; July 23.

Judge for the southern district of Florida, $42,000—**Sidney M. Aronovitz;** Miami, Fla.; senior partner in the law firm of Aronovitz, Silver and Booth, Miami (1970-76); June 20, 1920, in Key West, Fla.; Dem.; Sept. 17.

Judge for the district of Idaho, $42,000—**Marion J. Callister;** Boise, Idaho; U.S. attorney for the district of Idaho (1975-76); June 6, 1921, in Moreland, Idaho; Rep.; Aug. 26.

Judge for the northern district of Illinois, $42,000—**John P. Crowley,** Evanston, Ill.; senior partner in the law firm of Crowley, Burke, Nash and Shea Ltd., Chicago; Oct. 5, 1936, in Chicago, Ill.; Rep.; June 16.

Judge for the northern district of Illinois, $42,000—**George N. Leighton;** state justice, Illinois Appellate Court, (1969-76); Oct. 22, 1912, in New Bedford, Mass.; Dem.; Feb. 2.

Judge for the southern district of Illinois, $42,000—**J. Waldo Ackerman,** Springfield, Ill.; Illinois state judge, 7th judicial circuit (1971-76); Jan. 1, 1926, in Jacksonville, Fla.; Rep.; July 2.

Judge for the northern district of Indiana, $42,000—**Phil M. McNagny Jr.;** Columbia City, Ind.; partner in the law firm of Gates, Gates and McNagny, Columbia City; (1960-76); July 16, 1924, in Fort Wayne, Ind.; Rep.; May 6.

Judge for the eastern district of Louisiana, $42,000—**Charles Schwartz Jr.;** Metairie, La.; partner in the law firm of Little, Schwartz and Dussom, New Orleans; (1970-76); Aug. 20, 1922, in New Orleans, La.; Rep.; May 6.

Judge for the eastern district of Louisiana, $42,000—**Morey L. Sear;** New Orleans, La.; U.S. magistrate, eastern district of Louisiana (1971-76); Feb. 26, 1929, in New Orleans, La.; Rep.; May 6.

Judge for the western district of Louisiana, $42,000—**W. Eugene Davis;** New Iberia, La.; partner in the law firm of Caffery, Duhe and Davis, New Iberia (1964-76); Aug. 18, 1936, in Winfield, Ala.; Rep.; Sept. 17.

Judge for the eastern district of Michigan $42,000—**Ralph B. Guy Jr.;** Dearborn, Mich.; U.S. attorney, eastern district of Michigan (1970-76); Aug. 30, 1929, in Detroit, Mich.; Rep.; May 11.

Judge for the eastern district of New York, $42,000—**George C. Pratt;** Syosset, N.Y.; partner in the law firm of Farrell, Fritz, Pratt, Caemmerer and Cleary, Williston Park (1967-76); May 22, 1928, in Corning, N.Y.; Rep.; May 6.

Judge for the northern district of New York, $42,000—**Howard G. Munson;** Syracuse, N.Y.; member in the law firm of Hiscock, Lee, Rogers, Henley and Barclay, Syracuse (1952-76); July 26, 1924, in Claremont, N.H.; Rep.; Sept. 23.

Judge for the southern district of New York, $42,000—**Vincent L. Broderick;** New York, N.Y.; member in the law firm of Forsyth, Decker, Murray and Broderick, New York City (1971-76); April 26, 1920, in New York, N.Y.; Dem.; Sept. 23.

Judge for the southern district of New York, $42,000—**Gerard L. Goettel;** Rye, N.Y.; U.S. magistrate, southern district of New York (1971-76); Aug. 5, 1928, in New York, N.Y.; Rep.; March 26.

Judge for the southern district of New York, $42,000—**Charles S. Haight Jr.;** New York, N.Y.; senior partner in the law firm of Haight, Gardner, Poor and Havens, New York City; (1957-76); Sept. 23, 1930, in New York, N.Y.; Rep.; March 26.

Judge for the northern district of Ohio, $42,000—**John M. Manos;** Bay Village, Ohio; state court of appeals judge, 8th appellate district of Ohio; (1969-76); Dec. 8, 1922, in Cleveland, Ohio; Rep.; March 26.

Judge for the western district of Pennsylvania, $42,000—**Maurice B. Cohill Jr.;** Pittsburgh, Pa.; judge of the court of common pleas of Allegheny County, Pa.; (1969-76); Nov. 26, 1929, in Pittsburgh, Pa.; Rep.; May 18.

Judge for the southern district of Texas, $42,000—**Ross N. Sterling;** Houston, Texas; member in the law firm of Vinson, Elkins, Searls, Connally and Smith, Houston; (1958-76); Jan. 18, 1931, in Houston, Texas; Rep.; May 6.

Judge for the western district of Virginia, $42,000—**Glen M. Williams;** Jonesville, Va.; U.S. commissioner/magistrate, western district of Virginia (1963-75); Feb. 17, 1920, in Jonesville, Va.; Rep.; Sept. 17.

Judge for the southern district of West Virginia, $42,000—**John T. Copenhaver Jr.;** Charleston, W.Va.; referee in bankruptcy, U.S. district court, southern district of West Virginia (1958-76); Sept. 29, 1925, in Charleston, W.Va.; Rep.; Sept. 1.

U.S. Court of Military Appeals

Judge for the term expiring May 1, 1991, $44,600—**William Holmes Cook;** Carbondale, Ill.; reappointment (1974-76); June 2, 1920, in Carbondale, Ill.; Rep.; March 10. ▌

Presidential
Election

CQ

1976 Presidential Election

Ford Loses Close Race with Carter

The American electorate called for an end to eight years of divided government Nov. 2, selecting Democrat Jimmy Carter of Georgia as the 39th President and maintaining lopsided Democratic majorities in both houses of Congress.

Carter's victory over President Ford was narrow, achieved by a popular plurality of fewer than two million and an electoral count of only 297-240. The congressional decision was overwhelming, with Democrats keeping their 2-1 advantage in the House and their 62-38 margin over Republicans in the Senate.

But the combined result was Democratic control at both ends of Pennsylvania Avenue, the first such restoration since John F. Kennedy's election in 1960 and only the party's fourth in the 20th century. Despite the obvious differences between Kennedy and Carter, there were many similarities between the political climates of 1961 and 1977.

As in 1961, the nation inaugurated a President who campaigned on the promise of an aggressive and imaginative new government, but who had offered few specifics about what he would do. Carter's victory, like Kennedy's, was a triumph of party and region, with the nation's majority party drawing just what it had to draw, winning most of the South and losing most of the West.

The Solid South returned in 1976 for the first time since 1944. Oklahoma and Virginia were the only two of the 13 southern states that Carter failed to carry, and he came within a percentage point in both. The South gave Carter 115 of his 297 electoral votes.

The South not only voted for Carter; it voted for him in large numbers. Turnout was up virtually everywhere in the South, and Carter reaped the benefits. He won 11 of the 12 southern states which showed a higher percentage turnout in 1976 than in 1972.

But the Democratic successes would not have been possible without a strong party-line vote in New York and Pennsylvania, states that had shown no discernible fondness for Carter but that went heavily Democratic in 1960 and 1968—and did so again this time. A reversal in New York alone would have given Ford the election; but, as in Pennsylvania, labor unions worked hard to keep their constituency in line, and the majority eventually fell into place.

Even though Carter's national popular vote margin was more than 10 times greater than Kennedy's in 1960 and more than twice as great as Richard M. Nixon's in 1968, the electoral college system came closer to misfiring than it did in either of those two years. Carter's southern strength gave him millions of extra popular votes that were of no electoral value.

The election ended a lackluster campaign that saw Carter's lead in the polls drop from 33 points after the Democratic convention to the point where the race was considered too close to call. The campaign was notable for the first presidential debates since 1960. Carter's poor performance in the first debate was considered of major importance in Ford's rise in the polls; his improved showing in the remaining two debates may have saved the election for him.

Election Analysis

Jimmy Carter's rural southern background made him unique among Democratic presidential nominees, but his coalition was a lot like the ones used by his predecessors. He swept the South, took a majority in the East, and did well enough in the Midwest to struggle home with a victory.

But it was not easy. Carter won with the smallest electoral college margin since Woodrow Wilson won re-election in 1916.

In nearly half the states, the winner's popular plurality was less than 5 percentage points. In 11 of them, it was two or less. Carter won only three of the closest 11 states.

In several states, the independent candidacy of Eugene J. McCarthy appeared to have tipped the balance to Ford. McCarthy and his aides claimed that the former Democrat was aiming his appeal at dissatisfied independents, but McCarthy appeared to have drawn most of his votes from Carter.

In the national popular vote count McCarthy made little impact, receiving about 750,000 votes (less than 1 per cent of the total). Yet in four Ford carried—Iowa, Maine, Oklahoma and Oregon—the McCarthy vote was greater than the margin by which the President carried the states. The former Democratic senator also took nearly 60,000 votes in Ohio.

Carter won by welding together varying proportions of Roosevelt's New Deal coalition—the South, the industrial Northeast, organized labor, minorities, and the liberal community. Carter won majorities in each of these regions and voting groups and made a better than usual showing for a Democratic candidate in the rural Midwest.

South

Carter's near sweep of the South was the best showing by any Democrat in the region since Roosevelt carried all 13 southern states in 1944. Carter's success was also an abrupt

Electoral College Votes

(270 Electoral Votes Needed to Win)

State	VOTES Carter	VOTES Ford
Alabama	9	
Alaska		3
Arizona		6
Arkansas	6	
California		45
Colorado		7
Connecticut		8
Delaware	3	
District of Columbia	3	
Florida	17	
Georgia	12	
Hawaii	4	
Idaho		4
Illinois		26
Indiana		13
Iowa		8
Kansas		7
Kentucky	9	
Louisiana	10	
Maine		4
Maryland	10	
Massachusetts	14	
Michigan		21
Minnesota	10	
Mississippi	7	
Missouri	12	
Montana		4
Nebraska		5
Nevada		3
New Hampshire		4
New Jersey		17
New Mexico		4
New York	41	
North Carolina	13	
North Dakota		3
Ohio	25	
Oklahoma		8
Oregon		6
Pennsylvania	27	
Rhode Island	4	
South Carolina	8	
South Dakota		4
Tennessee	10	
Texas	26	
Utah		4
Vermont		3
Virginia		12
Washington*		8
West Virginia	6	
Wisconsin	11	
Wyoming		3
TOTALS	**297**	**240**

Even though Ford carried the state of Washington by more than 60,000 votes, one Republican elector who was pledged to Ford refused to vote for him. The elector cast his ballot instead for Ronald Reagan.

shift from 1972, when George McGovern received only 29 per cent of the southern vote.

Six of the 10 states in which Carter received more than 55 per cent of the vote were in the South: Georgia (67 per cent), Arkansas (65 per cent), Alabama (56 per cent), North Carolina (55 per cent), South Carolina (56 per cent) and Tennessee (56 per cent).

The base of Carter's southern strength was the black vote, which went up dramatically over 1972. But Carter's appeal in white rural counties of the South was also strong. In Cheatham County, Tennessee, for example, a county carried overwhelmingly by George C. Wallace in 1968, Carter rolled up a margin of more than 3-1. Carter's vote also exceeded 3-1 in some of the heavily Mexican-American counties of south Texas.

Ford did manage to run ahead in the traditionally Republican mountainous areas of the South and in the growing suburbs. In the region as a whole, Ford captured a majority of the white vote. But Carter's wide edge in the black community enabled him to score a regional landslide.

East

In the East, Carter depended on an urban base, as all Democratic nominees have done in the past 40 years. Carter drew 52 per cent of the popular vote in the East, and received 108 of the region's 144 electoral votes. But he ran weaker there than either Kennedy in 1960 or Hubert H. Humphrey in 1968, especially in heavily Catholic and ethnic Massachusetts, Rhode Island and Connecticut.

Carter lost primaries in Massachusetts and Rhode Island in the spring, and barely won in Connecticut. He did not campaign extensively in the New England industrial states, and though he carried both Massachusetts and Rhode Island, his margin of victory was only half that compiled by Humphrey.

In the largest cities of the East, though, Carter did tally nearly two-thirds of the vote, rolling up majorities similar to those enjoyed by Kennedy and Humphrey. Carter took New York City by more than 700,000 votes, Philadelphia by more than 250,000 and Baltimore by about 100,000.

Carter's strength among certain groups was evident in New York City. He carried Jewish areas of the city frequently with 75 per cent or more of the vote. His appeal among Puerto Ricans and blacks was even more impressive. He won Puerto Rican assembly districts in south Bronx and black districts in Manhattan and Brooklyn with upwards of 90 per cent of the vote. The strong black support for Carter was evident in Baltimore and the District of Columbia, both cities with majority black populations.

The heavy urban vote for Carter was augmented by strong support from organized labor. The labor effort proved significant in offsetting some of the ethnic dissatisfaction with Carter. In one such labor area, Scranton and Wilkes-Barre, Pa., Carter received more than 55 per cent of the vote. His margin of victory trailed both Kennedy and Humphrey but still was better than many Democrats had expected.

Liberal academic communities, about the only source of strong support for McGovern four years earlier, were again in the Democratic column in 1976. Cambridge, Mass., home of Harvard University, went to Carter by a wide margin. McCarthy, who had campaigned hard on college campuses, made a minimal impact.

Ford's eastern strength was in the traditionally Republican suburbs, small towns and rural areas. Ford carried nearly all the major suburban counties, but Carter made significant inroads in several. Prince George's County, Md., which includes many of the blue-collar suburbs of Washington, D.C., went to Carter by 30,000 votes. Nixon had carried the county in 1968. Ford carried both Nassau and Suffolk Counties in New York, but his margin was only half that rolled up by the Republicans in 1968. Ford's failure to build up wider leads in the New York and Maryland suburbs helped Carter carry both states.

In spite of his deficit in the South and East, Ford nearly won the election with strong showings in the Midwest and West. Except for 1964, the Republicans have carried both regions in every election since 1948. Ford received about 50 per cent of the popular vote in the Midwest and 87 of the region's 145 electoral votes.

Midwest

Carter took only four states in the region, but picked off a key industrial state, Ohio, and scored a surprise victory in Wisconsin. In spite of its progressive reputation, Wisconsin normally has been in the Republican column in presidential elections, and McCarthy's presence on the ballot in 1976 was expected to insure a Ford victory.

In both states Carter won with strong showings in normally Republican rural areas. Carter had shown strength in these areas during the primary season, when he emphasized his own rural background. His gains in the agricultural areas offset some declines in Democratic strongholds.

Elsewhere in the rural Midwest, Carter's rural background, plus dissatisfaction with the Ford administration's agricultural policy, apparently aided the Democrat.

Except for Minnesota and Wisconsin, Carter lost the farm belt, but his showing in four states was substantially better than that of Kennedy or Humphrey.

The state of Iowa, which went Republican by more than 140,000 votes in 1960 and 1968, went for Ford by less than

13,000. Kansas, despite the presence of Sen. Robert Dole as Ford's running mate, voted Republican by a plurality of about 72,000 votes, much smaller than Nixon's in either 1968 or 1972.

Carter also ran much better than his immediate Democratic predecessors in both North and South Dakota. He lost North Dakota by about 17,000 votes, about half the deficit of Kennedy and one-third that of Humphrey. Carter's loss in South Dakota was by less than 5,000 votes, a better showing than Kennedy, Humphrey or even native son George McGovern had made in the past.

In the industrial Midwest, the vote followed the pattern in the East, with Carter winning sizeable majorities in the large, traditionally Democratic cities, such as Chicago and Detroit, but losing the suburban and outstate vote to Ford.

West

Ford made his best showing in the West, winning 51 per cent of the popular vote and carrying all but one state, Hawaii. Neither Ford nor Carter ran well in the region during the primaries, but the President benefited from traditional Republican strength and the absence of an intensive Carter effort in the region to score a series of one-sided victories. Ford's best showing was in Utah, where he received 62.4 per cent of the vote.

Carter's margin of defeat in seven western states was actually worse than either Kennedy or Humphrey recorded. A growing perception of Carter as a liberal apparently hurt the Democratic standard-bearer in these states, most of all in the conservative Rocky Mountain region—Arizona, Colorado, Idaho, Utah and Wyoming.

Carter improved on the showing of both Kennedy and Humphrey in only one western state, Oregon. There, returns showed Carter losing by fewer than 2,000 votes, a substantial improvement over 1960 and 1968, when the Republicans carried the state by more than 40,000 votes.

The Presidential Election: Vote by Regions

The following chart is based on official presidential results obtained from the states. A breakdown of the states within each region is found in the voter turnout chart, page 63. All candidates are listed who were on the ballot in at least two states. A dash (—) indicates candidate received less than one-tenth of one per cent of the vote.

	East	South	Midwest	West	National Vote	National Per Cent
Jimmy Carter (D)	51.5%	53.7%	48.3%	45.7%	40,828,587	50.1%
Gerald R. Ford (R)	47.0	45.0	49.7	51.0	39,147,613	48.0
Eugene J. McCarthy (Ind.)	0.8	0.4	1.3	1.3	755,358	0.9
Roger MacBride (Lib.)	0.1	0.1	0.2	0.6	172,765	0.2
Lester G. Maddox (AIP)	0.2	0.2	0.1	0.5	170,887	0.2
Thomas Anderson (Amer.)	—	0.4	0.2	0.2	161,047	0.2
Peter Camejo (SWP)	0.1	0.1	0.1	0.2	91,228	0.1
Gus Hall (Communist)	0.1	0.1	0.1	0.1	59,119	0.1
Margaret Wright (People's)	—	—	—	0.3	49,025	0.1
Lyndon H. LaRouche (U.S. Labor)	0.1	—	—	—	40,046	—
Benjamin C. Bubar (Proh.)	—	—	—	—	15,898	—
Jules Levin (SLP)	—	—	—	—	9,610	—
Frank P. Zeidler (Soc.)	—	—	—	—	6,036	—

Official 1976 Presidential Vote

Total Popular Votes: 81,551,948
Carter's Plurality: 1,680,974

State	JIMMY CARTER (Democrat) Votes	%	GERALD R. FORD (Republican) Votes	%	OTHER Votes	%		Plurality
Alabama	659,170	55.7	504,070	42.6	19,610	1.7	C	155,100
Alaska	44,055	35.7	71,555	57.9	7,935	6.4	F	27,500
Arizona	295,602	39.8	418,642	56.4	28,475	3.8	F	123,040
Arkansas	498,604	65.0	267,903	34.9	1,028	0.1	C	230,701
California	3,742,284	47.6	3,882,244	49.3	242,515	3.1	F	139,960
Colorado	460,801	42.5	584,456	54.0	37,709	3.5	F	123,655
Connecticut	647,895	46.9	719,261	52.1	14,370	1.0	F	71,366
Delaware	122,559	52.0	109,780	46.6	3,403	1.4	C	12,779
Dist. of Columbia	137,818	81.6	27,873	16.5	3,139	1.9	C	109,945
Florida	1,636,000	51.9	1,469,531	46.6	45,100	1.4	C	166,469
Georgia	979,409	66.7	483,743	33.0	4,306	0.3	C	495,666
Hawaii	147,375	50.6	140,003	48.1	3,923	1.3	C	7,372
Idaho	126,549	36.8	204,151	59.3	13,387	3.9	F	77,602
Illinois	2,271,295	48.1	2,364,269	50.1	83,269	1.8	F	92,974
Indiana	1,014,714	45.7	1,185,958	53.4	21,690	1.0	F	171,244
Iowa	619,931	48.5	632,863	49.5	26,512	2.1	F	12,932
Kansas	430,421	44.9	502,752	52.5	24,672	2.6	F	72,331
Kentucky	615,717	52.8	531,852	45.6	19,573	1.7	C	83,865
Louisiana	661,365	51.7	587,446	46.0	29,628	2.3	C	73,919
Maine	232,279	48.1	236,320	48.9	14,610	3.0	F	4,041
Maryland	759,612	52.8	672,661	46.7	7,624	0.5	C	86,951
Massachusetts	1,429,475	56.1	1,030,276	40.4	87,807	3.4	C	399,199
Michigan	1,696,714	46.4	1,893,742	51.8	63,293	1.7	F	197,028
Minnesota	1,070,440	54.9	819,395	42.0	59,754	3.1	C	251,045
Mississippi	381,329	49.6	366,846	47.7	21,205	2.8	C	14,483
Missouri	998,387	51.1	927,443	47.5	27,770	1.4	C	70,944
Montana	149,259	45.4	173,703	52.8	5,772	1.8	F	24,444
Nebraska	233,293	38.4	359,219	59.2	14,237	2.3	F	125,926
Nevada	92,479	45.8	101,273	50.2	8,124	4.0	F	8,794
New Hampshire	147,645	43.5	185,935	54.7	6,047	1.8	F	38,290
New Jersey	1,444,653	47.9	1,509,688	50.1	60,131	2.0	F	65,035
New Mexico	201,148	48.3	211,419	50.7	4,023	1.0	F	10,271
New York	3,389,558	51.9	3,100,791	47.5	43,851	0.7	C	288,767
North Carolina	927,365	55.2	741,960	44.2	9,589	0.6	C	185,405
North Dakota	136,078	45.8	153,470	51.7	7,545	2.5	F	17,392
Ohio	2,011,621	48.9	2,000,505	48.7	99,747	2.4	C	11,116
Oklahoma	532,442	48.7	545,708	50.0	14,101	1.3	F	13,266
Oregon	490,407	47.6	492,120	47.8	47,306	4.6	F	1,713
Pennsylvania	2,328,677	50.4	2,205,604	47.7	86,506	1.9	C	123,073
Rhode Island	227,636	55.4	181,249	44.1	2,285	0.6	C	46,387
South Carolina	450,807	56.2	346,149	43.1	5,627	0.7	C	104,658
South Dakota	147,068	48.9	151,505	50.4	2,105	0.7	F	4,437
Tennessee	825,879	55.9	633,969	42.9	16,498	1.1	C	191,910
Texas	2,082,319	51.1	1,953,300	48.0	36,265	0.9	C	129,019
Utah	182,110	33.6	337,908	62.4	21,200	3.9	F	155,798
Vermont	78,789	42.8	100,387	54.6	4,726	2.6	F	21,578
Virginia	813,896	48.0	836,554	49.3	46,644	2.7	F	22,658
Washington	717,323	46.1	777,732	50.0	60,479	3.9	F	60,409
West Virginia	435,864	58.0	314,726	41.9	290	0.0	C	121,138
Wisconsin	1,040,232	49.4	1,004,987	47.8	58,956	2.8	C	35,245
Wyoming	62,239	39.8	92,717	59.3	1,387	0.9	F	30,478
Totals	**40,828,587**	**50.1**	**39,147,613**	**48.0**	**1,575,748**	**1.9**	**C**	**1,680,974**

NOTE: This chart is based on official results obtained from the states in December 1976. The "other" vote listed after Carter and Ford is a combination of third party and scattered write-in votes.

McCarthy made his best showing in Oregon, and apparently cost Carter the state. McCarthy, who won the Oregon Democratic primary in 1968, received more than 40,000 votes, 3.9 per cent of the state total.

Another prominent third-party candidate, former Georgia Gov. Lester Maddox, received fewer than 200,000 votes nationally. He made his best showing in Idaho, where he received 1.7 per cent of the vote.

Turnout Rate Declines

Carter is only the third presidential candidate to ever receive more than 40 million votes in a general election. Richard M. Nixon, with 47.2 million votes in 1972, and Lyndon B. Johnson, with 43.1 million votes in 1964, were the others. Ford's 39.1 million votes is the most ever received by a losing candidate, easily eclipsing Nixon's old mark of 34.1 million set in 1960.

More than 81.5 million Americans voted in the 1976 presidential election, a figure that can be deceptive. On one hand, it was a record turnout, nearly four million more voters than 1972. The turnout was up over four years ago in more than half the states and nearly 30 million more voters participated in this election than in the 1974 congressional election.

On the other hand, the turnout rate was only 54.4 per cent, a full percentage point below 1972 and the lowest rate of voter participation since the Dewey-Truman contest in 1948, which drew only 53 per cent of the voters to the polls. The turnout rate was down from 1972 in eight of the 10 largest states, with only Texas (up 2.6 per cent) and Florida (up .5 per cent) showing increases. *(Box, this page)*

The turnout rate also dropped in three of the four regions, increasing only in the South. Ironically, while the rate in the South jumped from 45.3 per cent in 1972 to 48.1 per cent this year, the region's voter participation rate remained lower than any other region.

As in 1972 the turnout rate was highest in the Midwest, although there was a slight decline from 60.8 per cent four years ago to 60.4 per cent this year. In the other two regions the decline was more precipitous.

The turnout in the East dropped from 57.7 per cent to 55.0 per cent, with the fall off due primarily to a decrease in the turnout rate in the major industrial states—New York, Pennsylvania and New Jersey. In spite of relaxed registration requirements, the rate declined most sharply in New York, with the turnout dropping six percentage points to 50.6 per cent. Outside the South, only three other states had a lower turnout rate than New York.

The decline in the turnout rate was even sharper in California—7.7 per cent below 1972. California's fall off was the largest of any state in the nation and contributed to a massive decline in the voter participation rate in the entire western region. The turnout dropped from 59.9 per cent of the eligible western voters in 1972 to 54.4 per cent this year.

The states compiling the best turnout rates were in the upper Midwest and the Rocky Mountains. In 1972 five states recorded a turnout rate above 65 per cent: South Dakota (68.7 per cent), Minnesota and Utah (68.4 per cent), North Dakota (68.0 per cent) and Montana (67.8 per cent). Three of these states were among the top five this year, led by Minnesota with 71.6 per cent and followed by Utah, North Dakota, Wisconsin and Maine. ∎

Voter Turnout

The figures below are based on official presidential returns from the states compiled by Congressional Quarterly. The columns for 1972 and 1976 represent the percentage of the voting age population which voted.

	1976 Turnout	1976	1972
EAST			
Connecticut	1,381,526	62.5%	66.3%
Delaware	235,742	58.5	62.4
District of Columbia	168,830	32.8	30.8
Maine	483,209	65.2	61.1
Maryland	1,439,897	50.3	50.3
Massachusetts	2,547,558	61.0	62.0
New Hampshire	339,627	59.2	64.2
New Jersey	3,014,472	58.5	60.0
New York	6,534,200	50.6	56.6
Pennsylvania	4,620,787	54.7	56.0
Rhode Island	411,170	63.5	62.0
Vermont	183,902	56.2	60.8
West Virginia	750,590	58.6	62.4
SOUTH			
Alabama	1,182,850	47.3	43.5
Arkansas	767,535	51.1	47.9
Florida	3,150,631	49.8	49.3
Georgia	1,467,458	43.5	37.9
Kentucky	1,167,142	49.2	48.4
Louisiana	1,278,439	50.5	44.3
Mississippi	769,380	49.8	45.0
North Carolina	1,678,914	43.6	43.4
Oklahoma	1,092,251	56.4	56.9
South Carolina	802,583	41.5	38.6
Tennessee	1,476,346	49.9	43.6
Texas	4,071,884	47.9	45.3
Virginia	1,697,094	48.1	45.5
MIDWEST			
Illinois	4,718,833	61.1	62.7
Indiana	2,222,362	61.1	60.8
Iowa	1,279,306	63.6	63.3
Kansas	957,845	59.5	59.0
Michigan	3,653,750	58.3	59.5
Minnesota	1,949,589	71.6	68.4
Missouri	1,953,600	58.4	57.3
Nebraska	606,749	56.2	55.9
North Dakota	297,093	68.8	68.0
Ohio	4,111,873	55.1	57.5
South Dakota	300,678	64.1	68.7
Wisconsin	2,104,175	65.5	62.0
WEST			
Alaska	123,545	53.5	48.2
Arizona	742,719	47.8	50.5
California	7,867,043	51.4	59.1
Colorado	1,082,966	61.1	60.2
Hawaii	291,301	48.6	50.4
Idaho	344,087	60.7	63.1
Montana	328,734	63.5	67.8
Nevada	201,876	47.6	51.0
New Mexico	416,590	54.0	57.5
Oregon	1,029,833	62.3	61.7
Utah	541,218	69.1	68.4
Washington	1,555,534	61.3	63.8
Wyoming	156,343	58.8	63.8

Ford's Campaign for GOP Nomination

Gerald Ford ran his primary campaign on his two-year performance record as President.

The plan was to cultivate the image of an America healed of its divisive internal wounds, involved in a promising economic recovery and at peace both at home and abroad. In doing this, Ford had many of the incumbent's powers of policy-making, media access and patronage. All of these were to be used against Reagan, who announced his candidacy Nov. 20, 1975.

Ford was not an incumbent in the traditional sense. Having risen to the nation's highest office through presidential appointment and congressional confirmation, he had never faced national election and had no national constituency.

To overcome this drawback, Ford began early to capitalize on his position, spending considerable time in the fall of 1975 traveling across the country. Knowing that Reagan would have to make bold stands on key issues, Ford hoped to remain presidential in his own low-key manner.

And at first, the plan seemed to work. Ford won New Hampshire by about 1,500 votes, for his first election victory ever outside Michigan's 5th Congressional District. In Florida, where he was once thought far behind, the President was helped by older voters' fears that Reagan would alter the Social Security system. Ford scored a convincing victory. Following a big win in Illinois March 16, Ford strategists hoped to build a party consensus that would force Reagan to withdraw and support the President's nomination before the campaign moved into Reagan's Sun-Belt strongholds. As they had done privately before the campaign had begun, Ford's supporters began publicly urging Reagan to pull out of the race in the name of party unity.

Ford Campaign Problems

It was at that point that the plan, as scheduled, began to bog down.

Of course, all had not run smoothly to that point. Vice President Nelson Rockefeller had become a political casual-

1976 Republican Primary Results

Following are the official results from the Republican presidential preference primaries. Not included are returns from delegate selection primaries in Alabama, New York and Texas.

Primary	Turnout	Ford	Reagan	Plurality		Primary	Turnout	Ford	Reagan	Plurality	
New Hampshire (Feb. 24)	111,674	49.4%	48.0%	F	1,587	Arkansas (May 25)	32,526	35.1	63.4	R	9,182
Massachusetts (March 2)	188,449	61.2	33.7	F	51,820	Idaho (May 25)	89,793	24.9	74.3	R	44,420
Vermont (March 2)	32,157	84.0	15.2*	F	22,122	Kentucky (May 25)	133,528	50.9	46.9	F	5,293
Florida (March 9)	609,819	52.8	47.2	F	34,145	Nevada (May 25)	47,749	28.8	66.3	R	17,890
Illinois March 16)	775,893	58.9	40.1	F	145,455	Oregon (May 25)	298,528	50.3	45.8	F	13,490
North Carolina (March 23)	193,727	45.9	52.4	R	12,571	Tennessee (May 25)	242,535	49.8	49.1	F	1,688
Wisconsin (April 6)	591,812	55.2	44.3	F	64,743	Montana (June 1)	89,779	34.6	63.1	R	25,583
Pennsylvania (April 27)	796,660	92.1	5.1*	F	692,962	Rhode Island (June 1)	14,352	65.3	31.2	F	4,885
Georgia (May 4)	188,472	31.7	68.3	R	68,870	South Dakota (June 1)	84,077	44.0	51.2	R	6,092
Indiana (May 4)	631,354	48.7	51.3	R	16,190	California (June 8)	2,336,121	34.3	65.7	R	735,869
Nebraska (May 11)	208,414	45.4	54.5	R	18,951	New Jersey (June 8)	242,122	100.0	--	F	242,122
West Virginia (May 11)	155,692	56.8	43.2	F	21,080	Ohio (June 8)	935,757	55.2	44.8	F	96,465
Maryland (May 18)	165,971	58.0	42.0	F	26,611						
Michigan (May 18)	1,062,814	64.9	34.3	F	326,128	TOTAL	10,259,775	53.5%	45.7%	F	794,978

* Write-in votes.

ty late in 1975 when he removed himself from consideration as Ford's 1976 running mate. The former New York governor was thought to have taken himself out of the race to undercut conservative hostility toward him and toward a Ford-Rockefeller ticket.

Another member of the Ford team turned out to be a political liability. Campaign Director Howard H. (Bo) Callaway resigned March 30 after being charged with using improper influence with government agencies to benefit a Colorado ski resort of which he was part owner. The abuses were said to have taken place while the former Georgia representative was Secretary of the Army. Callaway had been blamed for the early inefficiency of the Ford campaign. Since late 1975, he had been acting as titular head of the campaign while more of the day-to-day decisions fell to his deputy, California campaign consultant Stuart Spencer. Callaway was replaced after his resignation by Rogers C. B. Morton.

The Ford campaign had continually been accused of being inefficient and ineffective. In the early stages, Ford was said to be spending too much time shaking hands and smiling at crowds and not enough time talking about serious political problems with party leaders and campaign workers. Partially because of these campaign problems and partially because of Reagan's effective television campaign, the Ford strategy ran into major snags in North Carolina on March 23.

Reagan Closes Gap

In that primary, Reagan recovered. Proving he could win there, he survived until May when his Sun-Belt strategy could finally come into play against Ford's incumbency.

A series of important victories followed for Reagan in the South and Southwest. By mid-May, the Ford candidacy had fallen behind in the convention delegate count. Ford survived with a large victory in his home state May 18, breaking the Californian's momentum. Added to that victory were stepped up efforts to cash in on Ford's incumbency with a flurry of patronage in key primary states and more effective usage of Ford's access to the press. The two candidates split the six May 25 primaries evenly, with Ford taking Kentucky, Tennessee and Oregon. The border state wins were interpreted as a success for Ford, showing he could compete with Reagan for conservative votes.

The President finally regained the edge in the delegate count in late May by persuading his technically uncommitted supporters in New York and Pennsylvania to declare for him. Ford ended the primary season with an easy win in New Jersey and a hefty margin in Ohio. Reagan kept close with a landslide victory in California, assuring that the nomination would turn on the status of the uncommitted delegates to the convention.

Convention Victory Uncertain

From June 8, the date of those final primaries, until the convention balloting, the Ford campaign concentrated on wooing those crucial uncommitted votes. Scattered throughout the states, the uncommitted delegates were afforded instant VIP status by the President who had all along seen his incumbency as his strongest card. Special phone calls, White House visits and fulfillment of other political favors were all included in the package used by Ford to win votes.

The Ford campaign received an unexpected shot in the arm when Reagan announced that liberal Senator Richard S. Schweiker (R Pa.) would be his running mate. Reagan alienated many of his conservative backers in this quest for a wider appeal, and a package of northeastern delegates. Some dismayed uncommitted delegates and party leaders began to move into the Ford corner.

John B. Connally announced his support for the President, perhaps in hopes of being Ford's own vice-presidential choice. Most importantly, Clarke Reed, leader of the crucial Mississippi delegation, announced his support for the President, although the disposition of the entire delegation was then still uncertain.

Ford approached the convention with guarded optimism, buoyed by reaction to Reagan's Schweiker selection, but still uncertain of victory. Hoping to avoid any open hostility with Reagan forces which would either jeopardize Ford's shaky lead or destroy chances for a post-convention unified party, Ford strategists backed away from major confrontations on platform planks, even on one that implied criticism of the Ford-Kissinger foreign policy. ∎

1976 Republican Convention

Divided Republicans Nominate Ford and Dole

The 31st quadrennial National Convention of the Republican party, meeting in Kansas City, Mo., Aug. 16-19, chose President Gerald R. Ford, 63, to run for election to the presidency in his own right. Ford was nominated on the first ballot by a 1,187-1,070 vote, surviving a remarkably close challenge from his persistent opponent, former California Gov. Ronald Reagan. The conservative platform which was also adopted at the convention showed the nearly equal influence of Ford and Reagan.

Reagan, who had lost to Ford in the early New Hampshire and Florida primaries and had been almost counted out of the race, had been resuscitated by major primary wins in Texas and Indiana. When the primaries ended Ford was only slightly ahead in the delegate count, and he and Reagan fought throughout the summer for votes at state caucuses and among the uncommitted. They went to Kansas City with Ford still slightly ahead but the outcome in some doubt.

After Reagan ruled out acceptance of the second spot, Ford selected Robert Dole, 53, senator from Kansas since 1969 and a former Republican national chairman, to be his running mate. Dole was widely considered to be an effective gut fighter. He had been little mentioned during earlier speculation about Ford's vice presidential choice. Tennessee Sen. Howard H. Baker, the convention keynoter, had been considered the likeliest nominee.

In addition to the Ford-Reagan struggle, the 1976 Republican convention was characterized by the unmitigated abuse heaped on the Democrats. Speaker after speaker—and the generally conservative platform—blamed long-time Democratic control of Congress for an intolerable level of federal spending, escalating government control of individual freedom and proliferation of the federal bureaucracy. In many ways, the Republicans took the tone of the party out of power in the White House, battling to regain its control. But most speakers made only indirect references to the Watergate scandal which had unseated President Richard M. Nixon in 1974 and any problems it may have caused the Republicans; Nixon's name was not mentioned.

To the Last Delegate

The Republican delegates arrived in Kansas City more evenly split than they had been since 1952, when Dwight D. Eisenhower edged Sen. Robert A. Taft (Ohio 1939-53) for the GOP nomination. Both Ford, breaking with tradition, and Reagan arrived in town three days before the balloting to continue their pursuit of delegates.

Ford, relying heavily on the prestige of the presidency that sometimes had failed to produce results during the seven-month campaign, invited a number of wavering delegates to his hotel suite in the new Crown Center Hotel while Reagan also courted delegates personally.

Campaign strategists and conservative supporters pursued other maneuvers that either fizzled or could not break Ford's scanty but solid delegate margin. Early in the week, conservative House members tried unsuccessfully to convince Sen. James L. Buckley (Cons-R N.Y.) to seek the nomination in an effort to draw off enough votes to deny Ford a first-ballot victory.

But the contest in fact ended a night before the presidential balloting when delegates defeated 1,069-1,180 a move by the Reagan team to force Ford to name his vice presidential choice by 9 a.m. the next morning. Reagan staff members, down to their last tactic, hoped Ford's choice might disgruntle delegates before the nomination vote.

A conservative-backed addition to the foreign policy planks of the party platform provoked no Ford-Reagan fight after the vote on the vice presidential rule. Jubilant with their earlier victory, the Ford team quietly accepted the amendment.

The outcome thus assured, delegates the following night gave Ford the nomination on the first ballot by the 1,187-1,070 vote.

The Rules Fight

By a margin of 112 votes on Aug. 17, the Reagan forces lost the first and probably the most important roll call of the convention. The vote came on a Reagan-sponsored amendment to the Rules Committee report that would have required all presidential candidates to disclose the name of their running mate before the presidential balloting the next night.

The final count stood at 1,068 in favor of the amendment and 1,180 against, with 11 abstentions. The vote was the first tangible evidence of Ford strength at the convention and seemed to pave the way for his first-ballot nomination.

The idea of a test vote on the vice presidential question was sprung by Reagan's campaign manager, John Sears, barely a week before the convention, when on Aug. 9 he appeared before the Rules Committee of the Republican National Committee and urged that the proposal be included as Section C of Rule 16. The amendment was clearly aimed at throwing Ford on the defensive, because Reagan had designated Pennsylvania Sen. Richard S. Schweiker as his running mate on July 26.

Under the proposal, failure of a candidate to comply would have freed all delegates from any commitments to vote for him.

The Reagan proposal was handily defeated in the preconvention Rules Committee, where Ford supporters predominated. But Sears was publicly confident that the Reagan forces could carry the issue on the convention floor. Victory on the rules question, he predicted, would be a stepping stone to Reagan's nomination.

The convention debate and vote on Rule 16 was the focal point of the Aug. 17 session and was treated as such by many in the gallery and on the floor, who interrupted the proceedings several times with loud chanting. Vociferous cheers and boos erupted from the Ford and Reagan sections of the hall as speeches were delivered for or against their positions.

Debate

An agreement between the campaign leaders of the two candidates allowed for 30 minutes of debate, with conven-

---

Rules Changes

The dramatic contest over vice presidential selection overshadowed the approval of the entire Rules Committee report with its changes in Republican Party rules.

A major change was the creation of two new committees under the auspices of the Republican National Committee. One was a direct outgrowth of Watergate—a seven-member select committee to monitor and review the expenses of the Republican presidential candidate in the fall campaign.

The other committee would review party rules and make recommendations for structural changes. The new committee could take up such issues as vice presidential selection and delegate apportionment, but changes it proposed could not be approved formally until the next convention in 1980.

The establishment of this new rules review committee within the national committee was a defeat for party liberals. They wanted a continuation of the inactive Rule 29 Committee, which was mandated by the 1972 convention to review party rules but operated independently of the national committee and had a membership with considerable liberal representation.

Supporters of the Rule 29 Committee made their appeal Aug. 15 before the convention Rules Committee. Led by Rep. William A. Steiger of Wisconsin, the chairman of the Rule 29 Committee, they argued that an independent-minded panel was the best vehicle for reform.

Conservative opponents countered that the broad-based Rule 29 Committee had run wild, suggesting rules changes that looked as if they were copied from the Democrats. Clarke Reed, outgoing chairman of the Mississippi Republican Party, said: "What we need is the dispassionate review of changes." Reed favored limiting membership on future rules review committees to national committee members. An amendment to that effect was approved, 65-27, which established a new committee under the National Committee.

Other major rules changes involved the petition requirements for platform minority reports and increased delegate apportionment for Puerto Rico. The minority report issue brought little discussion. The new rule required minority reports from the Platform Committee to have the support of 25 per cent of the Platform Committee members. Previous rules did not specify any figure. The new figure was identical to the amount of support required by the Democrats, who adopted the 25 per cent figure in 1976 to curtail debate on frivolous issues.

The number of delegates for Puerto Rico was increased from eight in 1976 to 14 in 1980. The increase came on an appeal from the Puerto Rican member of the Rules Committee, Patrick Wilson, who argued that the island, with three million inhabitants, was underrepresented. By a vote of 55-42, the committee approved the increased delegate allocation.

---

tion Rules Committee Chairman Kent B. McGough, the Ohio state chairman, controlling the time for the Ford forces and former Missouri Rep. Thomas B. Curtis, the sponsor of the amendment, leading the Reagan side.

Supporters of the proposals characterized it as a "right to know" amendment. "A presidential candidate must tell us who's on his team before we are expected to join him," Curtis argued. "The delegates have the right to be consulted for a day of decision that will have an impact for years to come." Other Reagan supporters claimed that the proposal was a needed reform of the vice presidential selection process and was a striking contrast to the position of the Democrats, who had done nothing on the subject.

Speakers against the amendment countered that it was solely a maneuver of the Reagan forces and that any vice presidential selection reform should be deliberately considered on its merits.

The amendment, declared Dorann H. Gunderson of Wisconsin, "smacks of desperation and political opportunism. This is an amendment for one time, one place and one candidate."

Other speakers noted that under the proposal, the Ford-Reagan ticket desired by many Republicans would be impossible. Michigan Sen. Robert P. Griffin concluded: "I see it as a basically divisive proposal. It would drive a wedge in our party and prevent the unity we must achieve. I see no merit in a proposal that locks Sen. Schweiker in and Gov. Reagan out."

Roll Call

The roll call began at 10:13 p.m. with Alabama, solid for Reagan, casting all of its 37 votes for the amendment. The Reagan forces held the lead throughout the early going, losing the advantage about halfway through the roll call when New York went 134-20 against the amendment.

The deficit of the Reagan backers increased after Ohio went 7-90 against and Pennsylvania 14-89 against. The Pennsylvania result was a clear indication that state leaders in the Ford campaign remained in control of the delegation, despite Schweiker's effort to woo their support.

Reagan strength near the end of the roll call tightened the count, but Florida and Mississippi, which had passed when first called, cast heavy votes against the amendment. Florida's 28-38 vote against sealed the amendment's defeat. Mississippi, under the unit rule, cast its entire 30 votes against the Reagan proposal, padding the Ford margin.

The casting of the Mississippi vote followed several hours of strategy sessions in which Ford and Reagan partisans within the delegation argued whether the unit rule should be used. The rule was traditional in Mississippi GOP convention voting, but the nearly even Ford-Reagan split within the state in 1976 made its imposition controversial. The final decision was to use the rule, and Ford was the beneficiary, taking 31 of the Mississippi delegates and alternates, to 28 for the Reagan position on 16C, and one abstention.

The close vote gave the Ford side all 30 Mississippi convention votes. Sears later told reporters that word of Mississippi's decision to stick with unit rule and support Ford had led to erosion of Reagan's strength on 16 C in other key delegations.

None of the other parts of the Rules Committee report were debated, including the "justice resolution" (Rule 18), which binds delegates elected in primary states according to state law. Fearing a defection of "closet" Reagan delegates

(Continued on p. 69)

Balloting for Republican Nominations

(Before switches)

		Presidential[1]		Vice Presidential		
		Ford	Reagan	Dole	Others[2]	Abstensions
Alabama	37		37	30	7	
Alaska	19	17	2	19		
Arizona	29	2	27	29		
Arkansas	27	10	17	19	7	1
California	167		167	80	3	84
Colorado	31	5	26	27	3	1
Connecticut	35	35		34		1
Delaware	17	15	2	17		
Florida	66	43	23	35	31	
Georgia	48		48	40	8	
Hawaii	19	18	1	19		
Idaho	21	4	17	20	1	
Illinois	101	86	14	101		
Indiana	54	9	45	54		
Iowa	36	19	17	36		
Kansas	34	30	4	33		1
Kentucky	37	19	18	32	5	
Louisiana	41	5	36	34	6	1
Maine	20	15	5	19	1	
Maryland	43	43		40	3	
Massachusetts	43	28	15	39	2	2
Michigan	84	55	29	67	14	3
Minnesota	42	32	10	40	1	1
Mississippi	30	16	14	30		
Missouri	49	18	31	47	1	1
Montana	20		20	20		
Nebraska	25	7	18	19	6	
Nevada	18	5	13	17		1
New Hampshire	21	18	3	19	2	
New Jersey	67	63	4	67		
New Mexico	21		21	17	4	
New York	154	133	20	152	2	
North Carolina	54	25	29	54		
North Dakota	18	11	7	18		
Ohio	97	91	6	97		
Oklahoma	36		36	17	19	
Oregon	30	16	14	26	3	1
Pennsylvania	103	93	10	96	7	
Rhode Island	19	19		17		2
South Carolina	36	9	27	36		
South Dakota	20	9	11	20		
Tennessee	43	21	22	41	2	
Texas	100		100	26	73	1
Utah	20		20	17	3	
Vermont	18	18		18		
Virginia	51	16	35	41	8	2
Washington	38	7	31	32	6	
West Virginia	28	20	8	17	1	
Wisconsin	45	45		44	1	
Wyoming	17	7	10	13	4	
District of Columbia	14	14		14		
Puerto Rico	8	8		8		
Guam	4	4		3	1	
Virgin Islands	4	4		4		
TOTAL	2,259	1,187	1,070	1,921	235	103

1. Other presidential votes as follows: Elliot L. Richardson 1—N.Y.; abstension 1—Ill.

2. Other vice presidential votes as follows:

Jesse Helms 103—Ala. 4; Calif. 1; Colo. 2; Ga. 4; Guam 1; La. 1; Mich. 12; Minn. 1; Neb. 5; N.M. 2; Okla. 4; Ore. 2; Pa. 2; Tenn. 1; Texas 43; Utah 3; Va. 8; Wash. 5; Wyo. 2.

Ronald Reagan 27—Ala. 1; Ky. 5; La. 2; Mo. 1; N.H. 2; Pa. 3; Texas 9; Wash. 1; W.Va. 1; Wyo. 2.

Phillip M. Crane 23—Ark. 4; Ga. 2; Okla. 15; Pa. 1; Texas 1.

John L. Grady 19—Fla. 19.

Louis Frey Jr. 9—Fla. 9.

Anne Armstrong 6—Fla. 2; Texas 4.

Howard H. Baker Jr. 6—Ala. 1; Ark. 1; Neb. 1; N.Y. 2; Ore. 1.

William F. Buckley Jr. 4—Colo. 1; Mich. 2; N.M. 1.

John B. Connally 4—Maine 1; Pa. 1; Texas 2.

David C. Treen 4—Ga. 1; La. 3.

Alan Steelman 3—Texas 3.

Robert E. Bauman 2—Md. 2.

Bill Brock 2—Fla. 1; Tenn. 1.

George Bush 2—Texas 2.

Paul Laxalt 2—Calif. 1; Texas 1.

Elliot L. Richardson 2—Mass. 2.

Richard S. Schweiker 2—Ark. 2.

William E. Simon 2—Md. 1; Texas 1.

Jack Wellborn 2—Texas 2.

Receiving one vote each: James B. Allen—Ala.; Ray Barnhart—Texas; Pete V. Domenici—N.M.; James B. Edwards—Ga.; Frank Glenn—Texas; James A. McClure—Idaho; Nancy Palm—Texas; Donald H. Rumsfeld—Wis.; John Sears—Calif.; Roger Staubach—Texas; Steven D. Symms—Texas.

(Continued from p. 67)

in several primary-state delegations, Ford leaders had pushed for the amendment. In contrast to their attitude toward Rule 16, the Reagan forces did not order a fight on the "justice" resolution, although it was extensively debated in committee deliberations. After the roll-call vote on Rule 16, the Rules Committee report was adopted by a voice vote.

Platform Debate

By the time the convention got around to debating the platform, about 1:15 a.m., an expected bitter struggle between Ford and Reagan forces had been deflated by the earlier vote on rules. The arena, which had been packed two hours earlier, held a somewhat smaller crowd after midnight. Many Ford delegates in particular, confident that they had won the main event, left while members of the Platform Committee presented the 65-page document.

Two minority planks were offered, in accordance with Platform Committee rules that required petitions signed by 25 per cent of the members. The first, sponsored by Ann F. Peckham of Wisconsin, called for deleting all platform references to abortion. The committee-approved section supported a constitutional amendment "to restore protection of the right to life of unborn children."

The 12-minute debate on the abortion plank did not split along Ford-Reagan lines. Supporters of the minority report argued that abortion was not a suitable topic for a party document. Opponents insisted that the anti-abortion language should be retained. The minority report was defeated clearly by voice vote, and the language stayed in.

Foreign Policy

The second minority report, a six-paragraph addition to the foreign policy section, was sponsored by 34 Reagan supporters on the Platform Committee. Without mentioning names, it criticized President Ford and Secretary of State Henry A. Kissinger for losing public confidence, making secret international agreements and discouraging the hope of freedom for those who do not have it—presumably captive nations.

Many of Ford's supporters, including Rep. John B. Anderson (Ill.) and Senate Minority Leader Hugh Scott (Pa.), earlier had expressed strong opposition to the "morality in foreign policy" plank, as it came to be called. Ford's floor leader, Sen. Griffin, and Rep. David C. Treen (La.) sought compromise language in informal negotiations on the floor. But the Reagan forces, led by Sen. Jesse A. Helms (N.C.), were adamant.

Not wishing to offend the Reagan forces further, Ford's supporters decided not to fight. Sen. Roman L. Hruska (Neb.) announced from the podium that there would be no organized opposition to the plank. It was passed by voice vote at 1:52 a.m. The convention then approved the platform, as amended.

Ford's Nomination

Whatever enthusiasm the Reagan supporters had lost after their defeat on the vice presidential rule had returned by presidential nominating night Aug. 18.

Two and one-half hours of the six-hour session were consumed in demonstrations. Reagan's supporters were by far the most boisterous. But it was the Californian's last hurrah.

As razor-thin as Ford's margin on the final vote was, it remained solid. Despite every tactic and every argument the Reagan forces employed, they found few soft spots in the tiny majority the incumbent President had been building for six months.

Early in the evening, as New York Sen. Jacob K. Javits, one of his party's most liberal senators, was telling the largely conservative convention that the party must broaden its base by appealing to shop stewards as well as business executives, the first demonstration broke out. The delegates were in no mood for long speeches.

Michigan Rep. Guy Vander Jagt, chairman of the Republican Congressional Campaign Committee, continued a theme worked and reworked throughout the convention—that the Democrats in Congress, who had enjoyed a majority for 40 of the past 44 years, were responsible for spending too much, interfering too much in people's lives and adding too many employees to the federal payroll.

Filibuster

Finally came the nomination, and a Reagan demonstration that was, in effect, a filibuster. Some delegates claimed the series of outbursts, the longest of which lasted 45 minutes, was designed to keep Ford's nominating speeches from being carried on prime-time television.

The behavior of many Reagan supporters, particularly those in the galleries, contrasted with the conciliatory attitude many had demonstrated earlier in the convention. Most Reaganites had made it clear that they wanted their man but were willing to take Ford. But as the final roll call neared after a long and sometimes bitter battle for the nomination, the frustrated Reagan forces decided to go down for the final time in a sea of noise.

For what seemed an interminable period, they blew their horns, waved their banners, shouted their chants and snake-danced in the aisles. Ford's supporters sat silently. Betty Ford left the hall as Reagan's nomination speeches began. And despite Convention Chairman John J. Rhodes' admonition that "you're acting like a bunch of Democrats," the Reaganites were intransigent.

Occasionally the demonstration was interrupted by a speaker. Nevada Sen. Paul Laxalt, Reagan's campaign chairman, nominated the Californian. "There is no more effective campaigner in this country than Ronald Reagan," Laxalt said, a statement Ford himself concurred in hours later when he met with his vanquished opponent.

Even the hero of the conservatives, North Carolina Sen. Jesse A. Helms, had difficulty beginning his seconding address for Reagan.

When the hall finally quieted, Ford was nominated by Michigan Gov. William G. Milliken, who praised the President for re-establishing leadership, reviving the economy and restoring faith in government. "He first became President without our nomination," Milliken reminded the convention, "and without the American mandate. Now he has earned both."

The Ford nomination was seconded from the floor by 19 delegates.

Roll Call

By the time the secretary began calling the role of the states, the mood began to change. The tension of the

(Continued on p. 73)

Texts of GOP Acceptance Speeches

Ford Address

Following is the text, as delivered, of President Ford's Aug. 19 speech accepting the Republican presidential nomination.

Mr. Chairman,

Delegates and alternates to this Republican convention:

I am honored by your nomination—and I accept it.

I accept with pride, with gratitude, and with a total will to win a great victory for the American people.

We will wage a winning campaign in every region of this country—from the snowy banks of Minnesota to the sandy plains of Georgia. We concede not a single state. We concede not a single vote.

This evening I am proud to stand before this great convention as the first incumbent President since Dwight D. Eisenhower who can tell the American people: America is at peace.

Tonight I can tell you straight away—This nation is sound.

This nation is secure.

This nation is on the march to full economic recovery and a better quality of life for all Americans.

And I'll tell you one more thing. This year the issues are all on our side. I'm ready, I'm eager to go before the American people and debate the real issues face to face with Jimmy Carter. The American people have the right to know first-hand where both of us stand.

I am deeply grateful to those who stood with me in winning the nomination of the party whose cause I have served all my adult life.

I respect the convictions of those who want a change in Washington. I want a change, too. After 22 long years of majority misrule, let's change the United States Congress.

My gratitude tonight reaches far beyond this arena, to countless friends whose confidence, hard work, and unselfish support have brought me to this moment.

It would be unfair to single out anyone. But may I make an exception for my wonderful family, Mike, Jack, Steve and Susan—and especially my dear wife, Betty.

We Republicans have had some tough competition. We not only preach the virtues of competition; we practice them.

But tonight we come together, not on a battlefield to conclude a cease-fire, but to join forces on a training field that has conditioned us all for the rugged contest ahead.

Let me say this, from the bottom of my heart: After the scrimmages of the past few months, it really feels good to have Ron Reagan on the same side of the line.

To strengthen our championship lineup, the convention has wisely chosen one of the ablest of Americans as our next Vice President, Senator Bob Dole of Kansas.

With his help, with your help, with the help of millions of Americans who cherish peace, who want freedom preserved, prosperity shared, and pride in America, we will win this election.

I speak not of a Republican victory, but a victory for the American people.

You at home, listening tonight—you are the people who pay the taxes and obey the laws. You are the people who make our system work. You are the people who make America what it is. It is from your ranks that I come, and on your side I stand.

Something wonderful happened to this country of ours these past two years. We all came to realize it on the Fourth of July.

Together, out of years of turmoil and tragedy, wars and riots, assassinations and wrongdoing in high places, Americans recaptured the spirit of 1776. We saw again the pioneer vision of our revolutionary founders and our immigrant ancesors.

Their vision was of free men and free women enjoying limited government and unlimited opportunity.

The mandate I want in 1976 is to make this vision a reality. But it will take the voices and the votes of many more Americans, who are not Republicans, to make that mandate binding and my mission possible.

I have been called an unelected President, an accidental President. We may even hear that again from the other party despite the fact that I was welcomed and endorsed, by an overwhelming majority of their elected representatives in the Congress, who certified my fitness to our highest office.

Having become Vice President and President without expecting or seeking either, I have had a special feeling toward those high offices.

To me, the presidency and the vice presidency were not prizes to be won, but a duty to be done.

So tonight, it is not the power and glamour of the presidency that leads me to ask for another four years. It is something every hard-working American will understand—the challenge of a job well begun, but far from finished.

Two years ago, on Aug. 9, 1974, I placed my hand on the Bible which Betty held and took the same constitutional oath that was administered to George Washington. I had faith in our people, in our institutions and in myself.

"My fellow Americans," I said, "our long national nightmare is over."

It was an hour in our history that troubled our minds and tore at our hearts; anger and hatred had risen to dangerous levels, dividing friends and families. The polarization of our political order had aroused unworthy passions of reprisal and revenge.

Our governmental system was closer to stalemate than at any time since Abraham Lincoln took that same oath of office.

Our economy was in the throes of runaway inflation, taking us headlong into the worst recession since Franklin D. Roosevelt took the same oath.

On that dark day I told my fellow-countrymen: "I am acutely aware that you have not elected me as your President by your ballots, so I ask you to confirm me as your President with your prayers."

On a marble fireplace in the White House is carved a prayer which John Adams wrote. It concludes, "May none but honest and wise men ever rule under this roof."

Since I have resided in that historic house, I have tried to live by that prayer.

I faced many tough problems. I probably made some mistakes, but on balance, America and Americans have made an incredible comeback since August 1974.

Nobody can honestly say otherwise.

And the plain truth is that the great progress we have made, at home and abroad, was in spite of the majority who run the Congress of the United States.

For two years, I have stood for all the people against the vote-hungry, free-spending congressional majority on Capitol Hill.

Fifty-five times I vetoed extravagant and unwise legislation. Forty-five times I made those vetoes stick. Those vetoes have save American taxpayers billions and billions of dollars.

I am against the big tax spender and for the little taxpayer.

I called for a permanent tax cut coupled with spending reductions to stimulate the economy and relieve hard-pressed middle income taxpayers. Your personal exemption must be raised from $750 to $1,000.

But the other party's platform talks about tax reform, but there's one big problem—their own Congress won't act.

I called for reasonable, constitutional restrictions on court-ordered busing of school children.

The other party's platform concedes that busing should be a "last resort" but there's the same problem—their own Congress won't act.

I called for a major overhaul of criminal laws to crack down on crime and illegal drugs.

The other party's platform deplores America's $90-billion cost of crime. There's the problem again—their own Congress won't act.

The other party's platform talks about a strong defense. Now here's the other side of the problem again—their own Congress did act. They slashed $50-billion from our national defense needs in the last 10 years.

My friends, Washington is not the problem—their Congress is the problem.

You know the President of the United

States is not a magician who can wave a wand, or sign a paper that will instantly end a war, cure a recession or make a bureaucracy disappear. A President has immense powers under the Constitution, but all of them ultimately come from the American people, and their mandate to him.

That is why, tonight, I turn to the American people and ask not only for your prayers, but also for your strength and your support...for your voice and for your vote.

I come before you with a two-year record of performance, without your mandate. I offer you a four-year pledge of greater performance, with your mandate.

As Governor Al Smith used to say, "Let's look at the record."

Two years ago, inflation was 12 per cent.

Sales were off, plants were shut down, thousands were being laid off every week.

Fear of the future was throttling down our economy and threatening millions of families.

Let's look at the record since August 1974.

Inflation has been cut in half.

Payrolls are up, profits are up, production is up, purchases are up.

Since the recession was turned around, almost four million of our fellow Americans have found new jobs or got their old jobs back. This year more men and women have jobs than ever before in the history of the United States.

Confidence has returned and we are in the full surge of sound recovery to steady prosperity.

Two years ago, America was mired in withdrawal from Southeast Asia. A decade of Congresses had shortchanged our global defenses and threatened our strategic posture. Mounting tension between Israel and the Arab nations made another war seem inevitable.

The whole world watched and wondered where America was going. Did we in our domestic turmoil have the will, the stamina, and the unity to stand up for freedom?

Look at the record since August two years ago.

Today America is at peace and seeks peace for all nations. Not a single American is at war anywhere on the face of this earth tonight.

Our ties with Western Europe and Japan, economic as well as military, were never stronger. Our relations with Eastern Europe, the Soviet Union and Mainland China are firm, vigilant and forward-looking. Policies I have initiated offer sound progress for the peoples of the Pacific, Africa and Latin America.

Israel and Egypt, both trusting the United States, have taken an historic step that promises an eventual just settlement for the whole Middle East.

The world now respects America's policy of peace through strength. The United States is again the confident leader of the free world.

Nobody questions our dedication to peace, but nobody doubts our willingness to use our strength when our vital interests are at stake. And we will.

I called for an up-to-date, powerful Army, Navy, Air Force and Marines that will keep America secure for decades.

A strong military posture is always the best insurance for peace.

But America's strength has never rested on arms alone. It is rooted in our mutual commitment of our citizens and leaders in the highest standard of ethics and morality and in the spiritual renewal which our nation is undergoing right now.

Two years ago people's confidence in their highest officials, to whom they had overwhelmingly entrusted power, had twice been shattered. Losing faith in the word of their elected leaders, Americans lost some of their own faith in themselves.

Again, let's look at the record since August 1974.

From the start, my administration has been open, candid, forthright.

While my entire public and private life was under searching examination for the vice presidency, I reaffirmed my lifelong conviction that truth is the glue that holds government together—not only government, but civilization itself.

I have demanded honesty, decency and personal integrity from everybody in the executive branch of the government. The House and Senate have the same duty. The American people will not accept a double standard in the United States Congress.

Those who make our laws today must not debase the reputation of our great legislative bodies that have given us such giants as Daniel Webster, Henry Clay, Sam Rayburn and Robert A. Taft. Whether in the nation's capital, the state capital or city hall, private morality and public trust must go together.

From Aug. 9, 1974, to August of 1976 the record shows steady progress upward toward prosperity, peace and public trust.

My record is one of progress, not platitudes.

My record is one of specifics, not smiles.

My record is one of performance, not promises.

It is a record I am proud to run on.

It is a record the American people—Democrats, independents and Republicans alike—will support on November 2nd.

For the next four years I pledge to you that I will hold to the steady course we have begun.

But I have no intention of standing on the record alone.

We will continue winning the fight against inflation.

We will go on reducing the deadweight and impudence of bureaucracy.

We will submit a balanced budget by 1978.

We will improve the quality of life at work, at play and in our homes and in our neighborhoods.

We will not abandon our cities. We will encourage urban programs which assure safety in the streets, create healthy environments, and restore neighborhood pride.

We will return control of our children's education to parents and local school authorities.

We will make sure that the party of Lincoln remains the party of equal rights.

We will create a tax structure that's fair for all of our citizens, one that preserves the continuity of the family home, the family farm and the family business.

We will ensure the integrity of the Social Security system and improve Medicare so that our older citizens can enjoy the health and the happiness that they have earned. There is no reason that they should have to go broke just to get well.

We will make sure that this rich nation does not neglect citizens who are less fortunate, but provides their needs with compassion and with dignity.

We will reduce the growth and the cost of government, and allow individual breadwinners and businesses to keep more of the money that they earn.

We will create a climate in which our economy will provide a meaningful job for everyone who wants to work and a decent standard of life for all Americans.

We will ensure that all of our young people have a better chance in life than we had—an education they can use and a career they can be proud of.

We will carry out a farm policy that assures a fair market price for the farmer, encourages full production, leads to record exports, and eases the hunger within the human family.

We will never use the bounty of America's farmers as a pawn in international diplomacy; there will be no embargoes.

We will continue our strong leadership to bring peace, justice and economic progress where there is turmoil, especially in the Middle East.

We will build a safer and saner world, through patient negotiations and dependable arms agreements, which reduce the danger of conflict and the horror of thermonuclear war. While I am President we will not return to a collision course that could reduce civilization to ashes.

We will build an America where people feel rich in spirit as well as in worldly goods. We will build an America where people feel proud, about themselves and about their country.

We will build on performance, not promises; experience, not expediency; real progress instead of mysterious plans to be revealed in some dim and distant future.

The American people are wiser than our opponents think. They know who pays for every campaign promise. They are not afraid of the truth. We will tell them the truth.

From start to finish, our campaign will be credible. It will be responsible. We will come out fighting. And, we will win.

Yes, we have all seen the polls and the pundits who say our party is dead. I've heard that before. So did Harry Truman.

I'll tell you what I think. The only polls that count are the polls the American people go to on November 2.

Right now, I predict right now that the American people are going to say that night—Jerry, you've done a good job. Keep right on doing it.

As I try, in my imagination, to look into all the homes where families are watching the end of this great convention, I can't tell which faces are Republicans, which are Democrats and which are independents. I cannot see their color or creed. I see only Americans.

I see Americans who love their husbands, their wives and their children.

I see Americans who love their country for what it has been and what it must become.

I see Americans who worked hard but who are willing to sacrifice all they have worked for to keep their children and their country free.

I see Americans who in their own quiet way pray for peace among nations and peace among themselves. We do love our neighbors and we do forgive those who have trespassed against us.

I see a new generation that knows what is right and knows itself—a generation determined to preserve its ideals, its environment, our nation and the world.

My fellow Americans, I like what I see. I have no fear for the future of this great country. And as we go forward, together, I promise you once more what I promised before: To uphold the Constitution; to do what is right, as God gives me to see the right, and to do the very best I can for America.

God helping me, I won't let you down. ∎

Dole Address

Following is the text, as delivered, of Sen. Robert Dole's Aug. 19 speech accepting the Republican vice presidential nomination.

Mr. Chairman, fellow Republicans—fellow Americans: Let me say, at the outset when I was here as temporary chairman, I didn't plan on coming back this evening—I'm very happy to be here.

Needless to say, I want to express my thanks to President Ford for calling me this morning. I'm most pleased that I was in the room when he called. I want to thank Vice President Rockefeller for that very wonderful nomination speech and, of course, Peggy Pinder and Art Fletcher and Paul Laxalt for their seconding speeches. I want to thank Mrs. Williams for being here tonight and assisting me and assisting other Americans.

I listened to the earlier newscasts, and many were saying that Dole is not a household word. But it is a four-letter word you can get used to.

I stand before you tonight proud of the confidence our President has shown in me, gratified by your trust, humbled by this new opportunity to serve the nation we love and determined to work with all my heart to insure four more years of Republican leadership in the White House.

President Ford's administration began with prayer. Trusting in a just and beneficient God, and in the courage and wisdom and good will of our people, the President accepted stewardship of our Nation in one of the most difficult times in our history.

With the help of God, with the goodwill of our people and with his courage, compassion and wisdom, America has weathered the storm.

Today, there are those who tell Americans to lower their expectations. America was not built by men and women with limited vision and small hopes and low expectations.

It was built by men and women with tomorrow on their minds. It was built by believers—by those who could look across the broad sweep of a bounteous land of unbounded opportunity and see possibilities none before had ever dreamed of.

In their eyes, the future gleamed brightly, and upon their achievements we live today—with more freedom, more opportunity, more dignity, more wealth and with greater obligations than any people before in history.

My fellow Republicans—we need not ask the American people to lower their expectations.

Rather let us ask them to raise their sights ever higher—as they always have done in the past—let us do so with that confidence which comes with the knowledge that we have a President who has met and will continue to meet the highest expectations of the American people.

We have heard much about offering the American people a choice this year. I believe we should. I believe we do.

The eyes of the world—and the hopes of those who are free and those who wish to be free—focus on this country.

Wherever tyranny reigns in this world, it reigns through the instruments of government.

All history tells us that to maximize government is to minimize human freedom.

I believe that the promise of America is not told, nor shall it be fulfilled, through the oppressive constraints of government.

The question and the purpose of human liberty are not the rights of government, the dignity of government, or the future of government. Rather they are the rights of the individual, the hopes and dreams of the individual, the dignity of the individual and the future of humanity itself.

We have written a long and noble chapter in the history of human liberty. We have proved that it works—that the powerful engines of freedom push mankind further toward justice, toward equality, toward prosperity and security than ever government managed to drag humanity in those directions.

And so, my fellow Republicans, let us not define ourselves in terms of what we stand against—but in terms of what we stand for.

The wisdom of what we stand for is demonstrated in the record of the great and good man who leads this nation today.

In the wake of Vietnam, many felt that the will of our people was so sorely tried that we would not soon have the strength to wage peace in the world—to halt aggression before it began.

But President Ford understood that a free people are never too tired to defend their freedom. And so where our rights and interests have been threatened, he has responded—and upon the evidence of America's will to stand fast for what it believes, a structure of peace is being erected in the world.

And in the wake of a continued inflation and recession, there are those who argued that the best medicine for a crippled economy was to cripple it further. They advocated the short-term solution for long-term disaster, believing the American people were unwilling to make the necessary sacrifices to restore prosperity to our land. They were wrong. President Ford knows the way back to prosperity is through persistence and perseverance. Yes, and through sacrifice.

The way back to a healthy economy has been difficult and painful. But by refusing to resign us to the seductive panaceas of more government spending, President Ford has persisted, he has persevered—and he has prevailed.

He has suffered abuse, he has endured accusations about his concern for the jobless; he has borne with patience those who have questioned his compassion for the poor, and he has put this economy back on the road to good health.

The shrill denunciations of those who oppose his economic policies come not from concern that he might fail, but from desperation at the fact that he is succeeding.

And he is succeeding, my friends, because he has placed his faith in the American people, and not in the discredited gimmicks of government.

My fellow Americans, President Ford has begun the great work of building peace, renewing prosperity and restoring confidence in the basic institutions of freedom in America.

But there is much more to be done.

We are at peace with the world, but the world is not at peace with itself. We live in a dangerous world, and the danger for us is lessened only by the fact that those whose ambitions might exceed their common sense know what the President of the United States of America stands for.

Here at home, there are still those who believe in government rather than in people. We have, for example, a Congress which lurches along in a search for more and more ways to gain control not merely over the way we live, but over the purposes for which we live—which ought to be left to the decisions of the hearts and minds of each single individual.

The freedom and sovereignty of our land count for nothing if they are not matched equally by the freedom and sovereignty of every American.

Today, our business and industry continue to be burdened by endless, confusing government regulation. Certainly we must have laws that govern the private sector and how it conducts itself, just as we have laws that govern how our people conduct themselves.

But just as we must avoid legislating freedom, creativity and initiative out of the lives of our people, so we must also avoid legislating these virtues out of our system of free enterprise.

And, in my opinion, we have to free the free enterprise system.

Until we get government out of the business sector, we are going to have difficulty getting people back into jobs that are real and productive.

Until we get government out of the credit markets, business will be unable to expand as it ought to and employ more people.

Yes, ladies and gentlemen, there is work to be done.

Until we break the stranglehold of the party of big government over the Congress of the United States, we are going to have more federal spending, more federal control over our private lives and more empty promises that leave our people disillusioned and frustrated.

And let us not be deterred or discomfited by those who interpret the long and hard-fought primary campaign as a sign of division in Republican ranks. Let us rather take pride in the knowledge that the battle was honorably waged—and honorably won. Let us rather take pride in the fact that we had two such men as President Ford and Governor Reagan to contend for this nation's leadership.

I mean to be worthy of that honor.

In this bicentennial year, we have the opportunity to restore those principles upon which America was founded 200 years ago. It is for us now to determine whether we shall be the designers of our destiny—or the victims of it.

America was founded upon the belief that men and women had the right to be free.

Our Republican Party was born in the struggle to preserve and extend freedom.

Our task today and tomorrow and the week following and the month following is nothing less than to further the principles of freedom upon which our nation and our party were established. Our task today and in the days and weeks ahead must be to insure the election of a President who understands those principles, and lives by them—and leads this nation by them. With our help, with the help of the American people, and with the help of almighty God, we shall succeed, and I again thank you very much.∎

(Continued from p. 69)

previous night's vote on the vice presidential rule was missing. As the clerk confirmed the vote of each state delegation, the end drew nearer for the party's conservative wing, much as it had 24 years earlier when Dwight D. Eisenhower squeaked past Ohio Sen. Robert A. Taft.

At first, Reagan, bolstered by the votes in California and some Deep South states, took a healthy lead. But, as everyone expected, Ford's strength in the big northeastern states—New York, New Jersey, Pennsylvania, Connecticut, Ohio—and others such as Minnesota and Illinois pushed Ford ahead.

There was a pause as the Virginia delegation was individually polled. Then West Virginia, voting 20 to 8 in favor of Ford, put the President over the top. On a voice vote, the convention made the nomination unanimous by acclamation.

The final vote was 1,187 for Ford, 1,070 for Reagan, one vote from the New York delegation for Commerce Secretary Elliot L. Richardson and one abstention. *(See chart)*

Acceptance Speeches

Reagan's supporters gave their candidate a warm welcome during his first appearance at the convention hall Aug. 19, but the crowd that gathered to hear Ford's acceptance speech was quieter than it had been earlier in the week. Blue and white "Ford and Dole" signs blanketed most of the hall.

Well-delivered, Ford's speech concentrated on his record since taking office in mid-1974 and his future goals. The President took credit for cutting inflation in half, increasing employment to a record level and bringing the country to peace. Many observers felt the carefully rehearsed Ford speech was the best of his political career.

He touched several times on the restoration of confidence in the White House and the return of personal integrity to the executive branch of government. His administration, Ford said, had been "open, candid and forthright" from the beginning.

Needling his opponent, Ford concluded to applause: "My record is one of specifics, not smiles."

For the future, Ford promised continued economic recovery, less "impudence" from bureaucracy and a balanced federal budget by 1978.

"We will build on performance, not promises; experiences, not expediency; real progress instead of mysterious plans to be revealed in some dim and distant future," Ford said in another reference to Carter.

While primarily positive in tone, Ford's speech did rebuke the Democratic Congress for its passage of bills he has vetoed and its obstruction of his proposals to revise tax rules, restrict busing and overhaul criminal laws.

Going to the convention platform at Ford's beckoning after his acceptance speech—after first resisting determined calls from his supporters to address the crowd—Reagan asked for conciliation. "We must go forth from here united and determined," he said. "What a great general said long ago is true: there is no substitute for victory."

Dole's Remarks

Dole's vice presidential speech, in contrast to a biting address he had delivered to the convention Aug. 16, developed the same themes as the Ford speech with only slightly tougher attacks on Congress.

"Let us not define ourselves in terms of what we stand against," he urged, "but in terms of what we stand for."

The crowd received the speech politely, but the response was pale compared with the rousing cheer for Reagan when he arrived on the platform as the band played his convention theme song, "California Here We Come."

The final vote, after switches, for Dole as the vice presidential nominee was 1,981. Another 278 delegates abstained or voted for numerous favorite sons. Vice President Nelson A. Rockefeller nominated his own potential successor, telling the crowd that the Kansas senator not only could stand the heat of political battle, but also could "really dole it out." ∎

Dole Profile:

Dole: A Seasoned Political Infighter

In naming Robert Dole as his vice presidential running mate, President Ford chose a hardened party warrior who could be expected to carry an aggressive political fight to the Democrats in the fall election.

In his 16 years in Congress, the Kansas senator earned a reputation not so much for his legislative skills as for his zest for political warfare. He emerged on the national political stage as the acid-tongued Republican national chairman who led the party during the 1972 Nixon re-election campaign and the early stages of Watergate.

As chairman from 1971 to 1973, Dole earned the respect of Nixon and other party regulars for his personal loyalty and his dedication to the Republican cause. But his blunt, sometimes abrasive outspokenness also embroiled him in controversy, eventually causing him to be dumped as chairman and nearly costing him re-election to the Senate in 1974. Former Sen. William B. Saxbe (R Ohio), another Nixon loyalist who also was outspoken, criticized Dole as "a hatchet man" who was "out of the mainstream" of Republican politics.

Dole also went to the Republican ticket as a conservative not likely to antagonize disappointed backers of Ronald Reagan. He supported the Vietnam War right up to its end. He opposed Democratic social welfare spending programs. And as a midwesterner who fought indefatigably in Congress to protect programs such as crop subsidies, which are dear to farmers, he could be counted on to help repair political damage suffered by Ford in 1975 when he clamped an embargo on grain exports to the Soviet Union.

Background

Dole, 53, was born in Russell, Kan., his voting residence in 1976. He attended public schools there and went to the University of Kansas for two years before joining the Army during World War II.

Dole bears the marks of his war service. He was severely wounded on April 14, 1945, when he led an infantry charge on a machine-gun nest in Italy. His right shoulder bone was shattered and several vertebrae were cracked. Doctors feared that he would never walk again, but after more than three years in Army hospitals, he regained use of his legs. The injuries left his right arm useless.

For those injuries, Dole earned a Purple Heart, his second of the war. The experience led him in his Senate career to push for federal programs for the handicapped.

In 1948, Dole married Phyllis Holden, the physical therapist who had attended him while he was bedridden. When he returned to Topeka's Washburn University after the war to get his B.A. and law degree, his wife served as his substitute right hand, taking notes, transcribing lectures and writing his answers on exams.

In 1972 they were divorced. Dole was married again on Dec. 6, 1975, to Federal Trade Commissioner Mary E. Hanford.

Political Career

When he was chosen to run for Vice President, Dole had never lost an election. At age 26, he won election in 1950 to the Kansas Legislature. In 1952 he was elected to the first of four terms as the Russell County prosecutor, a post he held until 1960.

Dole won election to the U.S. House in 1960 and served there for four terms. As the representative of a large wheat-growing district in Kansas, he devoted most of his efforts to agricultural issues.

In the House, he showed early glimmerings of the hard-line partisanship for which he came to be known. In 1962, he set himself up as a one-man watchdog for signs of Kennedy administration involvement in the Billy Sol Estes grain storage scandal. In 1964, he served as chairman of a Republican committee formed to investigate the Bobby Baker scandal. Baker was a protege of Lyndon B. Johnson, who parlayed the post of secretary to the Senate majority leader into a personal fortune.

Also in 1964, a presidential election year, Dole led an effort to prohibit Johnson, then the President, from issuing memorial certificates to relatives of deceased veterans. Dole complained that the documents were political campaign literature.

When Republican Sen. Frank Carlson (1950-69) retired in 1968, Dole ran against former Kansas Gov. William H. Avery for the GOP nomination to replace him. Dole won with a comfortable 68.5 per cent, then went on to defeat a moderate Democrat in the general election. He won with a 60.5 per cent plurality.

Senate Record

Almost from the day he entered the Senate, Dole made waves. Consigned by the seniority system to obscurity in his committee assignments, Dole virtually set up camp on the Senate floor. He assumed for himself the role of Nixon

---

Dole's Background

Profession: Lawyer.

Born: July 22, 1923, Russell, Kan.

Home: Russell.

Religion: Methodist.

Education: University of Kansas, University of Arizona; Washburn University, Topeka, Kan., B.A., 1949, LL.B., 1952.

Public Offices: Kansas Legislature, 1951-53; Russell County prosecuting attorney, 1953-60; U.S. House, 1961-69; Senate since 1969; Republican national chairman, 1971-73.

Military: Army, discharged as captain; Bronze Star, Purple Heart.

Memberships: Russell, Kansas and American Bar Associations; past president, Kansas County Attorneys' Association and Washburn Alumni Association; American Legion; Disabled American Veterans; VFW; Kappa Sigma; Masons; Shrine; Kiwanis; Elks; 4-H Fair Association.

Family: Married Phyllis E. Holden, 1948; divorced in 1972; one child, Robin. Married Mary Elizabeth Hanford, a federal trade commissioner, Dec. 6, 1975.

Senate Committees: Agriculture and Forestry; Budget; Finance; Post Office and Civil Service; Select Committee on Nutrition and Human Needs.

defender in Senate debates, rising automatically to answer Democratic attacks on the administration. He offended some senior senators by prowling the Capitol hallways between debates, seeking to engage them in further discussion of issues.

The Kansas senator was one of the Nixon administration's most vocal defenders in some of the Senate's most heated battles. Among other issues, he helped lead Republican fights for the Supreme Court nominations of G. Harrold Carswell and Clement F. Haynsworth and for the construction of the Safeguard anti-ballistic missile system.

In 1971, Nixon rewarded Dole for his loyalty with the GOP chairmanship, an unusual honor for a freshman senator. Dole had lobbied actively for the job and won it over the protests of senior Republicans, including Minority Leader Hugh Scott (Pa.), who were concerned that Dole was too aggressive and too abrasive for the job. A White House staff member said at the time that the Kansan had been chosen because he "looks good on television" and could "say things which the President himself cannot."

As chairman during a turbulent period in the party's history, Dole was the forceful spokesman that Nixon apparently had sought. In 1971, he joined with Vice President Spiro T. Agnew in attacking the news media, and especially television networks, for biased reporting of the Vietnam War. When Sen. Edmund S. Muskie (D Maine) was trying to build a campaign for President in 1971 by attacking the FBI for domestic spying, Dole compared what he called "Muskieism" with "the McCarthyism of the 50s."

When the Democrats began attacking the administration in the summer and fall of 1972 for the Watergate break-in, Dole dismissed the issue as a diversionary tactic concocted in desperation by Democrats on the verge of defeat. He accused *The Washington Post,* which uncovered much of the scandal, of trying to conduct a "rescue operation" for Democratic candidate George McGovern (D S.D.). "The greatest political scandal of this campaign," Dole charged, "is the brazen manner in which, without benefit of clergy, *The Washington Post* has set up housekeeping with the McGovern campaign."

Dole's blistering attacks on the Democrats at times caused consternation in some wings of his own party. In July 1972, he received letters from several Republican governors urging him, for the sake of party wholeness, to tone down his attacks. He came under criticism from local and state party members who felt that the party had not supplied them with enough concrete help, such as money and organization, in the 1972 elections below the presidential level. Dole also incurred trouble from above by criticizing Nixon for not campaigning actively in the 1972 election, especially for Republican Senate candidates.

Shortly after the election, the controversial Kansan was removed as chairman, despite his stated desire to stay on. He denied that his relationship with Nixon had soured, however, blaming his ouster instead on "a faceless nameless few in the White House...the gutless wonders who seem to take personal satisfaction in trying to do somebody in."

Dole remained loyal to Nixon during most of the Watergate affair. In the summer of 1973, during the hearings by the Senate Watergate Committee, he introduced in the Senate an unsuccessful resolution to end the hearings, saying the public was tired of them and the matter should be settled in court.

He stated in February of the next year that there was no legal case against the President. But by June he had softened somewhat, saying he hoped Nixon was not involved and criticizing the President for secluding himself away from the public in the White House.

Watergate and Dole's tie to the administration almost cost him the election. At one time he was rated 12 points in the polls behind his popular opponent, U.S. Rep. William R. Roy (D 1971-74).

Nor did Nixon's Aug. 9 resignation bring him much comfort in the race. For, although Gerald Ford's accession to the Presidency boosted Republican stock generally, the new President's first actions did not go down well with Dole's conservative Kansas constituency. "President Ford has tried to help me," Dole remarked jokingly. "First there was the Nixon pardon, then there was amnesty and last week the cancellation of the wheat to the Russians."

Immediately after the Nixon pardon, Dole issued a statement criticizing Ford for the action. Under increasing attack from Roy in Kansas, Dole characteristically went on the offensive himself. Instead of trying to defend his Watergate record, he portrayed Roy as a "mudslinger" for trying to associate Dole with the scandal. And he imported Sen. Lowell P. Weicker Jr. (R Conn.), a member of the Senate Watergate Committee, to testify to his character.

In the November election, Dole surprised the experts, coming from behind to win with a bare 50.9 per cent majority.

Voting Record

Dole and Sen. Walter F. Mondale of Minnesota, the Democratic vice presidential nominee, were the first senators to oppose each other on the second spots of Republican and Democratic tickets since 1952, when Republican Nixon ran against Democrat John Sparkman of Alabama.

The voting records of Dole and Mondale could hardly have been more different. Whereas Mondale had one of the Senate's most liberal overall records, Dole's was decidedly more conservative.

The conservative Americans for Constitutional Action (ACA) gave Dole an average rating of 75 per cent for his voting record over the seven-year period 1969-75. Conversely, the liberal Americans for Democratic Action (ADA) never gave him a rating higher than 19 per cent. His highest rating with the AFL-CIO Committee on Political Action (COPE) was 27 per cent.

Although Dole kept a special eye out for the needs of his Kansas farm constituency, he did not win particularly high ratings from farm groups. His ratings from the National Farmers Union ranged from a low of 25 per cent in 1969, Dole's first year in the Senate, to 78 per cent in 1975. His 1974 rating was 35 per cent.

On partisan issues, Dole was a loyal Republican and supporter of Presidents Nixon and Ford. In almost every year since 1969, he voted with the majority of his party on more than 80 per cent of issues voted on in the Senate.

On issues on which the two Presidents indicated their positions, Dole supported them on at least 71 per cent of the votes in every year except 1974, when the figure fell to 63 per cent.

Dole was usually present in the Senate to vote on at least 90 per cent of roll-call votes, a record neither better nor worse than that of most of his colleagues.

Discussing his political philosophy during a 1976 press conference, Dole said, "I consider myself to be fairly conservative, just as conservative as some of those who worry about Ford being too liberal—which is hard to believe." ∎

Text of 1976 Republican Platform

Preamble

To you, an American citizen:

You are about to read the 1976 Republican Platform. We hope you will also find time to read the Democrats' Platform. Compare. You will see basic differences in how the two parties propose to represent you.

"The Platform is the Party's contract with the people." This is what it says on the cover of the official printing of the Democrat Platform. So it should be. The Democrats' Platform repeats the same thing on every page: More government, more spending, more inflation. Compare. This Republican Platform says exactly the opposite—less government, less spending, less inflation. In other words, we want you to retain more of your own money, money that represents the worth of your labors, to use as you see fit for the necessities and conveniences of life.

No matter how many statements to the contrary that Mr. Carter makes, he is firmly attached to a contract with you to vastly increase the powers of government. Is bigger government in Washington really what you want?

Make no mistake: You cannot have bigger programs in Washington and less government by Washington. You must choose.

What is the cost of these added or expanded programs? The Democrats' Platform is deliberately vague. When they tell you, as they do time after time, that they will "expand federal support," you are left to guess the cost. The price tag of five major Democrat Platform promises could add as much as $100-billion to the annual cost of government. But the Democrats' Platform proposes over 60 new or expanded spending programs and the expansion or creation of some 22 Washington agencies, offices or bureaus. In fact, the total of all Democrat proposals can be as high as $200-billion a year. While this must be a rough estimate, it does give you a clue to the magnitude and direction of these commitments: *The Democrats' Platform can increase federal spending by 50 percent.* If a Democrat Congress passes the Democrat Platform and it is signed by a Democrat President, what happens then? The Democrats could raise your taxes by 50 per cent to pay for the new programs. Or the Democrats could *not* raise taxes and the result would be a runaway inflation. Of course, contract or no contract, the Democrats may not honor their promises. Are you prepared to risk it?

In stark contrast to the Democrats' Platform, we offer you a responsive and moderate alternative based on these principles:

—We believe that liberty can be measured by how much freedom you have to make your own decisions—even your own mistakes. Government must step in when your liberties impinge on your neighbor's.

Government must protect your constitutional rights. Government must deal with other governments and protect you from aggressors. Government must assure equal opportunity. And government must be compassionate in caring for those citizens who are unable to care for themselves.

—Our federal system of local-state-national government is designed to sort out on what level these actions should be taken. Those concerns of a national character—such as air and water pollution that do not respect state boundaries or the national transportation system or efforts to safeguard your civil liberties—must, of course, be handled on the national level.

—As a general rule, however, we believe that government action should be taken first by the government that resides as close to you as possible. Governments tend to become less responsive to your needs the farther away they are from you. Thus, we prefer local and state government to national government, and decentralized national government wherever possible.

—We also believe that you, often acting through voluntary organizations, should have the opportunity to solve many of the social problems of your community. This spirit of freely helping others is uniquely American and should be encouraged in every way by government.

—Every dollar spent by government is a dollar earned by you. Government must always ask: Are your dollars being wisely spent? Can we afford it? Is it not better for the country to leave your dollars in your pocket?

—Your elected officials, their appointees, and government workers are expected to perform their public acts with honesty, openness, diligence, and special integrity. At the heart of our system must be confidence that these people are always working for you.

—We believe that your initiative and energy create jobs, our standard of living and the underlying economic strength of the country. Government must work for the goal of justice and the elimination of unfair practices, but no government has yet designed a more productive economic system or one which benefits as many people.

—The beauty of our land is our legacy to our children. It must be protected by us so that they can pass it on intact to their children.

—The United States must always stand for peace and liberty in the world and the rights of the individual. We must form sturdy partnerships with our allies for the preservation of freedom. We must be ever willing to negotiate differences, but equally mindful that there are American ideals that cannot be compromised. Given that there are other nations with potentially hostile designs, we recognize that we can reach our goals only while maintaining a superior

national defense that is second to none.

We support these principles because they are right, knowing full well that they will not be easy to achieve. Acting with restraint is most difficult when confronted by an opposition Congress that is determined to promise everything to everybody. And this is what the Democrat Congress has been doing. A document, such as this Platform, which refuses to knuckle under to special interest groups, will be accused of being "uncaring." Yet it is exactly because *we do care* about your basic freedom to manage your own life with a minimum of government interference, because *we do care* about encouraging permanent and meaningful jobs, because *we do care* about your getting paid in sound dollars, because *we do care* about resisting the use of your tax dollars for wasteful or unproven programs—it is for these reasons that we are proposing only actions that the nation can afford and are opposing excessive tinkering with an economic system that works better than any other in the world.

Our great American Republic was founded on the principle: "one nation under God, with liberty and justice for all." This bicentennial year marks the anniversary of the greatest secular experiment in history: That of seeking to determine that a people are truly capable of self-government: It was our "Declaration" which put the world and posterity on notice "that all Men are...endowed by their Creator with certain unalienable Rights" and that those rights must not be taken from those to whom God has given them.

Recently, Peggy Pinder, a 23-year-old student from Grinnell, Iowa, who is a delegate to this convention, said that she joined our party "because Republicans understand the place of government in the people's lives better than the Democrats. Republicans try to find ways to take care of needs through the private sector first while it seems automatic for Democrats to take care of them through the governmental system."

The perception of Peggy Pinder governs this Platform. Aren't these the principles that you want your elected representatives to have?

Jobs and Inflation

We believe it is of paramount importance that the American people understand that the number one destroyer of jobs is inflation. We wish to stress that the number one cause of inflation is the government's expansion of the nation's supply of money and credit needed to pay for deficit spending. It is above all else deficit spending by the federal government which erodes the purchasing power of the dollar. Most Republicans in Congress seem to understand this fundamental cause-and-effect relationship and their support in sustaining over 40 Presidential vetoes in the past two years has prevented over $13-billion in federal spending. It is clear that most of the Democrats do not understand this vital principle, or, if they do, they simply don't care.

Inflation is the direct responsibility of a spendthrift Democrat-controlled Congress that has been unwilling to discipline itself to live within our means. The temptation to spend and deficit spend for political reasons has simply been too great for most of our elected politicians to resist. Individuals, families, companies and most local and state governments must live within a budget. Why not Congress?

Republicans hope every American realizes that if we are to permanently eliminate high unemployment, it is essential to protect the integrity of our money. That means putting an end to deficit spending. The danger, sooner or later, is runaway inflation.

Wage and price controls are not the solution to inflation. They attempt to treat only the symptom—rising prices—not the cause. Historically, controls have always been a dismal failure, and in the end they create only shortages, black markets and higher prices. For these reasons the Republican Party strongly opposes any reimposition of such controls, on a standby basis or otherwise.

Unfortunately, the Democrat-controlled Congress now persists in attempting to obtain control over our nation's money creation policies by taking away the independence of the Federal Reserve Board. The same people who have so massively expanded government spending should not be allowed politically to dominate our monetary policy. The independence of the Federal Reserve System must be preserved.

Massive, federally-funded public employment programs, such as the Humphrey-Hawkins Bill currently embraced by the new National Platform of the Democrat Party will cost billions and can only be financed either through very large tax increases or through ever increasing levels of deficit spending. Although such government "make-work" programs usually provide a temporary stimulus to the economy, "quick-fix" solutions of this sort—like all narcotics—lead to addiction, larger and larger doses, and ultimately the destruction of far more jobs than they create. Sound job creation can only be accomplished in the private sector of the economy. Americans must not be fooled into accepting government as the employer of last resort. Nor should we sit idly by while 2.5 million American jobs are threatened by imports of textile products. We encourage the renewal of the GATT Multifiber Arrangement and the signing of other necessary bilateral agreements to protect our domestic textile industry.

In order to be able to provide more jobs, businesses must be able to expand; yet in order to build and expand, they must be profitable and able to borrow funds (savings) that someone else has been willing to part with on a temporary basis. In the long run, inflation discourages thrift, encourages debt and destroys the incentive to save which is the mainspring of capital formation. When our government—through deficit spending and debasement of the currency—destroys the incentive to save and to invest, it destroys the wellspring of American productivity. Obviously, when production falls, the number of jobs decline.

The American people are beginning to understand that no government can ever add real wealth (purchasing power) to an economy by simply turning on the printing presses or by creating credit out of thin air. All government can do is confiscate and redistribute wealth. No nation can spend its way into prosperity; a nation can only spend its way into bankruptcy.

Taxes and Government Spending

The Republican Party recognizes that tax policies and spending policies are inseparable. If government spending is not controlled, taxes will inevitably rise either directly or through inflation. By failing to tie spending directly to income, the Democrat-controlled Congress has not kept faith with the American people. Every American knows he cannot continually live beyond his means.

The Republican Party advocates a legislative policy to obtain a balanced federal budget and reduced tax rates. While the best tax reform is tax reduction, we recognize the need for structural tax adjustments to help the working men and women of our nation. To that end, we recommend tax credits for college tuition, post-secondary technical training and child care expenses incurred by working parents.

Over the past two decades of Democrat-control of the Congress, our tax laws have become a nightmare of complexity and unfair tax preferences, virtually destroying the credibility of the system. Simplification should be a major goal of tax reform.

We support economic and tax policies to insure the necessary job-producing expansion of our economy. These include hastening capital recovery through new systems of accelerated depreciation, removing the tax burden on equity financing to encourage more capital investment, ending the unfair double taxation of dividends, and supporting proposals to enhance the ability of our working and other citizens to own "a piece of the action" through stock ownership. When balanced by expenditure reductions, the personal exemption should be raised to $1,000.

Agriculture and Rural Development

The bounty of our farms is so plentiful that we may tend to forget what an amazing production achievement this really is. The American farmer and rancher produces enough food to feed over 56 people—a threefold increase in productivity in 20 years.

Rural America must be maintained as a rewarding place to live. To accomplish this, our rural areas are entitled to services comparable to their urban neighbors, such as water and sewer systems, improved electricity and telephone service, adequate transportation, available and adequate financial credit, and employment opportunities which will allow small farmers to supplement their incomes.

Farm exports have continued to expand under the policies of this Republican Administration—from a low of $6-billion in 1968, the last Democrat year, to $22-billion in 1975. These exports are not giveaway programs; most are earning dollars from the marketplaces of the world, establishing a favorable balance of trade and a higher standard of living for all. Through our farm exports we fight the problem of world hunger, especially with the humanitarian Food for Peace Program (Public Law 480) of the Eisenhower Administration and the Republican-controlled Congress of 1954.

Republican farm policy has permitted farmers to use their crop land fully. We are at last moving toward making effective use of our superb resources. Net farm income from 1972 through 1975 averaged $26-billion, more than double the average of the 1960's. Government should not dictate to the productive men and women who work the land. To assure this, we support the continuation of the central principles of the Agricultural Act of 1973, with adjustments of target prices and loan levels to reflect increased production costs.

We oppose government-controlled grain reserves, just as we oppose federal regulations that are unrealistic in farm practices, such as those imposed by the Occupational Safety and Health Administration (OSHA) and the Environmental Protection Agency (EPA).

We urge prompt action by Congress in amending the Grain Inspection Act to strengthen the present inspection system and restore its integrity.

We firmly believe that when the nation asks our farmers to go all out to produce as much as possible for world-wide markets, the government should guarantee them unfettered access to those markets. Our farmers should not be singled out by export controls. Also, when a foreign nation subsidizes its farm exports, our farmers deserve protection against such unfair practices. The federal government should assure that foreign imported commodities are equal in quality to our domestic commodities. Nations from whom we buy commodities should not be allowed to circumvent import restriction laws, such as the Meat Import Quota Act of 1964.

We recognize the importance of the multilateral trade negotiations now in progress and urge our representatives to obtain the most beneficial agreements for our farmers and the nation's economy.

In order to assure the consumers of America an uninterrupted source of food, it is necessary to pass labor relations legislation which is responsive to the welfare of workers and to the particular needs of food production. Such legislation should recognize the need to prevent work stoppages during critical harvest periods.

We must help farmers protect themselves from drought, flood and other natural disasters through a system of all-risk crop insurance through federal government reinsurance of private insurance companies combined with the existing disaster payment program.

As in 1972, we urge prompt passage of the Republican-sponsored legislation now pending in Congress which will increase the estate tax exemption to $200,000, allow valuation of farm property on a current use basis and provide for extension of the time of payment in the case of farms and small businesses. This overdue estate and gift tax legislation must be approved this year. We favor a liberalized marital deduction and oppose capital gains tax at death.

Innovations in agriculture need to be encouraged by expanding research programs including new pest and predator control measures, and utilization of crops as a new energy resource. If we expect our farmers to produce an abundant food supply, they must have all the energy they need to produce, market and process their crops and livestock.

We continue to support farmer cooperatives, including rural electric and telephone cooperatives, in their efforts to improve services to their members. We support the Capper-Volstead Act.

We believe that non-farm corporations and tax-loss farming should be prevented from unfairly competing against family farms, which we support as the preferred method of farm organization.

Since farmers are practicing conservationists, they should not be burdened with unrealistic environmental regulations. We are concerned about regulations issued by the Army Corps of Engineers that will regulate all "routine" agricultural and forestry activities on "all" our waters and wetland, and support legislation to exempt routine farming operations from these requirements. The adjudication of water rights should be a matter of state determination.

Small Business

Small business, so vital to our economic system, is free enterprise in its purest sense. It holds forth opportunity to the individual, regardless of race or sex, to fulfill the American dream. Small businesses are the base of our economy and its main source of strength. Some 9.6 million small firms generate 55 per cent of our private employment—or the livelihood of over 100 million Americans. Yet while small businesses have a unique place in our society, they also have unique problems that government must address. Therefore, we recommend that the Small Business Administration (SBA):
—Assure adequate financing to those credit worthy firms that cannot now obtain funds through conventional channels;
—Include the proper mix of loan programs to meet the needs of the

many different types of firms that constitute the American small business community;
—Serve as an aggressive advocate for small business and provide procurement, management and technological assistance.

For survival, small businesses must have relief from the overwhelming burden placed on them by many regulatory bodies. Paperwork proliferation has grown out of control, and small business is not equipped to deal with this aggravation.

The present tax structure does not allow small firms to generate enough capital to grow and create jobs. Estate taxes need liberalization to benefit the family business in the same manner as for the family farm. Encouraging investment in small businesses through more equitable tax treatment remains the best and least expensive method of creating productive employment.

The Republican Party, recognizing that small and independent business is the backbone of the American competitive system, pledges itself to strengthen this vital institution.

Antitrust

The Republican Party believes in and endorses the concept that the American economy is traditionally dependent upon fair competition in the marketplace. To assure fair competition, antitrust laws must treat all segments of the economy equally.

Vigorous and equitable enforcement of antitrust laws heightens competition and enables consumers to obtain the lowest possible price in the marketplace.

Bureaucratic Overregulation

We believe that the extent of federal regulation and bureaucratic interference in the lives of the American people must be reduced. The programs and activities of the federal government should be required to meet strict tests of their usefulness and effectiveness.

In particular, we consider essential an analysis of the extensive growth of laws and regulations governing production processes and conditions and standards for consumer products, so as to determine whether the services and benefits the American people receive are worth the price they are paying for these services in higher taxes and consumer prices.

We are intensely aware of the need to protect our environment and provide safe working conditions in American industry, while at the same time preventing the loss of jobs and the closing of small businesses through unrealistic or over-rigorous government regulations. We support a balanced approach that considers the requirements of a growing economy and provides jobs for American workers.

The average businessman and employer is being overwhelmed by government-required paperwork. We support legislation to control and reduce the burden of federal paperwork, particularly

that generated by the Internal Revenue Service and the Census Bureau.

Government That Works

We believe that Americans are fed up with and frustrated by national government that makes great promises and fails to deliver. We are. We think that Democrat Congresses—in control for 40 out of 44 years—are the grand masters of this practice. We think that national government that has grown so big that the left hand doesn't know what the right hand is doing has also caused the condition we are in.

What we now have is a government organization that doesn't make any sense. It has not developed by design. It just grew—by whim, bureaucratic fighting, and the caving in of Democratic Congresses to special interest demands. So today we find that nine federal departments and 20 independent agencies are involved in education; seven departments and eight agencies in health; federal recreation areas are administered by six agencies in three departments; and so forth.

What we need is a top-to-bottom overhaul. Two high level presidential commissions under two Presidents—one a Democrat, one a Republican—have investigated and come up with the same answer: There must be functional realignment of government, instead of the current arrangement by subject areas or constituencies.

We want federal domestic departments to reflect the major purposes of government, such as natural resources, human resources, community development and the economic affairs. Unfortunately, the Democrat Congress has refused to address this problem. Now we insist that attention must be paid.

Too often in the past, we have been content with organizational or procedural solutions to complex economic and social regulatory problems. We should no longer accept rhetoric as a substitute for concrete results. The President has proposed to Congress the Agenda for Government Reform Act, which would guarantee the systematic re-examination and reform of all federal regulatory activities within the next four years. This legislation requires Congress and the President to agree to undertake an exhaustive reassessment of the combined effects of all government regulations, and it requires them to adhere to a disciplined timetable to assure annual results. The American people deserve no less. Every agency of government must be made efficient, and every government regulation should be subjected to cost benefit analysis. The Occupational Safety and Health Administration (OSHA) is a typical example of a well-intentioned regulatory effort which has imposed large costs but has not solved our problems.

The beauty of America's original concept of government was its diversity, the belief that different purposes are best served by governments at different levels. In our lifetime, however, Democrat

Congresses have allowed this system to become warped and over-nationalized. As powers have flowed to Washington, the ability to attend to our problems has often dried up in our communities and states. This trend must be reversed. Local government is simply more accountable to the people, and local people are perfectly capable of making decisions.

We reaffirm the long standing principle of the Republican Party that the best government is the one closest to the people. It is less costly, more accountable, and more responsive to the people's needs. Our confidence in the people of this nation was demonstrated by initiating the Revenue Sharing Program. To date, $30-billion of federal tax dollars have been returned to the states and localities. This program is administered with fewer than 100 people and a computer. Revenue Sharing is an effort to reverse the trend toward centralization. Revenue Sharing must continue without unwarranted federal strictures and regulations.

As a further step in this direction, the Republicans in Congress promoted the new concept of federal block grants to localities for much greater flexibility. Under block grants, federal funds can be tailored by the states and localities to the wishes of each community. There are now two block grant programs—in community development and employment training. Block grant programs should be extended to replace many existing categorical health, education, child nutrition and social programs. The Democrat Congress stands guilty of failing to enact these vital reforms. Our ultimate goal is to restore taxing and spending to the local level.

The Republican Party has always believed that the proper role of government is to do only those things which individuals cannot do for themselves. We encourage individual initiative and oppose the trend of ever expanding government programs which is destroying the volunteer spirit in America. We firmly believe that community involvement is essential to the development of effective solutions to the problems confronting our country.

While we oppose a uniform national primary, we encourage the concept of regional presidential primaries, which would group those states which voluntarily agree to have presidential primaries in a geographical area on a common date.

We encourage full participation in our electoral process. We further recognize the sanctity and value of the ballot. In that regard, we oppose "federal post card registration." The possibilities could not only cheapen our ballot, but in fact threaten the entire electoral process.

Control of the United States Congress by the Democrat Party for 40 of the past 44 years has resulted in a system dominated by powerful individuals and riddled with corruption. Recent events have demonstrated an unwillingness and inability by the Democrat Party to cleanse itself. Selective morality has been the order of the day.

Positive Republican initiatives have languished in Democrat-controlled Congressional Committees while business as usual has continued in Washington. The American people demand and deserve reform of the United States Congress. We offer these proposals of far-reaching reform:

—Repeal of legislation which permits automatic increases in the salaries of Members of Congress, congressional staffs, and official expense allowances. Public accountability demands that Members publicly vote on increases on the expenses of their office. Members' salary increases should not become effective until a new Congress is elected.

—Elimination of proxy voting which allows Members to record votes in Committee without being present for the actual deliberations or vote on a measure.

—Elimination of Democrat Caucus rules which allow a Party to bind its Members' votes on legislation. Each Member of Congress represents his constituency and must be free to vote in accordance with the dictates of his constituency and individual conscience.

—A complete audit by the General Accounting Office of all congressional allowances and appropriate disciplinary measures for those who have violated the public trust.

—Full public disclosure of financial interests by Members and divestiture of those interests which present conflicts of interest.

—Changes in the House rules which would allow a House majority to require the House Ethics Committee to conduct an investigation into alleged misconduct by any Member of Congress if the Committee refuses to act on its own.

—A complete overhaul and streamlining of the system which has permitted the proliferation of subcommittees with overlapping responsibilities, vague jurisdictional definitions and a lack of legislative production.

—Quarterly publication of names, titles and salaries of all Congressional employees.

—Improved lobby disclosure legislation so that the people will know how much money is being spent to influence public officials.

Citizens are demanding the end to the rapid and wasteful increase in the size of Washington government. All steps must be taken to insure that unnecessary federal agencies and programs are eliminated and that Congress carefully scrutinize the total budget of each agency. If it is determined that sunset laws and zero-based budgeting can accomplish these ends then they will have our support. Washington programs must be made as cost-effective as those in the states and localities. Among the many serious complaints that we wish to register on behalf of the American people is the poor operation of the United States Postal Service.

We note the low respect the public has for Congress—a Democrat-controlled institution—and wonder how the Democrats

can possibly honor their pledge to reform government when they have utterly failed to reform Congress.

A Safe and Just Society

Every American has a right to be protected from criminals. Violence has no place in our land. A society that excuses crime will eventually fall victim to it. The American people have been subjected to an intolerable wave of violent crime.

The victim of a crime should be treated with compassion and justice. The attacker must be kept from harming others. Emphasis must be on protecting the innocent and punishing the guilty. Prevention of crime is its best deterrent and should be stressed.

Fighting crime is—and should be—primarily a local responsibility. We support the continuation of the federal help given through the Law Enforcement Assistance Administration to law enforcement officials in our states, counties and municipalities. Each state should have the power to decide whether it wishes to impose the death penalty for certain crimes. All localities are urged to tighten their bail practices and to review their sentencing and parole procedures.

The federal criminal code should include automatic and mandatory minimum sentences for persons committing offenses under federal jurisdiction that involve the use of a dangerous weapon; that involve exceptionally serious crimes, such as trafficking in hard drugs, kidnapping and aircraft hijacking; and that involve injuries committed by repeat offenders.

The work presently being done to tighten the anti-obscenity provisions of the criminal code has our full support. Since the jurisdiction of the federal government in this field is limited to interstate commerce and the mails, we urge state and local governments to assume a major role in limiting the distribution and availability of obscene materials.

We support the right of citizens to keep and bear arms. We oppose federal registration of firearms. Mandatory sentences for crimes committed with a lethal weapon are the only effective solution to this problem.

Sure and swift justice demands additional judges, United States Attorneys and other court workers. The Democrat Congress has created no new federal judgeships since 1970; we deplore this example of playing politics with the justice system.

Drug abuse is not simply a health problem, but also a very real law enforcement concern and a problem of worldwide dimension. Controlling drug abuse calls for the ratification of the existing international treaty on synthetic drugs, increased emphasis on preventing the diversion of amphetamines and barbiturates into illegal markets, and intensive efforts to keep drugs out of this country. Heroin continues to come across our borders. Drug enforcement agents and international cooperation must cut off this supply. We say: Treat the addicts, but, at the same time, remove the pushers from the street and give them mandatory sentences.

Juveniles now account for almost half the arrests for serious crimes—murder, rape, robbery and aggravated assault. The cost of school violence and vandalism is estimated at $600 million annually, about what is spent on textbooks. Primary responsibility for raising our children, instilling proper values and thus preventing juvenile delinquency lies with the family, not the government. Yet when families fail, local law enforcement authorities must respond. Law enforcement block grant funds can be used by states in correcting and preventing juvenile delinquency. The LEAA should promote additional research in this area. The structure of the family must be strengthened. All enterprises have to be encouraged to find more jobs for young people. A youth differential must be included in the minimum wage law. Citizen action should let the television industry know that we want it to curb violence in programming because of its effect on our youth.

The criminal justice system must be more vigilant in preventing rape, eliminating discrimination against the victim and dealing with the offenders.

States should recognize that antiquated and overcrowded prisons are not conducive to rehabilitation. A high priority of prison reform should be to help the young first-time offender. There should be adequate separation of young from adult offenders, more relevant prison industries, better counseling, community-based alternatives and more help in getting a job for the offender who has served his or her time.

Terrorism—both domestic and international—must be stopped. Not only must the strongest steps be taken in the United States, but collective action must come from all nations. Deterring every form of hijacking calls for sanctions against countries that aid terrorists. The world community should take appropriate action to deal with terrorist organizations. We applaud the daring rescue by Israel of innocent civilian hostages who were kidnapped by terrorists. While we regret that loss of life was involved, the courageous manner in which the hostages were freed speaks eloquently to our abhorrence of world bandits.

The Right to Privacy

Liberty depends in great measure on the privacy that each American retains.

We are alarmed by Washington's growing collection of information. The number of federal data banks is now estimated at between 800 and 900 and more than 50 agencies are involved. We question the need for all these computers to be storing records of our lives. Safeguards must protect us against this information being misused or disclosed. Major changes, for example, are needed to maintain the confidentiality of tax returns and Social Security records.

Recent Supreme Court decisions have held that an individual has no constitutional right to the privacy of records held in banks or other depository institutions and that they can be readily obtained by law enforcement agencies without a person's consent or knowledge. Law enforcement authorities must be able to pursue criminal violators, yet, at the same time, there should be reasonable controls imposed to protect the privacy of law-abiding citizens. We support legislation, now pending, to assure this protection.

Too many government records, on the other hand, are unnecessarily classified. Congress and the Executive should devise a more reasonable system for classifying and handling government information.

The President's achievements in protecting privacy are unequalled by past administrations and must be built upon in the future. We particularly note changes in federal record-keeping systems, the appointment of the Commission on the CIA, the reorganization of the intelligence community and the restriction of White House access to income tax returns.

The American Family

Families must continue to be the foundation of our nation.

Families—not government programs—are the best way to make sure our children are properly nurtured, our elderly are cared for, our cultural and spiritual heritages are perpetuated, our laws are observed and our values are preserved.

If families fail in these vitally important tasks, there is little the government, no matter how well-intentioned, can do to remedy the results. Schools cannot educate children adequately if families are not supportive of the learning process. Law enforcement authorities are nearly helpless to curb juvenile delinquency without family cooperation in teaching young people respect for property and laws. Neither medicine nor school feeding programs can replace the family's ability to provide the basis for good health. Isolation from meaningful family contact makes it virtually impossible for the elderly to avoid loneliness or dependence. The values of hard work and responsibility start with the family.

As modern life brings changes in our society, it also puts stresses on families trying to adjust to new realities while maintaining cherished values. Economic uncertainty, unemployment, housing difficulties, women's and men's concerns with their changing and often conflicting roles, high divorce rates, threatened neighborhoods and schools, and public scandal all create a hostile atmosphere that erodes family structures and family values. Thus it is imperative that our government's programs, actions, officials and social welfare institutions never be allowed to jeopardize the family. *We fear the government may be powerful enough to destroy our families; we know that it is not powerful enough to replace them.*

Because of our concern for family values, we affirm our beliefs, stated elsewhere in this Platform, in many elements that will make our country a more hospitable environment for family life—neighborhood schools; educational systems that include and are responsive to parents' concerns; estate tax changes to establish more realistic exemptions which will minimize disruption of already bereaved families; a position on abortion that values human life; a welfare policy to encourage rather than discourage families to stay together and seek economic independence; a tax system that assists rather than penalizes families with elderly members, children in day care or children in college; economic and employment policies that stop the shrinkage of our dollars and stimulate the creation of jobs so that families can plan for their economic security.

Education

Our children deserve quality education.

We believe that segregated schools are morally wrong and unconstitutional. However, we oppose forced busing to achieve racial balances in our schools. We believe there are educational advantages for children in attending schools in their own neighborhoods and that the Democrat-controlled Congress has failed to enact legislation to protect this concept. The racial composition of many schools results from decisions by people about where they choose to live. If Congress continues to fail to act, we would favor consideration of an amendment to the Constitution forbidding the assignment of children to schools on the basis of race.

Our approach is to work to eradicate the root causes of segregated schools, such as housing discrimination and gerrymandered school districts. We must get on with the education of all our children.

Throughout our history, the education of our children has been a community responsibility. But now federal categorical grant programs pressure local school districts into substituting Washington-dictated priorities for their own. Local school administrators and school boards are being turned into bookkeepers for the federal government. Red tape and restrictive regulations stifle imagination and creativity. We are deeply concerned about the decline in the performance of our schools and the decline in public confidence in them.

We favor consideration of tax credits for parents making elementary and secondary school tuition payments.

Local communities wishing to conduct non-sectarian prayers in their public schools should be able to do so. We favor a constitutional amendment to achieve this end.

We propose consolidating federal categorical grant programs into block grants and turning the money over to the states to use in accordance with their own needs and priorities and with minimum bureaucratic controls. A single program must preserve the funding that is directed at the needs of such special groups as the handicapped and the disadvantaged.

Primary responsibility for education, particularly on the elementary and secondary levels, belongs to local communities and parents. Intrusion by the federal government must be avoided. Bureaucratic control of schools by Washington has the potential for destruction of our educational system by taking more and more decisions away from parents and local school authorities. Total financial dependence on the federal government inevitably leads to greater centralization of authority. We believe, therefore, that a study should be authorized concerning funding of elementary and secondary education, coupled with a study regarding return to the states of equivalent revenue to compensate for any loss in present levels of federal funding.

Unless steps are taken immediately, soaring prices will restrict a college education to the rich and those poor enough to qualify now for government aid. Federal higher education policy should continue to focus on financial aid for needy individuals, but because the financial ability to go to college is fast slipping out of the grasp of middle income families, more realistic eligibility guidelines for student aid are essential.

Government interference in the management of colleges and universities must be stopped. Federal support to assist in meeting the grave financial problems of higher education should be forthcoming, but such funds should never be used as devices for imposing added controls.

Diversity in education has great value. Public schools and non-public schools should share in education funds on a constitutionally acceptable basis. Private colleges and universities should be assisted to maintain healthy competition and to enrich diversity. The cost of expanding public campuses can be kept down if existing private institutions are helped to accommodate our student population.

We favor continued special federal support for vocational education.

Health

Every American should have access to quality health care at an affordable price.

The possibility of an extended illness in a family is a frightening prospect, but, if it does happen, a person should at least be protected from having it wipe out lifetime savings. Catastrophic expenses incurred from major illnesses and accidents affect only a small percentage of Americans each year, but for those people, the financial burden can be devastating. We support extension of catastrophic illness protection to all who cannot obtain it. We should utilize our private health insurance system to assure adequate protection for those who do not have it. Such an approach will eliminate the red tape and high bureaucratic costs inevitable in a comprehensive national program.

The Republican Party opposes compulsory national health insurance.

Americans should know that the Democrat Platform, which offers a government-operated and financed "comprehensive national health insurance system with universal and mandatory coverage," will increase federal government spending by more than $70-billion in its first full year. Such a plan, could require a personal income tax increase of approximately 20 per cent. We oppose this huge, new health insurance tax. Moreover, we do not believe that the federal government can administer effectively the Democrats' cradle-to-grave proposal.

The most effective, efficient and economical method to improve health care and extend its availability to all is to build on the present health delivery and insurance system, which covers nine out of every ten Americans.

A coordinated effort should be mounted immediately to contain the rapid increase in health care costs by all available means, such as development of healthier life styles through education, improved preventive care, better distribution of medical manpower, emphasis on out-of-hospital services and elimination of wasteful duplication of medical services.

We oppose excessive intrusions from Washington in the delivery of health care. We believe in preserving the privacy that should exist between a patient and a physician, particularly in regard to the confidentiality of medical records.

Federal health programs should be consolidated into a single grant to each state, where possible, thereby allowing much greater flexibility in setting local priorities. Our rural areas, for example, have different health care delivery needs than our cities. Federal laws and regulations should respect these differences and make it possible to respond differently to differing needs. Fraud in Medicare and Medicaid programs should be exposed and eliminated.

We need a comprehensive and equitable approach to the subject of mental health. Such a program should focus on the prevention, treatment and care of mental illness. It should cover all aspects of the interrelationships between emotional illness and other specific disabilities.

The Republican Party applauds the enlightened programs that address mental retardation, cerebral palsy, epilepsy, and other developmental disabilities that seek to remove us from the dark ages in these areas.

Alcoholism and drug abuse, growing problems in America today, should receive the utmost attention.

While we support valid medical and biological research efforts which can produce life-saving results, we oppose any research on live fetuses. We are also opposed to any legislation which sanctions ending the life of any patient.

Child Nutrition

Every child should have enough to eat. Good nutrition is a prerequisite of a healthy life. We must focus our resources on feeding *needy* children. The present school lunch programs provide a 20 per cent subsidy to underwrite the meals of children from middle- and upper-income families.

The existing 15 child nutrition programs should be consolidated into one program, administered by the states, and concentrated on those children truly in need. Other federal programs should assure that low-income people will be able to purchase a nutritionally adequate food supply.

Equal Rights and Ending Discrimination

Roadblocks must be removed that may prevent Americans from realizing their full potential in society. Unfair discrimination is a burden that intolerably weighs morally, economically and politically upon a free nation.

While working to eradicate discriminatory practices, every citizen should be encouraged to take pride in and foster the cultural heritage that has been passed on from previous generations. Almost every American traces ancestry from another country; this cultural diversity gives strength to our national heritage.

There must be vigorous enforcement of laws to assure equal treatment in job recruitment, hiring, promotion, pay, credit, mortgage access and housing. The way to end discrimination, however, is not by resurrecting the much discredited quota system and attempting to cloak it in an aura of new respectability. Rather, we must provide alternative means of assisting the victims of past discrimination to realize their full worth as American citizens.

Wiping out past discrimination requires continued emphasis on providing educational opportunities for minority citizens, increasing direct and guaranteed loans to minority business enterprises, and affording qualified minority persons equal opportunities for government positions at all levels.

Women

Women, who comprise a numerical majority of the population, have been denied a just portion of our nation's rights and opportunities. We reaffirm our pledge to work to eliminate discrimination in all areas for reasons of race, color, national origin, age, creed or sex and to enforce vigorously laws guaranteeing women equal rights.

The Republican Party reaffirms its support for ratification of the Equal Rights Amendment. Our Party was the first national party to endorse the E.R.A. in 1940. We continue to believe its ratification is essential to insure equal rights for all Americans. In our 1972 Platform, the Republican Party recognized the great contributions women have made to society as homemakers and mothers, as contributors to the community through volunteer work, and as members of the labor force in careers. The Platform stated then, and repeats now, that the Republican Party "fully endorses the principle of equal rights, equal opportunities and equal responsibilities for women." The equal Rights Amendment is the embodiment of this principle and therefore we support its swift ratification.

The question of abortion is one of the most difficult and controversial of our time. It is undoubtedly a moral and personal issue but it also involves complex questions relating to medical science and criminal justice. There are those in our Party who favor complete support for the Supreme Court decision which permits abortion on demand. There are others who share sincere convictions that the Supreme Court's decision must be changed by a constitutional amendment prohibiting all abortions. Others have yet to take a position, or they have assumed a stance somewhere in between polar positions.

We protest the Supreme Court's intrusion into the family structure through its denial of the parents' obligation and right to guide their minor children. The Republican Party favors a continuance of the public dialogue on abortion and supports the efforts of those who seek enactment of a constitutional amendment to restore protection of the right to life for unborn children.

The Social Security System, our federal tax laws, and unemployment and disability programs currently discriminate against women and often work against married couples as well. These inequities must be corrected. We recognize that special support must be given to the increasing number of women who have assumed responsibility as the heads of households while also being wage earners. Programs for job training, counseling and other services should be established to help them attain their dual role in society.

We reiterate the pledges elsewhere in this platform of support for child care assistance, part-time and flexible-time work that enables men and women to combine employment and family responsibilities, estate tax reform, small business assistance for women, rape prevention and elimination of discriminatory housing practices.

Ethnic Americans

Ethnic Americans have enriched this nation with their hard work, self-reliance and respect for the rights and needs of others. Ethnic groups reaching our shores at various times have given our country its unique identity and strength among the nations of the world. We recognize and value the contributions of Ethnic Americans to our free and democratic society.

Hispanic-Americans

When language is a cause of discrimination, there must be an intensive educational effort to enable Spanish-speaking students to become fully proficient in English while maintaining their own language and cultural heritage. Hispanic-Americans must not be treated as second-class citizens in schools, employment or any other aspect of life just because English is not their first language. Hispanic-Americans truly believe that individual integrity must be paramount; what they want most from government and politics is the opportunity to participate fully. The Republican Party has and always will offer this opportunity.

Indians and Alaska Natives

We have a unique commitment to Native Americans; we pledge to continue to honor our trust relationship with them, and we reaffirm our federal Indian policy of self-determination without termination. This means moving smoothly and quickly away from federal domination to effective participation and communication by Indians in the political process and in the planning, content and administration of federal programs. We shall pursue our joint effort with Indian leaders to assist in the orderly development of Indian and native-owned resources and to continue to attack the severe health, education and unemployment problems which exist among Indians and Alaska Natives.

Puerto Rico, The District of Columbia and the Territories

The principle of self-determination also governs our positions on Puerto Rico and the District of Columbia as it has in past platforms. We again support statehood for Puerto Rico, if that is the people's choice in a referendum, with full recognition within the concept of a multicultural society of the citizens' right to retain their Spanish language and traditions; and support giving the District of Columbia voting representation in the United States Senate and House of Representatives and full home rule over those matters that are purely local.

We will continue to negotiate with the Congress of Micronesia on the future political status of the Trust Territories of the Pacific Islands to meet the mutual interests of both parties. We support a plebiscite by the people of American Samoa on whether they wish to elect a territorial governor. We favor whatever action necessary to permit American citizens resident in Guam, Puerto Rico and the Virgin Islands to vote for President and Vice President in national elections.

Responsibilities

Finally, the most basic principle of all: Achievement and preservation of human rights in our society is based on the willing acceptance by millions of Americans of their responsibilities as free citizens. Instead of viewing government programs with ever increasing expectations, we must readily assume the obligations of wage-earners, taxpayers and supporters of our government institution and laws. This is often forgotten, and so it is appropriate to remind ourselves in this Platform that this is why our society works.

Handicapped Citizens

Handicapped persons must be admitted into the mainstream of our society.

Too often the handicapped population of the nation—over 30 million men, women and children—has been denied the rights taken for granted by other citizens. Time after time, the paths are closed to the handicapped in education, employment, transportation, health care, housing, recreation, insurance, polling booths and due process of law. National involvement is necessary to correct discrimination in these areas. Individual incentive alone cannot do it.

We pledge continued attention to the problems caused by barriers in architecture, communication, transportation and attitudes. In addition, we realize that to deny education and employment simply because of an existing disability runs counter to our accepted belief in the free enterprise system and forces the handicapped to be overly dependent on others. Similarly, the denial of equal access to credit and to acquisition of venture capital on the basis of a handicap or other disability conflicts with Republican philosophy. We advocate the elimination of needless barriers for all handicapped persons.

Working Americans

Free collective bargaining remains the best way to insure that American workers receive a fair price for their labors.

The special problems of collective bargaining in state and local government should be addressed at those levels. Washington should not impose its standards on local governments. While we oppose strikes by public employees, we recognize that states have the right to permit them if they choose.

Union membership as a condition of employment has been regulated by state law under Section 14(b) of the Taft-Hartley Act. This basic right should continue to be determined by the states. We oppose strikes by federal employees, the unionization of our military forces and the legalization of common-situs picketing.

Employees of the federal government should not engage in partisan politics. The Civil Service system must remain non-partisan and non-political. The Hatch Act now protects federal employees; we insist that it be uniformly administered.

Among the rights that are the entitlement of every American worker is the right to join a union—large, small or independent; the right to be protected against racial discrimination and misuse of dues; the right to union elections that are fair and democratic; and the right to be assured of ultimately receiving his or her promised pension benefits.

Safe and healthful working conditions are goals of utmost importance. We should expect the Occupational Safety and Health Administration to help employers, particularly in small businesses, comply with the law, and we will support legislation providing on-site consultation.

There should be considerable concern over the presence of several million illegal aliens in the country who fill jobs that otherwise would be available to American workers. We support increased efforts to deal more effectively with this problem and favor legislation prohibiting employers from knowingly hiring illegal aliens. The Democrat leaders in Congress have systematically killed every attempt to debate this legislation in recent years.

Increased part-time and flexible-hour work should be encouraged wherever feasible. In keeping with our belief in family life, we want to expand more opportunities for men and women to combine family responsibilities and employment.

Welfare Reform

The work of all Americans contributes to the strength of our nation, and all who are able to contribute should be encouraged to do so.

In every society there will be some who cannot work, often through no fault of their own. The measure of a country's compassion is how it treats the least fortunate.

We appreciate the magnificent variety of private charitable institutions which have developed in the United States. The Democrat-controlled Congress has produced a jumble of degrading, dehumanizing, wasteful, overlapping and inefficient programs failing to assist the needy poor. A systematic and complete overhaul of the welfare system should be initiated immediately.

The following goals should govern the reform of the welfare system: (1) Provide adequate living standards for the truly needy; (2) End welfare fraud and prevent it in the future with emphasis on removing ineligible recipients from the welfare rolls, tightening food stamp eligibility requirements, and ending aid to illegal aliens and the voluntarily unemployed; (3) Strengthen work requirements, particularly directed at the productive involvement of able-bodied persons in useful community work projects; (4) Provide educational and vocational incentives to allow recipients to become self-supporting; (5) Better coordinate federal efforts with local and state social welfare agencies and strengthen local and state administrative functions. We oppose federalizing the welfare system; local levels of government are most aware of the needs of their communities. Consideration should be given to a range of options in financing the programs to assure that state and local responsibilities are met. We also oppose the guaranteed annual income concept or any programs that reduce the incentive to work.

Those features of the present law, particularly the food stamp program, that draw into assistance programs people who are capable of paying for their own needs should be corrected. The humanitarian purpose of such programs must not be corrupted by eligibility loopholes. Food stamp program reforms proposed by Republicans in Congress would accomplish the twin goals of directing resources to those most in need and streamlining administration.

We must never forget that unemployment compensation is insurance, not a welfare program. It should be redesigned to assure that working is always more beneficial than collecting unemployment benefits. The benefits should help most the hard-core unemployed. Major efforts must be encouraged through the private sector to speed up the process of finding jobs for those temporarily out of work.

Older Americans

Older Americans constitute one of our most valuable resources.

Families should be supported in trying to take care of their elderly. Too often government laws and policies contribute to the deterioration of family life. Our tax laws, for example, permit a deduction to the taxpayer who gives a contribution to a charitable institution that might care for an elderly parent, but offer little or no incentive to provide care in the home. If an elderly parent relinquishes certain assets and enters a nursing home, the parent may qualify for full Medicaid coverage, but if parents live with their children, any Supplemental Security Income benefit for which they are eligible may be reduced. Incentives must be written into law to encourage families to care for their older members.

Along with loneliness and ill health, older Americans are deeply threatened by inflation. The costs of the basic necessities of life—food, shelter, clothing, health care—have risen so drastically as to reduce the ability of many older persons to subsist with any measure of dignity. In addition to our program for protecting against excessive costs of long-term illness, nothing will be as beneficial to the elderly as the effect of this platform's proposals on curbing inflation.

The Social Security benefits are of inestimable importance to the well-being and financial peace-of-mind of most older Americans. We will not let the Social Security system fail. We will work to make the Social Security system actuarily sound. The Social Security program must not be turned into a welfare system, based on need rather than contributions. The cost to employers for Social Security contributions must not be raised to the point where they will be unable to afford contributions to employees' private pension programs. We will work for an increase in the earned income ceiling or its elimination so that, as people live longer, there will not be the present penalty on work. We will also seek to correct those provisions of the system that now discriminate against women and married couples.

Such programs as Foster Grandparents and Senior Companions, which provide income exempt from Social Security limitations, should be continued and extended to encourage senior citizens to continue to be active and involved in society. Appropriate domiciliary care programs should be developed to enable senior citizens to receive such care without losing other benefits to which they may be entitled.

We favor the abolition of arbitrary age levels for mandatory retirement.

The Medicare program must be improved to help control inflation in health care costs triggered by present regulations.

Other areas of concern to the elderly that need increased attention are home and outpatient care, adequate transportation, nutrition, day care and homemaker care as an alternative to costly institutional treatment.

A nation should be judged by its ability to help make all the years of life as productive and gainful as possible. This nation still has a job to do.

Veterans

The nation must never forget its appreciation and obligation to those who have served in the armed forces.

Because they bear the heaviest burdens of war, we owe special honor and compensation to disabled veterans and survivors of the war dead.

We are firmly committed to maintaining and improving our Veterans Administration hospital system.

Younger veterans, especially those who served in the Vietnam conflict, deserve educational, job and housing loan benefits equivalent to those of World War II and the Korean conflict. Because of our deep and continuing concern for those still listed as Prisoners of War or Missing in Action in Vietnam, the Foreign Policy section of this Republican Platform calls for top priority actions.

And we must continue to provide for our veterans at their death a final resting place for their remains in a national cemetery and the costs of transportation thereto.

A National Urban Strategy

The decay and decline of communities in this country is not just a physical and economic crisis, but traceable to the decline of a real "sense of community" in our society. Community development cannot be achieved merely by throwing dollars and mortar at our community problems; what must be developed is a new sense of mutual concern and responsibility among all members of a community for its improvement.

We recognize the family, the neighborhood and the private volunteer sector to be the most basic and vital units within our communities and their central role in revitalizing our communities. We propose a strategy for urban revitalization that both treats our urban areas as social organisms and recognizes that the family is the basic building block in these organisms.

Effectively helping our cities now requires a coordinated National Urban Policy. The cornerstone of this policy must be to curb inflation. This policy must be based on the principle that the levels of government closest to the cities' problems are best able to respond. Thus federal and state assistance to cities and counties should give the greatest flexibility to those directly on the scene, the local elected officials. Such a policy should replace grant programs—the approach of the Democrat Congress—with block grant programs that allow cities and counties to set their own priorities.

Without an urban policy, the Democrat-controlled Congress has created a hodge podge of programs which have all but destroyed our once vital cities. At the same time, urban crime rates have skyrocketed and the quality and promise of metropolitan education systems have plummeted. All this has happened during the years that the number of federal urban programs has increased almost tenfold: from 45 in 1946 to 435 in 1968; and expenditures have increased 3000 per cent: from $1-billion to $30-billion.

The Republican programs of revenue sharing and block grants for community development and manpower have already immensely helped our cities and counties. We favor extension of revenue sharing and the orderly conversion of categorical grants into block grants. When federal assistance programs for general purpose local governments are administered through the states, there should be direct passthrough and an effective role for cities and counties in the planning, allocation and use of the funds.

Federal, state and local government resources combined are not enough to solve our urban problems. The private sector must be the major participant. Economic development is the best way to involve business and industry; government support should emphasize capital formation and technical assistance for small and minority businesses.

We can bring about a new "birth of freedom" by following the example of those individuals, organizations and community leaders who have successfully solved specific undesirable conditions and problems through private efforts. Government officials should be aware of these successes in developing new approaches to public problems.

Financial institutions should be encouraged to participate in the financial requirements of urban development. Each institution should recognize its responsibility in promoting and maintaining economic growth and stability in the central cities.

Our urban policies should encourage families and businesses to improve their neighborhoods by means of participation in neighborhood self-help groups, improving

and rehabilitating their homes and businesses, and investing in and managing local businesses. We support the revision of federal business assistance programs to encourage joint efforts by local merchants' associations.

We need a comprehensive approach to plan, develop and implement a variety of programs which take into account the many diverse needs of each neighborhood. The establishment of a National Neighborhood Policy will signal a commitment to the improvement of the quality of our life in our neighborhoods.

We call for an expansion of the President's Committee on Urban Development and Neighborhood Revitalization to include representatives of elected state and local officials and the private sector.

Taken together, the thrust of the proposals in this section and in such related areas as housing, transportation, safety and taxes should contribute significantly to again making our cities a pleasant place to live. The Republican National Urban Strategy has been formed in the realization that when the bell tolls for the cities it tolls for all of America.

Housing

In the United States today we are the best housed nation in the history of world civilization. This accomplishment was achieved by a private enterprise system using free market concepts.

All of our citizens should be given the opportunity to live in decent, affordable housing.

We believe that we should continue to pursue the primary goal of expanding housing opportunities for all Americans and we should pursue the companion goal of reducing the degree of direct federal involvement in housing.

To most Americans the American Dream is a home of their own. The time has come to face some hard realities, primarily that the greatest impediment to decent and affordable housing is inflation. It logically follows that one effective housing program would be simply to elect a Republican Congress which would balance the federal budget.

To meet the housing needs of this country there must be a continuous, stable and adequate flow of funds for the purpose of real estate mortgages at realistic interest rates.

To continue to encourage home ownership which now encompasses 64 per cent of our families, we support the deductibility of interest on home mortgages and property taxes.

We favor the concept of federal revenue sharing and block grants to reduce the excessive burden of the property tax in financing local government.

We are concerned with the excessive reliance of financing welfare and public school costs primarily by the property tax.

We support inflation-impact studies on governmental regulations, which are inflating housing costs.

Current economic problems and environmental concerns must be balanced in each community by a policy of "Sensible Growth."

We oppose discrimination in housing, whether by individuals or by institutional financing policies.

We urge continued incentives to support the development of low and moderate income housing in order to assure the availability of adequate shelter for the less fortunate.

Rehabilitation and preservation of existing housing stock should be given high priority in federal housing policy.

We urge the continuation of the self-help restoration of housing, such as urban homesteading, which is providing housing for low-income families.

Transportation

The federal government has a special responsibility to foster those elements of our national transportation system that are essential to foreign and interstate commerce and national defense. In other transportation systems that primarily support local needs, the federal government's responsibility is to encourage the greatest possible decision-making and flexibility on the part of state and local governments to spend funds in ways that make the best sense for each community. Thus all levels of government have an important role in providing a balanced and coordinated transportation network.

In keeping with national transportation goals, the Railroad Revitalization and Regulatory Reform Act of 1976 has begun the task of removing regulatory constraints of the Interstate Commerce Commission on America's ailing railroads. Now we should carefully assess the need to remove many of the regulatory constraints imposed on the nation's airlines and motor carriers. Consumers pay too high a price for the artificial fare and rate structures imposed by federal regulations.

The great Interstate Highway System, initiated by President Eisenhower, has brought new freedom of travel to every American and must be completed and maintained. Our road network should always stress safety through better design as well as bridge maintenance and replacement.

We must also have a safe and efficient aviation system capable of responding to the air transportation needs of the future and of reducing exposure to aircraft noise. This includes airport development, navigational and safety facilities, and the design and adequate staffing of advanced air traffic control systems. In airplane use as in other modes of transportation, the impact on the physical environment must always be a basic consideration in federal decisions and such decisions should also include appraisals of impact on the economy. We deplore unfair treatment of United States airlines under foreign landing regulations.

Research must be continued to find safe, more fuel-efficient automobile motors and airplanes; safer, faster rail service; and more convenient, less expensive urban transportation. Tax policies should be considered which would stimulate the development and installation of new energy sources in transportation, such as railroad electrification.

The disorganization of a Democrat-controlled Congress frustrates the coordination of transportation policy. Currently there are more than 50 congressional subcommittees with independent jurisdiction in the transportation field. This hopelessly disjointed and disorganized approach must be reformed.

In keeping with the local goal setting in transportation, the Republican Party applauds the system under which state and local governments can divert funds from interstate highway mileage not essential to interstate commerce or national defense to other, more pressing community needs, such as urban mass transit.

We support the concept of a surface transportation block grant which would include the various highway and mass transit programs now in existence. This will provide local elected officials maximum flexibility in selecting and implementing the balanced transportation systems best suited to each locality. It will encompass both capital and operating subsidies for urban mass transit. It will eliminate red tape and over-regulation. We regret that the Democrat-controlled Congress has not adopted such a reform.

Energy

In 1973, Americans were shocked to discover that a plentiful supply of energy could no longer be assumed. Unfortunately, the Democrat majority in Congress still has not responded to this clear and urgent warning. The United States is now consuming more imported oil than it was three years ago and our dependence on foreign sources has continued to increase to the point where we now import more than 40% of our oil.

One fact should now be clear: We must reduce sharply our dependence on other nations for energy and strive to achieve energy independence at the earliest possible date. We cannot allow the economic destiny and international policy of the United States to be dictated by the sovereign powers that control major portions of the world's petroleum supplies.

Our approach toward energy self-sufficiency must involve both expansion of energy supply and improvement of energy efficiency. It must include elements that insure increased conservation at all levels of our society. It must also provide incentives for the exploration and development of domestic gas, oil, coal and uranium, and for expanded research and development in the use of solar, geothermal, co-generation, solid waste, wind, water, and other sources of energy.

We must use our non-renewable resources wisely while we develop alternative supplies for the future. Our standard of living is directly tied to a continued supply of energy resources. Without an adequate supply of energy, our entire economy will crumble.

Unwise government intervention in the marketplace has caused shortage of supply, unrealistic prices and increased dependence on foreign sources. We must immediately eliminate price controls on oil and newly-discovered natural gas in order to increase supply, and to provide the capital that is needed to finance further exploration and development of domestic hydrocarbon reserves.

Fair and realistic market prices will encourage sensible conservation efforts and establish priorities in the use of our resources, which over the long run will provide a secure supply at reasonable prices for all.

The nation's clear and present need is for vast amounts of new capital to finance exploration, discovery, refining, and delivery of currently usable forms of energy, including the use of coal as well as discovery and development of new sources. At this critical time, the Democrats have characteristically resorted to political demagoguery seeking short-term political gain at the expense of the long-term national interest. They object to the petroleum industry making any profit. The petroleum industry is an important segment of our economy and is entitled to reasonable profits to permit further exploration and development.

At the height of the energy crisis, the Republican Administration proposed a strong, balanced energy package directed at both expansion of supply and conservation of energy. The response from the Democrats in Congress was to inhibit expanded production through artificially set price and allocation controls, thereby preventing market forces from working to make energy expansion economically feasible.

Now, the Democrats proposed to dismember the American oil industry. We vigorously oppose such divestiture of oil companies—a move which would surely result in higher energy costs, inefficiency and under-capitalization of the industry.

Democrats have also proposed that the federal government compete with industry in energy development by creating a national oil company. We totally oppose this expensive, inefficient and wasteful intrusion into an area which is best handled by private enterprise.

The Democrats are playing politics with energy. If they are permitted to continue, we will pay a heavy price in lost energy and lost jobs during the decades ahead.

Immediate removal of counter-productive bureaucratic redtape will eliminate hindrances to the exploration and development of hydrocarbons and other energy resources. We will accelerate development of oil shale reserves, Alaskan petroleum and the leasing of the Outer Continental Shelf, always within the context of preserving the fullest possible protection for the environment. We will reduce complexity and delays involved in siting, licensing and the regulatory procedures affecting power generation facilities and refineries.

Coal, America's most abundant energy resource, is of inestimable value to the American people. It can provide the energy needed to bridge the gap between oil and gas and nuclear and other sources of energy. The uncertainties of governmental regulation regarding the mining, transportation and use of coal must be removed and a policy established which will assure that governmental restraints, other than proper environmental controls, do not prevent the use of coal. Mined lands must be returned to beneficial use.

Uranium offers the best intermediate solution to America's energy crisis. We support accelerated use of nuclear energy through processes that have been proven safe. Government research on the use of nuclear energy will be expanded to include perfecting a long-term solution to the problems of nuclear waste.

Among alternative future energy sources, fusion, with its unique potential for supplying unlimited clean energy and the promise of new methods of natural resource recovery, warrants continued emphasis in our national energy research program and we support measures to assure adequate capital investment in the development of new energy sources.

Environment and Natural Resources

A clean and healthy natural environment is the rightful heritage of every American. In order to preserve this heritage, we will provide for proper development of resources, safeguards for clean air and water, and protection and enhancement of our recreation and scenic areas.

As our environmental sophistication grows, we must more clearly define the role of the federal government in environmental protection.

We believe that it is a national responsibility to support scientific and technological research and development to identify environmental problems and arrive at solutions.

We are in complete accord with the recent Supreme Court decision on air pollution that allows the level of government closest to the problem and the solution to establish and apply appropriate air quality standards.

We are proud of the progress that the current Republican Administration has made toward bringing pollution of water, land and air under control. We will meet the challenges that remain by stepping up efforts to perfect our understanding of pollutants and the means for reducing their effects. Moreover, as the nation develops new energy sources and technologies, we must insure that they meet safe environmental standards.

We renew our commitments to the development of additional water supplies by desalinization, and to the more efficient use and re-use of waters currently available.

We are determined to preserve land use planning as a unique responsibility of state and local government.

We take particular pride in the expanded use of the National Park system in recent years, and will provide for continued improvement of the national parks and historic sites.

We support establishment of a Presidential Panel, including representatives of environmental groups, industry, the scientific community and the public to assist in the development of national priorities on environmental and energy issues. This panel will hear and consider alternative policy recommendations set forth by all of the interested groups, and then develop solutions that represent the overall public interest on environmental and energy matters.

One of this nation's greatest assets has been our abundant natural resources which have made possible our strong economic and strategic role in the world. We still have a wealth of resources, but they are not of infinite quantity. We must recognize that our material blessings stem from what we grow in the soil, take from the sea, or extract from the ground. We have a responsibility to future generations to conserve our non-renewable natural resources. Consistent with our needs, conservation should remain our national policy.

The vast land holdings of the federal government—approximately one-third of our nation's area—are the lands from which much of our future production of minerals must come. Public lands must be maintained for multiple use management where such uses are compatible. Public land areas should not be closed to exploration for minerals or for mining without an overriding national interest.

We believe Americans want their resources developed properly, their environment kept clean and their recreational and scenic areas kept intact. We support appropriate measures to achieve these goals.

We also believe that Americans are realistic and recognize that the emphasis on environmental concerns must be brought into balance with the needs for industrial and economic growth so that we can continue to provide jobs for an ever-growing work force.

The United States possesses the most productive softwood forests in the world, as well as extensive hardwood forests. Demands for housing, fuel, paper, chemicals and a multitude of other such needs require that these renewable resources be wisely managed on both public and private forest lands—not only to meet these needs, but also to provide for soil conservation, wildlife habitats and recreation.

Recognizing that timber is a uniquely renewable resource, we will use all scientifically sound means to maximize sustained yield, including clear-cutting and replanting where appropriate. We urge the Congress to strengthen the National Forest Service so that it can realize its potential in becoming an effective participant in the reforestation program.

We will support broader use of resource recovery and recycling processes through removal of economic disincentives caused by unnecessary government regulation.

One of the important issues at stake in the United Nations Law of the Sea Conference is access to the mineral resources in and beneath the sea. Technology, developed by United States industry, is at hand which can unlock resources of petroleum, manganese, nickel, cobalt, copper and other minerals. We will safeguard the national interest in development and use of these resources.

Science and Technology

Every aspect of our domestic economy and well-being, our international competitive position, and national security is related to our past and present leadership in basic and applied research and the development of our technology. But there can be no complacency about our continued commitment to maintain this leadership position.

In the past, most of these accomplishments have been achieved through a unique partnership between government and industry. This must continue and be expanded in the future.

Because our society is so dependent upon the advancement of science and the development of technology, it is one of the areas where there must be a central federal policy. We support a national science policy that will foster the public-private partnership to insure that we maintain our leadership role.

The national space program plays a pioneer role in exploring the mysteries of our universe and we support its expansion.

We recognize that only when our technology is fully distributed can it be assimilated and used to increase our productivity and our standard of living. We will continue to encourage young Americans to study science and engineering.

Finally, we support new initiatives to utilize better the recoverable commodities from solid waste materials. We can no longer afford the luxury of a throw-away world. Recycling offers environmental benefits, economic expansion, resource conservation and energy savings. We support a policy which will reward it and economic incentives which will encourage its expansion.

Arts and Humanities

The arts and humanities offer an opportunity for every American to become a participant in activities that add fullness, expression, challenge and joy to our daily lives. We Republicans consider the preservation of the rich cultural heritages of our various ethnic groups as a priority goal.

During our bicentennial year we have celebrated our anniversary with cultural activities as varied and colorful as our cultural heritage. The Republican Party is proud of its record of support to the arts and humanities during the last eight years. We are committed to steadily increase our support through the National Endowments for the nation's museums, theaters, orchestras, dance, opera and film centers as well as for individual artists and writers.

This upward trend in funding for the National Arts and Humanities Endowments deserves to continue. But Washington's presence should never dominate; it must remain limited to supporting and stimulating the artistic and cultural lives of each community.

We favor continued federal assistance to public broadcasting which provides us with creative educational and cultural alternatives. We recognize that public broadcasting is supported mainly through private sector contributions and commend this policy as the best insurance against political interference.

In 1976 we have seen vivid evidence that America's history lives throughout the nation. We support the continued commemoration throughout the bicentennial era by all Americans of those significant events between 1776 and 1789 which contributed to the creation of this nation. We support the efforts of both the public and private sectors, working in partnership, for the historic preservation of the unique and irreplaceable historic sites and buildings.

We propose safeguarding the rights of performing artists in the copyright laws, providing tax relief to artists who contribute their own talents and art works for public enjoyment, and encouraging the use of one per cent of the cost of government buildings for art works.

Much of the support of the arts and humanities comes from private philanthropy. This generosity should be encouraged by government policies that facilitate charitable donations.

Fiscal Responsibility

As Republicans, we are proud that in this Platform we have urged tax reductions rather than increased government spending. With firm restraint on federal spending this Platform pledges that its proposals for tax changes—reductions, structural adjustments, differentials, simplifications and job-producing incentives—can all be achieved within the balanced federal budgets we also demand as vital to the interests of all Americans. Without such spending restraint, we cannot responsibly cut back taxes. We reaffirm our determination that any net reduction of revenues must be offset by reduced government spending.

Foreign Policy, National Defense and International Economic Policy

Prologue

The foreign policy of the United States defines the relationships we seek with the world as a whole, with friends and with adversaries. Our policy must be firmly rooted in principle and must clearly express our goals. Our principles cannot be subject to passing whim; they must be true, strong, consistent and enduring.

We pledge a realistic and principled foreign policy designed to meet the needs of the nation in the years ahead. The policies we pursue will require an informed consensus; the basis of that consensus will be the American people, whose most cherished desire is to live in freedom and peace, secure from war or threat of war.

The United States is a world power with world-wide interests and responsibilities. We pledge the continuation of efforts to revitalize our traditional alliances and to maintain close consultation with our friends. International cooperation and collaboration is required because we can achieve neither our most important objectives nor even our own security in the type of "splendid isolation" which is urged upon us by so many strident voices. The regrettable emergence of neo-isolationism often expressed in Congress and elsewhere is detrimental, we believe, to a sound foreign policy.

The branches of government can and should work together as the necessary prerequisite for a sound foreign policy. We lament the reckless intrusion of one branch into the clear constitutional prerogative of another. Confronted by so many challenges and so many crises, the United States must again speak with one voice, united in spirit and in fact. We reject partisan and ideological quarrels across party lines and urge Democrats to join with us to lay the foundations of a true bipartisan spirit. Let us speak for this country with one voice, so that our policies will not be misunderstood by our allies or our potential adversaries.

Effective policy must rest on promises which are understood and shared, and must be defined in terms of priorities. As the world has changed in a dynamic fashion, so too have our priorities and goals, and so too have the methods of debating and discussing our objectives. When we assumed Executive office eight years ago, we found the national security and foreign policy machinery in shambles. Last-minute reactions to crises were the practice. The National Security Council, so effective under President Eisenhower, had fallen into disuse. As an important first step, the National Security Council machinery was streamlined to cope with the problems of the moment and long-range planning. This restored process allows once again for exhaustive consideration of all the options from which a President must choose. Far from stifling internal debate and dissent as had been the practice in the past, Republican leadership now invites and stimulates evaluation of complex issues in an orderly decision-making process.

Republican leadership has also taken steps to report comprehensively its foreign policy and national security objectives. An annual "State of the World" message, designed to increase communication with the people and with Congress, has become a permanent part of Presidential practice.

A strong and effective program of global public diplomacy is a vital component of U.S. foreign policy. In an era of instant communications, the world is infinitely and forever smaller, and we must have the capacity to communicate to the world—to inform, to explain and to guard against accidental or willful distortion of United States policies.

Interdependence has become a fact of international life, linking our actions and policies with those of the world at large. The United States should reach out to other nations to enrich that interdependence. Republican leadership has demonstrated that recognition of the ties that bind us to our friends will serve our mutual interests in a creative fashion and will enhance the chances for world peace.

Morality in Foreign Policy

The goal of Republican foreign policy is the achievement of liberty under law and a just and lasting peace in the world. The principles by which we act to achieve peace and to protect the interests of the United States must merit the restored confidence of our people.

We recognize and commend that great beacon of human courage and morality, Alexander Solzhenitsyn, for his compelling message that we must face the world with no illusions about the nature of tyranny. Ours will be a foreign policy that keeps this ever in mind.

Ours will be a foreign policy which recognizes that in international negotiations we must make no undue concessions; that in pursuing detente we must not grant unilateral favors with only the hope of getting future favors in return.

Agreements that are negotiated, such as the one signed in Helsinki, must not take from those who do not have freedom the hope of one day gaining it.

Finally, we are firmly committed to a foreign policy in which secret agreements, hidden from our people, will have no part.

Honestly, openly, and with firm conviction, we shall go forward as a united people to forge a lasting peace in the world based upon our deep belief in the rights of man, the rule of law and guidance by the hand of God.

National Defense

A superior national defense is the fundamental condition for a secure America and for peace and freedom for the world. Military strength is the path to peace. A sound foreign policy must be rooted in a superior defense capability, and both must be perceived as a deterrent to aggression and supportive of our national interests.

The American people expect that their leaders will assure a national defense posture second to none. They know that planning for our national security must be a joint effort by the President and Congress. It cannot be the subject of partisan disputes. It should not be held hostage to domestic political adventurism.

A minimum guarantee to preserve freedom and insure against blackmail and threats, and in the face of growing Soviet military power, requires a period of sustained growth in our defense efforts. In constant dollars, the present defense budget will no more than match the defense budget of 1964, the year before a Democrat Administration involved America so deeply in the Vietnam War. In 1975 Soviet defense programs exceeded ours in investment by 85 per cent, exceeded ours in operating costs by 25 per cent, and exceeded ours in research and development by 66 per cent. The issue is whether our forces will be adequate to future challenges. We say they must be.

We must always achieve maximum value for each defense dollar spent. Along with the elimination of the draft and the creation, under a Republican President, of all-volunteer armed services, we have reduced the personnel requirements for support functions without affecting our basic posture. Today there are fewer Americans in the uniformed services than at any time since the Fall of 1950. Substantial economies have been made in weapons procurement and we will continue to act in a prudent manner with our defense appropriations.

Our national defense effort will include the continuation of the major modernization program for our strategic missile and bomber forces, the development of a new and intercontinental ballistic missile, a new missile launching submarine force and a modern bomber—the B-1—capable of penetrating the most sophisticated air defenses of the 1980's. These elements will comprise a deterrent of the first order.

We will increase our army to 16 divisions, reinforce our program of producing new tanks and other armored vehicles, and support the development of new, highly accurate precision weapons.

Our Navy, the guarantor of freedom of the seas, must have a major shipbuilding program, with an adequate balance between nuclear and non-nuclear ships. The composition of the fleet must be based on a realistic assessment of the threat we face, and must assure that no adversary will gain naval superiority.

An important modernization program for our tactical air forces is under way. We will require new fighters and interceptor aircraft for the Air Force, Navy and Marines. As a necessary component of our long-range strategy, we will produce and deploy the B-1 bomber in a timely manner, allowing us to retain air superiority.

Our investments in military research and development are of great importance to our future defense capabilities. We must not lose the vital momentum.

With increasing complexity of weapons, lead times for weapons systems are often as long as a decade, requiring careful planning and prudent financial decisions. An outstanding example of this process is the development and deployment of the cruise missile, which incorporates pinpoint precision by means of sophisticated guidance systems and is an exceptionally economical weapon to produce.

Security assistance programs are important to our allies and we will continue to strengthen their efforts at self-defense. The improvement of their capabilities can help to ensure that the world balance is not tipped against us and can also serve to lessen chances for direct U.S. involvement in remote conflicts.

As a vital component of our over-all national security posture, the United States must have the best intelligence system in the world. The effectiveness of the intelligence community must be restored, consonant with the reforms instituted by President Ford. We favor the creation of an independent oversight function by Congress and we will withstand partisan efforts to turn any part of our intelligence system into a political football. We will take every precaution to prevent the breakdown of security controls on sensitive intelligence information, endangering the lives of U.S. officials abroad, or affecting the ability of the President to act expeditiously whenever legitimate foreign policy and defense needs require it.

NATO and Europe

Fundamental to a stable, secure world is the continuation of our traditional alliances. The North Atlantic Treaty Organization, now approaching the end of its third decade, remains healthy and vigorous.

The threat to our mutual security by a totalitarian power bent on expansion brought 15 nations together. The expression of our collective will to resist resulted in the creation and maintenance of a military deterrent which, while not without occasional strains, has served our vital interests well. Today that threat continues.

We have succeeded in extending our cooperation within NATO and have taken bold new steps in economic cooperation with our partners. Faced with a serious crisis in the energy field following the imposition of the oil boycott, we demonstrated that it was possible to coordinate our joint activities with the other NATO nations.

The economic strength of Western Europe has increased to the point where our NATO partners can now assume a larger share of the common defense; in response to our urging, our allies are demonstrating a greater willingness to do so. This is not the time to recommend a unilateral reduction of American military forces in Europe. We will, however, pursue the balanced reduction of forces in both Western and Eastern Europe, based on agreements which do not jeopardize the security of the Alliance. With our Alliance partners, we affirm that a strong NATO defense, based on the United States military presence, is vital to the defense of Western Europe.

Some of our NATO allies have experienced rapid and dynamic changes. We are encouraged by developments in the Iberian peninsula, where both Portugal and Spain now face more promising futures. Early consideration should be given to Spain's accession to the North Atlantic Treaty Organization.

At the same time we would view with concern any political developments elsewhere in Europe which are destabilizing to NATO interests. We support the right of all nations to choose their leaders. Democracy and freedom are best served by ensuring that those fundamental rights are preserved and extended for future generations to choose in freedom.

The difficult problem of Cyprus, which separates our friends in Greece and Turkey, should be addressed and resolved by those two countries. The eastern flank of NATO requires restored cooperation there and, eventually, friendly relations between the two countries.

Republican leadership has strengthened this nation's good relations with the European Economic Community in an age of increasing competition and potential irritations. We will maintain and strengthen the excellent relations we have achieved with the EEC.

In the final analysis, the NATO Alliance will be as effective as our will and determination, as well as that of our allies, to support it. The function of collective security is to deter wars and, if necessary, to fight and win those wars not successfully deterred. Our vigilance is expecially required during periods of prolonged relaxation of tensions with our adversaries because we cannot permit ourselves to accept words and promises as a substitute for deeds. We are determined that the NATO Alliance shall not be lulled into a false sense of security. It can and must respond vigorously when called upon to act.

Asia and the Pacific

The United States has vital interests in the entire Pacific Basin and those interests lie foremost in Asian tranquility and stability.

The experience of ending direct American involvement in a difficult and costly war initiated during Democrat Administrations has taught us a great deal about how we ought to define our interests in this part of the world. The United States is indisputably a Pacific power. We have sought to express our interests in the area through strengthening existing friendly ties and creating new ones.

Japan will remain the main pillar of our Asian policy. We have helped to provide the framework, over the course of thirty years, for the development of the Japanese economy, which has risen to second place among free world nations. This nation, without natural resources, has maximized its greatest resource, the Japanese people, to achieve one of the world's most significant economic advances. We will continue our policy of close consultation and cooperation with this valued friend. We have succeeded in establishing an exceptional relationship with Japan. Our long-range goals of stability and economic cooperation are identical, forming the essential strength of a relationship which both countries seek actively to deepen.

With respect to the Republic of Korea, a nation with which we have had traditionally close ties and whose economy has grown rapidly in recent years, we shall continue our policy of military and economic assistance. United States troops will be maintained in Korea so long as there exists the possibility of renewed aggression from North Korea. Time has not dimmed our memories of the sudden assault against South Korea. We reaffirm the commitment of the United States to the territorial integrity and the sovereignty of the Republic of Korea. Simultaneously we encourage the Governments of South Korea and North Korea to institute domestic policy initiatives leading to the extension of basic human rights.

When Republicans assumed executive office in 1969, we were confronted with a war in Vietnam involving more than 500,-000 U.S. troops, and to which we had committed billions of dollars and our national honor and prestige. It was in the spirit of bipartisan support for Presidential foreign policy initiatives, inaugurated in the postwar era by Senator Arthur Vandenberg, that most Republicans support the United States commitment to assist South Vietnam resist Communist-sponsored aggression. The human cost to us was great; more than 55,000 Americans died in that conflict, and more than 300,000 were wounded.

A policy of patient, persistent and principled negotiations extricated the United States from that ill-fated war with the expectation that peace would prevail. The refusal of the Democrat-controlled Congress to give support to Presidential requests for military aid to the beleaguered nations of South Vietnam, Cambodia and Laos, coupled with sustained military assaults by the Communists in gross violation of the Paris Peace Accords, brought about the collapse of those nations and the subjugation of their people to totalitarian rule.

We recognize that there is a wide divergence of opinion concerning Vietnam, but we pledge that American troops will never again be committed for the purpose of our own defense, or the defense of those to whom we are committed by treaty or other solemn agreements, without the clear purpose of achieving our stated diplomatic and military objectives.

We must achieve the return of all Americans who may be held in Southeast Asia, and a full accounting for those listed as Missing in Action. We strongly urge continued consultation between the President and the National League of Families of American Prisoners and Missing in Southeast Asia. This country owes at least this much to all of these courageous people who have anguished so long over this matter. To this end, and to underscore our top priority commitment to the families of these POWs and MIAs, we recommend, among other actions, the establishment of a Presidential Task Force headed by a special Presidential representative.

We condemn the inhumane and criminal retributions which have taken place in Cambodia, where mass executions and forced resettlements have been imposed on innocent civilians.

The important economic developments taking place in Singapore, Indonesia, Malaysia, the Philippines and other Asian countries will lead to much improved living standards for the people there. We reaffirm our friendship with these nations. Equally, our relationships with Australia and New Zealand are historic and important to us; they have never been better and provide a firm base on which to build.

United States-Chinese Relations

A development of significance for the future of Asia and for the world came to fruition in 1972 as our communications were restored with the People's Republic of China. This event has allowed us to initiate dialogue with the leaders of a quarter of the earth's population, and trade channels with the People's Republic have been opened, leading to benefits for each side.

The People's Republic of China can and will play an increasingly important role in world affairs. We shall seek to engage the People's Republic of China in an expanded network of contacts and trade. Such a process cannot realistically proceed at a forced or incautious pace; the measured but steady growth of our relations best serves our interests. We do not ignore the profound differences in our respective philosophies, governmental institutions, policies and views on individual liberty, and we are hopeful that basic human rights will be extended to the Chinese people. What is truly fundamental is that we have established regular working channels with the People's Republic of China and that this process can form an important contribution to world peace.

Our friendly relations with one great power should not be construed as a challenge to any other nation, large or small. The United States government, while engaged in a normalization of relations with the People's Republic of China, will continue to support the freedom and independence of our friend and ally, the Republic of China, and its 16 million people. The United States will fulfill and keep its commitments, such as the mutual defense treaty, with the Republic of China.

The Americas

The relations of the United States with the Americas are of vital and immediate importance. How we conduct our affairs with our neighbors to the North and South will continue to be a priority.

In the recent past our attention has at times been diverted to more distant parts of the world. There can be no sensible alternative to close relationships and understanding among the nations of this hemisphere.

It is time for a series of new departures in our relations with Canada. Canada is our most important trading partner, and we are hers. We, as Americans, feel a deep affinity for our Canadian friends, and we have much at stake in the development of closer relationships based on mutual understanding and complete equality.

To our neighbors in Mexico, Central America and South America, we also say that we wish the opportunity to expand our dialogue. The needs of our friends are great, but this must not serve as an obstacle for a concerted effort to work together more closely. The United States has taken steps to adjust tariffs so as to maximize access to our markets. We recognize that our neighbors place no value on complex and cumbersome aid schemes; they see self-help, modernization, and expanded trade as the main sources of economic progress. We will work with them to define specific steps that we can take to help them achieve greater economic strength, and to advance our mutual interests.

By continuing its policies of exporting subversion and violence, Cuba remains outside the Inter-American family of nations. We condemn attempts by the Cuban dictatorship to intervene in the affairs of other nations; and, as long as such conduct continues, it shall remain ineligible for admission to the Organization of American States.

We shall continue to share the aspirations of the Cuban people to regain their liberty. We insist that decent and humane conditions be maintained in the treatment of political prisoners in the Cuban jails, and we will seek arrangements to allow international entities, such as the International Red Cross, to investigate and monitor the conditions in those jails.

The present Panama Canal Treaty provides that the United States has jurisdictional rights in the Canal Zone as "if it were the sovereign." The United States intends that the Panama Canal be preserved as an international waterway for the ships of all nations. This secure access is enhanced by a relationship which commands the respect of Americans and Panamanians and benefits the people of both countries. In any talks with Panama, however, the United States negotiators should in no way cede, dilute, forfeit, negotiate or transfer any rights, power, authority, jurisdiction, territory or property that are necessary for the protection and security of the United States and the entire Western Hemisphere.

We reaffirm our faith in the ability of the Organization of American States, which remains a valuable means of inter-American consultation.

The Middle East

The preservation of peace and stability in the Middle East is a paramount concern.

The efforts of two Republican Administrations, summoning diplomatic and political skills, have been directed toward reduction of tensions and toward avoiding flashpoints which could serve as an excuse for yet another round of conflict between Israel and the Arab countries.

Our commitment to Israel is fundamental and enduring. We have honored and will continue to honor that commitment in every way—politically, economically and by providing the military aid that Israel requires to remain strong enough to deter any potential aggression. Forty per cent of all United States' aid that Israel has received since its creation in 1948 has come in the last two fiscal years, as a result of Republican initiatives. Our policy must remain one of decisive support for the security and integrity of Israel.

An equally important component of our commitment to Isreal lies in continuing our efforts to secure a just and durable peace for all nations in that complex region. Our efforts have succeeded, for the first time since the creation of the state of Israel, in moving toward a negotiated peace settlement which would serve the interests and the security of all nations in the Middle East. Peace in the Middle East now requires face-to-face, direct negotiations between the states involved with the recognition of safe, secure and defensible borders for Israel.

At the same time, Republican Administrations have succeeded in reestablishing communication with the Arab countries, and have made extensive progress in our diplomatic and commercial relations with the more moderate Arab nations.

As a consequence of the Middle East conflict of 1973, the petroleum producing states imposed an embargo on the export of oil to most of the advanced industrial countries. We have succeeded in creating numerous cooperative mechanisms to protect ourselves, working in concert with our allies, against any future embargoes. The United States would view any attempt to reimpose an embargo as an essentially hostile act. We will oppose discriminatory practices, including boycotts of any type.

Because we have such fundamental interests in the Middle East, it will be our policy to continue our efforts to maintain the balance of power in the Mediterranean region. Our adversaries must recognize that we will not permit a weakening of our defenses or any attempt to disturb valued Alliance relationships in the Eastern Mediterranean.

We shall continue to support peace initiatives in the civil war in Lebanon; United States envoys engaged in precisely such an initiative were murdered, and we express our sorrow for their untimely deaths and for all other dedicated government employees who have been slain elsewhere while in service to their country. In Lebanon, we stand ready to provide food, medical and other humanitarian assistance.

Africa

The United States has always supported the process of self-determination in Africa. Our friendship for the African countries is expressed in support for continued peaceful economic development, expansion of trade, humanitarian relief efforts and our belief that the entire continent should be free from outside military intervention. Millions of Americans recognize their historical and cultural ties with Africa and express their desire that United States policy toward Africa is a matter of great importance.

We support all forces which promote negotiated settlements and racial peace. We shall continue to deplore all violence and terrorism and to urge all concerned that the rights of tribal, ethnic and racial minorities be guaranteed through workable safeguards. Our policy is to strengthen the forces of moderation, recognizing that solutions to African problems will not come quickly. The peoples of Africa can coexist in security, work together in freedom and harmony, and strive together to secure their prosperity. We hope that the Organization of African Unity will be able to achieve mature and stable relationships within Africa and abroad.

The interests of peace and security in Africa are best served by the absence of arms and greater concentration on peaceful development. We reserve the right to maintain the balance by extending our support to nations facing a threat from Soviet-supplied states and from Soviet weapons.

United States-Soviet Relations

American foreign policy must be based upon a realistic assessment of the Communist challenge in the world. It is clear that the perimeters of freedom continue to shrink throughout the world in the face of the Communist challenge. Since 1917, totalitarian Communism has managed through brute force, not through the free electoral process, to bring an increasingly substantial portion of the world's land area and peoples under its domination. To illustrate, most recently South Vietnam, Cambodia, and Laos have fallen under the control of Communist dictatorships, and in that part of the world the Communist pressure mounts against Thailand, the Republic of China, and the Republic of Korea. In Africa, Communist Cuban forces, brazenly assisted by the Soviet Union, have recently imposed a Communist dictatorship upon the people of Angola. Other countries in Africa and throughout the world generally await similar fates. These are the realities of world power in our time. The United States is thoroughly justified in having based its foreign policy upon these realities.

Thirty years ago relations between [the] United States and the Soviet Union were in a phase of great difficulty, leading to the tensions of the Cold War era. Although there have been changes in this crucial superpower relationship, there re-

main fundamental and profound differences between us. Republican Presidents, while acknowledging the depth of the gulf which separates our free society from Soviet society, have sought methodically to isolate and develop those areas of our relations which would serve to lessen tension and reduce the chance of unwanted conflict.

In a world beset by countless opportunities for discord and armed conflict, the relationship between the United States and the Soviet Union is critically important; on it rests the hopes of the world for peace. We offer a policy that maintains our fundamental strength and demonstrates our steadfast determination to prevent aggressive use of Soviet power.

The role of a responsible, participating Congress in maintaining this diplomatic and military posture is critical to success. The United States must remain a loyal and dependable ally, and must be prepared to carry out commitments and to demonstrate a willingness to act. Resistance to open aggression, such as the Soviet-sponsored Cuban intervention in Angola, must not be allowed to become the subject of a partisan debate, nor can it be allowed to become an unchallenged and established pattern of international behavior, lest our credibility and deterrent strength be greatly diminished.

Soviet military power has grown rapidly in recent years, and while we shall prevent a military imbalance or a sudden shift in the global balance of power, we shall also diligently explore with the Soviet Union new ways to reduce tensions and to arrive at mutually beneficial and self-enforcing agreements in all fields of international activity. Important steps have been taken to limit strategic nuclear arms. The Vladivostok Agreement of November 1974 placed a ceiling on the strategic forces of both the United States and the Soviet Union. Further negotiations in arms control are continuing. We shall not agree for the sake of agreement; on the contrary, we will make sure that any agreements yield fundamental benefits to our national security.

As an example of hardheaded bargaining, our success in concluding agreements limiting the size of peaceful nuclear explosions and nuclear weapons tests will, for the first time, permit the United States to conduct onsite inspections in the Soviet Union itself. This important step can now be measured in practical terms. All such agreements must stand the test of verification. An agreement that does not provide this safeguard is worse than no agreement at all.

We support the consolidation of joint efforts with our allies to verify that our policies regarding the transfer of technology to the Soviet Union and its allies are in concert and that consultation will be designed to preclude the sale of those technology-intensive products to the Soviet Union by the United States and our allies which will directly or indirectly jeopardize our national security.

Our trade in nonstrategic areas creates jobs here at home, substantially improves our balance-of-payments position, and can contribute to an improved political climate in the world. The overseas sale of our agricultural products benefits American farmers and consumers. To guard against any sudden shift in domestic prices as the consequence of unannounced purchases, we have instituted strict reporting procedures and other treaty safeguards. We shall not permit concessional sales of agricultural products to the Soviet Union, nor shall we permit the Soviet Union or others to determine our agricultural export policies by irregular and unpredictable purchases.

The United States and the Soviet Union remain ideological competitors. We do not shrink from such a challenge; rather, we welcome the opportunity to demonstrate that our way of life is inherently preferable to regimentation and government-enforced orthodoxy. We shall expect the Soviet Union to implement the United Nations Declaration on Human Rights and the Helsinki Agreements, which guarantee the conditions for the free interchange of information and the right to emigrate, including emigration of Soviet Jews, Christians, Moslems and others who wish to join close relatives abroad. In this spirit we shall expect the immediate end of all forms of harassment, including imprisonment and military service, aimed at preventing such emigration. America must take a firm stand to bring about liberalization of emigration policy in countries which limit or prohibit free emigration. Governments which enjoy the confidence of their people need have no fear of cultural, intellectual or press freedom.

Our support for the people of Central and Eastern Europe to achieve self-determination will continue. Their ability to choose their future is of great importance to peace and stability. We favor increasing contact between Eastern and Western Europe and support the increasing economic ties of all the countries of Europe. We strongly support the continuation of the Voice of America, Radio Free Europe and Radio Liberty with adequate appropriations. Strict reciprocity must govern our diplomatic relations with the Soviet Union. We express our concern for the safety of our diplomatic representatives in the Soviet Union, and we insist that practices such as microwave transmissions directed at the United States Embassy be terminated immediately.

Thus our relations with the Soviet Union will be guided by solid principles. We will maintain our strategic and conventional forces; we will oppose the deployment of Soviet power for unilateral advantages or political and territorial expansion; we will never tolerate a shift against us in the strategic balance; and we will remain firm in the face of pressure, while at the same time expressing our willingness to work on the basis of strict reciprocity toward new agreements which will help achieve peace and stability.

International Cooperation

Strong support for international cooperation in all fields has been a hallmark of United States international policy for many decades. Two Republican Administrations have strengthened agencies of international cooperation not only because of our humanitarian concern for others, but also because it serves United States interests to be a conscientious member of the world community.

The political character of the United Nations has become complex. With 144 sovereign members, the U.N. experiences problems associated with a large, sometimes cumbersome and diverse body. We seek to accommodate to these changes in the spirit of friendly concern, but when the United Nations becomes arrayed against the vital interest of any of its member states on ideological or other narrow grounds, the very principles of the organization are threatened. The United States does not wish to dictate to the U.N., yet we do have every right to expect and insist that scrupulous care be given to the rights of all members. Steamroller techniques for advancing discriminatory actions will be opposed. Actions such as the malicious attempt to depict Zionism as a form of racism are inconsistent with the objectives of the United Nations and are repugnant to the United States. The United States will continue to be a firm supporter and defender of any nation subjected to such outrageous assaults. We will not accept ideological abuses in the United States.

In the many areas of international cooperation which benefit the average American—elimination of terrorism, peacekeeping, nonproliferation of nuclear weapons, termination of the international drug trade, and orderly use of ocean resources—we pledge to build new international structures of cooperation. At the same time, we shall seek to insure that the cost of such new structures, as well as the cost of existing structures, are more equitably shared among participating nations. In the continued tradition of American concern for the quality of human life everywhere, we shall give vigorous support to the non-political work of the specialized agencies of the United Nations which deal with such areas as nutrition and disaster relief for the world's poor and disadvantaged.

The United States should promptly withdraw from the International Labor Organization if that body fails to stop its increasing politicization.

Eight years ago we pledged to eliminate waste and to make more business-like the administration of United States foreign aid programs. We have endeavored to fulfill these pledges. Our foreign economic assistance programs are now being operated efficiently with emphasis on helping others to help themselves, on food production and rural development, on health programs and sound population planning assistance, and on the development of human resources.

We have sought to encourage others, including the oil producing countries, to assume a larger share of the burden of assistance. We shall continue our efforts to secure adequate sources of financing for economic projects in emerging countries.

The world's oceans, with their vast resources, must become areas of extended cooperation. We favor a successful conclusion to the Law of the Sea Conference provided it will suitably protect legitimate national interests, freedom of the seas and responsible use of the seas. We are determined to maintain the right of free and unmolested passage for ships of all nations on the high seas and in international waterways.

We favor an extension of the territorial sea from three to twelve miles, and we favor in principle the creation of a 200 mile economic zone in which coastal states would have exclusive rights to explore and develop natural resources.

We strongly condemn illegal corporate payments made at home and abroad. To eliminate illegal payments to foreign officials by American corporations, we support passage of President Ford's proposed legislation and the OECD Declaration on Investment setting forth reasonable guidelines for business conduct.

The growth of civilian nuclear technology, and the rising demand for nuclear power as an alternative to increasingly costly fossil fuel resources, combine to require our recognition of the potential dangers associated with such developments. All nations must work to assure that agreements and treaties currently governing nuclear technology and nuclear exports are carefully monitored. We shall work to devise new multilateral policies governing the export of sensitive nuclear technologies.

International Economic Policy

The tumultuous events of the past several years in the world economy were an enormous challenge to our creativity and to our capacity for leadership. We have emerged from this difficult period in a new position in the world, and we have directed and guided a sound recovery.

To assure the permanence of our own prosperity, we must work with others, demonstrating our leadership and the vitality of our economy. Together with the industrial democracies, we must ensure steady, non-inflationary growth based on expanded international cooperation.

The Republican Administration will cooperate fully in strengthening the international trade and monetary system, which provides the foundation for our prosperity and that of all nations. We shall bargain hard to remove barriers to an open economic system, and we shall oppose new restrictions to trade. We shall continue to represent vigorously our nation's economic interests in the trade negotiations taking place in Geneva, guard against protectionism, and insist that the principles of fair trade be scrupulously observed. When industries and jobs are adversely affected by foreign competition, adjustment assistance under the Trade Act of 1974 is made available. This Act must be under continuous review to ascertain that it reflects changing circumstances.

The Republican Party believes that cooperation in the energy field is indispensable to international stability. Most of the industrial democracies and the less developed countries are increasingly dependent on imported oil, which causes them to be politically, economically and strategically vulnerable. Through the establishment of the International Energy Agency, steps have been taken to expand consumer cooperation. We shall also continue the dialogue with the oil producing countries.

We shall continue to work closely with the less-developed countries to promote their economic growth. Those countries will be encouraged to enter into mutually beneficial trade relationships with us that contribute to world peace. To achieve this, we must strengthen the confidence of the major industrial countries as they take part in discussions with less-developed countries. There is no reason for us to be defensive; our combined assets can be used in a coordinated strategy to make our influence effective. We will not yield to threats or confrontational politics.

While we shall support a global increase of investment in natural resources of all types, we shall also oppose the replacement of the free market mechanism by cartels, price-fixing arrangements or commodity agreements. We shall continue policies designed to assure free market consumers abroad that the United States will remain a dependable supplier of agricultural commodities.

Conclusion

The American people can be proud of our nation's achievements in foreign policy over the past 8 years.

We are at peace.

We are strong.

We re-emphasize the importance of our ties with the nations of the Americas.

Our relations with allies in the Atlantic community and with Japan have never been closer.

Significant progress has been made toward a just and durable settlement in the Middle East.

We have sought negotiation rather than confrontation with our adversaries, while maintaining our strategic deterrent.

The world economic recovery, led by the United States, is producing sustainable growth.

In this year of our nation's bicentennial, the American people have confidence in themselves and are optimistic about the future.

We, the Republican Party, proudly submit our record and our platform to you.

August 17, 1976 ▌

Transcript of First Ford-Carter Debate

Following is a transcript of the first election debate between President Gerald R. Ford and Democratic challenger Jimmy Carter. The debate took place Sept. 23, 1976, at the Walnut Street Theater in Philadelphia, Pa. The moderator was Edwin Newman of NBC News. Panelists were Frank Reynolds of ABC News, James P. Gannon of The Wall Street Journal *and Elizabeth Drew of* The New Yorker.

Unemployment

Reynolds: Mr. President, Governor Carter: Governor, in an interview with the Associated Press last week, you said you believed these debates would alleviate a lot of concern some voters have about you. Well, one of those concerns, not an uncommon one about candidates in any year, is that many voters say they don't really know where you stand. Now you have made jobs your number one priority and you have said you are committed to a drastic reduction in unemployment. Can you say now, Governor, in specific terms, what your first step would be next January, if you are elected, to achieve that?

Carter: First of all, is to recognize the tremendous economic strength of this country and to set the putting back to work of our people as a top priority. This is an ef-

fort that ought to be done primarily by strong leadership in the White House, the inspiration of our people, the tapping of business, agriculture, industry, labor and government at all levels to work on this project. We will never have an end to the inflationary spiral and we will never have a balanced budget until we get our people back to work.

There are several things that can be done specifically that are not now being done. First of all is to channel research and development funds into areas that will provide a large number of jobs. Secondly, we need to have a commitment in the private sector to cooperate with government in matters like housing. Here, a very small investment of taxpayers money in the housing field can bring large numbers of extra jobs and the guarantee of mortgage loans and the putting forward of "202" programs for housing for older people, and so forth, to cut down the roughly 20 per cent unemployment now existing in the construction industry.

Another thing is to deal with our needs in the central cities where the unemployment rate is extremely high—sometimes among minority groups, those who don't speak English, or who are black, or young people—are 40 per cent of the unemployment. Here a CCC type program would be appropriate to channel money into the sharing with the private sector and also local and state governments to employ young people who are now out of work.

Another very important aspect of our economy would be to increase production every way possible; to hold down taxes on individuals; and to shift the tax burdens onto those who have avoided paying taxes in the past. These are kind of specific things, none of which are being done now, and would be a great help in reducing unemployment.

There is an additional factor that needs to be done and covered very succinctly, and that is to make sure that we have a good relationship with management: business on the one hand, and labor on the other. In a lot of places where unemployment is very high, we might channel specific targeted job opportunities by paying part of the salary of unemployed people, and also sharing with local governments the payment of salaries, which would enable us to cut down the unemployment rate much lower before we hit the inflationary level. But I believe that by the end of the first four years of the next term, we could have the unemployment rate down to three per cent adult unemployment, which is about four—four and a half per cent overall; control the inflation rate, and have a balanced growth of about four to six per cent, around 5 per cent, which would give us a balanced budget.

Reynolds: Governor, in the event you are successful, and you do achieve a drastic drop in unemployment, that is likely to create additional pressure on prices. How willing are you to consider an income policy: in other words, wage and price controls?

Carter: Well, we now have such a low utilization of productive capacity, about 73 per cent—I think it is about the lowest since the Great Depression years—and such a high unemployment rate, now 7.9 per cent, that we have a long way to go in getting people to work before we have the inflationary pressures; and I think this would be easy to accomplish, to get jobs down without having the strong inflationary pressures that would be necessary. I would not favor the payment of a given fixed income to people unless they are not able to work. But with tax incentives for the low income groups, we could build up their income levels above the poverty level, and not rate welfare more profitable than work.

Newman: Mr. President, your response.

Ford: I don't believe that Mr. Carter has been any more specific in this case than he has been on many other instances. I noticed particularly that he didn't endorse the Humphrey-Hawkins bill, which he has on occasions, and which is included as a part of the Democratic platform. That legislation allegedly would help our unemployment. But we all know that it would have controlled our economy. It would have added $10- to $30-billion each year in additional expenditures by the federal

Debaters Carter and Ford wait patiently as moderator Edwin Newman discusses an audio problem with a technician during the first presidential debate.

government. It would have called for export controls on agricultural products.

In my judgment, the best way to get the jobs is to expand the private sector, where five out of six jobs today exist in our economy. We can do that by reducing federal taxes, as I proposed about a year ago when I called for a tax reduction of $28-billion, three-quarters of it to go to private taxpayers and one-quarter to the business sector.

We could add to jobs in the major metropolitan areas by a proposal that I recommended that would give tax incentives to business to move into the inner city, and to expand or to build new plants, so that they would take a plant or expand a plant where people are and people are currently unemployed. We could also help our youth with some of the proposals that would give to young people an opportunity to work and learn at the same time, just as we give money to young people who are going to college.

Those are the kind of specifics that I think we have to discuss on these debates, and these are the kinds of programs that I will talk about on my time.

Newman: Mr. Gannon, your question to President Ford.

Taxes

Gannon: Mr. President, I would like to continue for a moment on this question of taxes, which you have just raised. You have said that you favor more tax cuts for middle-income Americans, even those earning up to $30,000 a year. That, presumably, would cost the Treasury quite a bit of money in lost revenue. In view of the very large budget deficits that we have accumulated, and that are still in prospect, how is it possible to promise further tax cuts and to reach your goal of balancing the budget?

Ford: At the time, Mr. Gannon, that I made the recommendation for a $28-billion tax cut, three-quarters of it to go to individual taxpayers and 25 per cent to American business, I said at the same time that we had to hold the lid on federal spending; that for every dollar of a tax reduction we had to have an equal reduction in federal expenditures—a one-for-one proposition; and I recommended that to the Congress with a budget ceiling of $395-billion; and that would have permitted us to have a $28-billion tax reduction.

In my tax reduction program for middle-income taxpayers, I recommended that the Congress increase personal exemptions from $750 per person to $1,000 per person. That would mean, of course, that for a family of four, that family would have $1,000 more personal exemption—money that they could spend for their own purposes, money that the government wouldn't have to spend. But if we keep the lid on federal spending, which I think we can, with the help of the Congress, we can justify fully a $28-billion tax reduction.

In the budget that I submitted to the Congress in January of this year, I recommended a 50 per cent cutback in the rate of growth of federal spending. For the last ten years, the budget of the United States has grown from about 11 per cent per year. We can't afford that kind of growth in federal spending. And in the budget that I recommended, we cut it in half, a growth rate of five to five and a half per cent. With that kind of limitation on federal spending we can fully justify the tax reductions that I have proposed. And it seems to me with the stimulant of more money in the hands of the taxpayer, and with more money in the hands of business to expand, to modernize, to provide more jobs, our economy will be stimulated so that we will get more revenue, and we will have a more prosperous economy.

Gannon: Mr. President, to follow up a moment, the Congress has passed a tax bill which is before you now, which did not meet, exactly, the sort of outline that you requested. What is your intention on that bill, since it doesn't meet your requirements? Do you plan to sign that bill?

Ford: That tax bill does not entirely meet the criteria that I established. I think the Congress should have added another $10-billion reduction in personal income taxes, including the increase of personal exemptions from $750 to $1,000. And Congress could have done that if the budget committees of the Congress and the Congress as a whole had not increased the spending that I recommended in the budget. I am sure you know that in the resolutions passed by the Congress, they have added about $17-billion in more spending by the Congress over the budget that I recommended; so that I would prefer in that tax bill to have an additional tax cut, and a further limitation on federal spending. Now, this tax bill that hasn't reached the White House yet, but is expected in a day or two, it is about 1,500 pages. It has some good provisions in it. It has left out some that I have recommended, unfortunately. On the other hand, when you have a bill of that magnitude, with those many provisions, a President has to sit and decide if there are more good than bad. And from the analysis that I have made so far, it seems to me that that tax bill does justify my signature and my approval.

Newman: Governor Carter, your response.

Carter: Well, Mr. Ford is changing considerably his previous philosophy. The present tax structure is a disgrace to this country. It is just a welfare program for the rich. As a matter of fact, 25 per cent of the total tax deductions go for only 1 per cent of the richest people in this country, and over 50 per cent of the tax credits go for the 14 per cent of the richest people in this country.

When Mr. Ford first became President, in August of 1974, the first thing he did in October was to ask for a $4.7-billion increase in taxes on our people, in the midst of the heaviest recession since the Great Depression of 1940s. In January of 1975, he asked for a tax change of $5.6-billion increase on low- and middle-income private individuals, a $6.5-billion decrease on the corporations and the special interests. In December of 1975 he vetoed the roughly $18- $20-billion tax reduction bill that had been passed by the Congress. And then he came back later on, in January of this year, and he did advocate a $10-billion tax reduction. But it would be offset by a $6-billion increase this coming January, and deductions and social security payments and for unemployment compensation.

The whole philosophy of the Republican Party, including my opponent, has been to pile on taxes for low-income people, to take them off on the corporations. As a matter of fact, since the late sixties, when Mr. Nixon took office, we have had a reduction in the percentage of taxes paid by corporations from 30 per cent down to about 20 per cent. We have had an increase in taxes paid by individuals, payroll taxes from 14 per cent up to 20 per cent, and this is what the Republicans have done to us, and this is why a tax reform is so important.

Newman: Mrs. Drew, your question to Gov. Carter.

Surplus

Drew: Governor Carter, you have proposed a number of new or enlarged programs, including jobs, health, welfare reform, child care, aid to education, aid to cities, changes in social security, and housing subsidies. You have also said that you want to balance the budget by the end of your first term. Now, you haven't put a price tag on those programs, but even if we priced them conservatively, and we account for full employment by the end of your first term, and we account for the economic growth that would occur during that period, there still isn't enough money to pay for those programs and balance the budget by any estimates that I have been able to see. So in that case, what would give?

Carter: Well, as a matter of fact, there is. If we assume a rate of growth of our economy equivalent to what it was during President Johnson, President Kennedy—even before the Vietnamese War; and if we assume that at the end of the four-year period we can cut our unemployment rate down to four to four and a half per cent, under those circumstances, even assuming no elimination of unnecessary programs, and assuming an increase in the allotment of money to finance programs, increasing as the inflation rate does, my economic projections—confirmed by the House and the Senate Committees—have been with a $60-billion extra amount of money that can be spent in fiscal year '81, which would be the last year of this next term, within that $60-billion increase, they would befit the programs that I promise the American people.

I might say, too, that if we see that these goals cannot be reached, and I believe that they are reasonable goals, that I would cut back on the rate of implementation of new programs in order to accommodate a balanced budget by fiscal year '81, which is the last year of the next term. I believe we ought to have a balanced budget during normal economic circumstances, and these projections have been very carefully made. I stand behind them, and if they should be in error, slightly on the down side, then I will phase in the programs that we have so advocated more slowly.

Drew: Governor, according to the budget committees of the Congress that you referred to, if we get the full employment, would they project a 4 per cent unemployment, and as you say, even allowing for the inflation in the programs, there would not be anything more than a surplus of $5-billion by 1981, and conservative estimates of your programs would be that they would be about $85- to $100-billion. So how do you say that you are going to be able to do these things and balance the budget.

Carter: Well, the assumption that you have described as different is in the rate of growth of our economy.

Drew: No, but we took that into account in those figures.

Carter: I believe that it is accurate to say that the committees to whom you refer, the employment rate that you state and with the five to five and a half per cent growth rate in our economy, that the projections would be a $60-billion increase in the amount of money that we have to spend in 1981, compared to now, and with that framework would befit any improvements in the program.

Now, this does not include extra control over unnecessary spending, the weeding out of obsolete or obsolescent programs. We will have a safety version built in, with complete reorganization of the executive branch of government, which I have pledged to do. The present bureaucratic structure of the federal government is a mess. And if I am elected President, that is going to be a top priority of mine: to completely revise the structure of the federal government to make it economical, efficient, purposeful and manageable for a change. And also, I am going to institute zero-base budgeting, which I used four years in Georgia, which assesses every program every year, and eliminates those programs that are obsolete or obsolescent.

With these projections, we will have a balanced budget by fiscal year 1981, if I am elected President. I keep my promises to the American people and it is just predicated on very modest, but, I think, accurate projections of employment increases and a growth in our national economy equal to what was experienced under Kennedy-Johnson before the Vietnam War.

Newman: President Ford.

Ford: If it is true that there will be a $60-billion surplus by fiscal year 1981, rather than spend that money for all the new programs that Governor Carter recommends and endorses, and which are included in the Democratic platform, I think that the American taxpayer ought to get an additional tax break—a tax reduc-

tion of that magnitude. I feel that the taxpayers are the ones that need the relief. I don't think that we should add additional programs of the magnitude that Governor Carter talks about.

It seems to me that our tax structure, today, has rates that are too high. But I am very glad to point out that since 1969, during a Republican administration, we have had 10-million people taken off the tax rolls at the lower end of the taxpayer area, and at the same time, assuming that I sign the tax bill that was mentioned by Mr. Gannon, we will, in the last two tax bills, have increased the minimum tax of all wealthy taxpayers. And I believe that by eliminating 10-million taxpayers in the last eight years, and by putting a heavier tax burden on those in the higher tax brackets, plus the other actions that have been taken, we can give taxpayers adequate tax relief.

Now, it seems to me that as we look at the recommendations of the budget committees, and our own projections, there isn't going to be any $60-billion dividends. I have heard of those dividends in the past. It always happens. We expected one at the time of the Vietnam War, but it was used up before we ever ended the war, and taxpayers never got the adequate relief they deserved.

Newman: Mr. Reynolds.

Draft Resisters

Reynolds: Mr. President, when you came into office, you spoke very eloquently of the need for a time for healing; and very early in your administration you went out to Chicago, and you announced, you proposed a program of case-by-case pardons for draft resisters, to restore them to full citizenship. Some 14,000 young men took advantage of your offer, but another 90,000 did not. In granting the pardon to former President Nixon, sir, part of your rationale was to put Watergate behind us: to, if I might quote you, again, truly end our long, national nightmare. Why does not the same rationale apply, now, today in our bicentennial year to the young men who resisted in Vietnam, and many of them still in exile abroad?

Ford: The amnesty program that I recommended in Chicago in September of 1974 would give to all draft evaders and military deserters the opportunity to earn their good record back. About 14-15,000 did take advantage of that program. We gave them ample time. I am against an across-the-board pardon of draft evaders or military deserters.

Now, in the case of Mr. Nixon, the reason that the pardon was given was that when I took office, this country was in a very, very divided condition. There was hatred. There was divisiveness. People had lost faith in their government in many, many respects. Mr. Nixon resigned, and I became President. It seemed to me that if I was to adequately and effectively handle the problems of high inflation, a growing recession, the involvement of the United States still in Vietnam, that I had to give

100 per cent of my time to those two major problems. Mr. Nixon resigned. That is disgrace, the first President out of 38 that ever resigned from public office under pressure. So when you look at the penalty that he paid and when you analyze the requirements that I had—to spend all of my time working on the economy, which was in trouble that I inherited, working out our problems in Southeast Asia, which were still plaguing us, it seemed to me that Mr. Nixon had been penalized enough by his resignation in disgrace, and the need and necessity for me to concentrate on the problems of the country fully justified the action that I took.

Reynolds: I take it, then, sir, that you do not believe that it is—that you are going to reconsider and think about those 90,000 who are still abroad? Have they not been penalized enough? Many of them have been there for years.

Ford: Well, Mr. Carter has indicated that he would give a "blanket" pardon to all the draft evaders. I do not agree with that point of view. I gave, in September of 1974, an opportunity for all draft evaders, all deserters to come in, voluntarily, clear their records by earning an opportunity to restore their good citizenship. I think we gave them a good opportunity. I don't think we should go any further.

Newman: Governor Carter.

Carter: Well, I think it is very difficult for President Ford to explain the difference between the pardon of President Nixon and his attitude toward those who violated the draft laws. As a matter of fact, now I don't advocate amnesty. I advocate pardon. There is a difference, in my opinion and in accordance with the ruling of the Supreme Court and, of course, the definition in the dictionary. Amnesty means that what you did was right. Pardon means that what you did—whether it was right or wrong—you are forgiven for it. And I do advocate a pardon for draft evaders. I think it is accurate to say that in two years ago when Mr. Nixon, Mr. Ford put in this amnesty that three times this many deserters were excused as were the ones who evaded the draft.

But I think that now is the time to heal our country after the Vietnam War, and I think that what the people are concerned about is not the pardon or the amnesty of those who evaded the draft, but whether or not our crime system is fair. We have got a sharp distinction drawn between "white-collar crime," the big shots who are rich, who are influential very seldom go to jail. Those who are poor and who have no influence quite often are the ones who are punished. And the whole subject of crime is one that concerns our people very much, and I believe the fairness of it is what is a major problem and addresses our leader, and this is something that hasn't been addressed adequately by this administration. But I hope to have a complete responsibility on my shoulders to help bring about a fair criminal justice system and also to bring about an end to divisiveness that has occurred in our country as a result of the Vietnam War.

Newman: Mr. Gannon.

Government Reorganization

Gannon: Governor Carter, you have promised a sweeping overhaul of the federal government, including a reduction in the number of government agencies, you say it would go down to about 200 from some 1,900. That sounds, indeed, like a very deep cut in the federal government. But isn't it a fact that you are not really talking about fewer federal employees, or less government spending, but rather that you are talking about reshaping the federal government, not making it smaller?

Carter: Well, I have been through this before, Mr. Gannon, as the governor of Georgia. When I took over, we had a bureaucratic mess like we have in Washington, now. And we had 300 agencies, departments, bureaus, commissions, some fully budgeted, some not, but all having responsibility to carry out. There was conflict. And we cut those 300 agencies and so forth down substantially. We eliminated 278 of them. We set up a simple structure of government that could be administered fairly, and it was a tremendous success. It hasn't been undone since I was there. It resulted also in an ability to reshape our court system, our prison system, our educational system, our mental health programs and a clear assignment of responsibility and authority, and also to have our people understanding controlling our government.

I intend to do the same thing if I am elected President. When I get to Washington, coming in as an outsider, one of the major responsibilities that I will have on my shoulder is a complete reorganization of the executive branch of the government.

We now have a greatly expanded White House staff. When Mr. Nixon went in office, for instance, we had three and a half million dollars spent on the White House and the staff. That has escalated, now, to sixteen and a half million dollars in the last Republican administration. This needs to be changed. We need to put the responsibilities back on the Cabinet members.

We also need to have a great reduction in agencies and programs. For instance, we now have in the health area 302 different programs administered by 11 major departments and agencies; 60 other advisory commissions responsible for this, Medicaid through one agency, Medicare is in a different one, the check on the quality of health care is in a different one, none of them are responsible for health care, itself. This makes it almost impossible for us to have a good health program.

We have just advocated this past week consolidation of the responsibilities for energy. Our country now has no comprehensive energy program or policy. We have 20 different agencies in the federal government responsible for the production, the regulation, the information about energy, the conservation of energy, spread all over government. This is a gross waste of money. So tough, competent management of government, giving us a simple, efficient, purposeful and manageable government would be a great step forward; and if I am elected, and I intend to be, then it is going to be done.

Gannon: Well, I would like to press my question on the number of federal employees: whether you would really plan to reduce the overall number or merely put them in different departments and re-label them. In your energy plan you consolidate the number of agencies into one, or you would; but does that really change the overall?

Carter: I can't say for sure that we would have fewer government employees when I go out of office than when I come in. It took me about three years to completely reorganize the Georgia government. The last year I was in office, our budget was actually less than it was a year before, which showed a great improvement. Also, we had a two per cent increase in the number of employees the last year, but it was a tremendous shift from administrative jobs into the delivery of services. For instance, we completely revised our prison system. We established 84 new mental health treatment centers, and we shifted people out of administrative jobs into the field to deliver better services. The same thing would be done at the federal government level.

I accomplished this with substantial reductions in employees in some departments. For instance, in the transportation department, we cut back about 25 per cent of the total number of employees. In giving our people better mental health care, we increased the number of employees, but the efficiency of it, the simplicity of it, the ability of people to understand their own government and control it, was a substantial benefit derived from complete reorganization.

We have got to do this at the federal government level. If we don't, the bureaucratic mess is going to continue. There is no way, now, for people to understand what their government is. There is no way to get the answer to a question. When you come to Washington as a governor to try to begin a new program for your people, like the treatment of drug addicts, I found there was thirteen different federal agencies that I had to go to, to manage the drug treatment program. In the Georgia government, we only had one agency responsible for drug treatment. This is the kind of change that would be made, and it would be of tremendous benefit in long-range planning and tight budgeting or saving the taxpayers money, making the government more efficient, cutting down on bureaucratic wastes, having a clear delineation of authority, responsibility of employees, and giving our people a better chance to understand and control their government.

Newman: President Ford.

Ford: I think the record should show, Mr. Newman, that the Bureau of Cen-

sus—we checked it just yesterday—indicates that in the four years that Governor Carter was governor of the state of Georgia, expenditures by the government went up over 50 per cent. Employees of the government of Georgia, during his term of office, went up over 25 per cent, and the figures also show that the bonded indebtedness of the state of Georgia during his governorship went up over 20 per cent.

And there was some very interesting testimony given by Governor Carter's successor, Governor Busbee, before a Senate committee a few months ago on how he found the Medicaid program when he came in to office following Governor Carter. He testified, and these are his words, the present governor of Georgia, he says he found the Medicaid program in Georgia a shambles.

Now let me talk about what we have done in the White House as far as federal employees are concerned. The first order that I issued after I became President was to cut or eliminate the prospective 40,000 increase in federal employees that had been scheduled by my predecessor. And in the term that I have been President—some two years—we have reduced federal employment by 11,000. In the White House staff, itself, when I became President, we had, roughly, 540 employees. We now have about 485 employees. So we made a rather significant reduction in the number of employees in the White House staff working for the President. So I think our record in cutting back employees, plus the failure on the part of the governor's program to actually save employment in Georgia, shows which is the better plan.

Newman: Mrs. Drew.

Ford Initiatives

Drew: Mr. President, at Vail, after the Republican convention, you announced that you would now emphasize five new areas. Among those were jobs in housing and health, improved recreational facilities for Americans, and you also added crime. You also mentioned education. For two years you were telling us that we couldn't do very much in these areas because we couldn't afford it, and in fact we do have a $50-billion deficit now. In rebuttal to Governor Carter a little bit earlier, you said that if there were to be any surplus in the next few years you thought it should be turned back to the people in the form of tax relief. So how are you going to pay for any new initiatives in these areas you announced at Vail you were going to now stress?

Ford: Well, in the last two years, as I indicated before, we had a very tough time. We were faced with heavy inflation—over 12 per cent. We were faced with substantial unemployment. But in the last 24 months we have turned the economy around and we have brought inflation down to under six per cent and we have reduced the—well, we have added employment of about four million in the last 17 months to the point where we have 88 million people working in America today—the most in the history of the country.

The net result is, we are going to have some improvements in our receipts. And I think we'll have some decrease in our disbursement.

We expect to have a lower deficit in fiscal year 1978. We feel that with this improvement in the economy, we feel with more receipts and fewer disbursements we can, in a moderate way, increase, as I recommended, over the next ten years, a new parks program that would cost $1.5-billion, doubling our national parks system. We have recommended that in the housing program we can reduce down payments and moderate monthly payments. But that doesn't cost any more as far as the federal treasury is concerned.

We believe that we can do a better job in the area of crime. But that requires a tougher sentencing, mandatory certain prison sentences for those who violate our criminal laws. We believe that you can revise the federal criminal code, which has not been revised in a good many years. That doesn't cost any more money. We believe that you can do something more effectively with a moderate increase in money in the drug abuse program. We feel that in education we can have a slight increase—not a major increase. It's my understanding that Governor Carter has indicated that he approves of a $30-billion expenditures by the federal government as far as education is concerned. At the present time we are spending roughly $3.5-billion. I don't know where that money would come from. But if we look at the quality of life programs—jobs, health, education, crime, recreation—we feel that as we move forward with a healthier economy we can absorb the small necessary costs that will be required.

Drew: Sir, in the next few years would you try to reduce the deficit, would you spend money for these programs that you have just outlined, or would you, as you said earlier, return whatever surplus you got to the people in the form of tax relief?

Ford: We feel that the programs that I have recommended, the additional $10-billion tax cut, with the moderate increases in the quality of life area, we can still have a balanced budget, which I will submit to the Congress in January of 1978. We won't wait one year or two years longer, as Governor Carter indicates.

As the economy improves and it is improving, our gross national product this year will average about six per cent increase over last year. We will have a lower rate of inflation for the calendar year this year of something slightly under six per cent. Employment will be up, revenues will be up. We'll keep a lid on some of these programs that we can hold down as we have a little extra money to spend for those quality of life programs which I think are needed and necessary.

Now, I cannot and would not endorse the kind of programs that Governor Carter recommends. He endorses the Democratic

platform, which as I read it calls for approximately 60 additional programs. We estimate that those programs would add a $100-billion minimum and probably $200-billion maximum each year to the federal budget. Those programs you cannot afford and give tax relief. We feel that you can hold the line and restrain federal spending, give a tax reduction and still have a balanced budget by 1978.

Newman: Governor Carter?

Carter: Mr. Ford takes the same attitude that the Republicans always take. In the last three months before an election, they are always for the programs that they fight the other three and a half years. I remember when Herbert Hoover was against jobs for people, I remember when Alf Landon was against Social Security, and later President Nixon 16 years ago was telling the public that John Kennedy's proposal would bankrupt the country and would double the cost.

The best thing to do is to look at the record of Mr. Ford's administration and Mr. Nixon's before his. We had last year a $65-billion deficit, the largest deficit in the hisory of the country. More of a deficit spending than we had in the entire eight-year period under President Johnson, President Kennedy. We've got a 500,000 more Americans out of jobs today than were out of work three months ago; and since Mr. Ford has been in office in two years we've had a 50 per cent increase in unemployment from five million people out of work, to two-and-a-half million more people out of work, a total of seven-and-a-half million.

We've also got a comparison between himself and Mr.Nixon. He's got four times the size of a deficit that Mr. Nixon even had himself. This talking about more people at work is distorted because with the 14 per cent increase in the cost of living in the last two years it means that women and young people have had to go to work when they didn't want to, because their fathers couldn't make enough to pay the increased cost of food and housing and clothing. We have had in the last two years alone $120-billion total deficits under President Ford, and at the same time we have had in the last eight years a doubling in the number of bankruptcy for small business. We've had a negative growth in our national economy measured in real dollars. The take-home pay for a worker in this country is actually less now than it was in 1968, measured in real dollars. This is the kind of record that's there, and talk about the future and a drastic change or conversion on the part of Mr. Ford in the last minute is one that just doesn't go.

Energy Policy

Reynolds: Governor Carter, I'd like to turn to what we used to call the energy crisis. Yesterday, a British government commission on air pollution, one headed by a nuclear physicist, recommended that any further expansion of nuclear energy be delayed in Britain as long as possible. Now, this is a subject that is quite controversial

among our own people, and there seems to be a clear difference between you and the President on the use of nuclear power plants, which you say you would use as a last priority. Why, sir? Are they unsafe?

Carter: Well, among my other experiences in the past I have been a nuclear engineer and did graduate work in this field. I think I know the capabilities and limitations of atomic power. But the energy policy of our nation is one that has not yet been established under this administration.

I think almost every other developed nation in the world has an energy policy except us. We have seen the Federal Energy Agency established, for instance, in the crisis of 1973, which was supposed to be a temporary agency. Now it's permanent, it's enormous, it's growing every day. I think *The Wall Street Journal* reported not too long ago that they have 112 public relation experts working for the Federal Energy Agency to try to justify to the American people its own existence.

We've got to have a firm way to handle the energy question. The reorganization proposal that I put forth is one, a first step. In addition to that we need to have a realization that we've got about 35 years' worth of oil left in the whole world. We are going to run out of oil. When Mr. Nixon made his famous speech on Operation Independence we were importing about 35 per cent of our oil. Now we have increased that amount by 25 per cent. We now import about 44 per cent of our oil.

We need to shift from oil to coal. We need to concentrate our research and development effort on coal burning and extraction, safer mines that also is clean burning. We need to shift very strongly towards solar energy, and have strict conservation measures, and as the last resort only, continue to use atomic power.

I would certainly not cut out atomic power altogether. We cannot afford to give up that opportunity until later; but to the extent that we continue to use atomic power, I will be responsible as President to make sure that the safety precautions were initiated and maintained. For instance, some that have been forgotten. We need to have the reactor coil below ground level. The entire power plant that uses atomic power tightly sealed and a heavy vacuum maintained. There ought to have a standardized design. There ought to be a full-time atomic energy specialist, independent of the power company, in the control room full time, 24 hours a day, to shut down the plant if an abnormality develops. These kinds of procedures, along with evacuation procedures, adequate insurance ought to be initiated.

So, shift from oil to coal, emphasize research and development of coal use and also on solar power, strict conservation measures—not yield every time that the special interest groups put pressure on the President, like this administration has done—and use atomic energy only as the last resort, with the strictest possible safety precautions. That's the best overall energy policy in the brief time we have discussed it.

Reynolds: Governor, on that same subject, would you require mandatory conservation efforts to try to conserve fuel?

Carter: Yes, I would. Some of the things that can be done about this is a change in the rate structure of the electric power companies. We now encourage people to waste electricity. And by giving the lowest rates to the biggest users, we don't do anything to cut down on peak load requirements. We don't have an adequate requirement for the insulation of homes, for the efficiency of automobiles. And whenever the automobile manufacturers come forward and say they can't meet the limits that the Congress has put forth, this Republican administration has delayed the implementation date.

In addition to that we ought to have a shift of the use of coal, particularly in the Appalachian regions, where the coal is located. A lot of very high quality, low carbon coal...uh...I mean, low sulphur coal is there. It's where our employment is needed. This would help a great deal.

So, mandatory conservation measures, yes. Encouragement by the President for people to voluntarily conserve, yes. And also the private sector ought to be encouraged to bring forward to the public the benefits from efficiency. One bank in Washington, for instance, gives lower interest loans for people who adequately insulate their homes and who buy efficient automobiles. And some major manufacturing companies like Dow Chemical have through very effective efficiency mechanisms cut down the use of energy by as much as 40 per cent with the same outproduct. These kinds of things ought to be done. They ought to be encouraged and supported and even required by the government, yes.

Newman: President Ford?

Ford: Governor Carter skims over a very serious and very broad subject. In January of 1975 I submitted to the Congress and to the American people the first comprehensive energy program recommended by any President. It called for an increase in the production of energy in the United States. It called for conservative measures so that we would save the energy that we have. If you are going to increase domestic oil and gas production, and we have to, you have to give those producers an opportunity to develop their land or their wells. I recommended to Congress that we should increase coal production in this country from 600 million tons a year to 1.2 billion tons by 1985. In order to do that we have to improve our extraction of coal from the ground, we have to improve our utilization of coal, make it more efficient, make it cleaner.

In addition, we have to expand our research and development in the program for energy independence. We have increased, for example, solar energy research from about $84-million a year to about $120-million a year. We are going as fast as the expert says we should. In nuclear power we have increased the research and development under the Energy Research and Development Agency very substantially to ensure that our nuclear power plants are safer, that they are more efficient and that we have adequate safeguards. I think you have to have greater oil and gas production, more coal production, more nuclear production, and in addition you have to have energy conservation.

Jobs

Gannon: Mr. President, I'd like to return for a moment to this problem of unemployment. You have vetoed or threatened to veto a number of job bills passed or in development in the Democratic Congress, Democratic-controlled Congress. Yet, at the same time, the government is paying out, I think it is $17-billion, perhaps $20-billion a year in unemployment compensation caused by the high unemployment. Why do you think it is better to pay out unemployment compensation to idle people than to put them to work in public service jobs?

Ford: The bills that I have vetoed, the one for an additional $6-billion, was not a bill that would have solved our unemployment problems. Even the proponents of it admitted that no more than 400,000 jobs would be made available. Our analysis indicates that something in the magnitude of about 150,000 to 200,000 jobs would be made available. Each one of those jobs would have cost the taxpayer $25,000. In addition, the jobs would not be available right now. They would have not materialized for about nine to 18 months. The immediate problem we have is to stimulate our economy now so that we can get rid of unemployment.

What we have done is to hold the lid on spending in an effort to reduce the rate of inflation, and we have proven, I think very conclusively, that you can reduce the rate of inflation and increase jobs. For example, as I have said, we have added some four million jobs in the last 17 months. We have now employed 88 million people in America, the largest number in the history of the United States. We've added 500,000 jobs in the last two months.

Inflation is the quickest way to destroy jobs, and by holding the lid on federal spending we have been able to do a good job, an affirmative job in inflation and as a result have added to the jobs in this country.

I think it is also appropriate to point out that through our tax policies we have stimulated added employment throughout the country, through investment tax credits, the tax incentive for expansion and modernization of our industrial capacity. It is my opinion that the private sector, where five out of the six jobs are, where you would have permanent jobs, with an opportunity for advancement, is a better place than make-work jobs under the program recommended by the Congress.

Gannon: Just a follow up, Mr. President. The Congress has just passed a $3.7-billion appropriation bill which would provide money for the public works jobs program that you earlier tried to kill by your veto of the authorization legislation. In the light of the fact that unemployment again is rising, or has in the past three months, I wonder if you have re-thought that question at all, whether you would consider allowing this program to be funded, or will you veto that money bill?

Ford: That bill has not yet come down to the Oval Office, so I am not in a position to make any judgment on it tonight. But that an extra $4-billion that would add to the deficit, which would add to the inflationary pressures, would help to destroy jobs in the private sector, not make jobs where the jobs really are. These make-work temporary jobs, dead-end as they are, are not the kind of jobs that we want for our people.

I think that it is interesting to point out that in the two years that I've been President, I have vetoed 56 bills. Congress has sustained 42 vetoes. As a result, we have saved over $9-billion in federal expenditures. And the Congress, by overriding the bills that I did veto, the Congress has added some $13-billion to the federal expenditures and to the federal deficit.

Now, Governor Carter complains about the deficit that this administration has had, and yet he condemns the vetoes that I have made that have saved the taxpayers $9-billion, and could have saved an additional $13-billion. Now, he can't have it both ways. And therefore, it seems to me that we should hold the lid, as we had to, to the best of our ability, so we stimulate the private economy and get the jobs where the jobs are—five out of six—in this economy.

Newman: Governor Carter?

Carter: Well, Mr. Ford doesn't seem to put into perspective the fact that 500,000 more people are out of work than there were three months ago, while we have two and a half million more people out of work than were when he took office.

This touches human beings. I was in a city in Pennsylvania not too long ago, near here, and there were about four or five thousand people in the audience—that was a train trip. Now, I said, 'how many adults here are out of work?' About a thousand raised their hands.

Mr. Ford actually has fewer people now in the private sector and non-farm jobs than when he took office. And still he talks about a success. Seven point nine per cent unemployment is a terrible tragedy in this country. He says he has learned how to match unemployment with inflation. That's right. We got the highest inflation we've had in 25 years right now, except under this administration and that was 50 years ago. And we got the highest unemployment we've had under Mr. Ford's administration since the Great Depression. This affects human beings, and his insensitivity in providing those people a chance to work has made this a welfare administration and not a work administration.

He hasn't saved $9-billion with his vetoes. It's only been a net saving of $4-

billion, and the cost in unemployment compensation, a welfare compensation and lost revenues has increased $23-billion in the last two years.

This is a typical attitude that really causes havoc in people's lives. And then its covered over by saying that our country has naturally got a six per cent unemployment rate or seven per cent unemployment rate or six per cent inflation. It's a travesty. It shows a lack of leadership.

We've never had a President since the war between the states that vetoed more bills. Mr. Ford has vetoed four times as many bills as Mr. Nixon per year, and 11 of them have been overridden. One of his bills that was overridden, he only got one vote in the Senate and seven votes in the House from Republicans. So this shows a breakdown in leadership.

Newman: Mr. Carter, under the rules I must stop you. Mrs. Drew?

Tax Reform

Drew: Governor Carter, I'd like to come back to the subject of taxes. You have said that you want to cut taxes for the middle and lower income groups. But unless you're willing to do such things as reduce the itemized deductions for charitable contributions or home mortgage payments or interest or taxes or capital gain, you can't really raise sufficient revenue to provide an overall tax cut of any size. So how are you going to provide that tax relief that you're talking about?

Carter: Now we have such a grossly unbalanced tax system as I said earlier, that it is a disgrace. Of all the tax benefits now 25 per cent of them goes to the one per cent richest people in this country. Over 50 per cent, 53 to be exact, of the tax benefits go the the 14 per cent richest people in this country. And we've had a 50 per cent increase in payroll deductions since Mr. Nixon went into office eight years ago.

Mr. Ford has advocated, since he has been in office, over $5-billion in reductions for corporations, special interest groups and the very, very wealthy who drive their income not from labor but from investments. That has got to be changed.

A few things that can be done: we have now a default system so that the multinational corporations who invest overseas, if they make a million dollars in profits overseas, they don't have to pay any of their taxes unless they bring their money back into this country. When they don't take their taxes, the average American pays their taxes for them. Not only that, but it robs this country of jobs because instead of coming back with that million dollars and creating a shoe factory, say in New Hampshire or Vermont, if the company takes its money down to Italy and builds a shoe factory, they don't have to pay any taxes on the money.

Another thing is the system called "DISC," which was originally designed, proposed by Mr. Nixon to encourage exports. This permits a company to create a dummy corporation to export their products and then not to pay the full amount of taxes only. This costs our government about $1.4-billion a year. And when those rich corporations don't pay that tax, the average American taxpayer pays it for them.

Another one that is very important is the business deductions. Jet airplanes, first-class travel, the fifty-dollar martini lunch. The average working person can't take advantage of that, but the wealthier people can.

Another system is where a dentist can invest money in, say raising cattle, and can put in $100,000 of his own money, borrow $900,000—that makes a million—and mark off a great amount of loss through that procedure. There was one example, for instance, where somebody produced pornographic movies...they put in $30,000 of their own money and got $120,000 in tax savings.

Well, these special kinds of programs have robbed the average taxpayer and have benefitted those who are powerful and who can employ lobbyists and who can have their CPAs and their lawyers to help them benefit from their roughly 8,000 pages of a tax code. The average American person can't do it. You can't hire a lobbyist out of unemployment compensation checks.

Drew: Governor, to follow up on your answer, in order for any kind of tax relief to really be felt by the middle- and lower-income people, you need about, according to congressional committees on this, you need about $10-billion. Now you listed some things, the deferral on foreign income as estimated, would save about $500-million. This you said was $1.4-billion. The estimate of the outside, if you eliminated all tax shelters, is $5-billion. So where else would you raise the revenue to provide this tax relief? Would you in fact do away with all business deductions, and what other kinds of preferences would you do away with?

Carter: No, I wouldn't do away with all business deductions. I think that would be a very serious mistake. But if you could just do away with the ones that are unfair, you could lower taxes from everyone.

I would never do anything that would increase the taxes for those who work for a living, or who are presently required to list all their income; but what I want to do is not to raise taxes but to eliminate loopholes. And this is the point of my first statistic that I gave you, that the present tax benefits that have been carved out over a long period of years—50 years—by sharp tax lawyers and by lobbyists, have benefited just the rich. These programs that I described to you earlier, the tax deferrals for overseas, the DISC, and the tax shelters, they only apply to people in the $50,000-a-year bracket or up. And I think that this is the best way to approach it, is to make sure that everybody pays taxes on the income that they earn and make sure that you take whatever savings that there is from the higher income levels and give it to the lower- and middle-income families.

Newman: President Ford.

Ford: Governor Carter's answer tonight does not coincide with the answer that he gave in an interview to the Associated Press a week or so ago. In that interview, Governor Carter indicated that he would raise the taxes on those in the median or middle-income brackets or higher. Now if you take the median or middle-income taxpayer, that is about $14,000 per person. Governor Carter has indicated publicly in an interview that he would increase the taxes on about 50 per cent of the working people of this country.

I think the way to get tax equity in this country is to give tax relief to the middle-income people who have an income of from roughly $8,000 up to $25-30,000. They have been short-changed as we have taken 10 million taxpayers off the tax rolls in the last eight years, and as we have added to the minimum tax provision to make all people pay more taxes.

I believe in tax equity for the middle-income taxpayers, increasing the personal exemption. Mr. Carter wants to increase taxes for roughly half of the taxpayers of this country.

The governor has also played a little fast and loose with the facts about vetoes. The records show that President Roosevelt vetoed on an average of 55 bills a year. President Truman vetoed on the average, while he was President, about 38 bills a year. I understand that Governor Carter, when he was governor of Georgia, vetoed between 35 and 40 bills a year. My average in two years is 26. But in the process of that we have saved $9-billion. And one final comment, Governor Carter talks about the tax bills and all the inequities that exist in the present law. I must remind him the Democrats have controlled the Congress for the last 22 years and they wrote all the tax bills.

Anti-Washington Mood

Reynolds: I suspect that we could continue on with this tax argument for some time, but I'd like to move to another area. Mr. President, everybody seems to be running against Washington this year, and I'd like to raise two coincidental events and ask you whether you think perhaps they may have a bearing on the attitude throughout the country. The House Ethics Committee has just now ended its investigation of Daniel Schorr. After several months and many thousands of dollars, trying to find out how they obtained and caused to be published a report of the Congress that probably is the property of the American people. At the same time, the Senate Select Committee on Standards and Conduct has voted not ready to begin an investigation of a United States senator because of allegations against him that he may have been receiving corporate funds illegally over a period of years. Do you suppose sir, that things like this contribute to the feeling in the country that maybe there's something wrong in Washington, and I don't mean just in the executive branch, but throughout the whole government.?

Ford: There is a considerable anti-Washington feeling throughout the country. But I think the feeling is misplaced. In the last two years we have restored integrity in the White House. And we've set high standards in the executive branch of the government. The anti-Washington feeling, in my opinion, ought to be focused on the Congress of the United States.

For example, this Congress very shortly will spend a billion dollars a year for its housekeeping, its salaries, its expenses and the like. The next Congress will probably be the first billion-dollar Congress in the history of the United States. I don't think the American people are getting their money's worth from the majority party that runs this Congress.

We in addition see that in the last four years the number of employees hired by the Congress has gone up substantially. Much more than the gross national product, much more than any other increase throughout our society. Congress is hiring people by the droves. And the cost, as a result, has gone up.

I don't see any improvement in the performance under the present leadership, so it seems to me instead of the anti-Washington being aimed at everybody in Washington, it seems to me that the focus should be where the problem is, which is in the Congress of the United States. And particularly in the majority in the Congress. They spend too much money on themselves, they have too many employees, there's some question about their morality. It seems to me that in this election the focus should not be on the executive branch but the correction should come as the voters vote for their members of the House of Representatives or for their United States senator. That's where the problem is and I hope there will be some corrective action taken so we can get some new leadership in the Congress of the United States.

Reynolds: Mr. President, if I may follow up, I think you've made it plain that you take a dim view of the majority in the Congress. Isn't it quite likely sir, that you will have a Democratic Congress in the next session, if you are elected President, and hasn't the country a right to ask whether you can get along with that Congress, or whether we'll have continued confrontation?

Ford: Well, it seems to me that we have a chance, the Republicans, to get a majority in the House of Representatives. We will make some gains in the United States Senate. So there will be different ratios in the House as well as in the Senate. And as President I will be able to work with that Congress.

But let me take the other side of the coin, if I might. Supposing we have had a Democratic Congress for the last two years, and we've had Governor Carter as President. He has in effect said that he would agree with all of.... He would disapprove of the vetoes that I have made and would have added significantly to expenditures and the deficit of federal government. I think it would be contrary to one of the basic concepts in our system of government, a system of checks and balances. We have a Democratic Congress today and fortunately we've had a Republican President to check their excesses with my vetoes. If we have a Democratic Congress next year and a President who wants to spend an additional $100-billion dollars a year, or maybe $200-billion a year, with more programs, we will have, in my judgment, greater deficits with more spending, more dangers of inflation. I think the American people want a Republican President to check on any excesses that come out of the next Congress, if it is a Democratic Congress.

Newman: Governor Carter?

Carter: Well, it's not a matter of a Republican or Democrat. It's a matter of leadership or no leadership. President Eisenhower worked with a Democratic Congress very well. Even President Nixon, because he was a strong leader, at least, worked with a Democratic Congress very well.

Mr. Ford has vetoed, as I said earlier, four times as many bills per year as Mr. Nixon. Mr. Ford quite often puts forth a program just as a public relations stunt and never tries to put it through the Congress by working with the Congress. I think under Ford or Nixon and Eisenhower they passed about 60 to 75 per cent of their legislation. This year Mr. Ford will not pass over 26 per cent of all the legislative proposals he put forward. This is goverment by stalemate, and we've seen almost a complete breakdown in the proper relationship between a President who represents his country and a Congress who collectively also represents this country.

We've had Republican Presidents before who've tried to run against a Democratic Congress. And I don't think it's the Congress who's Mr. Ford's opponent; but if he insists that I be responsible for the Democratic Congress, of which I have not been a part, then I think it's only fair that he be responsible for the Nixon administration in its entirety, of which he was a part. That, I think, is a good balance.

But the point is, that the President ought to lead this country. Mr. Ford, so far as I know, except for avoiding another Watergate, has not accomplished one single major program for this country; and there's been a constant squabbling between the President and the Congress, and that's not the way this country ought to be run. I might go back to one other thing. Mr. Ford has misquoted an AP news story that was in error to begin with, that the story reported several times that I would lower taxes for low and middle income families. And that correction was delivered to the White House, and I'm sure that the President knows about this correction, but he still insists on repeating an erroneous statement.

Newman: President Ford, Governor Carter, we no longer have enough time for two complete sequences of questions. We have only about six minutes left for questions and answers. For that reason we will drop the follow-up questions at this point but each candidate will still be able to respond to the other's answers. To the extent that you can, gentlemen, please keep your remarks brief.

Federal Reserve Board

Gannon: Governor Carter, one important part of the government's economic policy, an apparatus we haven't talked about, is the Federal Reserve Board. I'd like to ask you something about what you said, and that is that you believe that a President ought to have a chairman of the Federal Reserve Board whose views are compatible with his own. Based on the record of the last few years, would you say that your views are compatible with those of Chairman Arthur Burns? And if not, would you seek his resignation if you are elected?

Carter: What I have said is that the President ought to have a chance to appoint a chairman of the Federal Reserve Board to have a co-terminous term: in other words, both of them serve the same four years. The Congress can modify the supply of money by modifying the income tax laws. The President can modify the economic structure of our country by public statements and general attitudes on the budget that he proposes. The Federal Reserve has an independent status that ought to be preserved. I think that Mr. Burns did take a typical erroneous Republican attitude in the 1973 year when inflation was so high. They assume that the inflation rate was because of excessive demand, and therefore put into effect tight constraint on the economy, very high interest rates, which is typical also of a Republican administration, tried to increase the tax payments by individuals, cut the tax payments by corporations.

I would have done the opposite. I think the problem should have been addressed by increasing productivity, by putting people back to work so they could purchase more goods; lower income taxes on individuals, perhaps raise them if necessary on corporations in comparison. But Mr. Burns, in that respect, made a very serious mistake.

I would not want to destroy the independence of the Federal Reserve Board, but I do think that we ought to have a cohesive economic policy with at least a chairman of the Federal Reserve Board and the President's terms being the same, and then the Congress, of course be the third entity with independence, subject only to the President's veto.

Newman: President Ford, your response?

Ford: The chairman of the Federal Reserve Board should be independent. Fortunately, he has been during Democratic as well as Republican administrations. As a result, in the last two years, we have had a responsible monetary policy.

The Federal Reserve Board indicated that the supply of money would be held between four to four and a half per cent and seven to seven and a half per cent. They have done a good job in integrating the money supply with the fiscal policy of the executive and legislative branches of the government.

It would be catastrophic if the chairman of the Federal Reserve Board became the tool of the political party that was in power. It's important for our future economic security that that job be non-political, and separate from the executive and the legislative branches

Intelligence Agency Abuses

Drew: Mr. President, the real problem with the FBI, in fact all of the intelligence agencies, there are no real laws governing them. Such laws as there are tend to be vague and open-ended. Now, you have issued some executive orders, but we've learned that leaving these agencies to executive discretion and direction can get them and in fact the country in a great deal of trouble. One President may be a decent man, the next one might not be. So, what do you think about trying to write in some more protection by getting some laws governing these agencies?

Ford: You are familiar, of course, with the fact that I am the first President in 30 years who has reorganized the intelligence agencies in the federal government, the CIA, the defense intelligence agency, the National Security Agency and the others. We've done that by executive order, and I think we've tightened it up. We've straightened out their problems developed over the last few years. It doesn't seem to me that it's needed or necessary to have legislation in this particular regard.

I have recommended to the Congress, however, I'm sure you're familiar with this, legislation that would make it very proper in the right way that the attorney general could go in and get the right for wiretapping under security cases. This was an effort that was made by the attorney general and myself, working with the Congress. But even in this area, where I think new legislation, where I think new legislation would be justified, the Congress has not responded. So I feel in that case, as well as in the reorganization of the intelligence agencies, as I've done, we have to do it by executive order.

And I'm glad that we have a good director in George Bush, we have good executive orders and the CIA and the DIA and NASA, or NSA are now doing a good job under proper supervision.

Newman: Governor Carter?

Carter: Well, one of the very serious things that's happened in our government in very recent years, and it's continued to mount up until now—is the break-down in the trust among our people in that....

(Here the audio was lost for 28 minutes.)

Carter: There has been too much government secrecy and not enough respect for the personal privacy of American citizens.

Concluding Statements

Newman: It is now time for the closing statements, which can be up to four minutes long. Governor Carter, by the same toss of the coin that directed to you, you are to go first now.

Carter: Well, tonight we've had a chance to talk a lot about the past. But I think it's time to talk about the future. Our nation in the last eight years has been divided as never before. It's a time for unity, it's a time to draw ourselves together. To have a President and a Congress that can work together with mutual respect for a change. Cooperating for a change. And open for a change, so the people can understand their own government.

It's time for government, industry and labor, manufacturing, agriculture, education, all the entities in our society, to cooperate. It's a time for government to understand and to cooperate with our people.

For a long time our American citizens have been excluded, sometimes misled, sometimes have been lied to. This is not compatible with the purpose of our nation.

I believe in our country. It needs to be competent, the government needs to be well-managed efficient, economical. We need to have a government that's sensitive to our people's needs, to those who are old and poor, who don't have adequate health care, who have been cheated too long with our tax programs, who've been out of jobs, whose families have been torn apart.

We need to restore the faith and the trust of the American people in their own government. In addition to that, we've suffered because we haven't had leadership in this administration. We've got a government of stalemate, with loss of vision of what our country can and ought to be. This is not the America that we've known in the past. It's not the America that we have to have in the future.

I don't plan to know all the answers, but I've got confidence in my country, our economic strength is still there. Our system of government, in spite of Vietnam, Cambodia, CIA, Watergate, has still the best system of government on earth.

And the greatest resources of all are the 215-million Americans who still have within us the strength, the character, the intelligence, the experience, the patriotism, the idealism, the compassion, the sense of brotherhood, all of which we can rely on the future to restore the greatness to our country. We ought not to be excluded from our government any more. We need a President who can go in, who derives a strength from the people.

I owe of the special interests nothing. I owe everything to you, the people of this country. And I believe we can bind our wounds, I believe that we can work together, and I believe that if we can tap the tremendous untapped reservoir of innate strength in this country, then we can once again have a government as good as our people. And let the world know what we still know and hope for, that we still live in

the greatest and the strongest and the best country on earth.

Newman: President Ford?

Ford: On November 2nd, all of you will make a very, very important decision. One of the major issues in this campaign is trust. A President should never promise more than he can deliver. And a President should always deliver everything that he's promised. A President can't be all things to all people, a President should be the same thing to all people.

Another issue in this campaign, Governor Carter has endorsed the Democratic Platform, which calls for more spending, bigger deficits, more inflation, and more taxes. Governor Carter has embraced the record of the present Congress dominated by his political party. It calls for more of the same. Governor Carter in his acceptance speech called for more and more programs which means more and more government.

I think the real issue in this campaign, that which you must decide on November 2nd, is whether you should vote for his promises or my performance in two years in the White House.

On the 4th of July we had a wonderful 200th birthday for our great country. It was a superb occasion, it was a glorious day. In the first century of our nation's history, our forefathers gave us the finest form of government in the history of mankind. In the second century of our nation's history our forefathers developed the most productive industrial nation in the history of the globe.

Our third century should be the century of individual freedom for all our 215-million Americans today and all that join us. In the last few years government has gotten bigger and bigger, industry has gotten larger and larger, labor unions have gotten bigger and bigger. And our children have been the victims of mass education. We must make this next century the century of the individual. We should never forget that a government big enough to give us everthing we want is a government big enough to take from us everything we have. The individual worker in the plants throughout the United States should not be a small cog in a big machine. The member of a labor union must have his rights strengthened and broadened, and our children in their education should have an opportunity to improve themselves, based on their talents and their abilities.

My mother and father, during the depression, worked very hard to give me an opportunity to do better in our great country. Your mothers and fathers did the same thing for you and others. Betty and I have worked very hard to give our children a brighter future in the United States, our beloved country. You and others in this great country have worked hard and done a great deal to give your children and your grandchildren the blessings of a better America. I believe we can all work together to make the individual in the future have more, and all of us working together can build a better America. ∎

Transcript of Second Ford-Carter Debate

Following is the United Press International transcript of the second election debate between President Gerald R. Ford and Democratic challenger Jimmy Carter. The debate took place Oct. 6, 1976, at the Palace of Fine Arts in San Francisco. The moderator was Pauline Frederick of The Public Broadcasting System. The panelists were Max Frankel of The New York Times, *Henry Trewhitt of* The Baltimore Sun *and Richard Valeriani of NBC News.*

Carter Statement

Q: Governor since the Democrats last ran our foreign policy, including many of the men who are advising you, the country has been relieved of the Vietnam agony and the military draft, we've started arms control negotiations with the Russians, we've opened relations with China, we've arranged the disengagement of the Middle East, we've regained influence with the Arabs without deserting Israel. Now, maybe, we've even begun a process of peaceful change in Africa. Now you've objected in this campaign to the style with which much of this is done and you've mentioned some other things that you think ought to have been done. But do you really have a quarrel with this Republican record? Would you not have done any of those things?

Carter: Well, I think the Republican administration has been almost all style and spectacular and not substance. We've got a chance tonight to talk about first of all leadership, the character of our country and a vision of the future. And in every one of these instances the Ford administration has failed. And I hope tonight that I and Mr. Ford will have a chance to discuss the reason for those failures. Our country is not strong anymore. We're not respected anymore. We can only be strong overseas if we're strong at home. And when I become President, we'll not only be strong in those areas but also in defense. A defense capability second to none.

We've lost in our foreign policy the character of the American people. We've ignored or excluded the American people and Congress from participation in shaping of our foreign policy. It has been one of secrecy or exclusion. In addition to that we've had a chance to become now, contrary to our longstanding beliefs and principles, the arms merchant of the whole world. We've tried to buy success from our enemies at the same time we've excluded from the process the normal friendship of our allies. In addition to that, we've become fearful to compete with the Soviet Union on an equal basis. We talk about detente. The Soviet Union knows what they want in detente,

and they've been getting it. We have not known what we've wanted and we've been out-traded in almost every instance.

The other point I want to make is about our defense. We've got to be a nation blessed with a defense capability—efficient, tough, capable, well organized, narrowly focused fighting capability. The ability to fight, if necessary, is the best way to avoid the chance for or the requirement to fight.

And the last point I want to make is this. Mr. Ford and Mr. Kissinger have continued on with the policies of Richard Nixon. Even the Republican platform has criticized the lack of leadership in Mr. Ford and they criticized the foreign policy of his administration. This is one instance in which I agree with the Republican platform.

I might say this in closing, and that is that as far as foreign policy goes, Mr. Kissinger has been the President of this country. Mr. Ford has shown an absence of leadership, and an absence of a grasp of what this country is and what it ought to be. That's got to be changed, and that is one of the major issues of this campaign in 1976.

Ford: Gov. Carter again is talking in broad generalities. Let me take just one question that he raises: The military strength and capability of the United States. Gov. Carter in November of 1975 indicated that he wanted to cut the defense budget by $15-billion. A few months later he said he wanted to cut the defense budget by $8-billion or $9-billion. And more recently he talks about cutting the defense budget by $5-billion to $7-billion. There is no way you can be strong militarily and have those kind of reductions in our military appropriations.

Now let me tell you a little story. About late October of 1975, I asked the then Secretary of Defense, Mr. Schlesinger, to tell me what had to be done if we were going to reduce the defense budget by $3-billion to $5-billion.

A few days later Mr. Schlesinger came back and said if we cut the defense budget by $3-billion to $5-billion, we will have to cut military personnel by 250,000; civilian personnel by 100,000; jobs in America by 100,000. We would have to stretch out our aircraft procurement. We would have to reduce our naval construction program. We would have to reduce our research and development for the Army, the Navy, the Air Force and Marines by 8 per cent. We would have to close 20 military bases in the United States immediately. That's the kind of a defense program that Mr. Carter wants.

Let me tell you this straight from the shoulder: You don't negotiate with Mr. Brezhnev from weakness, and the kind of a defense program that Mr. Carter wants will mean a weaker defense and a poor negotiating position.

Q: Mr. President, my question is really the other side of the coin. For a generation, the United States has had a foreign policy based on containment of communism. Yet we have lost the first war in Vietnam. We lost a shoving match in Angola. The Communists threatened to come to power by peaceful means in Italy and relations generally have cooled with the Soviet Union in the last few months. So let me ask you first, what do you do about such cases as Italy? And secondly, does this general drift mean that we're moving back toward something of a cold war relationship with the Soviet Union?

Ford: I don't believe we should move to a cold war relationship. I think it's in the best interest of the United States, and the world as a whole, that the United States negotiate rather than go back to the cold war relationship with the Soviet Union.

I don't look at the picture as bleakly as you indicated in your question, Mr. Trewhitt. I believe that the United States has had many successes in recent years, in recent months as far as the Communist movement is concerned. We have been successful in Portugal, where a year ago it looked like there was a very great possibility that the Communists would take over in Portugal. It didn't happen. We have democracy in Portugal today.

A few months ago, I should say maybe two years ago, the Soviet Union looked like they had continued strength in the Middle East. Today, according to Prime Minister Rabin, the Soviet Union is weaker in the Middle East than they have been in many, many years. The facts are the Soviet Union relationship with Egypt is at a low level. The Soviet Union relationship with Syria is at a very low point. The United States today, according to Prime Minister Rabin of Israel, is at a peak in its influence and power in the Middle East.

But let's turn a minute to the southern African operations that are now going on. The United States of America took the initiative in southern Africa. We wanted to end the bloodshed in southern Africa. We wanted to have the right of self-determination in Africa. We wanted to have majority rule with the full protection of the rights of the minority. We wanted to preserve human dignity in southern Africa. We have taken the initiative, and in southern Africa today the United States is trusted by the black front line nations and black Africa. The United States is trusted by the other elements in southern Africa.

The United States' foreign policy under this administration has been one of progress and success. And I believe that instead of talking about Soviet progress we can talk about American successes. And may I make an observation part of the question you asked, Mr. Trewhitt. I don't believe it's in the best interest of the United States and the NATO nations to have a Communist government in NATO. Mr. Carter has said he would look with sympathy to a Communist government in NATO. I think that would destroy the integrity and the strength of NATO and I am totally opposed to it.

Carter: Unfortunately, he's just made a statement that's not true. I have never advocated a Communist government for Italy. That would obviously be a ridiculous thing for anyone to do who wanted to be President of this country. I think that this is an instance of deliberate distortion, and this has occurred also in the question about defense.

As a matter of fact, I've never advocated any cut of $15-billion in our defense budget. As a matter of fact, Mr. Ford has made a political football out of the defense budget. About a year ago, he cut the Pentagon budget $6.8-billion. After he fired James Schlesinger, the political heat got so great that he added back about $3-billion. When Ronald Reagan won the Texas primary election, Mr. Ford added back another $1.5-billion. Immediately before the Kansas City convention he added back another $1.8-billion in the defense budget.

And his own Office of Management and Budget testified that he had a $3-billion cut insurance added to the defense budget under pressure from the Pentagon. Obviously this is another indication of trying to use the defense budget for political purposes, like he's trying to do tonight.

Now we went into South Africa late; after Great Britain, Rhodesia, the black nations had been trying to solve this problem for many years. We didn't go in until right before the election, similar to what had taken place in 1972 when Mr. Kissinger announced peace was at hand just before the election at that time. And we have weakened our position in NATO because the other countries in Europe supported the democratic forces in Portugal long before we did. We stuck to the Portugal dictatorships much longer than other democracies did in this war.

Experience, Secrecy

Q: Gov. Carter, much of what the United States does abroad is done in the name of the national interest. What is your concept of the national interest? What should the role of the United States be and in that connection, concerning your limited experience in foreign affairs and the fact that you take some pride in being a Washington outsider, don't you think it would be appropriate to tell the American voters, before the election, the people you would like to have in key positions such as Secretary of State, Secretary of Defense, national security affairs adviser at the White House?

Carter: Well, I'm not going to name my Cabinet before I get elected. I've got a little ways to go before I start doing that. But I have an adequate background I believe. I am a graduate of the U.S. Naval Academy, the first military graduate since Eisenhower. I served as governor of Georgia and have traveled extensively in foreign

countries and South America, Central America, Europe, the Middle East and in Japan. I've traveled the last 21 months among the people of this country. I've talked to them and I've listened. And I've seen it first hand in a very vivid way the deep hurt that's come to this country in the aftermath of Vietnam and Cambodia and Chile and Pakistan and Angola and Watergate, CIA revelations.

What we were formerly so proud of—the strength of our country, its moral integrity, the representation in foreign affairs of what our people or what our Constitution stands for has been gone in the secrecy that has surrounded our foreign policy in the last few years. The American people, the Congress have been excluded.

I believe I know what this country ought to be. I've been one who's loved my nation as many Americans do and I believe there's no limit placed in what we can do in the future if we can harness the tremendous resources, militarily, economically and the stature of our people, the meaning of our Constitution in the future.

Every time we've had a serious mistake in foreign affairs, it's been because the American people have been excluded from the process. If we can just tap the intelligence and ability, the sound common sense and the good judgment of the American people, we can once again have a foreign policy to make us proud instead of ashamed, and I'm not going to exclude the American people from that process in the future as Mr. Ford and Kissinger have done.

This is what it takes to have a sound foreign policy—strong at home, strong defense, permanent commitments, not betray the principles of our country, and involve the American people and the Congress in the shaping of our foreign policy. Everytime Mr. Ford speaks from a position of secrecy in negotiations and secret treaties that have been pursued and achieved, in supporting dictatorships, in ignoring human rights, we are weak and the rest of the world knows it.

So these are the ways that we can restore the strength of our country, and they don't require a long experience in foreign policy. Nobody has that except a President who's served a long time or a Secretary of State. But my background, my experience, my knowledge of the people of this country, my commitment to our principles that don't change, those are the best bases to correct the horrible mistakes of this administration and restore our own country to a position of leadership in this world.

Q: How specifically, governor, are you going to bring the American people into the decision-making process in foreign policy? What does that mean?

Carter: First of all, I would quit conducting the decision-making process in secret, as has been the characteristic of Mr. Kissinger and Mr. Ford. In many instances we've made agreements, like in Vietnam, that have been revealed later on to our embarrassment.

Recently Ian Smith, the president of Rhodesia, announced that he had unequivocal commitments from Mr. Kissinger that he could not reveal. The American people don't know what those commitments are. We've seen in the past a destruction of the elected governments like in Chile and the strong support of military dictatorship there. These kinds of things have hurt us very much.

I would restore the concept of the fireside chat, which was an integral part of the administration of Franklin Roosevelt, and I would also restore the involvement of the Congress.

When Harry Truman was President he was not afraid to have a strong Secretary of Defense. Dean Acheson, George Marshall were strong Secretaries of Defense, excuse me, State. But he also made sure that there was a bipartisan support. The members of Congress—Arthur Vandenburg, Walter George—were part of the process. And before our nation made a secret agreement, before we made a bluffing statement, we were sure that we had the backing not only of the President and the Secretary of State but also of the Congress and the people. This is the responsibility of the President, and I think it's very damaging to our country that Mr. Ford has turned over this responsibility to the Secretary of State.

Ford: Governor Carter again contradicts himself. He complains about secrecy and yet he is quoted as saying that in the attempt to find a solution in the Middle East that he would hold unpublicized meetings with the Soviet Union, I presume for the purpose of imposing a settlement on Israel and the Arab nations.

But let me talk just a minute about what we've done to avoid secrecy in the Ford administration. After the United States took the initiative in working with Israel and with Egypt in achieving the Sinai II Agreement—and I'm proud to say that not a single Egyptian or Israeli soldier has lost his life since the signing of the Sinai Agreement. But at the time that I submitted the Sinai Agreement to the Congress of the United States, I submitted every single document that was applicable to the Sinai II Agreement. It was the most complete documentation by any President of any agreement signed by a President on behalf of the United States.

Now as far as meeting with the Congress is concerned, during the 24 months that I've been the President of the United States, I have averaged better than one meeting a month with responsible groups or committees of the Congress, both House and Senate. The Secretary of State has appeared in the several years that he's been the Secretary before 80 different committee hearings in the House and in the Senate. The Secretary of State has made better than 50 speeches all over the United States explaining American foreign policy. I have made myself at least 10 speeches in various parts of the country where I have discussed with the American people defense and foreign policy.

Soviets, Eastern Europe

Q: Mr. President, I'd like to explore a little more deeply our relationship with the Russians. Now, they used to brag during Kruschev's day that because of their greater patience and because of our greed for business deals that they would sooner or later get the better of us. Is it possible that, despite some setbacks in the Middle East, they've proved their point? Our allies in France and Italy are now flirting with Communism. We've recognized a permanent Communist regime in East Germany. We've virtually signed in Helsinki an agreement that the Russians have dominance in Eastern Europe. We've bailed out Soviet agriculture with our huge grain sales, we've given them large loans, access to our best technology, and if the Senate hadn't interfered with the Jackson amendment, maybe you would have given them even larger loans. Is that what you call a two-way street of traffic in Europe?

Ford: I believe that we've negotiated with the Soviet Union since I've been President from a position of strength. And let me cite several examples.

Shortly after I became President, in December of 1974, I met with General Secretary Breshnev in Vladivostok, and we agreed to a mutual cap on ballistic missile launchers at a ceiling of 2,400, which means that the Soviet Union, if that becomes a permanent agreement, will have to make a reduction in their launchers that they now have or plan to have. I've negotiated at Vladivostok with Mr. Breshnev a limitation on the MIRVing of their ballistic missiles at a figure of 1,320, which is the first time that any President has achieved a cap, either on launchers or on MIRVs.

It seems to me that we can go from there to the grain sales. The grain sales have been a benefit to American agriculture. We have achieved a 5¾ year sale of a minimum of 6 million metric tons, which means that they have already bought about 4 million metric tons this year and are bound to buy another 2 million metric tons, to take the grain and corn and wheat that American farmers have produced in order to have full production, and these grain sales to the Soviet Union have helped us tremendously in meeting the costs of the additional oil, and the oil that we have bought from overseas.

If we turn to Helsinki, I'm glad you raised it Mr. Frankel. In the case of Helsinki, 35 nations signed an agreement, including the Secretary of State for the Vatican. I can't under any circumstances believe that his Holiness the Pope would agree by signing that agreement that the 35 nations have turned over to the Warsaw Pact nations the domination of Eastern Europe. It just isn't true, and if Mr. Carter alleges that His Holiness, by signing that has done, he is totally inaccurate.

Now what has been accomplished by the Helsinki agreement—number one—we have an agreement where they notify us and we notify them of any military maneuvers that are to be undertaken. They have done

it in both cases where they've done so. There is no Soviet domination of Eastern Europe and there never will be under a Ford administration.

Q: I'm sorry, could I just follow? Did I understand you to say, sir, that the Russians are not using Eastern Europe as their own sphere of influence and occupying most of the countries there and making sure with their troops that it's a Communist zone, whereas on our side of the line, the Italians and the French are still flirting with communism?

Ford: I don't believe, Mr. Frankel, that the Yugoslavians consider themselves dominated by the Soviet Union. I don't believe that the Romanians consider themselves dominated by the Soviet Union. I don't believe that the Poles consider themselves dominated by the Soviet Union. Each of those countries is independent or autonomous. It has its own territorial integrity, and the United States does not concede that those countries are under the domination of the Soviet Union. As a matter of fact, I visited Poland, Yugoslavia and Romania to make certain that the people of those countries understood that the President of the United States and the people of the United States are dedicated to their independence, their autonomy and their freedom.

Carter: Well, in the first place, I'm not criticizing His Holiness the Pope. I was talking about Mr. Ford. The fact is that secrecy has surrounded the decisions made by the Ford administration.

In the case of the Helsinki agreement—it may have been a good agreement at the beginning, but we have failed to enforce the so-called basket three part, which ensures the right of people to migrate, to join their families, to be free, to speak out. The Soviet Union is still jamming Radio Free Europe. Radio Free Europe is still being jammed. We have also seen a very serious problem with the so-called Sonnenfeld document—which apparently Mr. Ford has just endorsed—which says there is an organic linkage between the Eastern European countries and the Soviet Union. And I would like to see Mr. Ford convince the Polish Americans and the Czech Americans and the Hungarian Americans in this country that those countries don't live under the domination and the supervision of the Soviet Union behind the Iron Curtain.

We also have seen Mr. Ford exclude himself from access to the public. He hasn't had a tough, cross examination press conference in over 30 days. One press conference he had without sound.

He's always shown a weakness in yielding to pressure. The Soviet Union, for instance, put pressure on Mr. Ford and he refused to see a symbol of human freedom recognized around the world, Aleksandr Solzhenitzyn. The Arabs have put pressure on Mr. Ford, and he's yielded and has permitted a boycott by the Arab countries of American businesses who trade with Israel or have American Jews owning or taking

part in the management of American companies. His own Secretary of Commerce had to be subpoenaed by the Congress to reveal the names of businesses who were subject to this boycott. They didn't volunteer the information: he had to be subpoenaed.

And the last thing I'd like to say is this. This grain deal with the Soviet Union in '72 was terrible, and Mr. Ford made up for it with three embargoes, one against our own ally Japan. That's not the way to run our foreign policy, including international trade.

Middle East Arms

Q: Governor, I'd like to pick up on that point, actually, and on your appeal for a greater measure of American idealism in foreign affairs. Foreign affairs come home to the American public in such issues as oil embargoes and grain sales—that sort of thing. Would you be willing to risk an oil embargo in order to promote human rights in Iran, Saudi Arabia, withhold arms from Saudi Arabia for the same purpose—or I think, for a matter of fact you've perhaps answered this final part, but would you withhold grain from the Soviet Union in order to promote civil rights in the Soviet Union?

Carter: I would never single out food as a trade embargo item. If I ever decided to impose an embargo because of a crisis in international relationships, it would include all shipments of all equipment. For instance, if the Arab countries ever again declare an embargo against our nation on oil, I would consider that not a military but an economic declaration of war. And I would respond instantly and in kind. I would not ship that Arab country anything—no weapons, no spare parts for weapons, no oil drilling rigs, no oil pipe, no nothing. I wouldn't single out just food.

Another thing that I'd like to say is this: in our international trade, as I said in my opening statement, we have become the arms merchant of the world. When this Republican administration came into office we were shipping about $1-billion worth of arms overseas. Now, $10- to $12-billion worth of arms overseas to countries, which quite often use these arms to fight each other. This shift in emphasis has been very disturbing to me.

Speaking about the Middle East, under the last Democratic administration, 60 per cent of all weapons that went into the Middle East were for Israel. Nowadays—75 per cent went for Israel before—now, 60 per cent go to the Arab countries, and this does not include Iran. If you include Iran, our present shipment of weapons to the Middle East, only 20 per cent goes to Israel.

This is a deviation from idealism; it's a deviation from our commitment to our major ally in the Middle East, which is Israel; it's a yielding to economic pressure on the part of the Arabs on the oil issue and it's also a tremendous indication that under the Ford administration we have not addressed the energy policy adequately. We still have no comprehensive energy policy in this country. And it's an overall sign of weakness.

When we are weak at home economically—high unemployment, high inflation, a confused government, a wasteful defense establishment—this encourages the kind of pressure that has been put on us successfully. It would have been inconceivable 10 or 15 years ago for us to be brought to our knees with an Arab oil embargo. But it was done three years ago and they're still putting pressure on us from the Arab countries to our discredit around the world. These are the weaknesses that I see and I believe it is not just a matter of idealism, it's a matter of being tough, it's a matter of being strong, it's a matter of being consistent. Our priorities ought to first of all be to meet our own military needs, secondly to meet the needs of our allies and friends and only then should we ship military equipment to foreign countries.

As a matter of fact, Iran is going to get 80 F-14s before we even meet our own Air Force orders for F-14s, and the shipment of Spruance class destroyers to Iran are much more highly sophisticated than the Spruance class destroyers that are presently delivered to our own Navy. This is ridiculous and it ought to be changed.

Q: Governor, let me pursue that if I may. If I understand you correctly, you would, in fact, to use my examples, withhold arms from Iran and Saudi Arabia even if the risk was an oil embargo and they should be securing those arms from somewhere else and then if the embargo came, then you'd respond in kind. Do I have it correctly?

Carter: If—Iran is not an Arab country, as you know, it's a Moslem country—but if Saudi Arabia should declare an oil embargo against us, then I would consider that an economic declaration of war and I would make sure that the Saudians understood this ahead of time so that there would be no doubt in their mind. I think that under those circumstances they would refrain from pushing us to our knees as they did in 1973 with their previous oil embargo.

Ford: Governor Carter apparently doesn't realize that since I've been President we have sold to the Israelis over $4-billion in military hardware, we have made available to the Israelis over 45 per cent of the total economic and military aid since the establishment of Israel 27 years ago. So the Ford administration has done a good job in helping our good ally Israel and we're dedicated to the survival and security of Israel.

I believe that Governor Carter doesn't realize the need and necessity for arms sales to Iran. He indicates he would not make those. Iran is bordered very extensively by the Soviet Union. Iran has Iraq as one of its neighbors. The Soviet Union and the Communist-dominated government of Iraq are neighbors of Iran and Iran is an ally of the United States. It's my strong feeling that we ought to sell arms to Iran for its own national security and as an ally, a strong

ally of the United States. The history of our relationship goes back to the days of President Truman when he decided it was vitally necessary for our own security as well as for that of Iran that we should help that country, and Iran has been a good ally. In 1973 when there was an oil embargo, Iran did not participate. Iran continued to sell oil to the United States. I believe that it's in our interest and in the interest of Israel and Iran and Saudia Arabia to sell arms to those countries. It's for their security as well as ours.

China

Q: Mr. President, the policy of your administration is to normalize relations with mainland China. That means at some time establishing full diplomatic relations, and obviously doing something about the mutual defense treaty with Taiwan. If you are elected will you move to establish full diplomatic relations with Peking and will you abrogate the mutual defense treaty with Taiwan, and as a corollary would you provide mainland China with military equipment if the Chinese were to ask for it?

Ford: Our relationship with the People's Republic of China is based upon the Shanghai Communique of 1972 and that communique calls for the normalization of relations between the United States and the People's Republic. It doesn't set a time schedule, it doesn't make a determination as to how that relationship should be achieved in relationship to our current diplomatic recognition and obligations to the Taiwanese government. The Shanghai Communique does say that the differences between the People's Republic on the one hand and Taiwan on the other shall be settled by peaceful means. The net result is that this administration, and during my time as the President for the next four years, we will continue to move for normalization of relations in the traditional sense and we will insist that the disputes between Taiwan and the People's Republic be settled peacefully, as was agreed in the Shanghai Communique of 1972.

The Ford administration will not let down, will not eliminate or forget our obligations to the people of Taiwan. We feel that there must be a continued obligation to the people, the some 19 or 20 million people in Taiwan, and as we move during the next four years, those will be the policies of this administration.

Q: And, sir, the military equipment for the mainland Chinese?

Ford: There is no policy of this government to give to the People's Republic or to sell to the People's Republic of China military equipment. I do not believe that we, the United States, should sell, give or otherwise transfer military hardware to the People's Republic of China or any other Communist nation such as the Soviet Union and the like.

Q: Governor Carter?

Carter: Well, I'd like to go back just one moment to the previous question where Mr. Ford I think confused the issue by try-

ing to say that we were shipping Israel 40 per cent of our aid. As a matter of fact, during this current year we are shipping Iran, have contracted to ship to Iran, about $7.5-billion worth of arms, and also to Saudi Arabia about $7.5-billion worth of arms.

Also, in 1975 we almost brought Israel to their knees, after the Yom Kuppur war, by the so-called reassessment of our relationship to Israel. We in effect tried to make Israel the scapegoat for the problems in the Middle East and this weakened our relationship with Israel a great deal and put a cloud on the total commitment that our people feel toward the Israelis. There ought to be a clear, unequivocal commitment, without change, to Israel.

In the Far East I think we need to continue to be strong and I would certainly pursue the normalization of relationships with the People's Republic of China. We opened up a great opportunity in 1972, which pretty well has been frittered away under Mr. Ford, that ought to be a constant inclination towards friendship. But I would never let that friendship with the People's Republic of China stand in the way of the preservation of the independence and freedom of the people of Taiwan.

'Guns and Butter'

Q: Governor, we always seem in our elections, and maybe in between, too, to argue about who can be tougher in the world. Give or take a few billion dollars, give or take one weapons system, our leading politicians and I think you two gentlemen seem to settle roughly on the same strategy in the world at roughly the same Pentagon budget cost. How bad do things have to get in our own economy or how much backwardness and hunger would it take in the world to persuade you that our national security and our survival required very drastic cutbacks in arms spending and dramatic new efforts in other directions?

Carter: Well, always in the past we've had the ability to have a strong defense and also have a strong domestic economy and also to be strong in our reputation and influence within the community of nations. These characteristics of our country have been endangered under Mr. Ford. We are no longer respected. In a showdown vote in the United Nations or in any other international council, we are lucky to get 20 per cent of the other nations to vote with us. Our allies feel that we've neglected them. The so-called Nixon shock against Japan has weakened our relationships there. Under this administration, we've also had an inclination to keep separate the European countries, thinking that if they are separate then we can dominate them and proceed with our secret, Lone Ranger-type diplomatic efforts.

I would also like to point out that we in this country have let our economy go down the drain. The worst inflation since the Great Depression. The highest unemployment of any developed nation in the world. We have a higher unemployment rate in this country than Great Britain, than West

Germany. Our unemployment rate is twice as high as it is in Italy, it's three or four times as high as it is in Japan, and that terrible circumstance in this country is exported overseas. We comprise about 30 per cent of the world economic trade power influence. And when we're weak at home, weaker than all our allies, that weakness weakens the whole free world. So a strong economy is very important.

Another thing that we need to do is re-establish the good relationship that we ought to have between the United States and our natural allies in France. They have felt neglected. And using that base of strength, and using the idealism, the honesty, the predictability, the commitment and the integrity of our own country, that's where our strength lies. And that would permit us to deal with the developing nations in a position of strength.

Under this administration we've had a continuation of a so-called balance of power politics where everything is looked on as a struggle between us on the one side and the Soviet Union on the other. Our allies, the smaller countries, get trampled in the rush. What we need is to try to seek individualized bilateral relationships with countries regardless of their size and to establish world order politics, which means that we want to establish peace through strength. We also want to revert back to the stature. and the respect that our country had in previous administrations. Now, I can't say when this can come, but I can guarantee it will not come if Gerald Ford is re-elected and his present policies continue. It will come if I'm elected.

Q: If I hear you right, sir, you're saying guns and butter both. But President Johnson also had trouble keeping up Vietnam and his domestic program. I'm really asking when do the needs of the cities and our own needs, and those of other backward and even more needy countries and societies around the world take precedence over our own military spending? Ever?

Carter: Well, let me say very quickly that under President Johnson, in spite of the massive investment in the Vietnam War, he turned over a balanced budget to Mr. Nixon. The unemployment rate was less than 4 per cent, the inflation rate under Kennedy and Johnson was about 2 per cent—one-third what we have under this administration. So we did have at that time with good management the ability to do both. I don't think anybody can say that Johnson and Kennedy neglected the poor and destitute people in this country or around the world.

But I can say this, the number one responsibility of any President, above all else, is to guarantee the security of our nation. An ability to be free of the threat of attack or blackmail and to carry out our obligations to our allies and friends and to carry out a legitimate foreign policy. They must go hand in hand, but the security of this nation has got to come first.

Ford: Let me say very categorically, you cannot maintain the security and the

strength of the United State with the kind of defense budget cuts that Governor Carter has indicated. In 1975 he wanted to cut the budget $15-billion. He's now down to a figure of $5-billion to $7-billion. Reductions of that kind will not permit the United States to be strong enough to deter aggression and maintain the peace.

Governor Carter apparently doesn't know the facts. As soon as I became President, I initiated meetings with the NATO heads of state and met with them in Brussels to discuss how we could improve the defense relationship in western Europe. In November of 1975 I met with the leaders of the five industrial nations in France for the purpose of seeing what we could do, acting together, to meet the problems of the coming recession. In Puerto Rico this year, I met with six of the leading industrial nations' heads of state to meet the problem of inflation, so we would be able to solve it before it got out of hand.

I have met with the heads of government bilaterally as well as multilaterally. Our relations with Japan have never been better. I was the first United States President to visit Japan. And we had the Emperor of Japan here this past year, and the net result is Japan and the United States are working more closely together now than at any time in the history of our relationship.

You can go around the world, and let me take Israel for example. Just recently President Rabin said that our relations were never better.

SALT Negotiations

Q: Mr. President, you referred earlier to your meeting with Mr. Brezhnev at Vladivostok in 1974, and you agreed on that occasion to try to achieve another Strategic Arms Limitation SALT agreement within the year. Nothing happened in 1975, or not very much publicly at least, and those talks are still dragging and things got quieter as the current season approached. Is there a bit of politics involved there perhaps on both sides or, perhaps more important, are interim weapons developments—and I'm thinking of such things as the cruise missile and the Soviet SS20, intermediate range rocket—making SALT irrelevant, bypassing the SALT negotiations?

Ford: First we have to understand that SALT I expires Oct. 3, 1977. Mr. Brezhnev and I met in Vladivostok in December of 1974 for the purpose of trying to take the initial step so we could have a SALT II agreement that would go through 1985. As I indicated earlier, we did agree on a 2,400 limitation on launchers of ballistic missiles. That would mean a cutback in the Soviet program that would not interfere with our own program. At the same time we put a limitation of 1,320 on MIRV.

Our technicians have been working since that time in Geneva trying to put into technical language an agreement that can be verified by both parties, and in the meantime there has developed the problem of the Soviet Backfire, their high-

performance aircraft, which they say is not a long-range aircraft and which some of our people say is an intercontinental aircraft. In the interim, there has been the development on our part primarily the cruise missile. Cruise missiles that could be launched from land-based mobile installations. Cruise missiles which could be launched high performance aircraft like the B-52s or the B-1s, which I hope we proceed with. Cruise missiles which could be launches from either surface or submarine naval vessels.

Those gray area weapon systems are creating some problems in that the agreement for a SALT II negotiation. But I can say that I am dedicated to proceeding and I met just last week with the foreign minister of the Soviet Union and he indicated to me that the Soviet Union was interested in narrowing the differences and making a realistic and a sound compromise.

I hope and trust, in the best interests of both countries and in the best interests of all peoples throughout this globe, that the Soviet Union and the United States can make a mutually beneficial agreement. Because if we do not and SALT I expires on Oct. 3, 1977, you will unleash an all-out nuclear arms race with the potential of a nuclear holocaust of unbelievable dimension. So it is the obligation of the President to do just that, and I intend to do so.

Q: Mr. President, let me follow that up. I'll submit that the cruise missile adds a whole new dimension to the arms competition, and then cite a statement by your office to the Arms Control Association a few days ago in which you said that the cruise missile might eventually be included in a comprehensive arms limitation agreement, but that in the meantime it was an essential part of the American strategic arsenal. Now, may I assume from that you're intending to exclude the cruise missile from the next SALT agreement? Or is it still negotiable?

Ford: I believe that the cruise missiles which we are now developing in research and development across the spectrum, from the air, sea or from the land, can be included in a SALT II agreement. They are a new weapon system that has a great potential, both convention and nuclear arms. At the same time, we have to make certain the Soviet Union's Backfire, which they claim is not an intercontinental aircraft and which some of our people contend is, must also be included if we are to get the kind of agreement which is in the best interest of both countries. And I really believe that it's far better for us, and for the Soviet Union, and more importantly for the people around the world, that these two super powers find an answer for a SALT II agreement before Oct. 3, 1977. I think goodwill on both parts, hard bargaining by both parties and a reasonable compromise will be in the best interest of all parties.

Carter: Well, Mr. Ford acts like he's running for President for the first time. He's been in office two years, and there has been absolutely no progress made toward a new

SALT agreement. He has learned the date of the expiration of SALT I apparently. We've seen in this world a development of a tremendous threat to us. As a nuclear engineer myself, I know the limitations and capabilities of atomic power. I also know that as far as the human beings on this earth are concerned, that the nonproliferation of atomic weapons is number one.

Only in the last few days, with the election approaching, has Mr. Ford taken any interest in the nonproliferation movement. I advocated last May in a speech at the United Nations that we move immediately as a nation to declare a complete moratorium on the testing of all nuclear devices, both weapons and peaceful devices—that we not ship any more atomic fuel to a country which refuses to comply with strict controls over the waste, which can be reprocessed into explosives. I've also advocated that we stop the sale by Germany and France of reprocessing plants to Pakistan and Brazil, and Mr. Ford hasn't moved on them. We also need to provide an adequate supply of enriched uranium. Mr. Ford again, under pressure from the atomic energy lobby, has insisted that this reprocessing or rather re-enrichment be done by private industry and not by the existing government plants.

This kind of confusion and absence of leadership has let us drift now for two years, with the constantly increasing threat of atomic weapons throughout the world. We now have five nations that have atomic bombs that we know about. If we continue under Mr. Ford's policy, by 1985 or '90 we'll have 20 nations that have the capability of exploding atomic weapons. This has got to be stopped. That is one of the major challenges and major undertakings I will assume as the next President.

U.S. Strength

Q: Governor Carter, earlier tonight you said America is not strong anymore; America is not respected any more. I must ask you, do you really believe that the United States is not the strongest country in the world? Do you really believe that the United States is not the most respected country in the world? Or is that just campaign rhetoric?

Carter: No, it's not just campaign rhetoric. I think that militarily we are as strong as any nation on earth. I think we've got to stay that way and to continue to increase our capabilities to meet any potential threat. But as far as strength derived from commitment to principle; as far as strength derived from the unity within our country, as far as strength derived from the people, the Congress, the Secretary of State, the President, sharing in the evolution and carrying out of our foreign policy, as far as strength derived from the respect of our own allies and friends—so they're assured that we will be staunch in our commitment and will not deviate and will give them adequate attention—as far as strength derived from doing what is right, caring for the poor, providing food and becoming the bread-

basket of the world instead of the arms merchant of the world, in those respects we're not strong.

Also, we'll never be strong again overseas unless we're strong at home. And with our economy in such terrible disarray and getting worse by the month, we've got 500,000 more Americans unemployed today than we had three months ago. We've got 2.5 million Americans out of work now than we had when Mr. Ford took office. This kind of deterioration in our economic strength is bound to weaken us around the world.

And we not only have problems at home, but we export those problems overseas. So as far as respect of our own people toward our own government, as far as participation in shaping of concepts and commitments, as far as the trust of our country among the nations of the world, as far as dependence of our country in meeting the needs and obligations that we have expressed to our allies, as far as the respect of our country even among our particular adversaries, we are weak. Potentially, we are strong. Under this administration, that strength has not been realized.

Ford: Governor Carter brags about the unemployment during Democratic administrations, and condemns the unemployment of the present time. I must remind him that we're at peace, and during the period that he brags about unemployment being low the United States was at war.

Now let me correct one other comment that Governor Carter just made. I have recommended to the Congress that we develop the uranium enrichment plant at Portsmouth, Ohio, which is a publicly-owned, U.S. government facility. I have indicated that the private program which would follow on in Alabama is one that may or may not be constructed. But I am committed to the one at Portsmouth, Ohio.

The governor also talks about morality in foreign policy. The foreign policy of the United States meets the highest standards of morality. What is more moral than peace, and the United States is at peace today. What is more moral in foreign policy than for the administration to take the lead in the World Food Conference in Rome in 1974, when the United States committed 6 million metric tons of food—over 60 per cent of the food committed for the disadvantaged and underdeveloped nations of the world. The Ford administration wants to eradicate hunger and disease in our underdeveloped countries throughout the world. What is more moral than for the United States under the Ford administration to take the lead in southern Africa, in the Middle East? Those are initiatives in foreign policy which are of the highest moral standard, and that is indicative of the foreign policy of this country.

Morality

Q: Mr. President, can we stick with morality? For a lot of people, it seems to cover a bunch of sins. Mr. Nixon and Mr. Kissinger used to tell us that instead of

morality we had to worry in the world about living with and letting live all kinds of governments that we really didn't like—North and South Korean dictators, Chilean fascists, Chinese Communists, Iranian emperors and so on. They said the only way to get by in the wicked world is to treat others on the basis of how they treated us, and not how they treated their own people. But, more recently, we seem to have taken a different tack. We seem to have decided that it is part of our business to tell the Rhodesians, for instance, that the way they are treating their own black people is wrong and they've got to change their own government and put pressure on them. We're rather liberal in our advice to the Italians as to how to vote. Is this a new Ford foreign policy in the making? Can we expect that you are now going to turn to South Africa, force them to change their government, intervene in similar ways to end the bloodshed as you called it, say in Chile or Chilean prisons, or to throw our weight around for the values that we hold dear in America?

Ford: I believe that our foreign policy must express the highest standards of morality and the initiates that we took in southern Africa are the best examples of what this administration is doing and will continue to do in the next four years.

If the United States had not moved as we did in southern Africa, there's no doubt there would have been an acceleration of bloodshed in that part of the world. If we had not taken our initiative, it's very, very possible that the government of Rhodesia would have been overrun and that the Soviet Union and the Cubans would have dominated southern Africa. So the United States, seeking to preserve the principle of self-determination, to eliminate the possibility of bloodshed, to protect the rights of the minority as we insisted upon the rights of the majority, I believe followed the good conscience of the American people in foreign policy. And I believe that we have used our skill.

Secretary of State Kissinger has done a superb job in working with the black African nations' so-called front line nations. He has done a superb job in getting the prime minister of South Africa, Mr. Vorster, to agree that the time had come for a solution to the problem of Rhodesia. Secretary Kissinger in his meeting with Prime Minister Smith of Rhodesia was able to convince him that it was in the best interests of whites as well as blacks in Rhodesia to find an answer for a transitional government and then a majority government. This is a perfect example of the kind of leadership that the United States under this administration has taken. And I can assure you that this administration will follow that high moral principle in our future efforts in foreign policy.

Including our efforts in the Middle East, where it is vitally important because the Middle East is the crossroads of the world. There have been more disputes and it's an area where there's more volatility than any other place in the world. But because the Arab nations and the Israelis trust the United States we were able to take the lead in the Sinai II Agreement. And I can assure you the United States will take the leadership role in moving toward a comprehensive settlement of the Middle Eastern problems. I hope and trust as soon as possible and we will do with the highest moral principles.

Q: Mr. President, just clarify one point. There are lots of majorities in the world that feel they're being pushed around by minority governments. Are you saying they can not expect to look to us for, not just good cheer, but throwing our weight on their side in South Africa, or in Taiwan, or in Chile, to help change their governments as in Rhodesia?

Ford: I would hope that as we move to one area of the world from another...and the United States must not spread itself too thinly. That was one of the problems that helped to create the circumstances in Vietnam. But as we as a nation find that we are asked by the various parties, either one nation against another or individuals within a nation, that the United States will take the leadership and try to resolve the differences.

Let me take South Korea as an example. I have personally told President Park that the United States does not condone the kind of repressive measures that he has taken in that country. But I think in all fairness and equity we have to recognize the problem that South Korea has. On the north they have North Korea with 500,000 well-trained, well-equipped troops. They are supported by the People's Republic of China. They are supported by the Soviet Union.

South Korea faces a very delicate situation. Now the United States in this case, this administration has recommended a year ago and we have reiterated it again this year, that the United States, South Korea, North Korea and the People's Republic of China sit down at a conference table to resolve the problems of the Korean peninsula. This is a leadership role that the United States under this administration is carrying out. And if we do it, and I think the opportunities and the possibilities are getting better, we will have solved many of the internal domestic problems that exist in South Korea at the present time.

Carter: I noticed that Mr. Ford did not comment on the prisons in Chile. This is a typical example, maybe of many others, where this administration overthrew an elected government and helped to establish a military dictatorship. This has not been an ancient history story. Last year under Mr. Ford, of all the Food for Peace that went to South America, 85 per cent went to the military dictatorship in Chile.

Another point I want to make is this. He says we have to move from one area of the world to another. That's one of the problems with this administration's so-called shuttle diplomacy. While the Secretary of State's in one country, there are

almost 150 others wondering what we're going to do next; what will be the next secret agreement. We don't have a comprehensible, understandable foreign policy that deals with world problems or even regional problems.

Another thing that concerned me was what Mr. Ford said about unemployment, insinuating that under Johnson and Kennedy, that unemployment could only be held down when this country is at war. Karl Marx said that the free enterprise in a democracy can only continue to exist when they are at war or preparing for war. Karl Marx was the grandfather of communism. I don't agree with that statement. I hope Mr. Ford doesn't either.

He has put pressure on the Congress, and I don't believe Mr. Ford will even deny this, to hold up on non-proliferation legislation until the Congress agrees for an $8-billion program for private industry to start producing enriched uranium.

And the last thing I want to make is this. He talks about peace, and I'm thankful for peace. We were peaceful when Mr. Ford went into office. But he and Mr. Kissinger and others tried to start a new Vietnam in Angola and it was only the outcry of the American people and the Congress when this secret deal was discovered that prevented our renewed involvement in that conflagration which was taking place there.

Panama Canal

Q: Gov. Carter, before this event, the most communications I received concerned Panama. Would you, as President, be prepared to sign a treaty which at a fixed date yields the administrative and economic control of the Canal Zone, and shared defense, which as I understand, was the position the United States took in 1974?

Carter: Well, here again, the Panamanian question is one that's been confused by Mr. Ford. He had directed his diplomatic representatives to yield to the Panamanians full sovereignty over the Panama Canal Zone at the end of a certain period of time. When Mr. Reagan raised this question in Florida, Mr. Ford not only disavowed his instructions, but he also even dropped parenthetically his use of the word detente. I would never give up complete control or practical control of the Panama Canal Zone. But I would continue to negotiate with the Panamanians.

When the original treaty was signed back in the early 1900s, Theodore Roosevelt was President, Panama retained sovereignty over the Panama Canal Zone. We retained control as though we had sovereignty. Now I would be willing to go ahead with negotiations. I believe that we can share more fully responsibilities for the Panama Canal Zone with Panama. I would be willing to continue to raise the payment for shipment of goods through the Panama Canal Zone. I might even be willing to reduce to some degree our military emplacements in the Panama Canal Zone. But I would not relinquish the practical

control of the Panama Canal Zone anytime in the foreseeable future.

Ford: The United States must and will maintain complete access to the Panama Canal. The United States must maintain a defense capability of the Panama Canal and the United States will maintain our national security interest in the Panama Canal.

The negotiations for the Panama Canal started under President Johnson and have continued up to the present time. I believe those negotiations should continue but there are certain guidelines that must be followed and I just defined them.

Let me take just a minute to comment on something that Gov. Carter said on non-proliferation. In May of 1975, I called for a conference of nuclear suppliers. That conference has met six times. In May of this year, Gov. Carter took the first initiative, approximately 12 months after I had taken my initiative a year ago.

Mayaguez Episode

Q: Mr. President, the Government Accounting Office has just put out a report suggesting that you shot from the hip in the Mayaguez rescue mission, that you ignored diplomatic messages that a peaceful solution was in prospect. Why didn't you do more diplomatically at the time? And a related question: Did the White House try to prevent the release of that report?

Ford: The White House did not prevent the release of that report. On July 12 of this year, we gave full permission for the release of that report. I was very disappointed in the fact that the GAO released that report because I think it interjected political partisan politics at the present time.

But let me comment on that report. Somebody who sits in Washington, D.C., 18 months after the Mayaguez incident can be a very good grandstand quarterback. And let me make another observation. This morning I got a call from the skipper of the Mayaguez. He was furious because he told me it was the action of me, President Ford, that saved the lives of the crew of the Mayaguez. And I can assure you if we had not taken the strong and the forceful action that we did, we would have been criticized very, very severely for sitting back and not moving.

Capt. Miller is thankful. The crew is thankful. We did the right thing. It seems to me that those who sit in Washington 18 months after the incident are not the best judges of the decision-making process that had to be made by the National Security Council and by myself at the time the incident was developing in the Pacific. Let me assure you that we made every possible overture to the People's Republic of China and through them to the Cambodian government. We made diplomatic protest to the Cambodian government through the United Nations. Every possible diplomatic means was utilized. But at the same time, I had a responsibility—so did the National Security Council—to meet the problem at hand. And we handled it responsibly and I think Capt. Miller's testimony to that effect is the best evidence.

Carter: Well, I'm reluctant to comment on the recent report. I haven't read it. I think the American people have only one promise—that the facts about the Mayaguez be given to them accurately and completely.

Mr. Ford has been there for 18 months. He had the facts that were released today immediately after the Mayaguez incident. I understand that the report today is accurate. Mr. Ford has said, I believe, that it was accurate. That the White House made no attempt to block the issuing of that report, I don't know if that is exactly accurate or not. I understand that both the Secretary of the Department of State and the Defense Department have approved the accuracy of today's report, or yesterday's report, and also the National Security Agency.

I don't know what was right or what was wrong or what was done. The only thing I believe is that whatever the knowledge was that Mr. Ford had should have been given to the American people 18 months ago, after the Mayaguez incident occurred. This is what the American people want. When something happens and it endangers our national security, or when something happens that threatens our stature in the world, or when American people are endangered by the actions of a foreign country or just 40 sailors on the Mayaguez, we have to move aggressively and quickly to rescue them. But then after the immediate action was taken, I believe the President has an obligation to tell the American people the truth and not wait 18 months later for the report to be issued.

Boycott of Israel

Q: Governor Carter, if the price of gaining influence among the Arabs is closing our eyes a bit to their boycott against Israel, how would you handle it?

Carter: I believe that the boycott of American businesses by the Arab countries because those businesses trade with Israel or because they have American Jews who are owners or directors in the company is an absolute disgrace. This is the first time that I remember in the history of our country that we've let a foreign country circumvent or change our Bill of Rights. I'll do everything I can as President to stop the boycott of American businesses by the Arab countries.

It's not a matter of diplomacy or trade. It's a matter of morality. And I don't believe the Arab countries will pursue when we have a strong President who will protect the integrity of our country, the commitment of our constitutional Bill of Rights and protect people in this country who happen to be Jews. It may later be Catholics, it may later be Baptists who are threatened by some foreign country. But we ought to stand staunch. I think it's a disgrace that so far Mr. Ford's administration has blocked the passage of legislation that would have

revealed by law every instance of the boycott and it would have prevented the boycott from continuing.

Ford: Again Governor Carter is inaccurate. The Arab boycott action was first taken in 1952 and in November of 1975 I was the first President to order the executive branch to take action, affirmative action, through the Department of Commerce and other Cabinet departments, to make certain that no American businessman or business organization should discriminate against Jews because of an Arab boycott.

And I might add that my administration, and I'm very proud of it, is the first administration that has taken an antitrust action against companies in this country that have allegedly cooperated with the Arab boycott. Just on Monday of this week, I signed a tax bill that included an amendment that would prevent companies in the United States from taking a tax deduction if they have in any way whatsoever cooperated with the Arab boycott. And last week when we were trying to get the Export Administration Act through the Congress, necessary legislation, my administration went to Capitol Hill and tried to convince the House and the Senate that we should have an amendment on that legislation which would take strong and effective action against those who participate or cooperate with the Arab boycott.

One other point. Because the Congress failed to act, I am going to announce tomorrow that the Department of Commerce will disclose those companies that have participated in the Arab boycott. This is something that we can do, the Congress failed to do it and we intend to do it.

Q: Mr. President, if you get the accounting of missing in action you want from North Vietnam or Vietnam—I'm sorry—would you then be prepared to reopen negotiations for restoration of relations with that country?

Ford: Let me restate our policy. As long as Vietnam, North Vietnam, does not give us a full accounting of our missing in action, I will never go along with the admission of Vietnam to the United Nations. If they do give us a bona fide, complete accounting of the 800 MIAs, then I believe the United States should begin negotiation for the admission of Vietnam to the United Nations. But not until they have given us the full accounting of our MIAs.

Carter: One of the most embarrassing failures of the Ford administration and one that touches specifically on human rights is his refusal to appoint a presidential commission to go to Vietnam, to go to Laos, to go to Cambodia and try to trade for release of information on those who are missing in action in those wars. This is what the families of the MIAs want. So far, Mr. Ford has not done it. We've had several fragmentary efforts by members of the Congress, and by private citizens.

Several months ago, the Vietnam government said, 'We are ready to sit down

and negotiate for release of information on MIAs.' So far, Mr. Ford has not responded. I also would never normalize relationships with Vietnam nor permit them to join the United Nations until they've taken this action. But that's not enough. We need to have an active and aggressive action on the part of the President, the leader of this country, to seek out every possible way to get that information, which has kept the MIA families in despair and doubt, and Mr. Ford has just not done it.

Concluding Statements

Carter: The purpose of this debate and the outcome of this election will determine three basic things: leadership, upholding the principles of this country and proper priorities and commitments for the future. This election will also determine what kind of world we leave our children. Will it be a nightmare world, threatened with the proliferation of atomic bombs not just in five major countries but dozens of smaller countries that have been permitted to develop atomic weapons because of a failure of our top leadership to stop proliferation? Will we have a world of hunger and hatred? And will we be living in an armed camp, stripped of our friendship and allies, hiding behind a tight defense that's been drawn in around us because of fear from the outside world? Will we have a government of secrecy that excludes the American people from participation in making basic decisions and therefore covers up mistakes and makes it possible for our government, our government, to depart from the principles of our Constitution's Bill of Rights? Or will we have a world of peace, with the threat of atomic weapons eliminated, with full trade, with our people at work, inflation controlled, openness in government, our people proud once again, Congress, citizens, President, Secretary of State working in harmony, in unity toward a common future? A world where people have enough to eat, a world where we care about those who don't?

Can we become a breadbasket of the world instead of the arms merchant of the world? I believe we can and we ought to. And we've been hurt in recent years in this country, in the aftermath of Vietnam, Cambodia, Chile, Pakistan, Angola, Watergate, CIA, we've been hurt. Our people feel that we've lost something precious. That's not necessary. I want to see our nation return to a posture, an image, a standard to make us proud once again. I remember the world of NATO and a world of Point Four and a world of the Marshall Plan and a world of Peace Corps. Why can't we have that once again? We ought to be a beacon for nations who search for peace and who search for freedom, who search for individual liberty, who search for basic human rights. We haven't been lately. We can be once again. We'll never have that world leadership until we're strong at home, and we can have that strength if we return to the basic principles. It ought not to be a strength of bombastic threats. It ought to be a quiet strength, based on the integrity of our people, the vision of the Constitution, an innate strong will and purpose that God's given us in the greatest nation on earth.

Ford: As we have seen tonight, foreign policy and defense policy are difficult and complex issues. We can debate methods, we can debate one decision or another. But there are two things which cannot be debated: experience and results.

In the last two years I have made policy decisions involving long range difficulties in policy, and made day-to-day judgments, not only as President of the United States, but as leader of the free world. What is the result of that leadership? America is strong, America is free, America is respected. Not a single young American today is fighting or dying on any foreign battlefield. America is at peace with freedom. Thank you. ∎

Transcript of Third Ford-Carter Debate

Following is the transcript of the third debate. It took place at William and Mary College Oct. 22. The moderator was Barbara Walters of ABC. Panelists were columnist Joseph Kraft, Robert Maynard of The Washington Post *and Jack Nelson of* The Los Angeles Times.

Future Sacrifices

Q: Mr. President, I assume that the Americans all know that these are difficult times and that there's no pie in the sky and that they don't expect something for nothing. So, I'd like to ask you as a first question as you look ahead in the next four years, what sacrifices are you going to call on the American people to make, what price are you going to ask them to pay to realize your objectives? Let me add, Gov. Carter, that if you felt that it was appropriate to answer that question in your comments as to what price it would be appropriate for the American people to pay for a Carter administration, I think that would be proper, too. Mr. President?

Ford: Mr. Kraft [columnist Joseph Kraft], I believe that the American people in the next four years under a Ford administration will be called upon to make those sacrifices to preserve the peace which we have. Which means of course that we will have to maintain an adequate military capability, which means of course that I think we will have to add a few billion dollars to our defense appropriations to make certain that we have adequate strategic forces—adequate conventional forces.

I think the American people will be called upon to be in the forefront in getting leadership to the solution of those problems which must be solved in the Middle East, in southern Africa and any problems that might arise in the Pacific. The American people will be called upon to tighten their belts a bit in meeting some of the problems we face domestically.

I don't think that America can go on a big spending spree with a whole lot of new programs that would add significantly to the federal budget. I believe that the American people, given the leadership that I expect to give, would be willing to give this trust to preserve the peace and the necessary restraint at home to hold the lid on spending so that we, I think, could have a long-overdue and justified tax reduction for the middle-income people. Then I think the American people would be willing to make those sacrifices for peace and prosperity in the next four years.

Q: Mr. President, doesn't your policy really imply that we're going to have to have a fairly high rate of unemployment over a fairly long time, that growth is going to be fairly slow, and that we're not going to be able to do very much in the next four or five years to meet the basic agenda of our national needs in the cities, in health, in transit and a whole lot of things like that, aren't those the real costs?

Carter: Well, I must say first of all that I think in [the] case of the Carter administration the sacrifices will be much less. Mr. Ford's own environmental agency has projected a 10 per cent unemployment rate by 1978 if he's President. The American people are ready to make sacrifices if they are part of the process, if they know that [they] will be helping to make decisions and won't be excluded from being an involved party to the national purpose. The major effort we must put forward is to put our people back to work.

And I think that this is one example where a lot of people have selfish, grasping ideas now. I remember 1973 and the dark of the energy crisis, when President Nixon told the American people to make a sacrifice, to cut down on the waste of gasoline, to cut down on the speed of automobiles. There was a tremendous surge of patriotism, that "I want to make a sacrifice for my country." I think we can call together, with strong leadership from the White House, business, industry and labor, and say, "Let's have voluntary price restraints. Let's lay down some guidelines so we don't have continuing inflation."

We can also have an end to the extremes. We now have one extreme, for instance, of some welfare recipients who, by taking advantage of the welfare laws, the housing laws, the Medicaid laws and the food stamp laws, make over $10,000 a year, and they don't have to pay any taxes on it. At the other extreme, just 1 per cent of the richest people in our country derive 25 per cent of all the tax benefits. So both those extremes grasp for advantage, and the person who has to pay that expense is the middle-income family who's still working for a living, and they have to pay for the

Ford: No, Mr. Kraft, we're spending very significant amounts of money now, some $200-billion a year, almost 50 per cent of the total federal expenditure by the federal government at the present time for human needs. Now we will probably need to increase that to some extent. But we don't have to have growth in spending that will blow the lid off and add to the problems of inflation.

I believe that we can meet the problems within the cities of this country, and still give a tax reduction. I proposed, as you know, a reduction to increase the personal exemption from $750 to $1,000. With the fiscal program that I have, and if you look at the projection, it shows that we will reduce unemployment, that we will continue to win the battle against inflation, and at the same time give the kind of quality of life that I believe is possible in America. A job, a home for all those that'll work and save for it, safety in the streets, health care that is affordable. These things can be done if we have the right vision and the right restraint and the right leadership. rich who have privilege and for the poor who are not working.

But I think a balanced approach, with everybody being part of it and a striving for unselfishness, could help, as it did in 1973, to let people sacrifice for their own country. I know I'm ready for it. I think the American people are, too.

Level of the Campaign

Q: By all indications, the voters are so turned off by this election campaign so far that only half intend to vote. One major reason for this apathetic electorate appears to be the low level at which this campaign has been conducted. It has digressed frequently from important issues into allegations of blunder and brainwashing and fixations on lust and *Playboy*. What responsibility do you accept for the low level of this campaign for the nation's highest office?

Carter: I think the major reason for a decrease in participation that we have experienced ever since 1960 has been a deep discouragement of the American people about the performance of public officials. When you got 7½ to 8 million people out of work, and you've got three times as much inflation as you had during the last eight-year Democratic administration, and you have the highest deficits in history; when you have it becoming increasingly difficult for a family to put a child through college or to own a home, there's a natural inclination to be turned off. Also, in the aftermath of Vietnam and Cambodia and Watergate and the CIA revelations, people have felt that they've been betrayed by public officials.

I have to admit that in the heat of the campaign—I've been in 30 primaries during the springtime, I've been campaigning for 22 months—I've made some mistakes. And I think this is part of just being a human being. I have to say that my campaign has been an open one, and the *Playboy* interview has been of very great concern to me. I don't know how to deal with it exactly. I agreed to give the interview to *Playboy*. Other people have done it and are notable—Gov. Jerry Brown; Walter Cronkite; Albert Schweitzer; Mr. Ford's own Secretary of the Treasury, Mr. Simon; William Buckley; many other people. But they weren't running for President, and in retrospect, from hindsight, I would not have given that interview had I to do it over again.

If I should ever decide in the future to discuss my deep Christian beliefs and condemnation and sinfulness, I'll use another forum besides *Playboy*. But I can say this: I'm doing the best I can to get away from that, and during the next 10 days, the American people will not see the Carter campaign running television advertisements and newspaper advertisements based on a personal attack on President Ford's character.

I believe that the opposite is true with President Ford's campaign, and I hope that we can leave those issues in this next 10 days about personalities and mistakes of the past—we've both made some mistakes—and talk about unemployment, inflation, housing, education, taxation, government organization, stripping away of secrecy and the things that are crucial to the American people. I regret the things in my own long campaign that have been mistaken, but I'm trying to do away with those in the last 10 days.

Ford: I believe that the American people have been turned off in this election, Mr. Maynard [Robert Maynard of *The Washington Post*], for a variety of reasons. We have seen on Capitol Hill, in the Congress, a great many allegations of wrongdoing, of alleged immorality. Those are very disturbing to the American people. They wonder how an elected representative can serve them and participate in such activities serving in the Congress of the United States. Yes, and I'm certain many, many Americans were turned off by the revelations of Watergate, a very, very bad period of time in American political history. Yes, and thousands and maybe millions of Americans were turned off because of the problems that came out of our involvement in Vietnam.

But on the other hand, I found on July 4 of this year a new spirit born in America. We were celebrating our bicentennial, and I find that there is a movement as I travel around the country of greater interest in this campaign. Like many hard-working persons seeking public office in the campaign, inevitably sometimes you will use rather graphic language, and I'm guilty of that, just like I think most others in the political arena [are]. But I do make a pledge that in the next 10 days when we're asking the American people to make one of the most important decisions in their lifetime, because I think this election is one of the most vital in the history of America, that we do together what we can to stimulate voter participation.

House Watergate Investigation

Q: Mr. President, you mentioned Watergate, and you became President because of Watergate, so do you owe the American people a special obligation to explain in detail your role in limiting one of the original investigations of Watergate, that was the one by the House Banking Committee? Now I know you've answered questions on this before, but there are questions that still remain, and I think people want to know what your role was. Will you name the persons you talked to in connection with that investigation, and since you say you have no recollection of talking to anyone from the White House,

would you be willing to open for examination the White House tapes of conversations during that period?

Ford: Mr. Nelson [Jack Nelson of *The Los Angeles Times*], I testified before two committees, House and Senate, on precisely the questions that you have asked. And the testimony under oath was to the effect that I did not talk to Mr. Nixon, to Mr. Haldeman, to Mr. Ehrlichman or to any of the people at the White House. I said that I had no recollection whatsoever of talking with any of the White House legislative liaison people. I indicated under oath that the initiative that I took was at the request of the ranking members of the House Banking and Currency Committee on the Republican side, which was a legitimate request and a proper response by me.

Now that was gone into by two congressional committees, and following that investigation, both committees overwhelmingly approved me, in both the House and the Senate did likewise. Now, in the meantime, the special prosecutor, within the last few days, after an investigation himself, said there was no reason for him to get involved, because he found nothing that would justify it. And then just a day or two ago, the Attorney General of the United States made a further investigation and came to precisely the same conclusion.

Now, after all of those investigations by objective, responsible people, I think the matter is closed once and for all. But to add one other feature, I don't control any of the tapes. Those tapes are in the jurisdiction of the courts and I have no right to say yes or no. But all the committees, the Attorney General, the special prosecutor, all of them have given me a clean bill of health. I think the matter is settled once and for all.

Q: Well, Mr. President, if I do say so, though, the question is that I think that you still have not gone into details about what your role in it was. I don't think there is any question about whether or not there was criminal prosecution, but whether you have told the American people your entire involvement, and whether you would be willing, even if you don't control the tapes, whether you would be willing to ask that the tapes be released for examination.

Ford: That's for the proper authorities who have control over those tapes to make that decision. I have given every bit of evidence, answered every question that's been asked me by any senator or any member of the House. Plus the fact that the special prosecutor, on his own initiation, and the Attorney General on his initiation, the highest law enforcement official in this country, all of them have given me a clean bill of health. And I've told everything I know about it. I think the matter is settled once and for all.

Walters [moderator Barbara Walters of ABC]: Gov. Carter, your response.

Carter: I don't have a response.

Yugoslavia

Q: Gov. Carter, the next big crisis spot in the world may be Yugoslavia. President Tito is old and sick, and there are divisions in his country. It's pretty certain that the Russians are going to do everything they possibly can after Tito dies to force Yugoslavia back into the Soviet camp. But last Saturday you said, and this is a quote, "I would not go to war in Yugoslavia even if the Soviet Union sent in troops." Doesn't that statement practically invite the Russians to intervene in Yugoslavia? Doesn't it discourage Yugoslavs who might be tempted to resist? And wouldn't it have been wiser on your part to say nothing and to keep the Russians in the dark as President Ford did and as I think every President has done since President Truman?

Carter: Over the last two weeks, I've had a chance to talk to two men who have visited the Soviet Union, Yugoslavia and China. One is Gov. Averell Harriman, who visited the Soviet Union and Yugoslavia, and the other one is James Schlesinger, whom I think you accompanied to China. I got a complete report back from those countries from these two distinguished gentlemen.

Mr. Harriman talked to the leaders in Yugoslavia, and I think it's accurate to say that there is no prospect, in their opinion, of the Soviet Union invading Yugoslavia should Mr. Tito pass away. The present leadership there is fairly uniform in their purpose, and I think it's a close-knit group, and I think it would be unwise for us to say that we will go to war in Yugoslavia if the Soviets should invade, which I think would be an extremely unlikely thing.

I have maintained from the very beginning of my campaign, and this was a standard answer that I made in response to the Yugoslavian question, that I would never go to war, become militarily involved, in the internal affairs of another country unless our own security was directly threatened. And I don't believe that our security would be directly threatened if the Soviet Union went into Yugoslavia. I don't believe it will happen. I certainly hope it won't. I would take the strongest possible measures, short of actual military action there by our own troops, but I doubt that that would be an eventuality.

Q: One quick follow-up question. Did you clear the response you made with Secretary Schlesinger and Gov. Harriman?

Carter: No, I did not.

Ford: Well, I firmly believe, Mr. Kraft, that it's unwise for a President to signal in advance what options he might exercise if any international problem arose.

I think we all recall with some sadness that the period of the late 1940s, early 1950, there were some indications that the United States would not include South Korea in their area of defense. There are some who allege, I can't prove it true or untrue, that such a statement in effect invited the North Koreans to invade South Korea. It's a fact they did.

But no President of the United States, in my opinion, should signal in advance to a prospective enemy what his decision might be or what option he might exercise. It's far better for a person sitting in the White House, who has a number of options, to make certain that the other side, so to speak, doesn't know precisely what you're going to do. And therefore, that was the reason that I would not identify any particular course of action when I responded to a question a week or so ago.

Gen. Brown's Remarks

Q: Sir, this question concerns your administrative performance as President. The other day, Gen. George Brown, the chairman of the Joint Chiefs of Staff, delivered his views on several sensitive subjects, among them Great Britain, one of this country's oldest allies. He said, and I quote him now, "Great Britain, it's a pathetic thing. It just makes you cry. They're no longer a world power. All they have are generals, admirals and bands." Since Gen. Brown's comments have caused this country embarrassment in the past, why is he still this nation's leading military officer?

Ford: I have indicated to Gen. Brown that the words that he used in that interview, in that particular case and in several others, were very ill-advised. And Gen. Brown had indicated his apology, his regrets, and I think that will, in this situation, settle the matter.

It is tragic that the full transcript was not released and that there were excerpts. Some of the excerpts [were] taken out of context. Not this one, however, that you bring up. Gen. Brown has an exemplary record of military performance. He served this nation with great, great skill and courage and bravery for 35 years. And I think it's the consensus of the people who are knowledgeable in the military field that he is probably the outstanding military leader and strategist that we have in America today.

Now he did use ill-advised words, but I think in the fact that he apologized, that he was reprimanded, does permit him to stay on and continue that kind of leadership that we so badly need as we enter into negotiations under the SALT II agreement or, if we have operations that might be developing in the Middle East or in southern Africa, in the Pacific, we need a man with that experience, that knowledge, that know-how, and I think in light of the fact that he has apologized, would not have justified my asking for his resignation.

Carter: Well, just briefly, I think this is the second time that Gen. Brown has made a statement for which he did have to apologize. And I know that everybody makes mistakes. I think the first one was related to the unwarranted influence of American Jews on the media and in the Congress. This one concerned Great Britain. I think he said that Israel was a military burden on us and that Iran hoped to re-establish the Persian empire. I'm not sure that I remembered earlier that President Ford had expressed his concern about the statement or apologized for it.

This is something, though, that I think is indicative of the need among the American people to know how its Commander in Chief, the President, feels and I think the only criticism that I would have of Mr. Ford is that immediately when the statement was revealed, perhaps a statement from the President would have been a clarifying and a very beneficial thing.

Doubts About Carter

Q: Governor, despite the fact that you have been running for President a long time now, many Americans still seem to be uneasy about you. They don't feel that they know you or the people around you. One problem seems to be that you haven't reached out to bring people of broad background and national experience into your campaign or your presidential plans. Most of the people around you on a day-to-day basis are the people you have known in Georgia. Many of them are young and relatively inexperienced in national affairs. Doesn't this raise a serious question whether you would bring into a Carter administration people with the necessary background to run the federal government?

Carter: I don't believe it does. I began campaigning 22 months ago. At that time, nobody thought I had a chance to win. Very few people knew who I was. I came from a tiny town, as you know, Plains, and didn't hold public office, didn't have very much money. And my first organization was just four or five people plus my wife and my children, three sons and their wives.

And we won the nomination by going out into the streets—barbershops, beauty parlors, restaurants, stores, in factory shift lines, also in farmers' markets and livestock sale barns—and we talked a lot and we listened a lot and we learned from the American people. And we built up an awareness among the voters of this country, particularly those in whose primaries I entered—30 of them, nobody's ever done that before—about who I was and what I stood for.

Now we have a very, very wide-ranging group of advisers who help me prepare for these debates and who teach me about international economics, foreign affairs, defense matters, health, education, welfare, government reorganization. I'd say several hundred of them, and they're very fine and very highly qualified.

The one major decision that I have made since acquiring the nomination, and I share this with President Ford, is the choice of a Vice President. I think this should be indicative of the kind of leaders I would choose to help me if I am elected. I chose Sen. Walter Mondale. And the only criterion I ever put forward in my own mind was who among the several million people in this country would be the best person qualified to be President if something should happen to me and to join me in being Vice President if I should win that in return. And I'm convinced now, more than I was when I got the nomination, that Walter Mondale was the right choice.

And I believe this is a good indication of the kind of people I would choose in the future. Mr. Ford has had that same choice to make. I don't want to say anything critical of Sen. Dole, but I've never heard Mr. Ford say that that is his primary consideration—who is the best person to choose in this country to be President of the United States. I feel completely at ease knowing that someday Sen. Mondale might very well be President. In the last vice presidential nominees, incumbents, three of them have become President. But I think this is indicative of what I would do.

Ford: The governor may not have heard my established criteria for the selection of the Vice President, but it was a well-established criteria that the person I selected would be fully qualified to be President of the United States. And Sen. Bob Dole is so qualified. Sixteen years in the House of Representatives and in the Senate. Very high responsibilities and important committees.

I don't mean to be critical of Sen. Mondale, but I was very, very surprised when I read that Sen. Mondale made a very derogatory, very personal comment about Gen. Brown after the news story that broke about Gen. Brown. If my recollection is correct, he indicated that Gen. Brown was not qualified to be a sewer commissioner. And I don't think that's a proper way to describe a chairman of the Joint Chiefs of Staff who has fought for his country for 35 years, and I'm sure the governor would agree with me on that.

I think Sen. Dole would show more good judgment and discretion than to so describe a heroic and brave and very outstanding leader of the military. So I think our selection of Bob Dole as Vice President is based on merit. And if he should ever become the President of the United States, with his vast experience as a member of the House and a member of the Senate, as well as a Vice President, I think he would do an outstanding job as President of the United States.

Environmental Issues

Q: Mr. President, let me assure you and maybe some of the viewing audience that being on this panel hasn't been as it may seem, all torture and agony. One of the heartening things has been that I and my colleagues have received literally hundreds and maybe even thousands of suggested questions from ordinary citizens across the country who want answers.

Ford: That's a tribute to their interest in this election.

Q: I'll give you that. But, let me go on, because one main subject on the minds of all of them has been the environment. They're particularly curious about your record. People really want to know why you vetoed the strip-mining bill. They want to know why you worked against strong controls on auto emissions. They want to know why you aren't doing anything about pollution of the Atlantic Ocean. They want to know why a bipartisan organization such as the National League of Conservation Voters says that when it comes to environmental issues, your are—and I'm quoting—"hopeless."

Ford: First, let me set the record straight. I vetoed the strip-mining bill, Mr. Kraft, because it was the overwhelming consensus of knowledgeable people that that strip-mining bill would have meant the loss of literally thousands of jobs, something around 140,000 jobs. Number two, that strip-mining bill would have severely set back our need for more coal, and Gov. Carter has said repeatedly that coal is the resource that we need to use more in the effort to become independent of the Arab oil supply. So, I vetoed it because of a loss of jobs and because it would have interfered with our energy independence program.

The auto emissions: It was agreed by Leonard Woodcock, the head of the UAW, and by heads of all the automobile industry, with labor and management together saying that those auto emission standards had to be modified.

But let's talk about what the Ford administration has done in the field of environment. I have increased as President by over 60 per cent the funding for water treatment plants in the United States, the federal contribution.

I have fully funded the land and water conservation program. In fact, I've recommended and the Congress approved a substantially increased land and water conservation program. I have added in the current year's budget the funds for the National Park Service—for example, the proposed about $12-million to add between 400 and 500 more employees for the National Park Service.

And a month or so ago I did likewise, [saying] over the next 10 years, we should expand—double—the national parks, the wilderness areas, the scenic river areas. And then of course, the final thing is that I have signed and approved of more scenic rivers, more wilderness areas, since I've been President than any other President in the history of the United States.

Carter: Well, I might say that I think the League of Conservation Voters is absolutely right. This administration's record on environment is very bad.

I think it's accurate to say that the strip-mining law which was passed twice by the Congress—and was only like two votes, I believe, of being overridden—would have been good for the country. The claim that it would have put 140,000 miners out of work is hard to believe, when at the time Mr. Ford vetoed it, the United Mine Workers was supporting the bill. And I don't think they would have supported the bill had they known that they would lose 140,000 jobs.

There has been a consistent policy on the part of this administration to lower or to delay enforcement of air pollution standards and water pollution standards. And under both President Nixon and Ford,

moneys have been impounded that would have gone to cities and others to control water pollution.

We have no energy policy. We, I think, are the only developed nation in the world that has no comprehensive energy policy, to permit us to plan in an orderly way, have no way of increasing the scarce energy forms, oil, and have research and development concentrated on the increased use of coal, which I strongly favor—the research and development to be used primarily to make the coal-burning to be clean.

We need a heritage trust program, similar to the one we had in Georgia, to set aside additional lands that have geological and archeological importance, natural areas for enjoyment. The lands that Mr. Ford brags about having approved are in Alaska and they are enormous in size, but as far as accessibility of them by the American people are fairly far in the future.

We've taken no strong policy in control of the pollution of our oceans, and I would say the worst threat to our environment of all is nuclear proliferation, and this administration, having been in office now for two years or more, has still not taken strong or bold action to stop the proliferation of nuclear waste around the world, particularly plutonium. Those are some brief remarks about the failures of this administration. I would do the opposite in every respect.

Programs for Cities

Q: Governor, federal policy in this country since World War II has tended to favor the development of suburbs at the great expense of central cities. Does not the federal government now have an affirmative obligation to revitalize the American city? We have heard little in this campaign to suggest that you have an urban reconstruction program. Would you please outline your urban intentions for us tonight?

Carter: Yes I'd be glad to. In the first place, as is the case with the environmental policy and the energies policies I've just described, and the policy for nonproliferation of nuclear waste, this administration has no urban policy. It's impossible for mayors or governors to cooperate with the President, because they can't anticipate what's going to happen next. A mayor of a city like New York, for instance, needs to know 18 months or two years ahead of time what responsibilities the city will have in administration and in financing things like housing, pollution control, crime control, education, welfare and health.

This has not been done, unfortunately. I remember the headline in the *Daily News* that said, "Ford to New York: Drop Dead." I think it's very important that our cities know that they have a partner in the federal government.

Quite often Congress has passed laws in the past designed to help people with the ownership of homes and with the control of crime and with adequate health care and education programs and so forth. Those programs were designed to help those who

need it most. And quite often this has been the very poor people and neighborhoods in the downtown urban centers. Because of the greatly advantaged persons who live in the suburbs, better education, better organization, more articulate, more aware about what the laws are, quite often this money has been channeled out of the downtown centers where it's needed.

Also I favor all revenue-sharing money being used for local governments and also to remove prohibitions in the use of revenue-sharing money so that it can be used to improve education and health care. We have now, for instance, only 7 per cent of the total education cost being financed by the federal government. When the Nixon-Ford administration started, it was 10 per cent. That's a 30 per cent reduction in the portion that the federal government contributes to education in just eight years. And as you know, the cost of education has gone up tremendously.

The last point is that the major thrust has got to be to put people back to work. We've got an extraordinarily high unemployment rate among downtown urban ghetto areas, particularly among the very poor and particularly among minority groups—sometimes 50 or 60 per cent. And the concentration of employment opportunities in those areas would help greatly not only to reestablish the tax base, but also to reduce the extraordinary welfare cost. One of the major responsibilities on the shoulders of New York City is to finance welfare. And I favor a shifting of the welfare cost away from the local governments altogether, and over a longer period of time, let the federal government begin to absorb part of it that's now paid by the state governments. Those things would help a great deal with the cities, but we still have a very serious problem there.

Ford: Let me speak up very strongly. The Ford administration does have a very comprehensive program to help the urban areas. I fought for, and the Congress finally went along with, a general revenue-sharing program whereby cities and states, the cities two-thirds and the states one-third, get over $6-billion a year in cash through which they can provide many services, whatever they really want. In addition, we in the federal government make available to cities about $3.3-billion in what we call community development.

In addition, as a result of my pressure on the Congress, we got a major mass transit program over a four-year period, $11.8-billion. We have a good housing program that will result in cutting the down payments by 50 per cent and having mortgage payments lower at the beginning of any mortgage period. We're expanding our homestead housing program.

The net result is, we think under Carla Hills, who's the chairman of my urban development and neighborhood revitalization program, we will really do a first-class job in helping the communities throughout the country. As a matter of fact, that committee under Secretary Hills released about a 75-page report with specific recommendations so we can do a better job in the weeks ahead. And in addition, the tax program of the Ford administration, which provides an incentive for industry to move into our major metropolitan areas, into the inner cities, will bring jobs where people are and help to revitalize those cities as they can be.

Civil Rights

Q: Mr. President, your campaign has been running ads in black newspapers saying that, quote, for black Americans, President Ford has quietly [been] getting the job done. Yet study after study has shown little progress in desegregation and in fact actual increases in segregated schools and housing in the Northeast. Now, civil rights groups have complained repeatedly that there's been lack of progress and commitment to an integrated society during your administration. So how are you getting the job done for blacks and other minorities, and what programs do you have in mind for the next four years?

Ford: Let me say at the outset: I'm very proud of the record of this administration. In the Cabinet I have one of the outstanding, I think, administrators as the Secretary of Transportation, Bill Coleman.

You're familiar, I'm sure, with the recognition given in the Air Force to Gen. James, and there was just approved a three-star admiral, the first in the history of the United States Navy. So we are giving full recognition to individuals of quality in the Ford administration in positions of great responsibility.

In addition, the Department of Justice is fully enforcing, and enforcing effectively, the Voting Rights Act, the legislation that involves jobs, housing for minorities, not only blacks but all others. The Department of HUD is enforcing the new legislation that outlaws, that takes care of, red-lining.

What we're doing is saying that there are opportunities, business opportunities, educational opportunities, responsibilities where people with talent, black or any other minority, can fully qualify for offers of minority business. And the Department of Commerce has made available more money in trying to help black businessmen or other minority businessmen than any other administration since the office was established. The Office of Small Business, under Mr. Kobelinski, has a very massive program trying to help the black community. The individual who wants to start a business or expand his business as a black businessman is able to borrow, either directly or with guaranteed loans. I believe that on the record that this administration has been responsive and we have carried out the law to the letter, and I am proud of the record.

Carter: The description just made of this administration's record is hard to recognize. I think it's accurate to say that Mr. Ford voted against the Voting Rights Acts and against the Civil Rights Acts in the debating stage. I think once it was assured they were going to pass, he finally voted for it.

This country changed drastically in 1969 when the terms of John Kennedy and Lyndon Johnson were over and Richard Nixon and Gerald Ford became the Presidents. There was a time when there was hope for those who are poor and downtrodden and who are elderly or who are ill or who were in minority groups, but that time has been gone.

I think the greatest thing that ever happened to the South was the passage of the Civil Rights Act and the opening up of opportunities to black people—the chance to vote, to hold a job, to buy a house, to go to school and to participate in public affairs, and not only liberate our black people but it also liberated the whites.

We've seen in many instances in recent years in minority affairs a section of the small loan administration, Small Business Administration, lend a black entrepreneur just enough money to get started and then to go bankrupt. The bankruptcies have gone up in an extraordinary degree.

FHA, which used to be a very responsible agency, who everyone looked to to help on a home, lost $600-million last year. There have been over 1,300 indictments in HUD, over 800 convictions. Well, those were just in home loans. And now the federal government has become the world's largest slum landlord.

We've got a 30 per cent or 40 per cent unemployment rate among minority young people, and there has been no concerted effort given to the needs of those who are both poor and black, or who are poor and speak a foreign language. And that's where there has been a great generation of despair and ill health and lack of education, lack of purposefulness and lack of hope for the future. But it doesn't take just a quiet or minimum enforcement of the law. It requires an aggressive searching out and reaching out to help people who especially need it. And that's been lacking in the last eight years.

Constitutional Amendments

Q: Gov. Carter, in the nearly 200-year history of the Constitution, there've been only, I think it's 25, amendments, most of them on issues of the very broadest principle. Now we have proposed amendments in many highly specialized causes, like gun control, school busing, balanced budgets, school prayer, abortion, things like that. Do you think it's appropriate to the dignity of the Constitution to tack on amendments in wholesale fashion? And which of the ones that I listed—that is, balanced budgets, school busing, school prayer, abortion, gun control—which of those would you really work hard to support if you were President?

Carter: I would not work hard to support any of those. We've always had, I think, a lot of constitutional amendments proposed, but the passage of them has been fairly slow and few and far between. In the 200-year history there's been a very cautious approach to this with whatever we have a transient problem.

Now I'm strongly against abortion. I think abortion's wrong. I don't think the government ought to do anything to encourage abortion. But I don't favor a constitutional amendment on the subject. But short of a constitutional amendment, even in the confines of the Supreme Court rulings, I'll do everything I can to minimize the need for abortions with better sex education, family planning, with better adoptive procedures. I personally don't believe the federal government ought to finance abortions, but I draw the line and don't support a constitutional amendment. However, I honor the right of people to seek the constitutional amendments on school busing, on prayer in the schools and on abortion. But among those you named, I won't actively work for the passage of any of them.

Ford: I support the Republican platform, which calls for the constitutional amendment that would outlaw abortions. I favor the particular constitutional amendment that would turn over to the states the individual right of the voters in those states the chance to make a decision by public referendum. I call that the people's amendment. I think if you really believe that the people of a state ought to make a decision on a matter of this kind, that we ought to have a federal constitutional amendment that would permit each one of the 50 states to make the choice. I think this is a responsible and a proper way to proceed.

I believe also that there is some merit to an amendment that Sen. Everett Dirksen proposed very frequently, an amendment that would change the court decision as far as voluntary prayer in public schools. It seems to me that there would be an opportunity, as long as it's voluntary, as long as there is no compulsion whatsoever, that an individual ought to have that right. So in those two cases, I think such a constitutional amendment would be proper, and I really don't think in either case they're trivial matters. I think they're matters of very deep convictions as far as many, many people in this country believe, and therefore, they shouldn't be treated lightly, that they're matters that are important. And in those two cases, I would favor them.

Gun Control

Q: Mr. President, twice you have been the intended victim of would-be assassins using handguns. Yet you remain a steadfast opponent of substantive handgun control. There are now some 40 million handguns in this country, going up at the rate of 2.5 million a year. And tragically, those handguns are frequently purchased for self-protection and wind up being used against a relative or a friend. In light of that, why do you remain so adamant in your opposition to substantive gun control in this country?

Ford: Mr. Maynard, the record of gun control, whether it is one city or another or in some states, does not show that the registration of a gun, a handgun, or the registration of the gun owner has in any way whatsoever decreased the crime rate or the use of that gun in the committing of a crime. The record just doesn't prove that such legislation or action by a local city council is effective.

What we have to do, and this is the crux of the matter, is to make it very, very difficult for a person who uses a gun in the commission of a crime to stay out of jail. If we make the use of a gun in the commission of a crime a serious criminal offense, and that person is prosecuted, then, in my opinion, we are going after the person who uses the gun for the wrong reason.

I don't believe in the registration of handguns or the registration of the handgun owner. That has not proven to be effective, and therefore, I think the better way is to go after the criminal, the individual who commits the crime in the possession of a gun and uses that gun for a part of his criminal activity. Those are the people who ought to be in jail. And the only way to do it is to pass strong legislation so that once apprehended, indicted, convicted, they'll be in jail and off the streets and not using guns in the commission of a crime.

Q: But Mr. President, don't you think that the proliferation of the availability of handguns contributes to the possibility of those crimes being committed? And there's a second part to my follow-up, very quickly. There are, as you know and as you've said, jurisdictions around the country with strong gun-control laws. The police officials in those cities contend that if there were a national law, to prevent other jurisdictions from providing the weapons that then come into places like New York, that they might have a better handle on the problem. Have you considered that in your analysis of the handgun proliferation problem?

Ford: Yes, I have. And the individuals with whom I've consulted have not convinced me that a national registration of handguns or handgun owners will solve the problem you're talking about. The person who wants to use a gun for an illegal purpose can get it whether it's registered or outlawed. They will be obtained. And they are the people who ought to go behind bars. You should not in the process penalize the legitimate handgun owner. And when you go through the process of registration you, in effect, are penalizing that individual who uses his gun for a very legitimate purpose.

Carter: I think it's accurate to say that Mr. Ford's position on gun control has changed. Earlier, Mr. Levi, his Attorney General, put forward a gun control proposal which Mr. Ford later, I believe, espoused, that called for a prohibition against a sale of so-called Saturday night specials. And it would have put very strict control over who owned a handgun. I have been a hunter all my life and happen to own both shotguns, rifles and a handgun. The only purpose I would see in registering handguns and not

long guns of any kind would be to prohibit the ownership of those guns by those who have used them in the commission of a crime, who have been proven to be mentally incompetent to own a gun. I believe that limited approach to the question would be advisable and, I think, adequate. But that's as far as I would go with it.

Supreme Court

Q: Governor, you've said the Supreme Court of today is, as you put it, moving back in a proper direction in rulings that have limited the rights of criminal defendants. And you've compared the present Supreme Court under Chief Justice Burger very favorably with the more liberal court we had under Chief Justice Warren. So exactly what are you getting at, and can you elaborate on the kind of court you think this country should have? And can you tell us the kind of qualifications and philosophy you would look for as President in making Supreme Court appointments?

Carter: While I was governor of Georgia, although I'm not a lawyer, we had complete reform of the Georgia court system. We streamlined the structure of the court, put in administrative officers, put a unified court system in, required that all severe sentences be reviewed for uniformity. And, in addition to that, put forward a proposal that was adopted and used throughout my own term of office of selection of, for all judges and district attorneys or prosecuting attorneys, on the basis of merit.

Every time I had a vacancy on the Georgia Supreme Court—and I filled five of those vacancies out of seven total and about half the court of appeals judges, about 35 per cent of the trial judges—I was given from an objective panel the five most highly qualified persons in Georgia. And from those five, I always chose the first or second one.

So merit selection of judges was the most important single criterion. And I would institute the same kind of procedure as President, not only in judicial appointments but also in diplomatic appointments.

Secondly, I think that the Burger court has fairly well confirmed the major and most far-reaching and most controversial decisions of the Warren court. Civil rights has been confirmed by the Burger court, hasn't been reversed, and I don't think there's any inclination to reverse those basic decisions. The one-man, one-vote rule, which is a very important one that struck down the unwarranted influence in the legislature of sparsely populated areas of the states. The right of indigent or very poor accused persons to legal counsel. I think the Burger court has confirmed that basic and very controversial decision of the Warren court. Also the protection of an arrested person against unwarranted persecution in trying to get a false confession.

But now I think there have been a couple of instances where the Burger court has made technical rulings where an obviously guilty person was later found to be guilty [innocent]. And I think that in that case, some of the more liberal members of the so-called Warren court agreed with those decisions. But the only thing I have pointed out was, what I've just said, and that there was a need to clarify the technicalities so that you couldn't be forced to release a person who was obviously guilty just because of a small technicality in the law. And that's a reversal of position by the Burger court with which I do agree.

Q: Governor, I don't believe you answered my question, though, about the kinds of people you would be looking for the court, the type of philosophy you would be looking for if you were making appointments to the Supreme Court as President.

Carter: Okay, I thought I answered it by saying that it would be on the basis of merit. Once the search and analysis procedure had been completed, and once I'm given a list of the five or seven or 10 best-qualified persons in the country, I would make a selection from among those persons. If the list was, in my opinion, fairly uniform, that there was no outstanding person, then I would undoubtedly choose someone who would most accurately reflect my own basic political philosophy as best I could determine it.

Q: Which would be?

Carter: To continue the progress that has been made under the last two courts—the Warren court and the Burger court.

I would also like to completely revise our criminal justice system—to do some of the things at the federal level in court reform that I've just described, as has been done in Georgia and other states. And I would like to appoint people who would be interested in helping with that. I know that Chief Justice Burger is. He hasn't had help yet from the administration, from the Congress, to carry this out.

The emphasis, I think, of the court system should be to interpret the Constitution and the laws equally between property protection and personal protection. But when there's a very narrow decision—which quite often there's one that reaches the Supreme Court—I think the choice should be with human rights. And that would be another factor that I would follow.

Ford: Well, I think the answer as to the kind of person that I would select is obvious. I had one opportunity to nominate an individual to the Supreme Court and I selected the Circuit Court of Appeals judge from Illinois, John Paul Stevens. I selected him because of his outstanding record as a Circuit Court of Appeals judge, and I was very pleased that an overwhelmingly Democratic United States Senate, after going into his background, came to the conclusion that he was fit and should serve, and the vote on his behalf was overwhelming.

So I would say somebody in the format of Justice Stevens would be the kind of an individual that I would select in the future, as I did him in the past.

I believe, however, a comment ought to be made about the direction of the Burger court, vis-a-vis the court that preceded it. It seems to me that the Miranda case was a case that really made it very, very difficult for the police, the law enforcement people in this country to do what they could to make certain that the victim of a crime was protected and that those that commit crimes were properly handled and sent to jail. The Miranda case the Burger court is gradually changing, and I'm pleased to see that there are some steps being made by the Burger court to modify the so-called Miranda decision.

I might make a correction of what Gov. Carter said, speaking of gun control. Yes, it is true I believe that the sale of Saturday night specials should be cut out, but he wants the registration of handguns.

Economic Conditions

Q: Mr. President, the country is now in something that your advisers call an economic pause. I think to most Americans that sounds like an antiseptic term for low growth, unemployment standstill at a high level, decline in take-home pay, lower factory earnings, more layoffs. Isn't that really a rotten record, and doesn't your administration bear most of the blame for it?

Ford: Let me talk about the economic announcements that were made just this past week. Yes, it was announced that the GNP real growth in the third quarter was at 4 per cent. But do you realize that over the last 10 years that's a higher figure than the average growth during that 10-year period? Now it's lower than the 9.2 per cent growth in the first quarter, and it's lower than the 5 per cent growth in the second quarter. But every economist—liberal, conservative—that I'm familiar with—recognizes that in the fourth quarter of this year and in the first quarter of next year that we'll have an increase in real GNP.

And now let's talk about the pluses that came out this week. We had an 18 per cent increase in housing starts. We had a substantial increase in new permits for housing. As a matter of fact, based on the announcement this week, there will be at an annual rate 1.8 million new houses built, which is a tremendous increase over last year and a substantial increase over the earlier part of this year.

Now in addition, we had a very, some very good news, in the reduction in the rate of inflation. And inflation hits everybody, those who are working and those who are on welfare. The rate of inflation as announced just the other day is under 5 per cent, and the 4.4 per cent that was indicated at the time of the 4 per cent GNP was less than the 5.4 per cent. It means that the American buyer is getting a better bargain today because inflation is less.

Q: Mr. President, let me ask you this. There has been an increase in layoffs, and that's something that bothers everybody, because even people that have a job are afraid that they're going to be fired. Did you predict that layoff, that increase in layoffs? Didn't that take you by surprise, hasn't your administration been surprised by this pause? In fact, haven't you been so obsessed with saving money that you didn't even push the government to spend funds that were allocated?

Ford: Mr. Kraft, I think the record can be put in this way, which is the way that I think satisfies most Americans: Since the depths of the recession, we have added four million jobs. Most importantly, consumer confidence as surveyed by the reputable organization at the University of Michigan is at the highest since 1972.

In other words, there is a growing public confidence in the strength of this economy. And that means that there will be more industrial activity. It means that there will be a reduction in the unemployment. It means that there will be increased hires. It means that there will be increased employment.

Now we've had this pause, but most economists, regardless of their political philosophy, indicate that this pause for a month or two was healthy, because we could not have honestly sustained a 9.2 per cent rate of growth, which we had in the first quarter of this year.

Now, I'd like to point out as well that the United States' economic recovery from the recession of a year ago is well ahead of the economic recovery of any major free industrial nation in the world today. We're ahead of all the Western European countries. We're ahead of Japan. The United States is leading the free world out of the recession that was serious a year, year and a half ago. We're going to see unemployment going down, more jobs available and the rate of inflation going down. And I think this is a record the American people will understand and appreciate.

Carter: With all due respect to President Ford, I think he ought to be ashamed of mentioning that statement, because we have the highest unemployment rate now than we had at any time since the Great Depression caused by Herbert Hoover and the time President Ford took office. We've got 7½ million people out of jobs. Since he's been in office, 2½ million more American people have lost their jobs. In the last four months alone, 500,000 Americans have gone on the unemployment rolls. In the last month, we've had a net loss of 163,000 jobs.

Anybody who says that the inflation rate is in good shape now ought to talk to the housewives. One of the overwhelming results that I've seen in polls is that people feel that you can't plan any more. There's no way to make a prediction that my family might be able to own a home or to put my kid through college. Savings accounts are losing money instead of gaining money. Inflation is robbing us. Under the present

administration—Nixon's and Ford's—we've had three times the inflation rate that we experienced under President Johnson and President Kennedy.

The economic growth is less than half today what it was at the beginning of this year. And housing starts—he compares the housing starts to the last year. I don't blame him, because in 1975 we had fewer housing starts in this country, fewer homes built, than any year since 1940. That's 35 years. And we've got a 35 per cent unemployment rate in many areas of this country among construction workers. Now Mr. Ford hasn't done anything about it, and I think this shows a callous indifference to the families that have suffered so much. He has vetoed bills passed by Congress within the congressional budget guidelines—job opportunities for two million Americans.

We'll never have a balanced budget, we'll never meet the needs of our people, we'll never control the inflationary spiral as long as we have 7½ or eight million people out of work, who are looking for jobs. And we've probably got 2½ more million people who are not looking for jobs any more because they've given up hope. That is a very serious indictment of this administration. It's probably the worst one of all.

Carter's Decreasing Lead

Q: Gov. Carter, you entered this race against President Ford with a 20-point lead or better in the polls. And now it appears that this campaign is headed for a photo finish. You've said how difficult it is to run against a sitting President. But Mr. Ford was just as much an incumbent in July when you were 20 points ahead as he is now. Can you tell us what caused the evaporation of that lead in your opinion?

Carter: Well, that's not exactly an accurate description of what happened. When I was that far ahead, it was immediately following the Democratic convention and before the Republican convention. At that time, 25 or 30 per cent of the Reagan supporters said that they would not support President Ford. But as occurred at the end of the Democratic convention, the Republican Party unified itself.

And I think immediately following the Republican convention, there was about a 10-point spread. I believe that to be accurate, I had 49 per cent, President Ford 39 per cent. The polls are good indications of fluctuations, but they vary one from another.

And the only poll I've ever followed is the one that, you know, is taken on election day. I was in 30 primaries in the spring, and at first it was obvious that I didn't have any standing in the poll. As a matter of fact, I think when Gallup ran their first poll in December of 1975 they didn't put my name on the list. They had 35 people on the list. My name wasn't even there. At the beginning of the year I had about 2 per cent. So the polls to me are interesting, but they don't determine, you know, my hopes or my despair.

117

I campaign among people. I've never depended on powerful political figures to put me in office. I have a direct relationship with hundreds of people around the—hundreds of thousands around the country who actually campaign for me.

In Georgia alone, for instance, I got 84 per cent of the vote, and I think there were 14 people in addition to myself on the ballot, and Gov. Wallace had been very strong in Georgia.

That's an overwhelming support from my own people who know me best. And today, we have about 500 Georgians at their own expense—just working people who believe in me—spread around the country involved in the political campaign.

So the polls are interesting, but I don't know how to explain the fluctuation. I think a lot of it depends on current events—sometimes foreign affairs, sometimes domestic affairs.

But I think our hold of support among those who are crucial to the election has been fairly steady. And my success in the primary season was, I think, notable for a newcomer, for someone who's from outside of Washington, who never has been a part of the Washington establishment. And I think that we'll have good result[s] November the 2nd for myself and I hope for the country.

Ford: I think the increase in the prospects as far as I'm concerned and the less favorable prospects for Gov. Carter reflect that Gov. Carter is inconsistent in many of the positions that he takes. He tends to distort on a number of occasions.

Just a moment ago, for example, he was indicating that in the 1950s, for example, unemployment was very low. He fails to point out that in the 1950s we were engaged in the war in Vietnam, I mean in Korea, we had 3,500,000 young men in the Army, Navy, Air Force and Marines. That's not the way to end unemployment or to reduce unemployment.

At the present time we're at peace. We have reduced the number of people in the Army, Navy, Air Force and Marines from 3,500,000 to 2,100,000. We are not at war, we have reduced the military manpower by 1,400,000. If we had that many more people in the Army, Navy, Air Force, Marines, our unemployment figure would be considerably less. But this administration doesn't believe the way to reduce unemployment is to go to war or to increase the number of people in the military. So you can't compare unemployment, as you sought to, with the present time, with the 1950s, because the then administration had people in the military. They were at war, they were fighting overseas, and this administration has reduced the size of the military by 1,400,000. They're in the civilian labor market and they're not fighting anywhere around the world today.

Concluding Statements

Ford: For 25 years I served in the Congress, under five Presidents. I saw them work, I saw them make very hard decisions. I didn't always agree with their decisions, whether they were Democratic or Republican Presidents.

For the last two years, I've been the President, and I have found from ex-perience that it's much more difficult to make those decisions than it is to second-guess them. I became President at the time the United States was in a very troubled time. We had inflation of over 12 per cent, we were on the brink of the worst recession in the last 40 years, we were still deeply involved in the problems of Vietnam. The American people had lost faith and trust and confidence in the presidency itself. That situation called for me to first put the United States on a steady course and to keep our keel well-balanced, because we had to face the difficult problems that had all of a sudden hit America.

I think most people know that I did not seek the presidency. But I am asking for your help and assistance to be President for the next four years. During this campaign we've seen a lot of television shows, a lot of bumper stickers and a great many slogans of one kind or another. But those are not the things that count. What counts is that the United States celebrated its 200th birthday on July 4. As a result of that wonderful experience all over the United States, there is a new spirit in America. The American people are healed, are working together. The American people are moving again and moving in the right direction.

We have cut inflation by better than half. We have come out of the recession, and we're well on the road to real prosperity in this country again. There has been a restoration of faith and confidence and trust in the presidency because I've been open, candid and forthright. I have never promised more than I could produce, and I have produced everything that I promised. We are at peace. Not a single American is fighting or dying.

We have peace with freedom. I've been proud to be President of the United States during these very troubled times. I love America, just as all of you love America. It would be the highest honor for me to have your support on Nov. 2 and for you to say, "Jerry Ford, you've done a good job. Keep on doing it." Thank you, and good night.

Carter: The major purpose of an election for President is to choose a leader, someone who analyzes the depths of feeling in our country, to set a standard for our people to follow, to inspire our people to reach for greatness, to correct our defects, to answer difficult questions, to bind ourselves together in a spirit of unity. I don't believe the present administration has done that.

We have been discouraged and we have been alienated. Sometimes we've been embarrassed and sometimes we've been ashamed that people are out of work, and there's a sense of withdrawal.

But our country is innately very strong. Mr. Ford is a good and decent man, but he's been in office now more than 800 days, approaching almost as long as John Kennedy was in office. I'd like to ask the American people what's been accomplished. A lot remains to be done.

My own background is different from his. I was a school board member, a library board member. I served on a hospital authority. I was in the state senate and I was governor and I'm an engineer, a naval officer, a farmer, a businessman. And I've learned that it will require someone who can work harmoniously with the Congress, who can work closely with the people of this country and who can bring a new image and a new spirit to Washington.

Our tax structure is a disgrace and needs to be reformed. I was governor of Georgia for four years. We never increased sales taxes or income tax or property tax. As a matter of fact, the year before I went out of office we gave a $50-million refund to the property tax payers of Georgia.

We spend $600 per person in this country, every man, woman and child, for health care. We still rank 15th among all the nations of the world in infant mortality. And our cancer rate is higher than any country in the world. We don't have good health care. We could have it.

Employment ought to be restored to our people. We've become almost a welfare state. We spend now 700 per cent more on unemployment compensation than we did eight years ago when the Republicans took over the White House. Our people want to go back to work.

Our education system can be improved. Secrecy ought to be stripped away from government, and a maximum of personal privacy ought to be maintained.

Our housing programs have gone bad. It used to be that the average family could own a house. But now less than a third of our people can afford to buy their own homes.

The budget was more grossly out of balance last year than ever before in the history of our country—$65-billion—primarily because our people are not at work.

Inflation is robbing us, as we've already discussed, and the government bureaucracy is just a horrible mess. This doesn't have to be.

Now I don't know all the answers. Nobody could. But I do know that if the President of the United States and the Congress of the United States and the people of the United States said, "I believe our nation is greater than what we are now," I believe that if we are inspired, if we can achieve a degree of unity, if we can set our goals high enough and work toward recognized goals with industry and labor and agriculture along with government at all levels, then we can achieve great things.

We might have to do it slowly. There are no magic answers to it. But I believe together we can make great progress. We can correct our difficult mistakes and answer those very tough questions. I believe in the greatness of our country, and I believe the American people are ready for a change in Washington.

We've been drifting too long. We've been dormant too long. We've been discouraged too long. And we have not set an example for our own people.

But I believe that we can now establish in the White House a good relationship with Congress, a good relationship with our people, set very high goals for our country and with inspiration and hard work, we can achieve great things and let the world know. That's very important, but more importantly, let the people in our own country realize that we still live in the greatest nation on earth. Thank you very much. ∎

Presidential Messages

CQ

Text of Ford's 1976 State of the Union Message

Following is the White House text of President Ford's Jan. 19 State of the Union message to Congress:

**TO THE CONGRESS OF
THE UNITED STATES:**

As we begin our Bicentennial, America is still one of the youngest Nations in recorded history. Long before our forefathers came to these shores, men and women had been struggling on this planet to forge a better life for themselves and their families.

In man's long upward march from savagery and slavery—throughout the nearly 2000 years of the Christian calendar, the nearly 6000 years of Jewish reckoning—there have been many deep, terrifying valleys, but also many bright and towering peaks.

One peak stands highest in the ranges of human history. One example shines forth of a people uniting to produce abundance and to share the good life fairly and in freedom. One Union holds out the promise of justice and opportunity for every citizen.

That Union is the United States of America.

We have not remade paradise on earth. We know perfection will not be found here. But think for a minute how far we have come in 200 years.

We came from many roots and have many branches. Yet all Americans across the eight generations that separate us from the stirring deeds of 1776, those who know

no other homeland and those who just found refuge on our shores, say in unison:

I am proud of America and proud to be an American. Life will be better here for my children than for me.

I believe this not because I am told to believe it, but because life has been better for me than it was for my father and my mother.

I know it will be better for my children because my hands, my brain, my voice and my vote, can help make it happen.

And it has happened here in America.

It happened to you and to me.

Government exists to create and preserve conditions in which people can translate their ideals into practical reality. In the best of times, much is lost in translation. But we try.

Sometimes we have tried and failed.

Always we have had the best of intentions. But in the recent past we sometimes forgot the sound principles that had guided us through most of our history. We wanted to accomplish great things and solve age-old problems. And we became over-confident of our own abilities. We tried to be a policeman abroad and an indulgent parent here at home. We thought we could transform the country through massive national programs;

• But often the programs did not work; too often, they only made things worse.

• In our rush to accomplish great deeds quickly, we trampled on sound principles of restraint, and endangered the rights of individuals.

• We unbalanced our economic system by the huge and unprecedented growth of Federal expenditures and borrowing. And we were not totally honest with ourselves about how much these programs would cost and how we would pay for them.

• Finally, we shifted our emphasis from defense to domestic problems while our adversaries continued a massive buildup of arms.

New Balance

The time has now come for a fundamentally different approach—for a new realism that is true to the great principles upon which this nation was founded.

We must introduce a new balance to our economy—a balance that favors not only sound, active government but also a much more vigorous, healthier economy that can create new jobs and hold down prices.

We must introduce a new balance in the relationship between the individual and the Government—a balance that favors greater individual freedom and self-reliance.

We must strike a new balance in our system of Federalism—a balance that favors greater responsibility and freedom for the leaders of our State and local governments.

We must introduce a new balance between spending on domestic programs and spending on defense—a balance that ensures we fully meet our obligations to the needy while also protecting our security in a world that is still hostile to freedom.

And in all that we do, we must be more honest with the American people, promising them no more than we can deliver, and delivering all that we promise.

The genius of America has been its incredible ability to improve the lives of its citizens through a unique combination of governmental and free citizen activity.

History and experience tell us that moral progress comes not in comfortable and complacent times, but out of trial and confusion. Tom Paine aroused the troubled Americans of 1776 to stand up to the times that try men's souls, because the harder the conflict the more glorious the triumph.

A Better Year

Just a year ago I reported that the State of the Union was not good.

Tonight I report that the State of our Union is better—in many ways a lot better—but still not good enough.

To paraphrase Tom Paine, 1975 was not a year for summer soldiers and sunshine patriots. It was a year of fears and alarms and of dire forecasts—most of which never happened and won't happen.

As you recall, the year 1975 opened with rancor and bitterness. Political misdeeds of the past had neither been forgotten nor forgiven.

Federal Budget Outlays, 1950-1977

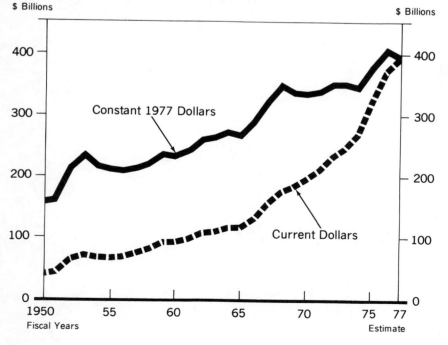

$ Billions

$ Billions

Constant 1977 Dollars

Current Dollars

400 — 400
300 — 300
200 — 200
100 — 100
0 — 0

1950   55   60   65   70   75 77
Fiscal Years   Estimate

The longest, most divisive war in our history was winding toward an unhappy conclusion. Many feared that the end of that foreign war of men and machines meant the beginning of a domestic war of recrimination and reprisal.

Friends and adversaries abroad were asking whether America had lost its nerve.

Finally, our economy was ravaged by inflation—inflation that was plunging us into the worst recession in four decades.

At the same time, Americans became increasingly alienated from all big institutions. They were steadily losing confidence not just in big government, but in big business, big labor and big education, among others.

Ours was a troubled land.

And so, 1975 was a year of hard decisions, difficult compromises, and a new realism that taught us something important about America.

It brought back a needed measure of common sense, steadfastness and self-discipline. Americans did not panic or demand instant but useless cures. In all sectors people met their difficult problems with restraint and responsibility worthy of their great heritage.

Add up the separate pieces of progress in 1975, subtract the setbacks, and the sum total shows that we are not only headed in the new direction I proposed 12 months ago, but that it turned out to be the right direction.

It is the right direction because it follows the truly revolutionary American concept of 1776 which holds that in a free society, the making of public policy and successful problem-solving involves much more than government. It involves a full partnership among all branches and levels of government, private institutions and individual citizens.

Common sense tells me to stick to that steady course.

Economy

Take the state of our economy.

Last January most things were rapidly getting worse.

This January most things are slowly but surely getting better.

The worst recession since World War II turned around in April. The best cost of living news of the past year is that double digit inflation of 12% or higher was cut almost in half. The worst—unemployment remains too high.

Today nearly 1.7 million more Americans are working than at the bottom of the recession. At year's end people were again being hired much faster than they were being laid off.

Yet let us be honest: many Americans have not yet felt these changes in their daily lives. They still see prices going up too fast, and they still know the fear of unemployment.

And we are a growing Nation. We need more and more jobs every year. Today's economy has produced over 85 million jobs for Americans, but we need a lot more jobs, especially for the young.

My first objective is to have sound economic growth without inflation.

We all know from recent experience what runaway inflation does to ruin every other worthy purpose. We are slowing it; we must stop it cold.

For many Americans the way to a healthy non-inflationary economy has become increasingly apparent; the government must stop spending so much and borrowing so much of our money; more money must remain in private hands where it will do the most good. To hold down the cost of living, we must hold down the cost of government.

In the past decade, the Federal budget has been growing at an average rate of over 10 percent every year. The budget I am submitting Wednesday cuts this rate of growth in half. I have kept my promise to submit a budget for the next fiscal year of $395 billion. In fact, it is $394.2 billion.

By holding down the growth in Federal spending, we can afford additional tax cuts and return to the people who pay taxes more decision-making power over their own lives.

Tax Cut

Last month I signed legislation to extend the 1975 tax reductions for the first six months of this year. I now propose that effective July 1, 1976, we give our taxpayers a tax cut of approximately $10 billion more than Congress agreed to in December.

My broader tax reduction would mean that for a family of four making $15,000 a year there will be $227 more in take home pay annually. Hard-working Americans caught in the middle can really use that kind of extra cash.

My recommendations for a firm restraint on the growth of Federal spending and for greater tax reduction are simple and straightforward: For every dollar saved in cutting the growth in the Federal budget we can have an added dollar of Federal tax reduction.

We can achieve a balanced budget by 1979 if we have the courage and wisdom to continue to reduce the growth of Federal spending.

One test of a healthy economy is a job for every American who wants to work.

Government—our kind of government—cannot create that many jobs. But the Federal Government can create conditions and incentives for private business and industry to make more and more jobs.

Five out of six jobs in this country are in private business and industry. Common sense tells us this is the place to look for more jobs and to find them faster.

I mean real, rewarding, permanent jobs.

To achieve this we must offer the American people greater incentives to invest in the future. My tax proposals are a major step in that direction.

To supplement these proposals, I ask that Congress enact changes in Federal tax laws that will speed up plant expansion and the purchase of new equipment. My recommendation will concentrate this job-creation tax incentive in areas where the unemployment rate now runs over 7 percent. Legislation to get this started must be approved at the earliest possible date.

Within the strict budget total I will recommend for the coming year, I will ask for additional housing assistance for 500,-000 families. These programs will expand housing opportunities, spur construction and help to house moderate and low income families.

We had a disappointing year in the housing industry in 1975 but it is improving. With lower interest rates and available mortgage money, we can have a healthy recovery in 1976.

A necessary condition of a healthy economy is freedom from the petty tyranny of massive government regulation. We are wasting literally millions of working hours costing billions of consumers' dollars because of bureaucratic red tape. The American farmer, who not only feeds 215 million Americans but also millions worldwide, has shown how much more he can produce without the shackles of government control.

Now, we need reforms in other key areas in our economy—the airlines, trucking, railroads, and financial institutions. I have concrete plans in each of these areas, not to help this or that industry, but to foster competition and to bring prices down for the consumer.

This Administration will strictly enforce the Federal antitrust laws for the same purpose.

Energy

Taking a longer look at America's future there can be neither sustained growth nor more jobs unless we continue to have an assured supply of energy to run our economy. Domestic production of oil and gas is still declining. Our dependence on foreign oil at high prices is still too great, draining jobs and dollars away from our own economy at the rate of $125 per year for every American.

Last month I signed a compromise national energy bill which enacts a part of my comprehensive energy independence program. This legislation was late in coming, not the complete answer to energy independence, but still a start in the right direction.

I again urge the Congress to move ahead immediately on the remainder of my energy proposals to make America invulnerable to the foreign oil cartel. My proposals would:

Reduce domestic natural gas shortages.

Allow production from national petroleum reserves;

Shares of the Budget

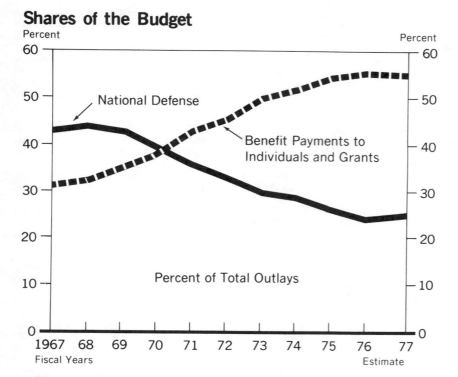

Percent

60

50 — National Defense

40 — Benefit Payments to Individuals and Grants

30

20

10 — Percent of Total Outlays

0

1967 68 69 70 71 72 73 74 75 76 77
Fiscal Years   Estimate

Percent

60

50

40

30

20

10

0

Stimulate effective conservation, including revitalization of our railroads and the expansion of our urban transportation systems;

Develop more and cleaner energy from our vast coal resources;

Expedite clean and safe nuclear power production;

Create a new national Energy Independence Authority to stimulate vital energy investment;

And accelerate development of technology to capture energy from the sun and the earth for this and future generations.

Also for the sake of future generations we must preserve the family farm and family-owned small businesses. Both strengthen America and give stability to our economy.

I will propose estate tax changes so that family businesses and family farms can be handed down from generation to generation without having to be sold to pay taxes.

I propose tax changes to encourage people to invest in America's future, and their own, through a plan that gives moderate income families income tax benefits if they make long-term investments in common stock in American companies.

Health

The Federal Government must and will respond to clearcut national needs—for this and future generations.

Hospital and medical services in America are among the world's best but the cost of a serious and extended illness can

quickly wipe out a family's lifetime savings. Increasing health costs are of deep concern to all and a powerful force pushing up the cost of living.

The burden of a catastrophic illness can be borne by very few in our society. We must eliminate this fear from every family.

I propose catastrophic health insurance for everybody covered by Medicare. To finance this added protection, fees for short-term care will go up somewhat, but nobody after reaching age 65 will have to pay more than $500 a year for covered hospital or nursing home care nor more than $250 for one year's doctors' bills.

We cannot realistically afford Federally dictated national health insurance providing full coverage for all 215 million Americans. The experience of other countries raises questions about the quality as well as the cost of such plans. But I do envision the day when we may use the private health insurance system to offer more middle income families high quality health services at prices they can afford and shield them also from catastrophic illnesses.

Using the resources now available, I propose improving the Medicare and other Federal health programs to help those who really need more protection: older people and the poor. To help States and local governments give better health care to the poor I propose that we combine 16 existing Federal programs including Medicaid into a single $10 billion Federal grant.

Funds would be divided among the States under a new formula which provides a larger share of Federal money to those states that have a larger share of low income families.

I will take further steps to improve the quality of medical and hospital care for those who have served in our armed forces.

Social Security

Now let me speak about Social Security.

Our Federal Social Security system for people who have worked hard and contributed to it all their lives is a vital part of our economic system. Its value is no longer debatable. In my budget for fiscal year 1977 I am recommending that the full cost of living increase in Social Security benefits be paid during the coming year.

But I am concerned about the integrity of our Social Security Trust Fund that enables people—those retired and those still working who will retire—to count on this source of retirement income. Younger workers watch their deductions rise and wonder if they will be adequately protected in the future.

We must meet this challenge head-on.

Simple arithmetic warns all of us that the Social Security Trust Fund is headed for trouble. Unless we act soon to make sure the fund takes in as much as it pays out, there will be no security for old or young.

I must therefore recommend a 3/10 of one percent increase in both employer and employee Social Security taxes effective January 1, 1977. This will cost each covered employee less than one extra dollar a week and will ensure the integrity of the trust fund.

As we rebuild our economy, we have a continuing responsibility to provide a temporary cushion to the unemployed. At my request the Congress enacted two extensions and expansions in unemployment insurance which helped those who were jobless during 1975. These programs will continue in 1976.

In my fiscal 1977 budget, I am also requesting funds to continue proven job training and employment opportunity programs for millions of other Americans.

Welfare

Compassion and a sense of community—two of America's greatest strengths throughout our history—tell us we must take care of our neighbors who cannot take care of themselves. The host of Federal programs in this field reflect our generosity as a people.

But everyone realizes that when it comes to welfare, government at all levels is not doing the job well. Too many of our welfare programs are inequitable and invite abuse. Worse, we are wasting badly needed resources without reaching many of the truly needy.

Complex welfare programs cannot be reformed overnight. Surely we cannot simply dump welfare into the laps of the 50 States, their local taxpayers or private charities, and just walk away from it. Nor is it the right time for massive and sweeping changes while we are still recovering from a recession.

Nevertheless, there are still plenty of improvements we can make. I will ask Congress for Presidential authority to tighten up rules for eligibility and benefits.

Last year I twice sought long overdue reform of the scandal riddled Food Stamp program. This year I say again: Let's give Food Stamps to those most in need. Let's not give any to those who don't need them.

Crime

Protecting the life and property of the citizen at home is the responsibility of all public officials but is primarily the job of local and State law enforcement authorities.

Americans have always found the very thought of a Federal police force repugnant and so do I. But there are proper ways in which we can help to ensure domestic tranquility as the Constitution charges us.

My recommendations on how to control violent crime were submitted to the Congress last June with strong emphasis on protecting the innocent victims of crime.

To keep a convicted criminal from committing more crimes we must put him in prison so he cannot harm more law-abiding citizens. To be effective, this punishment must be swift and certain.

Too often criminals are not sent to prison after conviction but are allowed to return to the streets.

Some judges are reluctant to send convicted criminals to prison because of inadequate facilities. To alleviate this problem at the Federal level, my new budget proposes the construction of four new Federal facilities.

To speed Federal justice, I propose an increase this year in U.S. Attorneys prosecuting Federal crimes and reinforcement of the number of U.S. Marshals.

Additional Federal judges are needed, as recommended by me and the Judicial Conference.

Another major threat to every American's person and property is the criminal carrying a handgun. The way to cut down on the criminal use of guns is not to take guns away from the law-abiding citizen, but to impose mandatory sentences for crimes in which a gun is used, make it harder to obtain cheap guns for criminal purposes, and concentrate gun control enforcement in high crime areas.

My budget recommends 500 additional Federal agents in the 11 largest metropolitan high crime areas to help local authorities stop criminals from selling and using handguns.

The sale of hard drugs is on the increase again. I have directed all agencies of the Federal Government to step up enforcement efforts against those who deal in drugs. In 1975, Federal agents seized substantially more heroin coming into our country than in 1974.

As President, I have talked personally with the leaders of Mexico, Colombia and Turkey to urge greater efforts by their Governments to control effectively the production and shipment of hard drugs.

I recommended months ago that the Congress enact mandatory fixed sentences for persons convicted of Federal crimes involving the sale of hard drugs. Hard drugs degrade the spirit as they destroy the body of their users.

It is unrealistic and misleading to hold out the hope that the Federal Government can move in to every neighborhood and clean up crime. Under the Constitution, the greatest responsibility for curbing crime lies with State and local authorities. They are the frontline fighters in the war against crime.

There are definite ways in which the Federal Government can help them. I will propose in the new budget that the Congress authorize almost $7 billion over the next five years to assist State and local governments to protect the safety and property of all citizens.

As President I pledge the strict enforcement of Federal laws and—by example, support, and leadership—to help State and local authorities enforce their laws. Together we must protect the victims of crime and ensure domestic tranquility.

Last year I strongly recommended a five-year extension of the existing revenue sharing legislation which thus far has provided $23.5 billion to help State and local units of government solve problems at home. This program has been effective with decision-making transferred from the Federal Government to locally elected officials. Congress must act this year or State and local units of government will have to drop programs or raise local taxes.

Including my health care reforms, I propose to consolidate some 59 separate Federal programs and provide flexible Federal dollar grants to help States, cities and local agencies in such important areas as education, child nutrition, and social services. This flexible system will do the job better and do it closer to home.

National Security

The protection of the lives and property of Americans from foreign enemies is one of my primary responsibilities as President.

In a world of instant communications and intercontinental missiles, in a world economy that is global and interdependent, our relations with other nations become more, not less, important to the lives of Americans.

America has had a unique role in the world since the day of our independence 200 years ago. And ever since the end of World War II, we have borne—successfully—a heavy responsibility for ensuring a stable world order and hope for human progress.

Today, the state of our foreign policy is sound and strong.

● We are at peace—and I will do all in my power to keep it that way.

● Our military forces are capable and ready; our military power is without equal. And I intend to keep it that way.

● Our principal alliances, with the industrial democracies of the Atlantic Community and Japan, have never been more solid.

● A further agreement to limit the strategic arms race may be achieved.

● We have an improving relationship with China, the world's most populous nation.

● The key elements for peace among the nations of the Middle East now exist.

● Our traditional friendships in Latin America, Africa, and Asia, continue.

● We have taken the role of leadership in launching a serious and hopeful dialogue between the industrial world and the developing world.

● We have achieved significant reform of the international monetary system.

We should be proud of what the United States has accomplished.

The American people have heard too much about how terrible our mistakes, how evil our deeds, and how misguided our purposes. The American people know better.

The truth is we are the world's greatest democracy. We remain the symbol of man's aspirations for liberty and well-being. We are the embodiment of hope for progress.

I say it is time we quit downgrading ourselves as a nation. Of course it is our responsibility to learn the right lessons from past mistakes. It is our duty to see that they never happen again. But our greater duty is to look to the future. The world's troubles will not go away.

The American people want strong and effective international and defense policies.

In our Constitutional system, these policies should reflect consultation and accommodation between the President and Congress. But in the final analysis, as the framers of our Constitution knew from hard experience, the foreign relations of the United States can be conducted effectively only if there is strong central direction that allows flexibility of action. That responsibility clearly rests with the President.

I pledge to the American people policies which seek a secure, just, and peaceful world. I pledge to the Congress to work *with* you to that end.

We must not face a future in which we can no longer help our friends, such as in Angola—even in limited and carefully controlled ways. We must not lose all capacity to respond short of military intervention. Some hasty actions of the Congress during the past year—most recently in respect to Angola—were in my view very short-sighted. Unfortunately, they are still very much on the minds of our allies and our adversaries.

A strong defense posture gives weight to our values and our views in international negotiations; it assures the vigor of our alliances; and it sustains our efforts to promote settlements of international conflicts. Only from a position of strength can we negotiate a balanced agreement to limit the growth of nuclear arms. Only a balanced agreement will serve our interest and minimize the threat of nuclear confrontation.

The Defense Budget I will submit to the Congress for fiscal 1977 will show an essential increase over last year. It provides for a real growth in purchasing power over last year's Defense Budget, which includes the costs of our All-Volunteer Force.

We are continuing to make economies to enhance the efficiency of our military forces. But the budget I will submit represents the necessity of American strength for the real world in which we live.

As conflict and rivalries persist in the world, our United States intelligence capabilities must be the best in the world.

The crippling of our foreign intelligence services increases the danger of American involvement in direct armed conflict. Our adversaries are encouraged to attempt new adventures, while our own ability to monitor events, and to influence events short of military action—is undermined.

Without effective intelligence capability, the United States stands blindfolded and hobbled.

In the near future, I will take actions to reform and strengthen our intelligence community. I ask for your *positive* cooperation. It is time to go beyond sensationalism and ensure an effective, responsible, and responsive intelligence capability.

Future

Tonight I have spoken of our problems at home and abroad. I have recommended policies that will meet the challenge of our third century.

I have no doubt that our Union will endure—better, stronger and with more individual freedom.

We can see forward only dimly—one year, five years, a generation perhaps. Like our forefathers, we know that if we meet the challenges of our own time with a common sense of purpose and conviction—if we remain true to our Constitution and our ideals—then we can know that the future will be better than the past.

I see America today crossing a threshold, not just because it is our Bicentennial, but because we have been tested in adversity. We have taken a new look at what we want to be and what we want our nation to become.

I see America resurgent, certain once again that life will be better for our children than it is for us, seeking strength that cannot be counted in megatons and riches that cannot be eroded by inflation.

I see these United States of America moving forward as before toward a more perfect Union where the government serves and the people rule.

We will not make this happen simply by making speeches, good or bad, yours, or mine, but by hard work and hard decisions made with courage and common sense.

I have heard many inspiring Presidential speeches, but the words I remember best were spoken by Dwight D. Eisenhower.

"America is not good because it is great," the President said. "America is great because it is good."

President Eisenhower was raised in a poor but religious home in the heart of America. His simple words echoed President Lincoln's eloquent testament that "right makes might." And Lincoln in turn evoked the silent image of George Washington kneeling in prayer at Valley Forge.

So all these magic memories, which link eight generations of Americans, are summed up in the inscription just above me.

How many times have we seen it?—"In God We Trust."

Let us engrave it now in each of our hearts as we begin our Bicentennial.

GERALD R. FORD

Text of President's Fiscal '77 Budget Message

Following is the text of President Ford's fiscal 1977 budget message to Congress, released Jan. 21:

To the Congress of the United States:

The Budget of the United States is a good roadmap of where we have been, where we are now, and where we should be going as a people. The budget reflects the President's sense of priorities. It reflects his best judgment of how we must choose among competing interests. And it reveals his philosophy of how the public and private spheres should be related.

Accordingly, I have devoted a major portion of my own time over the last several months to shaping the budget for fiscal year 1977 and laying the groundwork for the years that follow.

As I see it, the budget has three important dimensions. One is the budget as an element of our economic policy. The total size of the budget and the deficit or surplus that results can substantially affect the general health of our economy—in a good way or in a bad way. If we try to stimulate the economy beyond its capacity to respond, it will lead only to a future whirlwind of inflation and unemployment.

The budget I am proposing for fiscal year 1977 and the direction I seek for the future meet the test of responsible fiscal policy. The combination of tax and spending changes I propose will set us on a course that not only leads to a balanced budget within three years, but also improves the prospects for the economy to stay on a growth path *that we can sustain.* This is not a policy of the quick fix; it does not hold out the hollow promise that we can wipe out inflation and unemployment overnight. Instead, it is an honest, realistic policy—a policy that says we can steadily reduce inflation and unemployment if we maintain a prudent, balanced approach. This policy has begun to prove itself in recent months as we have made substantial headway in pulling out of the recession and reducing the rate of inflation; it will prove itself decisively if we stick to it.

A second important dimension of the budget is that it helps to define the boundaries between responsibilities that we assign to governments and those that remain in the hands of private institutions and individual citizens.

Over the years, the growth of government has been gradual and uneven, but the trend is unmistakable. Although the predominant growth has been at the State and local level, the Federal Government has contributed to the trend too. We must not continue drifting in the direction of bigger and bigger government. The driving force of our 200-year history has been our private sector. If we rely on it and nurture it, the economy will continue to grow, providing new and better choices for our people and the resources necessary to meet our shared needs. If, instead, we continue to increase government's share of our economy, we will have no choice but to raise taxes and will, in the process, dampen further the forces of competition, risk, and reward that have served us so well. With stagnation of these forces, the issue of the future would surely be focused on who gets what from an economy of little or no growth rather than, as it should be, on the use to be made of expanding incomes and resources.

As an important step toward reversing the long-term trend, my budget for 1977 proposes to cut the rate of Federal spending growth, year to year, to 5.5%—less than half the average growth rate we have experienced in the last 10 years. At the same time, I am proposing further, permanent income tax reductions so that individuals and businesses can spend and invest these dollars instead of having the Federal Government collect and spend them.

A third important dimension of the budget is the way it sorts out priorities. In formulating this budget, I have tried to achieve fairness and balance:

—between the taxpayer and those who will benefit by Federal spending;

—between national security and other pressing needs;

—between our own generation and the world we want to leave to our children;

—between those in some need and those most in need;

—between the programs we already have and those we would like to have;

—between aid to individuals and aid to State and local governments;

—between immediate implementation of a good idea and the need to allow time for transition;

—between the desire to solve our problems quickly and the realization that for some problems, good solutions will take more time; and

—between Federal control and direction to assure achievement of common goals and the recognition that State and local governments and individuals may do as well or better without restraints.

Clearly, one of the highest priorities for our Government is always to secure the defense of our country. There is no alternative. If we in the Federal Government fail in this responsibility, our other objectives are meaningless.

Accordingly, I am recommending a significant increase in defense spending for 1977. If in good conscience I could propose less, I would. Great good could be accomplished with other uses of these dollars. My request is based on a careful assessment of the international situation and the contingencies we must be prepared to meet. The amounts I seek will provide the national defense it now appears we need. We dare not do less. And if our efforts to secure international arms limitations falter, we will need to do more.

Assuring our Nation's needs for energy must also be among our highest priorities. My budget gives that priority.

While providing fully for our defense and energy needs, I have imposed upon these budgets the same discipline that I have applied in reviewing other programs. Savings have been achieved in a number of areas. We cannot tolerate waste in any program.

In our domestic programs, my objective has been to achieve a balance between all the things we would like to do and those things we can realistically afford to do. The hundreds of pages that spell out the details of my program proposals tell the story, but some examples illustrate the point.

I am proposing that we take steps to address the haunting fear of our elderly that a prolonged, serious illness could cost them and their children everything they have. My medicare reform proposal would provide protection against such catastrophic health costs. No elderly person would have to pay over $500 per year for covered hospital or nursing home care, and no more than $250 per year for covered physician services. To offset the costs of

Budget Totals Since 1975

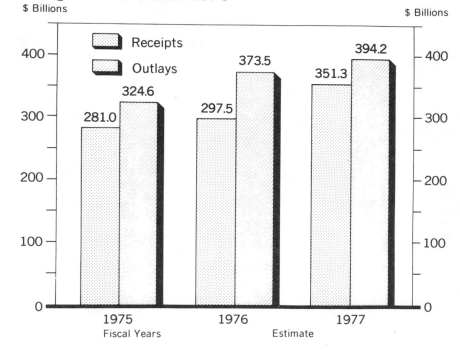

this additional protection and to slow down the runaway increases in federally funded medical expenses, I am recommending adjustments to the medicare program so that within the new maximums beneficiaries contribute more to the costs of their care than they do now.

My budget provides a full cost-of-living increase for those receiving social security or other Federal retirement benefits. We must recognize, however, that the social security trust fund is becoming depleted. To restore its integrity, I am asking the Congress to raise social security taxes, effective January 1, 1977, and to adopt certain other reforms of the system. Higher social security taxes and the other reforms I am proposing may be controversial, but they are the right thing to do. The American people understand that we must pay for the things we want. I know that those who are working now want to be sure that the money will be there to pay their benefits when their working days are over.

My budget also proposes that we replace 59 grant programs with broad block grants in four important areas:

—A health block grant that will consolidate medicaid and 15 other health programs. States will be able to make their own priority choices for use of these Federal funds to help low-income people with their health needs.

—An education block grant that will consolidate 27 grant programs for education into a single flexible Federal grant to States, primarily for use in helping disadvantaged and handicapped children.

—A block grant for feeding needy children that will consolidate 15 complex and overlapping programs. Under existing programs, 700,000 needy children receive no benefits. Under my program, all needy children can be fed, but subsidies for the nonpoor will be eliminated.

—A block grant that will support a community's social service programs for the needy. This would be accomplished by removing current requirements unnecessarily restricting the flexibility of States in providing such services.

These initiatives will result in more equitable distribution of Federal dollars, and provide greater State discretion and responsibility. All requirements that States match Federal funds will be eliminated. Such reforms are urgently needed, but my proposals recognize that they will, in some cases, require a period of transition.

These are only examples. My budget sets forth many other recommendations. Some involve new initiatives. Others seek restraint. The American people know that promises that the Federal Government will do more for them every year have not been kept. I make no such promises. I offer no such illusion: This budget does not shrink from hard choices where necessary. Notwithstanding those hard choices, I believe this budget reflects a forward-looking spirit that is in keeping with our heritage as we begin our Nation's third century.

GERALD R. FORD

January 21, 1976.

Military Assistance

Following is the White House text of President Ford's Jan. 20 message to Congress on the military assistance program.

TO THE CONGRESS OF
THE UNITED STATES:

The Foreign Assistance Act of 1974, enacted by the 93rd Congress on December 30, 1974, expresses the sense of the Congress that the policies and purposes of the military assistance program should be "reexamined in light of changes in world conditions and the economic position of the United States in relation to countries receiving such assistance." Section 17(a) of the act expresses the view that the program, except for military education and training activities, "should be reduced and terminated as rapidly as feasible consistent with the security and foreign policy requirements of the United States."

To give effect to section 17(a) of the act, the Congress directed that I submit to the first session of the 94th Congress a detailed plan for the "reduction and eventual elimination of the present military assistance program." In the intervening period, the two foreign affairs committees are considering draft legislation that would arbitrarily terminate grant military assistance programs after September 30, 1977, unless authorized by the Congress.

I have stressed repeatedly in my messages to the Congress and in my reports to the American people, the need for constancy and continuity in our foreign policy, and, in particular, in our relationship with nations which turn to us for necessary support in meeting their most pressing security needs. Since World War II, the United States has extended such assistance to friends and allies. This policy has contributed immeasurably to the cause of peace and stability in the world. Many countries which once received grant military assistance have achieved self-sufficiency in providing for their security interests, and grant military assistance to a number of current recipients is being reduced or eliminated.

I firmly believe that grant military assistance in some form will remain a basic requirement for an effective U.S. foreign policy for the foreseeable future. In the Middle East and elsewhere, we must maintain our flexibility to respond to future assistance requirements which cannot now be reckoned with precision. It will continue to be in our interest to be able to meet the legitimate security requirements of countries who cannot shoulder the full burden of their own defense and grant assistance will continue to be needed to assist countries that provide us essential military bases and facilities. These requirements will not disappear; they are the necessary result of the unsettled state of the world and of our role as a world power.

Nevertheless, in recognition of the expressed sense of the Congress, I have, in preparing the 1977 budget and legislative program, reexamined the policies, purposes, and scope of the military assistance program with a view to reducing or terminating any country programs no longer essential to the security and foreign policy interests of the United States. As a consequence of this review, the 1977 military assistance budget request will reflect a 28 percent reduction below the 1976 request, the termination of grant materiel assistance to Korea, and elimination of five small grant programs in Latin America. Furthermore, our preliminary estimate of the 1978 requirements indicates that additional reductions and some additional program terminations should be feasible in the absence of unfavorable security or economic development in the countries concerned.

I must emphasize, however, that offsetting increases in foreign military sales credits will be required in most instances to meet the legitimate military needs of our friends and allies at a time when much of their military equipment is reaching obsolescence and prices of new equipment are increasing drastically. Moreover, the capacities of many of these grant military aid recipients to assume additional foreign exchange costs because of reduced military aid are limited by the necessity to cope with higher oil prices as well as the impact of the recession in the developed countries on their exports. In these circumstances, I believe the interests of the United States in the continued security of these countries are better served by a gradual reduction of grant military assistance attuned to the particular circumstances of each country than by an arbitrary termination of all such assistance on a given date.

Finally, I must emphasize that in this uncertain and unpredictable era we must maintain our national strength and our national purposes and remain faithful to our friends and allies. In these times, we must not deny ourselves the capacity to meet international crises and problems with all the instruments now at our disposal. I urge the Congress to preserve the authorities in law to provide grant military aid, an instrument of our national security and foreign policy that has served the national interest well for more than 30 years.

GERALD R. FORD

The White House,
January 20, 1976.

Programs for Elderly

Following is the White House text of President Ford's Feb. 9 message to Congress on programs for the elderly:

TO THE CONGRESS OF
THE UNITED STATES:

I ask the Congress to join with me in making improvements in programs serving the elderly.

As President, I intend to do everything in my power to help our nation demonstrate by its deeds a deep concern for the dignity and worth of our older persons. By so doing, our nation will continue to benefit from the contributions that older persons can make to the strengthening of our nation.

The proposals being forwarded to Congress are directly related to the health and security of older Americans. Their prompt enactment will demonstrate our concern that lifetimes of sacrifice and hard work conclude in hope rather than despair.

The single greatest threat to the quality of life of older Americans is inflation. Our first priority continues to be the fight against inflation. We have been able to reduce by nearly half the double digit inflation experienced in 1974. But the retired, living on fixed incomes, have been particularly hard hit and the progress we have made in reducing inflation has not benefited them enough. We will continue our efforts to reduce federal spending, balance the budget, and reduce taxes. The particular vulnerability of the aged to the burdens of inflation, however, requires that specific improvements be made in two major Federal programs, Social Security and Medicare.

We must begin by insuring that the Social Security system is beyond challenge. Maintaining the integrity of the system is a vital obligation each generation has to those who have worked hard and contributed to it all their lives. I strongly reaffirm my commitment to a stable and financially sound Social Security system. My 1977 budget and legislative program include several elements which I believe are essential to protect the solvency and integrity of the system.

First, to help protect our retired and disabled citizens against the hardships of inflation, my budget request to the Congress includes a full cost of living increase in Social Security benefits, to be effective with checks received in July 1976. This will help maintain the purchasing power of 32 million Americans.

Second, to insure the financial integrity of the Social Security trust funds, I am proposing legislation to increase payroll taxes by three-tenths of one percent each for employees and employers. This increase will cost no worker more than $1 a week, and most will pay less. These additional revenues are needed to stabilize the trust funds so that current income will be certain to either equal or exceed current outgo.

Third, to avoid serious future financing problems I will submit later this year a change in the Social Security laws to correct a serious flaw in the current system. The current formula which determines benefits for workers who retire in the future does not properly reflect wage and price fluctuations. This is an inadvert error which could lead to unnecessarily inflated benefits.

The change I am proposing will not affect cost of living increases in benefits after retirement, and will in no way alter the benefit levels of current recipients. On the other hand, it will protect future generations against unnecessary costs and excessive tax increases.

I believe that the prompt enactment of all of these proposals is necessary to maintain a sound Social Security system and to preserve its financial integrity.

Income security is not our only concern. We need to focus also on the special health care needs of our elder citizens. Medicare and other Federal health programs have been successful in improving access to quality medical care for the aged. Before the inception of Medicare and Medicaid in 1966, per capita health expenditures for our aged were $445 per year. Just eight years later, in FY 1974, per capita health expenditures for the elderly had increased to $1218, an increase of 174 percent. But despite the dramatic increase in medical services made possible by public programs, some problems remain.

There are weaknesses in the Medicare program which must be corrected. Three particular aspects of the current program concern me: 1) its failure to provide our elderly with protection against catastrophic illness costs, 2) the serious effects that health care cost inflation is having on the Medicare program, and 3) lack of incentives to encourage efficient and economical use of hospital and medical services. My proposal addresses each of these problems.

In my State of the Union Message I proposed protection against catastrophic health expenditures for Medicare beneficiaries. This will be accomplished in two ways. First, I propose extending Medicare benefits by providing coverage for unlimited days of hospital and skilled nursing facility care for beneficiaries. Second, I propose to limit the out-of-pocket expenses of beneficiaries, for covered services, to $500 per year for hospital and skilled nursing services and $250 per year for physician and other non-institutional medical services.

This will mean that each year over a billion dollars of benefit payments will be targeted for handling the financial burden of prolonged illness. Millions of older persons live in fear of being stricken by an illness that will call for expensive hospital and medical care over a long period of time. Most often they do not have the resources to pay the bills. The members of their families share their fears because they also do not have the resources to pay such large bills. We have been talking about this problem for many years. We have it within our power to act now so that today's older persons will not be forced to live under this kind of a shadow. I urge the Congress to act promptly.

Added steps are needed to slow down the inflation of health costs and to help in the financing of this catastrophic protection. Therefore, I am recommending that the Congress limit increases in Medicare payment rates in 1977 and 1978 to 7% a day for hospitals and 4% for physician services.

Additional cost-sharing provisions are also needed to encourage economical use of the hospital and medical services included under Medicare. Therefore, I am recommending that patients pay 10% of hospital and nursing home charges after the first day and that the existing deductible for medical services be increased from $60 to $77 annually.

The savings from placing a limit on increases in Medicare payment rates and some of the revenue from increased cost sharing will be used to finance the catastrophic illness program.

I feel that, on balance, these proposals will provide our elder citizens with protection against catastrophic illness costs, promote efficient utilization of services, and moderate the increases in health care costs.

The legislative proposals which I have described are only part of the over-all effort we are making on behalf of older Americans. Current conditions call for continued and intensified action on a broad front.

We have made progress in recent years. We have responded, for example, to recommendations made at the 1971 White House Conference on Aging. A Supplemental Security Income program was enacted. Social Security benefits have been increased in accord with increases in the cost of living. The Social Security retirement test was liberalized. Many inequities in payments to women have been eliminated. The 35 million workers who have earned rights in private pension plans now have increased protection.

In addition we have continued to strengthen the Older Americans Act. I have supported the concept of the Older Americans Act since its inception in 1965, and last November signed the most recent amendments into law.

A key component of the Older Americans Act is the National Network on Aging which provides a solid foundation on which action can be based. I am pleased that we have been able to assist in setting up this network of 56 State and 489 Area Agencies on Aging, and 700 local nutrition agencies. These local nutrition agencies, for example, provide 300,000 hot meals a day five days a week.

The network provides a structure which can be used to attack other important problems. A concern of mine is that the voice of the elderly, as consumers, be heard in the governmental decision-making process. The Network on Aging offers opportunities for this through membership on advisory councils related to State and Area

Agencies on Aging, Nutrition Project Agencies and by participation in public hearings on the annual State and Area Plans. Such involvement can and will have a significant impact on determining what services for the aging are to be given the highest priorities at the local level.

The principal goal of this National Network on Aging is to bring into being coordinated comprehensive systems for the provision of service to the elderly at the community level. I join in the call for hard and creative work at all levels—Federal, State and Area—in order to achieve this objective. I am confident that progress can be made.

Toward this end, the Administration on Aging and a number of Federal Departments and agencies have signed agreements which will help to make available to older persons a fair share of the Federal funds available in such areas as housing, transportation, social services, law enforcement, adult education and manpower—resources which can play a major role in enabling older persons to continue to live in their own homes.

Despite these efforts, however, five percent of our older men and women require the assistance provided by skilled nursing homes and other long term care facilities. To assist these citizens, an ombudsman process, related solely to the persons in these facilities, is being put into operation by the National Network on Aging. We believe that this program will help to resolve individual complaints, facilitate important citizen involvement in the vigorous enforcement of Federal, State and local laws designed to improve health and safety standards, and to improve the quality of care in these facilities.

Today's older persons have made invaluable contributions to the strengthening of our nation. They have provided the nation with a vision and strength that has resulted in unprecedented advancements in all of the areas of our life. Our national moral strength is due in no small part to the significance of their contributions. We must continue and strengthen both our commitment to doing everything we can to respond to the needs of the elderly and our determination to draw on their strengths.

Our entire history has been marked by a tradition of growth and progress. Each succeeding generation can measure its progress in part by its ability to recognize, respect and renew the contributions of earlier generations. I believe that the Social Security and Medicare improvements I am proposing, when combined with the action programs under the Older Americans Act, will insure a measure of progress for the elderly and thus provide real hope for us all.

GERALD R. FORD

The White House,
February 9, 1976.

Federal Election Commission

Following is the White House text of President Ford's proposal for continuing the Federal Election Commission:

TO THE CONGRESS OF
THE UNITED STATES:

In only two weeks time, unless there is affirmative action by the Congress, the Federal Election Commission will be stripped of most of its powers.

We must not allow that to happen. The American people can and should expect that our elections in this Bicentennial year, as well as other years, will be free of abuse. And they know that the Federal Election Commission is the single most effective unit for meeting that challenge.

The Commission has become the chief instrument for achieving clean Federal elections in 1976. If it becomes an empty shell, public confidence in our political process will be further eroded and the door will be opened to possible abuses in the coming elections. There would be no one to interpret, advise or provide needed certainty to the candidates with regard to the complexities of the Federal Election law. If we maintain the Commission, we can rebuild and restore the public faith that is essential for a democracy.

The fate of the Commission has been called into question, of course, by the decision of the Supreme Court on January 30. The Court ruled that the Commission was improperly constituted. The Congress gave the Commission executive powers but then, in violation of the Constitution, the Congress reserved to itself the authority to appoint four of the six members of the Commission. The Court said that this defect could be cured by having all members of the Commission nominated by the President upon the advice and consent of the Senate. Under the Court's ruling, the Commission was given a 30-day lease on life so that the defect might be corrected.

I fully recognize that other aspects of the Court's decision and that, indeed, the original law itself have created valid concerns among Members of Congress. I share many of those concerns, and I share in a desire to reform and improve upon the current law. For instance, one section of the law provides for a one-House veto of Commission regulations, a requirement that is unconstitutional as applied to regulations of an agency performing Executive functions. I am willing to defer legislative resolution of this problem, just as I hope the members of Congress will defer adjustment of other provisions in the interest of the prompt action which is now essential.

It is clear that the 30-day period provided by the Court to reconstitute the Commission is not sufficient to undertake a comprehensive review and reform of the campaign laws. And most assuredly, this 30-day period must not become a convenient excuse to make ineffective the campaign reforms that are already on the books and have been upheld by the Court. There is a growing danger that opponents of campaign reform will exploit this opportunity for the wrong purposes. This cannot be tolerated; there must be no retreat from our commitment to clean elections.

Therefore, I am today submitting remedial legislation to the Congress for immediate action. This legislation incorporates two recommendations that I discussed with the bipartisan leaders of the Congress shortly after the Court issued its opinion.

First, I propose that the Federal Election Commission be reconstituted so that all of its six members are nominated by the President and confirmed by the Senate. This action must be taken before the February 29 deadline.

Second, to ensure that a full-scale review and reform of the election laws are ultimately undertaken, I propose that we limit through the 1976 elections the application of those laws administered by the Commission. When the elections have been completed and all of us have a better understanding of the problems in our current statutes, I will submit to the Congress a new, comprehensive election reform bill to apply to future elections. I also pledge that I will work with the Congress to enact a new law that will meet many of the objections of the current system.

I know there is widespread disagreement within the Congress on what reforms should be undertaken. That controversy is healthy; it bespeaks of a vigorous interest in our political system. But we must not allow our divergent views to disrupt the approaching elections. Our most important task now is to ensure the continued life of the Federal Election Commission, and I urge the Congress to work with me in achieving that goal.

GERALD R. FORD

The White House,
February 16, 1976

Social Services

Following is the White House text of President Ford's proposal for providing block grants to the states for community services:

TO THE CONGRESS OF
THE UNITED STATES:

Today the Secretary of the Department of Health, Education, and Welfare is transmitting my proposed Financial Assistance for Community Services Act to the Congress.

This proposal is in keeping with my philosophy of reducing unnecessary and burdensome Federal restrictions while increasing State and local flexibility and responsibility in the administration of social programs.

This reform proposal will improve and strengthen the program of social services established under Title XX of the Social Security Act. It will provide a $2.5 billion block grant annually to the States on a population basis. It will eliminate the requirement for State matching funds, as well as most Federal requirements and prohibitions on the use of Federal funds.

These changes are an important step toward an improved Federal-State relationship in the social services field. Enactment of Title XX in January, 1975, was a beginning. That law eliminated many of the problems of the past by giving States broad authority to allocate resources within a general framework. Rather than making States responsible to the Federal government, accountability for social services was made a matter between each State and its citizens through an open planning process—a process which has shown great promise.

Title XX, however, did not go far enough. It added new restrictions which interfere with effective delivery of services. Officials at State and local levels of government indicate that they are willing and able to assume greater responsibility to gain greater flexibility in meeting local needs.

The proposed Financial Assistance for Community Services Act will:

—Eliminate the requirement that States must match one State dollar for three Federal dollars.

—Eliminate numerous restrictive conditions on how Federal funds may be used: burdensome Federal requirements for child day care; limitations on social services funding for health and institutional care; and procedures for the imposition of fees and the determination of eligibility.

—Concentrate Federal dollars on people most in need, those under the poverty threshold and those receiving public assistance.

—Assure that no State will receive less money as a result of this legislation than it received in fiscal year 1976.

—Decrease Federal monitoring and oversight of State plan requirements and expenditures of funds with the States assuming greater responsibility in this area.

—Improve the public planning process by which citizens and local governments participate in identifying needs and establishing priorities.

I ask Congress to enact this legislation promptly so that States may begin to use Federal and local money more effectively.

GERALD R. FORD

The White House,
February 23, 1976

Health Block Grants

Following is the White House text of President Ford's proposal for giving block grants to the states for health programs:

TO THE CONGRESS OF
THE UNITED STATES:

The health of our people is one of our Nation's most vital resources.

Significant progress has been made in improving the health of the Nation's people during the last 25 years, as can be seen in the reductions in the infant mortality rate, increases in life expectancy, and the conquering of some communicable diseases. This progress has come under a largely private health care system with the support of public funds.

In the past 10 year period (1965-1975) Federal spending for health has increased from $5 billion to $37 billion. With greater Federal funding has come a multitude of Federal programs, regulations and restrictions—all motivated by the best of intentions but each adding to the confusion and overlap and inequity that now characterizes our efforts at the national level.

Today I am proposing to the Congress legislation that addresses these problems. I am asking Congress to enact the Financial Assistance for Health Care Act which will consolidate Medicaid and 15 categorical Federal health programs into a $10 billion block grant to the States. I am proposing that future Federal funding for this new program be increased annually in increments of $500 million plus the amounts needed after 1980 to ensure that no State will in the future receive less under this proposal than it received in fiscal year 1976.

The Financial Assistance for Health Care proposal is being submitted after extensive consultation with organizations representing the publicly elected officials who will be responsible for administering the program. I believe this proposal represents a major step toward overcoming some of the most serious defects in our present system of Federal financing of health care.

My proposal is designed to achieve a more equitable distribution of Federal health dollars among States and to increase State control over health spending. My proposal also recognizes the appropriate Federal role in providing financial assistance to State and local governments to improve the quality and distribution of health services.

The enactment of this legislation will achieve a more equitable distribution of Federal health dollars by providing funds according to a formula giving primary weight to a State's low-income population. The formula also takes into account the relative "tax effort" made by a State and the per capita income of that State.

Let me emphasize that every State will receive more Federal funds in fiscal years 1977, 1978 and 1979 under the block grant than it received in fiscal year 1976. My proposal also allows for a gradual phase-in of the distribution formula in future years to insure a systematic, orderly transition that will permit States to adjust to the new program.

To assure accountability and responsiveness to the public, my proposal requires each State to develop an annual health care plan as a condition to receiving Federal funds. This plan will be developed through a Statewide public review and comment process which will assure participation by all concerned parties. Thus, increased State responsibility will be coupled with expanded public participation, and accountability in the development of State health policies.

This proposed consolidation of health programs is essential to continue our national progress in the field of health. It is designed to permit States greater flexibility in providing for delivery of health care services to those with low income. It eliminates the requirements for State matching. And it recognizes the need for a cooperative relationship among governments at all levels. My proposal would reduce Federal red tape, increase local control over health spending, and expand public participation in health planning.

While I am proposing to increase State control over health spending, we will continue to concentrate our efforts in areas of appropriate Federal responsibility. For example, my budget proposals for 1977 include the following:

—In food and drug safety, I have asked for $226 million in 1977, an increase of $17 million, to enable further progress in priority areas;

—In the area of drug abuse prevention, I propose almost $500 million for prevention and treatment to expand national drug abuse treatment capacity to meet the current need;

—My budget requests more than $3 billion for health research, including continued support of major national efforts in cancer and heart disease research and support for new scientific opportunities in the fields of environmental health, aging, and immunology;

—In our effort to improve the training and utilization of doctors and other health professionals, I have requested new legislation and funding of $319 million, designed to concentrate on the problems of geographic and specialty maldistribution of health professionals;

—To assist local communities to attract physicians, dentists and other health professionals to underserved areas, I am proposing to expand the National Health Service Corps demonstration program 38 percent from $18 million to $25 million;

—To assist the development of a strong health maintenance alternative, I have directed HEW to move rapidly in administering the dual option provisions of the HMO Act. And, to complete the 5-year effort to demonstrate and test the health maintenance organization concept, I have requested an additional year's authorization for new commitments. As of last June, there were 10 health maintenance organizations certified through the dual option provisions;

—To provide improved health services to American Indians and Alaska Natives, I am asking for $355-million. Spending by the Indian Health Service alone in 1977 will result in over $685 per beneficiary, or over $2,740 per Indian family of four;

—In the area of veterans' health care, I have requested $4.5-billion to assure continued quality care by providing for increases in medical staff and research related to VA health care delivery.

A realistic assessment of the present health care programs and the responsibilities of Federal, State, and local governments fully demonstrates that the reforms I am proposing in Federal health care are needed now. The Medicare Improvements of 1976 that I recommended to the Congress on February 11 also represents a balanced response to needed program reforms. This proposal is designed to improve catastrophic health cost protection for our aged and disabled, restrain cost increases in the Medicare program and provide training for the hospital insurance trust fund.

I request that the Congress give both these measures the earliest possible consideration.

GERALD R. FORD

The White House,
February 25, 1976

Education Block Grants

Following is the White House text of President Ford's message to Congress requesting financial assistance to the states for education in the form of block grants rather than the 24 existing categorical programs:

TO THE CONGRESS OF
THE UNITED STATES:

The education of our children is vital to the future of the United States. From the start, our Founding Fathers knew that ignorance and free government could not co-exist. Our nation has acted from the beginning on the sound principle that control over our schools should remain at the State and local level. Nothing could be more destructive of the diversity of thought and opinion necessary for national progress than an excess of control by the central government.

In recent years, our national sense of fairness and equity has led to an increasing number of Federal programs of aid to education. The Federal government has recognized a responsibility to help ensure adequate educational opportunities for those with special needs, such as the educationally deprived and the handicapped. We have appropriately provided States and localities with added resources to help them improve opportunities for such students. At the same time, we have channeled our aid into too many narrow and restrictive categorical programs. As a result, we have made it more difficult for the schools to educate.

It is time that we reconcile our good intentions with the recognition that we at the Federal level cannot know what is best for every school child in every classroom in the country.

In my State of the Union address, I spoke of the need for a new realism and a new balance in our system of Federalism—a balance that favors greater responsibility and freedom for the leaders of our State and local governments.

Our experience in education demonstrates that those principles are not abstract political philosophy, but guides to the concrete action we must take to help assure the survival of our system of free government. We must continually guard against Federal control over public schools.

I am proposing today the Financial Assistance for Elementary and Secondary Education Act which will consolidate 24 existing programs into one block grant. The focus of this block grant will be on improved educational opportunities for those with special needs—the handicapped and educationally deprived. Federal funds will be provided with a minimum of Federal regulation and a maximum of local control. My proposal is based on the conviction that education needs can be most effectively and creatively met by allowing States greater flexibility in the use of Federal funds.

I am particularly pleased at the extent to which my proposal reflects extensive consultations with individuals, organizations representing publicly elected officials and leaders in the education community. The proposal has been modified and strengthened since the time of my State of the Union message as a result of suggestions we received. I am convinced it represents essential changes in our system of providing aid to education.

My proposals will consolidate programs in the following areas:
—Elementary and Secondary Education
—Education for the Handicapped
—Adult Education
—Vocational Education

To assure that students with special needs receive proper attention, the proposed legislation provides that 75 percent of a State's allocation be spent on the educationally deprived and handicapped, and that vocational education programs continue to be supported. The same strong civil rights compliance procedures that exist in the programs to be consolidated are included in this legislation.

Under the proposed legislation, funds will be allocated to States based on a formula which takes into account the number of school-aged children and the number of children from low-income families. No State will receive less money than it did in Fiscal Year 1976 under the programs to be consolidated. Further, local education agencies will be assured that the funds will reach the local level, where children are taught and where control should be exercised.

Vocational education is an important part of our total education system. Here, too, my proposal seeks greater flexibility at the local level while maintaining Federal support. States would be required to spend a portion of the funds they receive on vocational education, giving special emphasis to the educationally deprived and the handicapped.

Non-public school and Indian tribal children would continue to be eligible for assistance under this proposal. Where States do not serve such children, the Commissioner of Education will arrange to provide funds directly, using the appropriate share of the State's funds.

The proposed legislation will require States to develop a plan, with public participation, for the use of Federal funds. All interested citizens, students, parents and appropriate public and private institutions will participate in the development of the plan. States will be required to develop procedures for independent monitoring of compliance with their plan. State progress will be measured against the plan, but the plan itself will not be subject to Federal approval.

For Fiscal Year 1977 I am requesting $3.3 billion for the education block grant. For the next three fiscal years, I am proposing authorizations of $3.5 billion, $3.7 billion and $3.9 billion. For too long the real issue in our education programs—Federal versus State and local control—has been obscured by endless bickering over funding levels. Hopefully, with these request levels, we can focus the attention where it belongs, on reform of our education support programs.

Enactment of this legislation will allow people at the State and local level to stop worrying about entangling Federal red tape and turn their full attention to educating our youth.

I urge prompt and favorable consideration of the Financial Assistance for Elementary and Secondary Education Act.

GERALD R. FORD

The White House,
March 1, 1976

Energy Proposals

Following is the White House text of President Ford's legislative proposals for achieving U.S. energy independence.

TO THE CONGRESS OF
THE UNITED STATES:

A little over two years ago, the Arab embargo proved that our Nation had become excessively dependent upon others for our oil supplies. We now realize how critical energy is to the defense of our country, to the strength of our economy, and to the quality of our lives.

We must reduce our vulnerability to the economic disruption which a few foreign countries can cause by cutting off our energy supplies or by arbitrarily raising prices. We must regain our energy independence.

During the past year, we have made some progress toward achieving our energy independence goals, but the fact remains that we have a long way to go. However, we cannot take the steps required to solve our energy problems until the Congress provides the necessary additional authority that I have requested. If we do not take these steps, our vulnerability will increase dramatically.

In my first State of the Union Address last year, I pointed out that our vulnerability would continue to grow unless a comprehensive energy policy and program were implemented. I outlined these goals for regaining our energy independence:
—First, to halt our growing dependence on imported oil during the next few critical years.
—Second, to attain energy independence by 1985 by achieving invulnerability to disruption caused by oil import embargoes. Specifically, we must reduce oil imports to between 3 and 5 million barrels a day, with an accompanying ability to offset any future embargo with stored petroleum reserves and emergency standby measures.
—Third, to mobilize our technology and resources to supply a significant share of the free world's energy needs beyond 1985.

In pursuing these goals, we have sought to provide energy at the lowest cost consistent with our need for adequate and secure supplies. We should rely upon the private sector and market forces since it is the most efficient means of achieving these goals. We must also achieve a balance between our environmental and energy objectives.

These goals were reasonable and sound a year ago and they remain so today.

Since January of 1975, this Administration has initiated the most comprehensive set of energy programs possible under current authority. This includes actions to conserve energy, to increase the production of domestic energy resources, and to develop technology necessary to produce energy from newer sources.

During this time, I have also placed before the Congress a major set of legislative proposals that would provide the additional authority that is needed to achieve our energy independence goals.

Thus far, the Congress has completed action on only one major piece of energy legislation—the Energy Policy and Conservation Act— which I signed into law on

December 22, 1975. That law includes four of the original proposals I submitted to the Congress over a year ago. Eighteen other major legislative proposals still await final action by the Congress.

Natural Gas

The need for Congressional action is most critical in the area of natural gas. We must reverse the decline in natural gas production and deal effectively with the growing shortages that face us each winter.

Deregulating the price of new natural gas remains the most important action that can be taken by the Congress to improve our future gas supply situation. If the price of natural gas remains under current regulation, total domestic production will decline to less than 18 trillion cubic feet in 1985. However, if deregulation is enacted, production would be about 25 per cent higher by 1985. Natural gas shortages mean higher costs for consumers who are forced to switch to more expensive alternative fuels and mean, inevitably, an increasing dependence on imported oil. Curtailment of natural gas to industrial users in the winters ahead means more unemployment and further economic hardships.

Therefore, I again urge the Congress to approve legislation that will remove Federal price regulation from new natural gas supplies and will provide the added short-term authorities needed to deal with any severe shortages forecast for next winter.

I also urge prompt action by the Congress on a bill I will be submitting shortly which is designed to expedite the selection of a route and the construction of a transportation system to bring the vast supplies of natural gas from the North Slope of Alaska to the "lower 48" markets. This legislation would make possible production of about 1 trillion cubic feet of additional natural gas each year by the early 1980s.

We expect imports of liquefied natural gas (LNG) to grow in the next several years to supplement our declining domestic supply of natural gas. We must balance these supply needs against the risk of becoming overly dependent on any particular source of supply.

Recognizing these concerns, I have directed the Energy Resources Council to establish procedures for reviewing proposed contracts within the Executive Branch, balancing the need for supplies with the need to avoid excessive dependence, and encouraging new imports where this is appropriate. By 1985, we should be able to import 1 trillion cubic feet of LNG to help meet our needs without becoming overly dependent upon foreign sources.

Nuclear Power

Greater utilization must be made of nuclear energy in order to achieve energy independence and maintain a strong economy. It is likewise vital that we continue our world leadership as a reliable supplier of nuclear technology in order to assure that worldwide growth in nuclear power is achieved with responsible and effective controls.

At present 57 commercial nuclear power plants are on line, providing more than 9 per cent of our electrical requirements, and a total of 179 additional plants are planned or committed. If the electrical power supplied by the 57 existing nuclear power plants were supplied by oil-fired plants an additional one million barrels of oil would be consumed each day.

On January 19, 1975, I activated the independent Nuclear Regulatory Commission (NRC) which has the responsibility for assuring the safety, reliability, and environmental acceptability of commercial nuclear power. The safety record for nuclear power plants is outstanding. Nevertheless, we must continue our efforts to assure that it will remain so in the years ahead. The NRC has taken a number of steps to reduce unnecessary regulatory delays and is continually alert to the need to review its policies and procedures for carrying out its assigned responsibilities.

I have requested greatly increased funding in my 1977 budget to accelerate research and development efforts that will meet our short-term needs to:

—make the safety of commercial nuclear power plants even more certain;

—develop further domestic safeguards technologies to assure against the theft and misuse of nuclear materials as the use of nuclear-generated electric power grows;

—provide for safe and secure long-term storage of radioactive wastes;

—and encourage industry to improve the reliability and reduce the construction time of commercial nuclear power plants.

I have also requested additional funds to identify new uranium resources and have directed ERDA to work with private industry to determine what additional actions are needed to bring capacity online to reprocess and recycle nuclear fuels.

Internationally, the United States in consultation with other nations which supply nuclear technology has decided to follow stringent export principles to ensure that international sharing of the benefits of nuclear energy does not lead to the proliferation of nuclear weapons. I have also decided that the U.S. should make a special contribution of up to $5-million in the next 5 years to strengthen the safeguards program of the International Atomic Energy Agency.

It is essential that the Congress act if we are to take timely advantage of our nuclear energy potential. I urge enactment of the Nuclear Licensing Act to streamline the licensing procedures for the construction of new powerplants.

I again strongly urge the Congress to give high priority to my Nuclear Assurance Act to provide enriched uranium needed for commercial nuclear powerplants here and abroad. This proposed legislation, which I submitted in June 1975, would provide the basis for transition to a private competitive uranium enrichment industry and prevent the heavy drain on the Federal budget. If the Federal Government were required to finance the necessary additional uranium enrichment capacity, it would have to commit more than $8-billion over the next 2 to 3 years and $2-billion annually thereafter. The taxpayers would eventually be repaid for these expenditures but not until sometime in the 1990's. Federal expenditures are not necessary under the provisions of this act since industry is prepared to assume this responsibility with limited Government cooperation and some temporary assurances. Furthermore, a commitment to new Federal expenditures for uranium enrichment could interfere with efforts to increase funding for other critical energy programs.

Coal

Coal is the most abundant energy resource available in the United States, yet production is at the same level as in the 1920s and accounts for only about 17 per cent of the Nation's energy consumption. Coal must be used increasingly as an alternative to scarce, expensive or insecure oil and natural gas supplies. We must act to remove unnecessary constraints on coal so that production can grow from the 1975 level of 640 million tons to over 1 billion tons by 1985 in order to help achieve energy independence.

We are moving ahead where legislative authority is available.

The Secretary of the Interior has recently adopted a new coal leasing policy for the leasing and development of more coal on Federal lands. To implement this policy, regulations will be issued governing coal mining operations on Federal lands, providing for timely development, and requiring effective surface mining controls which will minimize adverse environmental impacts and require that mined lands be reclaimed. As a reflection of the States' interests, the Department proposes to allow application on Federal lands of State coal mine reclamation standards which are more stringent than Federal standards, unless overriding National interests are involved.

I have directed the Federal Energy Administration and the Environmental Protection Agency to work toward the conversion of the maximum number of utilities and major industrial facilities from gas or oil to coal as permitted under recently extended authorities.

We are also stepping up research and development efforts to find better ways of extracting, producing and using coal.

Again, however, the actions we can take are not enough to meet our goals. Action by the Congress is essential.

I urge the Congress to enact the Clean Air Act amendments I proposed which will provide the balance we need between air quality and energy goals. These amendments would permit greater use of coal without sacrificing the air quality standards necessary to protect public health.

Oil

We must reverse the decline in the Nation's oil production. I intend to implement the maximum production incentives that can be justified under the new Energy Policy and Conservation Act. In addition, the Department of the Interior will continue its aggressive Outer Continental Shelf development program while giving careful attention to environmental considerations.

But these actions are not enough. We need prompt action by the Congress on my proposals to allow production from the Naval Petroleum Reserves. This legislation is now awaiting action by a House-Senate Conference Committee.

Production from the reserves could provide almost 1 million barrels of oil per day by 1985 and will provide both the funding and the oil for our strategic oil reserves.

I also urge the Congress to act quickly on amending the Clean Air Act auto emission standards that I proposed last June to achieve a balance between objectives for improving air quality, increasing gasoline mileage, and avoiding unnecessary increases in costs to consumers.

Building Energy Facilities

In order to attain energy independence for the United States, the construction of numerous nuclear power plants, coal-fired power plants, oil refineries, synthetic fuel plants, and other facilities will be required over the next two decades.

Again, action by the Congress is needed.

I urge Congress to approve my October 1975 proposal to create an Energy Independence Authority, a new Government corporation to assist private sector financing of new energy facilities.

This legislation will help assure that capital is available for the massive investment that must be made over the next few years in energy facilities, but will not be forthcoming otherwise. The legislation also provides for expediting the regulatory process at the Federal level for critical energy projects.

I also urge Congressional action on legislation needed to authorize loan guarantees to aid in the construction of commercial facilities to produce synthetic fuels so that they may make a significant contribution by 1985.

Commercial facilities eligible for funding under this program include those for synthetic gas, coal liquefaction and oil shale, which are not now economically competitive. Management of this program would initially reside with the Energy Research and Development Administration but would be transferred to the proposed Energy Independence Authority.

My proposed energy facilities siting legislation and utility rate reform legislation, as well as the Electric Utilities Construction Incentives Act complete the legislation which would provide the incentives, assistance and new procedures

needed to assure that facilities are available to provide additional domestic energy supplies.

Energy Development Impact Assistance

Some areas of the country will experience rapid growth and change because of the development of Federally-owned energy resources. We must provide special help to heavily impacted areas where this development will occur.

I urge the Congress to act quickly on my proposed new, comprehensive, Federal Energy Impact Assistance Act which was submitted to the Congress on February 4, 1976.

This legislation would establish a $1 billion program of financial assistance to areas affected by new Federal energy resource development over the next 15 years. It would provide loans, loan guarantees and planning grants for energy-related public facilities. Funds would be repaid from future energy development. Repayment of loans could be forgiven if development did not occur as expected.

This legislation is the only approach which assures that communities that need assistance will get it where it is needed, when it is needed.

Energy Conservation

The Nation has made major progress in reducing energy consumption in the last two years but greatly increased savings can yet be realized in all sectors.

I have directed that the Executive Branch continue a strong energy management program. This program has already reduced energy consumption by 24 percent in the past two years, saving the equivalent of over 250,000 barrels of oil per day.

We are moving to implement the conservation authorities of the new Energy Policy and Conservation Act, including those calling for State energy conservation programs, and labeling of appliances to provide consumers with energy efficiency information.

I have asked for a 63 percent increase in funding for energy conservation research and development in my 1977 budget.

If the Congress will provide needed legislation, we will make more progress. I urge the Congress to pass legislation to provide for thermal efficiency standards for new buildings, to enact my proposed $55 million weatherization assistance program for low-income and elderly persons, and to provide a 15 percent tax credit for energy conservation improvements in existing residential buildings. Together, these conservation proposals can save 450,000 barrels of oil per day by 1985.

International Energy Activities

We have also made significant progress in establishing an international energy policy. The U.S. and other major oil consuming nations have established a com-

prehensive long-term energy program through the International Energy Agency (IEA), committing ourselves to continuing cooperation to reduce dependence on imported oil. By reducing demand for imported oil, consuming nations can, over time, regain their influence over oil prices and end vulnerability to abrupt supply cutoffs and unilateral price increases.

The International Energy Agency has established a framework for cooperative efforts to accelerate the development of alternative energy sources. The Department of State, in cooperation with FEA, ERDA, and other Federal agencies, will continue to work closely with the IEA.

While domestic energy independence is an essential and attainable goal, we must recognize that this is an interdependent world. There is a link between economic growth and the availability of energy at reasonable prices. The United States will need some energy imports in the years ahead. Many of the other consuming nations will not be energy independent. Therefore, we must continue to search for solutions to the problems of both the world's energy producers and consumers.

The U.S. delegation to the new Energy Commission will pursue these solutions, including the U.S. proposal to create an International Energy Institute. This Institute will mobilize the technical and financial resources of the industrialized and oil producing countries to assist developing countries in meeting their energy problems.

1985 and Beyond

As our easily recoverable domestic fuel reserves are depleted, the need for advancing the technologies of nuclear energy, synthetic fuels, solar energy, and geothermal energy will become paramount to sustaining our energy achievements beyond 1985. I have therefore proposed an increase in the Federal budget for energy research and development from $2.2 billion in 1976 to $2.9 billion in the proposed 1977 budget. This 30 percent increase represents a major expansion of activities directed at accelerating programs for achieving long-term energy independence.

These funds are slated for increased work on nuclear fusion and fission power development, particularly for demonstrating the commercial viability of breeder reactors; new technology development for coal mining and coal use; enhanced recovery of oil from current reserves; advanced power conversion systems; solar and geothermal energy development; and conservation research and development.

It is only through greater research and development efforts today that we will be in a position beyond 1985 to supply a significant share of the free world's energy needs and technology.

Summary

I envision an energy future for the United States free of the threat of embargoes and arbitrary price increases by foreign governments. I see a world in which all nations strengthen their cooperative efforts to solve critical energy problems. I envision a major expansion in the production and use of coal, aggressive exploration for domestic oil and gas, a strong commitment to nuclear power, significant technological breakthroughs in harnessing the unlimited potential of solar energy and fusion power, and a strengthened conservation ethic in our use of energy.

I am convinced that the United States has the ability to achieve energy independence.

I urge the Congress to provide the needed legislative authority without further delay.

GERALD R. FORD

The White House,
February 26, 1976

Regulatory Reform

Following is the White House text of President Ford's May 13 message to Congress on regulatory reform:

TO THE CONGRESS OF
THE UNITED STATES:

Our American economic system has been built upon individual initiative and freedom to strive to achieve our economic goals. In an increasingly complex society, however, the role of government has been to assist in the search for solutions to our National problems. But in many cases, government imposed solutions have created new problems and mandated excessive costs on our society. Over the years, we have departed from the reliance on individual initiative and consumer choice. We have expanded government's role and created a rigid system which has become less able to respond to changing conditions.

The growth of government expanded rapidly in the Depression era. New government agencies were created to resolve our economic and social problems—to help reduce unemployment, to stabilize financial markets, and to protect failing businesses. As a result of a proliferation of such government agencies since then—all designed to solve an increasing variety of problems—we have come to expect the Federal Government to have all the answers—more and better housing—an efficient transportation system—improved health care—and equal opportunities in the job market.

In our compassionate desire to solve urgent human problems, we have given the Federal Government the power to regulate more and more of our economy and our way of life. Over the years, regulation has been considered an inexpensive, easy answer to some very complex problems. Now, we are beginning to realize how high the costs are of what appeared to be the easy solutions of the past.

Federal programs and bureaucracies have grown geometrically. In the last fifteen years 236 departments, agencies, bureaus and commissions have been created while only 21 have been eliminated. Today we have more than a thousand different Federal programs, more than 80 regulatory agencies, and more than 100,000 government workers whose primary responsibility is to regulate some aspect of our lives.

My Administration has made the reform of government regulation one of its highest priorities. We have initiated a national debate on the role that government regulation should play in our economy. In the past year, we have achieved the most significant and comprehensive progress toward reform in three decades. At the same time we have moved toward a more open and vigorous free market in which consumers have available a wider range of goods and services to choose from and where businessmen have a greater opportunity to run their own businesses.

For example:

● We have reversed the trend of paperwork growth and reduced regulatory delays.

● We have repealed the Federal fair trade laws which created artificially high consumer prices.

● The Senate has passed the Financial Institutions Act which is the most sweeping reform of banking regulation in over 40 years.

● We have increased civil and criminal penalties for antitrust violations to insure that competition flourishes.

● We have interjected competition into the setting of stock brokerage fees for the first time since the major stock exchanges were established almost 200 years ago.

● We have reduced the amount of ICC regulation of railroads for the first time since the creation of that agency in 1887, and have proposed comprehensive and long overdue reforms of airline and motor carrier regulation.

These are important steps, but they are only a beginning. We need a better understanding of the combined effects of all government regulatory activities on our economy and our lives. We need to eliminate contradictions and overlaps. We need to abolish outdated and unnecessary regulation. We need to strengthen the effectiveness of Congressional oversight of government operations.

To meet these needs, I am today submitting the Agenda for Government Reform Act which would establish a four-year action program to work toward these goals. It would produce comprehensive reforms to:

● Guarantee that government policies do not infringe unnecessarily on individual choice and initiative nor intervene needlessly in the market place.

● Find better ways to achieve our social goals at minimal economic cost.

● Insure that government policies and programs benefit the public interest rather than special interests.

● Assure that regulatory policies are equitably enforced.

This legislation would require the President to develop legislative reform proposals by January 31 of each year, and Congress would be required to act upon them. Such a disciplined approach will help focus attention on major, yet often neglected, aspects of government activities. This Agenda will require the assessment of the cumulative impact of government actions on major sectors of the economy and build a rational basis for more informed trade-offs between broad economic goals, such as more jobs and lower prices, and specific regulatory objectives, such as cleaner air and adequate rural services. And it will help identify the hidden costs imposed on the economy by government regulation.

This legislation is the product of joint Congressional and Executive branch interest in seeking long term solutions to our regulatory problems. Senators Charles Percy and Robert Byrd have been leaders in pressing for comprehensive reforms. In the House of Representatives, Congresswoman Barbara Jordan and Congressman John Anderson have also introduced systematic reform legislation. My legislation addresses similar concerns. I look forward to working with Congress to achieve our common goals.

Let me stress that this new program must *not* delay reform efforts now underway. This new legislation is a complement not a substitute for the on-going administrative improvements and legislative proposals I have already announced. My Administration will continue to press forward with reduction of unnecessary and burdensome regulation and elimination of government-imposed paperwork and red tape. We will continue to make administrative improvements wherever possible, and to obtain congressional action on proposals for increased competition in regulated industries.

This is an ambitious program. But I believe it possible to make our regulatory system responsive to the concerns of all Americans. They demand and deserve nothing less. I ask the Congress to act quickly on this legislation so that together we may begin to create a legacy of economic prosperity for future generations.

GERALD R. FORD

The White House,
May 13, 1976

Busing Legislation

Following is the White House text of President Ford's June 24 message to Congress proposing legislation to limit court-ordered desegregation plans and establish a National Community and Education Committee:

TO THE CONGRESS OF
THE UNITED STATES:

I address this message to the Congress, and through the Congress to all Americans, on an issue of profound importance to our domestic tranquility and the future of American education.

Most Americans know this issue as busing—the use of busing to carry out court-ordered assignment of students to correct illegal segregation in our schools.

In its fullest sense the issue is how we protect the civil rights of all Americans without unduly restricting the individual freedom of any American.

It concerns the responsibility of government to provide quality education, and equality of education, to every American.

It concerns our obligation to eliminate, as swiftly as humanly possible, the occasions of controversy and division from the fulfillment of this responsibility.

At the outset, let me set forth certain principles governing my judgments and my actions.

First, for all of my life I have held strong personal feelings against racial discrimination. I do not believe in a segregated society. We are a people of diverse background, origins and interests; but we are still one people—Americans—and so must we live.

Second, it is the duty of every President to enforce the law of the land. When I became President, I took an oath to preserve, protect and defend the Constitution of the United States. There must be no misunderstanding about this: I will uphold the constitutional rights of every individual in the country. I will carry out the decisions of the Supreme Court. I will not tolerate defiance of the law.

Third, I am totally dedicated to quality education in America—and to the principle that public education is predominantly the concern of the community in which people live. Throughout the history of our Nation, the education of our children, especially at the elementary and secondary levels, has been a community endeavor. The concept of public education is now written into our history as deeply as any tenet of American belief.

In recent years, we have seen many communities in the country lose control of their public schools to the Federal courts because they failed to voluntarily correct the effects of willful and official denial of the rights of some children in their schools.

It is my belief that in their earnest desire to carry out the decisions of the Supreme Court, some judges of lower Federal courts have gone too far. They have:

—resorted too quickly to the remedy of massive busing of public school children;

—extended busing too broadly; and

—maintained control of schools for too long.

It is this overextension of court control that has transformed a simple judicial tool, busing, into a cause of widespread controversy and slowed our progress toward the total elimination of segregation.

As a President is responsible for acting to enforce the Nation's laws, so is he also responsible for acting when society begins to question the end results of those laws.

I therefore ask the Congress, as the elected representatives of the American people, to join with me in establishing guidelines for the lower Federal Courts in the desegregation of public schools throughout the land—acting within the framework of the Constitution and particularly the Fourteenth Amendment to the Constitution.

It is both appropriate and constitutional for the Congress to define by law the remedies the lower Federal Courts may decree.

It is both appropriate and constitutional for the Congress to prescribe standards and procedures for accommodating competing interests and rights.

Both the advocates of more busing and the advocates of less busing feel they hold a strong moral position on this issue.

To many Americans who have been in the long struggle for civil rights, busing appears to be the only way to provide the equal educational opportunity so long and so tragically denied them.

To many other Americans who have struggled much of their lives and devoted most of their energies to seeking the best for their children, busing appears to be a denial of an individual's freedom to choose the best school for his or her children.

Whether busing helps school children get a better education is not a settled question. The record is mixed. Certainly, busing has assisted in bringing about the desegregation of our schools. But it is a tragic reality that, in some areas, busing under court order has brought fear to both black students and white students—and to their parents.

No child can learn in an atmosphere of fear. Better remedies to right Constitutional wrongs must be found.

It is my responsibility, and the responsibility of the Congress, to address and to seek to resolve this situation.

In the twenty-two years since the Supreme Court ordered an end to school segregation, this country has made great progress. Yet we still have far to go.

To maintain progress toward the orderly elimination of illegal segregation in our public schools, and to preserve—or, where appropriate, restore—community control of schools, I am proposing legislation to:

1. Require that a court in a desegregation case determine the extent to which acts of unlawful discrimination have caused a greater degree of racial concentration in a school or school system than would have existed in the absence of such acts;

2. Require that busing and other remedies in school desegregation cases be limited to eliminating the degree of student racial concentration caused by proven unlawful acts of discrimination;

3. Require that the utilization of court-ordered busing as a remedy be limited to a specific period of time consistent with the

legislation's intent that it be an interim and transitional remedy. In general, this period of time will be no longer than five years where there has been compliance with the court order.

4. Create an independent National Community and Education Committee to help any school community requesting citizen assistance in voluntarily resolving its school segregation problem.

Almost without exception, the citizens' groups both for and against busing with which I have consulted told me that the proposed National Community and Education Committee could be a positive addition to the resources currently available to communities which face up to the issue honestly, voluntarily and in the best spirit of American democracy.

This citizens' Committee would be made up primarily of men and women who have had community experience in school desegregation activities.

It would remain distinct and separate from enforcement activities of the Federal Courts, the Justice Department and the Department of Health, Education and Welfare.

It is my hope that the Committee could activate and energize effective local leadership at an early stage:

—To reduce the disruption that would otherwise accompany the desegregation process; and

—To provide additional assistance to communities in anticipating and resolving difficulties prior to and during desegregation.

While I personally believe that every community should effectively desegregate on a voluntary basis, I recognize that some court action is inevitable.

In those cases where Federal court actions are initiated, however, I believe that busing as a remedy ought to be the last resort, and that it ought to be limited in scope to correcting the effect of previous Constitutional violations.

The goal of the judicial remedy in a school desegregation case ought to be to put the school system, and its students, where they would have been if the acts which violate the Constitution had never occurred.

The goal should be to eliminate "root and branch" the Constitutional violations and all of their present effects. This is the Constitutional test which the Supreme Court has mandated—nothing more, nothing less.

Therefore, my bill would establish for Federal courts specific guidelines concerning the use of busing in school desegregation cases. It would require the court to determine the extent to which acts of unlawful discrimination by governmental officials have caused a greater degree of racial concentration in a school or school system than would have existed in the absence of such acts. It would further require the court to limit the relief to that necessary to correct the racial imbalance actually caused by those unlawful acts. This would prohibit a court from ordering busing throughout an entire school system simply for the purpose of achieving racial balance.

In addition, my bill recognizes that the busing remedy is transitional by its very nature and that when a community makes good faith efforts to comply, busing ought to be limited in duration. Therefore, the bill provides that three years after the busing remedy has been imposed a court shall be required to determine whether to continue the remedy. Should the court determine that a continuation is necessary, it could do so only for an additional two years. Thereafter, the court could continue busing only in the most extraordinary circumstances, where there has been a failure or delay of other remedial efforts or where the residual effects of unlawful discrimination are unusually severe.

Great concern has been expressed that submission of this bill at this time would

encourage those who are resisting court-ordered desegregation—sometimes to the point of violence.

Let me here state, simply and directly, that this Administration will not tolerate unlawful segregation.

We will act swiftly and effectively against anyone who engages in violence.

I assure the people of this Nation that this Administration will do whatever it must to preserve order and to protect the Constitutional rights of our citizens.

The purpose of submitting this legislation now is to place the debate on this controversial issue in the halls of Congress and in the democratic process—not in the streets of our cities.

The strength of America has always been our ability to deal with our own problems in a responsible and orderly way. We can do so again if every American will join with me in affirming our historic

commitment to a Nation of laws, a people of equality, a society of opportunity.

I call on the Congress to write into law a new perspective which sees court-ordered busing as a tool to be used with the highest selectivity and the utmost precision.

I call on the leaders of all the Nation's school districts which may yet face court orders to move voluntarily, promptly, objectively and compassionately to desegregate their schools.

We must eliminate discrimination in America.

We must summon the best in ourselves to the cause of achieving the highest possible quality of education for each and every American child.

GERALD R. FORD

The White House,
June 24, 1976

International Economic Report

Following is the White House text of President Ford's March 17 message accompanying the fourth annual International Economic Report:

TO THE CONGRESS OF THE UNITED STATES:

America in 1975 renewed and strengthened its commitment to pursue the traditional U.S. goals of freer trade and enhanced global economic stability and prosperity. The United States has proposed a series of major economic initiatives providing leadership in efforts to improve trade and monetary arrangements, to establish cooperative mechanisms for dealing with the problems of food and energy, and to offer effective international responses to those nations in greatest need. 1975 was a year of achievement which produced new and more effective international economic policies, as the following highlights indicate.

Economic Summit Meeting

In November I met with the heads of the governments of France, West Germany, Italy, Japan and the United Kingdom at Rambouillet, France to discuss the world economic situation and economic problems common to our countries. The Summit Meeting concentrated on the need for new efforts in the areas of world trade, monetary matters and raw materials, including energy. We agreed that sustained, stable economic growth in the industrial nations will be facilitated by our cooperative efforts. This Meeting, and the accompanying bilateral talks I had with leaders of the major industrialized democracies, established a new spirit of cooperation and confidence stemming from a deeper understanding of our common destiny. They set the stage for our efforts to deal with a variety of specific

international economic challenges facing us in 1976.

Monetary Affairs

Efforts to revise the international monetary system resulted in major reforms. At the recent meeting of the International Monetary Fund's Interim Committee in Jamaica, we reached agreement on amendments to the IMF Articles of Agreement with respect to quotas, exchange rates, and the role of gold. The negotiations resulted in the first major revision of the international monetary system since the 1944 Bretton Woods Conference. The exchange rate provisions of the IMF Articles of Agreement will be amended to provide a flexible framework for the future evolution of the system. The Interim Committee also reached agreement on steps to phase gold out of the international monetary system.

Multilateral Trade Negotiations

The Multilateral Trade Negotiations in Geneva have gained momentum since early 1975. At the Rambouillet Summit we unanimously agreed to seek a successful conclusion of these negotiations by 1977. The United States will continue to provide strong support and leadership to the effort to reduce trade barriers and otherwise improve the world trading system.

Energy

The establishment of the International Energy Agency by the United States and its OECD partners constituted a major response to the economic imbalance in the vital area of energy. The IEA has developed the details of an International Energy Program designed to limit the vulnerability of the participating nations to supply interruptions. Agreement was also reached on longer-term cooperation to reduce consumption and develop alternative energy

sources in order to lessen dependence on imported energy. We have established emergency arrangements providing for energy reserves, consumption restraint measures, and allocation procedures.

Developing Countries

The United States is committed to assisting developing countries in their efforts to achieve economic progress. Our response to the needs of the less developed countries was expressed clearly and positively at the Seventh Special Session of the United Nations in September. We proposed a new development security facility in the IMF to stabilize overall export earnings in developing countries, and numerous other ideas—including trade preferences—to achieve mutually beneficial solutions to the problems of economic development.

Commodities

At the Seventh Special Session of the United Nations we indicated that we will consider participating in various commodity agreements on a case-by-case basis. We also announced that we intend to join the Fifth International Tin Agreement, subject to Congressional approval. The need, value and structure of commodity agreements vary for different commodities. In considering commodity agreements on a case-by-case basis, we will oppose concerted efforts to manipulate supplies and prices which ignore the interests of consuming countries while seeking to assure developing countries adequate income from their natural resources.

Food and Agriculture

The United States in 1975 continued its vital leadership in seeking strengthened cooperation to increase world food production and trade. We proposed an expanded international grain reserve system and enlarged our food aid assistance. We will continue our policy of encouraging maximum agricultural production, and our efforts to achieve an efficient distribution system to assure that hungry people will be fed.

U.S.-Soviet Agreements on Grain and Oil

Last October, the United States and the Soviet Union signed an agreement providing for regular and orderly sales of American wheat and corn during the next five years. The American people—our farmers, our workers, and our consumers—will benefit from this agreement. The Soviet Union is committed to purchasing at least six million metric tons of grain per year, representing one billion dollars in annual export earnings.

In signing this agreement, we have assured a stable, long-term foreign market for our grain, and a more reliable flow of payments from abroad. We have assured American farmers that the Soviet Union will be a regular buyer of grain at market prices, thereby increasing the incentive for full production. We have provided jobs for American transportation workers and seamen. We have neutralized a great destabilizing factor in our grain markets. Perhaps most importantly, we have preserved our private marketing system, permitting us to maintain our highly successful policy of all-out production and open markets.

In the same constructive spirit, the governments of the United States and the Soviet Union have also committed themselves to negotiations on a five-year agreement for the purchase of Soviet oil. These negotiations are currently underway.

Multinational Corporations

Multinational corporations (MNC's) continue to be a highly visible and controversial factor in international affairs. MNC's have made major contributions to world economic development and will continue to do so in the future. While the major portion of foreign investment by multinational corporations is concentrated in industrial nations, many developing countries actively seek investments by MNC's, recognizing their potential contribution to economic development. Recognizing the generally positive impact of MNC's on world trade and production, I am distressed by reports of corrupt practices by some companies. For that reason, I have directed that members of my Administration undertake efforts, both domestically and internationally, to assure that multinational corporations obey the laws and conform with the public policies of the countries in which they do business.

We are participating in the development of an international code to provide guidelines for responsible corporate behavior. The Organization for Economic Cooperation and Development has made substantial progress toward drafting a code, and similar efforts will be undertaken in the United Nations and the Organization of American States in 1976. It is highly important that such codes of conduct provide that both multinational corporations and host governments share the responsibility for eliminating abuses.

Investment

The United States policy on international investment is based on our belief that a free market system without artificial barriers or incentives leads to the most efficient allocation of capital in the world economy. Accordingly we provide "national treatment" of foreign investors in the United States, treating them equally with domestic firms, and we expect similar treatment of U.S. companies investing abroad.

Following a comprehensive review of Administration policy toward inward investment, we concluded that it would be desirable to establish arrangements to monitor the flow of foreign investments in the United States. By Executive Order, I established the Committee on Foreign Investment in the United States, to monitor the impact of foreign investment in the United States and coordinate the implementation of U.S. policy on such investment. A new Office of Foreign Investment was established in the Department of Commerce. We have also asked foreign governments contemplating significant investments in this country to consult with us prior to making such investments.

Export Policy

U.S. exports continue to play a vital role in strengthening our domestic economy. We are continuing our efforts to expand U.S. exports by providing competitive export financing, improved market information, and an increased foreign awareness of U.S. products. The United States prefers not to interfere with competitive markets. We oppose the use of export subsidies and similar measures which artificially distort trading relationships. At the same time, we must realistically take into account export policies of competitive countries, and we will continue to promote U.S. exports by insuring that competitive credit terms are available through the Export-Import Bank and the Commodity Credit Corporation of the Department of Agriculture, and sufficient tax incentives are available through the Domestic International Sales Corporation mechanism to meet foreign competition.

As we enter the last quarter of the twentieth century, our policies are directed toward working with others to ensure that the world's talents and resources better serve the well-being of mankind. We continue to seek a world in which all people can prosper, a world without hunger or severe want, a world in which the best efforts of all nations are prized and rewarded, so that their progress and health are ensured.

My Council on International Economic Policy plays a significant role in the development of America's international economic policies to meet immediate needs and guide our future course. Through its participation on the Economic Policy Board we have achieved better coordination of U.S. domestic and international economic policy than ever before in our history.

This, the fourth International Economic Report of the President, measures the range of the Administration's concerns and the character of the American response to major international economic issues. I am proud of our progress and accomplishments in 1975. I am confident that they will lead toward a more free and open world of international economic relations benefitting the American people and all people.

GERALD R. FORD

The White House,
March 17, 1976

Legislative Priorities

Following is the White House text of President Ford's July 22 message to Congress on his legislative priorities:

TO THE CONGRESS OF
THE UNITED STATES:

In the weeks remaining in this session of the 94th Congress there is an opportunity to write a legislative record of which we can all be proud. Over the past 23 months I have sent legislative proposals to the Congress dealing with many vital areas of national concern. Some of these proposals have been enacted, some are nearing enactment, but many others have been stalled in the legislative process.

Today I am calling on the Congress to turn its full and undivided attention to this unfinished agenda of legislative business. If you do, the record you will take to the people will be a good one.

The agenda is long, even though it does not include everything that should be passed by the Congress before it goes home. For example, I have not included here the appropriation bills which must be passed. Most of the agenda items have been debated at length by the Congress and the time for action has arrived.

The priority categories for action are familiar ones:
—tax reductions coupled with spending restraint
—crime control
—restoring the integrity of the Social Security System
—catastrophic health care protection for those covered by Medicare
—restrictions on forced, court ordered busing
—revenue sharing and block grants
—regulatory reform
—energy
—indemnification of swine flu manufacturers

—the remainder of my defense program plus defense cost saving legislation —and other legislation ranging from agriculture to the environment; from higher education to reform of the Federal retirement system.

In the agenda that follows, I have listed the specific legislation that needs to be passed by the Congress. I am convinced that the passage of these bills is in the real interest of all the American people.

Taxes

Permanent Tax Reduction

This proposal would provide a $28-billion permanent income tax reduction effective July 1, 1976. Major provisions affecting individual income taxes include an increase in personal exemptions from $750 to $1,000, a reduction in tax rates, and substitution of a flat standard deduction for the low income allowance and percentage standard deduction.

Estate and Gift Tax Adjustment Act

This legislation would raise the estate tax exemption from $60 thousand to $150 thousand and make all transfers of assets between spouses exempt from estate and gift taxes. The estate tax rate structure would be altered so that taxes on the largest estates would remain unchanged.

In addition, this legislation would make it easier to continue the family ownership of a small farm or business following an owner's death. This would be accomplished by liberalizing present rules governing installment payments of estate taxes attributable to a small family farm or closely-held business by providing a 5-year "grace" period before such payments must begin, reducing the interest rate on those payments, and by extending the installment period from 10 to 20 years.

Jobs Creation Incentive Act

This legislation would encourage construction of new facilities and expansion of old facilities in areas experiencing unemployment in excess of 7 per cent in order to increase employment opportunities in these areas. The increased construction would be encouraged by allowing very rapid amortization for nonresidential buildings and capital equipment.

Broadened Stock Ownership

Tax incentives to encourage broader ownership of common stock by working men and women would be provided by this proposal. Taxes on funds invested in stock-purchase plans established by employers or directly by individuals would be deferred provided such funds are invested for at least 7 years.

Crime Control

Amendments to the Criminal Code

Amendments would provide for the imposition of a mandatory term of imprisonment in certain cases. A mandatory term of imprisonment would be imposed if the offender: (1) commits an extraordinarily serious crime involving kidnapping, aircraft hijacking, or trafficking in hard drugs; (2) commits a violent offense after previously having committed a violent offense. A separate amendment would provide mandatory prison sentences for anyone who uses a gun in the commission of a crime. This amendment would also ban the importation, manufacture, assembly, sale or transfer of cheap, easily concealable handguns (the so-called "Saturday Night Specials").

Narcotic Sentencing and Seizure Act of 1976

This legislation would improve the ability of law enforcement officials to put traffickers of hard drugs into prison, take the easy profits out of drug trafficking, and improve the capacity of law enforcement officials to detect and apprehend drug smugglers. Major features of the proposal would require (1) minimum mandatory prison sentences for persons convicted of opiate (heroin and similar narcotic drugs) trafficking, (2) denial of bail to persons arrested for opiate trafficking, (3) the forfeiture under certain conditions of negotiable instruments used or intended to be used in illegal opiate trafficking, and (4) masters of boats—including pleasure vessels—to report their arrival to Customs authorities within 24 hours.

Crime Control Act

The Administration's proposal would extend the Law Enforcement Assistance Administration (LEAA) for five years, place LEAA under the general policy direction of the Attorney General, authorize LEAA to allocate up to $50-million annually to high crime impact areas, eliminate provisions in current law which require maintenance of previous LEAA spending for juvenile delinquency programs at the 1972 level, and place special emphasis on improving the operation of State and local court systems. This legislation is designed to continue a vital Federal financial and technical assistance program to State and local governments so that they can improve their ability to enforce the law.

Justice Department Reorganization and Reform Act

The proposed legislation would provide a constitutional means of helping curb corruption in Government. It would establish within the Department of Justice a permanent Office of Special Prosecutor, whose head would be appointed by the President

with Senate confirmation, and a Government Crimes Section in the Criminal Division to investigate and prosecute job-related criminal violations of Federal law committed by any elected or appointed Federal Government officer or employee. A proposed Government Crimes Section in Justice would have responsibility for investigating criminal violations of Federal lobbying and campaign laws. This legislation would also require designated officers and employees of the Federal Government to file comprehensive annual financial statements.

Social Security

Social Security Improvement Amendments

Two legislative proposals have been submitted to Congress to help insure a secure and viable Social Security System.

The "Social Security Amendments of 1976" would increase Social Security payroll contributions and thereby stop the immediate, short-term drain on the Social Security trust funds—which are now expected to pay out about $4-billion more in benefits each year than they take in.

The "Social Security Benefit Indexing Act" would correct a serious flaw in the method of computing benefits which, if left unchanged, would create severe long-range financial pressures on the trust funds. The two measures are necessary first steps to solve both the short and long-range financial problems of the Social Security system.

Catastrophic Health Protection

Medicare Improvements of 1976

The proposed "Medicare Improvements of 1976" is designed to provide greater protection against catastrophic health costs for the 25 million aged and disabled Americans eligible for Medicare. An estimated 3 million beneficiaries would pay less in 1977 as a result of the proposed annual limits of $500 for hospital services and $250 for physician services. The legislation would also provide for moderate cost-sharing for Medicare beneficiaries to encourage economical use of medical services and would slow down health cost inflation by putting a limit on Federal payments to hospitals and physicians.

Busing

School Desegregation Standards and Assistance Act

The purpose of this legislation is to maintain progress toward the orderly elimination of illegal segregation in public schools while preserving community control of schools. The legislation would set guidelines for Federal courts concerning the use of busing in school desegregation cases. It would require that courts determine the extent to which acts of unlawful discrimination have caused a greater degree of racial concentration in a school or school system that would have existed otherwise and to confine the relief provided to correcting the racial imbalance caused by those unlawful acts. The legislation would also limit the duration of court-ordered busing, generally to a period of no longer than five years.

General Revenue Sharing And Block Grants

General Revenue Sharing: Extension and Revision of the State and Local Fiscal Assistance Act

This proposal would extend and revise the highly successful general revenue sharing program which expires on December 31, 1976. The program would be extended for five and three-quarters years, and the current method of funding with annual increases of $150-million would be retained. The basic revenue sharing formula would be retained but the existing per capita restraint would be eased. Civil rights and public participation provisions would be strengthened while reporting requirements would be made more flexible.

Federal Assistance for Community Services Act

This proposal would improve and strengthen the program of social services established under Title XX of the Social Security Act. The $2.5-billion provided annually by the Federal Government would be distributed as a block grant to the States, with no requirement for State matching funds. Most Federal requirements and prohibitions on the use of Federal funds would be eliminated. Services to low-income Americans would be emphasized; Federal funds would be focused on those whose incomes fall below the poverty income guidelines.

Financial Assistance for Elementary and Secondary Education

This proposal would consolidate 24 programs of Federal assistance to State and local education agencies for non-postsecondary education purposes into one block grant. Three-quarters of the Federal support would have to be used for disadvantaged and handicapped students, with greater flexibility for States to target funds among programs in accordance with their own priorities. Administrative requirements on the States would be greatly reduced through reduction of Federal regulations and simplification of reporting procedures, and public participation would be required in the State planning process.

Financial Assistance for Health Care Act

This proposal would consolidate Medicaid and 15 categorical Federal health programs into a single $10-billion block grant to the States. The proposal is designed to overcome some of the most serious defects in the present system of Federal financing of health care and to permit States to meet their citizens' health needs in a more effective manner. It would achieve a more equitable distribution of Federal health dollars among States, and eliminate the present State matching requirements. It would also reduce Federal red tape, give States greater flexibility in providing for delivery of health care services to those with low income, and expand public participation in health planning.

Child Nutrition Reform Act of 1976

This proposal would establish a single comprehensive block grant to provide Federal funds for States to feed needy children. It would consolidate into a single authority the fifteen complex and overlapping child nutrition programs currently administered by the Department of Agriculture. This new approach would concentrate Federal spending on the nutritional needs of poor children, while eliminating the substantial Federal subsidies now provided for non-needy children. It would also ease the heavy administrative burden being imposed on State and local governments by the complicated requirements and inflexible mandates of the present programs.

Regulatory Reform

Agenda for Government Reform Act

The Agenda for Government Reform Act would authorize a major review of Federal regulatory activities. It would require the President, over a four-year period, to submit specific proposals to the Congress for the reform of Federal regulatory activities affecting certain sectors of the American economy (e.g., transportation, agriculture, public utilities, etc.). It is designed to produce reforms to guarantee that government policies do not infringe unnecessarily on individual choices and initiative nor intervene needlessly in the marketplace, to find better ways to achieve our social goals at minimal economic cost, to insure that government policies and programs benefit the public interest rather than special interests, and to assure that regulatory policies are equitably enforced.

Aviation Act of 1975

The Aviation Act is designed to provide consumers better air transportation services at a lower cost by increasing real competition in the airline industry, removing artificial and unnecessary regulatory constraints and ensuring continuance of a safe and efficient air transportation system. It would introduce and foster price competition in the airline industry; provide for the entry of new airline service; eliminate anticompetitive air carrier agreements; and ensure that the regulatory system protects consumer interests rather than special industry interests.

Motor Carrier Reform Act

The Motor Carrier Reform Act would benefit the consuming public and the users of motor carrier services by eliminating excessive and outdated regulations affecting trucking firms and bus companies. It would stimulate competition in these industries, increase their freedom to adjust rates and fares to changing economic conditions, eliminate restrictions requiring empty backhauls, underloading, or circuitous routing, and enhance enforcement of safety regulations.

Financial Institutions Act

The Financial Institutions Act is intended to remove Federal restrictions on the interest rates and services banks and savings and loan associations can offer to the public. It is designed to offer more competitive returns to small savers and a more diversified range of services to all banking customers.

Energy

New Natural Gas Deregulation

This bill is designed to reverse the declining natural gas supply trend as quickly as possible and to insure increased supplies of natural gas at reasonable prices to the consumer. Under the proposal, wellhead price controls over new natural gas sold in interstate commerce would be removed. This action will enable interstate pipelines to compete for new onshore gas and encourage drilling for gas onshore and in offshore areas.

Alaskan Natural Gas Transportation System

This bill was designed to expedite the selection and construction of a system for the transportation of natural gas from the North Slope of Alaska to the lower 48 States through the establishment of new administrative and judicial procedures. The bill is necessary because of expected prolonged litigation of any Federal Power Commission decision and to assure that all necessary considerations are brought to bear in selecting a system. The bill would enable reaching a decision on this vital issue by no later than October 1, 1977, while still providing adequately for the detailed technical, financial and environmental studies that must be completed to assure a decision in the public interest, with participation by both the Congress and the Executive.

Nuclear Fuel Assurance Act

This legislation would authorize the Energy Research and Development Administration to enter into cooperative agreements with private firms wishing to finance, build, own and operate uranium enrichment plants and authorize work on an addition to a government-owned enrichment plant. Existing capacity is fully committed. Additional capacity is needed to meet domestic demands for fuel for commercial nuclear power plants and to enable the U.S. to maintain its position as a leading world supplier of nuclear fuel and equipment for peaceful purposes. This legislation would permit a transition to a private competitive uranium enrichment industry, ending the government monopoly and avoiding the need to spend Federal funds for capacity that can be provided by private industry.

Commercial Pricing for Uranium Enrichment Service

This legislation would permit the Energy Research and Development Administration (ERDA) to revise the basis for establishing its prices for uranium enrichment services to domestic and foreign customers. It would enable ERDA to include cost elements in its price which should be associated with a commercial-industrial activity (e.g., provisions for taxes, insurance, and return on equity). The bill would end an unjustifiable subsidy by the taxpayers to domestic and foreign customers.

Synthetic Fuels

The Administration supports legislation to amend the Energy Research and Development Administration's existing authorities to provide $2-billion in loan guarantees during 1977 for the commercial demonstration of synthetic fuel production from coal, oil shale, and other domestic resources. A total of $6-billion in loan guarantees is expected to be necessary over the 1976 to 1978 period in order to reach the 1985 objective of 350,000 barrels per day of synthetic fuel production capacity. With the enactment of the Energy Independence Authority legislation these ERDA projects will be transferred to the Energy Independence Authority.

Winterization Assistance Act

This proposal would establish within the Federal Energy Administration, a grant program for States to assist low income persons, particularly the elderly, in winterizing their homes in order to reduce the long-term consumption of energy. The combined savings in fuel, estimated to be thousands of barrels a day, would not only lessen America's dependence on imported fuels, but would also lower heating bills of low-income persons and families.

Building Energy Conservation Standards Act of 1975

This proposal would establish thermal (heating and cooling) efficiency standards for all new homes and commercial buildings to conserve energy. It is anticipated that this program will save the equivalent of 350,000 barrels of oil per day in 1985. Stan-

dards would be promulgated by HUD and primary responsibility for enforcement would be with State and local governments through building codes.

Utilities Act of 1975

This bill is designed to help restore the financial health of electric utilities. It would eliminate undue regulatory lags involved in approving proposed rate changes and assure that rates adequately reflect the full cost of generating and transmitting electricity. Though many States have already adopted similar programs, enactment of the bill would establish certain standard regulatory procedures across the Nation, resulting in more equitable treatment of utilities.

Federal Energy Administration Extension Act

The Administration has proposed a simple extension of the Federal Energy Administration for 18 months. This will provide the continuity needed to insure FEA's ability to implement the complex programs contained in the Energy Policy and Conservation Act of 1975 and to adequately administer oil price controls.

Energy Independence Authority of 1975

This Act would establish a $100-billion Energy Independence Authority, a self-liquidating corporation designed to encourage the flow of capital and provide financial assistance, through loans and loan guarantees, to private enterprise engaged in the development of energy sources and supplies important to the attainment of energy independence but which would not otherwise be financed.

This bill also seeks to expedite and facilitate the Federal regulatory and licensing process and to hasten the commercial operation of new energy technologies subsequent to the research and development phase.

Nuclear Powerplant Siting and Licensing Procedures

This legislation is intended to shorten and improve the licensing process for nuclear facilities by allowing licensing procedures for reactor sites and standardized reactor designs to be completed at an earlier point in time. It would require the Nuclear Regulatory Commission to assure expeditious reactor siting and licensing hearings consistent with the public safety, exclude from consideration any issue which has either been decided or which could have been raised and decided in previous proceedings, and coordinate planning and scheduling of siting and licensing procedures with State agencies.

Electric Power Facility Construction Incentive Act

This legislation is designed to provide tax incentives to stimulate the construction

of new electric power generating facilities other than petroleum fueled generating plants. Construction costs of electric utilities would be reduced through changes in the investment tax credit and allowances for amortization and depreciation. These provisions would encourage utilities to reactivate their plans for the construction of nuclear plants and coal-fired plants that were cancelled or deferred in 1974 and 1975.

Energy Facilities Planning and Development Act

This bill is designed to expedite the development of energy facilities. The Federal Energy Administration would be required to develop a National Energy Site and Facility Report with appropriate Federal, State, industry and public input. Information in this report would be utilized by the Federal Government, the States and industry in developing and implementing plans to insure that needed energy facilities are sited, approved and constructed on a timely basis. At the Federal level, FEA would be responsible for coordinating and expediting the processing of applications to construct energy facilities.

Natural Gas Emergency Standby Act

This legislation would provide a limited exemption from the regulation of natural gas in interstate commerce. It would grant the Federal Power Commission authority to allow companies which transport natural gas in interstate commerce to meet the natural gas requirements of their high priority users by purchasing natural gas (a) from sources not in interstate commerce and (b) from other companies on an emergency basis free from the provisions of the Natural Gas Act, except for reporting requirements.

Clean Air Act Amendments

The Administration favors legislation which would stabilize auto emission standards at the levels specified by EPA for model year 1977 for three years and imposes stricter standards for two years thereafter. With respect to significant deterioration and stationary source standards, changes are needed to achieve a better balance among environmental, energy and economic needs.

Defense

Proposed changes to the Defense budget will be transmitted to the Congress in a separate message. These changes will include revised authorization and appropriation requests. These changes will:

1. Request approval of vital Defense programs deleted in Congressional action thus far.

2. Request deletion of unneeded increases the Congress added to the Defense program.

3. Request approval of a series of legislative proposals which would produce

major economies without impairing our national defense capabilities.

In addition to changes in the Defense budget, the Congress should enact the following legislation.

Military Construction Appropriation Authorization, Fiscal Year 1977

This legislation authorizes fiscal year 1977 appropriations for new construction for Defense, the military departments and the Reserve Components. On July 2, 1976, HR 12384 was vetoed because it contained a provision which would have seriously restricted the Executive's ability to carry out certain military base closures and reductions. Congress should reenact this otherwise acceptable legislation without the objectionable base closure provision.

Uniformed Services Retirement Modernization Act

The Administration's legislation proposes substantial revisions to the uniformed services nondisability retirement system designed to increase its effectiveness both as an element of the compensation system and as an element of the personnel management system. These revisions would be phased in gradually with appropriate provisions for saved-pay. Major features of the proposal include:

—increased multipliers for members with long service (over 24 years).

—an early retirement annuity for members who retire short of a full career (less than 30 years) with an increased annuity when they would have reached 30 years of service.

—use of the highest average basic pay for one year instead of terminal basic pay in computing retirement benefits at age 65.

—integration of military and social security retirement benefits at age 65.

—payments to both voluntary and involuntary separatees who leave before completing 20 years of service.

Restraint Items Requiring Permanent Legislation

1. Wage Board pay reform.
2. Phase out commissary direct labor subsidy.
3. Eliminate 1% "kicker" from retired pay adjustment compensation.
4. Eliminate administrative duty pay for Reserve and National Guard Commanders.
5. Reduce the number of annual paid drills for the National Guard.
6. Eliminate dual compensation of Federal employees for National Guard and Reserve annual training.
7. Revise cadet and midshipman pay policy.

International

Bretton Woods Agreement Act Amendments

This legislation would authorize the United States to accept fundamental amendments to the Articles of Agreement of the International Monetary Fund. The amendments to the Articles generally concern: members' exchange arrangements; reduction in the role of gold in the international monetary system; changes in the characteristics and uses of the special drawing right; and simplification and modernization of the Fund's financial operations and transactions. The bill would also authorize the United States to consent to an increase in its quota in the Fund equivalent to 1,705 million Special Drawing Rights.

Protection of Intelligence Sources and Methods

This legislation is designed to protect intelligence sources and methods from unauthorized disclosures. It provides for criminal and civil sanctions against those who are authorized access to such intelligence information and who reveal it to unauthorized persons. The bill contains provisions to prevent damaging disclosures of intelligence sources and methods in the course of prosecution and also includes safeguards to adequately protect the rights of an accused. Injunctive relief would be provided in those instances in which unauthorized disclosure is threatened and serious damage to intelligence collection efforts would result.

Foreign Intelligence Surveillance Act

This legislation is designed to ensure that the Government will be able to collect necessary foreign intelligence while at the same time providing assurances to the public that electronic surveillance for foreign intelligence purposes will not be abused. The proposed bill would provide a procedure for seeking a judicial order approving the use, in a particular case, of electronic surveillance to obtain foreign intelligence information. It also would establish standards that must be satisfied before any such order could be entered. The bill follows the framework of existing law governing such surveillance undertaken for criminal law enforcement purposes, with appropriate adjustments to meet the special needs and purposes of foreign intelligence investigations.

Export Administration Act Extension

This legislation would extend the Export Administration Act from September 30, 1976, to September 30, 1979. The Act authorizes the President to regulate exports of U.S. goods and technology to the extent necessary to protect the domestic economy from an excessive drain of scarce materials, to further the foreign policy of the United States and to control exports when necessary for purposes of national security. The Administration also has requested that the maximum civil penalty under the Act be raised from $1,000 to $10,000 and that criminal penalties be raised from $10,000 to more meaningful levels.

Financial Support Fund

This legislation would authorize the President to accept membership for the United States in a new, $25-billion Financial Support Fund agreed to by the Organization for Economic Cooperation and Development (OECD). The Fund would be available for a period of two years to provide short to medium-term financing to participating OECD members faced with extraordinary financing needs. The proposal for the Fund was developed as part of a comprehensive response to the economic and financial problems posed by severe increases in oil prices.

The Administration's proposal would permit U.S. participation in the Fund by authorizing the Secretary of the Treasury to issue guarantees. The bill would authorize appropriations of such sums as are necessary to meet obligations on guarantees issued by the Secretary but not to exceed an amount equivalent to approximately $7-billion.

International Bank for Reconstruction and Development (IBRD), Increased United States Participation

This legislation would authorize the Secretary of the Treasury as the United States Governor to the IBRD (World Bank) to vote for an increase of $8.4-billion in the authorized capital stock of the Bank. It would also authorize him to subscribe, on behalf of the United States, to an additional 13,005 shares of capital stock and authorize appropriations of approximately $1.57-billion for the increase in United States participation.

Implement Agreement Between The United States and Turkey

This proposed joint resolution would approve the new Defense Cooperation Agreement with the Government of Turkey and authorize the President to implement the Agreement.

Economic Coercion Act of 1975

This proposal would prohibit any business enterprise from using economic means to coerce any person or entity to fail to do business with or otherwise to discriminate against any United States person on the ground of race, color, religion, sex or national origin. The prohibition would be enforced by civil actions brought by aggrieved persons or by the Attorney General.

Increased Participation in the Asian Development Fund

This legislation would authorize appropriations of $50-million which would permit the United States to make the first of three scheduled contributions to a multi-donor replenishment of the Asian Development Fund.

Agriculture

U.S. Grain Standards Act Amendments

The Administration proposed a bill to amend the United States Grain Standards Act to improve the grain inspection system. Specifically, the bill would:

—retain the Federal, State and private grain inspection system now in effect, but authorizes USDA to perform original inspection on an interim basis during suspension or revocation proceedings against an official inspection agency, or where other qualified agency or person is not willing or able to provide service;

—authorize USDA to conduct monitoring activities in foreign ports for grain officially inspected under the Act;

—eliminates the potential for conflict of interest from the present grain inspection system;

—require official inspection agencies to comply with certain training, staffing, supervisory and reporting requirements;

—provide for the suspension or revocation of official inspection agencies for violation of the Act;

—provide for the triennial designation of all official inspection agencies; and,

—require the payment of grain inspection fees which would make the program largely self-supporting.

Federal Crop Insurance Act

The Administration proposed a bill to amend the Federal Crop Insurance Act and to repeal the disaster payment provisions for feed grains, cotton, and wheat under the Agriculture Act of 1949. The proposed amendments would permit the Federal Crop Insurance Corporation to offer insurance on a nationwide basis on feed grains, cotton, and wheat and thus provide the producers of those commodities with protection from the financial losses attributable to crop failures. It would also permit the Corporation to reinsure policies written by private insurance companies thereby expanding the availability of this valuable service. This program would save an estimated $250-million in government outlays annually and place the cost of and responsibility for maintaining crop insurance on the producers who would benefit from it.

Restructure Agriculture Conservation Program

The Administration proposed a bill to update the conditions under which the Federal Government provides financial assistance to agricultural producers for needed soil, water, woodland, and wildlife conservation and environmental enhancement measures on agricultural lands. Specifically, the bill would:

—provide for financial assistance to those agricultural producers *who are financially unable* to fully carry out needed conservation practices; and,

—*limit financial assistance* under the Act to *enduring type* practices pertaining to soil, water, woodland, and wildlife conservation on agricultural lands and *emphasize long-term agreements* as opposed to *annual or short-term* conservation practices.

Environment

Federal Water Pollution Control Act Amendments

The 1976 amendments proposed to the Act would affect future funding of the waste water treatment grant program. They would focus Federal funding on the construction of treatment plants and associated interceptor sewers; eliminate the eligibility of that portion of each project designed to serve reserve capacity for future population growth; and authorize the Administrator of EPA to extend the July 1, 1977 deadline for compliance with secondary treatment and water quality standards on a case-by-case basis for periods not to exceed six years. In addition, extensions of appropriation authorizations were proposed for FY 76 and FY 77.

Comprehensive Oil Pollution Liability and Compensation Act

The Comprehensive Oil Pollution Liability and Compensation Act of 1975 would establish a $200-million domestic fund which would be available to compensate individuals who suffer damages from oil spills in U.S. waters. The bill would create a uniform nationwide system of strict liability for oil spill damages and a standard procedure for settlement of claims. It would also implement two international conventions which deal with oil pollution caused by tankers on the high seas.

Income Assistance

National Food Stamp Reform Act

This proposal would concentrate food stamp program benefits on those truly in need, significantly improve program administration, and correct abuses and inequities of the current program. A standard deduction would replace the present set of complex itemized deductions; eligibility would be limited to those whose net income is below the poverty level; families would be required to spend 30 per cent of household income for stamps; a more realistic measure of actual income over the preceding 90 days would be used to determine eligibility; categorical eligibility for public assistance recipients would be eliminated; and able-bodied recipients would be required to seek, accept, and retain gainful employment.

Work Incentive (WIN) Program Amendments of 1976

The purpose of the Work Incentive (WIN) program is to help recipients of Aid to Families with Dependent Children (AFDC) shift from welfare to self-support through employment. The proposed WIN amendments would redesign the program to help more AFDC applicants and recipients move into the mainstream of the economy with greater efficiency and less cost to the taxpayers. It would revise WIN to ensure that employable AFDC applicants and recipients in WIN areas are exposed to job opportunities, and will actively search for and accept suitable jobs. The legislation would extend to AFDC applicants the employment services presently provided only to AFDC recipients—i.e., direct placement and labor market exposure—and would terminate the less effective work and training components of the WIN program.

Aid to Families With Dependent Children (AFDC) Amendments of 1976

This proposal would simplify the administration of the Aid to Families with Dependent Children (AFDC) program and focus the resources devoted to this program on the most needy. For example, it would standardize the disregard for work-related expenses, thereby eliminating one of the troublesome inequities of the AFDC program, and it would eliminate the dual work registration requirement for unemployed fathers which would remove an extra burden on the individual and reduce administrative work. It would also require that an applicant for AFDC under the unemployed fathers program apply for and accept any unemployment compensation benefits to which he is entitled. Currently, as a result of a Supreme Court decision, an individual who is eligible for unemployment compensation benefits has the option of applying for either unemployment compensation benefits or AFDC benefits. An individual's first recourse should be to unemployment benefits for which his employer has contributed and to which he is entitled.

Low Income Housing Contributions

This proposal would amend the definition of "income" used in determining eligibility and maximum rental charges under the low-income public housing program, to conform the criteria used in public housing to those used in the lower-income housing assistance program under section 8 of the United States Housing Act of 1937. Present law provides for a number of exclusions from income, among which are exclusions for minor children, extraordinary medical or other expenses, and a flat deduction of 5 per cent of the family's gross income (10 per cent in the case of elderly households). The amendment would require exclusions only for the number of minor children in the household and for the extent of medical or other unusual expenses. This would promote equity between tenants and public housing authorities and between tenants and Federal taxpayers.

Unemployment Compensation Amendments

This proposal would expand coverage under the regular unemployment insurance system to additional groups of workers and would make urgently needed changes to strengthen the financing of the system. The permanent extended unemployment insurance program would be made more responsive to changes in the economy. A National Commission on Unemployment Compensation would be established to comprehensively study the system and proposed changes, and make recommendations for further improvements.

Veterans

Medical Insurance for VA Hospital Care

Many veterans who receive free medical care at VA hospitals have health insurance. This proposal would require the insurance companies to reimburse the VA for hospital care provided to veterans who do not have disabilities resulting from active military service. The proposal reflects the Administration's belief that the Federal taxpayer should not bear the cost of treating people with no service-connected disabilities when to do so will benefit only third parties, including insurance companies, who are legally liable for the disability or injury necessitating such treatment.

Termination of Veterans Educational Benefits

This proposal would terminate VA education benefits for those men and women who decide in the future to enter the peacetime All-Volunteer Force. The educational assistance programs for veterans, from their inception, were designed as readjustment benefits for those who served during wartime. They were never intended to be a continuing benefit and both the World War II and Korean conflict GI Bill programs were terminated within a reasonable period after the cessation of hostilities. The Vietnam conflict officially ended in May 1975; the draft, in June 1973. With the advent of a peacetime, All-Volunteer Force, GI Bill educational benefits are no longer appropriate for those who enter military service in the future.

Other

Indemnification of Swine Flu Manufacturers

This proposal is essential to implementation of the National Influenza Immunization Program. Current law bars the Federal Government from agreeing to indemnify vaccine manufacturers for losses from injuries which may result from the Federal Government's activities in the immunization program. The Administration proposal would enable HEW to agree to indemnify the manufacturers against claims attributable to inoculation with the vaccine, except claims arising out of the negligence of the manufacturer.

Student Loan Amendments

This proposal would correct certain abuses in the Federal guaranteed student loan program that have resulted in high default rates under that program. Specifically, the proposal would amend Title IV of the Higher Education Act to eliminate proprietary schools as eligible lenders, and amend the Bankruptcy Act to make student loans nondischargeable in bankruptcy during the five-year period after the first installment becomes due. The proposal would also prohibit borrowers who default on guaranteed loans from receiving a basic educational opportunity grant or any further guaranteed loans.

Federal Impact Aid Amendments of 1976

This bill would reform the impact aid program by targeting funds only on those school districts that are truly adversely affected by Federal activities. It would provide support to local education agencies only for those children whose parents both live and work on Federal property. These people do not pay property taxes, and the Administration believes that the Federal Government has a responsibility to help pay the cost of educating their children, but not to help pay the costs of educating other children whose parents pay local property taxes.

Comprehensive Health Professions Education Act

The Administration's proposal would provide Federal support to those medical and dental schools that agree to meet certain conditions. Unlike prior programs of Federal assistance which were directed toward increasing the aggregate numbers of doctors and dentists in the Nation, the Administration proposal would shift the emphasis of Federal support for health professions schools from merely increasing enrollments to addressing national problems of medical specialty and geographic maldistribution. The proposal is designed to produce more primary care physicians and to provide greater access to health professionals.

Higher Education Act Amendment and Extension

This bill would extend for four years those higher education programs which have demonstrated their effectiveness in meeting the post-secondary education needs of the Nation. The bill would extend the most effective student assistance programs, namely, the basic educational opportunity grant program, the work-study program, the State student incentive grant program, and the guaranteed student loan program. Programs to strengthen develop-ing institutions and the Teacher Corps program would also be extended. The bill would also simplify and clarify the requirements relating to accreditation and institutional eligibility.

Closure or Transfer of Public Health Service Hospitals

This proposal is one of several Administration initiatives designed to reform Federal financing and direct delivery of health care. It would authorize HEW to transfer to community use or close the eight Public Health Service hospitals which are underutilized and which essentially serve only one occupational group. The proposal reflects the conclusion that maintenance of a Federal hospital system for some 200,000 merchant seamen is an inappropriate and inefficient use of resources, particularly in light of low hospital occupancy rates, the excess supply of hospital beds, the availability of alternative health care facilities, and the substantial capital investment which would be required to continue operation of the hospitals.

Repeal the 1-Percent Add-On In The Cost-of-Living Adjustment Of The Civil Service Retirement System

Federal civilian and military retirement systems automatically increase benefits to compensate for changes in the Consumer Price Index (CPI). Since 1969, these automatic adjustments have included a 1% add-on which has been compounded with each subsequent CPI adjustment. This bill would eliminate the 1% add-on provision in the civil service retirement law which has been progressively over-compensating Federal retirees for changes in the cost of living. The Congress has passed legislation to eliminate the 1% add-on in the military, foreign service, and CIA retirement systems, but only if it is also eliminated for the civil service retirement system.

Wage Board Pay Reform

The basic principle governing Federal blue-collar employees' pay rates is that they should be comparable with prevailing rates and pay practices in the non-Federal sector in the same locality. This bill would eliminate aspects of present law governing wage board pay rates that are inconsistent with that principle and therefore result in Federal blue-collar workers earning more than their counterparts in the private sector. Among other things, the bill would eliminate use of wage rate data from outside the local area involved. It would also eliminate the present requirement for each grade to have five steps, and would substitute a step-rate structure that would accord with the predominant industry practice.

Increased Authorization For Certain Small Business Loan Programs

This legislation would increase the total amount of loan guarantees and other obligations which the Small Business Administration (SBA) may have outstanding at any one time. These revised ceilings will permit SBA to increase the number of loans made to those small businesses who otherwise would be unable to obtain credit in the private sector.

Federal Procurement Act

A number of recommendations made by the Commission on Government Procurement—including proposals to consolidate the basic Federal procurement acts and modernize the provisions for awarding contracts—would be implemented by this bill.

Reorganization Act Extension

This proposal would extend the President's authority to submit plans for the reorganization of executive agencies to the Congress. This authority expired on April 1, 1973. The legislation is designed to restore the authority necessary for the President to propose reorganization in order to foster both efficiency and flexibility in the structure of the Executive branch.

Stockpile Disposal

This legislation would authorize disposal from the national stockpile and supplemental stockpile of industrial diamond stones, antimony, tin, and silver. The amounts of these four materials recommended for disposal are in excess of adequate stockpile requirements, and their sale would result in estimated receipts of $746-million in fiscal year 1977.

Patent Modernization and Reform Act

This legislation would substantially strengthen the American patent system by improving the strength and reliability of issued patents through procedural reforms in the patent examination and issuance process. It would also simplify procedures for obtaining patents, make more complete and precise the disclosure of information about technology contained in patents, and add new provisions concerning enforcement of patents.

Winter Olympic Games Assistance

This legislation would authorize Federal financial assistance for the construction of certain permanent, unique sports facilities needed for the 1980 Winter Olympic Games at Lake Placid, New York. The total amount of special Federal assistance under both existing authorities and this legislation would not exceed $28-million plus the financing of certain increases in construction costs.

These are important legislative proposals dealing with matters of the National interest, and I urge the Congress to move with dispatch to enact them.

GERALD R. FORD

The White House,
July 22, 1976.

United States Foreign Intelligence Activities

Following is the White House text of President Ford's Feb. 18 message advising Congress of his intelligence community reorganization and proposing related legislation:

TO THE CONGRESS OF THE UNITED STATES:

By virtue of the authority vested in me by Article II, Section 2 and 3 of the Constitution, and other provisions of law, I have today issued an Executive Order pertaining to the organization and control of the United States foreign intelligence community. This order establishes clear lines of accountability for the Nation's foreign intelligence agencies. It sets forth strict guidelines to control the activities of these agencies and specifies as well those activities in which they shall not engage.

In carrying out my Constitutional responsibilities to manage and conduct foreign policy and provide for the Nation's defense, I believe it essential to have the best possible intelligence about the capabilities, intentions and activities of governments and other entities and individuals abroad. To this end, the foreign intelligence agencies of the United States play a vital role in collecting and analyzing information related to the national defense and foreign policy.

It is equally as important that the methods these agencies employ to collect such information for the legitimate needs of the government conform to the standards set out in the Constitution to preserve and respect the privacy and civil liberties of American citizens.

The Executive Order I have issued today will insure a proper balancing of these interests. It establishes government-wide direction for the foreign intelligence agencies and places responsibility and accountability on individuals, not institutions.

I believe it will eliminate abuses and questionable activities on the part of the foreign intelligence agencies while at the same time permitting them to get on with their vital work of gathering and assessing information. It is also my hope that these steps will help to restore public confidence in these agencies and encourage our citizens to appreciate the valuable contribution they make to our national security.

Beyond the steps I have taken in the Executive Order, I also believe there is a clear need for some specific legislative actions. I am today submitting to the Congress of the United States proposals which will go far toward enhancing the protection of true intelligence secrets as well as regularizing procedures for intelligence collection in the United States.

My first proposal deals with the protection of intelligence sources and methods.

The Director of Central Intelligence is charged, under the National Security Act of 1947, as amended, with protecting intelligence sources and methods. The Act, however, gives the Director no authorities commensurate with this responsibility.

Therefore, I am proposing legislation to impose criminal and civil sanctions on those who are authorized access to intelligence secrets and who willfully and wrongfully reveal this information. This legislation is not an "Official Secrets Act", since it would affect only those who improperly disclose secrets, not those to whom secrets are disclosed. Moreover, this legislation could not be used to cover up abuses and improprieties. It would in no way prevent people from reporting questionable activities to appropriate authorities in the Executive and Legislative Branches of the government.

It is essential, however, that the irresponsible and dangerous exposure of our Nation's intelligence secrets be stopped. The American people have long accepted the principles of confidentiality and secrecy in many dealings—such as with doctors, lawyers and the clergy. It makes absolutely no sense to deny this same protection to our intelligence secrets. Openness is a hallmark of our democratic society, but the American people have never believed that it was necessary to reveal the secret war plans of the Department of Defense, and I do not think they wish to have true intelligence secrets revealed either.

I urge the adoption of this legislation with all possible speed.

Second, I support proposals that would clarify and set statutory limits, where necessary, on the activities of the foreign intelligence agencies. In particular, I will support legislation making it a crime to assassinate or attempt or conspire to assassinate a foreign official in peacetime. Since it defines a crime, legislation is necessary.

Third, I will meet with the appropriate leaders of Congress to try to develop sound legislation to deal with a critical problem involving personal privacy—electronic surveillance. Working with Congressional leaders and the Justice Department and other Executive agencies, we will seek to develop a procedure for undertaking electronic surveillance for foreign intelligence purposes. It should create a special procedure for seeking a judicial warrant authorizing the use of electronic surveillance in the United States for foreign intelligence purposes.

I will also seek Congressional support for sound legislation to expand judicial supervision of mail openings. The law now permits the opening of United States mail, under proper judicial safeguards, in the conduct of criminal investigations. We need authority to open mail under the limitations and safeguards that now apply in order to obtain vitally needed foreign intelligence information.

This would require a showing that there is probable cause to believe that the sender or recipient is an agent of a foreign power who is engaged in spying, sabotage or terrorism. As is now the case in criminal investigations, those seeking authority to examine mail for foreign intelligence purposes will have to convince a federal judge of the necessity to do so and accept the limitations upon their authorization to examine the mail provided in the order of the court.

Fourth, I would like to share my views regarding appropriate Congressional oversight of the foreign intelligence agencies. It is clearly the business of the Congress to organize itself to deal with these matters. Certain principles, however, should be recognized by both the Executive and Legislative Branches if this oversight is to be effective. I believe good Congressional oversight is essential so that the Congress and the American people whom you represent can be assured that the foreign intelligence agencies are adhering to the law in all of their activities.

Congress should seek to centralize the responsibility for oversight of the foreign intelligence community. The more committees and subcommittees dealing with highly sensitive secrets, the greater the risks of disclosure. I recommend that Congress establish a Joint Foreign Intelligence Oversight Committee. Consolidating Congressional oversight in one committee will facilitiate the efforts of the Administration to keep the Congress fully informed of foreign intelligence activities.

It is essential that both the House and the Senate establish firm rules to insure that foreign intelligence secrets will not be improperly disclosed. There must be established a clear process to safeguard these secrets and effective measures to deal with unauthorized disclosures.

Any foreign intelligence information transmitted by the Executive Branch to the Oversight Committee, under an injunction of secrecy, should not be unilaterally disclosed without my agreement. Respect for the integrity of the Constitution requires adherence to the principle that no individual member nor committee, nor single House of Congress can overrule an act of the Executive. Unilateral publication of classified information over the objection of the President, by one committee or one House of Congress, not only violates the doctrine of separation of powers, but also effectively overrules the actions of the other House of Congress, and perhaps even the majority of both Houses.

Finally, successful and effective Congressional oversight of the foreign intelligence agencies depends on mutual trust between the Congress and Executive. Each branch must recognize and respect the rights and prerogatives of the other if anything is to be achieved.

In this context, a Congressional requirement to keep the Oversight Committee "fully" informed is more desirable and workable as a practical matter than formal requirements for notification of specific activities to a large number of committees.

Specifically, Section 662 of the Foreign Assistance Act, which has resulted in over six separate committee briefings, should be modified as recommended by the Commission on the Organization of the Government for the Conduct of Foreign Policy, and reporting should be limited to the new Oversight Committee.

Both the Congress and the Executive Branch recognize the importance to this Nation of a strong intelligence service. I believe it urgent that we take the steps I have outlined above to insure that America not only has the best foreign intelligence service in the world, but also the most unique—one which operates in a manner fully consistent with the Constitutional rights of our citizens.

GERALD R. FORD

The White House,
February 18, 1976.

Tax Cut Message

Following is the White House text of President Ford's Jan. 4, 1977, message to Congress on taxes:

TO THE CONGRESS OF
THE UNITED STATES:

In October 1975, I presented to the Congress a program of tax cuts and spending restraints that would have reduced the burden of government for all taxpayers. It would have given the American people more freedom to spend their incomes as they choose rather than as Washington chooses for them. However, Congress decided otherwise—to increase spending far more than I wanted and to cut taxes far less than I wanted.

My forthcoming 1978 Budget will provide a detailed blueprint for Federal spending. Today, as I promised, I am outlining my proposals for personal and business tax reductions in 1977. First, I again urge a permanent increase in the personal exemption from $750 to $1000 to replace the system of temporary tax credits that have so greatly complicated the individual income tax return. I am also recommending an increase in the low income allowance and a series of permanent tax rate reductions. In total, my proposals provide income tax relief for individuals of approximately $10 billion in 1977. The tax reductions of 1975 and 1976 focused tax relief on the lower income taxpayer. However, it is high time to focus substantial tax relief on middle income taxpayers. The tax relief I seek will cut the 1977 income taxes of a typical family with four with an income of $15,000 by $227.

In the long run, inflation and real economic growth constantly push taxpayers into higher and higher tax brackets if tax law remains unchanged. Some believe that these additional tax receipts should be spent on new Federal programs. I do not.

Instead, I believe that the Congress should periodically counteract the growing burden imposed by the tax system by providing offsetting tax cuts while continuing to restrain the rate of growth of Federal spending.

Corporate Tax Cut

The creation of good permanent jobs for our expanding labor force requires a higher level of private investment. I am, therefore, recommending again a permanent reduction in the corporate income tax from 48 to 46 percent. This would reduce business tax liabilities by $2.5 billion in 1977.

I also urge making permanent the 10 percent investment tax credit and the surtax exemption provisions of the Tax Reform Act of 1976. In the longer run we must eliminate the double taxation of dividend payments. I am, therefore, renewing my proposal to integrate corporate and personal income taxes gradually over a period of years beginning in 1978. All of these changes in the tax laws will increase the funds available, directly and indirectly, for new and better plants, machinery, stores and equipment.

I am again recommending accelerated depreciation for new plants and equipment installed in rural and urban labor market areas where unemployment is 7 percent or higher. I am firmly convinced that this is a far better way to help create jobs in those areas that have lagged behind in the economic recovery than adding layer upon layer of new hastily conceived spending programs.

A year ago, in my 1977 Budget, I noted that the old age, survivors and disability trust funds would be depleted in the early 1980's unless some action was taken. Therefore, much as I didn't like doing it, I felt compelled to recommend payroll tax rate increases beginning January 1, 1977. The employee share of this increase would have amounted to less than one dollar per week for taxpayers at the top end of the pay scale and a few cents per week for those at the bottom. Congress failed to act on this proposal. Partly because of the delay, a higher tax increase is now necessary if the social security system is to remain intact. Because current law already prescribes a four-tenths of one percent increase in the tax rate in 1978, I do not believe that a very large additional increase is appropriate in that year. I am therefore proposing an additional two-tenths of one percent rate increase in 1978 supplemented by a six-tenths of one percent rate increase in 1979 and a three-tenths of one percent rate increase in 1980. These increases will restore the fiscal integrity of the Social Security Trust Funds in the short run and, together with my proposals for correcting the inflation adjustment for future benefits for currently employed workers, will greatly reduce the long-run deficit faced by the social security system.

I have in the past urged several other changes in our tax laws which are both necessary and desirable. These will be proposed again in my budget, but need not be discussed in detail at this time. These include a tax credit for home insulation, exempting charitable contributions from the burden of the minimum tax, increasing the railroad retirement tax in a manner consistent with the recommended Social Security tax increases, and providing State and local governments with an option to issue taxable bonds subsidized in part by the Federal government.

I am also recommending repeal of the earned income credit and the provision for funding Employee Stock Ownership Plans through additional investment tax credits. The earned income credit is not integrated with the rest of our welfare system and makes future reform of that system even more difficult. The Employee Stock Ownership Plan provides a very large taxpayer subsidy to employers who wish to purchase stock in their firm for their employees. I do not believe that this is an equitable approach to the encouragement of stock ownership.

I urge that the Congress take prompt action on all of the above tax proposals.

GERALD R. FORD

The White House,
January 4, 1977

Text of Ford's 1977 State of the Union Message

Following is the text of President Ford's final State of the Union address, delivered to a joint session of Congress Jan. 12, 1977.

TO THE CONGRESS OF THE UNITED STATES:

In accordance with the Constitution, I come before you once again to report on the State of the Union.

This report will be my last, maybe.

But for the Union, it is only the first of such reports in our Third Century of Independence, the close of which none of us will ever see. We can be confident, however, that 100 years from now a freely elected President will come before a freely elected Congress chosen to renew our great Republic's pledge to Government of the people, by the people, and for the people.

For my part, I pray the Third Century we are beginning will bring to all Americans, our children and their children's children, a greater measure of individual equality, opportunity and justice, a greater abundance of spiritual and material blessings, and a higher quality of life, liberty and the pursuit of happiness.

The State of the Union is a measurement of the many elements of which it is composed—a political union of diverse states, an economic union of varying interests, an intellectual union of common convictions and a moral union of immutable ideals.

Taken in sum, I can report that the State of the Union is good. There is room for improvement as always, but today we have a more perfect union than when my stewardship began.

As a people, we discovered that our Bicentennial was much more than a celebration of the past; it became a joyous reaffirmation of all that it means to be Americans, a confirmation before all the world of the vitality and durability of our free institutions.

I am proud to have been privileged to preside over the affairs of our Federal Government during these eventful years when we proved, as I said in my first words upon assuming office, that "our Constitution works; our Great Republic is a Government of laws and not of men; here, the people rule."

The people have spoken; they have chosen a new President and a new Congress to work their will; I congratulate you—particularly the new members—as sincerely as I did President-elect Carter. In a few days, it will be his duty to outline for you his priorities and legislative recommendations. Tonight, I will not infringe on that responsibility, but rather wish him the very best in all that is good for our country.

During the period of my own service in this Capitol and in the White House I can recall many orderly transitions of governmental responsibility—of problems as well as of position, of burdens as well as of power. The genius of the American system is that we do this so naturally and so normally; there are no soldiers marching in the streets except in the Inaugural Parade; no public demonstrations except for some of the dancers at the Inaugural Ball; the opposition party doesn't go underground but goes on functioning vigorously in the Congress and the country; and our vigilant press goes right on probing and publishing our faults and our follies, confirming the wisdom of the framers of the First Amendment.

Because the transfer of authority in our form of government affects the state of the union, and of the world, I am happy to report to you that the current transition is proceeding very well. I was determined that it should; I wanted the new President to get off to an easier start than I had.

When I became President on August 9, 1974, our Nation was deeply divided and tormented. In rapid succession, the Vice President and the President had resigned in disgrace. We were still struggling with the after-effects of a long, unpopular and bloody war in Southeast Asia. The economy was unstable and racing toward the worst recession in 40 years. People were losing jobs. The cost of living was soaring. The Congress and the Chief Executive were at loggerheads. The integrity of our Constitutional process and of other institutions was being questioned.

For more than 15 years, domestic spending had soared as Federal programs multiplied and the expense escalated annually. During the same period, our national security needs were steadily shortchanged.

In the grave situation which prevailed in August 1974, our will to maintain our international leadership was in doubt.

I asked for your prayers, and went to work.

In January 1975, I reported to the Congress that the state of the union was not good. I proposed urgent action to improve the economy and to achieve energy independence in ten years. I reassured America's allies and sought to reduce the danger of confrontation with potential adversaries. I pledged a new direction for America.

Nineteen seventy-five was a year of difficult decisions, but Americans responded with realism, common sense and self-discipline.

By January 1976, we were headed in a new direction, which I hold to be the right direction for a free society. I was guided by the belief that successful problem-solving requires more than Federal action alone; that it involves a full partnership among all branches and levels of government, and public policies which nurture and promote the creative energies of private enterprises, institutions and individual citizens.

A year ago, I reported that the state of the union was better—in many ways a lot better—but still not good enough.

Common sense told me to stick to the steady course we were on, to continue to restrain the inflationary growth of government, to reduce taxes as well as spending, to return local decisions to local officials, to provide for long-range sufficiency in energy and national security needs. I resisted the immense pressures of an election year to open the floodgates of Federal money and the temptation to promise more than I could deliver. I told it as it was to the American people and demonstrated to the world that, in our spirited political competition, as in this chamber, Americans can disagree without being disagreeable.

Signs of Progress

Now, after 30 months as your President I can say that while we still have a way to go, I am proud of the long way we have come together.

I am proud of the part I have had in rebuilding confidence in the Presidency, confidence in our free system and confidence in our future. Once again, Americans believe in themselves, in their leaders, and in the promise that tomorrow holds for their children.

I am proud that today America is at peace. None of our sons are fighting and dying in battle anywhere in the world. And the chance for peace among all nations is improved by our determination to honor our vital commitments in the defense of peace and freedom.

I am proud that the United States has strong defenses, strong alliances and a sound and courageous foreign policy.

—Our alliances with our major partners, the great industrial democracies of Western Europe, Japan, and Canada, have never been more solid. Consultations on mutual security, defense and East-West relations have grown closer. Collaboration has branched out into new fields, such as energy, economic policy and relations with the Third World.

We have used many avenues for cooperation, including summit meetings held among major allied countries. The friendship of the democracies is deeper, warmer and more effective than at any time in 30 years.

—We are maintaining stability in the strategic nuclear balance, and pushing back the spectre of nuclear war. A decisive step forward was taken in the Vladivostok Accord which I negotiated with General Secretary Brezhnev—joint recognition that an equal ceiling should be placed on the number of strategic weapons on each side.

With resolve and wisdom on the part of both nations, a good agreement is well within reach this year.

—The framework for peace in the Middle East has been built. Hopes for future progress in the Middle East were stirred by the historic agreements we reached and the trust and confidence we formed.

—Thanks to American leadership, the prospects for peace in the Middle East are brighter than they have been in three decades. The Arab states and Israel continue to look to us to lead them from confrontation and war to a new era of accommodation and peace. We have no alternative but to persevere and I'm sure we will. The opportunities for a final settlement are great, and the price of failure is a return to the bloodshed and hatred that for too long have brought tragedy to all the peoples of this area, and repeatedly edged the world to the brink of war.

—Our relationship with the People's Republic of China is proving its importance and its durability. We are finding more and more common ground between our two countries on basic questions of international affairs.

In my two trips to Asia as President, we have reaffirmed America's continuing vital interest in the peace and security of Asia and the Pacific Basin, established a new partnership with Japan, confirmed our dedication to the security of Korea, and reinforced our ties with the free nations of Southeast Asia.

—An historic dialogue has begun between industrial nations and the developing nations. Most proposals on the table are the initiatives of the United States, including those on food, energy, technology, trade, investment and commodities. We are well launched on this process of shaping positive and reliable economic relations between rich nations and poor nations over the long-term.

—We have made progress in trade negotiations and avoided protectionism during recession. We strengthened the international monetary system. During the past two years the free world's most important economic powers have already brought about important changes that serve both developed and developing economies. The momentum already achieved must be nurtured and strengthened, for the prosperity of rich and poor depends upon it.

—In Latin America, our relations have taken on a new maturity and a sense of common enterprise.

—In Africa, the quest for peace, racial justice and economic progress is at a crucial point. The United States, in close cooperation with the United Kingdom, is actively engaged in that historic process. Will change come about by warfare and chaos and foreign intervention? Or will it come about by negotiated and fair solutions, ensuring majority rule, minority rights and economic advance? America is committed to the side of peace and justice, and to the principle that Africa should shape its own future free of outside intervention.

—American leadership has helped to stimulate new international efforts to stem the proliferation of nuclear weapons and to shape a comprehensive treaty governing the use of the oceans.

I am gratified by these accomplishments. They constitute a record of broad success for America, and for the peace and prosperity of all mankind. This Administration leaves to its successor a world in better condition than we found. We leave, as well, a solid foundation for progress on a range of issues that are vital to the well being of America.

What has been achieved in the field of foreign affairs, and what can be accomplished by the new administration, demonstrate the genius of Americans working together for the common good. It is this, our remarkable ability to work together, that has made us a unique nation. It is Congress, the President, and the people striving for a better world.

I know all patriotic Americans want this Nation's foreign policy to succeed.

I urge members of my party in this Congress to give the new President loyal support in this area.

I express the hope that this new Congress will re-examine its constitutional role in international affairs.

The exclusive right to declare war, the duty to advise and consent on the part of the Senate, and the power of the purse on the part of the House, are ample authority for the legislative branch and should be jealously guarded.

But because we may have been too careless of these powers in the past does not justify congressional intrusion into, or obstruction of, the proper exercise of Presidential responsibilities now or in the future. There can be only one Commander-in-Chief. In these times crises cannot be managed and wars cannot be waged by committee. Nor can peace be pursued solely by parliamentary debate. To the ears of the world, the President speaks for the Nation. While he is, of course, ultimately accountable to the Congress, the courts and the people, he and his emissaries must not be handicapped in advance in their relations with foreign governments as has sometimes happened in the past.

Economic Recovery

At home, I am encouraged by the Nation's recovery from the recession and our steady return to sound economic growth. It is now continuing after the recent period of uncertainty, which is part of the price we pay for free elections.

Our most pressing need today and in the future is more jobs—productive and permanent jobs created by a thriving economy.

We must revise our tax system both to ease the burden of heavy taxation and to encourage the investment necessary for the creation of productive jobs for all Americans who want to work. Earlier this month I proposed a permanent income tax reduction of ten billion dollars below current levels including raising the personal exemption from $750 to $1,000. I also recommended a series of measures to stimulate investment, such as accelerated depreciation for new plants and equipment in areas of high unemployment, a reduction in the corporate tax rate from 48 to 46 per cent, and eliminating the present double taxation of dividends. I strongly urge the Congress to pass these measures to help create the productive, permanent jobs in the private economy that are essential to our future. All of the basic trends are good; we are not on the brink of another recession or economic disaster. If we follow prudent policies that encourage productive investment and discourage destructive inflation, we will come out on top, and I'm sure we will.

We have successfully cut inflation by more than half: when I took office, the Consumer Price Index was rising at 12.2 per cent a year. During 1976, the rate of inflation was five per cent.

We have created more jobs. Over four million more people have jobs today than in the spring of 1975. Throughout this nation today we have over 88 million people in useful, productive jobs—more than at any other time in our nation's history. But, there are still too many Americans unemployed. This is the greatest regret that I have as I leave office.

We brought about with the Congress, after much delay, the renewal of general revenue sharing. We expanded community development and federal manpower programs. We began a significant urban mass transit program. Federal programs today provide more funds for our states and local governments than ever before—$70-billion for the current fiscal year.

Through these programs and others that provide aid directly to individuals we have kept faith with our tradition of compassionate help for those who need it. As we begin our third century we can be proud of the progress we have made in meeting human needs for all of our citizens.

We have cut the growth of crime by nearly 90 per cent. Two years ago, crime was increasing at a rate of 18 per cent annually. In the first three quarters of 1976, that growth rate had been cut to two per cent. But crime, and the fear of crime, remains one of the most serious problems facing our citizens.

We have had some successes. And there have been some disappointments.

Bluntly, I must remind you that we have not made satisfactory progress toward achieving energy independence.

Energy

Energy is absolutely vital to the defense of our country, to the strength of our economy, and to the quality of our lives. Two years ago I proposed to the Congress the first comprehensive national energy program:

A specific and coordinated set of measures that would end our vulnerability to embargo, blockade, or arbitrary price increases, and would mobilize U.S. technology and resources to supply a significant share of the free world's energy needs after 1985.

Of the major energy proposals I submitted two years ago, only half belatedly became law. In 1973, we were dependent upon foreign oil imports for 36 per cent of our needs. Today we are 40 per cent dependent, and we'll pay out 34 billion U.S. dollars for foreign oil this year. Such vulnerability at present or in the future is intolerable and must be ended.

The answer to where we stand on our national energy effort today reminds me of the old argument over whether the tank is half full or half empty. The pessimist will say we have half failed to achieve our ten-year energy goals, the optimist will say that we have half succeeded. I am always an optimist, but we must make up for lost time.

We have laid a solid foundation for completing the enormous task which confronts us. I have signed into law five major energy bills which contain significant measures for conservation, resource development, stockpiling and standby authorities.

We have moved forward to develop the Naval Petroleum Reserves; to build a five hundred-million barrel strategic petroleum stockpile; to phase-out unnecessary government allocation and price controls; to develop a lasting relationship with other oil consuming nations; to improve the efficiency of energy use through conservation in automobiles, buildings and industry; and

to expand research on new technology and renewable resources, such as wind power, geothermal and solar energy.

All these actions, significant as they are for the long term, are only the beginning. I recently submitted to the Congress my proposals to reorganize the federal energy structure, and the hard choices which remain if we are serious about reducing our dependence upon foreign energy.

These include programs to reverse our declining production of natural gas and increase incentives for domestic crude oil production. I propose to minimize environmental uncertainties affecting coal development, expand nuclear power generation and create an energy independence authority to provide government financial assistance for vital energy programs where private capital is not available.

We must explore every reasonable prospect for meeting our energy needs when our current domestic reserves of oil and natural gas begin to dwindle in the next decade.

I urgently ask Congress and the new Administration to move quickly on these issues. This Nation has the resources and capability to achieve our energy goals if its government has the will to proceed and I think we do.

Reorganization

I have been disappointed by inability to complete many of the meaningful organizational reforms which I contemplated for the Federal Government, although a start has been made.

For example, the Federal Judicial System has long served as a model for other courts. But today it is threatened by a shortage of qualified Federal judges and an explosion of litigation claiming Federal jurisdiction.

I commend to the new Administration and the Congress the recent report and recommendations of the Department of Justice, undertaken at my request, on "the needs of the Federal Courts." I especially endorse its proposals for a new commission on the judicial appointment process.

While the Judicial Branch of our Government may require reinforcement, the budgets and payrolls of the other branches remain staggering. I cannot help but observe that while the White House Staff and the Executive Office of the President have been reduced and the total number of civilians in the Executive Branch contained during the 1970s, the Legislative Branch has increased substantially, although the membership of the Congress remains at 535. Congress now costs the taxpayers more than a million dollars a year per member; the whole Legislative budget has passed the billion dollar mark.

I set out to reduce the growth in the size and spending of the Federal Government, but no President can accomplish this alone. The Congress sidetracked most of my requests for authority to consolidate overlapping programs and agencies, to

return more decision-making and responsibility to State and local governments through block grants instead of rigid categorical programs and to eliminate unnecessary red tape and outrageously complex regulations.

We have made some progress in cutting back the expansion of Government and its intrusion into individual lives—but believe me, there is much more to be done and you and I know it. It can only be done by tough and temporarily painful surgery by a Congress as prepared as the President to face up to this very real political problem.

Again, I wish my successor, working with a substantial majority of his own party, the best of success in reforming the costly and cumbersome machinery of the Federal Government.

The task of self-government is never finished. The problems are great; the opportunities are greater.

Defense

America's first goal is and always will be peace with honor. America must remain first in keeping peace in the world. We can remain first in peace only if we are never second in defense.

In presenting the State of the Union to the Congress and to the American people, I have a special obligation as Commander-in-Chief to report on our national defense. Our survival as a free and independent people requires, above all, strong military forces that are well-equipped and highly trained to perform their assigned mission.

I am particularly gratified to report that over the past two and a half years we have been able to reverse the dangerous decline of the previous decade in the real resources this country was devoting to national defense. This was an immediate problem I faced in 1974. The evidence was unmistakable that the Soviet Union had been steadily increasing the resources it applied to building its military strength.

During this same period the United States' real defense spending declined. In my three budgets, we not only arrested that dangerous decline, but we have established the positive trend which is essential to our ability to contribute to peace and stability in the world.

The Vietnam War both materially and psychologically affected our overall defense posture. The dangerous antimilitary sentiment discouraged defense spending and unfairly disparaged the men and women who served in our armed forces.

The challenge that now confronts this country is whether we have the national will and determination to continue this essential defense effort over the long term, as it must be continued. We can no longer afford to oscillate from year to year in so vital a matter. Indeed, we have a duty to look beyond the immediate question of budgets, and to examine the nature of the problem we will face over the next generation.

I am the first recent President able to address long-term basic issues without the burden of Vietnam. The war in Indochina consumed enormous resources, at the very time that the overwhelming strategic superiority we once enjoyed was disappearing. In past years, as a result of decisions by the United States, our strategic forces levelled off. Yet, the Soviet Union continued a steady, constant build-up of its own forces, committing a high percentage of its national economic effort to defense.

The United States can never tolerate a shift in the strategic balance against us, or even a situation where the American people or our allies believe the balance is shifting against us. The United States would risk the most serious political consequences if the world came to believe that our adversaries have a decisive margin of superiority. To maintain a strategic balance we must look ahead to the 1980s and beyond. The sophistication of modern weapons requires that we make decisions now if we are to ensure our security ten years from now.

Therefore I have consistently advocated and strongly urged that we pursue three critical strategic programs: the Trident missile launching submarine; the B-1 bomber, with its superior capability to penetrate modern air defenses; and a more advanced intercontinental ballistic missile that will be better able to survive nuclear attack and deliver a devastating retaliatory strike.

In an era where the strategic nuclear forces are in rough equilibrium, the risks of conflict below the nuclear threshold may grow more perilous. A major long-term objective, therefore, is to maintain capabilities to deal with, and thereby deter, conventional challenges and crises, particularly in Europe.

We cannot rely solely on strategic forces to guarantee our security or to deter all types of aggression. We must have superior Naval and Marine forces to maintain freedom of the seas, strong multi-purpose tactical Air Forces, and mobile, modern ground forces.

Accordingly: I have directed a long-term effort to improve our worldwide capabilities to deal with regional crises.

—I have submitted a five year Naval building program indispensable to the Nation's maritime strategy.

—Because the security of Europe and the integrity of NATO remain the cornerstone of American defense policy, I have initiated a special, long-term program to ensure the capacity of the alliance to deter or defeat aggression in Europe.

As I leave office, I can report that our national defense is effectively deterring conflict today. Our Armed Forces are capable of carrying out the variety of missions assigned to them. Programs are underway which will assure we can deter war in the years ahead.

But I also must warn that it will require a sustained effort over a period of years to maintain these capabilities. We must have the wisdom, the stamina and the courage to prepare today for the perils of tomorrow, and I believe we will.

As I look to the future—and I assure you I intend to go on doing that for a good many years—I can say with confidence that the State of the Union is good, but we must go on making it better and better.

This gathering symbolizes the Constitutional foundation which makes continued progress possible, synchronizing the skills of three independent branches of government, reserving fundamental sovereignty to the people of this great land.

It is only as the temporary representatives and servants of the people that we meet here—we bring no hereditary status or gift of infallibility and none follows us from this place. Like President Washington, like the more fortunate of his successors, I look forward to the status of private citizens with gladness and gratitude. To me, being a citizen of the United States of America is the greatest honor and privilege in this world.

From the opportunities which fate and my fellow citizens have given me, as a member of the House, as Vice President and President of the Senate, and as President of all the people, I have come to understand and to place the highest value on the checks and balances which our founders imposed on government through the separation of powers, among co-equal Legislative, Executive and Judicial Branches.

This often results in difficulty and delay, as I well know, but it also places supreme authority under God, beyond any one person, any one branch, any majority great or small, or any one party. The Constitution is the bedrock of all our freedoms; guard and cherish it; keep honor and order in your own house; and the Republic will endure.

It is not easy to end these remarks; in this chamber, along with some of you, I have experienced many, many of the highlights of my life. It was here that I stood 28 years ago with my freshman colleagues as Speaker Sam Rayburn administered the oath—I see some of you now, Charlie Bennett, Dick Bolling, Carl Perkins, Pete Rodino, Harley Staggers, Tom Steed, Sid Yates and Clem Zablocki, and I remember those who have gone to their rest.

It was here we waged many, many a lively battle, won some, lost some, but always remaining friends. It was here we surrounded by such friends, that the distinguished Chief Justice swore me in as Vice President on December 6, 1973. It was here I returned eight months later as your President to ask you not for a honeymoon, but for a good marriage.

I will always treasure those memories and the many, many kindnesses. I thank you for them.

My fellow Americans, I once asked for your prayers, and now I give you mine: May God guide this wonderful country, its people, and those they have chosen to lead them. May our third century be illuminated by liberty and blessed with brotherhood, so that we and all who come after us may be the humble servants of thy peace. Amen.

Good night and God bless you.

GERALD R. FORD

The White House,
January 12, 1977.

Text of President's Fiscal '78 Budget Message

Following is the text of President Ford's fiscal 1978 budget message to Congress on Jan. 17, 1977:

TO THE CONGRESS OF
THE UNITED STATES:

The budget is the President's blueprint for the operation of the Government in the year ahead. It records his views on priorities and directions for the future—balancing the American desire to solve every perceived problem at once with the practical reality of limited resources and competing needs.

The thirty budgets I have either shaped or helped to shape are a chronicle of our lives and times. They tell us what we have aspired to be and what we have been in fact. They tell us about the growing complexity of our society, about the changing and growing role of our Government, and about new problems we have identified and our attempts to solve them.

In shaping my budgets as President, I have sought to renew the basic questions about the composition and direction of the Government and its programs. In my reviews of existing and proposed programs and activities I have asked:

—Is this activity important to our national security or sense of social equity?

—Is this activity sufficiently important to require that we tax our people or borrow funds to pay for it?

—Must the federal government raise the taxes or borrow the funds or should state or local government do so?

—Should the federal government direct and manage the activity or should it limit its role to the provision of financing?

—How has the program performed in the past? Have the benefits outweighed the costs in dollars or other burdens imposed?

—Have the benefits gone to the intended beneficiary?

—Does this activity conflict with or overlap another?

As a result of these reviews I have proposed to reverse some trends and to accelerate others.

Government Spending Slowdown

I have proposed, and repropose this year, a marked slowdown in the rate of growth in government spending. Over the last three decades, federal, state, and local government spending has grown from 18 per cent of GNP to 34 per cent of GNP. Federal spending growth has averaged 10 per cent per year over the last decade. And even these percentages do not tell the whole story. As the budget documents illustrate, there has been a trend over the last few years toward so-called "off-budget" spending. This is an undesirable practice because it obscures the real impact of the federal government and makes it more difficult for any but the most technically knowledgeable citizens to understand what their government is doing. Therefore, I am calling for legislation to halt this practice so that our budget system will fully reflect the financial activities of the government.

In a related attempt to gain greater control over the rate of growth of government spending I have given special attention this year to spending plans for fiscal year 1979, the year after the budget year. For the first time, the federal budget shows detailed planning amounts for the year beyond the budget year. This innovation grows out of my conviction that our only real hope of curbing the growth of federal spending is to plan further in advance and to discipline ourselves to stick to those plans.

From the standpoint of deficits of most recent years the 1978 budget I present shows us fairly close to balance in 1979 and shows balanced budgets thereafter. The effects on 1978 and 1979 spending of congressional action in the last session rejecting many of the restraints I proposed for the current fiscal year, 1977, made total balance in 1979 impossible unless I was willing to abandon, at least in part, the further immediate tax relief I have advocated since October of 1975 and, for no reason other than being able to show such a 1979 balance, cut back from program levels I feel are justified. These alternatives were unacceptable, but given the greatly reduced deficit for 1979 this budget implies, congressional cooperation on the restraints I propose and a slightly better economic performance in the months ahead than we have used in preparing this 1978 budget, it is entirely possible that when the 1979 budget is due to be submitted, a year from now, it could be in total balance as I have strived to achieve.

Permanent Tax Cuts Sought

With restraint on the growth of federal spending, we can begin to provide permanent tax reductions to ease the burden on middle-income taxpayers and businesses. For too long government has presumed that it is "entitled" to the additional tax revenues generated as inflation and increases in real income push taxpayers into higher tax brackets. We need to reverse this presumption. We need to put the burden of proof on the government to demonstrate the reasons why individuals and businesses should not keep the income and wealth they produce. Accordingly, my long-term budget projections assume further tax relief will be provided, rather than presuming, as has been the practice in the past, that positive margins of receipts over expenditures that show up in projections are "surpluses" or "fiscal dividends" that must be used primarily for more federal spending, on existing or new programs or both.

One trend has been reversed in the past two years. After several years of decline in real spending for national security purposes the Congress has agreed in substantial part to my recommendations for increases in defense spending. The budget I propose this year and the planning levels for the succeeding four years assume a continuation of this real growth trend. My recommendations are the result of a careful assessment of our own defense posture and that of our potential adversaries. In this area as in all others, I am recommending spending I consider essential while at the same time proposing savings in outmoded or unwarranted activities. For the longer term, my recommendations recognize the simple fact that we must plan now for the defense systems we will need 10 years from now.

Higher R&D Spending Urged

This same approach was reflected last year in my recommendations for the federal government's basic research and development programs. In spite of the financial pressures on the federal budget, I recommended real growth. I am again proposing real growth for basic research and development programs this year because I am convinced that we must maintain our world leadership in science and technology in order to increase our national productivity and attain the better life we want for our people and the rest of the world.

I am also calling again for an end to the proliferation of new federal programs and for consolidation of many of the programs we now have. At last count there are 1,044 programs identified in the Catalog of Federal Domestic Assistance. While our nation has many needs, there is no rational justification for the maze that has been created.

Overlap and duplication are not the only defects of these programs; nor are they the most serious. More importantly the current programs too often fail to aid the intended beneficiaries as much as expected, rewarding instead those who have learned how to work the Washington system. Some of these programs fail to pinpoint responsibility and accountability for performance and too many impose a managerial and operating burden on the federal government, diverting attention from the functions that must be performed at the federal level and at the same time usurping the proper roles of state and local governments and the private sector.

Program Reforms Needed

If we could ever afford the "luxury" of this inefficiency and ineptitude, we can no longer. Federal programs for health services, elementary and secondary education, child nutrition and welfare, for example, are areas that desperately need reform. I called for action last year and prepared detailed legislative proposals. Those who truly care about the needs of our people will not let another year go by without reform. There is no excuse, for example, for the federal government to have 15 different child nutrition programs spending over $3-billion per year and still have 700,000 children from families below the poverty line who receive no aid. Nor is there any reason to take the money out of the taxpayers' pocket to subsidize their own children's school lunch.

It will take real courage to correct these problems and the others I have identified for congressional action without following the all too familiar pattern of the past—simply adding more programs. But, increasingly, courage is not a choice; it is an absolute requirement if we are to avoid ever larger, less responsive government.

The task ahead will not be easy because it will require some fundamental changes in our expectations for government. As a start, we need to understand that income and wealth are not produced in Washington, they are only redistributed there. As a corollary, we need to overcome the idea that members of the Congress are elected to bring home federal projects for their district or state. Until this idea is totally rejected, higher funding levels for old programs and more new programs will be enacted each year as members of the Congress seek to insure their re-election. We also need to overcome the prevalent attitude that only new programs with multibillion dollar price tags are worthy of media attention and public discussion and worthy of being judged bold and innovative. The multitude of programs already in a budget of more than $400-billion and initiatives to do something about them are worthy of intense public scrutiny, discussion and judgment in their own right.

These changes in attitude will require leadership not only by the executive branch, but, at least equally important, on the part of each member of the Congress. Members of the Congress must begin to share the burden of the President in saying no to special interest groups—even those in their own districts or states.

The changes that have occurred in the congressional budget-making process in recent years provide some basis for optimism for the future. The new budget committees have begun to provide a counterbalance to the spending and taxing committees, offering hope that the total effect of the splintered actions of the other committees will be given equal weight in the congressional process.

Special Task Forces Urged

But more progress is needed. Just as the budget process cannot do the whole job in the executive branch, it cannot in the Congress either. No matter how streamlined and properly organized the departments and agencies of the executive branch or the committees and subcommittees of the Congress become—and there is surely room for substantial improvement in this respect at both ends of Pennsylvania Avenue—the executive branch must continue to refine and the Congress must adopt processes whereby recommendations to the President or to the House or Senate, as the case may be, on major issues are developed by task force groups representing the competing priorities of various departments and agencies and of the various congressional committees and subcommittees. The reason is simply that most major issues cut across jurisdictional lines, no matter how well drawn—energy, international affairs, and welfare reform, to name but a few examples. I urge the new Administration to build on what has been accomplished in this regard in the executive branch. I urge the Congress promptly to put into place the necessary counterpart mechanisms. Such improvements in process, coupled with further progress in the development of the budget process, will help substantially in addressing and meeting our problems and attaining the goals we have set for our Nation.

The last thirty budgets record a turbulent period in our history; wars, domestic strife, and serious economic problems. In the last two years, we have laid the foundation for a positive future. We have stabilized international relationships and created the framework for global progress. At home, we have restored confidence in government while reversing the trends of inflation and unemployment. Building on this solid base, the policies and programs contained in this budget can help us to fulfill the promise of America.

GERALD R. FORD

January 17, 1977.

Texts of Twenty Presidential Vetoes

94th Congress, 2nd Session

Milk Price Supports

Following is the text of President Ford's Jan. 30 veto of S J Res 121, to provide for quarterly adjustments in the support price of milk and increase the support price to a minimum of 85 per cent of parity. It was the 18th veto of a public bill of the 94th Congress.

TO THE SENATE OF
THE UNITED STATES:

I am withholding my approval from S. J. Res. 121, which would increase the Federal support price for milk and require mandatory quarterly adjustments, for the following reasons:

1. It would saddle taxpayers with additional spending at a time when we are trying to cut the cost of government and curb inflation.

2. It would stimulate excessive production of milk, discourage consumption, force the Federal Government to increase purchases of dairy products under the milk support program and build up huge and costly surpluses.

3. It would result in unnecessarily high consumer prices.

Under this bill, government outlays would be increased by $530-million, including $180-million during the 1976-77 marketing year and $350-million during the subsequent 1977-78 marketing year. In addition, consumers would be required to pay an estimated $1.38-billion more at retail for dairy products over the next two years.

If S. J. Res became law, the support level for milk would be set at 85 per cent of parity, with adjustments at the beginning of each quarter, through March 31, 1978. This would result in substantial increases in the support level over the next two marketing years without taking into account either changing economic conditions or agricultural policies.

In disapproving similar legislation last January, I said: "To further reduce the demand for milk and dairy products by the increased prices provided in this legislation would be detrimental to the dairy industry. A dairy farmer cannot be well served by Government action that prices his product out of the market." This is still the case.

As far as this Administration is concerned, future changes in the price support level will be based, as in the past, on a thorough review of the entire dairy situation. Major economic factors, including the level of milk production, recent and expected farm prices for milk, the farm cost of producing milk, consumer prices and government price support purchases and budget outlays, will be considered. Elimination of this thorough review by mandating an inflexible support price would be inadvisable.

As you know, present legislation provides the Secretary of Agriculture with sufficient flexibility to increase the level of milk price supports between 75 and 90 percent of parity whenever the conditions indicate that an increase is necessary and advisable. The two increases announced by the Secretary of Agriculture last year—one in January and another in October—should make it clear that this Administration intends to provide the price assurance dairy farmers need.

In this regard, to ensure adequate milk price support levels, I have directed the Secretary of Agriculture to review support prices quarterly, starting April 1. If it appears necessary and advisable to make price support adjustments to ensure the supply of milk, the Secretary of Agriculture will do so.

In vetoing S. J. Res. 121, I urge the Congress to join me in this effort to hold down Federal spending, milk surpluses, and consumer prices.

GERALD R. FORD

The White House,
January 30, 1976.

First Jobs Bill

Following is the White House text of President Ford's Feb. 13 veto of HR 5247, the Public Works Employment Act. It was the 19th veto of a public bill of the 94th Congress.

TO THE HOUSE OF
REPRESENTATIVES:

I am returning without my approval H.R. 5247, the Public Works Employment Act of 1975.

Supporters of this bill claim that it represents a solution to the problem of unemployment. This is simply untrue.

The truth is that this bill would do little to create jobs for the unemployed. Moreover, the bill has so many deficiencies and undesirable provisions that it would do more harm than good. While it is represented as the solution to our unemployment problems, in fact it is little more than an election year pork barrel. Careful examination reveals the serious deficiencies in H.R. 5247.

First, the cost of producing jobs under this bill would be intolerably high, probably in excess of $25,000 per job.

Second, relatively few new jobs would be created. The bill's sponsors estimate that H.R. 5247 would create 600,000 to 800,000 new jobs. Those claims are badly exaggerated. Our estimates within the Administration indicate that at most some 250,000 jobs would be created—and that would be over a period of several years. The peak impact would come in late 1977 or 1978, and would come to no more than 100,000 to 120,000 new jobs. This would represent barely a one tenth of one percent improvement in the unemployment rate.

Third, this will create almost no new jobs in the immediate future, when those jobs are needed. With peak impact on jobs in late 1977 or early 1978, this legislation will be adding stimulus to the economy at precisely the wrong time: when the recovery will already be far advanced.

Fourth, Title II of the bill provides preferential treatment to those units of government with the highest taxes without any distinction between those jurisdictions which have been efficient in holding down costs and those that have not.

Fifth, under this legislation it would be almost impossible to assure taxpayers that these dollars are being responsibly and effectively spent.

Effective allocation of over $3 billion for public works on a project-by-project basis would take many months or years. The provision that project requests be approved automatically unless the Commerce Department acts within 60 days will preclude any useful review of the requests, and prevent a rational allocation of funds.

Sixth, this bill would create a new urban renewal program less than two years after the Congress replaced a nearly identical program—as well as other categorical grant programs—with a broader, more flexible Community Development block grant program.

I recognize there is merit in the argument that some areas of the country are suffering from exceptionally high rates of unemployment and that the Federal Government should provide assistance. My budgets for fiscal years 1976 and 1977 do, in fact, seek to provide such assistance.

Beyond my own budget recommendations, I believe that in addressing the immediate needs of some of our cities hardest hit by the recession, another measure already introduced in the Congress, H.R. 11860, provides a far more reasonable and constructive approach than the bill I am vetoing.

H.R. 11860 targets funds on those areas with the highest unemployment so that they may undertake high priority activities at a fraction of the cost of H.R. 5247. The funds would be distributed exclusively under an impartial formula as opposed to the pork barrel approach represented by the bill I am returning today. Moreover, H.R. 11860 builds upon the successful Community Development Block Grant program. That program is in place and working well, thus permitting H.R. 11860 to be administered

without the creation of a new bureaucracy. I would be glad to consider this legislation more favorably should the Congress formally act upon it as an alternative to H.R. 5247.

We must not allow our debate over H.R. 5247 to obscure one fundamental point: the best and most effective way to create new jobs is to pursue balanced economic policies that encourage the growth of the private sector without risking a new round of inflation. This is the core of my economic policy, and I believe that the steady improvements in the economy over the last half year on both the unemployment and inflation fronts bear witness to its essential wisdom. I intend to continue this basic approach because it is working.

My proposed economic policies are expected to foster the creation of 2 to 2.5 million new private sector jobs in 1976 and more than 2 million additional jobs in 1977. These will be lasting, productive jobs, not temporary jobs payrolled by the American taxpayer.

This is a policy of balance, realism, and common sense. It is an honest policy which does not promise a quick fix.

My program includes:

● Large and permanent tax reductions that will leave more money where it can do the most good: in the hands of the American people;

● Tax incentives for the construction of new plants and equipment in areas of high unemployment;

● Tax incentives to encourage more low and middle income Americans to invest in common stock;

● More than $21 billion in outlays for important public works such as energy facilities, wastewater treatment plants, roads, and veterans' hospitals representing a 17 percent increase over the previous fiscal year;

● Tax incentives for investment in residential mortgages by financial institutions to stimulate capital for home building.

I have proposed a Budget which addresses the difficult task of restraining the pattern of excessive growth in Federal spending. Basic to job creation in the private sector is reducing the ever-increasing demands of the Federal government for funds. Federal government borrowing to support deficit spending reduces the amount of money available for productive investment at a time when many experts are predicting that we face a shortage of private capital in the future. Less investment means fewer new jobs and less production per worker.

Last month, under our balanced policies, seasonally adjusted employment rose by 800,000. That total is almost three times as large as the number of jobs that would be produced by this legislation and the jobs those men and women found will be far more lasting and productive than would be created through another massive public works effort.

I ask the Congress to act quickly on my tax and budget proposals, which I believe

will provide the jobs for the unemployed that we all want.

GERALD R. FORD

The White House,
February 13, 1976

Day Care

Following is the White House text of President Ford's April 6 veto of HR 9803, a bill to give the states $125-million to help them comply with staffing, health and safety standards for federally funded day care centers. It was the 20th veto of a public bill of the 94th Congress.

TO THE HOUSE OF
REPRESENTATIVES:

I am returning without my approval H.R. 9803, a bill which would perpetuate rigid Federal child day care standards for all the States and localities in the Nation, with the cost to be paid by the Federal taxpayer.

I cannot approve legislation which runs directly counter to a basic principle of government in which I strongly believe—the vesting of responsibility in State and local government and the removing of burdensome Federal restrictions.

I am firmly committed to providing Federal assistance to States for social services programs, including child day care. But I am opposed to unwarranted Federal interference in States' administration of these programs.

The States should have the responsibility—and the right—to establish and enforce their own quality day care standards. My recently proposed Federal Assistance for Community Services Act would adopt this principle, and with it greater State flexibility in other aspects of the use of social services funds available under Title XX of the Social Security Act.

H.R. 9803 is the antithesis of my proposal. It would make permanent highly controversial and costly day care staff-to-children ratios. And it would deny the States the flexibility to establish and enforce their own staffing standards for federally assisted day care.

This bill would not make day care services more widely available. It would only make them more costly to the American taxpayer. It would demand the expenditure of $125 million over the next six months, and could lead to $250 million more each year thereafter.

H.R. 9803 would also specify that a portion of Federal social services funds be available under Title XX of the Social Security Act for a narrow, categorical purpose. In the deliberations leading to enactment of Title XX, a little over a year ago, the States and the voluntary service organizations fought hard to win the right to determine both the form and the content of services to be provided according to their own priorities. This bill would undermine the Title XX commitment to State initiative by dictating not only how day care services are to be provided, but also how they are to be financed under Title XX.

It would introduce two additional Federal matching rates for some day care costs that are higher than the rates for other Title XX-supported services, thereby further complicating the States' administration of social services programs. My proposal would, on the other hand, eliminate State matching requirements altogether.

Moreover, H.R. 9803 would create an unfair situation in which some child day care centers would operate under a different set of standards than other centers within the same State. Those day care centers in which fewer than 20 percent of those served are eligible under Title XX could be exempt from Federal day care standards. This provision would have the probable effect in some instances of reducing the availability of day care services by encouraging day care centers to reduce the proportion of children in their care who are eligible under Title XX in order to meet the "quota" set by H.R. 9803. In those centers not choosing to take advantage of this loophole, the effect could well be to increase day care costs to families who use these centers on a fee-paying basis. In effect, they would be helping to subsidize the high costs imposed on day care providers serving Title XX-eligible children.

There is considerable debate as to the appropriateness or efficacy of the Federal day care standards imposed by H.R. 9803. In fact, the bill recognizes many of these questions by postponing their enforcement for the third time, in this case to July 1 of this year. Fewer than one in four of the States have chosen to follow these standards closely in the administration of their day care programs. The Congress itself has required by law that the Department of Health, Education, and Welfare conduct an 18-month study ending in 1977, to evaluate their appropriateness.

Rather than pursue the unwise course charted in this bill, I urge that the Congress extend, until October 1, 1976, the moratorium on imposition of Federal day care staffing standards that it voted last October. This would give the Congress ample time to enact my proposed Federal Assistance for Community Services Act, under which States would establish and enforce their own day care staffing standards and fashion their social services programs in ways they believe will best meet the needs of their citizens.

GERALD R. FORD

The White House,
April 6, 1976

Hatch Act

Following is the White House text of President Ford's April 12 veto of HR 8617, a bill to give federal employees the right to participate in partisan political campaigns and to run for local, state or federal office. It was the 21st veto of a public bill of the 94th Congress.

TO THE HOUSE OF
REPRESENTATIVES:

I am today returning, without my approval, H.R. 8617, a bill that would essentially repeal the Federal law commonly known as the Hatch Act, which prohibits Federal employees from taking an active part in partisan politics.

The public expects that government service will be provided in a neutral, nonpartisan fashion. This bill would produce an opposite result.

Thomas Jefferson foresaw the dangers of Federal employees electioneering, and some of the explicit Hatch Act rules were first applied in 1907 by President Theodore Roosevelt. In 1939, as an outgrowth of concern over political coercion of Federal Employees, the Hatch Act itself was enacted.

The amendments which this bill makes to the Hatch Act would deny the lessons of history.

If, as contemplated by H.R. 8617, the prohibitions against political campaigning were removed, we would be endangering the entire concept of employee independence and freedom from coercion which has been largely successful in preventing undue political influence in Government programs or personnel management. If this bill were to become law, I believe pressures could be brought to bear on Federal employees in extremely subtle ways beyond the reach of any anti-coercion statute so that they would inevitably feel compelled to engage in partisan political activity. This would be bad for the employee, bad for the government, and bad for the public.

Proponents of this bill argue that the Hatch Act limits the rights of Federal employees. The Hatch Act does in fact restrict the right of employees to fully engage in partisan politics. It was intended, for good reason, to do precisely that. Most people, including most Federal employees, not only understand the reasons for these restrictions, but support them.

However, present law does not bar all political activity on the part of Federal employees. They may register and vote in any election, express opinions on political issues or candidates, be members of and make contributions to political parties, and attend political rallies and conventions, and engage in a variety of other political activities. What they may not—and, in my view, should not—do is attempt to be par-

tisan political activists and impartial Government employees at the same time.

The U.S. Supreme Court in 1973 in affirming the validity of the Hatch Act, noted that it represented "a judgment made by this country over the last century that it is in the best interest of the country, indeed essential, that federal service should depend upon meritorious performance rather than political service, and that the political influence of federal employees on others and on the electoral process should be limited."

The Hatch Act is intended to strike a delicate balance between fair and effective government and the First Amendment rights of individual employees. It has been successful, in my opinion, in striking that balance.

H.R. 8617 is bad law in other respects. The bill's provisions for the exercise of a Congressional right of disapproval of executive agency regulations are Constitutionally objectionable. In addition, it would shift the responsibility for adjudicating Hatch Act violations from the Civil Service Commission to a new Board composed of Federal employees. No convincing evidence exists to justify this shift. However, the fundamental objection to this bill is that politicizing the Civil Service is intolerable.

I, therefore, must veto the measure.

GERALD R. FORD

The White House,
April 12, 1976

Foreign Aid

Following is the White House text of President Ford's May 7 veto of S 2662, the fiscal 1976 foreign military aid and arms sales bill. The veto was the 22nd of a public bill of the 94th Congress.

TO THE SENATE OF
THE UNITED STATES:

I am returning, without my approval, S 2662, a bill that would seriously obstruct the exercise of the President's constitutional responsibilities for the conduct of foreign affairs. In addition to raising fundamental constitutional problems, this bill includes a number of unwise restrictions that would seriously inhibit my ability to implement a coherent and consistent foreign policy:

● By imposing an arbitrary arms sale ceiling, it limits our ability to respond to the legitimate defense needs of our friends and obstructs U.S. industry from competing fairly with foreign suppliers.

● By requiring compliance by recipient countries with visa practices or human rights standards set by our Congress as a condition for continued U.S. assistance, the bill ignores the many other complex factors which should govern our relationships with those countries; and it impairs our ability to deal by more appropriate means with objectionable practices of other nations.

• By removing my restrictions on trade with North and South Vietnam, S 2662 undercuts any incentive the North Vietnamese may have to provide an accounting for our MIAs.

• By mandating a termination of grant military assistance and military assistance advisory groups after fiscal year 1977 unless specifically authorized by Congress, the bill vitiates two important tools which enable us to respond to the needs of many countries and maintain vital controls over military sales programs.

The bill also contains several provisions which violate the constitutional separation of executive and legislative powers. By a concurrent resolution passed by a majority of both Houses, programs authorized by the Congress can be later reviewed, further restricted, or even terminated. Such frustration of the ability of the Executive to make operational decisions violates the President's constitutional authority to conduct our relations with other nations.

While I encourage increased Congressional involvement in the formulation of foreign policy, the pattern of unprecedented restrictions contained in this bill requires that I reject such Congressional encroachment on the Executive Branch's constitutional authority to implement that policy.

Constitutional Objections

With regard to the Constitutional issues posed by S 2662, this bill contains an array of objectionable requirements whereby virtually all significant arms transfer decisions would be subjected on a case-by-case basis to a period of delay for Congressional review and possible disapproval by concurrent resolution of the Congress. These provisions are incompatible with the express provision in the Constitution that a resolution having the force and effect of law must be presented to the President and, if disapproved, repassed by a two-thirds majority in the Senate and the House of Representatives. They extend to the Congress the power to prohibit specific transactions authorized by law without changing the law—and without following the constitutional process such a change would require. Moreover, they would involve the Congress directly in the performance of Executive functions in disregard of the fundamental principle of separation of powers. Congress can, by duly adopted legislation, authorize or prohibit such actions as the execution of contracts or the issuance of export licenses, but Congress cannot itself participate in the Executive functions of deciding whether to enter into a lawful contract or issue a lawful license, either directly or through the dis-

approval procedures contemplated in this bill.

The erosion of the basic distinction between legislative and Executive functions which would result from the enactment of S 2662, displays itself in an increasing volume of similar legislation which this Congress has passed or is considering. Such legislation would pose a serious threat to our system of government, and would forge impermissible shackles on the President's ability to carry out the laws and conduct the foreign relations of the United States. The President cannot function effectively in domestic matters, and speak for the nation authoritatively in foreign affairs, if his decisions under authority previously conferred can be reversed by a bare majority of the Congress. Also, the attempt of Congress to become a virtual co-administrator in operational decisions would seriously distract it from its proper legislative role. Inefficiency, delay, and uncertainty in the management of our nation's foreign affairs would eventually follow.

Apart from these basic constitutional deficiencies which appear in six sections of the bill, S 2662 is faulty legislation, containing numerous unwise restrictions.

Annual Ceiling on Arms Sales

A further objectionable feature of S 2662 is an annual ceiling of $9.0 billion on the total of government sales and commercial exports of military equipment and services. In our search to negotiate mutual restraints in the proliferation of conventional weapons, this self-imposed ceiling would be an impediment to our efforts to obtain the cooperation of other arms-supplying nations. Such an arbitrary ceiling would also require individual transactions to be evaluated, not on their own merits, but on the basis of their relationship to the volume of other, unrelated transactions. This provision would establish an arbitrary, overall limitation as a substitute for case-by-case analyses and decisions based on foreign policy priorities and the legitimate security needs of our allies and friends.

Discrimination and Human Rights

This bill also contains well-intended but misguided provisions to require the termination of military cooperation with countries which engage in practices that discriminate against United States citizens or practices constituting a consistent pattern of gross human rights violations. This Administration is fully committed to a policy of not only actively opposing but also seeking the elimination of discrimination by foreign governments against United States citizens on the basis of their race, religion, national origin or sex, just as the Administration is fully supportive of internationally recognized human rights as a standard for all nations to respect. The use of the proposed sanctions against sovereign nations is, however, an awkward and ineffective device for the promotion of those

policies. These provisions of the bill represent further attempts to ignore important and complex policy considerations by requiring simple legalistic tests to measure the conduct of sovereign foreign governments. If Congress finds such conduct deficient, specific actions by the United States to terminate or limit our cooperation with the government concerned would be mandated. By making any single factor the effective determinant of relationships which must take into account other considerations, such provisions would add a new element of uncertainty to our security assistance programs and would cast doubt upon the reliability of the United States in its dealings with other countries. Moreover, such restrictions would most likely be counterproductive as a means for eliminating discriminatory practices and promoting human rights. The likely result would be a selective disassociation of the United States from governments unpopular with the Congress, thereby diminishing our ability to advance the cause of human rights through diplomatic means.

Trade with Vietnam

The bill would suspend for 180 days the President's authority to control certain trade with North and South Vietnam, thereby removing a vital bargaining instrument for the settlement of a number of differences between the United States and these countries. I have the deepest sympathy for the intent of this provision, which is to obtain an accounting for Americans missing in action in Vietnam. However, the enactment of this legislation would not provide any real assurances that the Vietnamese would now fulfill their long-standing obligation to provide such an accounting. Indeed, the establishment of a direct linkage between trade and accounting for those missing in action might well only perpetuate Vietnamese demands for greater and greater concessions.

This Administration is prepared to be responsive to Vietnamese action on the question of Americans missing in action. Nevertheless, the delicate process of negotiations with the Vietnamese cannot be replaced by a legislative mandate that would open up trade for a specified number of days and then terminate that trade as a way to achieve our diplomatic objectives. This mandate represents an unacceptable attempt by Congress to manage the diplomatic relations of the United States.

Termination of Grant Military Assistance and Advisory Groups

The legislation would terminate grant military assistance and military assistance advisory groups after fiscal year 1977 except where specifically authorized by Congress, thus creating a presumption against such programs and missions. Such a step would have a severe impact on our relations with other nations whose security and well-being are important to our own national interests. In the case of grant assistance, it would limit our flexibility to assist countries whose national security is important to us but which are not themselves able to bear the full cost of their own defense. In the case of advisory groups, termination of missions by legislative fiat would impair close and longstanding military relationships with important allies. Moreover, such termination is inconsistent with increasing Congressional demands for the kind of information about and control over arms sales which these groups now provide. Such provisions would insert Congress deeply into the details of specific country programs, a role which Congress has neither the information nor the organizational structure to play.

I particularly regret that, notwithstanding the spirit of genuine cooperation between the Legislative and Executive Branches that has characterized the deliberations on this legislation, we have been unable to overcome the major policy differences that exist.

In disapproving this bill, I act as any President would, and must, to retain the ability to function as the foreign policy leader and spokesman of the Nation. In world affairs today, America can have only one foreign policy. Moreover, that foreign policy must be certain, clear and consistent. Foreign governments must know that they can treat with the President on foreign policy matters, and that when he speaks within his authority, they can rely upon his words.

Accordingly, I must veto the bill.

GERALD R. FORD

The White House,
May 7, 1976.

Military Construction

Following is the White House text of President Ford's July 2 veto of HR 12384, the fiscal 1977 military construction authorization bill. The veto was the 23rd of a public bill of the 94th Congress.

TO THE HOUSE OF
REPRESENTATIVES:

I am returning herewith without my approval HR 12384, a bill "To authorize certain construction at military installations and for other purposes."

I regret that I must take this action because the bill is generally acceptable, providing a comprehensive construction program for fiscal year 1977 keyed to recognized military requirements. One provision, however, is highly objectionable, thus precluding my approval of the measure.

Section 612 of the bill would prohibit certain base closures or the reduction of civilian personnel at certain military in-

stallations unless the proposed action is reported to Congress and a period of nine months elapses during which time the military department concerned would be required to identify the full range of environmental impacts of the proposed action, as required by the National Environmental Policy Act (NEPA). Subsequently, the final decision to close or significantly reduce an installation covered under the bill would have to be reported to the Armed Services Committees of the Congress together with a detailed justification for such decision. No action could be taken to implement the decision until the expiration of at least ninety days following submission of the detailed justification to the appropriate committees. The bill provides a limited Presidential waiver of the requirements of section 612 for reasons of military emergency or national security.

This provision is also unacceptable from the standpoint of sound government policy. It would substitute an arbitrary time limit and set of requirements for the current procedures whereby base closures and reductions are effected, procedures which include compliance with NEPA and adequately take into account all other relevant considerations, and afford extensive opportunity for public and congressional involvement. By imposing unnecessary delays in base closures and reductions, the bill's requirements would generate a budgetary drain on the defense dollar which should be used to strengthen our military capabilities.

Moreover, section 612 raises serious questions by its attempt to limit my powers over military bases. The President must be able, if the need arises, to change or reduce the mission at any military installation if and when that becomes necessary.

The Department of Defense has undertaken over 2,700 actions to reduce, realign, and close military installations and activities since 1969. These actions have enabled us to sustain the combat capability of our armed forces while reducing annual Defense costs by more than $4-billion. For realignment proposals already announced for study, section 612 could increase fiscal year 1978 budgetary requirements for defense by $150-million and require retention, at least through fiscal year 1977, of approximately 11,300 military and civilian personnel positions not needed for essential base activities.

The nation's taxpayers rightly expect the most defense possible for their tax dollars. I am certain Congress does not intend unnecessary or arbitrary increases in the tax burden of the American people. Numerous congressional reports on national defense demonstrate the desire by the Congress to trim unnecessary defense spending and personnel. I cannot approve legislation that would result in waste and inefficiency at the expense of meeting our essential military requirements.

GERALD R. FORD

The White House,
July 2, 1976

Coal Leasing

Following is the White House text of President Ford's July 3 veto of S 391, the Federal Coal Leasing Amendments Act. The veto was the 24th of a public bill of the 94th Congress.

TO THE SENATE OF
THE UNITED STATES.

I am returning to the Congress today without my approval S 391, the Federal Coal Leasing Amendments Act of 1975.

This bill addresses two essential issues: the form of Federal assistance for communities affected by development of Federally-owned minerals, and the way that Federal procedures for the leasing of coal should be modernized.

On the first of these issues, I am in total agreement with the Congress that the Federal Government should provide assistance, and I concur in the form of assistance adopted by the Congress in S 391. Specifically, I pledge my support for increasing the state share of federal leasing revenues from 37½ per cent to 50 per cent.

Last January I proposed to the Congress the Federal Energy Impact Assistance Act to meet the same assistance problem, but in a different way. My proposal called for a program of grants, loans and loan guarantees for communities in both coastal and inland states affected by development of federal energy resources such as gas, oil and coal.

The Congress has agreed with me that impact assistance in the form I proposed should be provided for coastal states, and I hope to be able to sign appropriate legislation in the near future.

However, in the case of states affected by S 391—most of which are inland, the Congress by overwhelming majority has voted to expand the more traditional sharing of Federal leasing revenues, raising the state share of those revenues by one-third. If S 391 were limited to that provision, I would sign it.

Unfortunately, however, S 391 is also littered with many other provisions which would insert so many rigidities, complications, and burdensome regulations into federal leasing procedures that it would inhibit coal production on federal lands, probably raise prices for consumers, and ultimately delay our achievement of energy independence.

I object in particular to the way that S 391 restricts the flexibility of the Secretary of the Interior in setting the terms of individual leases so that a variety of conditions—physical, environmental and economic—can be taken into account. S 391 would require a minimum royalty of 12½ per cent, more than is necessary in all cases. S 391 would also defer bonus payments—payments by the lessee to the government usually made at the front end of the lease—on 50 per cent of the acreage, an unnecessarily stringent provision. This bill would also require production within 10 years, with no additional flexibility. Furthermore it would require approval of operating and reclamation plans within three years of lease issuance. While such terms may be appropriate in many lease transactions—or perhaps most of them—such rigid requirements will nevertheless serve to set back efforts to accelerate coal production.

Other provisions of S 391 will unduly delay the development of our coal reserves by setting up new administrative roadblocks. In particular, S 391 requires detailed anti-trust review of all leases, no matter how small; it requires four sets of public hearings where one or two would suffice, and it authorizes states to delay the process where national forests—a federal responsibility—are concerned.

Still other provisions of the bill are simply unnecessary. For instance, one provision requires comprehensive federal exploration of coal resources. This provision is not needed because the Secretary of the Interior already has—and is prepared to exercise—the authority to require prospective bidders to furnish the department with all of their exploration data so that the secretary, in dealing with them, will do so knowing as much about the coal resources covered as the prospective lessees.

For all of these reasons, I believe that S 391 would have an adverse impact on our domestic coal production. On the other hand, I agree with the sponsors of this legislation that there are sound reasons for providing in federal law—not simply in federal regulations—a new federal coal policy that will assure a fair and effective mechanism for future leasing.

Accordingly, I ask the Congress to work with me in developing legislation that would meet the objections I have outlined and would also increase the state share of federal leasing revenues.

GERALD R. FORD

The White House,
July 3, 1976

2nd Jobs Bill

Following is the White House text of President Ford's July 6 veto of S 3201, the Public Works Employment Act of 1976. The veto was the 25th of a public bill of the 94th Congress.

TO THE SENATE OF
THE UNITED STATES:

I am today returning without my approval, S 3201, the Public Works Employment Act of 1976.

This bill would require $3.95-billion in federal spending above and beyond what is necessary. It sends a clear signal to the American people that four months before a national election, the Congress is enacting empty promises and giveaway programs. I

will not take the country down that path. Time and time again, we have found where it leads: to larger deficits, higher taxes, higher inflation and ultimately higher unemployment.

We must stand firm. I know the temptation, but I urge members of Congress to reconsider their positions and join with me now in keeping our economy on the road to healthy, sustained growth.

It was almost five months ago that the Senate sustained my veto of a similar bill, HR 5247, and the reasons compelling that veto are equally persuasive now with respect to S 3201. Bad policy is bad whether the inflation price tag is $4-billion or $6-billion.

Proponents of S 3201 argue that it is urgently needed to provide new jobs. I yield to no one in concern over the effects of unemployment and in the desire that there be enough jobs for every American who is seeking work. To emphasize the point, let me remind the Congress that the economic policies of this administration are designed to create 2-2.5 million jobs in 1976 and an additional 2 million jobs in 1977. By contrast, administration economists estimate that this bill, S 3201, will create at most 160,000 jobs over the coming years—less than 5% of what my own policies will accomplish. Moreover, the jobs created by S 3201 would reduce national unemployment by less than one-tenth of one per cent in any year. The actual projection is that the effect would be .06 per cent, at a cost of $4-billion. Thus, the heart of the debate over this bill is not over who cares the most—we all care a great deal—but over the best way to reach our goal.

When I vetoed HR 5247 last February, I pointed out that it was unwise to stimulate even further an economy which was showing signs of a strong and steady recovery. Since that time the record speaks for itself. The present 7.5 per cent unemployment rate is a full one per cent lower than the average unemployment rate of 8.5 per cent last year. More importantly, almost three and a half million more Americans now have jobs than was the case in March of last year. We have accomplished this while at the same time reducing inflation which plunged the country into the severe recession of 1975.

S 3201 would authorize almost $4-billion in additional federal spending—$2-billion for public works, $1.25-billion for countercyclical aid to state and local governments, and $700-million for EPA waste water treatment grants.

Beyond the intolerable addition to the budget, S 3201 has several serious deficiencies. First, relatively few new jobs would be created. The bill's sponsors estimate that S 3201 would create 325,000 new jobs but, as pointed out above, our estimates indicate that at most some 160,000 work-years of employment would be created—and that would be over a period of several years. The peak impact would come in late 1977 or 1978 and would add no more than 50,000 to 60,000 new jobs in any year.

Second, S 3201 would create few new jobs in the immediate future. With peak impact on jobs in late 1977 or early 1978, this legislation would add further stimulus to the economy at precisely the wrong time: when the economy is already far into the recovery.

Third, the cost of producing jobs under this bill would be intolerably high, probably in excess of $25,000 per job.

Fourth, this bill would be inflationary since it would increase federal spending and consequently the budget deficit by as much as $1.5-billion in 1977 alone. It would increase demands on the economy and on the borrowing needs of the government when those demands are least desirable. Basic to job creation in the private sector is reducing the ever increasing demands of the federal government for funds. Federal government borrowing to support deficit spending reduces the amount of money available for productive investment at a time when many experts are predicting that we face a shortage of private capital in the future. Less private investment means fewer jobs and less production per worker. Paradoxically, a bill designed as a job creation measure may, in the long run, place just the opposite pressures on the economy.

I recognize there is merit in the argument that some areas of the country are suffering from exceptionally high rates of unemployment and that the federal government should provide assistance. My budgets for fiscal years 1976 and 1977 do, in fact, seek to provide such assistance.

Beyond my own budget recommendations, I believe that in addressing the immediate needs of some of our cities hardest hit by the recession, another measure before the Congress, HR 11860 sponsored by Congressman Garry Brown and S 2986 sponsored by Senator Bob Griffin provides a far more reasonable and constructive approach than the bill I am vetoing.

HR 11860 would target funds on those areas with the highest unemployment so that they may undertake high priority activities at a fraction of the cost of S 3201. The funds would be distributed exclusively under an impartial formula as opposed to the pork barrel approach represented by the public works portions of the bill I am returning today. Moreover, HR 11860 builds upon the successful Community Development Block Grant program. That program is in place and working well, thus permitting HR 11860 to be administered without the creation of a new bureaucracy. I would be glad to accept this legislation should the Congress formally act upon it as an alternative to S 3201.

The best and most effective way to create new jobs is to pursue balanced economic policies that encourage the growth of the private sector without risking a new round of inflation. This is the core of my economic policy, and I believe that the steady improvements in the economy over the last half year on both the unemployment and inflation fronts bear witness to its essential wisdom. I intend to continue this basic approach because it is working.

My proposed economic policies are expected to produce lasting, productive jobs, not temporary jobs paid for by the American taxpayer.

This is a policy of balance, realism, and common sense. It is a sound policy which provides long term benefits and does not promise more than it can deliver.

My program includes:

● Large and permanent tax reductions that will leave more money where it can do the most good: in the hands of the American people;

● Incentives for the construction of new plants and equipment in areas of high unemployment;

● More than $21-billion in outlays in the fiscal year beginning October 1 for important public works such as energy facilities, waste water treatment plants, roads, and veterans' hospitals representing a 17 per cent increase over the previous fiscal year.

● And a five and three-quarter year package of general revenue sharing funds for state and local governments.

I ask Congress to act quickly on my tax and budget proposals, which I believe will provide the jobs for the unemployed that we all want.

GERALD R. FORD

The White House,
July 6, 1976

Fire Prevention

Following is the White House text of President Ford's July 7 veto of HR 12567, authorizing funds for fire prevention for fiscal 1977 and 1978. The veto was the 26th of a public bill of the 94th Congress.

TO THE HOUSE
OF REPRESENTATIVES:

I am returning, without my approval, HR 12567, a bill "to authorize appropriations for the Federal Fire Prevention and Control Act of 1974 and the Act of March 3, 1901, for fiscal years 1977 and 1978, and for other purposes."

I am disapproving HR 12567 because it contains a provision that would seriously obstruct the exercise of the President's constitutional responsibilities over Executive branch operations. Section 2 of the enrolled bill provides that Congress may, by concurrent resolution, "veto" a plan to commit funds for construction of the National Academy for Fire Prevention and Control. This provision extends to the Congress the power to prohibit specific transactions authorized by law, without changing the law and without following the constitutional process such a change would require. Moreover, it involves the Congress directly in the performance of Executive functions in disregard of the fundamental principle of separation of powers.

Provisions of this type have been appearing in an increasing number of bills which this Congress has passed or is considering. Most are intended to enhance the power of the Congress over the detailed execution of the laws at the expense of the President's authority. I have consistently opposed legislation containing these provisions, and will continue to oppose actions that constitute a legislative encroachment on the Executive branch.

I urge the Congress to reconsider HR 12567 and to pass a bill I can accept so that it will be possible for the National Fire Prevention and Control Administration to proceed with its important work.

GERALD R. FORD

The White House,
July 7, 1976.

Local Tax Exemptions

Following is the White House text of President Ford's Aug. 3 veto of S 2447, a bill exempting members of Congress (except those elected from Maryland) from paying state or local income taxes there. The veto was the 27th of a public bill of the 94th Congress.

TO THE SENATE OF
THE UNITED STATES:

I am returning today without my signature S 2447, which would exempt Members of Congress from certain local income taxes. This bill provides that a Member of Congress need not pay the income tax levied by a state or municipality in which the Member lives for the purpose of attending Congress.

Since Virginia and District of Columbia laws already exempt from paying of their income taxes Members living in such jurisdictions only while attending Congress, S 2447 would serve principally to prevent Maryland from levying such taxes on Members of Congress. However, it is one thing for a taxing jurisdiction voluntarily to exempt Members of Congress from its income tax laws and quite another for Congress to mandate a Federal exemption on a state income tax system. I believe such Federal interference is particularly objectionable where, as is the case in Maryland, a portion of the income tax is collected on behalf of counties to pay for local public services which all residents use and enjoy. It should also be noted that this bill would in effect freeze the exemptions now provided by Virginia and the District of Columbia, and they would then be powerless to change their tax laws in this regard.

Since this bill benefits a narrow and special class of person it violates, in my view, the basic concept of equity and fairness by creating a special tax exemption for Members of Congress while other citizens who are required to take up tem-

porary residence in the Washington area—or elsewhere—do not enjoy a similar privilege.

Finally, those who assert that there is a constitutional infirmity in applying a state income tax to Members while attending Congress may present the issue to the courts for resolution.

As the end of this session of Congress approaches, the American people would be better served if Congress would direct its attention to the important laws that should be passed this year—to cut taxes and spending; to expand catastrophic health care programs; to limit court ordered school busing; to attack crime and drugs; and to address many other important matters of concern to the American people—rather than by enacting legislation such as S 2447.

For these reasons, I am returning S 2447 and asking Congress to reconsider this bill.

GERALD R. FORD

The White House,
Aug. 3, 1976

Congressional Veto

Following is the White House text of President Ford's Aug. 13 veto of HR 12944 authorizing the EPA's pesticide program and containing a provision allowing congressional veto of any pesticide regulation issued by the EPA. The veto was the 28th public bill veto of the 94th Congress.

TO THE HOUSE OF
REPRESENTATIVES;

I am returning, without my approval, H.R. 12944, a bill "To extend the Federal Insecticide, Fungicide, and Rodenticide Act, as amended, for six months." If the only purpose of the bill were that set forth in its caption I would have no reservations about it.

The bill would, however, also make a serious substantive change in the law. It would subject rules and regulations issued under authority of the Act to a 60-day review period during which either House of Congress may disapprove the rule or regulation by simple resolution.

As I have indicated on previous occasions, I believe that provisions for review of regulations and other action by resolutions of one house or concurrent resolution are unconstitutional. They are contrary to the general principle of separation of power whereby Congress enacts laws but the President and the agencies of government execute them. Furthermore, they violate Article I, section 7 which requires that resolutions having the force of law be sent to the President for his signature or veto. There is no provision in the Constitution for the procedure contemplated by this bill.

Congress has been considering bills of this kind in increasing number. At my direction, the Attorney General moved recently to intervene in a lawsuit challenging the constitutionality of a comparable section of the federal election law. I hope that Congress will reconsider H.R. 12944 and pass a bill which omits this provision.

GERALD R. FORD

The White House
August 13, 1976

Electric Cars

Following is the White House text of President Ford's Sept. 13 veto of HR 8800 authorizing a federal program to develop electric cars. The veto was the 29th public bill veto of the 94th Congress.

TO THE HOUSE OF
REPRESENTATIVES:

I am returning, without my approval, HR 8800, the "Electric and Hybrid Vehicle Research, Development and Demonstration Act of 1976."

This bill would establish a five-year, $160 million research, development and demonstration project within the Energy Research and Development Administration (ERDA) to promote the development of an electric vehicle that could function as a practical alternative to the gasoline-powered automobile. One of the major objectives of the project would be the development and purchase by the Federal government of some 7,500 demonstration electric vehicles. Such development would cover some of the areas private industry stands ready to pursue.

It is well documented that technological breakthroughs in battery research are necessary before the electric vehicle can become a viable option. It is simply premature and wasteful for the Federal government to engage in a massive demonstration program—such as that intended by the bill—before the required improvements in batteries for such vehicles are developed.

ERDA already has adequate authority under the Energy Reorganization Act of 1974 and the Federal Non-nuclear Energy Research and Development Act of 1974 to conduct an appropriate electric vehicle development program. Under my fiscal year 1977 budget, ERDA will focus on the research areas that inhibit the development of practical electrical vehicles, for widespread use by the motoring public. Included is an emphasis on advanced battery technology.

Even assuming proper technological advances, the development of a completely new automobile for large-scale production is a monumental task requiring extensive investment of money and years of development. While the government can play an important role in exploring par-

ticular phases of electric vehicle feasibility—especially in the critical areas of battery research—it must be recognized that private industry already has substantial experience and interest in the development of practical electric vehicle transportation. I am not prepared to commit the federal government to this type of a massive spending program which I believe private industry is best able to undertake.

GERALD R. FORD

The White House
September 13, 1976

Retirement Benefits

Following is the White House text of President Ford's Sept. 24 veto of HR 5465, providing additional retirement benefits for certain employees of the Bureau of Indian Affairs and the Indian Health Service. It was Ford's 30th veto of a public bill during the 94th Congress.

TO THE HOUSE OF
REPRESENTATIVES:

I am returning, without my approval, H.R. 5465, a bill which would provide special retirement benefits to certain non-Indian employees of the Bureau of Indian Affairs (BIA) and the Indian Health Service (IHS) who are adversely affected by Indian preference requirements.

I strongly support the objective of having Indians administer the Federal programs directly affecting them. I am familiar with and understand the concern of non-Indian employees of these agencies about their long-term career prospects because of Indian preference. But H.R. 5465 is the wrong way to deal with this problem.

The bill is designed to increase employment opportunities for Indians by providing special compensation to non-Indian employees in BIA and IHS who retire early. It seeks to accomplish this purpose by authorizing payment of extraordinary retirement benefits under certain conditions to non-Indian employees of these agencies who retire before 1986—benefits more liberal than those available to any other group of Federal employees under the civil service retirement system. I believe that this approach will result in inequities and added costs that far exceed the problem it is attempting to solve—a problem which is already being addressed through administrative actions by the agencies involved.

H.R. 5465 would provide windfall retirement benefits to a relatively small number of the non-Indian employees of these agencies. The Indian employees and other non-Indian employees in these same agencies would not receive these benefits. The eligible employees are not in danger of losing their jobs. Because they may face a limited outlook for promotion, the bill would pay these employees costly annuities

even though they had completed substantially less than a full career. Payments could be made at age 50 after only 20 years of Federal service, of which as little as 11 years need be Indian-agency service. Their annuities would be equivalent to the benefits it would take the average Federal employee until age 60 and 27 years of service to earn.

This would seriously distort and misuse the retirement system to solve a problem of personnel management for which there are far more appropriate administrative solutions. The Departments of the Interior and Health, Education, and Welfare have established special placement programs to help non-Indian employees who desire other jobs. I am asking the Chairman of the Civil Service Commission to make certain that those placement efforts are rigorously pursued with all agencies of the Federal Government.

Further, these Departments assure me that many non-Indian employees continue to have ample opportunity for full careers with Indian agencies if they so desire. Accordingly, H.R. 5465 represents an excessive, although well-motivated, reaction to the situation. Indian preference does pose a problem in these agencies, but it can and should be redressed without resort to costly retirement benefits.

I am not prepared, therefore, to accept the discriminatory and costly approach of H.R. 5465.

GERALD R. FORD

The White House
September 24, 1976

Auto Engine Research

Following is the White House text of President Ford's Sept. 24 veto message of HR 13655, authorizing a five-year research program on auto engines. It was Ford's 31st veto of a public bill during the 94th Congress.

TO THE HOUSE OF
REPRESENTATIVES:

I am returning, without my approval, H.R. 13655, the "Automotive Transport Research and Development Act of 1976."

This bill would establish a five-year research and development program within the Energy Research and Development Administration (ERDA) leading to the development of advanced automobile propulsion systems, advanced automobile subsystems, and integrated test vehicles to promote the development of advanced alternatives to existing automobiles. The major objective of the program would be the development and construction of integrated test vehicles which would incorporate advanced automobile engines into complete vehicles conforming to Federal requirements for safety, emissions, damageability, and fuel economy. Such development would unnecessarily duplicate existing authorities and extend into areas private industry is best equipped pursue.

Both ERDA and the Department of Transportation (DOT), the two Federal agencies which would be most directly affected by this program, already have sufficient authority to accomplish the objectives of this bill. Under the authority of the Energy Reorganization Act of 1974 and the Federal Non-nuclear Energy Research and Development Act of 1974, ERDA's Highway Vehicle Systems program is presently proceeding with the development of new automobile engine systems to the point where several prototype systems can be demonstrated in vehicles on the road. Under my fiscal year 1977 budget, ERDA will continue to emphasize the development of such advanced engines designed to meet higher levels of fuel economy and lower emissions.

Ongoing DOT programs under the authority of the Department of Transportation Act, the National Traffic and Motor Vehicle Safety Act of 1966, and the Motor Vehicle Information and Cost Savings Act are currently sponsoring advanced automobile research that, except for advanced automobile engines, will achieve the purposes of this bill. Detailed design development for two versions of a Research Safety Vehicle should be completed before the end of this year. Under my fiscal year 1977 budget, DOT will have sufficient funds for its advanced automobile research and development activities.

The Federal government, through ERDA and DOT, can play an important role in exploring the research areas that must be developed before advanced automobiles are produced which meet the Nation's conservation goals—especially in the critical area of new engine research. However, it must be recognized that private industry has substantial expertise and interest in the development and production of advanced automobiles. The appropriate Federal role in this area should be confined to research and development only, and not extend into borderline commercial areas which private industry is best able to perform.

This highly complex technological program, moreover, would eventually require a massive spending program not reflected in the bill's $100 million start-up authorizations for the first two years of the program. This bill would unnecessarily expand research and development programs now underway, and would provide no commensurate benefit for the taxpayers who must pay for this program. I am therefore returning the bill without my approval.

GERALD R. FORD

The White House,
September 24, 1976.

Labor-HEW

Following is the White House text of President Ford's Sept. 29 veto of HR 14232, the fiscal 1977 appropriations bill for the Departments of Labor and Health, Education and Welfare. It was Ford's 32nd veto of a public bill during the 94th Congress.

TO THE HOUSE OF
REPRESENTATIVES:

Just before adjourning for the final weeks of the election campaign, the Congress has sent me H.R. 14232, the Departments of Labor and Health, Education and Welfare appropriations for fiscal year 1977 which begins Oct. 1. This last and second largest of the major Federal appropriation bills to be considered by this Congress is a perfect example of the triumph of election-year politics over fiscal restraint and responsibility to the hard-pressed American taxpayer.

Contained in this bill are appropriations for numerous essential domestic programs which have worthy purposes. My budget for these purposes totaled $52.5-billion, $700-million more than this year. Since 1970 expenditures for these programs have increased at a rate 75% greater than the rate of growth in the overall Federal Budget. Therefore, my 1977 proposals included substantial reforms in the major areas covered by these appropriations designed to improve their efficiency and reduce the growth of Federal bureaucracy and red tape.

The majority in control of this Congress has ignored my reform proposals and added nearly $4-billion in additional spending onto these programs.

The partisan political purpose of this bill is patently clear. It is to present me with the choice of vetoing these inflationary increases and appearing heedless of the human needs which these Federal programs were intended to meet, or to sign the measure and demonstrate inconsistency with my previous anti-inflationary vetoes on behalf of the American taxpayer.

It is to present me with the dilemma of offending the voting groups who benefit by these government programs, or offending those primarily concerned with certain restrictions embodied in the bill.

I am sympathetic to the purposes of most of these programs. I agree with the restriction on the use of Federal funds for abortion. My objection to this legislation is based purely and simply on the issue of fiscal integrity.

I believe the American people are wiser than the Congress thinks. They know that compassion on the part of the Federal Government involves more than taking additional cash from their paychecks. They know that inflationary spending and larger deficits must be paid for not only by all Federal taxpayers but by every citizen, including the poor, the unemployed, the retired persons on fixed incomes, through

the inevitable reduction in the purchasing power of their dollars.

I believe strongly in compassionate concern for those who cannot help themselves, but I have compassion for the taxpayer, too. My sense of compassion also says that we shouldn't ask the taxpayers to spend their money for a tangled mess of programs that the Congress itself has shown all too often to be wasteful and inefficient—programs which all too often fail to really help those in need.

The Congress says it cares about cutting inflation and controlling Federal spending.

The Congress says it wants to stop fraud and abuse in Federal programs.

The Congress says it wants to end duplication and overlap in Federal activities.

But when you examine this bill carefully you discover that what the Congress says has very little to do with what the Congress does.

If the Congress really cared about cutting inflation and controlling Federal spending, would it send me a bill that is $4-billion over my $52.5 billion request?

If the Congress really wanted to stop fraud and abuse in Federal programs like Medicaid, would it appropriate more money this year than it did last year without any reform?

If the Congress really wanted to end duplication and overlap in Federal activities, would it continue all of these narrow programs this year—at higher funding levels than last year?

If the Congress really wanted to cut the deficit and ease the burden on the taxpayer, would it ignore serious reform proposals?

The resounding answer to all of these questions is *no*.

Our longtime ally, Great Britain, has now reached a critical point in its illustrious history. The British people must now make some very painful decisions on government spending. As Prime Minister Callaghan courageously said just yesterday, "Britain for too long has lived on borrowed time, borrowed money and borrowed ideas. We will fail if we think we can buy our way out of our present difficulties by printing confetti money and by paying ourselves more than we earn."

I cannot ask American taxpayers to accept unwarranted spending increases without a commitment to serious reform. I do not believe the people want more bureaucratic business as usual. I believe the people want the reforms I have proposed which would target the dollars on those in real need while reducing Federal interference in our daily lives and returning more decision-making freedom to State and local levels where it belongs.

I therefore return without my approval H.R. 14232, and urge the Congress to enact immediately my budget proposals and to adopt my program reforms.

GERALD R. FORD

The White House,
September 29, 1976.

International Navigational Rules

Following is the White House text of President Ford's Oct. 10 veto of HR 5446, implementing the United States obligations under the Convention on the International Regulations for Preventing Collisions at Sea. It was Ford's 33rd veto of a public bill of the 94th Congress.

MEMORANDUM OF DISAPPROVAL.

I have withheld my signature from HR 5446, a bill to implement the United States obligations under the Convention on the International Regulations for Preventing Collisions at Sea, 1972.

The bill includes a provision which I believe to be unconstitutional. It would empower either the House of Representatives or the Senate to block amendments to the Convention's regulations merely by passing a resolution of disapproval.

This provision is incompatible with the express provision in the Constitution that a resolution having the force and effect of law must be presented to the President and, if disapproved, repassed by a two-thirds majority in the Senate and the House of Representatives. It extends to the Congress the power to prohibit specific transactions authorized by law without changing the law—and without following the constitutional process such a change would require. Moreover, it would involve the Congress directly in the performance of Executive functions in disregard of the fundamental principle of separation of powers.

I believe that this procedure is contrary to the Constitution, and that my approval of it would threaten an erosion of the constitutional powers and responsibilities of the President. I have already directed the Attorney General to become a party plaintiff in a lawsuit challenging the constitutionality of a similar provision in the Federal Election Campaign Act.

In addition, this provision would allow the House of Representatives to block adoption of what is essentially an amendment to a treaty, a responsibility which is reserved by the Constitution to the Senate.

This legislation would forge impermissible shackles on the President's ability to carry out the laws and conduct the foreign relations of the United States. The President cannot function effectively in domestic matters, and speak for the nation authoritatively in foreign affairs, if his decisions under authority previously conferred can be reversed by a bare majority of one house of the Congress.

The Convention—which has already been approved by the Senate—makes important changes in the international rules for safe navigation. It will enter into force in July of 1977. The United States should become a party to it. If the United States does not implement the Convention before it enters into force, there will be major differences between the navigational rules followed by U.S. ships and by the ships of many other countries. These differences will increase the danger of collisions at sea and create hazards to life and property at sea.

I strongly urge the 95th Congress to pass legislation early next year that will be consistent with our Constitution, so that the United States can implement the Convention before it enters into force.

GERALD R. FORD
October 10, 1976.

Rabbit Inspection

Following is the White House text of President Ford's Oct. 17 veto of HR 10073, requiring inspection of domesticated rabbit meat by the Department of Agriculture. It was Ford's 34th veto of a public bill passed by the 94th Congress.

MEMORANDUM OF DISAPPROVAL

I have withheld my approval from HR 10073, "An Act to provide for the mandatory inspection of domesticated rabbits slaughtered for human food, and for other purposes."

This bill would make applicable to domesticated rabbits, with minor exceptions, the provisions of the Poultry Products Inspection Act. It would require the Secretary of Agriculture to implement a mandatory inspection program for all domesticated rabbit meat sold in commerce, with certain exemptions related to type and volume of operations.

It should be noted that the Food and Drug Administration now inspects rabbit meat to ensure that it complies with Federal pure food laws. Thus, there is no health protection reason for requiring mandatory Agriculture Department inspection of rabbit meat.

The effect of this Act would be to substitute a mandatory taxpayer-financed Agriculture Department inspection program for a voluntary one that is now provided under another law and paid for by the processors and consumers of rabbit meat. Since the voluntary program already provides a means for certifying wholesomeness to those consumers who demand such protection for this specialty food and are willing to pay for the protection, I do not believe that a mandatory program is wise public policy.

In addition, it is estimated that the cost to the taxpayer of government inspection provided by this Act could be more than ten cents per pound.

The limited benefit to be derived by a relative few consumers of rabbit meat cannot be justified in terms of the cost to the taxpayer. I am therefore not approving HR 10073.

GERALD R. FORD

The White House,
October 17, 1976.

Agricultural Resources

Following is the White House text of President Ford's Oct. 19 veto of S 2081, the Agricultural Resources Conservation Act of 1976. It was his 35th veto of a public bill passed by the 94th Congress.

MEMORANDUM OF DISAPPROVAL

I am withholding my approval from S 2081, the "Agricultural Resources Conservation Act of 1976."

S 2081 would have required the Federal Government—the Soil Conservation Service of the Department of Agriculture—to appraise the land, water and related resources of the Nation, and to develop a plan and administer a program for the use of private and non-Federal lands.

I have several objections to S 2081. The bill would set the stage for the creation of a large and costly bureaucracy to "cooperate" with State and local governments and private landowners in an attempt to insure land use in compliance with the master plan. Too often Federal "cooperation"—when accompanied by vast amounts of Federal dollars and a large bureaucracy—becomes Federal "direction."

I am not opposed to providing technical assistance to those who need it. The Federal Government, including the Soil Conservation Service, already does a great deal in the management and protection of our natural resources. My 1977 budget proposal called for outlays in excess of $11-billion for these programs. Included in that amount is over $400-million for the very program administered by the Soil Conservation Service to which this bill is directed.

In addition, the bill would subject the President's statement of policy—a document that would be used in framing Executive Branch budget requests for this program—to a 60-day review period during which either House of Congress may disapprove the statement of policy by simple resolution. This would be contrary to the general principle of separation of power whereby Congress enacts laws but the President and the agencies of government execute them. Furthermore, it would violate Article I, section 7 which requires that resolutions having the force of law be sent to the President for his signature or veto.

In summary, S 2081 would violate the principles of fiscal responsibility, minimum Federal regulation, separation of powers, and constitutional government, and accordingly, I withhold my approval.

GERALD R. FORD

The White House,
October 19, 1976.

Foreign Immunity

Following is the White House text of President Ford's veto of S 3553, the

Foreign Sovereign Immunities Act of 1976. It was Ford's 36th veto of a public bill passed by the 94th Congress. (This veto was for technical reasons only, since Congress mistakenly had passed the same bill twice.)

MEMORANDUM OF DISAPPROVAL

I am withholding my approval from S 3553, the Foreign Sovereign Immunities Act of 1976, for technical reasons.

In its haste to adjourn, the Congress passed identical Senate and House bills on this subject. At the time the Senate passed the House bill, HR 11315, it attempted to vacate its earlier passage of S 3553 but was unable to do so because it had left the Senate's jurisdiction. The House, unaware that the Senate had passed the House bill, also passed the Senate bill.

In view of the Senate's action in attempting to vacate its passage of S 3553, there is doubt that S 3553 has been properly enrolled, and therefore I am separately approving HR 11315 and must withhold my approval from S 3553.

GERALD R. FORD

The White House,
October 21, 1976

Federal Grants

Following is the White House text of President Ford's veto of S 1437, the Federal Grant and Cooperative Agreement Act of 1976. It was Ford's 37th veto of a public bill passed by the 94th Congress.

MEMORANDUM OF DISAPPROVAL

I am withholding my approval of S 1437, the Federal Grant and Cooperative Agreement Act of 1976.

This legislation has a laudable goal—to clarify and rationalize the legal instruments through which the Federal Government acquires property and services and furnishes assistance to State and local governments and other recipients. The bill would establish three categories of legal instruments which Federal agencies would be required to use: procurement contracts, grant agreements, and cooperative agreements. These categories would be defined according to their different purposes.

S 1437 would also require the Director of the Office of Management and Budget to undertake a study which would (1) "develop a better understanding of alternative means of implementing Federal assistance programs...", and (2) "...determine the feasibility of developing a comprehensive system of guidance for Federal assistance programs."

The Office of Management and Budget completed a study, almost a year ago, of the definitions of "grant", "contract" and "cooperative agreement." That study, which has been reviewed by other Federal agencies, public interest groups, and other interested associations and groups, confirmed support for the objectives of this legislation but led to serious questions as to whether at this point legislation is necessary or desirable.

No matter how careful the drafting, a bill which requires thousands of transactions to be placed into one of three categories will probably result, in many cases, in limiting the flexibility of Federal agencies in administering their programs and creating a large number of technical difficulties for them. Federally supported basic research programs would be particularly difficult to classify in terms of the definitions in this bill.

The Office of Management and Budget is continuing to work in this area with the cooperation of other Federal agencies. It plans to issue policy guidance to Federal agencies that would more clearly distinguish between procurement and assistance transactions and to better define patterns of assistance relationships between Federal agencies and funding recipients.

In addition, OMB has been developing more comprehensive guidance for assistance programs, as indicated by the recent circulars issued by the agency establishing uniform administrative requirements for hospitals, universities, and non-profit grantees. I am directing OMB to continue to emphasize such activities.

Subsequent modifications and refinements can be made in these directives when further operating experience and evaluation suggest they are needed. Such an evolving set of activities in the Executive branch, a step-by-step process which learns from experience, is preferable to another lengthy study as required by this bill.

In view of the extremely complex and changing nature of Federal assistance programs, I believe that Congress should not legislate categories of Federal assistance relationships, but leave the number and nature of such classifications to the Executive branch to determine and implement. If experience from the studies and evaluations now underway demonstrates that legislation is required, that experience would also provide a better foundation for formulating legislation than we have now.

Accordingly, I must withhold my approval of S 1437.

GERALD R. FORD

The White House,
October 22, 1976

White House
News Conferences

Texts of Ford's 1976 White House News Conferences

February 17

Following is the White House text of President Ford's Feb. 17 news conference, his 27th since taking office.

THE PRESIDENT: Good evening. Won't you all sit down, please.

REORGANIZATION OF INTELLIGENCE COMMUNITY

For over a year the Nation has engaged in exhaustive investigations into the activity of the CIA and other intelligence units of our Government. Facts, hearsay, and closely held secrets—all have been spread out on the public record.

We have learned many lessons from this experience, but we must not become obsessed with the deeds of the past. We must act for the future.

Tonight I am announcing plans for the first major reorganization of the intelligence community since 1947.

First, I am establishing by Executive Order a new command structure for foreign intelligence. Henceforth, overall policy directions for intelligence will rest in only one place: the National Security Council, consisting of the President, the Vice President, the Secretary of State and Secretary of Defense. Management of intelligence will be conducted by a single new committee. That committee will be chaired by the Director of Central Intelligence, George Bush. To monitor the performance of our intelligence operations, I am creating a new independent Oversight Board to be made up of private citizens. Former Ambassador Robert D. Murphy will chair the Board and two other distinguished citizens—Stephen Ailes and Leo Cherne will be the members. All of these units, the National Security Council, the Committee on Foreign Intelligence and the Oversight Board—will be responsible to me, so that the President will continue to be ultimately accountable for our intelligence activities.

Second, to improve the performance of the intelligence agencies and to restore public confidence in them, I am issuing a comprehensive set of public guidelines which will serve as legally binding charters for our intelligence agencies. The charters will provide stringent protections for the rights of American citizens. I will soon meet with Congressional leaders to map out legislation to provide judicial safeguards against electronic surveillance and mail openings. I will also support legislation that would prohibit attempts on the lives of foreign leaders in peace time.

Third, tomorrow I will send to the Congress special legislation to safeguard critical intelligence secrets. This legislation would make it a crime for a Government employee who has access to certain highly classified information to reveal that information improperly.

I have been guided by two imperatives. As Americans we must not and will not tolerate action by our Government which will abridge the rights of our citizens. At the same time, we must maintain a strong and effective intelligence capability in the United States. I will not be a party to the dismantling of the CIA or other intelligence agencies.

To be effective, our foreign policy must be based upon a clear understanding of the international environment. To operate without adequate and timely intelligence information will cripple our security in a world that is still hostile to our freedoms.

Nor can we confine our intelligence to the question of whether there will be an imminent military attack. We also need information about the world's economy, about political and social trends, about food supply, population growth and certainly about terrorism.

To protect our security diplomatically, militarily and economically, we must have a comprehensive intelligence capability. The United States is a peace-loving nation and our foreign policy is designed to lessen the threat of war as well as aggression. In recent years we have made substantial progress toward that goal—in the Middle East, in Europe, in Asia and elsewhere throughout the world.

Yet, we also recognize that the best way to secure the peace is to be fully prepared to defend our interests. I believe fervently in peace through strength. A central pillar of our strength is, of course, our armed forces. But another great pillar must be our Intelligence Community—the dedicated men and women who gather vital information around the world and carry missions that advance our interests in the world.

The overriding task now is to rebuild the confidence as well as the capability of our intelligence services so that we can live securely in peace and freedom.

And now ladies and gentlemen, your questions.

Mr. Cormier.

George Bush

QUESTION: You have been talking lately, including tonight, about the need for a strong intelligence capability. You have appointed a Director of Central Intelligence who has little or no intelligence expertise that I am aware of and I wondered what do you see as the advantages of having a relative novice directing the intelligence community?

THE PRESIDENT: I respectfully disagree with your assessment of George Bush's capabilities and background. George Bush was our U.N. Ambassador and did a superb job at the United Nations. George Bush was our representative in the People's Republic of China and in that capacity did extremely well.

I have known George Bush for a number of years. I served with him in the House of Representatives where he did a very fine job. I am absolutely convinced he will perform superbly as the Director of the Central Intelligence Agency.

QUESTION: Mr. President, are you arguing that he has intelligence, an intelligence background?

THE PRESIDENT: I think he has the intelligence to do the job and the experience in foreign policy and I think these are major ingredients that make him an outstanding person for this responsibility.

Nixon Trip - 1

QUESTION: Robert Strauss has suggested that it might be good to ask former-President Nixon to postpone or cancel his trip to China. There are also reports that you are unhappy because it coincides with the New Hampshire primary. Do you have any plans to ask him to put off the trip?

THE PRESIDENT: I have no such plans. Mr. Nixon is going to the People's Republic of China as a private citizen at the invitation of that government. I don't believe for any alleged political purposes that I should intervene with the invitation of a foreign government to have a private American citizen visit that country.

QUESTION: But if the Chinese Government sends a special plane which lands at a military airport, asks for the top media in this country to cover him, some twenty representatives. You send your special briefing books on the change in leadership and it still is a private trip in their eyes?

THE PRESIDENT: Let me answer several of those questions. You have asked a good many of them.

First, there has been no special briefing given to Mr. Nixon. He has received periodic briefings or information concerning world affairs from the national or Federal Government. There was no special briefing given to him in relationship to this trip.

Whether or not he will land at a civilian or military airport has not been determined. It is a decision on the part of the Chinese Government as to where they would like to land and they have to ask us which of several airports. If and when we get a specific request, we will act on it.

CIA - 1

QUESTION: Mr. President, at first reading on your reform of the Central Intelligence Agency you seem to be putting the Agency more under the dominance and more under the control of the office of the Presidency and we know that office has abused the CIA in the past, and I am wondering what you have done to make sure that does not occur again since you are not apparently making an outside agent, outside of the White House, responsible for the CIA?

THE PRESIDENT: I think a President ought to be accountable, and what we have sought to do in this case is to make the process and the decision-making fall on the shoulders of the President, that he will be held accountable by the American people. In each of the cases, of the Director of the Central Intelligence Agency or any of the other intelligence agencies, the directives or the guidelines will hold special individuals accountable for what happens in their particular area of responsibility, but the final and the ultimate responsibility falls on the shoulders of the President and, in my case, I am willing to assume that responsibility and I can assure you it will be handled in the most appropriate way.

QUESTION: If you are setting a precedent, though, for future Presidents by giving them more authority over the CIA, would you also agree it also invites the prospect of a temptation for abuse of the CIA?

THE PRESIDENT: It should not happen, and I would hope that the American people will elect a President who will not abuse that responsibility. I certainly don't intend to.

GOP Politics - 1

QUESTION: Mr. President, last weekend in Florida you suggested that anyone to the right of you politically could not be elected as President. Newsmen assumed you were referring to Ronald Reagan but you were not entirely specific, and I would like to pin you down now.

Do you believe that Reagan is so far to the right that he cannot win a national election and, if you do believe that, I would like to know what you base your opinion on, especially in light of the fact that he was twice elected Governor of the most populous State in the country by a large margin?

THE PRESIDENT: I was referring to anybody in either political party who is to the right of me, and there are some in the Democratic Party and some—I think Governor Reagan is to the right of me philosophically. It seems to me that there are some differences, for example, between Governor Reagan and myself.

Let's take the issue of Social Security. He has suggested from time to time that it ought to be voluntary, not mandatory as it is under the existing law. He has suggested that maybe the funds from the Social Security program ought to be invested in the stock market. I disagree with both of those proposals. I believe in the firm integrity of the Social Security program and the way I have suggested, it seems to me, is the better approach.

Governor Reagan has suggested a $90 billion cut in Federal expenditures transferring the responsibilities and the programs to the local and State officials where they either have to abandon the programs or raise taxes to support them. I disagree with that approach.

I think that a better way to do it is to take the Federal funds and transfer them to the State and local units of government so that those services can be provided at the State and local level much more effectively.

These are some of the differences that exist between Mr. Reagan and myself. It is a somewhat different philosophy.

QUESTION: Specifically, do you believe he cannot win a national election?

THE PRESIDENT: I believe that anybody to the right of me, Democrat or Republican, can't win a national election.

GOP Politics - 2

QUESTION: Mr. President, are you ready to say now flatly that you are confident of winning the New Hampshire and/or the Florida primary?

THE PRESIDENT: I think we will do well in both. I certainly was greatly encouraged by the two days we were in Florida last weekend. The crowds were very large. The enthusiasm of not only my party workers but the public generally was extremely encouraging. We are going to New Hampshire on Thursday and Friday of this week and I am led to believe that we will be warmly received there. So I am encouraged in both cases.

QUESTION: Do you expect to win?

THE PRESIDENT: When I say I am encouraged, I think that is quite indicative that I think I will do very well.

CIA - 2

QUESTION: Mr. President, your opening remarks concerning the Central Intelligence Agency sounded considerably like an Official Secrets Act which applies in Great Britain. Now this Act has been criticized as being beyond the Constitutional realm that we apply here in the United States.

First of all, do you agree with that assessment? And secondly, wouldn't—if you received this kind of legislation, wouldn't this in the future present the kind of disclosures which have brought out the abuses in the Central Intelligence Agency?

THE PRESIDENT: I categorically disagree with your assessment. It is a great deal different from the Official Secrets Act that prevails in Great Britain. As a matter of fact, this is much more restrictive on the foreign intelligence community in the United States than anything that has been in existence in the past.

There are a number of specific limitations as to what foreign intelligence agencies in the United States can do. They are spelled out and there is an official charter for each one of the intelligence agencies.

I am recommending to the Congress several very specific pieces of legislation which are, I think, constructive and quite contrary to the impression you left with your question.

For example, I am recommending that the Attorney General proceed to work with the Congress to establish legislation for electronic surveillance so that he, representing the Administration, would have to go to the Court to get the authority even in national security matters. Under the present setup the Attorney General can simply do it without going to the Court if it involves national security. This is quite contrary to the impression that you raised with the question that you asked.

So I think we are going down the middle trying to make certain and positive that the intelligence capability of this country is first class and, at the same time, that the rights of individuals are adequately protected.

QUESTION: The second part of my question, Mr. President, was whether the legislation to prevent leaks in the third point of your opening remarks would not mean that the United States would once again be subjected perhaps in the future to abuses that had been exposed through the fact that people were not put in jail by leaking information?

THE PRESIDENT: Well, under the organization that I have established or will establish tomorrow, and under the legislation that I have recommended, there won't be any abuses and the people, if there are any abuses, will be held accountable. So I don't feel all that apprehensive that what happened in the past will be repeated in the future.

Ford Finances

QUESTION: Mr. President, your financial statement that was released earlier in the week shows that, despite some very heavy tax bites for Federal and State taxes, you ended up with about $135,000 in expendable income last year. It also showed that you made no investments and that you were not able to save any of that. Can you tell us how you can spend $2600 a week when you don't have to pay any rent or any mortgage payments? *(Laughter)*

THE PRESIDENT: I am glad that you were scrutinizing my complete and full disclosure of my financial activities. Let me say this: During that period of time, I had at least three of my four children in college and most of you know that that is not a cheap operation. I paid for it, they didn't borrow any money, they didn't get any scholarships, et cetera. That accounts for part of it.

And, quite frankly, I have sought to help my children so that at the time when I am no longer in a position to help them financially, I have made some investments for them, which is perfectly permitted under our laws of this country.

So between supporting them in college and trying to help them get a start when they get through college, I think we can account for every penny.

Intelligence Leaks - 1

QUESTION: Mr. President, you have not said anything about Members of Congress who reveal classified information. Does that concern you?

THE PRESIDENT: It does, and we have some experiences, and I am not pointing a finger at anybody, but certain information which we supplied to the Congress—to the House of Representatives—to a committee of the House—somehow either through a Member or through a staff member, highly classified material has been made public. This is something that the Congress, I think, has to address itself to. The Constitution protects a Member of the Congress, but it does not protect the illegal making of such information public for a staff member. I think the Congress has to clean up its own house and I have urged them to do so, and I hope they will.

QUESTION: Mr. President, will they take some steps in that direction—will this affect your providing classified information to Capitol Hill?

THE PRESIDENT: In the case of most committees, we have had no trouble whatsoever. There has been good cooperation. Arrangements have been lived up to. On the other hand, even after the House of Representatives, by almost a two to one margin, said a report that had highly classified information in it should not be released, it was leaked to certain individuals and to certain publications.

I think the House of Representatives ought to take some action. We have agreed to cooperate with them in whatever legal way they would ask us to do so, but I think it is a very serious matter, what happened in this one case.

CIA - 3

QUESTION: Mr. President, will your new Oversight Board supercede the 40 Committee?

THE PRESIDENT: No. We have an Oversight Committee composed of three members: Ambassador Murphy, Steve Ailes and Leo Cherne. That is a group that looks to make certain that there are no violations of the new restrictions and has an oversight responsibility working with the Inspector Generals in each of the intelligence agencies.

The 40 Committee is having a name change and some change in personnel. It will now be given a new name, but it will have on it the following people. It will have the Assistant to the President for National Security Affairs, it will have the Secretary of State, the Secretary of Defense, the Director of Intelligence, George Bush, the Chairman of the Joint Chiefs of Staff. It will have two observers—one, the Attorney General, and, two, the Director of the Office of Management and Budget.

So there are two separate organizations—the one I just described to handle covert operations recommended to the National Security Council and to me as President, and the Oversight Board, which will check up on any abuses.

QUESTION: Mr. President, in your opening statement on intelligence, you said that you would support legislation that would prohibit attempts on the lives of foreign leaders. Was it your intention to leave open the possibility of attempts on the lives of people in other cases, that is people who are not leaders and, if so, will your specific guidelines to the intelligence community address themselves to this problem?

THE PRESIDENT: I have said previously that I would not condone or authorize assassinations, period, certainly not in peace time. So the legislation I trust will follow those guidelines.

Unemployment

QUESTION: Mr. President, to turn to another subject, unemployment, in your State of Michigan, it covers around 13 percent, which is above the 8.5 national average, and you are vetoing the Public Works bill. As a compromise, do you smile upon Senator Griffin's bill as a compromise?

THE PRESIDENT: I think it is a far better piece of legislation than the legislation that the Congress passed and I have vetoed. The bill that came down to the White House really is a hoax. It is a campaign year document. It allegedly says it will provide 800,000 jobs. The truth is it will provide no more than 100,000 or 120,000 jobs at a cost, and this is the unbelievable part, of $25,000 per job.

Now, we can do a better job using that money elsewhere.

So I vetoed it. I hope that we can get it sustained and, if the Congress comes back with a proposal recommended by Senator Griffin and Congressman Gary Brown, which provides for the channelling of Federal funds of significantly less amounts into programs that are ready to go at local levels in areas where the unemployment is over eight percent and as long as the national unemployment is over seven percent, it would provide for about $750 million.

It could be done quickly. It could be done much more cheaply and it will be far more effective.

Now, it seems to me that the bill that I vetoed cannot be defended in any way whatsoever. The cost is higher per job. It will be late in being implemented. Actually the jobs won't be available for almost nine months to 18 months. We hope and expect to be out of the problems we are in, significantly by that time.

So the alternatives suggested by Senator Griffin and Congressman Brown are far better.

FBI Abuses

QUESTION: Mr. President, you made no reference in your opening statement to abuses by the FBI and some of the greatest abuses in the intelligence gathering were conducted by that agency. What do you have in mind for putting more severe controls on the FBI in intelligence gathering?

THE PRESIDENT: The Attorney General is in the process right now of writing very strict guidelines involving the activities of the FBI, and he expects to have those guidelines available and in place and effective within a relatively short period of time and those guidelines will take care of the problems that you have raised.

QUESTION: Mr. President, as I understand it then, those guidelines would be the result of Executive action and, as I understand it as well, much of what you propose here this evening will be the result of the Executive action, some of which you have already taken. Do you foresee no role for the Congress in oversight of intelligence-gathering activity at the time that it is going on, either foreign or domestic?

THE PRESIDENT: I will issue Executive Orders involving the foreign intelligence agencies. The Attorney General will do it as it affects the FBI. The Congress, I hope, will establish a Joint Committee along the format of the Joint Atomic Energy Committee and this committee called—if this is the proper title, it is up to the Congress, of course—the Joint Intelligence Committee, would have an oversight responsibility as to the programs and the performance of the intelligence communities in the Federal Government.

Nixon Trip - 2

QUESTION: Mr. President, following up on Helen's question, you were asked about the Nixon trip last weekend and you said in part that it was "wholesome and healthy for private citizens to make these sorts of trips to China." You have mentioned again tonight that former President Nixon is going as a private citizen. With all due respect, Richard Nixon is not exactly your run-of-the-mill private citizen. I would like to ask if you really think it is wholesome and healthy for the conduct of American foreign policy for Mr. Nixon to be making this trip?

THE PRESIDENT: He is not going there involving any foreign policy matters. He is going as a guest of the Chinese Government and he is going as a private citizen. He has not had any special briefings. He is going under the guidelines that I suggested.

QUESTION: You see no complications at all to foreign policy in his trip?

THE PRESIDENT: None whatsoever.

Intelligence Leaks - 2

QUESTION: Mr. President, you are concerned considerably over leaks of classified information, national security information and so on. I would like to ask what steps you are taking to assure the public that no one in your Administration misuses the classification system or the secrecy label to cover his own policy mistakes.

THE PRESIDENT: The recommendations that I will make include that every employee of the Executive Branch of the Government sign a statement to the effect that he will not divulge classified information and that he expects punishment for such a release of that information. In addition, I will ask for specific legislation making it a criminal offense for the release of such information and that, I think, protects the Government against any unauthorized leaks of classified secret information. Now, the Oversight Board and the NSC will take care of any failure to act properly in a non-criminal matter.

QUESTION: I would like to ask the question again because I think that perhaps we are talking about two different things.

Suppose, for example, a member of your Administration misused the label "Official Secrecy" to cover a policy error or a mistake that he made and clamped a secret label on it so that this mistake would not get out. What steps are you taking to assure the public that this does not happen?

THE PRESIDENT: We have made the head of the Central Intelligence Agency, the head of the Defense Intelligence Agency, the head of the other agencies responsible for the conduct of people working for them and we have an Inspector General system that I think will make sure that the other people do their jobs properly.

GOP Politics - 3

QUESTION: It is my recollection, Mr. President, that a couple of weeks ago in an interview with Walter Cronkite you said that there were no real philosophical differences between yourself and Ronald Reagan. I just wonder, when did you decide that there were some differences?

THE PRESIDENT: Fundamentally, I don't think there are any philosophical differences. There are some pragmatic differences, and these I tried to explain earlier today. I have to make hard decisions as to what legislation I will sign or what legislation I will recommend. That is quite different from being able to propose a plan or a program in words. One is a very hard decision; the other is very easy to say. And I tried to illustrate those pragmatic differences in the carrying out of a basic and moderate conservative philosophy.

QUESTION: But you are saying, when he is much to the right of you, that that is not a philosophical difference then?

THE PRESIDENT: I think he is to the right of me in a pragmatic and practical way.

Discriminatory Practices

QUESTION: Mr. President, during the Nixon Administration guidance was issued to Federal Executives that their activities should never support or appear to lend support to private organizations which practiced exclusionary discrimination. Does

your Administration follow that same rule?

THE PRESIDENT: Was that an Executive Order?

QUESTION: It was an order that Federal Executives' activities should never lend support or appear to lend support to private organizations which practiced exclusionary discrimination.

THE PRESIDENT: I would assume that we carry out the same policy.

QUESTION: Then, can I ask you, Mr. President, why, then, you lend the prestige of your high office to discrimination by golfing at Burning Tree Country Club which excludes women?

THE PRESIDENT: Well, there are no Federal funds go to Burning Tree.

Inflation

QUESTION: Mr. President, on food prices it is reality that each year, not seasonal and not monthly but each full year food prices go up as part of inflation. Now addressing yourself to the housewife and rising food prices, can you say to her that is something she should accept as a normal way of life or can you project one year, two years or what, that inflation will end on food and come back to what is called normal?

THE PRESIDENT: We have made some substantial progress in combatting inflation. When I became President the cost of living was over 12 percent. It is down in the range of about 6 percent at the present time.

We had some very good results announced last Friday in the wholesale price index. As a matter of fact, as I recall, the food factor in the wholesale price index as reported last Friday was a minus, not an increase. I think we are getting a good, effective handle on the question of inflation—not as good as we want but we have cut it over 50 percent since I have been President and we are making increased progress in this regard.

I think that we are achieving, particularly in the area of food, a better balance than we have had for a long, long time.

QUESTION: That is why in my original question I ruled out seasonal or monthly. The reality is that over the years food prices continue to go up. The price may remain the same, Mr. President, on an item, but the quantity has been diminished.

THE PRESIDENT: Well, when I became President, as I recall the food prices that year had gone up something like 20 percent. It is now estimated that food prices in this calendar year will increase somewhere between 4 and 5 percent. That is a significant improvement. I think it ought to get a little praise rather than condemnation. From 20 percent down to 4 or 5 percent is a lot of progress.

THE PRESS: Thank you. ∎

July 9

Following is the White House text of President Ford's July 9, 1976 news conference, his 34th since taking office.

THE PRESIDENT. We have no set format. I don't know whose turn it is—AP, UPI.

Bicentennial Celebration

Q. You have nothing in particular on your mind this morning, Mr. President?

THE PRESIDENT. No, I am just glad to see you all.

I feel very, very encouraged and very pleased with the results of the Bicentennial weekend. I was pleasantly surprised at the reaction throughout the country. I think it was well reported by the press that not only in Philadelphia, in Valley Forge, in New York, and Washington did everything move along extremely well, but it was reported all over the country that there was a real, genuine resurgence of good American feeling toward one another, toward the country, that I think augurs for a real good third century. So we are well on our way, and I think it will continue.

Frank [Frank Cormier, Associated Press], anything else?

Q. Not right offhand. *[Laughter]*

GOP Politics - 1

Q. Mr. President, how do you view your race for the nomination with Governor Reagan? How do you think you stand now in delegates? Are you confident of a victory, initially?

THE PRESIDENT. I am very confident. The projections clearly indicate to me that when we get to Kansas City we will have a first ballot victory. You can read all the numbers, but when you analyze them, I think, objectively the Ford nomination will prevail on the first ballot.

We have had some very good movement in individual States. We have had good results, of course, in North Dakota. We expect good results next week. And so when we go to Kansas City, I am very confident that we will prevail on the first ballot.

GOP Politics - 2

Q. Who do you want for a Vice-Presidential running mate?

THE PRESIDENT. Fran [Frances Lewine, Associated Press], I don't exclude anybody. We've got a wealth of talent, and I think it's premature to winnow that list down. We have to take into consideration a number of factors—the prime one, of course, being an individual who would be an excellent President. But there are other factors that have to be taken into consideration, and until we get closer to the convention, I think it is too early to make any real speculation.

Q. Would you rule anyone out like—would you rule Mr. Reagan out?

THE PRESIDENT. I repeat, I exclude nobody. And I hope that individuals in the meantime will not exclude themselves, because we want the best ticket we can get to win in November.

Ugandan Rescue - 1

Q. Mr. President, Governor Reagan made the statement when apprised of the Israeli rescue raid in Uganda, "This is what Americans used to do." And one of the hostages, who is an American citizen, said America didn't "give a damn about us, Israel freed us." I wonder, what is your reaction?

THE PRESIDENT. I can assure you that this administration has taken a firm action wherever we have been confronted with any illegal international action. The best illustration of course is what we did in 1975 in the *Mayaguez* incident. I think that was a clear warning to any nation that violates international law that this administration will act swiftly and firmly and, I think, successfully.

Q. If I could follow that up, the State Department said—when asked, "What is the United States doing?"—said that they had contacted numerous governments, as well as the International Red Cross. What else did we do to compare with the Israeli action?

THE PRESIDENT. We took whatever action we felt was appropriate at that time to indicate our strong feeling against international terrorism, and we asked for the full cooperation of all governments to make certain that the hostages were freed.

And as you know, we indicated to Prime Minister Rabin that we were gratified that the Israelis had taken the very specific action to free the hostages and, at the same time, we reiterated our firm opposition to international terrorism.

Q. Did we know in advance of that Israeli raid?

THE PRESIDENT. We did not.

Election Prospects - 1

Q. Mr. President, is there not concern that if you should win a narrow victory at the convention and receive the nomination by a small majority, that you will have some difficulty winning the election, being a member of the minority party?

THE PRESIDENT. Not at all. The competition has been close, controversial, and if you win, you win. I talk very affirmatively about the need and necessity for a unified party. I think we can leave Kansas City with a win and a unified party.

And once we get the nomination, we can start pointing out the distinct differences between the prospective Democratic nominee and myself; we can talk about the record that we have. It is a record that I think will be applauded objectively by 99 and 9/10 per cent of the delegates to the Republican Convention.

I think it will appeal to a good many Independents, and I have already had some indications that there are some Democrats

who think the record of the Ford administration is a good one. So we will enter the campaign after the convention with a good opportunity to prevail November 2.

Oil Prices

Q. Mr. President, when you met with the Saudi official [Prince Abdallah bin Abd al-Aziz-Saud, the Second Deputy Prime Minister and Commander of the National Guard of Saudi Arabia] this morning, did he indicate to you that oil prices will be going up again at the end of the year or didn't you discuss this at all?

THE PRESIDENT. There was no discussion of the prospect of any oil price increase. I expressed my appreciation for the action by OPEC in not increasing oil prices in their recent meeting. I pointed out I thought that was in the best interests of the free world and that it would be beneficial, not only to the oil consumers but the oil producers in the long run.

GOP Politics - 3

Q. Mr. President, this morning Tom Curtis, former FEC Chairman who, as you know, is now working for Ronald Reagan in his campaign, said that he feels the FEC should take action; that the White House is getting unfair treatment at Kansas City—you are getting more rooms—and specifically, according to Mr. Nofziger, 388 hotel rooms allotted to the Ford campaign and the White House, while only 100 rooms are allotted to the Reagan campaign; Ford groups have received 650 gallery passes, while the Reagan campaign has received only 300. And, because the conventions this time are using tax money, Curtis is saying that the FEC should take some action. How do you feel about it?

THE PRESIDENT. Of course, you have to recognize my good friend Tom Curtis is a Reagan delegate, so I would expect he would take that point of view. We are living up to the letter and the spirit of the law. The decisions in this case were made by the Republican National Committee. I understand they were made unanimously, and, as I am told, it doesn't fall within the jurisdiction of the Federal Election Commission.

But I reiterate that in every instance where there has been a ruling by the FEC, this administration has lived up to the letter as well as the spirit.

GOP Politics - 4

Q. Mr. President, do you plan to, in the interest of party unity, throw the Vice-Presidential nomination up to the convention; not mention any names, your preference, just let the convention delegates decide?

THE PRESIDENT. We haven't made any decision on that, Phil [Phil Jones, CBS News]. As I said, I have excluded no one from my consideration as far as a running mate is concerned. Whether that would be a possibility, it's just premature to make any commitment.

Taiwan Olympics Dispute

Q. Mr. President, what would you like for the International Olympic Committee to do to resolve the dispute between Canada and Taiwan?

THE PRESIDENT. I think it's tragic that international politics and foreign policy get involved in international sport competition. I strongly feel that the Olympics are a healthy thing for the world as a whole. Competition between athletes from all countries ought to be stimulated rather than curtailed. And so, I hope and trust that the diplomatic problems or the international foreign policy problems can be resolved so that this healthy competition can go on.

Q. Have you done anything about it? Have you contacted the Canadian Government?

THE PRESIDENT. I am being kept abreast of it, but this is a decision that gets involved in Canadian Government decisions on the one hand and the International Olympic Committee on the other. I have expressed myself very clearly that we hope they will continue as broadly based as possible.

Ugandan Rescue - 2

Q. Mr. President, do you believe that the Israeli violation of Uganda national sovereignty was justified?

THE PRESIDENT. The Department of State and our representatives to the United Nations will set forth our position very clearly in the debate that I think begins today, on one or more resolutions before the Security Council. I am told that our position is a firm one, on good legal grounds, and I will wait and let that be expressed by them during the debate.

GOP Politics - 5

Q. Mr. President, could we talk about the delegates once again? Do you believe that before you get to Kansas City you are going to have more than you need to get a first ballot victory—that you can cite and name?

THE PRESIDENT. I think, as I said a moment ago, we will have enough delegates to win on the first ballot, which I think infers certainly that we know who will be voting for President Ford's nomination.

Alaska Pipeline

Q. Mr. President, can you tell us what you've learned recently about the extent of the problems on the Alaska pipeline and what the penalties might be in terms of cost and delay?

THE PRESIDENT. I got a very complete report late yesterday afternoon from the Secretary of Interior and the Secretary of Transportation. I think you know that Under Secretary [Deputy Secretary] of Transportation John Barnum is either leaving or has left to go up there with a group of technical people to make an on-the-spot evaluation of the several reports as to the number of welds that are allegedly defective. I am going to be kept constantly advised as to what they recommend as to a procedure and as to the certainty that the pipeline meets all of the Department of Transportation's regulations for interstate pipeline safety.

We have not gotten into the added cost, whatever it might be, but I am confident that I will be fully advised at all times.

Q. Have you talked with any people from the Justice Department as to the possibility of criminality involved in falsification of records?

THE PRESIDENT. That is a matter for the Department of Justice to determine. I have not personally communicated with the Department, and I think they have to make any judgments over there, not myself.

Election Prospects - 2

Q. Mr. President, will Southern support be vital, and will it be absolutely necessary for your election in November?

THE PRESIDENT. I hope to get support in all 50 States, Dick [Richard Growald, United Press International]. We don't have any regional strategy. I have said repeatedly that I expect to run a national campaign and that certainly infers that we want support from the South; we want support from the other regions throughout the country.

Q. Do you think you can win without a good hunk of the South?

THE PRESIDENT. As I said, we want Southern support and I think we will get Southern support, and that will contribute to our victory in November.

GOP Politics - 6

Q. Mr. President, Jimmy Carter has been holding auditions for a running mate. Do you have a plan to do anything like that?

THE PRESIDENT. I think I know most of the people that are among those that we know would be a potential running mate. I am sure that I will have consultations, but we haven't set out any specific routine for it.

Q. Do you anticipate public announcements of people coming in for briefing sessions?

THE PRESIDENT. I don't anticipate that kind of a routine, so to speak. As I said, I know all the people quite intimately. I know their records. I know what they believe in. So I don't have to go through that experience such as Governor Carter is going through, because I don't think he knows some of these people that he is considering as well as I know all of the potential Republican running mates.

Q. Mr. President, I got the impression from what you said to Phil Jones that you might still be seriously considering throwing that choice open to the convention, or at least giving them a list of names. Are you seriously contemplating doing that?

THE PRESIDENT. I didn't mean to infer the conclusion you came to. I simply said that we have not made any firm commitment as to what procedure we would take at the time of the convention. I think a Presidential nominee ought to make his wishes known to the delegates. How he proceeds after that, we just haven't made a final decision on it.

HEW Ruling

Q. Mr. President, in light of your expressed displeasure over the decision by HEW regarding father-son/mother-daughter breakfasts, have you given any thought to perhaps curtailing the powers of the Office of Civil Rights in that Department?

THE PRESIDENT. We haven't given any thought to the curtailing of their overall responsibility. But, as President, I have a responsibility to review any decisions that they make, and when I saw that decision I was shocked—I go a little stronger than Ron reported yesterday—and I took immediate action because I think that was a very wrong decision. And if there are other decisions that I disagree with in the future, I will exercise my Presidential prerogative to suspend them or to change them. They have a responsibility to carry out what they think is the right determination, but if I disagree, I will certainly take affirmative action in the future, as I did in this case.

Wholesale Price Index

Q. Your reaction to the WPI figures, sir?

THE PRESIDENT. I think those WPI figures of .4 per cent fall within the guidelines that we have established. If you annualize that figure, it is less than 5 per cent, so it's within the overall expectations that we have for wholesale prices.

GOP Politics - 7

Q. Mr. President, after you have, through this campaign, made some harsh observations about Ronald Reagan, how could you seriously consider him as your running mate, a man who could become the President? You have had some pretty tough things to say about him. I can't quite see how you could possible consider him, if you feel that way.

THE PRESIDENT. I think we all have to understand in a very controversial political campaign you make a point, and sometimes with some political license. We have done that historically in this country. We can go back to the days of President Kennedy and the then Vice President Johnson. No one under any circumstances would have foreseen that that team would end up representing the Democratic Party.

All I am saying is that when you take a look at all of the Republican potentials, including Ronald Reagan, I think they all ought to be included for consideration.

Q. But would it be fair to say that you certainly wouldn't be as comfortable with Ronald Reagan as some others?

THE PRESIDENT. Phil [Phil Jones, CBS News], I am not going to get into degrees of comfort—*[laughter]*—with potential Republican candidates. When I pick that candidate, I expect him to be a good running mate and a good Vice President.

Q. But you said there are no retakes in the Oval Office, indicating that he doesn't have the experience to handle this office. And it just seems that you feel, or have indicated, that he is not qualified to be President.

THE PRESIDENT. I think when we pick the candidate, he will be a qualified person to be Vice President.

Mrs. Ford and Mrs. Nixon

Q. What can you tell us this morning about the health of Mrs. Ford? Is she feeling all right? Also, have you been in touch with the Nixon family about the former First Lady?

THE PRESIDENT. Mrs. Ford came down with a very bad cold yesterday following the church services at the Cathedral. She had a good night. She is going to take it easy for a day or so, and there is no concern, just a typical cold.

I stopped and saw Dr. Lukash when I came to the office this morning. He had not gotten any overnight reports on the condition of Mrs. Nixon. He is going to report to me as soon as he gets any information from her doctor.

Nixon Conversation

Q. Did you speak to President Nixon?

THE PRESIDENT. I called President Nixon.

Q. Can you tell us something of what he told you?

THE PRESIDENT. Well, he reported the sequence more or less as they have been reported in the press. I extended to him on behalf of Betty and myself our affection and best wishes for Mrs. Nixon's full and complete recovery.

Q. Did you talk about politics?

THE PRESIDENT. Not at all.

GOP Politics - 8

Q. Mr. President, as I understand it, the Republican National Committee is supposed to be neutral until there is a nominee; am I correct in that assumption?

THE PRESIDENT. That is a valid assumption.

Q. Thank you. Now then, why is Mrs. Smith [Mary Louise Smith, chairman, Republican National Committee] going to the convention as a Ford delegate?

THE PRESIDENT. Because she has an opportunity, like any other citizen of this country, to run and express her personal views. She is running the national committee on a very nonpartisan basis between my opponent and myself.

Trans-Canada Pipeline

Q. Mr. President, could we talk about the Alaska pipeline another time? You are from the Middle West, and when the pipeline act was passed in Congress—

THE PRESIDENT. I voted for it.

Q. Okay. There was quite a debate, though, about building a trans-Canada pipeline that would deliver oil to the Middle West where it is needed. There is still talk about that and, in fact, there is some legislation. Would you support legislation to build a pipeline from Valdez across Canada to the Middle West?

THE PRESIDENT. I don't believe that is an active possibility. I think you are referring to the possibility of a gas pipeline—

Q. They were going to double-truck it, apparently.

THE PRESIDENT. —from Northern Canada or Northern Alaska to the Middle West as one of several alternatives. There are other alternatives that would involve bringing the gas down to the Gulf of Alaska. That matter is before the Federal Power Commission at the present time. It is also before—in one way or another—before the comparable agency in the Canadian Government. There is legislation that is being sponsored which I think is good legislation, that would expedite the determination as to which route is the preferable one. It would be legislation much like that which was approved for the delivery of Alaskan oil. If that gas is badly needed in the United States—and I am not saying on the West Coast or the Middle West—but I think a decision has to be expedited. And so I would favor such legislation which would expedite the determination by the proper authorities as to which route was the better of the two or which is the best, if there are more than two.

Foreign Affairs

Q. Mr. President, since this is an election year, I wonder if you think there is not much chance of any startling developments in the area of foreign affairs, such as a SALT agreement or MBFR, or in any other area? Do you think it is very difficult to conduct negotiations at a time when frankly the occupancy of the White House is going to be uncertain for next year? Are we sort of at a standstill for the rest of the year in foreign affairs?

THE PRESIDENT. I have said specifically, as far as SALT is concerned, if we can get a good agreement I will make that agreement regardless of any political consequences. We are in the process of thoroughly analyzing our last proposal, the Soviet Union's reaction or last proposal. And if we can move forward on a good SALT agreement, I certainly will push for it, because I think it is in the national interest and in the best interest of mankind as a whole. So politics won't enter into any decision as far as SALT is concerned. I know of no other major areas that would have any political consideration as far as foreign policy.

SALT II Negotiations

Q. How about the SALT agreement?

THE PRESIDENT. I intend to push for it. I am not passing judgment as to whether it will come or won't come, but we are working on it, and I intend to push it. Whether we can achieve an agreement or not is uncertain. But it is in the best interest of the United States and mankind as a whole if we can get the right agreement. And I will do it regardless of the political atmosphere that may prevail here because of our election.

GOP Politics - 9

Q. Mr. President, can we pin something down? Is Ronald Reagan qualified to be President?

THE PRESIDENT. I said the person I select for the Vice Presidency will be qualified, and I don't exclude anybody.

Q. Therefore, he is qualified?

THE PRESIDENT. That's a fair conclusion—*[Laughter]*—if he is the nominee. *[Laughter]*

The President Ford Committee

Q. Mr. President, are you satisfied with the way your campaign committee has performed through the primary and convention State season? And after the convention, do you foresee at this point a substantial reorganization of your campaign?

THE PRESIDENT. I don't see any substantial reorganization. I have said, through Ron and otherwise, that Rog Morton is going to stay on. We intend to add people to the top echelon over there as the need arises for particular jobs that must be handled, such as the convention, such as other responsibilities. I see no anticipated major reorganization. Like any other organization, you look back in retrospect as a Monday morning quarterback you might have done a little better here and there. But I think the President Ford Committee, considering all the problems, has done a good job.

Q. Do you want Stu Spencer to stay on?

THE PRESIDENT. I certainly do. I think Stu Spencer is an extremely able person. He has done a good job.

Death Penalty Decision

Q. Mr. President, what was your reaction to the Supreme Court's decisions on the death penalty, and do you approve of the way they are going now?

THE PRESIDENT. I have stated on a number of occasions I support the death penalty at the Federal level for espionage, treason, et cetera. I support the death penalty for the kind of crimes that involve murder, et cetera. I support the direction in which the Supreme Court is going.

GOP Politics - 10

Q. Mr. President, one more question on Mr. Reagan, if you don't mind. At the end of your coming term—I presume that you are going to be elected—Mr. Reagan will be 70 years old. Do you still think he would be qualified at that time to replace you as President?

THE PRESIDENT. I would not speculate as to who the Republican candidate might be in 1980.

Q. It has become a custom for the Vice President to sort of—

THE PRESIDENT. I can only say I don't intend to be the candidate in 1980. *[Laughter]* But I expect to be the nominee in 1976, and I expect to hold office until January 20, 1981.

GOP Politics - 11

Q. Mr. President, to what extent do you personally get on the telephone and call delegates?

THE PRESIDENT. I do it occasionally.

Q. Well, once a night? Twice a night?

THE PRESIDENT. I don't keep a poll of it or a count, but I like to talk to people.

Q. What do you say to them?

THE PRESIDENT. Well, I thank them for their interest in the political system. I thank them that they are actively participating, and I compliment them on the job that I know they will do in Kansas City.

MR. CORMIER. Thank you, Mr. President. ∎

July 19

Following is the White House text of President Ford's July 19 news conference, his 35th since taking office.

THE PRESIDENT: Good afternoon.

Before responding to your questions, I have two announcements to make.

First, I am sending later this week a message to the Congress calling for prompt action on a number of legislative programs that Congress must act on before adjournment. I am recommending affirmative action, as quickly as possible, on my further tax reduction proposals, on the remaining portions of my energy independence recommendations, on my stronger anti-crime proposals, and, of course, general revenue sharing.

It seems to me that before Congress adjourns, it must undertake a vigorous legislative program if it is to maintain its credibility with the American people.

Secondly, I am sending to the Congress today a recommendation which would further advance our efforts to restore public confidence in the integrity of all three branches of the federal government, including the Executive Branch, the Legislative Branch, and the Judicial Branch. It is vitally important—I am determined and I trust the Congress is—to insure that those who hold public office maintain the highest possible standards and are fully accountable to the American people for their behavior while in public office. I hope the Congress will act very promptly on this legislation.

I will be glad to answer any questions. Helen?

Nomination - 1

QUESTION: Mr. President, do you think that you have the presidential nomination now locked up and, if not, do you think you will have it by the end of the week?

THE PRESIDENT: I am very encouraged with the results over the weekend. I believe that we are getting very close right now to the magic number of 1,130. I am confident by the time we get to Kansas City, we will have 1,130-plus.

QUESTION: How many delegates do you think you have now?

THE PRESIDENT: The best estimate, I think, is 1,103 and we expect some more good news this week. Therefore, by the time we get to Kansas City, I am confident we will have over 1,130.

Election

QUESTION: Mr. President, is Governor Carter beatable?

THE PRESIDENT: Absolutely.

QUESTION: And if so, how?

THE PRESIDENT: By the kind of an affirmative program that we have developed in the last 23 months here in the White House under the Ford administration. I intend to have an affirmative campaign based on the results of turning the economy around, achieving the peace and the restoration of public trust in the White House, itself.

QUESTION: Mr. President, Jimmy Carter has set forth some of his beliefs on foreign policy. Can you tell us whether you think there are major differences with what you are doing now in foreign policy and what they are?

THE PRESIDENT: Since I strongly believe that our foreign policy has been a successful one—we have achieved the peace, we have the military capability and the diplomatic skill to maintain that peace—I don't see, from what I have read, any legitimate complaints or objections by any of my Democratic friends, whether they are the candidates for the highest office or the members of the Congress.

Mondale

QUESTION: Mr. President, sir, do you feel that the selection of Walter Mondale as Vice President is going to change your selection of a vice presidential candidate?

THE PRESIDENT: I will make my choice known on the vice presidency based on the best person that could serve as President of the United States. My decision will not be predicated on my Democratic opponent's recommendation of Senator Mondale.

Vice President - 1

QUESTION: Mr. President, Mr. Carter took a month to select his vice presidential nominee. Will you be able to take very long? Will you have enough time to consider?

THE PRESIDENT: I have been thinking about this matter for some time. I know all of the individuals who are being considered very well. I have worked with them, know about them. I have studied carefully their records. Therefore, it won't be a last-minute analysis. It will be one based on a good many years of experience and opportunities to know how they performed in public office or otherwise. So, it is not going to be a last-minute decision where we winnow out the individuals in a 48-hour period.

Democratic Ticket

QUESTION: Mr. President, how do you assess the Carter-Mondale ticket?

THE PRESIDENT: I think it was obviously the choice of the Democratic Convention, which was well organized and well put together and well controlled. It is a ticket that can be beaten by an affirmative approach that I intend to have in setting forth the improvements that I have made domestically and in foreign policy during the time that I have been honored to be President of the United States.

It is a rather typical Democratic ticket when you add up the platform, its endorsement of the record of the Democratic Congress and the comments that I have heard, both in the acceptance speeches and in subsequent observations.

QUESTION: Can I follow up?

THE PRESIDENT: Sure.

QUESTION: You said that the ticket—on Saturday, I believe—that the ticket tries to be all things to all people. Just what do you mean by that?

THE PRESIDENT: If you look at the ticket itself, if you look at the platform and if you look at the record of the Democratic Congress, you can't help but come to the conclusion that they want to spend a lot of money on the one hand and they talk on the other about some restraint in federal spending.

You can take almost any one of the many issues, and they are on both sides of the issue. So, I think it fits in very precisely with my observation that I made on Saturday.

QUESTION: Mr. President, what is the biggest single issue between you and Governor Carter?

THE PRESIDENT: I am not going to discuss this campaign from that point of view. I think it is important for me to act affirmatively and indicating the results that we have accomplished. I will let Mr. Carter decide the issues where he has some differences.

Republican Issues

QUESTION: Mr. President, if you do go to the Convention with the number of delegates that you think you will go with now, is there anything else at the Convention that could really divide the Republicans there?

THE PRESIDENT: I would hope not because the Republican Party does have to be as unified as possible if we are going to win the election in 1976. I think that unity can be achieved at the Convention in Kansas City, and I will maximize my effort to accomplish that result. Therefore, we will have the job of picking the nominee and I expect to be the nominee. We have to write the platform. I hope the platform will be one that all can support, and not divisive. When we leave, we, as a party, must be united individually and collectively.

QUESTION: Mr. President, isn't that, sir, going to be easier said than done? These Reagan people are very committed. They have worked very hard. It is going to take more than just going into that Convention, isn't it, and saying, "Just come on and be on our side." What are you going to say to them?

THE PRESIDENT: I think these delegates, all of them, the ones that support me and the ones that support Mr. Reagan, have a philosophical identity. They do represent delegates, one group for me and the other for Mr. Reagan. But the identity of the philosophy is such that I think when the Convention is concluded, they can be together on the need and necessity for a candidate who will put forth their philosophy against that of the opposition.

Running-Mate - 1

QUESTION: Wouldn't they be a lot happier if you put Mr. Reagan on the ticket with you? There is going to be a lot of pressure on you to do that, is there not?

THE PRESIDENT: I am not going to make the judgment here as to who will be the vice presidential nominee. We will have a good vice presidential candidate and, as I said before, we are not going to exclude anybody.

Nixon Ties

QUESTION: Mr. President, the Democrats have already signaled what direction they are going to go by trying to tie your administration with close ties to the Nixon administration. How do you intend to handle that problem in the campaign and shed that yoke?

THE PRESIDENT: I am going to use the Ford record of 23 months, which is a good one, in turning the economy around, and achieving the peace and maintaining the peace, and the restoration of public confidence in the White House, and hopefully the restoration of public confidence in the other two branches of the federal government.

QUESTION: Excuse me. As a follow-up, inasmuch as you kept on such former Nixon intimates as Secretaries Kissinger, Simon and Butz and Messrs. Morton, Greenspan, Scowcroft and Rumsfeld, isn't their branding of your administration accurate?

THE PRESIDENT: Not at all because I have made the final decisions in each case.

Libya

QUESTION: Mr. President, does the United States have evidence or information that President Qadhafi of Libya is financing, planning, encouraging and serving as the central point of an international terrorist organization and conspiracy?

THE PRESIDENT: We do know that the Libyan government has in many ways done certain things that might have stimulated terrorist activity, but I don't think we ought to discuss any evidence that we have that might prove or disprove that.

QUESTION: In the light of what you had to say about the Israeli rescue mission, or mission in Uganda, if you have any reason to believe that the Libyan government is encouraging terrorist operations on an international basis, why, in the sort of classical phrase, why isn't the United States doing something about it?

THE PRESIDENT: We are working in the United Nations, we are working with many governments in trying to put forward a very strong, anti-terrorist effort in order to stop this kind of very unwarranted, unjustified action and will continue our efforts in that regard.

Running-Mate - 2

QUESTION: Mr. President, I would like to follow up on Ronald Reagan as a possible running mate. I am sure you read the paper every morning, and there is a quote in here today from Governor Reagan saying, "Once you become the vice presidential candidate, you have no authority over yourself," and he says, "I have expressed disagreement with a great many things with this administration. No, there is just no way, I wouldn't do it."

Doesn't that really close the door on Ronald Reagan as a running mate?

THE PRESIDENT: I am not going to pass judgment on what his attitude may be. I will simply reaffirm and reaffirm very strongly, I am not excluding any Republican from consideration as a potential running mate.

Italy - 1

QUESTION: Mr. President, has the United States decided, with or without the consent of Germany, France and Britain, not to extend any economic aid to Italy if the Communists join the government in Italy?

THE PRESIDENT: I have said on several occasions that the United States Government, under this administration, would be very disturbed by Communist participation in the government of Italy. For one reason, it would have a very, I think, unfortunate, impact on NATO which is, of course, a very vital part of our international defense arrangement. The United States does have apprehension on a broader basis for Communist participation in the Italian government.

Rockefeller

QUESTION: Mr. President, in view of Jimmy Carter's strength in the South and the Northeastern industrial states, possibly of crucial importance, do you now think it may have been unwise for the Republican high command and you to have told Vice President Nelson Rockefeller to get lost?

THE PRESIDENT: I certainly don't use those words when I describe the situation that you have sought to so dramatically describe. *[Laughter]*

The decision by Nelson Rockefeller was one that he made himself. He has been an outstanding Vice President. He has been a close personal friend and adviser and, I will, of course, abide by his decision, as I would by any others.

But, I repeat what I said a moment ago, in my looking around for a vice presidential running mate, I am not excluding anybody.

Nomination - 2

QUESTION: Mr. President, what do you feel your major problems are now to hold the nomination?

THE PRESIDENT: Getting a few more delegates.

QUESTION: Where specifically are the problems?

THE PRESIDENT: There are around 100 uncommitted delegates on a pretty wide geographical basis. Of course, Hawaii has 18, Mississippi has 30, and the others are spread through a number of other states. So, we are going to make a maximum effort to convince individual delegates who are uncommitted, as well as those two major states that have not yet committed themselves.

International Trade

QUESTION: Mr. President, a question on international trade. The American textile industry is very concerned about the increase in imports of textiles from the People's Republic of China. They would like you to negotiate a bilateral agreement with Peking. What is your view on that? Are you doing anything about it?

THE PRESIDENT: I made a statement about three months ago that fully covers that. If you will refer back to that, it will give you a detailed answer.

Vice President - 2

QUESTION: Mr. President, can you tell us some of the criteria that you will be using in selecting a Vice President? You have said here today that you will consider the vice presidential nominee only on his basis to become President should something happen to you, but will there be other criteria as well?

THE PRESIDENT: That is the principal one, of course, and any other criteria would have to be secondary to that. But, other criteria might be age, compatibility with my own philosophy, the experience both in domestic and international affairs. There are a whole raft of potential criteria that I think have to be put into the formula.

QUESTION: Let me ask you, if I can, then, about the process. As you know, Jimmy Carter had a well-publicized audition, if you will, of various candidates. Will you ask the people you have in mind to meet with you either here at the White House or a place of their choice so you can discuss with them their philosophy of government and any personal differences you may have?

THE PRESIDENT: Over the years I have done that with all or most of the people that are being considered, so I don't think we have to go through the similar kind of routine that Governor Carter went through.

As I understand it, he had never met several of the people that he considered. So, I could really understand why he went through that process. Because of my experience and knowledge about all of the individuals that I think are being considered, I don't think that kind of a process has to be carried out.

Italy - 2

QUESTION: Mr. President, if I may follow up on the question of Italy, since it is possibly related to other European countries, is there an American formula, should the Communists go to power in Italy, that will be applied?

THE PRESIDENT: We aren't going to dictate any formula to the government of Italy or to the people of Italy. That is a decision for them to make. But, I have expressed our views concerning Communist involvement in that government as far as its impact on NATO.

Swine Flu

QUESTION: Mr. President, can we ask you about the swine flu program? We understand it is in jeopardy now. The insurance companies will not insure the pharmaceutical companies which are making up the batch of vaccine. What can you do about it, can the government supply insurance?

THE PRESIDENT: Last week the Secretary of HEW and Dr. Cooper met with the four manufacturers and their legal counsel. I got a report Friday from Secretary Mathews. He was more optimistic than some of the press stories seemed to indicate. I have not talked to him today, but we are going to find a way, either with or without the help of Congress, to carry out their program that is absolutely essential, a program that was recommended to me unanimously by 25 or 30 of the top medical people in this particular field.

So, we are going to find a way, and I think we will eventually do it, and I expect the full cooperation of the industry and all other parties involved.

Watergate Reform

QUESTION: Mr. President, that Watergate reform bill, the Senate version of it goes to the floor today. Until last week the administration, I gather, was very much opposed to it. Now you are in with a major proposal to change it. Can you tell us how the administration came up with these proposals at the 11th hour?

THE PRESIDENT: The administration has had many reservations about several of the provisions in the bill that is on the floor of the Senate at the present time. One, the Senate bill provides, as we understand it—and we have gone into it with some outstanding legal scholars—an unconstitutional method of the appointment of a Special Prosecutor.

So, what we have recommended is a completely constitutional method of selecting a Special Prosecutor, one that would call for a Special Prosecutor recommended by the President, confirmed by the Senate for a three-year term with that particular Special Prosecutor being ineligible to serve other than the first three years.

That is definitely a constitutional way to have a Special Prosecutor who would have criminal authority over any allegations made against a President, a Vice President, high executive officials, all members of Congress and those involved in the judiciary.

Our reservation was not as to the thrust but as to the constitutionality of several provisions, including the one I have just described.

QUESTION: What is your proposal?

THE PRESIDENT: Well, it is our proposal that we feel would accomplish the job of restoring public confidence in all three branches of the federal government and do it in a constitutional way.

Nixon Pardon - 1

QUESTION: Mr. President, in his acceptance speech, Senator Mondale specifically attacked you for your pardon of Richard Nixon and received prolonged applause from the people in the hall. And later, Mr. Carter said it was an issue that ran deep in this country. Do you consider your pardon of Mr. Nixon a liability?

THE PRESIDENT: I decided to grant the pardon in the national interest. At that time, the United States was faced with serious economic problems and we were still involved in a long and difficult war in Southeast Asia. We have very important matters to face and to solve. We could not be involved in the Nixon matter and concentrate fully on the more important matters. I decided in the national interest. I would do it again.

Coalition

QUESTION: Mr. President, will you tell me, sir, what it is that you are accomplishing when you unite both wings of the party, when it is widely recognized that the party is a minority party in American politics and how do you win an election that way?

THE PRESIDENT: Well, we are going to unite the Republican Party and appeal to independent voters and a number of Democrats, just as the Republicans did in 1968 and 1972.

Nixon Pardon - 2

QUESTION: Mr. President, in connection with the pardon, in both Senator Mondale's speech and in Jimmy Carter's speech, there seemed to be a linkage between the pardon and Watergate, itself. Do you see any such linkage, number one, and secondly, do you think that Watergate should be an issue in the campaign?

THE PRESIDENT: I granted the pardon because I thought it was in the national interest. I think the American people will make the decision, not me, myself, whether it will be an issue or not.

Convention Rules

QUESTION: Mr. President, do you expect a rules fight at the Convention that will allow some delegates to abstain on the first ballot and possibly the second ballot?

THE PRESIDENT: Well, the Justice Amendment which we are proposing would require that all delegates vote according to the laws under which they were selected and I think that is a very proper amendment to carry out the wishes of the people that supported those individuals at the time they were chosen.

QUESTION: Can I follow up, sir? Do you have an indication from the Reagan people that they will not try and change the Justice Amendment?

THE PRESIDENT: To my knowledge, we have not consulted with them.

Vice President - 3

QUESTION: Mr. President, how many vice presidential possibilities do you have in mind?

THE PRESIDENT: Quite a few.

QUESTION: Like maybe a half dozen, a dozen?

THE PRESIDENT: I am not going to get into the numbers game. We have a fine, fine array of talent in the Republican Party and maybe elsewhere, and so we will just keep that open until we make the final choice.

QUESTION: When will you make that choice?

THE PRESIDENT: You heard me correctly.

QUESTION: Do your comments on the vice presidency here today rule out any possibility you will declare the nomination open and let the Convention in Kansas City decide the vice presidential selection?

THE PRESIDENT: I will certainly make a recommendation and I hope the Convention would follow my recommendation.

QUESTION: Mr. President, since you have known all of the people involved as a potential Vice President so long and so well, is it possible you have made your decision and are delaying the announcement until the convention?

THE PRESIDENT: Not at all.

QUESTION: Mr. President, can you tell us what elsewhere is?

THE PRESIDENT: Use your imagination.

Carter and Oil

QUESTION: Mr. President, Governor Carter has said that if the Arabs were to impose another oil embargo, he would treat that as an economic declaration of war and would cut off all U.S. trade with the Arab nations. What do you think of that proposal?

THE PRESIDENT: We have been able, through diplomatic successes, to avoid the possibility of a Middle Eastern war and thereby avoided the possibility of an oil embargo. I am confident that the Ford administration successes, diplomatically, in the Middle East, will preclude any such situation as was indicated by Mr. Carter.

If you are doing things right, if you have the trust of Arab nations, as well as Israel, I don't think we have to look forward to either a Middle Eastern war or an oil embargo.

Olympics

QUESTION: Mr. President, a question on the Olympics. Now that Taiwan and the African nations have pulled out, what is your assessment of the situation and what changes would you like to see made in the next Olympics?

THE PRESIDENT: I am very proud of the successes I read about of the American team there yesterday. They did very, very well in the 100-meter freestyle and several other events, and I think the American team has done well and will continue to do well.

QUESTION: Has it been over-politicized?

THE PRESIDENT: We have tried to keep the athletic competition at the international level away from being pawns in international politics. We did our very best to achieve that result and the net result was, with some unfortunate circumstances, that the athletes are able to compete, and I am proud of the American successes.

Race With Carter

QUESTION: Mr. President, will your race with Jimmy Carter be a conservative versus a liberal race? What is the difference between your philosophy and Mr. Carter's in those terms?

THE PRESIDENT: I am not going to pass judgment on my opponent's campaign. We are going to run our own campaign, which is one of a record of accomplishment in foreign policy, domestic policy and the restoration of trust in the White House. What they do is for them to decide.

QUESTION: You cannot then describe Carter as a liberal?

THE PRESIDENT: I am not going to pin a label on anybody. I am going to just say that we have done a good job and on the basis of doing a good job, I think the American people will want the same kind of a job done for the next four years.

Campaign Organization

QUESTION: Mr. President, when you were Vice President you said that you would not employ anything such as CREEP, as President Nixon had, that you would have no separate committee. Now we understand there will be a President Ford election committee and you will not be relying entirely on the Republican National Committee.

THE PRESIDENT: I think that is caused by the Election Reform Act that was passed late in 1974. When I made that speech out in Chicago—I think sometime in 1973 or early 1974—that election law had not been enacted. Once that law was enacted, it does require that you maintain a National Committee and that the candidate for the presidency have a separate organization.

So, as much as I might want to put the two together, it is precluded by the law itself.

Intelligence

QUESTION: Mr. President, Senator Mondale says that you don't have the intelligence to be a good President. What do you think?

THE PRESIDENT: I think the American people will judge that.

Uncommitted Delegates

QUESTION: Mr. President, can we assume that you will see all the noncommitted delegates by the time the convention begins?

THE PRESIDENT: I would hope I could, but I can't categorically promise that. I would like to, definitely.

Abortion

QUESTION: Mr. President, the Supreme Court recently handed down another decision on abortion essentially strengthening the first one. What does this do to your position that you would prefer a constitutional amendment turning it back to the states? Have you given up hope now for that?

THE PRESIDENT: I don't see how that recommendation on my part is undercut by the recent decisions of the Supreme Court. I do not believe in abortion on demand. I do think you have a right to have an abortion where the life of the mother is involved, where there was a rape. I don't go along with those who advocate an amendment that would be so ironclad you couldn't under any circumstances have an abortion.

I reiterate what I have said on a number of occasions. I think an amendment which permits the voters in a state to decide whether in that state they want or don't want, is a proper way to give the people of this country or in their respective states the decision-making power.

QUESTION: Mr. President, don't you think the Supreme Court decision is going to make it more difficult to get that amendment, however?

THE PRESIDENT: Not necessarily.

FBI

QUESTION: Mr. President, do you have any comment one way or another on that recent shake-up in the FBI on the Kelley dismissal of Mr. Callahan?

THE PRESIDENT: That was a decision by the Attorney General and by the FBI Director. Mr. Callahan was not a presidential appointee so it was handled by the proper authorities.

Carter's Personality

QUESTION: Mr. President, presumably you watched a little bit of the Democratic National Convention on television. If so, would you tell us how Jimmy Carter came across to you as a personality, as a potential campaigner and as an opponent?

THE PRESIDENT: I don't think I really had any impression of him. [Laughter]

QUESTION: You didn't watch enough to get an impression of him?

THE PRESIDENT: I was pretty busy.

New Jersey Delegation

QUESTION: Mr. President, all 67 members of the New Jersey delegation are already in your column.

THE PRESIDENT: I hope.

QUESTION: Why are you bringing them down here this afternoon to a private meeting from which the press has been barred?

THE PRESIDENT: I am inviting them down because I want to meet them personally. Just as I said a few moments ago, I would like very much to have the opportunity of meeting all of the delegates and alternates to the National Convention, and this is a good way for me to do with the New Jersey delegation as I have with the other delegations.

QUESTION: What will be the nature of this meeting and do you have any thoughts about the exclusion of the press from—

THE PRESIDENT: I didn't know until a few moments ago that members of the press were excluded.

QUESTION: Can we come?

THE PRESIDENT: We have had a number of such meetings, and the question never came up from the press before, and I just don't see why we should make an exception here.

Polls

QUESTION: Mr. President, why are you down so far in the polls when you are pitted against Jimmy Carter?

THE PRESIDENT: The only poll that really counts is the one that is going to come on November 2, when the voters of this country decide in all 50 states, and I will rely on that one.

QUESTION: But how can you account for the preferences there?

THE PRESIDENT: I don't think we should analyze the ups and downs of periodic public opinion polls. The real one

that counts—and that is the one that is going to decide this great election—is the one that comes November 2.

THE PRESS: Thank you, Mr. President.

THE PRESIDENT: Thank you all very much. It has been very pleasant out here. ∎

September 8

Following is the White House text of President Ford's Sept. 8, 1976 news conference, his 36th since talking office.

THE PRESIDENT. Good morning. I have a very short opening statement, and then we will get to the questions.

PROBLEMS IN SOUTHERN AFRICA

I met this morning with Secretary Kissinger to discuss his report on his meetings with Prime Minister Vorster and with European leaders. On the basis of this report, I believe that good progress has been made on the problems concerning southern Africa.

It is important to understand that in this diplomatic process now unfolding, the United States is offering its good offices as an intermediary. We are willing to present ideas on how progress can be achieved, but we are not—and I emphasize "not"—trying to develop a specific American plan.

We have three objectives: First, to prevent an escalation of the violence which in time could threaten our national security; second, to realize popular aspirations while guaranteeing minority rights and ensuring economic progress; third, to resist the intervention in the African situation by outside forces.

In his discussions with Prime Minister Vorster, the Secretary put forward some ideas conveyed to the United States by black African leaders, and Prime Minister Vorster gave us his reactions. As a result of these discussions, Assistant Secretary Schaufele is currently in Africa discussing the situation. On the basis of his report, I will decide whether further progress can be made through a visit by Secretary Kissinger to Africa, starting with black African countries most concerned. We want to create the opportunities and conditions for all races to live side-by-side.

The United States cannot solve by itself these complicated problems. We need the continued good will and dedication of the parties involved.

The process that is now beginning is an extremely important one. It is extremely complicated. There is no guarantee of success. But I believe the United States must now make a major effort because it is the right thing to do. It is in our national interest, and it is in the interest of world peace.

I will be glad to answer any questions.

Sen. Dole's Finances - 1

Q. Mr. President, when you selected Mr. Dole as your running mate, did you make a thorough check of his finances over and beyond, independently of what he gave you, and how was that done? Was it done through Justice, or where?

THE PRESIDENT. The office of White House counsel made a very thorough investigation of all of the individuals who were being considered for the office of Vice President. That was done by demanding that they send to us various information concerning their finances and related matters.

Subsequent to that information being furnished, a member of my staff at the office of the White House counsel interrogated the individuals who were being considered, including Senator Dole. As a result of that interrogation and information voluntarily supplied by Senator Dole, it was concluded by the office of the White House counsel that all things were in order.

Campaign Strategy - 1

Q. Mr. President, have we gotten a fair sample of your campaign this week, or do you have something else in mind for the future?

THE PRESIDENT. Let me say at the outset, Mr. Cormier, that I decided a long time ago—in fact, when I made my first announcement that I was a candidate—that the principal responsibility I had was that of being President of the United States. And I intend to carry out that responsibility. Secondly, we have a campaign strategy that will unfold in the days and weeks ahead. It is a strategy that we will adhere to and it is one that has been thoroughly worked out and definitely determined. And you will see how it evolves in the time ahead.

Presidential Debates - 1

Q. Mr. President, was it your suggestion that the first debate be held in Philadelphia and, if so, why?

THE PRESIDENT. Well, of course, I wanted the debates to start today, and we weren't too particular where the location might be. We are certainly in agreement with Philadelphia being the first site.

Abortion Issue - 1

Q. Mr. President, Jimmy Carter said today that your position on abortion and his are fundamentally the same. Do you agree with that? And, secondly, do you think the issue should be debated at all in the campaign?

THE PRESIDENT. First, the Democratic platform and the Republican platform on the issue of abortion are quite different. I subscribe to the Republican platform and Governor Carter subscribes to the Democratic platform. His position and mine are not identical. My position is that of the Republican platform, and I will stick with it.

Q. But that was not your position before.

THE PRESIDENT. I think—if I might correct you, Miss Thomas [Helen Thomas, United Press International]—the Republican platform is my platform. It is one that coincides with my long-held views.

Q. Do you think there should be a constitutional amendment against abortion?

THE PRESIDENT. I have had the position for some time that there should be a constitutional amendment that would permit the individual States to make the decision based on a vote of the people of each of the States.

Mr. Rodgers [Walter C. Rodgers, Associated Press Radio]?

SALT II Negotiations

Q. Mr. President, are we any closer to a second SALT agreement with the Russians and, if so, what are the prospects for such an agreement before the election?

THE PRESIDENT. We are continuing to work on the negotiations for a SALT II agreement. A good agreement would be in the best interest of the American people and the world as a whole. The decision on whether such an agreement is signed will have no relevance whatsoever to this current political campaign. We hope that such an agreement can be achieved as soon as possible.

Q. What would you say the prospects are, please, sir?

THE PRESIDENT. I think they are gradually improving, but we have some very difficult problems yet to resolve.

Campaign Laws

Q. Mr. President, don't you feel that there should be a law that limits what an incumbent President can do in the way of spending time, spending money, and use of employees of the White House and vehicles and other taxpayers' resources on his campaign?

THE PRESIDENT. I think the Congress has made its decision in that regard, Sarah [Sarah McClendon, McClendon News Service]. And I will, of course, always abide by the laws passed by the Congress.

Media in Campaign

Q. Mr. President, do you feel that you are in any way perhaps abusing the power of this office by controlling the media, to use the media as it were to make statements daily on one subject or another?

THE PRESIDENT. I apologize if I am using the American press. I am trying to do the job as President of the United States. And I hope that between the American press and the President we can convey important information to the American people.

Ford Economic Record

Q. Mr. President, Governor Carter and Senator Mondale and labor leader George Meany have all in recent speeches, in criticizing your economic record, referred to the Nixon-Ford administration, thus lumping the two together.

Would you prefer to run on your own economic record rather than being associated with the Nixon economic record, specifically, imposition of wage-price controls?

THE PRESIDENT. The Ford record is the record that I will run on, as far as foreign policy is concerned, as far as domestic policy is concerned. To take the particular matter that you mentioned, I have consistently said, and I reiterate, that wage and price controls will not be imposed by this administration.

This administration has had a good record in handling serious and difficult problems in the domestic economic field. We have added 4 million new people working in the last 12 months, 500,000 more in the last 2 months. So I will stand on my record, which I think it a good one.

Sen. Dole's Finances - 2

Q. Mr. President, there have been some questions in the last few days about Senator Dole. Have you had any contact with him on that subject, in particular about the control of money, or have you attempted to satisfy yourself anew about this, or perhaps your staff?

THE PRESIDENT. The statement made this morning by Mr. Wild, I think clarifies the situation very dramatically. Senator Dole was in the Cabinet meeting this morning and my staff has been in contact with his, and we are satisfied today, as we were at the time we made the initial investigation of his campaign finances.

Unemployment - 1

Q. Mr. President, the unemployment rate has gone up for 3 straight months. What, if any, plans do you have to deal with this problem should it continue to rise?

THE PRESIDENT. Our answer is to increase the number of people working. And as I indicated a moment ago, we have added 500,000 more people working in the last 60 days. In addition, we have 88 million people working today, an alltime high. We are going to continue to emphasize that more people are working and more jobs are available. And I am convinced that with our successful efforts against inflation and more jobs, the American people will subscribe to that economic policy.

Unemployment - 2

Q. May I follow up, Mr. President? Do you think the fact that unemployment is high in this particular period, just before the election, may harm you politically?

THE PRESIDENT. I think the American people are more knowledgeable, more sophisticated. They know that employment is going up every month, and that as long as there are people being hired and as long as the layoff rate continues to go down, the American people will be supportive of the economic policy of the Ford administration.

Urban Problems

Q. Mr. President, this afternoon 40 Congressmen from 14 States and the District of Columbia are meeting. This is the newly formed, as you know, Northeast Coalition. What can you say to them were you to send a message to them? They are concerned about industry leaving the Northeast. They are concerned about—I heard what you said to Aldo [Aldo B. Beckman, Chicago Tribune Press Service]—but they are concerned about joblessness, not people with jobs. They are concerned about urban blight. What do you say to that?

THE PRESIDENT. Well, we have a good program to try and rehabilitate our major urban cities all throughout the United States, including the Northeast—our revenue sharing program, our community development program.

I signed, after a great deal of work with the Congress, a mass transit bill that is very helpful and beneficial to major industrial centers throughout the United States. We will be glad to work with any group geographically or otherwise, including the Northeast group, to try and help in that regard.

Q. They also say, Mr. President, they are not getting a fair share of the Federal dollars. You mentioned mass transportation. They say that they are getting 15 per cent of the dollars whereas there was 40 per cent for mass transportation in the Northeast.

THE PRESIDENT. I am not familiar with those particular statistics but those funds are released based on laws passed by the Congress. So, if there is a problem in that regard, I think the basic law has to be amended.

Presidential Debates - 2

Q. Mr. President, how do you evaluate the debates as a factor in the campaign?

THE PRESIDENT. The American people will be the winner. And I am anxious that they get started as quickly as possible, and, as I indicated earlier, I proposed the first one be held today.

Prices on Industrial Goods

Q. Mr. President, a related economic question. The steel companies have rescinded a price increase on flat rolled steel which is a principal component of automobiles. Would you like to see this followed by a similar reduction or rescission of the increases in automobile prices recently announced by the automobile companies?

THE PRESIDENT. I would hope that the automobile manufacturers would take that into consideration.

Q. I would like to ask it in the framework of the fact that although you are claiming success against inflation, the industrial component of both wholesale and retail prices continues to rise, and this is the component that once it is up it does not go down. It is not volatile like food prices. With respect to the automobile companies, the other basic manufacturing segments of the economy, what would you like to see done? What do you think ought to be done? Or do you think anything needs to be done to try to stabilize the industrial component?

THE PRESIDENT. I belive that the wholesome competition in the American free enterprise system will solve that problem better than any other way.

Presidential Debates - 3

Q. Mr. President, what sort of preparations are you making for these debates? Do you, for instance, have one of your aides acting out the role of your opponent so you can get ready that way?

THE PRESIDENT. Not at all, Fred [Frederic W. Barnes, Washington Star]. I am obviously doing a great deal of study and preparation for these debates because I want the American people to know not only my own views but the views of Mr. Carter. And I think the best way for that to take place is for me and for himself to set forth those views, and that will be done in three debates.

Q. Mr. President, what is it you are doing in preparation? Are you studying some of Mr. Carter's statements? Are you watching videotapes of Governor Carter?

THE PRESIDENT. The matter is being thoroughly studied by me comprehensively.

Southern Africa

Q. Mr. President, you mentioned the African guaranteeing of minority rights. How many black governments in Africa do you regard as having shown minority rights—or respected them? Could you name some, and how could you go about guaranteeing such minority rights in the future?

THE PRESIDENT. I think in the plans that will evolve—and I hope they do—there will be adequate protection for minority rights in the two areas being considered at the present time.

FBI Director Kelley - 1

Q. Can you tell us what went into your judgment not to fire or reprimand the FBI Director in light of the questionable allegations raised against him?

THE PRESIDENT. Let me answer the Kelly matter this way: I was disappointed, to say the least, with the two responses given to the Kelley questions to Governor Carter. One, I think it showed a lack of compassion in the one statement, and a second statement that seemed to be contradictory of the first one.

I hope that Governor Carter understood that Mrs. Kelley at that time was suffering terminal cancer and that was a very sad and difficult time for the Director of the FBI. Number two, I was confused when in either Connecticut or Brooklyn he said that if he were President yesterday he would fire him, and then at the next stop he would not indicate whether he was going to fire him or keep him if he became President on January 21. So, I am confused on the one hand by his flip-flop on this issue, and I am very disappointed at his lack of compassion on the other.

Now the recommendation made to me by the Attorney General after thoroughly investigating the facts was that the circumstances were such that the FBI Director should be kept. He has reimbursed the Federal Government of $35 ($335), I think, for the furnishings for his apartment, and he has done a good job in my opinion in straightening out a very difficult situation in the FBI.

Abortion Issue - 2

Q. Mr. President, on the matter of abortion, do you feel that this issue, which is so semi-religious and so emotional, is a fit subject for a political debate, political discussion?

THE PRESIDENT. I don't think the American people expect candidates for office to duck any issues just because they are intense, with good people on both sides having different views. I think the American people ought to get an answer from Governor Carter and myself on this issue just like on any other issue.

Campaign Strategy - 2

Q. Mr. President, what do you think of Mr. Carter's characterization of you as "timid" in one statement and as "a captain hiding in a stateroom" in another?

THE PRESIDENT. That brings up an interesting point. I understand yesterday that Senator Mondale was complaining because I was not campaigning enough, and on August 4 of 1976, Governor Carter was complaining because I was campaigning too much. I wish they would get their act together. And it just seems to me that the American people want me first to be President and do the job here in the best way possible, and I intend to do it. And I will campaign at the proper time.

Q. Mr. President, in connection with that, if you find your campaign running in a dry gulch, won't you change your plans?

THE PRESIDENT. I don't expect the campaign on behalf of President Ford to run into a dry gulch. We are making good headway. I think the polls reflect it, and we expect to win.

Campaign Contributions

Q. Mr. President, sir, the reports of your campaign committee during the primaries indicate that approximately 100 Federal officials gave campaign contributions to the President Ford Committee, and some of them have subsequently said that they did so in response to solicitation letters from Mr. Mosbacher and other officials of the committee. Do you think it is proper for the President Ford Committee to keep those contributions, or should they be sent back?

THE PRESIDENT. I was not familiar with any solicitation of any Federal official on behalf of the President Ford Committee. And when I was shown that some individuals of this administration had voluntarily given to the President Ford Committee I did not know that they had done so beforehand. So I am sure there was no pressure, certainly none from me.

Nixon Pardon

Q. Mr. President, today, I believe, is the second anniversary of the pardon of Richard Nixon. I know you said in the past, under the same circumstances you would issue the pardon again. I wonder if you have any thoughts you would share with us about the impact the pardon will have on the election and how you plan to respond to any charges that are made?

THE PRESIDENT. If it is made a political issue, either subtly or directly, it is going to be very difficult to anticipate what the public reaction will be. But I made that judgment 2 years ago today on the basis of the circumstances at that time.

I thought it was in the national interest that I concentrate on the international problems, which were serious, and domestic problems, which were critical. And I felt at that time I should devote 100 per cent of my time to the problems both at home and abroad. And I think if the same circumstances prevailed today, I would do the same.

Soviet Defector

Q. Mr. President, this question is in two parts. Has the Soviet Union contacted you personally or this Government with regard to the pilot who has defected and asked for political asylum? And, secondly, are you concerned that your decision to grant political asylum will injure progress in our relations with the Soviet Union and specifically on SALT and matters of that kind?

THE PRESIDENT. I am not familiar with any inquiry by the Soviet Union. They may have, but I am just not informed as to that.

Number two, we have decided to grant asylum if the Soviet pilot asks for it. This is a tradition in the United States and as long as he wants such asylum, he will be granted it in the United States. I don't think that granting him asylum will interfere with our relations with the Soviet Union.

FBI Director Kelley - 2

Q. Mr. President, going back to the Kelley matter for a moment. Governor Carter said yesterday also that the FBI Director should be as pure as Caesar's wife. Do you agree with that statement, and in light of the allegations against Mr. Kelley, do you think he is?

THE PRESIDENT. On the basis of a thorough investigation by the Attorney General, an outstanding lawyer, and I think an outstanding Attorney General, he recommended that I take the action which I did which was to keep the FBI Director. And I have full faith in the analysis and the recommendations of the Attorney General, and therefore I think I made the right decision.

FRANK CORMIER, Associated Press. Thank you, Mr. President. ∎

September 30

Following is the White House text of President Ford's Sept. 30, 1976 news conference, his 37th since taking office.

Ford Finances

REPORTER. Mr. President, you are well aware of all the stories of allegations concerning your Grand Rapids past and the campaign financing, I know, and that the records allegedly have been subpoenaed by a Special Prosecutor. So this must be very disturbing, and I suppose you want it cleared up before the election.

I know that you believe that the Judiciary Committee covered it all. But can you say categorically that there has never been any misuse of any of your campaign funds when you ran for Congress?

THE PRESIDENT. First, let me say very emphatically that I strongly believe in the Special Prosecutor concept. I supported, the administration supports the continuation of a Special Prosecutor. I was pleased when the Senate passed a version that included such a provision. And I am disappointed that the House apparently is not going to do it. I should add that I have full confidence in the integrity of Mr. Ruff in his responsibilities as the Special Prosecutor.

Number two, I also believe in the full integrity of the Department of Justice, and I am certain that they will do whatever they are required to under their responsibilities.

Let me add that nobody on my staff has any authority whatsoever to contact either the Special Prosecutor or the Department of Justice to, in any way, hinder or impede whatever investigations are going on.

What I know about the Kent County situation I have picked up in reading the newspapers or seeing on television or radio what has been reported.

I, therefore, am not familiar with the precise charges, whatever they may be. But I can say with complete confidence that I am certain that when the investigation is completed, that I will be free of any allegations such as I've read about.

I would add this final comment: There is a saying that's prevalent in the law that "justice delayed is justice denied." And I am certain that the people responsible for any investigation will live up to the high standards required in the canon of ethics for

the legal profession, which does require that in any such investigations that they be full, complete, and concluded as readily as possible.

Q. Well, you don't know for certain whether there are charges or whether you are the target, or do you—

THE PRESIDENT. No.

Q. And doesn't your curiosity—even if you made public the fact that you were going to ask, I don't think that that would be undue pressure, would it?

THE PRESIDENT. We are trying to be so circumspect, so that we are not under any circumstances accused of any improprieties, that I have told members of my staff that under no circumstances should they make contacts with either the Special Prosecutor or the Department of Justice.

Q. Mr. President, don't you have the right under the current law to ask if you are the target of the Special Prosecutor's investigation. And, if that's the case, why don't you want to know that, at least?

THE PRESIDENT. I can't tell you whether under the law I can or can't. But, even if we do have that right, I think an inquiry by me or somebody on my staff would undoubtedly be misconstrued, and I just don't want any such allegation being made by anybody.

Speaker's Fees

Q. Mr. President, could you clear up a matter that has been pending for some time and was referred to in this investigation—or at least it was referred to in a newspaper article the other day—that when you were in the House you used to go down here to the Seamans Institute, I think 22nd Street or somewhere, like a lot of other House Members did of both parties, and read a little speech that they gave you to read at noon luncheons, and then they would give you a nice little check, maybe they would give you an extra $1,000 or $500 because you were majority—minority leader? I am sure this was probably done by a lot of other Congressmen, but was that true?

THE PRESIDENT. Any time I make a speech, Sarah [Sarah McClendon, McClendon News Service], I solicit from members of my staff—I did up in the House, and I asked any organization that I was speaking to to give me ideas on what they thought would be appropriate comments in speaking to that organization.

In the case of the meetings that you speak of, it was before the joint maritime labor organization—that's not the right term—but it's a combination of all the labor organizations that are involved in the maritime industry.

Yes, I asked them for suggestions as to what they thought would be appropriate for discussion before their group. And they, along with the executive branch of the government that had jurisdiction over shipbuilding or any aspects of the maritime industry—I also got recommendations from them. And this combination of ideas for a speech, people on my staff put together in a speech. But they were not the ones who wrote the speech that you are speaking of. They submitted what they thought would be appropriate, and we took their ideas with the suggestions from the staff committees on the House and Senate side, the executive department people, the labor organizations, from the maritime industry overall, and that combination of information went into whatever speeches I made. I think that's a very appropriate way to handle it.

Q. Did they give you a check for this, sir?

THE PRESIDENT. Oh, yes, and those checks were fully reported on my income tax returns. They were reported to any other authority that required it. And all of that matter was looked into by the House and Senate committees at the time of my Vice-Presidential hearing.

Q. But if they had matters pending before the Congress, did you think that was right to take that money when they had matters pending before the Congress?

THE PRESIDENT. Well, I was deeply interested in the new legislation that was before the House and the Senate to expand and upgrade our maritime industry. That was a group that likewise felt that way, and I think it was proper.

Social Outings

Q. Mr. President, in your golf outings, or social occasions, or other vacations with Rod Markley of Ford Motor Company or U.S. Steel, did you discuss Government business with them either when you were a Member of the House, or Vice President, or President?

THE PRESIDENT. Not to my best recollection.

Q. You never discussed business?

THE PRESIDENT. No.

Campaign Damage?

Q. Mr. President, do you think in the headlines that have run for about the last 10 days and the fact that some of these potential allegations have not been resolved, that there has been any damaging effect on your campaign, or would there be if "justice delayed" means that there is no resolution of this before November 2?

THE PRESIDENT. Well, I think it's vitally important that any aspects of either one of these matters be fully resolved as quickly as possible. I have no way of knowing what the impact is politically.

Campaign Money Use - 1

Q. Mr. President, one of the issues raised is whether any of this campaign money was actually ever diverted to your personal use. Would you like to say flatly whether that was so or not?

THE PRESIDENT. Well, I don't know whether that's an allegation that's being investigated by the Special Prosecutor's Office, but I can say that there was never money given to me by the Kent County Republican Committee. The Kent County Republican Committee may have done

some advertising on behalf of my candidacy or the candidacy of other Republican candidates running for public office. That's their function.

They, just for example, always the last week or so, would have a full-page ad with the gubernatorial candidate and the senatorial candidate, the congressional candidate, plus some State legislative officers, and so I suppose they spent their money on that, which is a perfectly proper function of the Kent County Republican Finance Committee and county organization. No money ever went to me personally.

Timing of Investigation

Q. Mr. President, does the timing of the Special Prosecutor's investigation seem strange to you, or do you question the motivation?

THE PRESIDENT. I would not under any circumstances question the motivation or the timing.

Q. Mr. President, are you holding this press conference because Jimmy Carter has accused you of keeping silent on these matters?

THE PRESIDENT. Not at all.

Travel Records

Q. Mr. President, your staff says they are having some trouble getting records of all these various golfing trips and what-not. Have you ever asked Mr. Whyte if he has records?

THE PRESIDENT. Well, it's my understanding that Mr. Whyte issued a two- or three-page statement a week or 10 days ago which outlined the circumstances of the three trips up to Pine Valley and the two down to Disneyland. I understand he issued that.

Q. I mean records of what it cost and who paid and all that sort of thing.

THE PRESIDENT. Well, I have no access to their records, so they will have to answer that.

Personal Integrity - 1

Q. Mr. President, you have said that it's vitally important that the matter be resolved as soon as possible. Is it your wish that it be resolved before the election? It is vitally important so the voters can see the full story, or the true story.

THE PRESIDENT. Well, it's more important to me personally that it be cleared up because I am very proud of my record of personal integrity. And I think that's more important than any impact it might have on the election.

Union Supporters

Q. Mr. President, may I ask you this question: Those marine unions, the Seafarers and the Marine Engineers, supported you down through the years. Then you vetoed a bill that they wanted—I forget the name of it, But I am sure you recall it. After that they shifted over to Jimmy Carter. Do you have any feeling that maybe

somebody in the Carter camp may have made some allegation to the Special Prosecutor and that's what triggered this, or is there a political motivation in there somewhere?

THE PRESIDENT. Bob [Bob Schieffer, CBS News], I wouldn't make any allegations of that kind. I don't think—since I don't know—I don't think I ought to make any comment.

Q. Well obviously, though, the Special Prosecutor wouldn't open an investigation, I would think, on just the basis of rumors. Somebody had to make an allegation there.

THE PRESIDENT. What impresses me the most is a statement by the former Special Prosecutor, Leon Jaworski, who has said, as I understand it, publicly, that before he left the office of Special Prosecutor he looked into such matters, and he came to the conclusion that there was no reason for action.

Now, that in no way challenges the right or the integrity of Mr. Ruff. But where any such charges came from, I would have no idea.

Q. Let me just make one follow-up. If I understand it, Mr. Jaworski said that he had investigated the Seafarers Union, and I think that was in relation to a $100,000 contribution they made to Richard Nixon. As far as I know, he's never said that he looked into MEBA—the Marine Engineers. Do you know in fact whether or not he did?

THE PRESIDENT. No, I can't be that precise.

Staff Contacts

Q. Mr. President, you said that you instructed that your staff shouldn't make any contacts to the Attorney General or to the prosecutor. Have there been any contacts made by any of these agencies to you so that you have any information at all either that this is going to be resolved quickly or any information at all?

THE PRESIDENT. I have no information whatsoever.

Q. Mr. President, do you have any information from people back in your old home district, the fifth district, that may have contacted you, presumably old friends of yours?

THE PRESIDENT. I read the Grand Rapids Press, which is a good newspaper, and I read stories concerning this and quotations from people who were former county chairmen or presently county chairmen, so I know what they've said. But they haven't talked extensively about the investigation. I guess they felt that they had testified or made their comments to whoever was investigating it, and they didn't really say very much.

Q. But you haven't talked to any of them personally?

THE PRESIDENT. No.

Pentagon Reprimands

Q. Mr. President, a number of Pentagon military officers have received disciplinary reprimands for accepting freebies, free weekends, hunting expeditions. If you think there is nothing improper about a Congressman accepting free golfing weekends, what distinction is there?

THE PRESIDENT. Well, the House passed a resolution sometime in 1968, as I understand it, which says nothing of significance or substance should be received. I do not feel that there was any impropriety on my part or any violation of that regulation.

I am an avid golfer. Most of you know it. I enjoy the company of people while I am playing golf. Every person that's been involved in these allegations I have reciprocated with as far as they coming either to my golf club or coming to our home.

There has been, I would say, substantial reciprocity. And whatever the circumstances of our getting together, has been in a proper way and in no way a violation, in my judgment, of any rule or ethical standard. These are close personal friends and have been for many years. And I have never accepted—or I don't believe they have tendered—any such things on the basis of seeking any special privilege or anything that was improper.

'Situation Ethics'

Q. Mr. President, on June 15, before the Southern Baptist Convention, you condemned very strongly what you call "situation ethics," and I was wondering why this golfing vacation wasn't really "situation ethics," when at that time you said the American people, particularly our young people, cannot be expected to take pride or even to participate in a system of government that is defiled and dishonored, whether in the White House or the halls of Congress.

My question is, do you feel that in view of what the White House has admitted, you have lived up to your own standards here?

THE PRESIDENT. I have said that I don't consider these infrequent weekends a violation of either the rules of the House or any ethical standards. I explained that these were longstanding personal relationships, where there has been virtual reciprocity, and I wouldn't have accepted if there had been any thought in my mind that it was improper or the violation of any code of ethics.

Q. Isn't that "situation ethics" though?

THE PRESIDENT. I don't think so.

Campaign Money Use - 2

Q. Mr. President, to follow up on Fran Lewine's question earlier, she asked you if any of the funds had been diverted for personal use, and your answer sir, was, that you had never received any funds from Kent County. Are we to understand that as a "no," that you have never used any of these funds for personal use?

THE PRESIDENT. From the Kent County Republican Committee?

Q. From any campaign fund?

THE PRESIDENT. I will say any campaign funds for personal use.

Personal Integrity - 2

Q. Do you find these stories personally painful, someone questioning your integrity?

THE PRESIDENT. Well, it naturally has some impact when I know that all of these things have been investigated by some 400 FBI agents and 5-to-6 Internal Revenue agents, with my income taxes going back to 8 or 9 years, when I know that I have been given a clean bill of health, not only by the FBI but the Internal Revenue Service, by the Senate and House committees, and an overwhelming vote in the House and Senate.

When I look at the investigation that was made of my personal life, the financial circumstances, probably more than anybody else in the history of this country, I know that there is no problem. So I guess to some extent one is bothered a bit. But as long as my conscience is clear I have no real problem.

Income Tax

Q. Sir, you brought up the matter of the income tax. It's proper, isn't it, if in case a person receives a gift, say of an airplane ticket or something of that sort, it has to be listed on their income tax as a gift. Or does reciprocity cover that when you buy a ticket later?

THE PRESIDENT. I am not familiar with the details of that, but the IRS went into all of these matters. They closed out my income-tax returns for back 8 or 9 years. They had people go into these with minute detail so I—

Q. Well, what I am asking is, actually I am asking for your legal advice.

THE PRESIDENT. Well, I am not here to give you any legal advice.

Longstanding Friendships

Q. Mr. President, is this longstanding personal relationship, personal and friendship though it may be—is nevertheless valuable to United States Steel and to the Ford Motor Company, much as the employers of other people who are friends of yours—for example, John Byrnes, who represents a great many interests in this town on tax reform, and—perhaps coincidentally, perhaps you believe this—your position is about like his on tax reform?

I asked you earlier whether you had discussed business with them during these social outings. Rod Markley said you and he discussed the Clean Air Act. I wonder, do you not see that it is to their benefit for you to have this personal relationship?

THE PRESIDENT. Let me modify what I said a moment ago. In a casual way, of course we might informally talk about certain matters, but I happen to feel that they were not asking me and I was not asking them. The times I've played with Rod have been at Burning Tree, where we are

both members and both pay our own way. John Byrnes, I played golf with him because he is a friend of 28-plus years. I don't see anything improper at all.

Q. Do you think that you can separate—

THE PRESIDENT. Absolutely.

Q. —their business as lobbyists and their representation of their corporations from your personal friendship?

THE PRESIDENT. As a matter of fact, some of their comments could be helpful in what the status is.

Q. Mr. President, yet that seems to be the issue that Carter is raising, though. He seems to be raising the old buddy system issue and saying, in fact, that you can't. Now what can you say to counter that? How can you?

THE PRESIDENT. Maybe he can't, but I can.

Q. Mr. President, may I ask you, you now are aware that some of these expenses were actually paid by the companies and not by your friends. But you were paying, when you had them to your home, you were paying yourself, the taxpayers were not taking care of this. So these companies in effect were financing some of this.

What is your thinking about why they wanted to do this, why they were willing to entertain you on these weekends?

THE PRESIDENT. I think you would have to ask the people who offered the invitation. These are personal friends, and I don't ask in advance why you want to pay my green fees. I think that's a matter for them on the basis of their own integrity.

Presidential Campaign

Q. Mr. President, you have been through one debate. Have you got any thoughts on the second one as to a change in format, or anything you would like to do differently?

THE PRESIDENT. We are very satisfied with the format that was used in the first debate. I thought it went very well.

Q. Mr. President, you look more worried than I've seen you in a long time.

THE PRESIDENT. Worried?

Q. Yes, sir. You haven't smiled very much in this news conference. You really look troubled, and I have known you for 10 years. Does this bother you? Is it something that's going to hurt you badly in the campaign?

THE PRESIDENT. I answered a moment ago I am more concerned about my personal reputation. But, I am not unhappy. I just am worried about getting over to the signing ceremony for one of these bill signings.

REPORTER. Thank you. ∎

October 14

Following is the White House text of President Ford's Oct. 14 news conference, his 38th since taking office:

THE PRESIDENT: Good evening. Will you please sit down.

I do have an opening statement. When I was chosen to be Vice President, I underwent the most intensive scrutiny of any man who has ever been selected for public office in the United States. My past life, my qualifications, my beliefs all were put under a microscope and in full public view. Nonetheless, all of you here tonight—and many of you in our listening audience—are aware of allegations that came forth in recent weeks involving my past political campaigns.

As I have said on several occasions, these rumors were false. I am very pleased that this morning the Special Prosecutor has finally put this matter to rest once and for all.

I have told you before that I am deeply privileged to serve as the President of this great nation. But, one thing that means more to me than my desire for public office is my personal reputation for integrity.

Today's announcement by the Special Prosecutor reaffirms the original findings of my vice presidential confirmation hearings. I hope that today's announcement will also accomplish one other major task—that it will elevate the Presidential campaign to a level befitting the American people and the American political tradition.

For too many days this campaign has been mired in questions that have little bearing upon the future of this nation. The people of this country deserve better than that. They deserve a campaign that focuses on the most serious issues of our time—on the purposes of government, on the heavy burdens of taxation, on the cost of living and on the quality of our lives and on the ways to keep America strong, at peace and free.

Governor Carter and I have profound differences of opinion on these matters. I hope that in the 20 days remaining in this campaign we can talk seriously and honestly about these differences so that on November 2 the American people can make a clear choice and give us, one of us, a mandate to govern wisely and well during the next four years.

Ladies and gentlemen, I will be glad to answer your questions.

Fran?

Q: Mr. President, would you also like to set the record straight tonight on an issue that John Dean has raised?

Did you at any time use your influence with any members of Congress or talk to lobbyist Richard Cook about blocking a 1972 Watergate break-in investigation by Wright Patman's House Banking Committee?

P: I have reviewed the testimony that I gave before both the House and the Senate committees and those questions were asked. I responded fully.

A majority of the members of the House committee and the Senate committee, after full investigation, came to the conclusion that there was no substance to those allegations.

I do not believe they are any more pertinent today than they were then, and my record was fully cleared at that time.

Arms to Israel, Farm Supports

Q: Mr. President in the past several days you have made two major decisions, one to sell Israel compression bombs, sophisticated weaponry, even though their request had been hanging fire for many months. You also decided to give the wheat price support, the 50 per cent boost, even though the Agriculture Department said the day before that there was no economic justification for these.

Can you state flatly that none of these decisions were designed to enhance you politically?

P: Categorically, those decisions were based on conditions I think justified fully the decisions that I made. In the case of the four items that were cleared for delivery to the government of Israel, those items have been on the list for consideration. Those items have been analyzed by the various departments in our government. And the net result was that I decided, after discussing the matter with my top advisers, that those items should be cleared for the government of Israel.

Q: On what justification do you give such weapons and why did you bypass the Pentagon and the State Department?

P: I made the decision, and that decision is mine—and they may have been a little disappointed that they did not have an opportunity to leak the decision beforehand—and I felt that it was a decision only for the Commander-in-Chief, and I made it as such, and based on recommendations that were made to me by responsible people, the top people, giving the advice in this regard.

On the other question regarding the increase in the loan rates, in May of 1975 I vetoed an agricultural bill on the basis that I thought it was not good legislation at that time. But I said at that time in the veto message that I would be very watchful to make certain that if conditions changed we would increase the loan rate.

In May of 1975, for example, the price of wheat was about $3.35 a bushel. Recently, the price of wheat was about $2.79 a bushel. There was a very severe drop. And in order to make certain that wheat will be marked properly and the farmer will have an opportunity to market that wheat which he produced at our request of full production, and in order for the farmers, the wheat farmers, to have adequate financing to proceed with their fall planting of winter wheat, I decided that it was in the best interest of full production for the American farmer that those loan rates be increased. They were based on a commitment I made in May of 1975, and changed conditions today.

Q: Mr. President, in the course of the Watergate Prosecutor's investigation of your income taxes, your taxes were made public, leaked to the press at one point, and in those taxes, it showed at one point you took money from your political organization and used over $1,000 for a family vacation to Vail and several hundred dollars for personal clothing.

I wonder if you would address the propriety of action like that.

P: I think you have to bear in mind, as I recall those initial payments, for airline tickets and for the others, were made out of what we call the Fifth District account, and within, I think it was a week, or two weeks at the most, I reimbursed that account fully in both cases.

Q: In the case of reimbursements, the tax information also showed that your personal bank account, as it were, went down in the red something like $3,000, but it was soon reimbursed, and there was a question left as to how you reimbursed that $3,000.

P: That was my next paycheck. *(Laughter)*

I think a few people in this country have written checks and then waited until the end of the month and then mailed the checks—maybe you haven't done it, but I suspect a few people have—and we mailed those checks after we had the money in the bank account. But I wrote the checks before the end of the month. It is a perfectly legitimate thing and there was never an overdraft in my account. *(Laughter)*

Accepting Gifts - 1

Q: Mr. President, there have been some questions a few weeks ago about your taking, accepting, golfing vacations and travel from lobbyists and corporations. It has been quite some time since these allegations were made. I wonder if you can clear this up tonight. Just how often, how many times, did you accept free travel and golfing vacations from lobbyists and corporations?

P: To the best of my recollection, the ones that came to light are the ones involved—there might be one or two more, but I can't recollect the instances.

Q: Mr. President, if I may follow up on Frances Lewine's first question, I don't think you quite answered the question. The question is not about your testimony at the time specifically, it is about the new allegations from John Dean that, in fact, you did discuss six times with Mr. Cook the matter of blocking the investigation by the House of Watergate and at the time you said, at the time that you went through your investigation, you mentioned, you said you did not recollect such discussions. Do you now recollect discussions with Mr. Cook on that subject?

P: I will give you exactly the same answer I gave to the House committee and the Senate committee. That answer was satisfactory to the House committee by a vote of 29 to eight, and I think a unanimous vote in the Senate committee.

The matter was fully investigated by those two committees and I think that is a satisfactory answer. I am not going to pass judgment on what Mr. Dean now alleges.

Q: Mr. President, would you oppose, on the Dean matter, would you oppose a review of White House tapes and investigation by the Special Prosecutor and investigation that has been called for by Congressman Conyers and Congresswoman Holtzman?

P: That is a decision for the Special Prosecutor to make, I have never, at any time, in the just previous investigations or at any other time, interfered with the judgment or the decisions of the Special Prosecutor, and I wouldn't in this case.

The Economy

Q: Mr. President, you have been going up and down the country, most recently in New York and New Jersey, saying things are getting better, things have improved and there is a definite difference between you and your other candidate, Mr. Carter.

There is a 7.8 per cent unemployment rate. The Commerce Department today announced that retail sales fell by 1.1 per cent. The stock market took a nose dive. Mr. Friedman, a conservative economist, says nothing that either you or Mr. Carter offers will cause a change in the rise of Federal spending, and finally, Mr. Greenspan—your own adviser—predicted today a continued 6 per cent inflation rate.

P: Let me set the record—

Q: I don't understand how things are getting better.

P: Let me set the record straight. There is a very distinct difference between Federal spending proposals by President Ford and those of Governor Carter. Governor Carter has endorsed, embraced, sponsored, 60-some new programs that will cost $100-billion a year at a minimum and $200-billion probably on an annual basis. So, there is a distinct difference between Governor Carter on the one hand and myself. He wants to spend more and I want to hold the lid on federal spending.

Let's talk about the status of the economy. In the first quarter of this calendar year, the rate of growth of GNP [gross national product] was 9.2 per cent. It fell in the second quarter to 4.5 per cent. It looks like the third quarter will be in the range of about 4 per cent.

I have checked with the responsible advisors to me in this area and they expect a resumption of the rate of growth of GNP in October, November and December of over 5 per cent and probably closer to 6 per cent, and they expect that same rate of growth in 1977.

We have had a pause, but we could not sustain the rate of growth of the first quarter of 1976, when it was 9.2 or [9.3]. We are now coming out of the dip or the pause that we had, and I believe that all, or practically all, economists recognize that the economy is continuing to improve and will get better in this quarter and in 1977.

Problems of Cities

Q: Mr. President?
P: Yes?
Q: Mr. President, in keeping the lid on federal spending, are you willing to accept the continued physical and social deterioration of the big cities of this country? A Marshall plan sort of approach has been offered. Would you, if elected, move in that direction?

P: I would not embrace any spending program that is going to cost the federal Treasury and the American taxpayers billions and billions and billions of dollars. We have good programs for the rehabilitation of our major metropolitan areas. I just signed a general revenue sharing bill. We fully fund the Community Development Act. We fully fund the mass transit legislation.

We have a number of very good programs that are in operation today, and about three months ago I appointed the Secretary of HUD, Carla Hills, to head a Cabinet Committee on Urban Development and Neighborhood Revitalization. That committee is working together very closely so that we get the full benefit out of all the federal dollars now available to help our inner cities and major metropolitan areas.

I think we are doing a good job and to all of a sudden just throw money in doesn't make any sense because you are bound to have more deficits, more taxes and more inflation.

So, I think we ought to make the programs we have today work and they are working and will solve the problem.

Yes?

Campaign Travels

Q: Mr. President, a review of your travel logs from this fall and last fall shows that for a comparable period last fall you spent exactly as much time on the road—15 days last fall—when there was no campaign and no election than you have this fall when there is a hotly contested presidential election.

Doesn't this lend a little bit of credence to Governor Carter's charge that you have been hiding in the White House for most of this campaign?

P: Tom, didn't you see that wonderful picture of me standing on the top of the limousine with the caption "Is He Hiding?" The truth is, we are campaigning when we feel that we can be away from the White House and not neglect the primary responsibilities that I have as President of the United States.

I think you are familiar with the vast number of bills that I have had to sign. We have done that. That is my prime responsibility, among other things. We do get out and campaign. We were in New York and New Jersey earlier this week. We are going to Iowa, Missouri and Illinois between now and Sunday.

We will be traveling when we can, but my prime responsibility is to stay in the White House and get the job done here, and I will do that and then we will campaign after that.

Q: Mr. President, how do you account for, at this rather late stage in the campaign, so many voters are telling pollsters that they remain undecided and many more are saying that they may not bother to vote at all?

P: It is disturbing that there are these statements to the effect that voters are apathetic. I believe we have tried to do everything we possibly can to stimulate voter participation. I want a maximum vote on this November 2 election and in every way I possibly can we are going to stimulate it between now and November 2.

I can't give you an answer as to why there is apathy. I am going to do what I can to overcome that apathy and, naturally, I hope to convince 51 per cent of the people in enough states so that we get enough electoral votes so that we can continue the policies of trust, peace and growing prosperity in the United States.

Accepting Gifts - 2

Q: Mr. President, do you think it is proper for a member of Congress to accept a golfing vacation or golfing weekend trip, and would you, now that you are in the White House, accept such a trip?

P: I have not accepted such a trip since I have been Vice President or President. And when I was in the Congress I have done as I said in the limited number of instances that have been in the paper.

Yes?

Q: Mr. President, you said that in your debate with Jimmy Carter, your statement on Eastern Europe demonstrated a certain lack of ability to think fast on your feet. Without intending to once again review the merits of that debate, how important, in your judgment, is it for a President to think fast on his feet to do his job properly?

P: I think it is vitally important for a President to make the right decisions in the Oval Office, and I think I have made the right decisions in the Oval Office. I have admitted that in that particular debate I made a slip in that one instance, but I would like to compare that one slip with the documented instances that we found in Governor Carter's presentation a week ago when he made some 14 either misrepresentations or inaccurate statements.

And while we are on that subject, I would like to say that I feel very strongly that the attitude that he took on that occasion, where he said America was not strong, where he said the United States Government had tried to get us into another Vietnam in Angola, and where he said the United States had lost respect throughout the world.

I don't approve of any candidate for office slandering the good name of the United States. It discourages our allies and it encourages our adversaries.

Yes?

Presidential Debates - 1

Q: Mr. President, on the debates, two of them have happened and one is to come. Do you have any thoughts perhaps on changing the rules for the third debate, and also, do you feel impeded since you are President and know more than you can say in public?

P: About the only improvement I would make is to get Mr. Carter to answer the questions. *(Laughter)*

Q: Mr. President, could you tell us why it took you six days and four clarifications before you finally admitted that you had in fact made a mistake in the debate in your remarks on Eastern Europe?

P: I think it took some thoughtful analysis because, as someone may have noticed, there was a letter to the editor in *The New York Times* a day or two ago by a very prominent ethnic, a man by the name of Janovitz, as I recall, who said that my answer was the right one. But it all depends on how you analyze the answer.

But I wanted to be very clear to make certain the Polish-Americans and other ethnics in this country knew that I knew that there are some 30 Soviet divisions in Poland and several of the other Eastern European countries.

On the other hand, I want to say very strongly that anybody who has been in Poland, for example, as I have in 1975, and seen the Polish people, the strong, courageous look in their face, the deep feeling that you get from talking with them, although they recognize that the Soviet Union has X number of divisions occupying their country, that freedom is in their heart and in their mind, and they are not going to be dominated over the long run by any outside power.

Now we concede for the time being the Soviet Union has that military power there, but we subscribe to the hopes and the aspirations of the courageous Polish people and their relatives here in the United States.

Q: Mr. President, if they tried to overthrow that power, would you look favorably on helping them in some way?

P: I don't think we should answer that question. I don't think it is going to happen. I don't think we should respond to that kind of a question in a press conference. Yes?

Presidential Debates - 2

Q: Mr. President, you have had some harsh words for your opponent's performance in the second debate, and yet every public opinion survey that I have seen showed you lost that debate and it was one that was on foreign and defense affairs, which are supposed to be your strong suit.

Do you agree that you lost that second debate and, if so, why? Or, if you think you won it, why do you think that happened?

P: I think there is a poll that shows the conclusion you have just set forth. I don't necessarily agree with that, but there were some very specific answers that were given by people who were interrogated afterwards. If you will look at that list of special questions that were asked of people who responded, it showed that in those cases—and I think they were the very fundamental ones on specific issues—firmness, strength—that a majority of people thought I had prevailed.

Natural Gas Prices

Q: Mr. President, the Federal Power Commission has authorized the increase in the price of new natural gas. That is something you favored. The original estimate was that it would cost the American consumer $1.3-billion a year. Now we are told that it may be as high or higher than $3-billion a year. Do you think that price increase should be rolled back or should it stand still?

P: The fundamental issue is, if you don't get a price increase you are not going to have any new natural gas. So, the question is, are you willing to pay for enough gas to heat our homes and to heat our factories so people will have jobs? We have to give an incentive to people to go out and find new natural gas sources, and if you don't give them that incentive, there won't be any heat for their homes or heat for their factories and we will lose the jobs.

Q: Are you willing to risk another jolt to the economy from this large price increase?

P: I think a bigger jolt would be to have the jobs lost and the houses cold.

Level of Campaign

Q: Mr. President, earlier in your campaign you said you intended to stress positive themes. Yet, in your most recent campaign appearance you concentrated on attacking Governor Carter. Tonight you accused him of slandering the name of the United States.

Do you think you have done all you can to elevate the level of this campaign and can we expect you to continue the way you have been in the last week or so?

P: I think it is very positive to talk about tax reductions, as I have recommended to the American people that we increase the personal exemption from $750 to $1,000. That is very positive and very affirmative, and certainly in contrast to what Mr. Carter wants, which is to increase taxes for people with a medium or middle income level, which is about $14,000. That is a distinct difference.

I am on the affirmative side. He is on the negative side.

President's Personal Expenses

Q: Mr. President?

P: Yes, Sarah? *(Laughter)* You knew I would get around to you.

Q: Thank you. When you were in Congress you filed an income tax return for those years saying that you had very little money left over. Like a lot of us, you have about $5 left over for spending money, I believe.

I wonder if you had included your golf fees and your dues at Congressional and Burning Tree? I believe you belonged to both of them, didn't you, and they are very expensive. You must have been strapped for funds. Who was helping you pay those large golfing expenses? You golfed three to five times a week, I believe.

P: First, that is an inaccurate statement and you know it, Sarah. *(Laughter)*

When you are the minority leader of the House of Representatives and on the job, you don't play golf three to five times a week. I am sorry you said that because you know that is not true.

Now, let me just say that I paid for those golfing dues or charges by check, and the committee and everybody else, the Internal Revenue Service, the Joint Committee on Internal Revenue Taxation, the FBI and now the Special Prosecutor have all looked into those in depth and in detail and they have given me a clean bill of health, and I thank them for it.

Ford Motor Company Taxes

Q: Mr. President, *The Washington Post* had an article today which noted that Ford Motor Company paid no taxes last year, paid no taxes the year before. Do you think that is fair and what are you going to do about it?

P: Well, I think it is proper to remind the American people that those tax laws which are on the statute books were written by the Democrats who controlled the Congress for the last 22 years. If they are wrong, it is the fault of the majority party in the Congress.

Q: What are you doing to change that?

P: We have made recommendations to the Congress over the last year and a half for some modifications in the income tax legislation, but how that would affect that particular company I can't give you the answer.

Presidential Debates - 3

Q: Mr. President, in a recent speech—I am afraid I don't recall where—you cut a line from your text in which you said something about the campaign should not be just a quiz show to see who gets to live in the White House for the next four years. And I assume you stand by that advance text. Were you trying to suggest that the debates have not been as effective as they should have been, they have not kept up the level of the campaign?

P: Ann, you know, you read the advance text. I hope you are listening when I speak. You know, on many occasions, I add a little here and I take something else out. Oftentimes, I don't get those texts until maybe a half, three-quarters of an hour before I make the speech. So, I make the judgment myself. Those are the recommendations of the speechwriters.

Now, I didn't think that was an appropriate thing to say and, therefore, I didn't include it in the text that I gave to the meeting that you referred to.

Q: Let me put it this way: Do you think the debates have helped keep up the level of the campaign?

P: I think the debates have been very wholesome. I think they have been constructive. I was the one that initiated the challenge. I believe that they ought to be an institution in future presidential campaigns. I really believe that. And for that reason, I didn't think that sentence in that prepared text which I deleted reflected my own views.

Q: Mr. President, thank you. A little while ago you gave us an idea of how you balance your family budget—you kite checks. *(Laughter)*

P: Oh, no, I don't. No, I don't. I have never been overdrawn, young lady.

Q: The question is, then, how is it that you are able to live on from $5 to $13 a week in cash as has been reported by *The Washington Post* and *The Wall Street Journal* in 1972?

P: I repeat that the Internal Revenue Service, the FBI, the Joint Committee on Taxation, two committees in the House and in the Senate, and an overwhelming majority of the members of the House and Senate, believed the testimony. They went back and checked every one of those income tax returns from 1973 back six years, and they gave me a clean bill of health. Now, it has been reinvestigated for the fourth time by the Special Prosecutor and he concurs with the previous investigations.

Those are the facts of life. I write checks.

Thank you all. Thank you very much.

THE PRESS: Thank you. ∎

October 20

Following is the White House text of President Ford's Oct. 20 news conference, his 39th since taking office.

THE PRESIDENT: Won't you all sit down.

It is easier to get in the Rose Garden. I guess we had better go back to it. We just had a door knob break off. *(Laughter)*

Q: That is a sign of the times.

P: You can't blame that on me. Helen?

Q: Mr. President, regardless of the allegations of influences at the time, and in view of the long national nightmare we went through, do you have any regrets, any remorse for the role that you played in helping to block the first investigation of one of the worst White House scandals in history? And I have a follow-up.

P: I don't believe what I did in working with the Republican Members of the House Committee on Banking and Currency was a blocking of an investigation of Watergate. I did that because the Republican Members of that committee specifically asked me to get them together.

Now what that committee would have done was, as I understood it, to investigate a very limited part of certain campaign activities. It didn't have any intention or have any program to do anything beyond that.

So, what I did was at the request of the responsible people on the Banking and Currency Committee and, under the circumstances, as I knew it then, I think I would do exactly the same thing.

Q: Well, Mr. President, there also is a

widespread speculation that you may pardon Mitchell, Haldeman and Ehrlichman as all part of the same package. Is there any validity to that?

P: There is absolutely no validity whatsoever to that rumor. In fact, you are the first one that has raised it with me, so I want you to know it and I want everybody else to know it. There is no credence whatsoever to it.

Q: Mr. President, in the past week, two top men in your administration—FBI Chief Clarence Brown, and General George—I mean Clarence Kelley and General George Brown, Chairman of the Joint Chiefs of Staff—have come under criticism for their comments involving curbs on the press and aid to Israel.

I want to know, have you made any comment on this? What is your view of this incident, and if you are elected would you keep these two men in these responsible jobs?

P: I am glad that the Counsel of the White House, through the Attorney General, did stop what I understood was to be a speech by Clarence Kelley. From what I know about the speech, I think it would have been ill-advised and would not reflect the views of President Ford in his relationship with the press.

Now, General Brown had an interview six or eight months ago. It was released at a time when I am certain that General Brown didn't anticipate it would be released, and it was released in part and not in whole.

General Brown, after consulting with Secretary of Defense Rumsfeld, did appear before the press, both of them, and explained the entire context of the interview. The total interview would lead any reasonable person to a different interpretation than the excerpts that were taken from it and were released to the press.

I happen to believe General Brown and I have reviewed the whole text of that interview myself. Some of those statements were impudent (imprudent) and were ill-advised, and I certainly don't believe that General Brown, in that position, ought to make those kind of comments in several instances, but I also don't believe it was fair in the prospective or released text that certain excerpts should be taken, and several of them taken out of context.

Now General Brown was just recommended by me and he was confirmed by the Senate for a two-year term as Chairman of the Joint Chiefs. I would expect him to stay. He has a superb military record—35 years of devoted service in wartime—and I think he has been a fine Chairman of the Joint Chiefs of Staff. But he made one or two ill-advised statements and I hope and trust that he won't do it again.

Q: Mr. President, you would keep both him and Mr. Kelley in their jobs?

P: Yes, because I think Clarence Kelley has taken a very serious situation in the F.B.I. I think he straightened it out and I think he is a person that all of us can have trust in as far as the job as the job as the

Director of the F.B.I.

Elevating Discourse

Q: Mr. President, at your last news conference you said that the campaign to date has been, quoting you, "mired in questions that have little bearing on the future of this nation," and that you would try to elevate the level of the discourse from there on. Subsequently you seemed to be preoccupied with suggesting that Mr. Carter was a dissembler and again to use your words, "an individual who waivers, wanders, wiggles and waffles," and your campaign organization has sponsored reproductions in advertisements of the front cover of Playboy Magazine. Is that what you meant by elevating the level of the discourse?

P: I think it is graphic and accurate to say that Mr. Carter does waiver, wander wiggle and waffle. There are plenty of illustrations, as a matter of fact, that that is true. Now the language is a little graphic, but there is nothing personal about it. I didn't attack his integrity or anything close to that. Now Mr. Carter did have an interview in Playboy Magazine. I haven't looked at the magazine. I am sure there are about seven million Americans, I understand, who will look at it and will probably read the article. *(Laughter)* But I reiterate what I said once before, I turned down an invitation by Playboy Magazine to have an interview such as Mr. Carter did. These are all factual statements either by myself or factual statements as to an interview that he had in a certain magazine.

Arab Boycott - 1

Q: Mr. President, Mr. Carter yesterday said that if he was elected he would end the Arab boycott. I wonder if you consider this a legitimate matter—

P: You mean the Arab oil embargo or the Arab boycott?

Q: The Arab boycott on Israel—I misspoke. I wonder if you consider this a legitimate objective and if you would like to do the same thing?

P: The Ford Administration is the only Administration since 1952 when the Arab boycott went into effect that has done anything in the Executive Branch of the government. Now Mr. Carter says that he would end it—very short sentence. I resent the inference of that. The Arab boycott was initiated in 1952. In effect he is saying that President Eisenhower didn't do anything, that President Kennedy didn't do anything about it, that President Johnson didn't do anything about it, President Nixon didn't do anything about it, and he infers I haven't, and of course he is inaccurate there. But I resent that he is challenging those other four Presidents—Eisenhower, Kennedy, Johnson and Nixon—because I know they opposed the Arab boycott just as much as I do and as much as Mr. Carter does. And I wonder if anybody can be so naive as to say in one sentence that he is going to do something that four other outstanding individuals didn't do even though they opposed the same thing, and I think it is ridiculous for him to make that kind of an allegation.

Dole's Record

Q: Mr. President, since your nomination, your decision to choose Robert Dole as Vice President has been one of the most important ones you have had to make. His record both during the campaign and in Congress has been one of extreme partisanship; for example, in his support of nominations to the Supreme Court of Haynesworth and Carswell and his actions on the Watergate investigation.

What can you point to in his career that shows that he has that judgment, that initiative and that leadership that Americans are looking for in a Vice President and potential President?

P: He served in the House of Representatives and in the United States Senate, I think, for 16 years. I believe that his record as a Representative and as a Senator is an excellent record. In fact, it is a record of longer tenure than Senator Mondale.

So, on that basis, he is better qualified than Senator Mondale. They have different philosophies. Mondale is a very liberal Senator, and Dole is a moderate to conservative, but I think Bob Dole, on the basis of his record of service in the Congress, is fully qualified to be Vice President.

Q: Mr. President, if I could go back to that Playboy interview for a moment sir, if you haven't read it or seen Playboy, why do you think it is fair to criticize Mr. Carter about it.

P: I have read the article. I haven't read it in the magazine.

Q: Well, if I could follow up on that, when you criticize him, is it because you specifically disagreed with some things that he said in that, or is it because of the political benefit that a person might be expected to get in criticizing Playboy Magazine?

Arab Boycott - 2

P: I don't know why Mr. Carter agreed to the interview. That is not for me to judge. That was a decision made by him. I don't think a President of the United States ought to have an interview in a magazine that has that format. It is a personal conviction.

Q: Mr. President, a moment ago, when you were talking about the Arab boycott, you were accusing Mr. Carter of inferring that previous Presidents had done nothing about it, but you prefaced that with a statement that the Ford Administration is the only one that had done anything about it since 1952. Aren't you and Mr. Carter making the same accusations.

P: I have done it. He says that he is going to end it. I think the affirmative action that I have taken—and it has been proven, I think, helpful, because of what has transpired since I think it was October 7 when the actual order was issued that would force

companies who had participated to have their names revealed—I think this will be a big deterrent. I hope it will.

I am against that Arab boycott, but I repeat, I am the first President that has taken any affirmative action, and I think the way that Mr. Carter stated it was a reflection on previous Presidents who I know felt as strongly as he does that an Arab boycott is contrary to the philosophy that we as Americans have.

Q: If you are saying that previous Presidents did nothing about it, aren't you, in effect, making the same accusation against him?

P: No, I said he said they had not done anything about it.

Q: You have said the Ford Administration is the only one that has done anything.

P: Anything that is required that companies put their name on the line that they participated or had received information, that is correct.

Q: During your last debate with Jimmy Carter, Mr. Carter stated that if there was another Arab oil boycott and he was President of the United States, he would break that boycott by countering it with a boycott of our own.

Mr. President, do you think this is a realistic possibility? Could the United States break down an Arab boycott or embargo by penalizing them by refusing to sell materials to them and, secondly, even if it is realistic, would it be in the best interest of the United States?

P: My answer would be that I would not tolerate an Arab oil embargo, but I add very quickly in the current atmosphere, because of the leadership of the Ford Administration, you aren't going to have an Arab oil embargo. Let me tell you why.

In 1973, we had the Yom Kippur War. That was settled. We had the Sinai I agreement, followed by the Sinai II agreement.

This Administration in the Sinai II agreement was able to expand the peace effort in the Middle East because the Arab nations on the one hand and Israel on the other trust the Ford Administration.

You won't find among Arab nations today the same attitude that prevailed at the time of the Yom Kippur War. You won't find the possibilities of another Middle East war today that you had in 1973. So, the probabilities of an Arab oil embargo are virtually nil because of the leadership of this Administration.

Now, furthermore, I do not agree with the proposed recommendation of Mr. Carter, if there was one. He said he would cut off food, he would cut off trade, he would cut off military arms.

I think we can avoid any Arab oil embargo and not have to resort to cutting off food that American farmers have produced and sell abroad in order to help our economy here at home.

Q: Mr. President, many people are saying that the candidates are showing no vision. What is your vision for America?

P: My vision for America, first, is that

we shall be a Nation at peace as we are today. My vision of the next four years is also that we will have a better quality of life; that we will have our younger people having a better opportunity for quality education; that every person who wants a job will have a job; that the best health care will be available, at prices people can afford; that we will have a record of safety and security in the streets of America for those 215 million Americans who ought to be able to walk in their community or any other part of the country without the threat of crime. My vision would also include an opportunity for greater recreation capability.

In other words, peace, a job, better health, better education, no crime or control over the criminal situation, and a better opportunity for recreation—those are the visions that I have.

Q: Many people, though, are asking whether you truly have a vision for the underprivileged, whether you really care.

P: When you say a job for everybody who wants to work, I think that certainly indicates that you have a deep concern for the people who are disadvantaged, unemployed.

Q: Mr. President, I wonder if you have made any wagers with your family, friends or staff about what the popular and electoral vote will be on November 2?

P: I haven't made any wagers with my family as to the outcome, but all of us—my four children, Betty and myself—believe that when the votes are finally counted, the American people will want four years of the progress we made in the last two, and a better America during that period. But there are no wagers as to whether we are going to win or not.

Q: Mr. President, the comment by Secretary Butz that led to his resignation was made in response to a question about this commitment of this Administration to blacks and other minorities. What is the commitment of this Administration? What plans do you have to expand the entering into the society of black and other minorities in the next four years if you are elected?

P: We have a number of good programs at the present time. We certainly will continue to enforce the Civil Rights Act that was passed when I was in Congress, which I supported. We will enforce it as to the right to vote, as to housing, as to the opportunity for minority business. We will cover the spectrum to make sure that any minority—not just blacks but any minority—Mexican-Americans, Chicanos, generally, blacks—all minorities in this country ought to be treated equitably and fairly, and they will under the existing laws as they have been for the last two-plus years.

Israeli Burden

Q: Mr. President, Barry Goldwater has said that he agrees with General Brown in the sense that Israel is a military burden of the United States and that we may deplete our own armor to supply Israel and we may give Israel too many arms, too much arms. Is Israel a burden in your opinion and will we deplete our own arms in giving Israel arms.

P: That is a very good question and I would like to expand a bit in my response, if I might. The United States is dedicated to the security and survival of Israel. The three million Israelis are a democratic state in an area where democracy doesn't flourish. We have many, many good firm fine ties with the people and with the Government of Israel. I want that to be understood very clearly.

Now you have to look at the broad picture when you look at the United States and Israel's military circumstances. At the time of the Yom Kippur War, the United States came immediately to the aid of Israel with substantial military hardware and military equipment. We drew down from our reserves in Western Europe, in the NATO forces, U.S. hardware that was sent to Israel. Now that was not an irreparable situation in NATO because in the interim, from 1973, we have virtually made up that drawdown but for a period of time one could say that the immediate needs of Israel in a crisis were a burden to the United States.

On the other hand, since I have been President, from August 9, 1974 to the present time, in order to make Israel strong militarily the Ford Administration has either granted or sold about $2½-billion worth of military equipment to the state of Israel. The net result is today Israel is stronger militarily than it was prior to the Yom Kippur War because of the support of the Ford Administration.

So today Israel is not a burden militarily to the United States because of the forthright action of the Ford Administration, and you have to take the comments that have been made in the proper context. Israel is a strong ally who doesn't want U.S. troops to be a participant in any future military engagement there because Israel is strong and the Ford Administration has contributed significantly to making them strong. But in the 1973 Yom Kippur War, some emergency actions had to be taken.

Now we have overcome it. Israel is strong and they are a good ally and we are dedicated to their security and survival.

Cities

Q: Mr. President, there has been a good deal of discussion, sir, and concern that the issues discussed in the campaign have been too narrow, and you and Mr. Carter haven't discussed a broad enough range of issues,

and that frankly very often during the debates you have been rattling off pre-rehearsed answers to questions regardless of the questions.

How about that large question, and would you have any particular initiative for America's troubled cities in another term.

P: Let me speak very forthrightly. I can't speak for Mr. Carter, but we don't anticipate what those questions are going to be from members of the press. We answer them based on our knowledge or our experience. In my case, they are not pre-rehearsed, and any allegations to that effect just aren't accurate.

Now let me say this about the Ford Administration and its reference to the needs and requirements of our major metropolitan areas. The Ford Administration, with general revenue sharing, with the Community Development Act, Mass Transit Act, with the LEAA program, and a number of other programs, has given more money to major metropolitan cities, to our big cities in this country than any previous Administration. That is a fact.

Now the net result is sometimes those programs have overlapped. And so about five months ago I asked Secretary of HUD, Carla Hills, to head a Cabinet-level committee called the Committee on Urban Development and Neighborhood Revitalization, and some time, I hope—maybe this week or next—we will have that Cabinet committee's recommendations so we could better utilize the vast amounts of money, the billions and billions of dollars that have gone from the Federal Treasury to our cities, so that they will be better utilized, and I am looking forward to that report. I am looking forward to having it published because I am told that it has some very good recommendations of how we can better utilize what we are making available.

Watergate Investigation

Q: Mr. President, in addition to doing what you did in connection with the Patman inquiry in 1972, at the request of the Republican Members of the Patman Committee, were you also asked by Mr. Nixon or anyone acting for him on the White House Staff to do that?

P: As I recall my testimony, John, before one—maybe both committees—I said I had never been contacted by President Nixon, by Mr. Ehrlichman, by Mr. Haldeman or by Mr. Dean, and I said that I had virtually daily contact with Mr. Timmons, who was the head of the Legislative Liaison Office. But, to the best of my

recollection, neither he nor anybody in his office asked me to take a hand in the Patman action or the committee action. That was my testimony in 1973; it is my testimony, or my answer to your question today.

Q: Mr. President, you stated that Governor Carter once advocated a $15 billion cut in the defense budget. He said that is not so, that he only wants to cut $5 billion or $7 billion out and he wants to take it all out of waste.

I would like to know, why don't you join Governor Carter in coming out in favor of cutting that much waste out of the defense budget?

P: First, the record is clear that on two occasions Governor Carter did say—once in Savannah, Georgia and once in Los Angeles—and he was quoted in reputable newspapers—that he would cut the defense budget $15 billion.

Now, it is true, according to what he says today, that he has gone from a $15 billion cut down to a $5 to $7 billion cut. I am glad to see that as he gets better educated in these matters that he understands that you can't do that to the Defense Department and be strong enough to meet the challenges of the Soviet Union or anybody else.

All right. The Ford Administration in January of this year recommended to the Congress the military budget that called for spending what we call obligational authority of about $112.5 billion. We said that you could keep the military strong and keep the peace as we have it with that kind of a military budget, providing the Congress would take certain other actions to improve the efficiency and achieve economies in the Defense Department, and I think those proposed economies totaled about $4-billion.

Now, the Congress, when they got all through, only approved about $1 billion and a half to $2 billion of those economies that the Ford Administration recommended for the Department of Defense. So, we were on record in January for some very specific economies and improved efficiencies in the Defense Department.

The net result is Congress wouldn't go along with it. They wouldn't change the laws. But, we are going to send up a budget in January for the Defense Department that will provide for the necessary funding to keep the peace, but we will also send up the kind of economy and efficiency recommendations that we made last January.

THE PRESS: Thank you.

P: Thank you all very much.

How do you like the afternoon shows? ∎

Index to Presidential Messages and News Conferences

278